OVER
THE MISTY
BLUE HILLS

The Story of
Cocke County,
Tennessee

by
RUTH WEBB O'DELL

Please Direct All Correspondence and Book Orders to:

Southern Historical Press, Inc.
PO Box 1267
375 West Broad Street
Greenville, S.C. 29602

ISBN # 0-89308-276-7

Printed in the United States of America

TABLE OF CONTENTS

ILLUSTRATIONS

*Notes by Pauline Shields Walker

The Author's Parents—1886
George W. Webb and Sarah K. McAndrew Webb.

To my parents, George W. and Sarah K. Mc-Andrew Webb, to my maternal grandparents, Reverend William Senter McAndrew and Martha J. Francis McAndrew, and to my paternal grandparents, Captain George W. Webb and Mary (Polly) Shrader Webb, I dedicate this story of Cocke County, Tennessee. They and their ancestors for generations back, contriouted all within their power to the upbuilding of this section of Tennessee.

Preface

For many reasons, the story of Cocke County, Tennessee, has never been published in book form. Several have endeavored to write it, but found the task either too difficult or died before having finished it.

Frequent courthouse fires destroyed early records of great value, a fact which has probably discouraged many others who might otherwise have undertaken the task. So far as dates and names are concerned, no one could write an accurate and complete history.

To piece together records from various sources, as I have done, requires much effort, will power, time and money for traveling to various county seats and libraries for original records. Finally, after several years, I have gathered what I hope is an interesting and informative volume. Later, I plan to treat more intensively those subjects and families which I can only touch in my allotted space.

To live a full and complete life, I have been told, it is necessary to teach a school or two, to write a book or two, and to build a house.

It has been my lot to keep many schools, and for several years it was my pleasure to superintend the teaching of one hundred and ten schools in Cocke County.

But this is my first effort at writing a book, and so it is in humility and in service to my fellow citizens that I have toiled to collect the information herein recorded, in order that they and their children will have a record of some of the activities of those who have preceded them.

Stories handed down by "word of mouth" from one generation to another are not always accurate. Each generation adds to or takes away from, as suits its fancy. Nevertheless, such a record is better than none and should be preserved, for knowledge that dies with us is forever lost.

To leave something behind that is lovely or worthwhile should be the aim of every person, each family, each generation. It is not always easy for each generation to realize that the dreams they dream, their fathers dreamed; the songs they sing, their fathers sang; the thoughts they think, their fathers thought. They like to think that they know much more than their forbears. According to Ridpath, all history is but one page, the same rehearsal of the past:

> *"First, freedom, then glory, when that fails,*
> *Wealth, corruption, barbarism at last,*
> *And history, in all her volumes vast,*
> *Hath but one page."*

Although it is impossible to list the names of all to whom I am indebted in compiling this volume, I must mention the following: Judge John H. DeWitt and wife of Nashville, whose kindly encouragement first gave me the idea of trying to assemble historical data on Cocke County; Mrs. John Trotwood Moore, for her untiring help; Judge Samuel Cole Williams of Johnson City, Vice-President for East Tennessee, Tennessee Historical Society, for his continuous research and willingness to assist me in this endeavor; Dr. Edmund C. Burnett, Carnegie Institute, Washington, D. C., for his continued encouragement and interest in having the history of Cocke County written; my late husband, George W. O'Dell, for his generosity in providing funds for research and travel; his mother, Mrs. Rita Jane Thomas O'Dell, for historical clippings, books, old newspapers, and court records from her ninety years of residence in Cocke County; my mother, Mrs. Sarah K. Webb, who reminded me daily over a period of years that I should be working on this history instead of doing other tasks; Jasper Gray, for the McSween articles; Tom Campbell, editor and owner of the *Newport Times,* who insisted that I submit material for publication in his paper that I might receive the benefit of constructive reader criticism; Robert P. Sulte, editor and owner of *The Newport Plain Talk,* for his recent publication of various chapters, and for editorial comment on the value of the work; Thomas Sandusky Gorman of Oceola, Missouri, for the story of the Gorman family; Mrs. Lennie Thomas Marshall and Elder W. C. McMillan, for original minutes of early churches; Lyle S. Moore, for Stokely Brothers information; Mrs. Lucile Smith Walker, for authentic family records of earliest settlers; to Miss Ethel Walker of Roanoke, Virginia, for various outlines of county histories; Miss Mae Walker of Lincoln Memorial University, Harrogate, Tennessee, for editing and typing manuscript; Judge Philip Cocke, for family data and unusual photograph of his ancestor, William, for whom Cocke County was named; Mrs. Lou Miller Robinson, for Napier information; Sam K. Leming, Waldron, Arkansas, for his valuable family records; Mrs. Charles Wayland, for Cocke County Seal and other historical data; Ann Bibee Mitchell, for courthouse records; Liston Lewis, for early sketch of present Newport; Mansfield McMahan, also W. J. Parks, Asheville, North Carolina, Caywood and Hamilton Mantooth, railroad officials; M. A. Roadman, for access to *Newport Herald* files; the Tennessee Valley Authority for the county survey, maps, and pictures; and to any one else who has in any way contributed to this or to the prospective second volume. To my daughter, Iris Ruth O'Dell Anderson and my son, Lynn S. O'Dell, for help and encouragement. To Mark and Mabel Raines for their generosity and encouragement. I wish also to thank the Justices of the Peace who made motions to give aid on this project; Esquires Estel Stokely, Charles Mantooth, Frank Stokely and the others, Esquires Guy Freshour, Dewey Strange, Clarence Scott, Burnett Dawson and James A. T. Wood, who stood with them.

—*Ruth W. O'Dell*

The arrival of the author in Cocke County with her mother, brother and sister, September, 1892.

The Scottish mansion home of Congressman William C. Anderson's family and where the author began housekeeping in 1905.

A SONG TO THE MOUNTAINS

By FRANCES BURNETT SWANN

O land of the misty blue mountains
Far away from the unresting sea,
Like a wandering dove seeking shelter,
My spirit finds refuge in thee.

O land of peaceful, deep valleys!
Green hills circling swift flowing streams
Soft winds from the heavens cool blowing—
O home of my visions and dreams!

Sublime in thy grandeur, O mountains,
Serene in thy calm majesty;
A temple whence strength ever cometh
To the eyes uplifted to thee.

O mountains; steadfast, enduring—
Full soon passes man's little day—
Sunrise and sunset beholding,
While time rolls the ages away.

Dear land of the misty blue mountains,
Secure from the turbulent sea
My spirit in longing wings homeward—
My heart still abideth with thee.

—From page 9 of *Garden Paths*

Foreword

By Edmund C. Burnett

In a recent survey of the conduct of the Southern states over a period of three hundred years in the matter of preserving (or failing to preserve) their historical records the author of that survey declares respecting the State of Tennessee: "Altogether it is the saddest story among the fourteen I am endeavoring to tell."* Tennessee has indeed had its full share of losses from all the calamities which may befall historical records— destruction by fire, wanton destruction, carelessness, indifference, incompetence, downright ignorance; and if degrees of guilt must be ascribed, fire would come off with the lightest sentence.

That survey does not in anywise concern itself with what has taken place in the state during the past half century, a period that records, happily, devoted efforts for the betterment of conditions, efforts notably successful upon the whole, even though now and again the sow has returned to her wallowing place in the mud. There is no purpose here either to rehearse the tale of woe—for it is a familiar enough tale to everyone who has concerned himself with the state's past—or to recount the eager endeavors to transform the tragic story into one with a happy ending.

There is another story of failure, of neglect, of indifference, even of deliberate though thoughtless destruction, with the consequent loss of the materials of our history scarcely secondary in importance to official records. Unofficial records, of which there are many categories, oftentimes possess a significance, a degree of revelation, surpassing that of the official record; and, because it is nobody's prescribed business to preserve them, oftener than otherwise they are not preserved. To point up this contention, a single example will suffice. One of the prime sources of our history has long been newspapers, and for local history in particular they are still a prime source; yet the preservation of local newspapers has for the most part been and remains spasmodic and accidental. The chief reason for these failures, as also for the failure to preserve business and private records and correspondence has been mainly the lack of what may be called the historical consciousness.

Tennesseans have not been too much but wholly lacking in historical consciousness. It has seemed to this observer that it has been chiefly a consciousness of the distant past, of pioneer times, of the legends and traditions of those days Tennesseans have been wont to drink deeply and with prideful satisfaction, little disturbed if those copious drafts have been asquirm with ingredients that could not stand up under the acid test of truth. It is much as if one took his stand upon an eminence on the brim of one of our broad valleys and gazed at the far horizon, hazy and beclouded, all unobservant of the stirring life in the valley that lies be-

---

* J. G. De Roulac Hamilton, "Three Centuries of Southern Records, 1607-1907," in *Journal of Southern History*, February, 1944.

tween. As for that dim horizon, it is to the credit of Judge Samuel C. Williams, more than to any other one person, that the air has been measurably cleared of the mists and what actually took place has been brought into true historic perspective.

If Tennesseans have manifested a laggardness in the preservation of their records and in making them available to the historian, it is for that very reason that the historical investigator has been slow to exploit the records that have survived, to draw them forth from their obscure and musty corners and bring them to the light of day, whether in documentary or interpretive form, that he that runs, or he that lolls, may read and be informed of what the state and its people have done and what manner of life they have lived. In short, in the writing of its history, our state is far, far behind; so far indeed that it is scarcely among the hopeful expectations that the next generation will see the gap even measurably closed.

When this observer has had occasion to turn his eye upon the historical activity in some of the younger states, states with no more than half of Tennessee's span of years, he has been reminded of the story of a fox chase somewhere in our mountains. The troop of hunters came upon a cabin in the woods and asked the denizen of the cabin, "Did the chase come by here?" "Right in front of this house," was the reply. "How was it going?" was the next eager question. "Wall," drawled the mountaineer, "when I seed 'em, the dogs wuz a leetle ahead." It has sometimes seemed as if the historians of some of these states had not merely brought their written history up to date, but had actually got a little ahead of events. Certainly there is no dearth there of historical consciousness. Indeed the state loyalty, the pride in their past manifested by the people of these artificially bounded segments of territory organized into states might well put to the blush of shame us Tennesseans, with our long and rich background.

Coming now to the more immediate purpose of these remarks, the historian nowadays is seldom content to delve in political annals only. Even political history, it is now recognized, rests upon a broad basis of social and economic fact; and, though the political historian may wring the official records dry, the historian in search of the economic and social springs of political action must fare farther afield and astream for the materials from which to fashion a true story of life and action. He must seek out the unofficial, the private, even the casual records of the time.

It is therefore that the life of communities, of towns, of counties, of geographical sections possessing a degree of unity, economic or other, constitute essential elements in the history of that larger entity that we call the state. It was a dictum of Plato that the state is the individual "writ large." In like manner it may be said that the history of a state, in the specific sense of a member of our federal union, is but the history of its component parts "writ large." Which is only to say that, for a full comprehension of the part played by a state as a whole it is essential to have an adequate knowledge, a firm grasp, of the life of its parts, whether those parts be natural geographic sections, the more or less artificial subdivisions called counties, or those community groups that, almost without exception, have a distinct unity of their own.

The Tennessee Historical Commission therefore, in its endeavor to promote the cause of history in our state, is acting with broad vision in encouraging the writing and publication of county histories, of which this volume of Mrs. O'Dell's is among the first. Geographically, Cocke County lies hard against the mountain range that was to become the western boundary of North Carolina and therefore became one of the early halting places of emigrants out of that state. Likewise, being on the edge of the great East Tennessee Valley, it received its share of migration down the valley from out Virginia. Necessarily, therefore, the history of Cocke County is an essential part of the history of the advancing frontier, which has come to be regarded as one of the most significant features of American history, so significant, in fact, that Professor Frederick J. Turner's "Frontier Hypothesis," advance a little more than half a century ago, has ever since run like a scarlet thread through nearly all writings on American history.

Moreover, Cocke County has had its parts, though minor ones they may be, in two of those experiments in self-government which constitute a unique chapter in the early history of Tennessee. The northern section of what came to be included within the boundaries of the county was for a time a frontier of the State of Franklin. Then, almost as the federal government was being organized, the southern section of the county was encompassed within the domain of what is sometimes called the Territory South of the French Broad River, sometimes the "Lesser Franklin," of whose history scarcely more than a tenuous shadow has survived.

To write the history of Cocke County has been no holiday excursion. Quite to the contrary, it has been an arduous, toilsome task, calling for a limitless pursuit of written records, prone oft times to play with the searcher the game of hide and seek, but likewise of those fading scrawls to be recovered only, perchance, from dimming recollections. It has been indeed a task comparable to the fabled search for the needle hidden in a haystack. Fortunately she has now and again been rewarded by finding the needle, and we are the beneficiaries. One with lesser determination and perseverance than Mrs. O'Dell would have fallen by the wayside and have plodded no farther on the journey. Or, like Faint-heart in *Pilgrim's Progress*, after floundering a while in the Slough of Despond, would have turned back and have sought no more to achieve the distant goal.

For the materials of Cocke County's history have suffered all the ills registered at the outset of this little excursion, and doubtless more besides—if any such there be. Notable among these calamities was the fire of 1876, when the courthouse was burned, and more than three-quarters of a century of the county's official records went up in smoke. This writer well remembers the occasion and the manner in which he learned of the fire. It was early in the morning after, and the man at whose side he chanced to be (James McKay) called to another, who had just appeared on the scene (John Pearson): "John, we can all get married again now, if we want to." "How's that?" queried John. "Why, the courthouse burned last night, so there's no record of our marriages." I wondered then, and I have wondered since, why that aspect of the disaster was the first to arise in Jim's mind. Very soon afterward I began to hear moanings over another aspect, the loss of the records of land transfers. This was a very practical aspect, and it was a serious one. That remoter phase of the disaster, the darkening of the county's history, probably weighed but lightly on most minds.

The present dearth of unofficial records, on the other hand, can be ascribed only to a minor extent to the chapter of accidents. This writer may, perhaps, be pardoned for mentioning here one instance of the sort that has lain like a leaden weight on his own mind and in some degree has even burdened his conscience, although it was not an accident for which he was in anywise responsible. Most of the merchant's books of account at what is now Del Rio (the ancient Big Creek), for a period of fifty years or more, beginning with 1867 or thereabouts, had been preserved intact, and this devotee of his state, his county, and his community, had long set his heart upon utilizing those books in telling the story of that section of the county in the last third of the nineteenth century—a story which he conceives to be, in some respects, unique. For it includes the story of the hog-driving business, for which old Big Creek was the funnel-mouth of the drive up French Broad River, the story of the coming of the railroad into the community and its pause there for a dozen years, the transformations in the life of the community in consequence of the coming of the railroad, and in particular the rise of the almost unique shaved-shingle business that flourished in that mountain section of the county for nearly a quarter of a century. For the telling of that story those account books would have been invaluable. Alas! Only a few short years ago they were consumed by fire, consequently that story never can be adequately told.

This is merely one of the handicaps Mrs. O'Dell has encountered in her endeavor to reconstruct the history of Cocke County. Her history has had to be constructed from such occasional and casual records as she has been able to unearth and from the recollections of the ancients. How many years of laborious and persistent probing she has devoted to the task of gathering her materials, probably she only knows, but there is scarcely a resident of the county who has not been made aware of her persistent and painstaking pursuit, expending without stint time, labor, travel, and all at her own expense. It goes without saying that she has rescued much of the history of the county and its people from threatened oblivion, and we, the people of the county, owe her a great debt of obligation.

—EDMUND C. BURNETT

Washington, February 28, 1946.

William Cocke, for whom Cocke County was named

The Political History of Cocke County

William Cocke and Early History

Over the misty blue hills came the pioneers from Virginia, North and South Carolina, into the "Wilderness Country" also known as the "Over Mountain Country of the Cherokees." They came long before the State of Franklin was organized—and among the first to come were William Cocke and John Clifton, two Revolutionary War Soldiers.

William Cocke was identified with every step of the early history of Cocke County. The original founder of the family of Cocke was Lieutenant Colonel Richard Cocke who came from Devonshire, England, in 1632, and brought with him twenty families, numbering sixty people. This entitled him to three thousand acres of land for which he received a grant from Sir John Harvey in March, 1636. Richard Cocke became County Lieutenant for Henrico County, Virginia, and represented it in the House of Burgesses from 1634 to 1654.

Descending in direct line from Richard Cocke were Thomas, Stephen, Abraham and then William Cocke, the last of whom was born near Upperville, in Fauquier, or Amelia County, Virginia, in 1747. This handsome youth, with dark piercing eyes and dark wavy hair, received the available educational advantages of a family of wealth and distinction.

Early in life, William Cocke married[1] Sarah Maclin of Nottoway of Brunswick County, Virginia. Soon after their marriage they left their Virginia home and emigrated westward to Sinking Creek, east of Bristol. Sarah accompanied her husband as far as the Watauga Settlement, from whence he continued on an exploring expedition into the wilderness with Daniel Boone. After several months, the young wife, fearing her husband had died, returned to her parents' home in Virginia, where her son, John Cocke, was born in 1772. Upon William's return, he brought his family back from Virginia.

At the age of twenty-seven years, William Cocke was offered an office in the Army by Lord Dunmore, the Colonial Governor of Virginia, provided he would espouse the cause of the crown against the colonists.

He replied, "The King does not have money enough to buy me. The cause of the colonies is just. I will devote my life to it." Immediately after this offer, he became an officer in the provincial militia.

Soon after the great victory for the Patriots at King's Mountain they returned to their homes and immediately called a Convention to form an Independent State. If they were strong and brave enough to establish their homes in the Indian Country, to set up an Independent Government of their own, to march to King's Mountain and turn the tide of the Revolutionary war, they reasoned that they were strong enough to form an Independent State and join the Union of States.

1. A copy of their marriage certificate is in possession of Judge Philip Cocke of Asheville, North Carolina.

The Watauga Men felt that North Carolina was not giving them a square deal, by ceding this territory to the general government which automatically relieved that state of any responsibility toward the settlers west of the Mountains. That meant they would have to protect their own territory against the Indians and manage their own affairs in every way, as they received no protection from the general government at that time, it moved as slowly then, as now and would be from 12 to 24 months accepting the responsibility given to their keeping by our Mother State. Our pioneers were in a terrible plight which they probably termed, "Between the Devil and the Deep Blue Sea." They felt they MUST do something to protect their own interests, their homes and their future. John Sevier pled with them to wait upon the general government, but the sentiment was exceedingly strong for an organization into a new state. Thus out of economic necessity, the idea of the State of Frankland came into existence. Frankland meant free land. The plan of government for the new state was formed by William Cocke, a brilliant student of government. The Head of the New State of Frankland was John Sevier. The name was soon changed to Franklin—with the hope that the venerable Benjamin would lend his influence toward helping the new state into the union. The following were instrumental in forming this organization, David Campbell, Samuel Houston, John Tipton, John Ward, Robert Love, David Craig, James Montgomery, John Strain, Robert Allison, David Looney, John Blair, James White, Samuel Menece, John Gilliland, James Stuart, George Maxwell, Joseph Tipton, Peter Parkinson.

According to Ramsey's Annals, when the early settlers heard of North Carolina ceding the Over-Mountain Counties of North Carolina to the Federal Government they realized that for two years time there would be lawlessness, as Congress had two years in which to decide whether to accept these counties or not. When deputies were elected to the Convention to adopt safety measures, William Cocke was among those from Sullivan County. These deputies met on August 23, 1784, at Jonesboro. The Committee on Public Affairs included William Cocke. This Committee decided that the

Convention had a right to adopt and prescribe such regulations as the particular exigencies of the time and the public good may require; that one or more persons ought to be sent to represent our situation in the Congress of the United States, and this Convention has just right and authority to prescribe a regular mode for his support.

This report was adopted by the convention and the question was carried in the affirmative, "on motion by Mr. Cocke, whether for or against forming ourselves into a separate and distinct state, independent of the State of North Carolina, at this time."

David Campbell and William Cocke were the chosen representatives of the Over-Mountain people to the North Carolina House of Commons. An accident prevented Campbell's appearance before the Assembly, but William Cocke in an impressive address called the attention of his listeners to the perilous condition in which the Over-Mountain inhabitants had been placed by the Cession Act of 1784. He concluded this speech with these words:

If the Mother shall judge the expense of adhesion too heavy to be borne, let us remain as we are, and support ourselves by our own exertions: if otherwise, let the means of the continuance of our connection be supplied with the degree of liberality which will demonstrate seriousness on one hand and secure affection on the other.

But this eloquence failed of its purpose, for the North Carolina legislature had brought on a crisis and had prevented the development of the State of Franklin.[2]

In the establishment of the State of Franklin, Cocke opposed the Houston Constitution and favored the adoption of the North Carolina Constitution, as presented by John Sevier.

In August 1786, Indian Chiefs, Hanging Maw and Old Tassel, wrote from Chota Ford to William Cocke, Alexander Outlaw, Samuel Wear, Henry Conway and Thomas Ingles, denying that their warriors had killed white people on the Kentucky or the Cumberland Road. They said, "They are not my people that spilt blood, and spoiled the good talk a little. I am glad to see my brothers and hold them fast by hand."

William Cocke answered from Coytoy in part as follows:

You all well know the great man over the water, King George, once commanded us all and then we were all brothers, and that the great man, the King, got angry with us and came over the water, killed our men and burnt some of our houses which caused a war, and all your people helped the great man over the water, gave up this land to us, the white people, and was at peace with us. We tell you plainly, our great counsellors have sold us the lands on the North side of the Tennessee to the Cumberland Mountains and we intend to settle and live on it.

("One Hundred Years in the Cumberland Mountains," by Hogue *American Historical Magazine* 1899.)

William Cocke journeyed to Philadelphia with the memorial of Franklin asking for recognition as a State,[3] but failed in his purpose.

On February 25, 1790, about three months after North Carolina entered the Union, she ceded to the General Government all her Western lands, and on May 26, 1790, an Act for the Government of the Territory of the United States South of the River Ohio was passed. William Blount became the Governor. William Cocke was a member of the House of Representatives that met in Knoxville, August 25, 1794. He introduced into the Assembly on September 4, 1794, the bill incorporating Blount College, the first non-sectarian College chartered in the United States, now the University of Tennessee.

---

2. J. J. Burnett's SKETCHES OF PIONEER BAPTIST PREACHERS states:
To many people, "The Lost State of Franklin," seems as unreal and mysterious as that of the fabled Atlantis, the imaginary prehistoric continent, or island, supposed to have been engulfed by an earthquake and swallowed up in the Atlantic Ocean. But the State of Franklin, bounded on the East by Asheville, N. C., on the West by Knoxville, Tennessee, lying under the shadow of the Great Smokies had an actual existence for three years and from 1785 to 1787 (Some historians give dates of State of Franklin 1784-1788.), with legislative, executive and judicial departments. A respectable militia and a population of several thousand mountaineers in a remote wilderness, "infused with the principles which inspired the Revolution," with John Sevier, an ideal frontiersman as its Governor.
3. According to J. T. McGill, in TENNESSEE HISTORICAL MAGAZINE, the *"State of Frankland"* was a proposed state; the *"State of Franklin," the state actually organized.* Also, the boundaries of the proposed state were much more inclusive than those of the actual state.

As soon as the citizens of "The Territory South of the River Ohio" discovered they had sixty thousand whites, the requisite population for a state, Governor Blount called a convention which adopted a constitution and the Lost State of Franklin became the State of Tennessee.

William Cocke was appointed on the Committee to prepare a device for the Great Seal of Tennessee. He was the Representative from Hawkins County and he and William Blount became the First United States Senators from the new state of Tennessee. The following letter clearly indicates their political acumen.

Philad. June 2nd. 1796.

Sir

We have the honor to enclose you herewith a printed copy of the proceedings of Congress respecting the State of Tennessee whereby your excellency will be informed of the necessity of convening the Legislature by proclamation at an early day for revising the law respecting the Election of Representatives to Congress and to elect Senators.

It is generally believed that the State of Tennessee would have experienced no difficulty in the admission of her Senators if it had not been understood that George Washington would not again accept the Presidency and that the State would throw its weight into the Southern Scale against John Adams whom it seems the northern people mean to run at the approaching Election.

The Legislature will also have to take measures for lessening the number of Electors for President and Vice President as we are told four have been appointed and the State can have but three.

We have the honor to be very respectfully

Your Excellencys most obedient Servants

WM BLOUNT,
WM COCKE.

His Excellency
John Sevier Esq
Gov in and over the State
Of Tennessee.

While in the United States Senate William Cocke did not affiliate with Thomas Jefferson and Aaron Burr, but acted with the brilliant Alexander Hamilton, George Washington, John Marshall and always as an ardent friend of John Sevier, the Governor of Tennessee.

After long years in the Senate, he refused to stand for re-election, but was appointed judge of the circuit court of Tennessee.

When William Cocke left the State (for interesting reasons) he re-newed many friendships of his early days, among them, W. C. C. Claiborne, Governor of Mississippi at that time.

In 1814 Cocke was appointed by President Madison, to the Chickasaw Indians, and his youngest son, Stephen, was made his Secretary. He was also elected to the Mississippi Legislature, in 1822 from Monroe and

Lowndes Counties. Stephen Cocke became first chancellor of Mississippi in 1845.

At the age of sixty-five years, William Cocke volunteered and as a private, marched under Colonel John Williams against the Seminole Indians in Florida, in a company organized in East Tennessee 1817-18. The Augusta, Georgia Chronicle has this to say of him:

"Among those exemplary citizens it is with admiration that one recognizes the venerable Judge Cocke, serving as a private under his respected friend and fellow citizen, Colonel Williams!"

It is interesting to know that John Cocke, the oldest son of William Cocke was the Major General at the time William served as a private.

In Columbus, Mississippi, is found the grave of this great pioneer, patriot and statesman, on whose tomb are these well-chosen words.

Here, lie the remains of William Cocke, who died in Columbus, Mississippi on 22 of August 1828. The deceased passed an active, eventual life. Was Captain in command during the Revolutionary struggle of 1776 and was distinguished for his bravery, daring and intrepidty. One of the pioneers who first crossed the Alleghaney mountains into the wilderness of Kentucky with Daniel Boone, took an active part in the formation of the Franklin Government, afterward the State of Tennessee. Was the delegate from that free State to the United States Congress for a period of twelve years and afterwards one of the Circuit Judges. He served in the Legislature of Virginia, North Carolina, Tennessee and Mississippi. At the age of sixty-five years was a Volunteer in the war of 1812-13 and again distinguished himself for his personal courage. He parted this life in the eighty-first year of his age, universally lamented.

Entombed with him is his second wife, Kissiah, widow of Parrish Sims, who departed this life at Columbus, Mississippi in 1820 in her fifty-second year.[4]

Thus ends the story of the brilliant man for whom Cocke County was named and we next take up the history of the area in which we find our county is located. We had many, many names before we were known by our present one but it is not possible to include the story of such names in this volume they can be easily found in any history of Tennessee.

Our Place In The History Of The Country

Few states in the American Union can boast of a more colorful, more interesting, or more significant history than that of Tennessee, and yet, he who seeks to study and understand the past finds himself baffled by the lack of an adequate history of the state. (William C. Binkley)

If we are to understand the value or significance of our own past we must possess the perspective to enable us to see the larger setting in which that past belongs.

History has always inevitably rested on investigation, and successful investigation depends upon the availability of records. If there are no records, there can be no history. And thus the first phase of historical work in this country, was of necessity, concerned primarily with the collection of records.

4. Judge Philip Cocke of Asheville, a descendant of William Cocke, through his son Sterling, furnished the information and photograph of his illustrious ancestor.

The second phase of historical writing was that in which the historian was trying to tell the people what he thought they wanted to hear about their past. He selected from the records the glorious or dramatic aspects of the past in a literary style that would appeal to a wide audience. (George Bancroft was this type.)

The third phase in historical writing is the one in which the historian conceives his function as that of telling the whole truth and nothing but the truth about some part of our past regardless of whether or not the general public wants to hear it.

One important effect of this method upon the writing of history, should not be overlooked. Because it is not humanly possible for any individual to apply the standards of critical scholarship to all the enormous mass of records that have been accumulated throughout the years. The historian has abandoned the idea of comprehensive treatment of the whole field of American history and has turned to specialization.

History often mentions both the Upper and the Lower War Fords on the Big Pigeon River. The following information clearly establishes the proper location of each ford.

"The first Church in Cocke County was organized at the home of James English, at the Upper War Ford." . . . near the home of the late Edd Burnett.

"The Court of Pleas and Quarter Sessions first held at Lower War Ford and at the House of Adams." The present home of W. D. McSween near Stokely Brothers factory. It was long the home of "The McSween Sisters" and now belongs to W. D. McSween's son, Donald McSween.

Cocke County History

Throughout the pages of this book it will be noted that many family names are spelled more than one way. Since there is no set rule for spelling proper names we must suppose that each scribe spelled to suit his own fancy.

In the spring of 1769, William Bean, from Pittsylvania County, Virginia, settled on Boone's Creek a tributary of the Watauga River; this formed the nucleus of the famous Watauga Settlement, followed by the Carter's Valley (now Hawkins County) settlement, and in turn the Brown settlement in 1775, which embraced land on both sides of the Nolachucky River (Nolachunheh River) Civilization pushed onward until it culminated in the settlement of the valleys of the Big Pigeon and the French Broad Rivers. The Indians called these rivers by other names given elsewhere in this volume.

From Ramsey's Annals of Tennessee, the first settlement of Cocke County was in the spring of 1783 when James Gilleland cleared the cane from a tract of ground in the fork of the French Broad and Big Pigeon Rivers at the mouth of the latter, and cultivated it in corn, but no cabin was built at that time.

This was followed by the location and clearing of land adjoining William Coleman, where the first cabin was built on the bank of (the Agiqua) French Broad River and this became a nucleus of the settlement of the Big Pigeon and the French Broad Rivers. These first men and women were of the Primitive Baptist Faith.

— 16 —

A part of Cocke County was the first to be opened to settlement south of the French Broad River, while the County's territory was yet in North Carolina. According to Ramsey's Annals, in 1783, the General Assembly of North Carolina designated the boundaries of the Cherokee hunting grounds making the Holston, the French Broad and the Big Pigeon Rivers a part of these boundaries. The lands down to the Big Pigeon were thereupon open to entry and were granted to purchasers by North Carolina, while lands below the French Broad at its mouth and below the Big Pigeon were not. Any settlement or entry there were by this legislative Act not declared to be void.

North Carolina had never acquired from the Cherokee Indians that part which it opened to entry, but it anticipated doing so, and acted as if it had. Not until 1791, in the treaty at White's Fort (Knoxville) was the Indians' claim reinstated. Long before that, North Carolina grantees had moved in and settled.

In 1787, a "Petition addressed to the General Assembly, and transmitted by Governor John Sevier, from the Western Country, asking that an organized government be set up to protect the settlers from Indians and to protect land claims, and to create a separate state." It was signed by Daniel Leming and Peter Fine and others. (North Carolina State Records).

Soon after the organization of the Church, due to the hostile incursions of the Indians, the inhabitants of the valleys of the Big Pigeon and the French Broad Rivers were compelled to shut themselves up in various forts in the County, and the Church had to be unattended for a while. The Forts were, William Whitson's situated on Big Pigeon River near the Wilton Springs, on the Campbell McNabb farm and near the Denton Mill, later owned by William Wood and now the property of Esquire Sam Rains. The Abraham McKay Fort was on the French Broad River not far from the George Susong residence. The Huff Fort was on the French Broad River not far from the rock falls on the Del Rio Road opposite the Holland farm and not far from the Frank Huff home. This fort stood until very recent years when it was burned. Wood's Fort stood on the French Broad near the J. H. Clark home.

The women and children of these settlements remained in these forts from January 1788 to September 1788 and again until 1789. There were constant Indian raids during these years.

These settlements were protected by the bravery of Colonel William Lillard, Lieutenant Colonel Abraham McKay, Major Peter Fine, Captain William Jobe, Captain John Fine, and Captain John McNabb, members of the Primitive Baptist Church. (W. J. McSween Papers)

On June 29, 1793, Cloyd's plantation on the south side of the Nolachucky River was the scene of an Indian raid, in which two children were killed and another dangerously wounded. Mrs. Cloyd was carried a half mile from the home and put to death, her body being horribly mangled. Colonel John McNabb with ninety-one volunteers assembled at the Big Pigeon and followed the trail of the Indians across the mountains to the Tuckasegee, where they killed two Indians. Other red men escaped because a member of the McNabb force thoughtlessly set up a war-hoop. (Judge Sam Cole Wiliams)

Is is claimed by some that the above name should be Loyd and not Cloyd. We are positive that the Loyd family lived in Cocke County from its earliest days to the present century, and that they were large land-owners adjoining the Humberd lands in Cocke County. J. W. Kyker and Dixie Denton Doak are descendants of the Loyd family.

As early as 1789, John Ellison, then of the Cocke County part of Greene County, represented the latter county in the House of Commons of North Carolina, and sat in the North Carolina Convention, which ratified the Federal Constitution of 1789.

Between Del Rio and Parrottsville is a small marker bearing the following inscription; John Ellason, died Feb. 13, 1846, aged 77 years . . . exactly 57 years after the first John sat in the House of Commons, probably he was the honored gentleman. Thus we come to appreciate the value of an authentic record because it forever removes our doubts about time, places, names and various activities.

In 1795 a communication addressed to Governor William Blount was submitted to the Territorial Legislature. It was from Vanderhorst of South Carolina and proposed that by joint action of that State and the Southwest Territory, a road be laid out and improved to run up the French Broad River and Little Pigeon into Buncombe County, N. C., thence on into South Carolina. This was the first effort to establish such a road.

It was needed to accommodate the passage of horses and livestock into South Carolina for sale there by residents in the lower part of the Territory. South Carolina was solicitous that this traffic be increased, since sellers of live-stock would invest the proceeds of sales in merchandise of various kinds in cities and towns of South Carolina. John Sevier and George Doherty were named by the Greene County Commission to examine and report on the project. (Williams)

In the census taken in 1795, Jefferson County, which then included Cocke County had a total of 7,840, including 1,706 free white males sixteen years of age and upwards. There were 776 slaves and 3,021 free white females. (Ramsey)

When Tennessee first became a State on June the 1, 1796, George Doherty was Senator and Alexander Outlaw and Adam Peck the Representatives for Jefferson County, of which Cocke County was then a part. In 1797 James Roddy was Senator and Adam Peck and William Lillard the Representatives. This was the Session that created Cocke County.

On October the 9, 1797, Jefferson County was divided and the County of Cocke laid off. It is thought that William Lillard, long a close friend to Cocke and the first Representative suggested that the new County be named for William Cocke.[5] Lillard represented the county for eighteen years. The longest record of any Representative.

---

5. Cocke County was created by an act passed October 9, 1797:
AN ACT TO DIVIDE THE COUNTY OF JEFFERSON INTO TWO SEPARATE AND DISTINCT COUNTIES
Whereas the citizens of Jefferson County, living on the waters of the French Broad and Big Pigeon above the mouth of Chucky River are so situated by rivers an mountains, that they cannot, with convenience, attend courts, general musters, or elections in said County; and it being made to appear to this General Assembly that the bounds required by the Constitution may be had in each County.
SECTION I. Be it enacted by General Assembly of the State of Tennessee that from and after the passing of this act the said County, shall be divided by a line to begin on the North Carolina boundary with this State on the South side of French Broad River, one mile from said River, thence down said River, one mile distance from the same to where it intersects the Greene County line;

Old Newport was located in the hollow and on the bank of the French Broad by reason of compromise. Upon the establishment of Cocke County by Act of the Tennessee General Assembly of October 9, 1797, there was a difference of opinion as to the location of the county seat. The first session of the Court of Pleas and Quarter Sessions was held on the site of the present town of Newport, on the south bank of the Big Pigeon, on the fourth Monday, in November, 1797, at the house of Daniel Adams, which was located in the garden, immediately west of the later dwelling house of the McSween sisters, and still later the property of W. D. McSween, at War Ford.

The same act creating the county provided that Henry Ragan, William Jobe, John Calfee, Peter Fine, John Keener, Reps Jones and John Mc-

---

thence with said line to Nolichucky River, a small distance below Captain William White's House; thence down the river to French Broad, leaving all the islands to Jeerson County; thence down the River French Broad in same manner, to the end of said River opposite Colonel Parmenas Taylor's and from thence a direct line to the top of English Mountain, within one mile of Sevier County line; thence parallel with that line to the uppermost House on Cozby's Creek, and from thence an Easterly line, to a point on the North Carolina Boundary line, as to leave 625 square miles in Jefferson County, and from thence with the said boundary line to the beginning, which bounds, so described shall, from and after the passage of this Act, be a separate and distinct County known by the name of Cocke.

SECTION II. Be it enacted that Henry Ragan, William Jobe, John Calfee, Peter Fine, John Keene, Reps Jones and John Glochien are hereby appointed commissioners, and authorized to lay off and appoint a place the most convenient in said County for the purpose of erecting a Court House, prison and stocks.

On January 2, 1799, an Act was passed to add part of Greene County to the County of Cocke.

SECTION I. Be it enacted by the General Assembly of the State of Tennessee, that from and after the passage of this Act, the line that divides the County of Greene from the County of Cocke shall begin at the corner of Greene and Jefferson Counties, on Nolichucky River, at the end of Bay's mountain, from thence up Nolichucky river to the mouth of Oven Creek, from thence a direct line to Major Gragg's plantation, so as to leave his plantation in Greene County. From thence a direct line to the Painted Rocks on French Broad River, below Warm Springs; from thence south to the Cocke County line, and all that part lying south of the said line shall be a part of Cocke County.

SECTION II. Be it enacted, that the Sheriff of Greene County shall have the same power and lawful authority to collect and receive all his arrearages of taxes and executions in that part of Cocke County that was formerly part of Greene County, in the same manner as if this Act had never been passed.

(Page 168, Chapter 13, Tennessee Acts, 1792-1803)

AN ACT TO APPOINT A COMMISSIONER TO RUN THE LINE BETWEEN THE COUNTIES OF GREENE AND COCKE

(Chapter 53, page 290. Passed October 29, 1801.)

SECTION I. Be it enacted by the General Assembly of the State of Tennessee, that David Stuart, be, and is hereby appointed a commissioner to run the line between the counties of Greene and Cocke agreeably to an act, entitled. "An Act to add a part of Greene County to the County of Cocke," passed at Knoxville the second day of January 1799.

SECTION II. Be it enacted that David Stuart shall receive "2 per day for running, and Thomas Holland $1 per day for marking said line, to be paid by the treasurer of Cocke County and their receipts shall be sufficient vouchers in the hands of the treasurer in the settlement of his accounts."

SECTION IV. Be it enacted, that the said David Stuart shall take an oath before some justice of the peace in Greene County that he will justly and truly run the aforesaid line accordingly to law.

Present Courthouse, two between these have burned.

Second Courthouse in Cocke County and remains of first hotel, probably the
original courthouse of hewn logs.

Glochlen should be commissioners and lay off and appoint a place, the most convenient in the county for prison and stocks, and to contract for the building of the same. After many heated meetings, John Gilleland donated the land upon which the houses of Old Newport used to stand, the capital of Cocke County was accordingly located there.

The preamble of an Act passed October 23, 1799, is as follows:

Whereas, John Gilleland having obligated himself to said commissioners to appropriate fifty acres of land aforesaid, for the purpose of laying out the town aforesaid, and having conveyed to the commissioners the said fifty acres of land for the purpose of erecting a court house, a prison and stocks and laying out a town to consist of half acre lots with proper street and alleys, and the commissioners having laid out the said fifty acres of land shall continue to be a town agreeable to the plan of said commissioners, by the name of Newport, and that the deed for said land shall be good and valid in law and equity for the purpose for which the said John Gilleland conveyed the same.

On the first of November, 1803, an Act was passed providing as follows: "That George H. Hynds, Augustine Jenkins and Jonathan Fine should be appointed as additional commissioners and that said commissioners, or a majority of them, shall make and execute deeds for conveying lots as heretofore by law laid out in said town." (McSween)

On October 3, 1805, an Act was passed appointing Isaac Leonard, Abraham McCoy (McKay) and John Inman as commissioners "to settle with the persons heretofore appointed commissioners in the County of Cocke to contract for the public and buildings and to regulate the town of Newport."

The first public building erected, the courthouse, was made of hewn logs, and located in the center of the street, southwest of where the courthouse later stood. (A Negro church now stands there.) The jail was an improvised log structure, back of the church building.

At that time, homicide was divided into murder and manslaughter, the former punishable by death, the latter when allowed by clergy, punishable by branding on such part of the body as the court might designate. Sometimes, the branding was on the forehead, but usually in the hand, the letter "M," the initial for manslaughter. The culprit was placed in the stocks, the letter "M" heated and placed and held there until the sheriff could repeat three times, the words, "God save the State."

An Act passed December 3, 1797, punished for the simple larceny of goods to the value of ten dollars, for the first offense, to receive not more than thirty-nine lashes on the bare back and to be imprisoned not more than twelve months. The punishment was hanging for the second offense.

If a person were convicted for stealing a horse, he was sentenced to receive the same number of lashes, to be imprisoned not less than six months and not more than two years, to sit in the pillory two hours on three different days and be branded with the letters "H.T." for Horse Thief. (McSween)

The stocks consisted of a frame of timber with holes in which the ankles and wrists were confined, the body placed in a sitting position and the limbs stretched to their limit. The pillory consisted of a frame of timber with holes for the head and wrists, placed on an upright beam, the head and wrists placed in the holes, the body and limbs stretched to their limit in standing posture. The whipping post was an upright beam securely placed in the ground. The culprit was stripped to the waist, the legs and arms securely fastened around the post and the lashes applied to the bare back.

Public days were always for inflicting the punishment at the whipping post, in order that the culprit might be humiliated. The stocks, pillory and whipping post for Cocke County were erected on the flat above and back of the ledge of limestone rock behind the old courthouse.

Prior to the Civil War there had been only one person executed for a capital offense in Cocke County, and that was a Negro woman convicted of killing her grandchild. She was executed north· of the whipping post on top of the hill, in a small sink, on the left hand side of the road leading from the site of the old courthouse in the direction of Fork Farm. (McSween). She merely lost him in French Broad River as she was swimming across it—with him on her back—rather than see him sold into slavery, as she had just witnessed.

A number of years after the organization of the State, officers elected by popular vote were presidential electors, members to Congress, and member of the General Assembly. The popular vote was not cast by civil districts, as now, but the entire voting population assembled at the county seat and cast their votes. All other officers of both State and County were appointed by either the legislature, the governor or the courts.

The justices of the peace were appointed by the legislature and when so appointed and qualified, they became justices of the peace and also justices of the County Court of Pleas and Quarter Sessions. This court appointed its own clerk, sheriff and register. In Cocke County, the Court of Pleas and Quarter Sessions was held on the fourth Monday in February, May, August, and November. The Court was to try all cases of law where the debt, damage, or cause of action, exceeded a certain sum of dollars, all action of trespass in ejectment, dower, and partition, and of trespass all cases of petit larcenies, assaults, batteries, criminal trespass, breaches of the peace, and other inferior misdemeanors. This court also had jurisdiction of the probate of wills and of the estates of idiots and lunatics, and appellate jurisdiction from the judgment of the justice of the peace.

The first Court of Pleas and Quarter Sessions was held at the house of Daniel Adams of Lower War Ford, and afterwards held in Newport. The justices were: John McNabb, Abednego Inman, Abraham McCoy (McKay), William Lillard, David Stuart, Samuel Jack, Peter Fine, William Jobe and James Lea. William Garrett was appointed clerk and remained its clerk for thirty years. The rules are similar as to those that govern our present day circuit court. (McSween)

On May 30, 1807, the number of commissioners for Old Newport was increased by the appointment of Henry Stephen, John Rice, John Gilleland, Blackman Jones, Roswell B. Kellogg, and William Garrett.

On October 19, 1812, by Act of General Assembly, Augustine Jenkins, Henry Stephen, William Garrett, Thomas Mitchell, Peter Fine, and William Jobe, were appointed commissioners for the town. This Act, in effect, made Newport a municipal incorporation, as Section 2 vested them with full power to pass all such ordinances, regulations and by-laws, not inconsistent with the laws and the Constitution of the State, as they might deem expedient and proper for the good government of the town. On November 14, 1817, Alexander Smith, Samuel Jenkins, Lewis Anderson, and John Fine were appointed additional commissioners. Section 3 of the Act provided that any monies in the county treasury might be appropriated to the building or repairing of the old courthouse.

In 1818, the First Congressional District of Tennessee was represented in Congress by John Rhea, and he procured an Act pensioning Revolutionary Soldiers. Under this Act, Cocke County had two pensioners, Jesse Bryant and Abraham Hembree. (McSween)

On October 12, 1819, the Legislature passed an Act, conferring upon the county court the power to levy a tax to build a new courthouse. This included twenty-five cents for each hundred acres of land; fifty cents for each slave between the ages of twelve and fifty years; five dollars on each retail store, ten dollars on each peddler and hawker and fifty cents for each four-wheeled pleasure carriage.

Since Old Newport never attained much importance except as the seat of justice, it never had more than one hundred fifty inhabitants.

The first houses in Old Newport were rude structures, of hewn logs, and there were no substantial buildings until about 1825. One of the largest buildings first erected in the town was used as a hotel, or an ordinary, and was kept by one Milligan. At that time, no one could run an ordinary without permission from the Court of Pleas and Quarter Sessions, and the keepers were allowed to charge no more than rates fixed by the court. The following were the tavern rates for 1797, the year that Cocke County came into existence:

It is ordered that they shall have the price following, Virginia money: for breakfast, one shilling; for dinner, one shilling and three pence; for supper, nine shillings; for rum, half pint, six shillings; for stable the night with forage, one shilling; for pasture, six shillings for 24 hours; for lodging, the night, for brandy, the half pint, eight shillings.

Whiskey and all other ardent spirits were sold at all ordinaries, and also by all merchants. Charlie Lewis was one of the first persons to sell goods in Old Newport. Lewis Anderson ran a blacksmith shop; Debby Milligan, the first barroom. The merchants of a later date were William C. Roadman, Sr., John and George Stuart, Smith and Siler, Rankin and Pulliam, James W. Rankin, and William McSween.

In 1831, the First Congressional District of Tennessee was represented in Congress by John Blair, who was instrumental in passing a law pensioning the soldiers of the Continental Army, which applied to a number of citizens of Cocke County: William Boydston, age 81; William Bragg, age 61 (?); Joseph Burke, age 72; Thomas Bibee, age 100; John Carmichael, age 77; William Coleman, age 72; John Henry, age 81; William Lufty, age 72; James Miliken, age 80; Samuel Martin, age 89; Thomas Palmer, age 73; James Potter, age 75; Lewis Sawyers, age 87; William Smallwood, age 74; Allen Serrett, age 71; Barlett Sisk, age 75; Peter Wise, age 81; Samuel Yates, age 77. The heirs of Alexander Smart, John Heath and Robert Jackson also drew pensions on account of services rendered by their fathers. (McSween)

The Mother of Ray County, Missouri

Cocke County in its early days became the "Mother" of Ray County, Missouri, organized in 1821, the same year the State of Missouri was taken from the Missouri Territory. Ray County had two settlements, both branches of the Missouri River: Crooked River and Fishing River, both made up mainly of East Tennessee people.

Fishing River Township, of which the O'Dell family was a component part, was organized in 1821, along with the new State and County. Earlier in 1818, Jacob Tarwater, a German from Tennessee, with his sons, Lewis, and Samuel Tarwater, chose Fishing River for his location. The next year, they were joined by the O'Dells, Clevengers, John Turner and wife Jane, John Hutchins and family, Mrs. Lucy Woods, Reuben Riggs and family, the Hightowers, Roes (Rowes), Rowlands and Van Sickles.

The O'Dell family made a large contingent, led by Isaac O'Dell, Sr., then a man seventy years old, born in New York, who came down through Pennsylvania into the Shenandoah Valley and on into Greene County and thence to Cocke County, Tennessee, from whence he removed to the West. Isaac (1778-1855), Caleb, Simon, and Nehemiah O'Dell and a large group of grandchildren, fifty in number, accompanying him were Solomon O'Dell of Cocke County, the son of Samuel of Cosby Creek, Simon O'Dell. One of the sons moved to Texas where many of Cocke County's early citizens went, to Denton County, which was established after Texas Independence, in 1845.

Richard Clevenger, with wife, Sarah Wood, born in New Jersey, traveled through Virginia and on into Cocke County about the beginning of 1800 and went on West with Jesse and Samuel Clevenger. John Clevenger, a natural leader, was born in 1798. While living in Cocke County, he with his brother, constructed a boat and traveled in it down the Big Pigeon to the French Broad River, thence onward on the Tennessee to the Ohio which carried them on to the Mississippi until they came to the mouth of the Missouri River, thence across the State to Ray County (Rhea) to the Excelsior Springs Community, where Reverend William Turnridge preached to the East Tennessee settlement. John Clevenger became justice of the peace and representative from Ray County in the Missouri Legislature. He was a charter member of the New Garden Baptist Church, and when necessity arose he could preach for the congregation. He was also sheriff and was still living in 1881.

The East Tennessee group held the tenets of the Separatist Baptist Church in their souls and the church formed for worship, in 1824, the group meeting previously in the home of Jacob Tarwater. The charter was granted to them by the Fishing River Association in 1823 from Mt. Pleasant Baptist Association farther East in Howard County, Missouri, which had its development under the leadership of William Lillard of Cocke County, Tennessee, and Madison County, Kentucky.

The new church in Ray County, called New Garden, was a few miles east of Excelsior Springs, Missouri. It is still active after a continuous history of 126 years (1950). Over its portals is the inscription "New Garden, 1824, Church, Primitive Baptist."

The first ministers were: James William and William Turnridge. Charter members were: J. Fletcher, Caleb O'Dell, Smith Hutchins, John Turner, Nehemiah O'Dell, John Hutchins, John Clevenger, Mrs. Elizabeth

Fletcher, Mrs. Rachel O'Dell, Mrs. Elizabeth Hutchins, Mrs. Jane Turner, Mrs. Mary O'Dell, Mrs. Patsy Turnridge, Mrs. Nancy Chapman, and Mrs. Lucy Woods. The first building was rudely constructed of logs but in 1852 a new one was erected.

The Civil War rent the New Garden congregation with the dissension within its fold. Most of the O'Dells were anti-slavery. The New Garden Church developed into two meetings, the pro-slavery one meeting on one Sunday and the anti-slavery on the other. The Pastor through these trying times was Isaac O'Dell, who had married Eleanor Riggs. He owned two slaves, a man and his wife. Years later this breach in the church was healed.

The graves in the New Garden churchyard are well marked. The oldest dates are those of Isaac O'Dell and wife, Nancy, though no doubt Isaac, Sr., and wife Alice were buried there.

The O'Dells in Missouri contributed five preachers: four Baptists and one Presbyterian: Isaac (1811-1890); Aaron (1837-1875); William Riggs (1852-1924), grandson of Isaac O'Dell; Caleb (1863-), great-grandson of Nehemiah O'Dell; Arthur Lee O'Dell (1877-), descendant of both Isaac and Caleb O'Dell, (June, 1942) pastor of House of Hope Presbyterian Church, St. Paul, Minnesota. Retired and lives in Hollywood, Calif., 1950.

A member of another Cocke County family furnished a pastor for the New Garden Church, Allen Sisk, born in 1833 near the Pleasant Grove Baptist Church. With his brother, he went to Missouri in 1853, where he married Nancy A. Smart. He united with the New Garden Church in 1860 and began the study for the ministry under Isaac O'Dell. He was ordained in 1866. He was endowed with a splendid singing voice, often putting the Scriptures into a singing metrical verse. Our present Allen Sisk was named for him.

The First Church in Cocke County, organized in the home of James English on Big Pigeon has lighted a torch that continues to burn, and says Ann, wife of Arthur Lee O'Dell, "From there they have journeyed[2] across our blessed land carrying the connecting link of family tie and name. Others of the O'Dell family have still held their torch aloft, on the old familiar ground, for the name still abides in Cocke County."

According to a *History of Saline County*, Missouri, published in 1881, there was a regular Cocke County settlement there known as Gwinntown, named for the three Gwinn brothers, Absolam, Bartholomew, and William, members of the migration of 1814 and 1816. Not all of the Cocke County migrants lived in this particular village. Mr. Dougherty believes that the McKissicks of Saline County went there from Cocke County.

The Democratic Party In Cocke County

In the early years of Cocke County, the majority of the citizens were adherents of the Anti-Federalist Party, which became the Democratic Party in Jackson's time. Until the Civil War period, it was the majority party in the County.

The Civil War made the Democratic Party the minority party and that it has been ever since. Among the reasons for this change were that the majority of the men joined the Confederate Army, due to sentiment and the fact that men had to travel across the State and also Kentucky into Ohio, to enlist, a hazardous journey. Three companies went into the Confederate Army. The first was organized with Thomas Gorman, Captain. When he was wounded A. L. Mims became Captain. The second company was organized by Edd Allen, who was made Captain. The third company was organized by Captain Wash. Out of the probably two thousand men who went away, not more than thirty from each company returned. Many of these did not remain in the County, due to animosities engendered between the two factions.

While the normal vote of the Democratic Party has been less than half that of the Republican Party, the Democrats have been able to elect one of their own number to various county offices at various times. Malcolm McNabb was a delegate of both Cocke and Sevier Counties to the Constitutional Convention in Nashville, 1871. James Netherton served as sheriff of the County in the early 70's. Flint Ray served two terms as sheriff at a rather recent period. John F. Stanberry, Sr. served as circuit court clerk in the 80's. Abe B. Weaver, at the same time, served as register of deeds. Allen Stokely served several terms as trustee of the County. Four times since the Civil War period, Democrats have represented the County in the General Assembly or Legislature, at Nashville; W. J. McSween, in the 80's; Robert B. Hickey, in 1890; and Geter Ray, in 1934. (Data by John Weaver.) James A. T. Wood served in 1941.

The Republican Party in Cocke County

Although in its early history, the Democratic or Jackson Party, was usually successful in Cocke County, the large majority of its citizens adhered to the Federal or Union Cause whenever the slavery question became the absorbing issue. Because slave labor was not profitable in the mountainous County, less than twenty per cent of the families of Cocke County owned slaves.

When a vote was taken concerning the calling of a convention to consider going out of the Union, Cocke County adhered to the Union cause. There were 510 votes in favor of secession and 1185 against it. More than double the number of soldiers joined the Union Army. Even when the second vote was taken, Cocke County stayed with the Union.

Since the Civil War, the Republican Party has been the major party in Cocke County, and in most cases has elected all county officials. The Republican Party in Cocke County in one presidential election gave more votes to the Grand Old Party than the states of Georgia, Alabama and Mississippi combined. (Information from Jacob L. Shults.)

Captain Edd Allen organized the first infantry that went out of Cocke County. Major Thomas Gorman, founder of Newport, decided that no Southern gentleman should walk and so he organized the fifth Tennessee Cavalry and after a few days drilling, decided he was too old to lead them. He called young Aaron Mims, a senior in Emory and Henry College to take command. Later he organized in Nashville the Edgefield School, now occupied by the East End Methodist Church of Nashville.

George W. Gorman of Cocke County was Captain of Company I, second infantry, East Tennessee Cavalry; George W. Webb of Jefferson County, his First Lieutenant; and his brother Andrew Jackson Webb,

Second Lieutenant. At the death of Captain Gorman, George W. Webb became Captain, thus being the youngest one in the Army, at twenty-one years of age.

It is said that Mary McSween was so in love with James Faubian that she took part of her mother's dress and made a flag for him. He and Sam Jack walked from Cocke County with one horse between them. Colonel Jack returned, but Colonel Faubian remained to become one of the builders of Texas.

Daniel Ellis, James Lane, A. C. Fondren, James Kinser, and David Fry were pilots for Union men in Cocke County. Robert Allen Ragan lived longer than any of the other pilots and lived a life that was unequaled for danger and thrills. His "Escape from East Tennessee to the Federal Lines," relates these experiences.

Soon after the advent of the railway into Cocke County, the people became divided over the location of the County seat. Those who lived in and around Parrottsville wanted to form a new County out of part of Greene and of Cocke Counties and have Parrotsville for the county seat. Dr. Bell and James La Rue prepared a petition to be circulated to secure money for a Courthouse and other town buildings. They first called upon Ezra Bible asking him to start the project with a generous donation. They were much chagrined when Ezra Bible replied, "I will give you twenty-five cents." They went directly toward Bridgeport to call upon Thomas O'Dell, who offered a beautiful site on his farm, on a hill just west of the Murray residence. When they came to Clifton, Major Thomas Gorman offered the present site.

After many months of discussion and viewing of sites, the people voted on the location, sometime during the 70's. This vote favored Clifton.

The first courthouse in Clifton (now Newport) was erected on the corner where the present Merchant and Planters Bank now stands. It burned along with several other buildings near it on the night of December 31, 1876. D. A. Mims, Colonel John F. Stanberry, W. H. Penland (county court clerk), worked all night helping M. A. Driskill, trustee, make his report for the County Court, which met the next day. Before they left, they cleaned out the stove and "laid the fire" for the next morning. They placed the wood ashes in a wooden box and went home for an hour or two of sleep. The ashes probably set the fire.

William McSween, father of the late W. J. McSween, had his law office next to the courthouse. It also burned to the ground and an adjoining store building, belonging to Dr. C. D. Fairfield. One day, a stranger appeared at the home of Major Baer, who had two sons and two daughters, the former named Bee and Will. Bee Baer escorted the man who was searching for a good doctor, to Dr. Fairfield. The visitor asked Dr. Fairfield if Dr. Hooper was a good doctor, whereupon he replied, "He says he is a good doctor."

After the courthouse burned, court was held in a shoeshop near the Mill for some time. This arrangement proved unsatisfactory, and the Courts were moved back to the banks of the French Broad. Again, the people were not pleased, and the Courts returned to Clifton, where they were held in a building owned by James A. Denton, located on the site of Ray Minnis' Drug Store, opposite the first location in Clifton. To attend the court sessions in Clifton, the people living in the northern part of the County had to "ford two rivers," and once again the Courts went to Newport. So anxious were the people of Clifton and the south side of the County to settle this moving, they subscribed enough money to build a wooden bridge over Big Pigeon River. C. F. Boyer suggested that the best way to please Parrottsville citizens was to build a bridge between the two rivers!

The Court let the bridge contract to John Cameron who lived in what is now the O'Dell House, built soon after 1814 and purchased from Alexander Stuart for ten thousand dollars and paid for, in notes, held by the O'Dells against various citizens.

Cocke County had no bridges until this one was constructed by Cameron in 1880 or 81, except a covered bridge at, or near, DeWitt Mill. at Bridgeport, which washed away in the great flood of 1867. The new bridge, replacing the old East Port one, cost $140,000 for right of way and improvements.

In 1873, the following was written of the towns in Cocke County:

There are four towns in the county—Newport, Parrottsville, Sweetwater and Clifton, the first having a population of eight hundred, the second of three hundred, the third of one hundred fifty, and Clifton about two hundred. Newport is an old town and has not improved any. Parrottsville is in the midst of good lands and has a fine population. Clifton is immediately upon the Cincinnati, Cumberland Gap and Charleston Railroad and is a flourishing place. More business, perhaps, is done there than by all the other places put together. The principal part of the trade of the County concentrates there.

It is interesting to know that "in the early days each County was to have, whether needed or not, a Sheriff, a Trustee, a Register, a Coroner, a Ranger, a set of Constables and a batch of Justices of the Peace."

The Magic of Cocke County Names

HISTORY—The various names given to Cocke County and its environs proclaim the colorful history of this particular area of Tennessee.

"The Wilderness Country West of the Alleghenies" applied to the entire state of Tennessee. At the time, Tennessee belonged to the wilderness country and it was thought to be included in Fincastle County, Virginia, and made up the present counties of Cocke, Greene, Hamblen, Hawkins, Jefferson and Sullivan.

"The Cherokee Country" was one of its most appropriate names and was applied to the entire eastern border of our present state which included Cocke County.

When Burke County, North Carolina, extended her border to the Mississippi River, Cocke County was a part of it.

In 1785, Caswell County, North Carolina, was its name, honoring Governor Richard Caswell. Joseph Hamilton became Clerk of the Court; George Doherty, Colonel of Militia; and John Zanhaun (Seahorn), Entry-Taker. It did not long remain Caswell County but soon became Greene County, in the Washington District of North Carolina. The other counties in the district were Hawkins, Sullivan, and Washington. This was the first area in the country to honor George Washington by taking his name. The remainder of Tennessee was known as Mero District.

An effort was made to name our state Frankland, meaning free land, each settler being entitled to a certain number of acres for himself, his wife receiving a certain number and one hundred acres for each child. When the time came for making the state name official, the name of Franklin, meaning free men, was chosen. It is surmised that the name was changed to Franklin in an effort to secure the support and influence of Benjamin Franklin toward statehood and admittance into the Union. This idea failed of fruition and the idea of a State of Franklin was given up.

After this episode, this country was known as "The Territory South of the River Ohio," and included eleven counties, Blount, Greene, Davidson, Hawkins, Jefferson, Knox, Sevier, Sullivan, Sumner, Tennessee, and Washington. It was known as Jefferson County as early as 1792. The country in general was known as "The Tennessee Country."

Henry Timberlake, a young British officer, visited the Cherokee Indians in 1761, and was the first to spell Tennessee as it is written today. The Indians spelled it "Tenasee" and gave the name to their most important town and two rivers, Big and Little Tennessee. Its meaning is unknown although some claim it means "the river with the big bend."

The pioneers residing in the Territory South of the River Ohio did not fancy remaining a territory. Three times they had made an effort toward statehood—Watauga, Cumberland, and "The Lost State of Franklin." Finally, the Territorial Legislature passed a law giving the territory the privilege of enumerating the citizenship. About 66,649 free people were listed and 10,613 slaves. Sixty thousand people would have been a sufficient number for statehood. The Constitutional Convention convened in Knoxville, January 11, 1796.

The Territorial Legislature remained in session twenty-seven days. Andrew Jackson suggested the name of Tennessee County for the new state. This was accepted and Tennessee County was then abolished and its area divided into parts known as Montgomery and Robertson counties.

On June 1, 1796, the new state of Tennessee was admitted into the Union and this area was then known as Jefferson County, William Blount and William Cocke became the first U. S. Senators.

The people of the Wilderness Country were early attached to William Cocke and John Clifton who were among the first pioneers to visit this particular area. William Cocke's first visit is said to have been made during the early 1770's when he was trying to find a suitable place to establish his home.

Immediately after the Revolutionary War, he was accompanied on a journey through what is now Cocke County, by another Revolutionary soldier, John Clifton, who became ill at War Ford and was compelled to remain there for a long while. The people who lived there found Clifton an agreeable, honorable gentleman. They loved him and wanted to show their appreciation of his fine qualities by "doing him an honor." They felt the same sense of obligation toward William Cocke who had taken such a prominent part in the formation of the State of Franklin and who had endeavored in every way to befriend the early pioneers and who had become their first United States Senator. Consequently, on October 9, 1797, when a new county was formed from Jefferson it was named for William Cocke, and the War Ford was known as Clifton, in honor of John Clifton. Clifton, it remained until a half century had passed when an effort was made to change the name of the County as follows.

By the Act of 1846, Chapter 123, it was provided that an election be held to decide upon a removal of the county seat, and "At the same time and place, for the purpose of changing the name of said county, from that of 'Cocke' to 'Union,' and if a majority of all qualified voters in said county shall be in favor of the name of 'Union,' then the name of Cocke County shall be known by the name of Union County."

The requirement that a majority of all qualified voters, and not of those voting, probably saved the name of Cocke County. The name of "Union" was a few years later given to a county adjoining Knox, Anderson, Campbell, Claiborne, and Grainger counties, a sort of "Union" of those counties it appears on the map. Many claim that "Union" would have been a misnomer for Cocke County as our citizenship then, as well as now, seldom agree on issues.

Many historians regret that many of the beautiful Indian names given to our rivers, ridges, mountains, caves, springs, valleys, and our eternal hills have been changed. The quaint and homemade names our early pioneers added to this list of Indian ones were also appropriate and should have been allowed to remain.

The origin of the word "Cherokee' is not known for a certainty. It came from the word "Tsalagi" which was later changed to "Chalaque" by the Portuguese. The French called it Cheraqui and the English thought it was "Cherokee" as early as 1708. Some claim it comes from the word

The Rev. J. M. Walters Bridge over the French Broad River

"Chera," meaning "Fire." Some tribes spoke of the Cherokees as Uplanders or Mountaineers. (Col. W. W. Stringfield article in the *Annals of Haywood County*.)

The most mysterious of these names is that of "The Great Smokies" which is as mystic as the blue veil of silvery mist that floats above them. The Cherokees tell that the name is "Giukoustee" which is Indian for "Smoke."

The first written reference to the name, Great Smoky, found by the author, is in an Act passed by the General Assembly of the State of North Carolina, in 1789. On maps of 1795 to 1930, the section of mountains between the Big Pigeon and French Broad Rivers, twenty-five bear no name; fifteen of the forty maps vary from Iron and Great Iron to Smoky and Great Smoky Mountains.

On February 6, 1930, the Congress of the United States settled the name as "The Great Smoky Mountains" and converted most of this highland region into a National Park. Some 17,170 acres of the park area lie within the borders of Cocke County. On February 2, 1938, Congress passed a bill authorizing the appropriation of sufficient funds with which to complete the purchase of the park, the remaining land to be purchased lying on the Tennessee side of the mountains. This was soon accomplished and the park dedicated just before the 1940 presidential election.

RIVERS—The French Broad River, known to the Cherokees as the Agiqua, Indian for "Broad" and also sometimes called Tah-kee-os-kee, Indian for "Racing waters," seems to have outwitted the historians. Some claim it was called by its present name because the French people claimed it as a tributary of the Tennessee, eventually flowing into the Ohio, and that they just added the "French" to the already "Broad" of the Indians, and thus French Broad.

Dr. Edmund C. Burnett, national historian of Del Rio, Tennessee, and of Washington, D. C., says there is no documentary evidence in support of the French claim to the region being the original idea of the name. He further states that William French once told him that he had seen deeds in which the river was called "John French's Broad River."

Others claim that hunters in the early days camped near the source of the French Broad River and in order to distinguish between the Broad rivers in South Carolina and in North Carolina referred to the stream in Cocke County as French Broad.

Charles Lanman refers in his letter (number 16) to the name as follows, "The origin of the name is obscure. It is often explained as a prefix to distinguish the river, east of the mountains, in the possession of the English. Another explanation is that 'French' was the name of a famous hunter."

Judge Samuel Cole Williams, Vice-President of the Tennessee Historical Society, believes that all waters flowing westward from the Blue Ridge Mountains were called French waters. For a while, the English almost conceded the western streams to the French.

Writing about 1770, James Adair, in his history of the American Indians, wrote of Herbert's spring on the western slope of the mountain: "It was natural for strangers to quench their thirst and have it to say they had drunk of the French Waters."

Many maps that ante-date John French give the name French Broad to the stream.

The cliffs near War Ford.

Big Pigeon River from the D. A. Mims Bridge back of Depot.

The Big Pigeon was known to the Indians as the Wayeh River, Indian for "beautiful maiden." Evidently the name, Big Pigeon, appealed more to their imagination than the other name, for it signifies rapidity. The big wild pigeon often lived along this particular stream. Its flight was so rapid, about a mile per minute, and the river likewise, the Indians thought that it "flew like a Big Pigeon."[1]

The Nolachucky, sometimes called Nollichucky, is another Indian name, and it means "dangerous stream," or "crooked waters." It is often shortened to Chucky River.

SPRINGS—Among the County's many fine springs, the best known are: Ailey, on the old stage coach road near Wilsonville; Stephens, on the Greeneville road, near Parrottsville; Carson Springs, the best known of all; Ellis, near the Old Inn in Parrottsville; Gum, on the Morristown highway, near the Dutch Bottoms; the unusual Huff spring, at Bridgeport, and almost in the middle of the French Broad River; Morel (Morrell) on the Morel farm, south of Newport. These springs have constantly been favorite picnic grounds from the Indian days to the present. Neddy's spring is often referred to by poets.

The O'Dell spring on the original homestead grounds of Benjamin and Mary McKay O'Dell is now owned by the fifth generation. Thomas O'Dell, Sr., a grandson, fourth generation, often related the story of the Indian battle fought near the spring. Arrowheads of flint are still found there. Several Indian braves are buried in the cemetery on the bluff nearby. This spring furnished water for an ancient distillery the government located in this area. For many years a tannery was operated just below the spring. Pioneers from North Carolina journeyed along this route from Bridgeport to the first Newport, the most noted of whom was "A. Johnson, Tailor," on his way to Greeneville. The old roadway ran along side the spring. Others claim he did not pass this way.

Powder springs are located in the Houston Valley community. The blue clay from this area is easily moulded into interesting designs by the school children, then baked and kept a long while for their amusement.

Rock springs received their name from the great abundance of rocks piled about them by the slaves of Major William Wilson, for whom Wilsonville was named. These springs were often visited because of their location on the old stage-coach road, for which the Wilson Inn was the stage terminal. The springs are north of the Old Inn.

The Samples springs are on the old Carson Springs road. One is on the present Edgar Sellers property and the other at Iris-Dell, home of the author. Two brothers settled the land around these springs.

Sulphur springs, once a health resort, is near Newport just off the Knoxville highway southwest of the Gospel Tabernacle. Yellow springs are near the Yellow Springs mountains in the Bridgeport area and were once patronized each summer by many families.

---

1. The flight of the passenger pigeon is a tragic story in American history (Information from Edwin C. Dixon, *Christian Observer*, September 23, 1942.). The width of a flying flock as observed by Audubon and Wilson was three miles, and the number was estimated at two billions. The last recorded great slaughter of these birds was in 1876, when one and one half millions were killed and sent from one state alone. In 1910, zoological authorities offered one thousand dollars for just one pair of these big wild pigeons, but none were found.

Wilton springs, on the original McNabb lands and not far from Denton Mills, have an interesting history. Fort Whitson, one of the three early forts, was located near the largest spring. Grannie Wilhite (Wilhoit), who lived in the fort related the following to the mother of John Weaver.

Two sons of the O'Dell family who lived on Cosby Creek, went across Big Pigeon in search of their cows at eventide. The lads failed to return. Their bodies were found at the foot of the hill where they had been scalped by the Indians. The next time the cows failed to appear at milking time, no one would volunteer to go after them. They were grazing near the mill and it was not necessary to cross the river. As soon as the twilight had merged into darkness, a cowbell was heard tinkling down the river-bank direction, just as the O'Dell boys had heard it and innocently followed the sound. One of the men left the fort with his gun. Quietly he slipped along some distance toward the "milk-gap" when he noticed the bell had ceased to tinkle. Being familiar with where the cows would be standing, he fired his gun in that direction. Next morning he found a dead Indian by the spring.

Wilton Springs was long a post office in the early days of the county's history. It continued to be such as late as 1867. Malcolm McNabb was the postmaster.

The Swaggerty spring, now known as the Wilds spring is not far from the Faubion spring now owned by Noga Susong Sheffey. In the same part of the county is the Nease spring. Probably the most visited of any of the springs in the Parrottsville section of the county is the Hale spring, which is in Parrottsville on the land originally entered by John Parrott shortly after the close of the Revolutionary War. Jacob Parrott built and operated the Tavern in the village, known as the Hale House, which stood until a few years ago. The Ellison spring was also known in early days as the Yett spring because a family of that name owned the property and built the house that later belonged to T. S. Ellison. On the Harned property not very far from Parrottsville are several good springs. One has been cared for by Bob Smith, who has had water forced from it into his home. The other springs on this place are known as the Swatzell and Ottinger springs. Near Harned's Chapel is a fine sulphur spring.

The Sisk spring and the one on the Isaac Stuart place form Sinking Creek, which has a surface flow of about four miles, sinking near the Good Hope Church. When the underground channel is closed, the water "backs up" and forms lakes, which beautify the Sisk and Tilman Blazer farms.

One of the largest springs in the Cosby section is known as Cold spring, and belongs to the Creed Denton family.

The best-known of Cocke County's springs has been known as a summer resort for more than one hundred years, and for hundreds of years before the white people so used Carson Springs, the Indians frequented that particular area of our mountain section. Many arrow-heads and other Indian relics have been found up and down the little valley below the springs and along the foot of the mountains. One of the springs contains lithia; the other, sulphur. The strong mineral waters of these springs are particularly effective in driving malaria out of the body, a fact that brought early settlers to the springs during the summer seasons.

The Carson family came to Cocke County from Jackson County, N. C., in the early 1800's. Two of the daughters of the family came along, one was Esther Carson. They settled in the Carson Springs area, hence the name.

Information given by Mrs. Bonnie Queen Roberts, whose father, Theodore Queen was a great grandson of the family.

Eleven acres of land, including the lower spring, were entered by the ancestor of Jennie St. Clair Carson, who later married a Felkner. Carson secured a grant for this land from Governor McMinn in 1816. Ex-Governor Ben W. Hooper, who now owns the lower spring, has the original grant, and his home and extensive orchards and gardens are near the spring.

In the early days, people flocked to this health resort. The Peterson Hotel was operated by C. T. Peterson and wife, Mattie B. Peterson, Massachusetts Yankees, who "sat" a sumptuous table. The coming of the automobile brought ruin to these summer resort hotels. The C C C boys made a trail from the old hotel to the fire tower on the top of English Mountain, a distance of six miles, beyond Camp Carson.

BRANCHES AND CREEKS—The early settlers always referred to small streams and brooks as branches or creeks. A branch was smaller than a creek, and Cocke County abounds in both. Caney Branch, between Newport and Greeneville, was named for the tremendous growth of canes along its banks. Grannie's Branch, three miles north of Newport, was named for a noted mid-wife and dancer, Grannie Gregg. She liked to smoke a clay pipe with a river cane stem of great length, and she lived to be very old.[2]

Grannie's Branch, that flows by the Harmony Grover schoolhouse, south of Del Rio, was named for Sallie Hayes Jones, wife of Russell Jones. She also smoked a clay pipe, wore lace caps, attended church at Beckie's Temple, and always carried her shoes almost to church. When she came to this stream of clear water she would wash her feet, put on her shoes and continue on her way to worship.

Nigger Branch is also located in the Del Rio area. It was so named because many colored men who worked by the day for John H. Stokely saved their money and purchased the land along this stream and there built their homes.

The best known of all these streams is Raven's Branch. Some claim it was named for Chief Raven, one of the highly-respected Cherokee chiefs who passed through the gap of the mountain, known as Raven's Gap, to fish in the French Broad River. On this mountain, also known as Raven's, the water divides, the western stream emptying into Lamb's Fork, the eastern one emptying into Laurel Fork of Big Creek. The Gulf is known as Lamb's Gulf and contains about eight to ten thousand acres. John Ford was offered this property for a gun and a horse. Ford refused the offer from A. Peck, saying, "What would I do with a bear den like that?" The Champion Paper and Fibre Company paid about one

2. Information by Pat Cureton, Sr., who remembered her.

hundred twenty thousand dollars for it. The mountain folk say, "That is where John Ford dropped his candy."

Esquire David L. Holt, born and reared in this section, claimed that this stream was named for Black Raven, an Indian brave who was killed in the gap of the mountain and his body buried near the headwaters of Raven's Branch.

"The name 'Raven' was used as a war-title and every tribe had a brave given the name for bravery in battle," writes Mrs. Charles Larew, authority on Indian legends. The most outstanding of the various "Ravens" was the Cherokee one who escaped from the removal in 1838 and settled in North Carolina. He was Savanukah, nephew of the great warrior, Oconostota, and generally recognized as the logical one to succeed his uncle as War Chief.[3]

Big Creek, in the Del Rio section, was named by the Indians. "Heap Big Creek" Cedar Creek, was so-called because of the abundant growth of cedars in that part of the county near the Greene County line.

J. W. D. Stokley said that Cosby Creek was named for Colonel Cosby, a Revolutionary soldier, who claimed government land along its banks and settled near where the Cosby Allen family established their residence. Clay Creek and Clear Creek received their names from their natural environment. Crippled Creek in the Hartford section is said to have been named by musical mountaineers who enjoyed banjo and guitar playing and the famous tune of "Cripple Creek."[4]

Crying Creek, tradition claims, was named for two devoted brothers who once went hunting along its course. Near the creek, one accidentally shot the other. His loud crying over the dead body of his brother was pathetic, and he frequently returned to the spot to grieve.

English Creek is thought to have been named for James English, who lived near the mouth of it and in whose home the first church in Cocke County was organized. This creek was known as Indian Creek in the early days.

Fine's Creek was known as Crystal Creek at first, then Twelve Mile Creek, because of its length of twelve miles. It was named for Vinet Fine was was buried in the creek to await removal later, but his body was never recovered.

Grassy Fork, of Lamb's Fork, of Big Creek, received its name, according to J. W. D. Stokely, when the old thirteenth district was formed from the first civil district.[5] The center of the district was the point where the Grassy Fork connects with the Lamb's Fork of Big Creek. This land is level and grassy. Later it became a voting place, the only one of the creeks so honored.

Indian Camp Creek was named because it was a favorite camping place for the Indians when they raided the white settlements. Many Indian relics have been found in this vicinity.

John's Creek and Tom's Creek were named for the two Holland brothers. Each time they went hunting one would follow one creek and the other would take a nearby creek and follow it to the source, which

---

3. John P. Brown, *Old Frontiers*, page 11.
4. There are other versions for this name.
5. Mr. Burnett is confident that the name long antedated creation of old thirteenth.

was one and the same spring. A mountain range divided the streams, which furnished sufficient hunting range for the boys.

Lamb's Fork and Laurel Fork of Big Creek were probably named because of the Lamb's Gulf and the Laurel thickets along the course of the stream. Long Creek was so-called for its length and Muddy Creek for its tendency to stay muddy or to become muddy.

Oven Creek was so-named for the natural bridge over it; in fact, there are two of these bridges. One is known as the Big Oven; the other, the Little Oven.

The Big Oven is of limestone and is about fifty feet across, approximately one hundred feet long, with a ceiling some ten or fifteen feet high over Oven Creek. Except in rainy seasons, this stream, disappears about two hundred yards above the bridge and reappears about the same distance below it on what appears to have been its regular course. Near the roadway over the bridge, one can walk down into the stream-bed and continue into the tunnel-like cavity one finds there for a distance of three hundred yards or more. From the ceiling of the tunnel is an opening to the surface like a chimney, known as The Roaring Hole, which is said to have been an ideal location for moonshiners of the early days. They used the chimney as a sort of elevator through which they drew their jugs by means of a rope secreted nearby. From this natural tunnel many other tunnels lead off in various directions. The second natural bridge over Oven Creek is much smaller than the one traversed by the highway. Only a farm road passes over it. It is a favorite fishing spot for the small boys around Harned's Chapel. The beautiful limestone rock formations along this creek extend beyond the Greene County line.

Rock Creek took its name from the numerous rocks in its bed and along its banks.

Rowdy Creek was the favorite haunt for many rowdy boys and men who gathered along its banks for ridiculous "carryings on." Fighting Creek was treated accordingly. Sinking Creek disappears and reappears in many places before it reaches its destination. Slate Creek is probably named for the slate rock through which it flows and for the knobs of slate rock in that section of the county.

Sweet-water Creek is now known as Edwina Creek. Some claim that the first Wood who rode into the Edwina area was so delighted with the sweet, cool water that he named it Sweet-water, but no one seems to know why it was changed to Edwina. Tobe Creek was named for a famous bear-hunter, Tobias Phillips, known as Tobe.

How Wolf Creek obtained its name seems to be shrouded in mystery. In 1859, it became a post office. Some claim the name was chosen because this region was the range for numerous packs of wolves. H. H. Gouchenour claims the Wolf tribe of Indians gave it their name. Hugh Allen insists it was named for the De Wolf family, who married into the O'Dell family in the early days.[6] Wolf Creek became Allendale during the sixties but the Allen family had it changed to its original name.

MOUNTAINS, GAPS, GROVES, HOLLOWS, KNOBS, VALLEYS—Chestnut Mountain is said to have been named on account of the abundance of chestnut trees on its sides. A Civil War story is told of two Hopkins brothers,

---

6. Wolf and his wife with daughter, Fannie, born in 1811, came from Virginia, and settled on the Creek later named for them. After his death, the widow married Henry O'Dell, son of William, II.

one from each army. The Confederate brother overtook the one in Union army, whose horse had fallen as though dead. The Confederate soldier dismounted and gave his horse to his brother of the Union army, so that he could escape. After a few hours, the horse revived.

English Mountain, according to John Weaver, was named for the man who lived near it and hunted on its slopes. One day he heard a turkey gobbler on the side of the mountain. Straightway he took his gun and his turkey caller (a small goose quill with which he could imitate the turkey-hen), and hid himself back of a log, imitated the turkey-hen, and watched for the gobbler until he came within range of his gun. English shot with true aim and a young Indian fell dead. English Mountain is also reported to be unique by geologists. Saltpeter caves and mineral springs abound there.

Mount Guyot (pronounced Gee-o), 6,621 feet above sea level, the highest of the County peaks was named for Arnold Guyot (1807-1884), a native of Switzerland. He was educated in Swiss and German colleges. He became a colleague of Agassiz in 1839 as Professor of Natural History and Geography at the College of Neuchatel, Switzerland. Guyot emigrated to America in 1846 and settled in Cambridge, Massachusetts. In 1854, he was appointed to the chair of Geology and Physical Geography at Princeton, a position he held until his death in 1884. He founded the museum at Princeton, in which are many specimens from his private collection. Under the auspices of the Smithsonian Institute, he perfected plans for a national system of meterological observations. In 1866-1874, he prepared a series of geographical maps and geographies, for which he received a medal in Vienna. Mount Guyot was given his name by S. B. Buckley before 1859.

Although Clingman's Dome[7] and Mount Le Conte[8] are not in Cocke County, they are the two other peaks, that with Mount Guyot, form what is known as a triangular mass.

In 1856, 1858, 1859, and 1860, Arnold Guyot made explorations in the Southern Applachian mountains for the U. S. Coast Survey. His

---

7. General Thomas Lanier Clingman, 1812-1897, graduated from the University of North Carolina in 1832, became a lawyer and a member of the North Carolina Legislature, 1836-1840. Was member of United States Congress, 1843-1858. Was appointed United States Senator, 1858. During the Civil War held the rank of Brigadier General in the Confederate Army. After the war he engaged in mining and scientific pursuits. He operated mica mines, made known the existence of diamonds, rubies and corundum in North Carolina. He spent much time in mountains because he loved them. Clingman's Dome was known to the Indians as "the home of the little people" and the four-footed beasts went there to heal their hurts. The Indian name of this peak was Kuwahi.

8. Mount Le Conte was named for Joseph Le Conte, 1823-1901. A physician and naturalist, he was born in Liberty County, Georgia. He graduated from Franklin College in 1841 and from the College of Physicians and Surgeons, New York, 1845. Following graduation, Dr. Le Conte practiced medicine in Macon, Georgia. In 1850, he became a pupil of Louis Agassiz at Cambridge, and accompanied him on many scientific expeditions. For a long while, Joseph Le Conte taught successfully at Oglethorpe University, Franklin College, University of Georgia and the University of South Carolina. During the Civil War, he was a chemist in the Confederate medical laboratory and later in the nitre and mining bureau at Columbia. From 1869 until his death, he held the chair of geology in the University of Southern California. He made many excursions into the mountains for the purpose of furthering his scientific experiments. Mount Le Conte is 6,593 feet high.

notes on these explorations and his map of the region came to light a few years ago and were published in the *North Carolina Historical Review*, July, 1938.

At one point in his notes he says:[9]

"When approaching the French Broad the chain is considerably depressed; but between this and the Big Pigeon it soon rises again to 4,703, in the High-Bluff, above Warm springs, and 4,336 feet in Walnut Mt., which as far as the Man (Max) Patch Peak (4,700) form the dividing ridge, together with many parallel ones of less elevation, and without general name."

At another point he has this statement:

"The New Found Mts. connect with the State Line Ridge near Max Patch Peak—4,700 feet—and terminate at Hominy Creek Gap."[10]

Hall's Top, one of the most easily reached peaks was named for the Hall family who once owned the Fork Farm, sold it for a rifle and a pony or mule and entered land on this mountain top and made a Hall settlement.[11] Rebeccah Hall (Freeman) Glenn claims the story is not true.

Jeff's Knob, at Del Rio, is named for Jefferson Burnett.

Max Patch, a mountain airport, is named for a family of McMahan's who once owned the peak. It was also owned by Mack Fox who cleared the part of it now in grass. Others claim it was known as Max Patch before Mack Fox owned it. Perhaps a government chronicler recorded the name of Mack's Patch and spelled it in the shortest way "Max."

Purty Holler Gap, in the Cosby section, proclaims the ability of the observing pioneer to recognize beauty of landscape when he saw it.

Big Snow Bird Mountain and Little Snow Bird Mountain received their names because the snow-birds[12] enjoyed nesting on these particular peaks. Some claim these birds visit the two peaks each winter because of a small snow-berry that grows in profusion there.

Snake-Den Mountain is what its name implies. Joseph Campbell discovered a snake-den on this particular mountain. He found so many rattlesnakes there that no one dared to visit the mountain for years afterwards. As late as 1932, a park ranger killed fourteen "rattlers," there and as many escaped.

Sulphur Spring Mountain, sometimes known as Yellow Springs Mountain, is crossed by a good road constructed by Frank Huff, Sr.

Sweet-tater Mountain and Tater Mountain, in the Del Rio area, were named by one of the Burnetts, all of whom had a fine sense of humor. Sweet-tater mountain is a little more pointed at the summit than the other.

Paint Rock was also an Indian name and was given to the place known as Unaka, which is Indian for "white man." It is said there is some substance near this area, which was used by the Indians for paint.

Sunset Gap means just that, and is the location of one of the best schools in the County, on the site given by Mrs. Elizabeth Williams, who wanted her grandchildren to receive instruction in the three R's.

---

9. Data furnished by Doctor Burnett.
10. After the word "Man" in the first passage, the editor has *sic* but brackets *Max* and cites the second passage.
11. See Chapter "Natural Setting and Resources."
12. Sometimes called snowflake, snow bunting, or junco.

Barker's Gap in the "Gulf" (Lamb's Gulf) near G. W. Freeman's store is named for John Barker, Civil War soldier, who came to the gulf to recuperate after his discharge. After ten days here he "headed for home" but was found with his boots, hat and coat gone, his discharge burned except for the word "discharge" and part of his name. A Mrs. Henderson and three Ford women hauled him to the gap on a sled, dug his grave, and buried him with bark around the quilts as a coffin.

Other picturesque names, many given by Swan Burnett, are Lemon's Gap, Houston Valley, the Slate Knobs, Blue Hill, Paris Hill, Irish Cut, Pig-Trot, Frog Pond, Blue Mill, Lundy's Lane, Scratch Ankle, Wash, Dutch Bottoms, Irish Bottoms.

Paris Hill, a long hill leading from Old Town to Clifton, was named for the Paris family who came from Virginia and evidently owned much of the land between the two towns. Great trees surrounded the home which once belonged to the father of George McClanahan, later to J. W. Kyker. Julian Paris and wife had several children: three girls— O'Dell, Julia and Rowena and four sons—Lon, Hugh,[13] Rufus, and Julian.

White Rock, considered one of the County's most sublime peaks, is of a sandstone formation resembling granite and gleams in the sunlight for many miles; hence its name. It was first known as Sharp Point and later Sharp's Peak, for at one place it has an area of less than twenty square feet. There are two springs on the top, one known as "the Bear Wash" and used as a bathing pool for birds and animals.[14] The peak is now Mt. Camerer, for one of the park officials.

The many groves in Cocke County played a part in the educational and religious development of the County.

Many of the citizens worshipped at Allen's Grove (named for the Allen family). It is located between Edwina and Cosby.

Bruner's Grover was named for Reverend Bruner who held a revival there a long time ago. He was from Monroe County and connected with Hiwassee College. In this grove was first erected a log house in the forks of the road below the present one. Known as "the Meadow School House," it was used for both church and school. Later a box-house was erected farther up the hill, where the Reverend Bruner preached. After this house was destroyed by fire, a new one was erected in 1870, and another one in 1907.

At the beginning of the present century, a new Methodist Episcopal Church was erected at this grove. The Odd Fellow Lodge helped with the finances and thus shared the building. The site was given by John Holt, the grandfather of Lennie Thomas Marshall.[15]

---

13. Mrs. Jane Thomas O'Dell told this story: Hugh Paris had difficulty getting the large Murry family to pass the pie to him. He had worked years for them. He was so fond of pie that the family decided to play a joke on him. As usual, he finished his dinner first and began by asking, "Mr. Murry please pass me the puie." (pronounced *pooie*.) Then he went on down the line calling on Harriet, George, Addie, Tom, Mrs. Murry, Lou, Kate, Nannie and finally back to Mr. Murry. Getting out of patience he raised his voice saying, "Harriet. darn you, pass me the puie." The family roared with laughter, but he got his pie.

14. See also chapter. "Natural Setting and Resources."

15. For a number of years the Methodist Church provided two additional teachers here.

Caton's Grove is another Methodist center and in the Cosby area. It was named for the Caton family and is the location of two school buildings, a church and a cemetery. For a number of years, the Methodist Church provided two teachers here in addition to the county teachers.

Fowler's Grove was named for Elijah Fowler during the seventies. Jobe Bible, a Lutheran, David Driskill, a Baptist, Moses Mims, a Southern Methodist, and Bird Palmer, a Northern Methodist, gave the land where the church stands as a union place of worship. Palmer later became a Southern Methodist. The building was used until 1905 for both school and church. At this time, R. P. Driskill gave a tract of land on the Creek Bank where a schoolhouse was erected. It was named Sycamore Dell by Rhoda Netherton. Clay Vinson was the first teacher. A few years later, A. M. Dawson of Parrottsville gave land across the stream for a new schoolhouse and the name went back to the original one of Fowler's Grove.[16]

Many of the County names begin with "B." Bat Harbor is said to have been so-named because it was a favorite hiding place for bats. Bison may have been named for the early America buffalo. Bogart must have been a family name. Boomer is said to have been named for a little squirrel of a brownish red color. It is odd that it is the size of a chipmunk and called "boomer" which is the Australian name for the male kangaroo.

Blufton is so-called from the picturesque bluffs near its location.

Bridgeport was named for the first bridge built in Cocke County. It was covered and placed at the old DeWitt Mill some distance above the present Major James T. Huff Bridge. It was built by David and John Stokely and washed away during the Civil War. Bridgeport became a post office in 1853, the third one established in Cocke County. Looking north from Bridgeport one sees Broad-Axe Hill, a field cleared in the shape of a broad axe, and edged with trees and small shrubs, since the oldest inhabitants can remember.

Briar Thicket was named by John Lovell, who had a retail store at Bybee. George Larkin, a revenue officer in 1885 had warrants for some of the men and asked Lovell about them. Lovell replied, "If we have anyone engaged in that sort of business you might find them in the briar thicket somewhere." Burnett and Bybee place names were for families who lived at each place. Burnett was for years known as Huckleberry; Bybee, as Lickskillet. Bybee was named for Tippecanoe Bibee (of Indian descent), known as "Uncle Tip."

VILLAGES—COSBY—There is a considerable difference of opinion as to the origin of the name Cosby. The English class of the Cocke County High School made a study of place names a few years ago and decided that it was named for Jonathan Cosby, who, they claimed, was the first government distiller in the Eastern part of Tennessee.

Ramsey's Annals states that Cosby was named for General Cosby (meaning the creek), as there was no white settlement in that section until after the first part of the last century. John Weaver claims that not until after 1807 or thereabouts was it possible for land to be entered beyond the Big Pigeon on the west side. Ramsey also makes mention of a Dr. John Cosby, whether he was the General or not is not clear. Inas-

---

16. According to Mrs. Lennie Thomas Marshall.

much as there are Cosby Creek, upper and Lower Cosby, the honors might be divided among the three Cosby's mentioned in history as having lived in this part of the wilderness country.

The author thinks of Cosby as having been named for Dr. James Cozby, one of the first doctors in this part of the country. He was a bosom friend of John Sevier and served with him for years in protecting the early settlers from the Indians. Dr. Cozby was a fearless Indian fighter and was the one who so skillfully threw the courtroom at Morganton, North Carolina, into confusion, when in his quick, alert, manner, he boldly walked in to rescue John Sevier, on trial for treason. It is said that the moment Sevier "caught Cozby's eye" or "Cozby caught Sevier's eye," Cozby merely turned his face toward the window where he had previously placed Sevier's trusty horse with the bridle carelessly thrown over its neck. By the time Dr. Cozby got the attention of the Judge by asking a simple question, Sevier was in the saddle and on his way to the over-mountain country.[17]

Dr. Cozby had a quick, energetic step and his manner of speech had the same characteristics. He was a member of the old stone Lebanon Church four and one half miles East of Knoxville. Rev. Samuel Carrick was his pastor. John Sevier, grave and reverential often sat in Dr. Cozby's pew.

Cosby, like Tennessee, is divided into three parts. Upper, Lower and Middle Cosby. Cosby Creek flows through all the different sections.

The Upper section, in the early days of the County, was much larger than the other sections. Half of it is now in the Great Smoky Mountains National Park. It was called the "UPPER" because in those days it was divided into two Civil Districts and the Upper district was known as "The Republican Gibraltar" of Cocke County. There was not even one Democratic voter living in this part of the section. Later a few moved in from North Carolina. It was a very popular saying in those days when election time came. . . . "As goes Cosby, so goes the County," and it was generally true.

For many years the Cosby Academy, owned and maintained by the Baptist Church, (but now owned by the County) has been one of the best schools in the county. It is attractive and well kept with dormitories and teachers cottage nearby.

Various Churches, both Baptist and Methodist dot this area which is more than fourteen miles in length and embraces many communities.

C C C 1462 was situated in the Cosby Section near the Valentine Nurseries. It was an attractive camp, well planned and beautifully planted.

Highway number 75 traverses the full length of this rugged, picturesque region and from it many wonderful views of the different mountain peaks can be enjoyed. Mount Guyot, the highest peak in the Great

---

17. Dr. James Cozby was a member of the old stone Lebanon Church, four and one-half miles East of Knoxville. Reverend Samuel Carrick was his pastor. John Sevier, grave and reverent, often sat in the Doctor's pew and worshipped with him. The story of how the Indians tried to attack Dr. Cozby's home and how he outwitted them proves his intelligence, his wisdom, and fearlessness. Almost single-handed he saved his home and family. Next morning, he went to see his nearest neighbors, found them murdered, except one little girl still breathing, whom he took home and treated until she recovered. Later, she became the mother of one of the leading families (Casteel) of Knoxville.

Jacob L. Shults

The Nolichucky River, northern boundary of Cocke County.

Smokies is easily distinguished from many points on this highway.

One of the most interesting characters living along the Highway, is Uncle Jakie Shults, known to the newspapers as RAZORBACK. He has the distinction of holding several different records. Besides being the UGLIEST MAN IN THE COUNTY, he is the only known person now living in the State who can boast the fact his father and himself have lived under the administration of every Governor of Tennessee from John Sevier to Governor Browning. Mr. Shults' father was Jacob W. Shults who was born in 1801.

On the head waters of Cosby Creek is the Elbert Carver apple orchard which is one of the finest in the County. It embraces several acres. The apples are mostly Starks Golden Delicious. It is now a part of the Park area.

Clevenger's Cross Roads, on the Knoxville Highway, was named for the Clevenger family. Zeb Clevenger was for many years a member of the County Court. His sons are Mack, Shell, and Walter.

CLIFTON—Clifton on the Big Pigeon later became the present Newport, Tennessee. Many people have thought that the name was chosen because of the mile of wonderful cliffs along the river at this point, but such is an error. Clifton was named for John Clifton, a beloved pioneer. The author believes that if it had been named for the cliffs it would have been spelled Cliffton. When the present railroad was being constructed, the Gorman Brothers gave the land for the present depot, which was known as Gorman's Depot for a long while, but the village remained Clifton.

On December 24, 1867, the Cincinnati, Cumberland Gap and Charleston Railroad was completed to Clifton at Gorman's Depot. It became such a great "drawing card," Newport, on the French Broad River, began to yearn to move itself over to Clifton on the Big Pigeon River. The question became the basis of "a long legal controversy," pending the settlement of which, the seat of justice vibrated between the two places."[18]

Stuart represented Newport (now Old Town) and Baer, the present Newport, then Clifton. Alex Stuart was the father of Mrs. Bessie T. Justus; Baer, the grandfather of Walter and Mayme Baer, formerly of Newport, but now of Knoxville.

The inhabitants of the then Newport devised a plan to extend the limits of their town of Newport on the French Broad River to include the town of Clifton on the Big Pigeon in order to secure a new jail for themselves. The old one was destroyed by fire during the Civil War.

At the July term of County Court in 1866, a committee of five persons was appointed to make this extension of Newport's limits. In 1867, the County Court appointed inspectors to hold an election to determine whether Newport's corporate limits should include Clifton. The purpose of this "evasion" was to get the jail and courthouse moved without having a county election, a requirement of the Constitution of Tennessee. Those people in Newport on the French Broad endeavored to hold the county seat at its original location. Those living in Clifton on the Big Pigeon were anxious to have the county seat in their midst.

18. Ex-Governor Ben W. Hooper published an excellent article in the *Newport Times*, November 23, 1938, which began with a Supreme Court decison rendered in 1874—"Alex Stuart et al vs. H. H. Baer et al."

As a result, the affair was carried to the Supreme Court. The Bill mentioned how on February 17, 1879, the defendants fraudulently procured an Act of Legislature extending the corporate limits of Newport to include Clifton for the purpose of removing the county seat; that Newport had no corporate limits, because no organization under this Act was ever had; that Newport and Clifton were two small villages two miles apart, separated by a river.

Complainants charge that all these Acts were done for the fraudulent purpose of effecting the removal of the Court House by indirect means and not in the mode prescribed by law."

The Bill enjoined the County Officers and the Chancellor, Honorable H. S. Smith, and Circuit Judge, Honorable J. H. Randolph, from removing records from Newport to Clifton, and from building Court House and other public buildings at Clifton.

The Supreme Court held that the various efforts to extend the corporate limits of Newport to include Clifton were illegal and utterly null and void and that the Act of the Legislature referred to was manifestly intended to effect a removal of the County Seat without holding the proper election.

After about seventeen years of confusion, the decision was finally in favor of Clifton. A courthouse was built under the supervision of C. F. Boyer, Joseph Morrell, and J. H. Fagala, completed in 1886, at a cost of ten thousand dollars. The people of Clifton "never dreamed" they would have to give up their beautiful name when the decision was finally made in their favor, but the population of Newport on the French Broad, being greater, the citizenry were naturally able to superimpose the name of Newport on Clifton. The only remains of the name is the residential section of Clifton Heights, a street that runs along the north bank of Big Pigeon, leading directly to the summit of the cliffs.

During the controversy, other names were suggested to settle the arguments peaceably, Gorman being one of the most popular. Gorman's Eddy was sometimes used in referring to the town, a whirlpool in the river suggesting the Eddy idea. The railway ran along on the Gorman land for quite a distance.[19]

The author has been told[20] that the O'Dell farm near Bridgeport lacked only one vote being chosen for the site of Newport when it was moved from its original location.

NEWPORT—In a biography of General William Conner of West Tennessee it is stated that one of the daughters, Sallie, of his great grandfather, John O'Conner (shortened to Conner), an emigrant from Ireland to Virginia, in 1745, married a man by the name of Newport, who removed to East Tennessee and settled at a town named for him. In January, 1946, a soldier named Newport published an interesting article in *Plain Talk* saying that his ancestors lived in Cocke County.

John O'Conner and eight sons were in the Revolutionary War, and all were Baptists. It is also stated that William Conner, Sallie's brother. settled in East Tennessee. Descendants of the Newports later settled in Lauderdale County, Tennessee.[21]

19. Gorman brothers story in "First Families of Cocke County."
20. Thomas O'Dell, Sr., owner of farm, and his wife, Mrs. Jane Thomas O'Dell.
21. *Prominent Tennesseans.*

In the early days, the name of Newport was written "New Port," the name given, no doubt, in anticipation that in time it would be the head of navigation and a "port" on the French Broad River. It was described in the *Tennessee Gazeteer* of 1834.

New Port was established in 1799 on the land of John Gilleland, on the bank of the French Broad River above the mouth of Big Pigeon. In 1833 it contained 150 inhabitants, two lawyers, two doctors, two clergymen, two churches, one school, two taverns, two stores, three blacksmiths, one cabinet maker, one tanner, one wagon maker, two hatters, two tailors, two shoe-makers, and two saddlers.

DEL RIO is in one of the most beautiful sections of Cocke County. It is twelve miles East of Newport on the Southern Railway, and but a "stone's throw" off the Dixie Highway or Federal Highway number 75. The French Broad River runs parallel with the Railway and the Highway at this point. Big Creek empties into the River at Del Rio and the place was known as Big Creek for many years. However, with the coming of the railway the freight shipments became often confused with those that were intended for Big Creek, North Carolina and for this reason it was thought advisable to change the name. The Post Office was known as Big Creek before the Station name was changed. It is said that the first suggestion for the name Del Rio for the station was given by the young doctor of that village at that time, Dr. Frank P. Robinson, who died Jan. 1946 in Greeneville. The citizens, led by Marve Stokely, Swann Burnett and J. J. Burnett, held a kind of "get-to-gether" meeting and agreed among themselves that it didn't seem right to have the station known as Del Rio and the P. O. as Big Creek and since the word Del Rio was supposed to mean, of the river, or by the river, they might as well choose the same for the P. O. and so they petitioned the Post Office authorities to change the name of the Post Office to that of the Station and thus the village became Del Rio.[22] Texas has a Del Rio but I am sure it has no more interesting history than that of our own Del Rio, by the French Broad River, in the Tennessee Mountains. I am sure that Del Rio, Texas is not to be compared with Del Rio, Tennessee in beauty. Before Del Rio was known as Big Creek the citizens got their mail addressed Parrottsville. It was also once known as Lucetta, later as Jonesville (Jonestown).

The altitude of the village is 1139.8 feet, it is surrounded by many mountain peaks that have interesting names that mean something to the residents of this particular section. Three fourths of a mile East of the station is Jeff's Knob. This beautiful peak was named for a beloved citizen, Jefferson Burnett. Stokely's Peak is for the Stokelys. The Rile knob, the Ball knob, Betty Kizzie knob each has its own interesting story. Kizzie Patch, the home of Kissiah Woody, who lived to be 110 years of age but died from excessive use of tobacco and coffee.

The Pond Ridge, on the top of which is a pond, that for ages has furnished the water for the cattle and sheep of the hills surrounding this particular one. Tater Hill, west of Del Rio, back of which the sun sets in the winter time, is not far from Sweet-tater Hill. Punch Bowl Mountain with its great bowl on the top is also visible from Del Rio Station.

22. Dr. Edmund C. Burnett claims he offered the name "Tokeeostee or Agiqua," the two Indian names by which the French Broad had long been known.

Snow Bird Mountain and Max Patch claim the attention of all visitors. It is the county's mountain airport and can be reached from both the Tennessee and North Carolina sides by automobile.

Middle Fork Knob has an intriguingly interesting story connected with it. On this mountain top, in the fifties, a "band of counterfeiters plied their trade." The stamp they used was called "Old Sook." The money they made was freely circulated in the State of Georgia. It is claimed they dug their silver from mines nearby, one of which is thought to have been the Buck Track Silver Mine, which was so named because of a deer track found in the rock near the entrance. The mine from which most of the silver came was discovered by a prospector from the West, who died without revealing its location so the story goes. This band of counterfeiters was connected with one John A. Murrell and their activities reached from Virginia to Missouri, and from New York and Philadelphia to New Orleans. They were captured in the year 1854. John Huff and Royal Stokely the second, were two of the officers who engaged in the capture. The molds used were placed in the vault of the Merchants and Planters Bank after being taken from river at Edwina. It is said that the band was about evenly divided between men of good reputation and men of bad character. Probably the good ones hadn't been with the "gang" very long. It is said that this leader, John A. Murrell once killed a man on horseback because he thought he had much money with him. To his disappointment he found twenty-five cents. He made the remark that anyone who carried no more than that ought to be killed. Several of the counterfeiters served terms in prison.

Southwest of Del Rio, near the M. S. Click place is a ledge of rock about four feet under ground, two hundred yards in length and four or five feet wide, which was discovered by TERA workers on Farm to Market road project.

From this ledge have been taken many interesting specimens of what appears to resemble etchings that are perfect representations of miniature trees, ferns, sunset scenes etc. The etching is of a different color to the rock. It is quite different to such formations found in coal. It is like an engraving or a glyptograph or something of that order. Some of the rocks picked up after blasting the road were perfect landscape scenes and in different colors.

Around the Del Rio section is found the rare yellow wood, called gopher. It is one of the rarest of the trees in Tennessee. It blooms in June, fragrant, showy white blossoms. They look something like sweet peas, and grow to a length of twelve or more inches. This tree is related to the locust. Its leaves are compound with five to eleven ovate leaflets, and the leaf stalks are hollowed at the base, there protecting the next year's buds. These blossoms come in great profusion every other year though a few come the year following the heavy bloom. It stays in bloom for about two weeks. The wood is rather yellow and brittle covered with a silver-gray bark. Only three or four of these handsome trees are to be found in Tennessee. There may be others not yet discovered. Two that stand together in the Great Smokies, eight miles from the foot of New Found Gap, the other between Blount County Tennessee and Swain County North Carolina in the corner where they meet.

"And God said unto Noah, make thee an ark of gopher wood." Genesis 6:13, 14.

This section of our county abounds in various herbs, roots, and medicinal plants, such as butterfly-root, rabbit's ear, "sang," properly known as ginseng, per coon root, iron weed, etc etc. Poison hemlock also grows in great abundance. It is the cicuta-virosa or water hemlock, which has fragrant white blossoms, which, if gathered while wet with dew, will poison the hands. If these flowers are placed in a room, those present will become nauseated with their sweet fragrance.

Long before the coming of the white people to the valley of the French Broad in the Del Rio Section, the Cherokee Indians, or some of their ancestors dwelt in a village in front of the present railway station. The soil at this point is full of fragments of pottery. Stone axes have been found there and other Indian relics. Arrowheads are quite numerous. When the Rail Road was being graded, skeletons were dug up at this particular spot, proving they had long slept in this Tokeostee's Land of the Sky. "Where the swift Agiqua's crystal stream curbs its impetuous course. As it threads its silvery gleam through this quiet, peaceful valley, Beautiful as an artist's dream" . . .

The Huff and Holland families were the first to come to the Del Rio section in 1784. Next came the Stokely family and the Jones Clan, the Burnetts arriving a bit later. Most of the land these first families entered or bought is still owned by their descendants.

In 1787, Captain John Waddle obtained from North Carolina, a grant for 600 acres, which included the best of the valley, that opens from Del Rio toward the south. The Holland family obtained many acres by grants, which extended East and West of Del Rio. In 1802, Captain Waddle sold a portion of his grant to Jehu Stokely, the ancestor of the Stokely family in Cocke County.

In 1834, Swan Pritchett Burnett came from Asheville, North Carolina to the Del Rio Valley and purchased the Nichols land that they had bought from Captain Waddle in 1815. There was something like 240 acres of this tract. To it was added another 100 by entry. Soon afterwards, Swann Burnett purchased the Holland lands and much of the Stokely holdings, much of which is owned today by one of his descendants, Honorable Edmund C. Burnett, of Washington, D. C. who spends his summers there.

Thus we see that Del Rio is still the home of the Huffs, the Stokeleys the Jones, Burnetts and their descendants, all of whom are kin by blood or marriage. Four of the children of Swann Burnett married four of the children of Stephen Huff. Jennie Huff, the girl scalped by Indians and left for dead recovered, grew to womanhood and married Royal Stokely, son of Jehu 1st.

Three daughters of Jehu Stokely and wife, Adaline Burnett married Susongs and many of the others married Jones mates. At least forty of them must have lived in the "Forty Log Houses" of John A. Jones interesting story by that title.

On August the 12, 1833, at the home of the Royal Stokely, was organized, the Big Creek Baptist Church. The First Missionary Baptist organization in the County. The leaders in this Church were, Joseph Manning, Ephraham Moore and Henry Hunt. Joseph Manning was the pastor for forty five years.

The first blacksmith in this part of the county was Jack Penland, father of Henry and James and Wesley Penland and several daughters elsewhere named.

Butler Dozier "set up" the first tannery in Cocke County, located near Nough. Aaron Bible owned it. Later one was operated at Parrottsville by Alex. McNabb.

Del Rio is a shipping point for various woods, such as chestnut, hemlock, jackpine, which is billed J.P., also much dogwood and gum. The Mead Corporation at Kingsport consumes a great quantity of this wood.

The State's best collection of native birds and animals, mounted and on display, eggs, reptiles and other collections of handmade articles of hair and glass, also bedspreads, coverlets, an originally designed mosaic made of seeds, and many old relics that belonged to the Indians are to be seen at the home of Frank Stokely and his mother Mrs. Marve Stokely. In addition to the native animals and birds we find here interesting specimens of mammoth deer, Rocky Mountain Sheep, caribou and elk, etc. Mr. Stokely has captured the various animals and his mother has served as the taxidermist. They have been more than fifty years developing this splendid museum. The collection of bedspreads, coverlets and other fancy handwork of Mrs. Melle Bell Stokely is unsurpassed.

Del Rio is the birthplace of many famous people who have made "THEIR MARK" in the world and who will leave their "footprints on the sands of time." Among such notables, we shall begin with the Bard of Cocke County, John A. Jones, a lineal descendant of the early pioneers of Jones and Nichols families. He is a pleasing, kindly, southern gentleman who enjoys living the quiet, peaceful life. His various and sundry bits of verse and poems make delightful reading. Sometimes he flavors them with a goodly dash of humor, as in his "Innocence Abroad," and "Annie Drew." His poem on "Remote Control" is one of my favorites but the children enjoy most, "With and Without Santa Claus." "Beautiful Land of the Mountains" is the favorite of most of our citizens.

May Justus, writer of books for children, was born near Del Rio, the daughter of Stephen and Margaret Brooks Justus. A sketch of her life and wonderful victory over many odds is given elsewhere in this story.

Edmund C. Burnett, one of our country's most brilliant and distinguished scholars, a lineal descendant of Swann Pritchett Burnett, spent his summers there near the original home of his forebears. He lived most of his time in Washington, D. C. where he worked in the Department of Historical Research in Carnegie.

Del Rio is the birthplace of two world famous people, a man and a woman. Captain John Floyd Arrowood, who was the FIRST AMERICAN BOY "CITED" for bravery in the World War. He was one of the OUTSTANDING soldiers of that War. The French Government decorated him with the Croix de Guerre for his heroic rescue of a number of men who were "hemmed in" and threatened with immediate annihilation by an attacking party of German soldiers who raided the trenches at night. From eight thousand to thirteen thousand shells were fired at this little group of men by the Germans. General John J. Pershing decorated Captain Floyd Arrowood, for his great bravery in face of battle in the Belleau Wood sector where his company came upon a "bunch" of sharpshooters who were stationed in the treetops, and literally mowing down the Americans. Captain Floyd Arrowood killed the leader, captured fourteen of the sharpshooters. Stories of his heroism and bravery were published in papers all over Europe. He was "dined and wined" and feted and honored everywhere, except at home, where his story is little known. He died in 1925, in the very prime of his young manhood, almost unknown, and wholly unsung, proving again that in one's own country it is often thus. We could and we should honor his memory by naming for him some kind of memorial, we have parks and mountain peaks yet unnamed. The bridge at Del Rio, and the Road across the mountains nearest the home of Captain Arrowood could perpetuate the memory of this young brave, whose record is said to be second only to that of Alvin C. York.

Outside of Cocke County, it is not generally known that Del Rio is the birthplace of Grace Moore, the World's Lady of Song. She was born on Big Creek, at the home of her maternal grandparents, William Stokely and wife, Emily Huff Stokely who lived near the present home of Grace Moore's mother's brother, Estel Stokely, Esquire. Grace Moore spent much of her early childhood at Del Rio and Nough where she enjoyed drifting and dreaming along the shores of the French Broad River or wading in Big Creek and climbing the mountain peaks nearby. Her mother, Jane Stokely Moore, went often to visit the home of her youth and the birthplace of her famous daughter, where most all the citizens were her kith and kin.

Thus you see that Del Rio, By the River, has produced distinguished citizens, of whom we are all justly proud. Wherever people eat, they are fed on Stokely Brothers choice vegetables. Wherever a radio is found people listen to the voice of Grace Moore, which has been heard the world around and those who read, claim that May Justus, Edmund Cody Burnett and John A. Jones have no superiors in the field of writing.

Mr. Jones is still living in 1950—more than 90 years of age.

While those who read history know that no soldier in the entire World War was accorded more honor than Captain John Floyd Arrowood of Del Rio, Tennessee.

DEL RIO

Del Rio is a mountain village;
　　It has two streets in one.
You can travel East one block, at least,
　　And, one west toward the setting sun.

It is ensconced on the bank of a stream,
　　From which it takes it name;
It numbers among those born of its womb,
　　Celebrities known to fame.

Del Rio will live in the annals of war
　　As long as the winds are free,
As long as Del Rio means "the river,"
　　And rivers run down to the sea.

It will live to tell of heroic deeds
  Of a native son o'er sea,
An American chap who put on the map,
  Del Rio, Tennessee.

It will tell how its boys on the fields of France,
  When the tide of war was in doubt,
Kindled a fire upon the altar of hope,
  Whose light will never go out.

I'm proud of the place where I was born;
  I've chosen to make it my home.
From its sacred retreat and two-way street
  I never again shall roam.

There, the streams are clear and placid;
  The hills are now touched with gold
The valleys are a tangle of native flowers,
  A heather of beauties untold.

I thrill at a glimpse of the sylvan screen
  That covers each mountain crest,
Where scenic beauty sits enthroned
  When nature is seen at its best.

I love to vision the old homestead,
  Where Grace Moore used to meet
With boys and girls from the countryside
  Ere she had the world at her feet.

In a land of Heroes matched by Stars,
  Where all may succeed who try,
I want to live by the side of the road
  And watch the world go by.

I want to live near the little town
  Of romance, song and thrills,
And, laid to rest, by the folks I love,
  Among my native hills.

———————

"Beautiful Land of the Mountains,
The place where I was born,
Land of perfect sunsets,
Land of perfect morn.
East Tennessee, I bless thee.
Where peaks of granite touch the sky
Around whose summits, eaglets fly,
And passing breezes whine and cry,
Then pause and purl but never die.
East Tennessee, I bless thee.
Where echo haunts enchanted hills
With voices of the rippling rills

— 48 —

And with the music, nature thrills
As every wooded cove it fills.
East Tennessee, I bless thee.
Where rushing rivers churn and foam
And race toward valleys, rich with loam
From which none ever care to roam
That is East Tennessee.
Where factories from North and East
Are setting up to share the feast
The touch of Midas has released
And with the passing years increased.
Where concrete roads extend apace
Communities to interlace,
And Model T's have lost the race.
That is East Tennessee.
Where education is the rule
And every child must be in school
Where University and College
Are filled with students seeking knowledge,
Where dwells the Anglo-Saxon race
With PROGRESS written on its face,
Where health and happiness abound
AND EVERY MAN IS KING UNCROWNED.
That is East Tennessee."

So says the BARD of the County and all agree that he is right. This lovely bit of verse was written by John A. Jones as he sat at his "House by the Side of the Road' from which he could see the "peaks of granite touch the sky," and the luxurious limousines passing by on the concrete highway in front of his home. We call it the Asheville Highway, the government calls it the Broadway of America.

Denton, of course, was named for the owner of the Denton Mill, Captain John Denton who was from Shenandoah County, Virginia, and settled here in 1785.

Edgemont was named because the first schoolhouse there seemed to rest on the edge of the mountain. Some claim the name was given the locality by ex-Governor and Mrs. Ben W. Hooper whose home is located near there.

Few of our present generation know that our present EDWINA was known as TAYLORSBURG prior to the Civil War and when it was Taylorsburg it was considered one of the most progressive and by far the largest of the communities in the entire County. It boasted a tannery, a shoe-shop, a store or two, owned by a man named Taylor, a Tavern and a Doctor's Office.

In the year 1859 Taylor sold his store to John F. Stanberry, also his home nearby which is known as the Old Samuel Stanberry Home, Samuel being the son of John F. the first.

The two doctors of Taylorsburg were Doctor Blackstock, who lived in the John Wood house at Edwina but later moved to Oregon. Mrs. Will Helm was his granddaughter.

Doctor Foreman came to this country from Syracuse, New York. He lived in an old loghouse near the home of Dr. Blackstock. He was the father of the late Joshua Foreman, a well known character of our county who was noted for his eccentricities, his scintillating wit and humor.

In the early days of Taylorsburg there came to the county a new settler. He was of Irish descent, he came from Shenandoah county, Virginia, to seek his fortune in this new country. He rode a bay mare, a few clothes were tied to the back of his saddle, on his shoulder he carried a muzzle-loading, flint-lock rifle. By his side trotted his faithful dog. He liked this country and most especially did he like Taylorsburg and there he "took up his abode." His name was John Wood. He married Fannie Grigsby of Grainger County. He built his first home in Cocke County about one and one half miles South of the present Ed Burnett Home on the Big Pigeon. It is still standing.

It is still in the hands of his descendants and is now owned by Carl Wood. John Wood and wife, Fannie Grigsby Wood had eight sons and no daughters. Two of the sons married Padgett sisters, two of them married Sisk sisters, two of them married Gillette sisters. One married a Kelly the first time, later, an Acton. One, (Abraham) died unmarried but was engaged to wed the sister of his brother William's wife. Later William's wife died and he wed a sister of his brother, Grigsby's wife, Mary Gillette.

Frog Pond means just that!

Fugate Siding was first known as Fugate, for an early settler, and we attached the "Siding" when the Railroad arranged a "siding" there. This community was settled by John Stokely, the first settlement on the south bank of the river. Across from his entry, a man by the name of Bileston had entered a small tract of land and built a strong log cabin on what was known as the finest fishing place on the French Broad River. As the Indians did not like the idea of white settlers occupying this territory, they decided to destroy the cabin of Bileston and camped nearby for that purpose. As soon as day began to break, Bileston made a noise in his house to see if the Indians were still watching it. Instantly the Chief raised his head and listened. From his port-hole, Bileston shot the Indian in the forehead, killing him instantly. The remaining Indians then attacked the house, but the barricades held fast. They picked up their chief's body and placed him on the back of a pony and left. Soon after this experience, Bileston sold his holdings to Evan Fugate, who later became the son-in-law of John Stokely, who lived and died just across the river from the farm of the late F. S. Huff, near Wolf Creek.

To Mrs. Fugate, the daughter of John Stokely, is credited the famous Fugate Apple. Some claim she raised the plant from a seed; others, that she found the seedling and cultivated it.

Gwinntown has long been forgotten. It was located on Big Pigeon, where the three Gwinn brothers, Alman, Bartholomew and Absolom once lived, near Kit Bullard's Old Mill. They went to Missouri and never tired of telling the people there about their mountain home and named their Missouri settlement Gwinntown for Absolom. (Some claim Kit Bullard's Old Mill was near Rogersville, but the three Gwinn brothers always referred to it as having been in Cocke County.)

Harmony Grove was named by S. L. Rollins who taught at what was then known as Jones' Chapel for several years. The people, being closely related, as Stokely's, Huffs, Jones's, Burnetts, and Rowes, and getting along so harmoniously together, and the schoolhouse being in a grove, Sol Rollins called the place Harmony Grove. It is located on the Max Patch Roadway.

Harned's Chapel, in the Parrottsville section, was named for Samuel Harned, one of the pioneers who came in 1800. His house is still standing. Samuel and his wife Rachel, entered about one thousand acres of virgin forest and did much to develop the community. They were the first persons buried in the Harned's Chapel Graveyard. A beautiful Methodist Church stands today as a monument to this courageous, pious couple. Mack Harned is a descendant and P. L. Harned of Nashville, was a relative.

Hartford was first known as Dryce, but when the Tennessee and North Carolina Railroad was being constructed into that part of the County, a John Hart, of Parkersburg, West Virginia, was instrumental in building the road through to Hartford or Dryce. He was one of the owners of the road. The people felt grateful for the railroad and wanted to show their appreciation by naming the village for him. There were more people in that area by the name of Ford than any other one name and it is said that John Hart suggested the idea of their adding Ford to his name and so it was that Dryce became Hartford.

Holt Community Center is located on the land of the Holt family, which has been handed down from generation to generation since the first one entered it long before 1805.

Inman was for the Inman family who once owned many acres of land in this neighborhood, also Inman Bend along Nolachucky River. They were known as "The Rich Inmans." Their ancestors were also great landowners in England. Among the first of this family to arrive in Cocke County were Shadrach, Meshack and Abednego Inman. Those three names were kept alive in the family over a long period of time. One of the oldest members now remembered was Esquire John Inman who had a store in the present Inman community. Another one now living recalls Shadrach, known as Shade, and George W. S. H., probably Shadrach, was representative in the Brownlow Session, 1865-67. During the same session, Charles Inman represented Sevier and Knox counties.

Jay Bird, one of the suburbs of Newport, was named this because it was the favorite haunt of the blue jay. Jim Town, a colored suburb, may have been named by C. F. Boyer, whose sense of humor often expressed itself in unusual ways, and the settlement is just across the river from his home. Leadvale is thought to have originally been "Lead-Vein" but if so, it is still hidden there. Liberty in the Cosby section and Liberty Hill on the Old Morristown Road probably had the same origin, the liberty idea. Long Creek took its name from the creek of the same name. Lundy's Lane was named by Swan L. Burnett. Naillon is said to have been named for a resident.

Paper prepared by the author several years ago for the Federal Government.

Name: NEWPORT, named for the first town of Newport located on the French Broad River in 1799.

Newport's First Board of Mayor and Aldermen. Left to right: Standing—J. P. Hedrick, Policeman Charles A. Robinson, Charlie B. Mims, Robert Dennis, Chief of Police. Seated—James I. Walers, Creed F. Boyer, Mayor Steven A. Burnett.

Population: 2,989 in city limits about the same number in suburbs.
Altitude: 930 ft. in business section 1200 in residential section.
Location: Newport is the county seat of Cocke County. It is located midway between Asheville, North Carolina and Knoxville, Tennessee, being 65 miles from each city by railway; 49 miles East of Knoxville by Dixie Highway Number 70 and 25; 27 miles South of Greeneville by Highway number 35; 22 miles South East of Morristown by Buffalo Trail number 25; 26 miles from North Carolina State line over Highway 75 by the way of Cosby.

Transportation: The Southern Railway passes through Newport with six passenger trains daily making important connections with all cities North or South, East or West. The fare is one and one-half cent per mile for day coaches.

Newport is approached from the East and the West by U. S. Highway number 70 and 25 which is also the Dixie Highway. From the North. by Highway 35 and the Buffalo Trail 25. To the South, Highway 75 leads to the State line. Greyhound busses pass through and stop at Newport on their Asheville to Knoxville run. Eight busses daily.

The nearest airports are Knoxville and Asheville, North Carolina.

Newport is also the junction point for the Tennessee and North Carolina Railroad which makes two trips daily to Crestmont, N. C. with bus.

Notes: Newport has one good hotel, the Rhea-Mims, located on Dixie Highway, directly opposite Masters and Myers Motor Company. It has 40 rooms and entirely modern.

Tourist Camps: The Smoky Mountains Tourist Camp and the Irish Cut Cabins are located two miles East of Newport on the Dixie Highway U. S. 70 and 25. They are constructed of natural field stone and have modern conveniences.

The Eureka Cabins located one mile East of Newport on the Dixie Highway, U. S. 70 and 25, have modern conveniences and a garage with each cabin.

Newport has many good Tourist Homes where lodging and meals can be secured at very reasonable rates.

Climate: The climate is delightful with long summers and short winters that are generally mild. The temperature averages 94.3 at the hottest and 8.2 at the coldest. The average rainfall for 35 years has been 34.16 inches. For 1934 it was 40.68 inches. Our great mountains protect us from strong winds.

History: Cocke County was first settled in 1785. The County was established by an act of the General Assembly Oct. 9, 1797. The County Seat was called Newport. It was located on the French Broad River about one and one half miles North of the present town of Newport. In 1867 when the Railroad came through Cocke County, the idea of moving the County seat to Gorman's Depot at Clifton became much agitated and a long drawn out legal battle ensued because the people North of the French Broad did not like the idea of having two rivers to "FORD" or "FERRY" to get to Clifton or Gorman's Depot. Finally in 1884 the County seat was moved and the town took the name of NEWPORT, giving up its beautiful and appropriate name of Clifton. The most desirable residential section is known as Clifton Heights and one of the first clubs organized in the County was known as the Clifton Club. The present U.D.C. club is known as THE CLIFTON CHAPTER.

Cocke County was named for General William Cocke one of the most distinguished of the pioneers and one of the first Senators.

Growth and Development: Newport has always enjoyed a slow and steady growth. It is a trading and business center, the fifth shipping point in the state, the home of the Mother plant of the world's largest cannery of choice vegetables.

Racial Groups: The white population is purest Anglo-Saxon descent. The only other racial group is the Negro which comprises a very small percent of the population; 21,035 are native born whites; 726 Negro; 9 foreign born; 28 mixed blood. Of the 6,804 males over 15 years of age, 2392 are unmarried (and it leap year) 278 men are widowers and 606 women are widows (which should prove something) 15,000 of the county's population are engaged in agricultural pursuits. The above applies to County.

Newport has within its city limits 1503 males, 1486 females; 5 Indians, 5 Englishmen, 2 Germans, 2 Poles, 1 Italian, 1 Canadian. The suburbs of Newport claim about the same number of citizens.

Industries: The Newport Cooperative Milling Association, The City Mill, The Parrott Bakery, Fielden Manufacturing Company, The Rice Ice Company, The Newport Laundry, The Dixie Hosiery Mills, The Chilhowee Extract Company, The A. C. Lawrence Leather Co., STOKELY BROTHERS AND COMPANY Canners. Many Railroad ties are yarded here and it is quite a lumber center, the Rhyne Lumber Company being the largest of the lumber companies. It is the shipping point for the Bush Brothers Cannery who have several plants in adjoining counties, canning all kinds of vegetables under their own label and pork and beans for Armour and Company.

Historic Remains: The region round about Newport was once the home of the Cherokee Indian tribes, one of their villages was near Wilton Springs. The Big Pigeon River was the border line until 1807. Many Indian relics have been found throughout the County. Indians are buried at different places in the County, the greatest number said to have been buried at the private burial grounds on the Thomas O'Dell Sr. farm on the French Broad River near Bridgeport. An Indian battle is said to have been fought there, hundreds of flint stones have been gathered from the field around the burial grounds. At Rankin and in the Dutch Bottoms are mounds said to be Indian Mounds.

Points of Interest: White Rock, Cocke County's most majestic Mountain peak, 5,100 feet high, densely wooded to the top save for the WHITE ROCK which is a mass of glistening, glazed sandstone formation several feet wide and extending down the North side of the peak for about 500 feet. From this peak one beholds the towns of Newport, Parrottsville, Whitepine, Morristown, Dandridge and with glasses Knoxville and Greeneville and other towns within this radius. This point is reached by taking Highway 75 to Cosby and low gap trail to the top of the mountain.

Max Patch, on the border between Tennessee and North Carolina is the most easily reached of any of the mountain peaks in the County; it has an excellent highway leading to the top from both the Tennessee and North Carolina sides. Airplanes land here upon occasion. The entire top was owned by a Mr. McMahan and cleared by a man named Mack Fox and was thus known by the mountaineers as Mack's patch, but why the secretary of the geodetic survey spelled it Max is not known, he was probably of German extraction and thought that the proper way to spell it or he may have thought it sounded like it should be so spelled.

Hall's Top: Six miles south east of Newport is Hall's Top, 3,609 feet high, named for a family of Halls who once owned the mountain. "Entered" it in 1795 by William Hall, whom it is said, traded the Fork Farm, which is the best farm in Cocke County for a Flint Lock Rifle that he might be able to hunt on this mountain of 700 acres. It is well supplied with water from several springs and for many years this colony of Halls lived there. The mountain now belongs to Everett Greer who plans to develop it into a private mountain resort for retired government employees.

Wilson Inn: Four miles West of Newport on the Dixie Highway, U. S. 70 an old Inn which was a popular tavern and relay station for the Stage Coaches in the early pioneering days of the County and State. Here lodged many notables of that day and time. Isham G. Harris, Felix Grundy, James C. Jones, Henry Clay, Sam Houston, Andrew Johnson, James K. Polk and Andrew Jackson. This property is now owned by Everett Greer of Washington, D. C. who plans to have it restored to its original dimensions and preserved in honor of Andrew Jackson and his kind who sought lodging there.

Carson Springs: Three miles south of the above Inn is Carson Springs famous for more than one hundred years for its fine water, the medicinal properties of which improve the health of most people. The hotel and summer cottages here are filled with visitors from June the first to October the first. Rates are reasonable and the water is free to all.

Natural Bridges: Three miles north of Parrotsville at Harned's Chapel, on the Warrensburg road is a natural bridge, called the BIG OVEN, it is about 50 ft. wide and 100 ft. long; about ¼ of a mile down the creek is another one not so large, it is the Little Oven.

High Oaks Tulip Gardens: These gardens so named because of the high oaks in front of the home at 218 North Street, Newport, Tennessee on State and Federal Highways 10-20-25 and 35. Open all the year to tourists and to the entire public at the tulip season which is generally the last week in April and the first week in May. Tulips of every known color and variety bloom here. They are imported by the thousands each year. In addition to the tulip gardens are the hanging rock gardens with rare and beautiful plants. Roses climb over trelliswork and artistic archways throughout the garden. Four hundred varieties of iris blooms in season and all spring bulbs native to this climate. This garden is a fairyland at any time during the blooming season from early spring to late frosts. Artistic seats in nooks and corners are inviting to all who wish to tarry and absorb this beauty and fragrance of Newport's most visited beauty spot. Thousands visit High Oaks Gardens each year. No charge is made at any time for this marvelous display of floral beauty, artistic landscaping and unusual rock masonry. This garden is the result of Mrs. Lillie E. Duncan's twelve years of tireless effort, careful planning and much expenditure of money.

Magnolia Terrace: On Woodlawn Avenue, between Church and Mill Streets is located the garden of Mrs. Fred Greer, known as Magnolia

The old Mims Hotel near the Depot

Magnolia Terrace, home of Kate Mims Greer, is noted for its collection of historic pictures and plates.

Terrace. In the part of the garden known as "Little Smoky" is a pioneer log cabin completely furnished as the pioneers furnished their cabins. This steep hillside represents the mountains and is densely planted with many native wild plants of the mountains. Artistic walkways and people adorn this garden which is a most unique one because of its setting.

Notables: Newport is the lifelong home of Ben W. Hooper twice elected Governor of Tennessee. Appointed member of U. S. Railway Labor Board in 1921 by President Harding where he served for five years with credit to himself and to the Board.

Cosby: The most beautiful and widely advertised section of Cocke County is Cosby divided into three parts, Lower Cosby, Middle Cosby, and Upper Cosby. Cosby Creek runs through the entire section which is many miles long and embraces several communities. From Highway 75 which traverses the fertile valley of Cosby Creek one beholds many wonderful views of the Great Smoky Mountains National Park of which Upper Cosby is a part. Mt. Guyot, the highest of the mountain peaks, is 6,636 feet high and is visible from many points along the highway. By gazing too long at this height one is certain to become dizzy along this route. However it is the most traveled of all our scenic drives. Cosby was named for Dr. James COZBY, one of the pioneer doctors and a fearless and brave Indian fighter with John Sevier.

The John Sevier Game Preserve: In this preserve are 135,000 acres of land. The most interesting part of it is Lamb's Gulf, a basin containing a small virgin forest of ten thousand acres. The home of the warden is in the basin, large enclosures for deer where they are fed until turned free to roam the mountains. Senate bill number 1005 (Chapter 638 Private Acts of 1933) by Senators O. L. McMahan and W. P. Monroe provides for the establishment and maintenance of this state game preserve which is on the Tennessee side of the North Carolina Border in the Great Smoky Mountains of Cocke County. This bill places full control of the preserve in department of game and fish of Tennessee.

The Great Smoky Mountains: The entire border line between Tennessee and North Carolina is characterized by a continuous high divide extending 60 miles in a southwest northeasterly direction, the crest of which falls below five thousand feet in only a few places, truly this boundary lies "majestically above the clouds in the land of the sky." The veil of silvery mist that floats constantly o'er this region reminds one of thin blue smoke.

Newport was the birthplace of Kiffin Rockwell who volunteered for the duration of the World War, enlisted Sept. 30, 1914. Was "ace" among allied aviators. Was shot down Sept. 23, 1916 in aerial battle in Alsace. He was in the heat of combat, 12,000 feet above the earth. His loss was an irreparable one to the Escadrille Lafayette.

May Justice, an interesting writer of Children's stories was born in Cocke County. She is a young author of much promise.

Education: Cocke County High School is located in Newport. The County has other high schools at Parrottsville and at Cosby. The Sunset Gap School on the line between Cocke and Sevier Counties is the most complete and most efficiently conducted of any of the rural grammar schools. It has its hospital and nursery departments, Teacher's Home and is well equipped with all necessities. Weaving and other arts are taught the children. Miss Sara Cochrine is its efficient executive. It belongs to the Presbyterian Church and is supported by it.

Civic Activities: The County has an active American Legion Post number 41 with an auxiliary that is unusually active. Some clubs are: The Mothers Club, The Parent-Teachers Association, The Young Artists Club, The Business and Professional Women's Club, The Clifton Chapter of the U. D. C., The Tax Payers League, The Kiwanis Club, The Medical Association, The Teacher's Association and various social clubs, The Masonic Lodge and the Eastern Star; The Junior Order of American Mechanics.

Publications: Newport has two papers to "disseminate useful knowledge" they are each published twice each week. One is the Newport Plain Talk the other is the Cocke County Tribune.

Newport's growth has been very gradual, which is always the way a growth should be. Our various changes have evolved from definite and comprehensible causes. We have had no cataclysmic transformations. Newport has never burned entirely out, neither has it been completely washed away though threatened a few times.

Newport's growth in the past should indicate its future possibilities if history repeats itself. We are now facing marvelous opportunities because of our 'strategic position' to the world's most picturesque region of mountain splendor and we should all co-operate to bring to this County a network of roads that will lead into the Great Smoky Mountains National Park. We should interest ourselves in instituting in every school in the County a revival of the handicrafts of our forebears and teach our boys and girls how to work with their hands in growing better farm products, more beautiful flowers and thereby making their homes more attractive to the millions of tourists that will pass our way leaving a stream of wealth that we have heretofore never dreamed would come to our people.

We are now living in the dawn of better hope for mankind, better health for our people, which insures happy, wholesome growth for our children free from many of the terrible diseases of childhood. Our scientists are rapidly moving toward such a new day by the hard work of thousands of research workers in various laboratories, together with the Doctors in their clinics and everyday practice. With infinite patience and devotions they search, not only in this country, but in many lands, with a united purpose, moving along in concerted action, endeavoring to help mankind to a more abundant life. Their victories over typhoid and scarlet fever, tuberculosis, diphtheria and smallpox, indicate their success. In the future our people shall live longer and enjoy better health. In this great service to the race, the women have a tremendous part to play.

Nough has had "enough" names to write a story. It was first known as End of the Road, Back of Beyond, Stump-town, Slab-town and finally Nough. As for Stump-town and Slab-town, the mill had been fed all the trees and left stumps everywhere, and the slabs from the lumber were piled high about the mill. The people resented these names and they suggested several names to the U. S. Post Office, among them Goodnough, for Charles Goodnough, a resident. Its author wrote a large and sprawling hand, the Good was at the end of the line and Nough began the next one. The Judge of the names chose "Nough" thinking it was a separate name. Thus the village was named Nough, through what is known as a fault of cacography. Charles Goodnough began his life work with John D. Rockefeller. J. L. Shults claims Mr. Goodnough was a "goodnough" inventor to make a biscuit cutter that would cut twenty-four biscuits at one "whack" and that he ate some of those biscuits; J. W. D. Stokely says that Charles Goodnough was a brilliant and beloved man. He was "goodnough" to represent his district in the County Court for more than twenty years.

Old Town was tacked on to Newport after it was moved to the new town of Clifton and became Newport number 2.

PARROTTSVILLE, named in honor of the first settlers by that name, is the third oldest town in the State. It is located seven miles north of Newport on the Greeneville Road or Highway 36. This section of our County was settled in 1769, by John Parrott, a Frenchman, son of Frederick Parrott who came from Alsace-Lorraine. After his arrival in America he married Barbara Edwards, an English lady. Five sons were born to this union, all of whom saw service in the Revolutionary War. One of the five sons, John Parrott, entered several hundred acres of land in the Parrottsville section. Jacob, the son of John Parrott built the first house erected in Parrottsville.

This first house in Parrottsville was built for a Tavern and of double hewn logs, was erected in 1830 and is in a fair state of preservation. It is now known as the Hale House. The Tavern operated by Jacob Parrott was patterned after the houses built by the Virginia gentry and was located on the old Stage Road which led from Washington to the South West, connecting Jonesboro, the State Capital, with the National Capital. Many of the pioneer Statesmen and celebrities of that day and time enjoyed stopping at this Tavern.

George Parrott, another son of John, built his home near the tavern, but on the bank of Clear Creek where the "Ford" was located. It was a two story log and frame house. George Parrott spent much of his time with the duties of the tavern which was connected with the Story Inn, sometimes called the Dry Fork Inn, located at what is now known as the Gillespie place. These two Inns seemed to have cooperated with the Wilson Inn at Wilsonville. The present Parrott family in Cocke County are the direct descendants of George Parrott.

The members of the original Parrott family' are buried in the old cemetery three miles East of Parrottsville on the present highway. Also Revolutionary Soldiers are interred there.

One of the few MANSIONS of that day and time was located in Parrotsville. It was the home of Robert Roadman, some claim, while others say it was the home of William Chesley Roadman. It was three stories high and stood where the M. E. Church now stands. It had twelve large rooms, three great dividing halls with a stairway in each hall.

On the second floor was the ballroom where much entertaining was enjoyed by guests from far and near. The entire front of the second story could be thrown into one long room by sliding partitions. From the outside two stairways led to a portico on the second floor which enabled guests to arrive and depart without having to go through the front entrance to the dwelling. A brick terrace was part of the front, from which brick paving extended to the street. This elegant old Southern Home of the Roadman family was sold after the War to a stock company made up of citizens who wished to establish a School. Later the company sold the property to the M. E. Church and for many years thereafter, a school was run by the M. E. Church. This came about by Parrottsville having been chosen as the site of the Old Camp Grounds where the Methodist preachers conducted Camp Meetings and so many members were added to the church that Parrottsville became not only the religious center of the county but also the educational center. Those who contributed most to the purchase of the old mansion of the Roadman family were John F. Ellison, J. Q. Easterly, Samuel D. Harned. The school was known as the Parrotsville Seminary and two years of college work were given in addition to the grammar and high school courses. The teachers of that period were, W. P. Monroe, James R. Penland, and George R. Stuart, who later became one of the outstanding preachers of his time. J. W. Lucas operated a private school for a year or two.

The commencement programs of the Parrottsville Seminary were attended by the young people and the older ones from all over the county and surrounding counties and from Western North Carolina. They came in wagons, in buggies, in carriages, on horseback and on foot. The programs were always held in springtime, along about the middle of May. They were held out in the open where an enclosure had been made of "BRUSH" as it was called, being limbs of cedar, pine, and any type of evergreen or greenery with roses and springtime blossoms intertwined. This made a most attractive and fragrant enclosure. For seats, slabs from the nearby mill were used by those who did not bring their own chairs.

At each end of Parrotsville is a good spring. The East end spring is known as the Ellison Spring, near the old brick dwelling that was erected before the Civil War and is now the home of T. S. Ellison. At the West end of the village is the Hale Spring.

After many years of school in the old mansion it was razed and the present M. E. Church built on the site.

In the early days when Parrottsville had several good stores, one owned by W. C. Roadman, another by a merchant named Duncan who had his salesroom and one or two or more warehouses set alongside his residence.

Rankin and Pulliam, McNabb and Faubion, Mims and Faubion were other firms. Newspapers were published from time to time. The *Reporter* by Joseph L. Bible in 1876.

Charles Huff and Hardin Kelley also published a paper.

The Argos was published by Nimrod Parker.

The first photographer was John Sterling Bushong of Virginia, who had learned the art in Knoxville, where he married Mary Harned, daughter of David and Polly Swaggerty Harned. When the Civil War "broke out" he took his young wife to the home of his parents in Virginia and joined the Confederate Army. After the war was over he brought her to her parents home in the Oven Creek section. He established his studio in a Cedar grove near the roadway that led to Warrensburg and on the farm now owned by the W. B. Smith family. People came from all over the county to have their pictures made.

When business seemed dull to the photographer he mounted his studio on a wagon and took it to different towns and communities throughout East Tennessee. On the back side of some of the pictures were the following lines;

"Pictures good and prices low
Now is your time, before we go."
Signed . . . J. S. Bushong, Traveling Photographer.

One of the outstanding women of the Parrottsville section in the early days was the wife of J. S. Bushong, Mary Harned Bushong who was a Community nurse, and her mother Polly Swaggerty Harned who was probably more active than her daughter. They were both cultured, intelligent, remarkable women who went about doing good, administering to the sick and dying. Polly Harned nursed all during the Civil War and afterwards. Her sons, William and Samuel fought in the Union Army.

Each of these women served their neighbors and friends without hope of reward. Each kept a saddle horse ever ready to go quickly when called. Mary always wore a black sun bonnet and in winter she wore a shawl of black and white wool, probably handmade. When she was called at night, she mounted her ready steed, "man fashion" and hurried quickly to the bedside of the suffering. Mary always wore the long black riding skirts that protected her feet and dress from the mud along the roadways.

The Parrotsville section has prided itself in its good homes and good citizens and it is a noticeable fact that very little of the "meanness" carried on in Cocke County has been "packed on" the Parrottsville section. The early settlers were the Parrotts, of French extraction, the Ottingers of German descent and the Nease families of French strain, while the Jones of that section were Welch. The Bell family was Scotch but this name did not arrive until 1872.

Parrottsville has produced many fine citizens, among them, Rev. Geo. R. Stuart, Prof. R. P. Driskill and Dr. Everett M. Ellison.

Peanut, Punkin Center, Punktown or Punkton are other villages without data as to their origin. Swan L. Burnett probably named Punkton.

Rankin was named in honor of Doctor Rankin, an early settler who lived on the hill where Doctor Roadman later lived. The last one of this particular family was Minerva Rankin. The Honorable Court Rankin of Jefferson County is a descendant and also Judge Lafayette Rankin of Jefferson County.

Redwine was named for the family with this lovely name. The Civil War had been fought before this family arrived in Cocke County. They lived in Lee County, Virginia, where James Redwine was a Circuit Rider. He took his sons, Elihu, Creed, Kane, Robert, Joseph, and joined the Union Army at Bloomington, Illinois. He became a chaplain. One of his sons was killed in the War. The others came with their father to Cocke County, Tennessee. Elihu, the best-known of the family, was the father of Mrs. Hugh Holder.

Read Hill is another name chosen through error. It is said that while Marve Stokely was postmaster at Del Rio a Government official came to accompany him into the community where Jack Click, Esquire, resided and to try to select an appropriate name for the post office there. A large red hill proclaimed its color. They decided to name the post office Red Hill, according to J. W. D. Stokely, but it was written down as Read Hill instead of Red. It is in the same locality as Sand Hill.

Reidville or Reidtown on the Knoxville Highway was named for David H. Reid, who was born in Cocke County, Dec 26, 1853, and died in Goodwell, Oklahoma, May 12, 1938. He was the son of Thomas and Nancy Anderson Reid and married Sallie Taylor, the only daughter of E. and Jane Taylor, October 25, 1877. As a descendant of the Gorman family she inherited money with which she and her husband established a store at the place now called Reidville. When they were married, Dave Reid had a shoe shop about where the Busy Bee Restaurant now stands. According to H. H. Gouchenour, Dave Reid had his home ready and furnished when he wed and Hugh ate supper with them on their wedding day. They became successful and built a large home near the Presbyterian Cemetery, which is still called The Reid House, (Sisk Apts.)

Saint Tide Hollow was named for "Tide" Holt, who was evidently named for Tidence Lane, one of the early preachers. Tide Holt was such a religous man that he was often called Saint Tide. The school in this locality was known as Possum College.[23]

Salem got its name from the members of the Lutheran Church who reside there. These Dutch people always centered their community life about their church, which usually had a biblical name. Salem is the Hebrew word Shalem, meaning security, the name of a city of which Melchizedek was king, located near "the King's Vale" in Palestine. Sardis and Syracuse were also probably biblical names.

Waterville, on the state line between Tennessee and North Carolina, where the North Carolina Power Company maintains a great power plant, evidently was named for the French "ville" and the word water.

Wilsonville was named for Major Wilson who once owned a vast plantation in this area extending from the top of English Mountain to the French Broad River. He also had the Stage Coach Terminal and an Inn, a part of which still stands near the Rock Spring where the Carson Springs Road joins with the Broadway of America. Wilsonville became our fourth post office in 1885. Miss Nina is a descendant of the Major.

Cato was established in 1853 with Andrew C. Huff as its first postmaster, and was where the John Huff store now stands.

Givens was located on the Joseph Fowler property. Wesley Givens was the postmaster and also a merchant. Some years later this post office was moved to Robert Wren's farm, now known as the Palmer Place. From the Palmer Place it was moved to the Dr. J. A. Thomas farm and he became postmaster until our present R. F. D. System was established.[24]

Drift was a post office located at the store of John Holt, the father-in-law of Doctor Thomas, and John Holt was its postmaster. Later this office was moved to the John Bible Place, which was then known as Help, with William Moore as postmaster. Help post office was then combined with Drift, and Minnie Bible became postmaster. This was in the Briar Thicket Community.

Driskill post office was named for the Driskill family and possibly was located on their lands. Jonesville was Del Rio. Ogdensville was a

23. Information from Lennie Thomas Marshall, daughter of Doctor Thomas.
24. According to C. F. Hughes.

post office in 1873 with Jesse J. O'Neil as postmaster. It was our present Wilsonville, and was named for George Ogden who married Elizabeth O'Neil, sister of the postmaster.

Shultsville was evidently in the Cosby area and may have meant the name as Shultsberg, which was once Hackletooth, now Cosby, which it became in 1862. Of course, Cosby has existed since the beginning of Cocke County.

It is not possible to list all the quaint names the people have given the various landmarks, but Del Rio seems to have had more than any of the other places, probably due to its being the home of the witty Burnett family. A descendant of this family, Burnett Rowe, of Charlotte, North Carolina, gives the following list: Rip Ship Thicket, Dog Hobble Ridge, Rough Arm Hollow, Bear Wallow, Woolly Ridge, Roaring Fork, Huggins Hell, Devil's Race Track, Devil's Den, Old Nick, Tear Britches Ridge, Chunky Gall, Shake a Rag, Turkey Trot, Broke Jug Creek, Long Nose Ridge, How Come You, Scat-Away, Dug Down, Stretch Yer Neck, Frog Level, Wear Hut, Big Soak, Desolation Gorge, Blue Hell, Daddy and Mammy's Creek, Rock House Mountain, Crestmont, Cataloochie.[25]

---

25. A few years ago, Thomas Weaver Sprinkle, nephew of Mrs. Mildred Weaver Burnett of Del Rio, prepared an original contest, the Cocke County Geography test, in which ex-Governor Ben W. Hooper and his contest partner, Mrs. Fred Graddon, won the first prize. It follows: by the river—Del Rio; fresh wine—Newport; a small stream with big name—Big Creek; plenty—Nough; a foul hotel—Rankin; an insect with a sting—Wasp; river with a homing instinct—Big Pigeon; perchance an industrious insect—Bybee; where Brer Rabbit was born and bred—Briar Patch; a heavy face covering—Leadvale; a bum measure—Punkton; a city of tropical birds—Parrotsville; notched citrus fruit—Lemon Gap; good when salted—Peanut; a dentist's hobby and a ship's haven—Bridgeport; a small rodent—boomer; a discouraged factory—Blue Mill—a vital organ and popular car—Hartford; where aviators and chauffeurs meet—Max Patch; named for the people who helped us win our independence—French Broad.

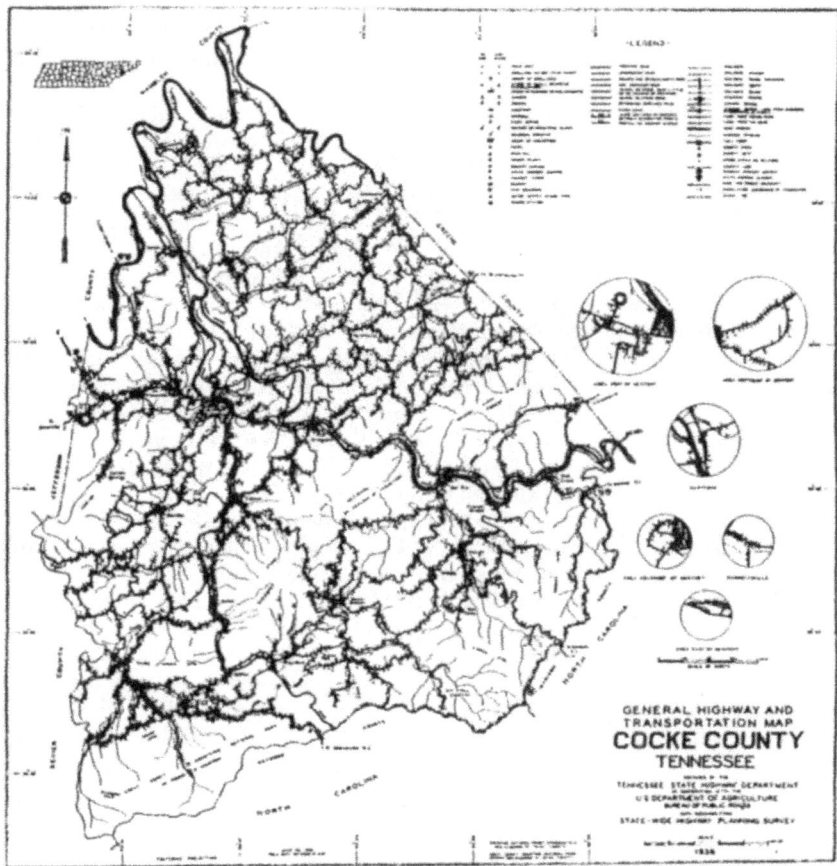

Map of Cocke County

Natural Setting and Resources

Cocke County, with its triangular outline, encloses about five hundred square miles of rugged mountains, rolling wooded hills and fertile valleys. The soil is bounded on the north by the Nolichucky River (Hamblen County), on the northeast by Greene County, on the southeast by North Carolina, and on the west by Sevier County. It has a temperate climate, with January the coldest month and July the hottest. Precipitation was 44.16 over a period of twenty-three years.

Cocke County's three rivers and many creeks not only add great beauty to the landscape but also offer hydro-electric power to an extent not surpassed by any other county in Tennessee. In one hundred miles they have a combined fall of six hundred feet of natural dam sites.[1]

The Big Pigeon rushes down the mountains to join the French Broad River as it crosses the county from the east to the northwest, for forty miles.[2] The Nolichucky (sometimes spelled Nolachucky), forming the northern boundary for twenty-four miles, is generally called Chucky.

The altitude of the county varies from 930 feet, in the business section of Newport, to 1200 feet in the residential sections, and to 6,636 feet at the highest point, Mount Guyot. (Pronounced Gee-o.) One of the highest peaks in the Smokies, it is on the county's southern boundary, and is located between Cocke and Sevier counties in Tennessee, and Haywood county in North Carolina. Newport is considered the northern doorway to the Great Smoky Mountains National Park, which is less than eighteen miles distant, over Highway 75 by way of Cosby, now (1950) known as the Governor Ben W. Hooper Highway. Newport has the nearest railroad to the park area, and is its most beautiful entrance.

Many of the county's peaks have Indian names and legends that cling to them.[3] Others have names of historical importance, as Tricorner Knob, 6,400 feet high, which was so named by Arnold Guyot, who made the first survey of this region. At that time, Tricorner Knob was the corner of three counties. It is one-half mile from Mount Guyot to the south, and lies at the junction of Balsam Mountain, the main divide of the Great Smokies. On the trail to these peaks, one passes the great grapevine, which measures sixty inches in circumference, three feet from the ground, and bears grapes each year. No one knows its age. It is on the watershed of Dunn's creek, off the new trail, but on the old one, and only one mile from the motor road that leads to Mount Guyot. Two other grapevines, measuring eighteen and twenty-one inches in circumference, grow near the huge vine. The largest tree in the smokies, a chestnut measuring twelve feet in diameter, grew at the same place.

---

1. A one-hundred foot dam could be built at Hartford, where the rock sides ascend at a steep angle, three hundred feet apart. (John Weaver, Engineer)

2. Sometimes called Black River, because the refuse from Champion Fiber Company in North Carolina makes it appear black and destroys many fish.

3. Most Cocke County citizens prefer these names to those given by various park officials.

The most sublime peak in the county is White Rock,[4] which towers 5,025 feet, and is a three-mile climb from the highway. A spring flows from near the summit and on the top of the peak is a pool known as Bear Wash. A white rock extends downward about five hundred feet on the north side. This glistening precipice is several feet wide and is of sandstone formation, with the appearance of granite. An adequate description of the view from White Rock has never been written, for it encompasses a vast aggregation of mountain splendor. The peaks and ridges are densely wooded with one hundred and fifty varieties of trees. From the stone fire tower on its top, all visitors enjoy a 360-degree view from the top of the world, far over our Misty Blue Hills.

Another beautiful peak is Hall's Top, 3,609 feet altitude, and only six miles southeast of Newport. It has an interesting history.[5] From Clover Hill, which is the heart of the "Top," once called Rich Top, "where the Devil had his race track and jumped off into the river,"[6] it is possible on a clear day to see the towns of Newport, Greeneville, Morristown, and Dandridge, also Cumberland and Clinch Mountains.

An orchard of Buff, Limbertwig and other varieties of apples known in 1800 were planted on Rich Top. These trees bore abundantly and apple houses of logs with underground pits were erected. The mountain land soon supported a Colony of Halls.[7]

---

4. The Board of Geographical Names at Washington has changed the name of White Rock or Sharp Top to Mount Cammerer, and the ridge will bear the same name, for Arno B. Cammerer, Director of the National Park Service from 1933 to 1941.

5. In 1795, mountain belonged to a Mr. Finney who exchanged it for a flint lock rifle and a small mule. William Hall offered the rifle for the mountain, but Mr. Finney refused to trade unless he could have the mule, valued at about fifty dollars.

6. From Malcolm McNabb, Cocke County member of First Convention that formed Constitution of State of Tennessee.

7. The Halls developed a shingle factory, which shingles they sold to the residents of Taylorsburg.

Samuel Hall, known as "Uncle Sammy," was born in 1802 on this mountain top, and is still remembered for his kindly deeds. Said he would give one thousand dollars to know the alphabet. One log house was converted into a schoolhouse and Allen Hall became its first teacher.

In the years, 1888 and 1889, Jasper Gray taught this school. He received twenty dollars per month and paid four of it for board. All children in school were Halls. Jasper boarded with a family who had ten children, the parents and teacher made thirteen people, all of whom lived in one room, cooking, eating, and sleeping in the same room. This family had seven cats and four hound dogs in the room.

Every autumn the Hall family would carry everything they had raised to market, three or four miles. Samuel Stanberry, the merchant, bought all the Halls could raise of food for thirty cents per bushel. In the spring, the people would again come to the store and purchase the same produce they had sold the previous fall, pay sixty cents a bushel and carry it back up the mountain. Expensive storage—then as now.

Sallie Hall (Aunt Sallie), was kindly. She often carried a "turn of corn" to Taylorsburg and brought it back as meal to her home, where she loaned "every dust" of it to her neighbors.

Sam Hoot Hall was known as "The Wild Man of the Mountains." Burnt-Faced Bill Hall enjoyed frightening members of his family. He followed his wife to "The Seven Oaks Grave Yard" where he rocked her and tied a band tightly around her neck. "I didn't think about killing her. I was just trying to scur her and hit her with rocks for about fifteen or seventy-five minutes and then tied her apron string around her neck to scur her good." Louranie's body was found by Clay Vinson, to whom Burnt-Faced Bill made the above remarks. He was sentenced to three years in prison, but was turned "loose." While a man who had stolen a horse had "to serve out" his sentence.

Hall's Top[8] has changed hands five times since 1795. Finney swapped it to the Halls. They sold it to Samuel Stanberry, the Taylorsburg merchant. The Stanberry family sold it to Harrison Sexton, trustee of Cocke County, who wanted to change the name to Mount Coolidge because it was so quiet and cool there. Mr. Sexton sold the mountain property to Col. Everett Greer, now of Washington, who intends (if he lives long enough) to develop it into a private mountain resort for retired government employees.

Max Patch raises its bald head 4,660 feet along the state line and belongs to the Bald Mountains, located in Greene, Cocke and Unicoi counties in Tennessee, and to Haywood, Madison and Yancey counties in North Carolina, which form the common boundary line of North Carolina and Tennessee and up until 1930 bore no name.[9]

Max Patch is about thirty miles southeast of Newport by way of Del Rio. Its name has never been confirmed and probably never will be.

The county's geological formations are of granite, quartzite, slate, and limestone,[10] which comprise the main and the outlying ranges of the Great Smokies. The rivers and creeks flowing across the county have eroded much sand and gravel, which the flood waters have carried to the lowlands. Its clays and shales compare favorably with any in America for the manufacturing of brick, both common and face, also for sewer pipe, wallcapping, and flue linings.

The ledges of stone along the Big Pigeon and French Broad Rivers and throughout the county are 98 per cent calcium carbonate, similar to the Lehigh Valley lime rock, the standard for Portland cements. This combined with alumina shales gives this section an opportunity for developing a cement-making industry. Large deposits of green slate compare favorably with those of the White Hall, New York, Districts, and abundant deposits of crystalline calcite are also found.

Deposits of iron ore in commercial quantities are found in the Del Rio and Wolf Creek sections, and they were operated on a small scale before the early 1900's. Ore from these districts was hauled by wagons to forges in Greene County. The Wolf Creek vein shows a width of four to eight feet and is traceable for 700 feet.[11]

In 1909, H. M. LaFollette, founder of the town by the same name, leased the Wolf Creek property and shipped out a quantity of ore. Barytes mines throughout this area have recently been worked for war production materials. These mines are on Mooneyham Creek and at Moccasin Gap. The Crehs mine has been reopened.

Kaolin in sufficient quantities for making crockery abounds near Del Rio. Manganese and barytes are also found near Del Rio and Hartford. Paint Rock has substantial deposits of Barytes.

---

8. Mr. Tracy, of Philadelphia, investigated the amount of chestnut oak and spruce on the mountains from this spot, in 1890, and the preparations for the erection of the Unaka Tannery began at once.

9. Data about White Top furnished by Everett Greer, owner; Jasper Gray, teacher; Mrs. Ethel Stanberry, widow of Dr. John F. Stanberry, and Mrs. Lawson D. Franklin.

10. T.V.A. claims the limestone in Cocke County tests about 90 per cent.

11. Nearly 40,000 acres of ore lands in Cocke and adjoining counties are owned by the Tennessee Iron, Coal, and Railway Company, a subsidiary of the United States Steel Company.

Near Waterville is a quartz vein three feet thick containing galena, copper, chalco-pyrite and traces of gold and silver.

For the most part, the rock formations consist of sedimentary rocks, sandstones, conglomerates, shales, slates, and limestones with pre-Cambrian and metamorphic rocks constituting the underlying basal members.

For almost a mile along the Big Pigeon River at Newport are beautiful cliffs that average one hundred feet in height, with some points one hundred fifty feet high. One that stands higher than the others is rather round and projects out of the water apparently alone. On its summit is a cross of immense size placed there by Robert Knowles years ago. The railway and highway run parallel with the river and the cliffs.[12]

Neddy's Mountain, beloved by Cocke countians, is three miles east of Bridgeport.

Along the Big Pigeon, near Bluffton, are other cliffs, more varied and beautiful in their color combinations than those on Clifton Heights.

On English Mountain, twelve miles southwest of Newport, is a ledge of sand cliffs, forty to fifty feet high and more than three miles in length, running northeast and southwest. The top of the ledge, shaped like a bench, is called the Benches. In them are located Maple Springs, one of sulphur and one of freestone water.

Numerous caves on this mountain, among them the saltpetre caves, are said to contain nitre in sufficient quantities to have attracted Civil War manufacturers of gunpowder. The Counterfeiter's Cave is located in Clifton Heights, cliffs near the white cross.

Rattling Cave near the eastern end of Clifton Heights is said to have been used as a sacrificial cave in prehistoric times. The geologists claim that the skeleton found imbedded in a ledge of rock is that of a Peruvian man. Hieroglyphics indicate some emblematic significance. The Mystery Cave has a sealed entrance.

Along the French Broad River are also numerous cliffs, caves, and mysterious fortifications, mounds and painted rocks. The ancient inhabitants perhaps built these pyramids on the earth as a homage to their Creator, showing their devotion to the universal laws of God ruling the heavens and the earth, desiring to bring the same harmony below which they saw above.

The fertility of the river valleys in the county naturally invited settlement of any race or tribe of people. Ethnologists have located mounds of an ancient race known as the Mound Builders. Remains of fortifications by that race are found about two miles below Newport.

North of Rankin on the east side of the French Broad River is a mound about twenty-five feet high, now overgrown. The first settlers, among them Joe Huff, entered this land about 1783.[13]

According to records in Raleigh, North Carolina, Peter Huff entered land on the east side of the French Broad River, opposite the mouth of Big Pigeon River, October 21, 1783.[14] John Huff entered land north of the French Broad River near Del Rio, October 14, 1783. The land, now valued at $50,000, on which the mound stands, was sold by Joe Huff, or

12. Vassar Brown, a small boy, drowned here. Five Indians are buried a few feet west of cliff, and in the early days a white man lost his life there.
13. Probably mound referred to in Goodspeed's HISTORY OF TENNESSEE.
14. H. W. Huff, in possession of land deeds, furnished information.

rather exchanged for a rifle gun. He entered another farm on the Big Pigeon, owned by "Big" Dave Williams until his recent death. (Bison Community)

Many Indian relics have been found on the Peter Huff Farm at Rankin, among them an Indian pipe of stone and in the image of a duck. Presumably it was the Big Chief's Pipe of Peace. Stone axe-heads and black and gray arrowheads, unlike any others in Tennessee, have also been found. William Huff, son of Peter Huff, while digging a cellar under the Peter Huff residence, found large human bones, probably Indian ones.[15]

In May, 1821, Robert Armstrong[16] of Knoxville, visited these ancient fortifications and made field notes and an accurate map of its outlines and exterior entrenchments, and these are the basis of his description:

> These works in Cocke County were located about one mile above the junction of Big Pigeon and French Broad Rivers, and on the north bank of Big Pigeon, on a bluff about one hundred and fifty feet above the level of the river, thus in the fork of the two rivers. From the summit of the bluff, a level plain extends out from the river, the place protected by the rivers on all sides except one. Eight and one half acres are enclosed by an entrenchment. The plain is supposed to have been the parade ground of the ancient warriors. The lower end was covered with the ruins of buildings of various sizes, stones still remain where the buildings stood, and these stones gave evidence of the fort having been destroyed by fire. From the lower end of the fort was a pass-way down the river, and gateways on the northern and eastern sides.

These venerable ruins were discovered in 1789 and at that time posts on one side of a gateway were still standing.

The county's two natural bridges, known as the Big Oven and the Little Oven, span Oven Creek in the northern part of the County. Interesting stories are told of Roaring Hole near these bridges. Liquor was passed up through it after the money came down.

Highways from all directions pass through the county and through Newport. Route 25 west to Knoxville is a part of the Dixie Highway to Miami. Route 25 east runs to Morristown and Middlesboro, Kentucky. Highway 25 runs to Asheville, North Carolina, also Highway 70. Highway 75, The Governor Ben W. Hooper Highway, goes to Cosby and the Great Smoky Mountains National Park.

The Southern railway winds its way across the county to the Carolinas. For many years, the Tennessee and North Carolina railway operated a line to Hartford and Mount Sterling. Later a bus line, owned by the same company, used the railroad track for several years for its daily runs to and from Crestmont, North Carolina. Now, a new roadway follows the old railroad bed through this rugged, picturesque section.

The Cherokee National Forest has within its established boundaries

---

15. Semi-civilized Indians often traveled over Cocke County between the years 1820 and 1930 selling cane-split baskets of various colors.

16. Armstrong, a military man, saw service in the regular army of the United States and in several campaigns against the Indians. In 1819, his cousin, John C. Calhoun, appointed him United States surveyor of the Indian line under the treaty of that year. He was a Knox County surveyor for over a generation.

The Broadway of America, Highway 75, just before it reaches Newport, Tenn.,
English Mountain to the right.

The John W. Fisher Bridge

1,204,000 acres. In the Unaka Division of this forest are the mountain regions. The net acreage of the Cherokee National Forest within the County is 35,076 acres, and the gross acreage is 119,000 acres. Handsome boundary markers have been placed near Bridgeport on the Asheville highway and at Edwina.

On the Tennessee side of the line between Tennessee and North Carolina is the John Sevier Game Preserve, which includes 135,000 acres of the county's mountain area. The boundary of this preserve is as follows: Beginning at the western border of the Pisgah National Forest on Highway No. 9, the line runs through Del Rio and Newport to Clevenger's Crossroads, four miles west of Newport, thence it follows the state Highway No. 35 to the Sevier County line, a little ways west of Chestnut Hill, thence south to the northern boundary of the Great Smoky Mountains National Park, thence with said boundary, east to the Tennessee and North Carolina state line near Waterville, to the beginning.

Lamb's Gulf, on Lamb's Fork of Big Creek, a basin of ten thousand acres, contains the home of the warden. Near it, deer are kept in an enclosure until they can be given free range.

Several thousands of Cocke County's acres are under water and 17,170 acres are in the Great Smoky Mountains National Park. The Pisgah Forest contains 6,000 acres. The net acreage of the Cherokee National Forest within the county's boundary is 35,076 acres. The John Sevier Game Preserve includes 135,000 acres. The Douglas Dam on the French Broad River covers 4,244 acres of rich river bottoms in Cocke County.

A unique dam is located on the Big Pigeon River about twenty-five miles southeast of Newport at Waterville, on the state line between North Carolina and Tennessee. From the dam to the turbines is a six-mile tunnel, fourteen feet wide, running through the mountains. The water passes through this tunnel with a drop of 861 feet, with but a 183-foot dam.[17]

The power plant is a few feet on the North Carolina side of the state line, but most of the power comes into Tennessee, from a modern plant, generating 100,000 kilowatts under an eight hundred foot head. Of the three generators, two run most of the time to furnish power for the Kingsport feeder line. From the remaining generator, 10,000 kilowatts are normally furnished the Knoxville line. The remaining current goes to Carolina consumers. Much of the power of the Kingsport line goes as far north as Ohio. The normal running capacity of the plant is about 90,000 kilowatts and is transmitted at 110,000 volts.

Trails, Travelers, Highways and Byways

The history of a people may be read by the roads they leave, because roads are silent messengers.

Since the earliest dawn of our State, the part of it now known as Cocke County has had numerous ways of travel and varied routes. Some

---

17. This project was undertaken and completed by the Carolina Power and Light Company, in charge of Mr. Dow, the engineer, who died suddenly from the strain about the time the dam was completed. No woman was allowed to enter the tunnel, which was begun on each side of the mountain. When the construction crews met they found they had varied in their calculations only a fraction of one inch from the specifications of the surveyor and engineers.

of them wind picturesquely around vine-clad hills, and others like silver ribbons encircle purple mountain peaks. Frequently, a road follows a meandering mountain stream. Sometimes, a highway runs boldly across one of the rivers by way of a beautiful new bridge. But in the beginning, the pioneers used trails and narrow roadways.

One of the earliest routes of travel was the Catawba Trail, used by the Catawba Indians of the Carolinas, who passed through the County on to Cumberland Gap. It was used as a path in warring with the tribes on and above the Ohio River. The trail followed the French Broad valley on the south side of that river.

The Great War Path of the Cherokees also passed through the county, and the Indians journeyed from north to south over it on their various wars. It was never more than three feet in width and generally only half that wide. It lead from the Chickamauga, near the present Chattanooga, through Ooltewah, crossed the Hiawassee River near its junction with the Tell, passed through or near where Maryville is now located, taking about the same course as the Maryville-Sevierville road now runs. It crossed Little River near the mouth of Ellijoy Creek. The trail then followed the creek over the ridge that divides the waters of Little River and that of the French Broad, thence with the course of Boyd's Creek, to its junction with the French Broad River. It divided near the Boyd's Creek battleground. The right hand or southern trail followed up the French Broad to near Sevierville, where it made another junction with a trail from Tuskegee that came by or near the present site of Townsend. This southern trail, after leaving Sevierville, divided again, one part going up the east prong of the Little Pigeon River, which is known as the East Fork of Little Pigeon. This trail led into the Great Smokies. The other trail followed what is now known as the Sevierville to Newport highway, number 35. It passed through Harrisburg, Republican, Fair Garden, Bird's Cross Roads, Chestnut Hill, Clevenger's Cross Roads, Wilsonville and Newport, Crossing Big Pigeon River at what was known as War Ford, sometimes called Lower War Ford, now Newport. The trail crossed directly opposite the residence of W. D. McSween, a few yards west of the present site of the home office of Stokely Brothers Canning Factory (known as "The House of Adams" during the early part of Cocke history.) Now the home of Donald McSween. From this Lower War Ford crossing, the trail wended its way through "the muster field" and evidently crossed the French Broad near the present bridge at Old Town, following the foot of the mountains south of Greeneville, and crossing the Nolachucky River near Brown's settlement, eight miles south of Jonesborough, the oldest town in Tennessee. From this point it followed the Cherokee Road by or near Garber's mill, passing through the southern suburbs of Johnson City to Sinking Creek, thence over the Buffalo Creek to its junction with the Watauga River.[18]

The first road constructed by white men in the county was built in 1784 while the county was part of Jefferson. It extended from War Ford to the Nolichucky river at the place where it was crossed by the Great War Path of the Cherokees.

---

18. This was the trail taken by the Indian Chief Abram when he made the attack on the white in 1776, made famous by the Battle of Sycamore Shoals.

The Knoxville Gazette of July 31, 1795, announced that "two wagons arrived here two days ago from South Carolina, having passed through the mountains."

On October 26, 1799, an act was passed by the Tennessee legislature authorizing the county court of Cocke to open "a road from near the town of Newport, to cross the mountains by the way of the old fields of Big Pigeon, into the state of Georgia."

When the turnpike shall be thus erected the said Court (Pleas and Quarter Sessions) shall appoint and employ a proper person to keep said turnpike had to give bond of $2000 for the faithful discharge of his duties, etc. He had to take oath not to take more money than provided by law.

Wagon and team and load, 75c; man and horse, 12½c; foot man, 6¼c; led horse, 6¼c; 4 wheel carriage of pleasure team and load, 150c; one chair horse and rider, 75c; cart team and load, 37½c.

The money collected was to be turned over to clerk of County for upkeep of road. The clerk got 2½% for his services each time the Court asked for settlement.

Page 126. AN ACT SUPPLEMENTARY TO AN ACT ENTITLED "An Act to Divide County of Jefferson into two Separate and Distinct Counties." No provision is made directing at what place the citizens of the new County of Cocke shall vote for Representative to Congress at the ensuing election to be held on the second Thursday and the day following of October instant—to remedy which—Be it enacted by the General Assembly, State of Tennessee, that the electors of the said County of Cocke shall be entitled to vote for a Representative to Congress at the said ensuing election on the second Thursday and day following of October instant at the Court House of Jefferson in same manner as heretofore used, anything in the said Act to the contrary notwithstanding.

Page 203, Chapter XXXII, records the act to establish town of Newport, which passed October 23, 1799, mentioning John Gilliand having donated "50 Acres of land for the purpose of laying out the town aforesaid lots to consist of one-half acre with proper streets and alleys.

Page 147, Act passed October 28, 1797, tells how census is first taken by Justice of the Peaces, who had to make full and complete lists of taxable property, polls, etc., by September of 1798.

Each was allowed $1.50 for each 100 taxable inhabitants enumerated as directed by this act, which same shall be appropriated for at next session of General Assembly.

William Maclean describes his journey from Lincoln, North Carolina, to Nashville, Tennessee, May-June, 1811, in the following extract:[19]

. . . Wednesday (May 15, 1811)—From this to Major David Jones 8 miles. Breakfasted here and fed my horse. From this to Asheville 10 miles. Arrived at Mjr. Erwins in this place 11 o'clock found Mr. Henry (Patrick Henry?—so the editor of the journal; but P. Henry died in 1799) and agreed to set out in Co. tomorrow morning.

---

19. *"William Maclean's Travel Journal,"* North Carolina Historical Review, October, 1938.

EXPENSE HERE

Self and horse 24 hours $1.00

1 sursingle 1.00

Thursday half after seven o'clock set out from this to Mr. Roberts 20 miles.

Dinner and horse feeding here $0.62½

From this to Barnells Station 1½ miles turnpike expense paid here $0.25

From this to Warm Springs 12 miles supper lodging and horse feeding $1.25

Friday from this to the ferry 1½ miles two ferries here ..$0.12½ (This was Hot Springs, N. C.)

From this to Hollands ferry 13 miles expense here $0.12½

From this to Mr. Walls on Long Creek 3 miles horse feeding and breakfast $0.50

From this to Fines ferry on French Broad 9 miles . . . this ferry is opposite to Newport the village of Cocke County, ferriage $0.12½

From this to Mr. Garretts one mile on Big Pidgeon where there is a Cotton Baging Manufactory erecting with machinery for breaking hemp—this is fixed with a spring pole to the Break and worked like the gate of a sawmill. Here I met with Col. Thomas Grey an old acquaintance who informed me he was seventy years old—Is yet firm, active and full of vivacity from thence we were piloted two miles by a Mr. *Hoskins* whose name is tatooed on his arm he is a blacksmith, five miles to Mr. McLenahans we arrived here at nine oclock. We forded Big Pidgeon which is about 150 yards wide or so near as I could estimate, Armstrongs ford supper, horse feeding and lodging $1.50

Saturday 18th. From this we proceeded early to Lownes Ferry upon French Broad 8 miles road good the river here said to be 200 yards wide and 20 feet deep at common water, it runs with an easy current and is furnished with a good ferry boat—At Lownes breakfast horse feeding and ferriage $0.56½ cents. From this to Dandridge 5¼ miles People flocking into this place to hear sermon—The Sacrament of the supper to be administered here to-morrow by Rev. Mr. Anderson. Dandridge is the County town of Jefferson county—Road good from Lownes ferry to this place and shorter than the way by Seahorns ferry which is the way commonly traveled—Seahorns ferry 5 miles above Lownes Nollachucky River empties into F. B. (French Broad) above Seahorns a little way.

At Dandridge we fell in company with Matthew Hurjess of York District So. Carolina going into West Tennessee from this place to Thompsons ten miles good road—land gravelly and poor generally—Limestone water—Fodder for our horses here and oats . . . $0.25 cents. From this to Cunningham 10 miles poor land generally road good there we stayed till Sunday afternoon. Mr. Cunninham is a sober religious sensible man Conversation on Politics Religion and natural Philosophy Expense here $1.50 and paid by me from this to the ferry at the mouth of the Holston 11 miles ferriage 6 pence Virginia money paid by me—from thence to Knoxville 5 miles. Here we put in at the James Darks—a good house but dear—Expense paid by Henry $3.25 (In Kingston) we put up at the house of Isaac Swan—a full cousin of Joseph Swans on Steel Creek—Horses fed with oats and fodder Dinner and Cyder to drink cost $0.75 paid by me . . .

Henry Ker gives an interesting account of his journey through this part of the country, prior to 1816:[20]

On the 27 of September, the weather being pleasant, I set out for Newport, a small town on the French Broad River. At sunset I arrived, having much difficulty in finding the town for it was hid in a deep valley. It is the most licentious place in the State of Tennessee, containing about twenty houses of sloth, indolence and dissipation. It is not my desire to stigmatize the character of any place; but when I discover people inhabiting a country of so much importance, and where they live in peace and plenty, subject only to wholesome laws, continually violating the laws of God and their country, I cannot avoid expressing my disgust, and considering them an injury to their country and a disgrace to the human family.

At Newport, I sold my horse, purchased an Ark, or flat bottomed boat, of about twelve tons burthen and hired three men to descend the river to New Orleans. On the first of October I began to descend French Broad. This river runs a North West Course about 25 or 30 miles and joins the Holston. It is very difficult for strangers to pass, in consequence of the number of rocks which lie scattered in the river. It is four or five hundred yards wide at its mouth. The next morning at sunrise, we entered the Holston, a considerable stream about 200 miles in length. In its course it receives the Watauga and French Broad and is navigable for crafts of thirty tons burthen one hundred miles from its mouth. Its shores abound with much valuable timber of all kinds. Many indolent people who inhabit these shores, who live solely by hunting and fishing, being very different from those who live in the inhabited parts of the State. There are several lead-mines on these rivers, one of them on the French Broad is very extensive.

Henry Ker also tells of his bear hunt and that he killed a 400 pound one as he journeyed along down the French Broad River.

John Silk Buckingham, Esquire, gives a contrasting picture to that of Ker of life in this county in his "Traveling in the Forties":[21]

At the foot of the mountain we met with the first log-hut in Tennessee, and it gave us, here, on the very threshold of the State, a favorable impression of its inhabitants. It was the neatest and cleanest we had seen in the country; though small, it had clean glass windows, without a single broken pane, neat white dimity curtains, on the inside clean though humble furniture, and industrious inmates, The children were all clean and well clad and the women were busily occupied. The cattle around the spot seemed numerous, and better fed than usual, though they live much less luxuriously than in England. There are here no rich pastures of meadow land, laid down in grass, such as one might suppose to be pasture grounds of the "fat bulls of Basham," but the cattle pick up such scanty subsistence as they may be able in the woods and along the way-side. As

20. *Ker's Travels,* published in 1816, at Elizabethton, New Jersey, page 20.
21. Buckingham's *Slave States of America.*

they thus wander several miles a day in search of provender, they are provided with a large metal bell hung under the neck, the heavy and dull sound of which is sufficiently loud to indicate where a wanderer who has strayed beyond his usual track may be found.

There are but few sheep seen anywhere along the road, as their flesh is not valued as food, but hogs were everywhere abundant. They are the ugliest of their species with long thin heads, long legs, arched backs, large lapping ears, lank bodies and long tails and they are among the filthiest of the filthy. I had never before thought there could be such difference in pigs; but I may now say, that the hog of England is as much superior in beauty of form and cleanliness of habit to the hog of America, as the Bucephalus and Alexander was to the Rosinante of Don Quixote, as superior, in short, as animals of the same race can be to each other.

About 7 o'clock we reached a clean and comfortable Inn at a station called Cave Hill, from a large cavern in the neighborhood; and as the coach was to halt here for sometime we availed ourselves of the assistance of the usual guides for such excursions and went to visit the cave by the bright light of a nearly full moon. (Here was a glowing description of the Cave, well known to the natives.)

We left the Inn at Cave Hill about 11 o'clock at night for Greeneville, but had scarcely gone a mile from thence, before the driver bade us roll our curtains of the coach up, and keep a good lookout, as an attempt had been made to rob the mail in this road only a few nights ago and the parties having been unsuccessful, he feared they would seek for some accession to their numbers and make another attempt. This was not very agreeable intelligence, but we put ourselves in a state of vigilance at least, so as to prepare for the worst; and tho we had not yet met with an instance of such an attack since we had been in the country, we thought the time might now have arrived and that we must brave it as well as we could, for we had never carried arms of defense of any kind whatsoever.

The road was a continual series of ascents and descents, to each of which, the driver had to adapt the coach, by locking and unlocking the wheels, as required. For this purpose he was obliged to get off every time with the reins in his hand, as there are no guards or other assistants sent with the mails here. We stopped, therefore, for this purpose fifty times at least, in our short journey of 13 miles. Besides he halted 4 times to water the horses, tying up the reins to the coach box, and requiring to go from 50 to 100 yards from the road for water, bringing it in the tin bucket, which coaches carry for the purpose, hung at one of the lamp posts, there being no watering troughs, as in England, on the road, and he had to bring a bucket for each of his four horses each time. A good hour was consumed in these four waterings.

The road, besides being thus hilly, had more than usually dense forests, especially in the bottoms of hollows, so that even the bright moon afforded us very little light, and the straining of the eyes in these dark places produced so many spectral illusions, that stumps of trees were perpetually taken for men on foot, waving boughs for horsemen in motion, but we encountered neither the one nor the other.

About an hour before reaching Greeneville, we forded the Noli-chucky river, a broad and clear but shallow stream, with high rocky banks, where another detention took place, so that we did not reach Greeneville till 4 o'clock, a little before daylight, having been there-fore 5 hours going a distance of 13 miles, over the most disagreeable road we had yet traveled.

The Greene County Court minutes of 1817-1819 speaks of "Reuben Allen, overseer of the road, from the ford of the river near George Farns-worth, to the road leading from Wilson's ford to Fine's Ferry."

An Act of the Assembly on November 1, 1833 authorized William P. Gillet "to open a turnpike road, commencing at Newport in the county of Cocke, and running up the south side of the French Broad River to Holland's ferry. Which road, when the situation of the ground will permit, shall be cut eighteen feet wide, clear of stumps and other ob-structions. And where said road, has to be cause wayed it shall, if the ground will permit, be twelve feet wide, and if there should be any creeks that require it there shall be good, sufficient and substantial bridges built over them."

The Acts of 1847-8 show that Benjamin Parker and William Tinker were given further time of two years to open and complete a turnpike road.

On January 18, 1848, the Assembly authorized Stephen Huff, Peter F. Kendrick and William Robinson to open a turnpike road and granted them a charter for thirty years to keep a toll gate on said road, and ap-pointed John P. Long, William Cumming, and Jeremiah Fryer, com-missioners of the aforesaid.

In the stage-coach period of the 1830's up the railroad era, Newport was one of the convenient points in Tennessee. Service lines operated through the town. One ran from North Carolina, through Shoun's cross-roads in Johnson County, through Newport to Knoxville, where con-nections were made to Nashville and numerous other points; another ran from Asheville, through Newport, to Nashville; and a third, from Warm Springs, through Newport and Maryville to Huntsville, Alabama. The coaches carried the mails, which were placed under the driver's seat. Their advent into a town was heralded by a blast of a trumpet. The town had two taverns in the 1830's, which gave entertainment to travelers.

As early as 1832 a stage-coach line ran from Wilkesboro, North Carolina, by way of Elizabethton, Jonesboro, Greeneville, through Newport and Dandridge to Knoxville. An early stage-mail line operated from Asheville, through Newport to Bean's Station in Grainger County and on through Cumberland Gap.

In addition to the two inns at Newport, there was one at Parrotts-ville, one at about midway between Parrottsville and Newport, known as "The Story Inn," owned and operated by Abraham McKay's family. It was on the high hill near the present Gillespie home, a site noted for the perfect view toward the south. The landscape is artistically perfect, mountains in the background, the French Broad and its rich valley that reaches back into the hills at the base of the mountains. Abraham Mc-Kay owned most of the land that was seen from this elevation. Hog-drivers, mule drivers, cattle drivers, on their way from Virginia and Kentucky to the Charleston markets stopped at this famous old inn be-cause of the lot room it afforded their stock. The various drivers claimed

The Abraham O'Dell home on the French Broad River sometimes called the Cameron house.

Part of the original Wilson Inn on Knoxville highway.

that on early mornings they could hear the "crack of the whips" from the drivers leaving the mouth of Chucky with their stock, they in turn "cracked their whips" so that the drivers, would know that the Story Inn would be prepared for them and so that those who had reached Hot Springs stands of Thomas Garrett and the ferryman Henry Ottinger would know to get ready for them, also Wash Allen at Wolf Creek. Of course, Peter Fine's Ferry at French Broad, at Old Town, had in all probability, become the Cureton Ferry by the time the vast droves of stock were on their way to Carolina markets. The ferryman there could be notified "by word of mouth" the night before.

The Wilson Inn also did a flourishing business in the early days and was a stage-coach terminal; part of it is still standing. It was built more than one hundred sixty years ago, west of Newport, where the Carson Springs road joins the highway. This property belonged to Major William Wilson, whose estate consisted of hundreds of acres of land designated, "From the top of the mountains on the South to bank of the Big Pigeon River on the North Side," in the section known as Wilsonville. It is so rocky in places that the oldest citizens claim that "when the Devil flew over this part of the country his apron string broke and down came the rocks." A few yards north of the highway near the Old Inn, is Rock Spring, near an immense pile of rocks placed there by the forty slaves of Major Wilson.

Distinguished citizens of Tennessee and the Nation stopped there in the early days. It was different then, about 100 by 200 feet, with the "L" part about 100 feet in length. Porches extended along the entire "L" side and all the way along the 200 foot front. The porch reached to the very edge of the stage roadway on the south side of the house. Among the visitors to the Wilson Inn were: Isham G. Harris, Felix Grundy, James C. Jones, Henry Clay, Sam Houston, President Andrew Johnson, who spoke for four hours at a nearby place, and James K. Polk.[22] Andrew Jackson was a frequent visitor to this Inn. Many years before he became President he held Court at Jonesboro and passed back and forth on such occasions. Sometimes he stopped at the Old Inn in Old Town,[23] from which he wrote the interesting letter to Rachel.

---

22. James K. Polk spent the night in this Inn with his opponent, "Lean Jimmy Jones" when they were running for Governor of Tennessee. Mrs. Wilson and the Major were delighted with Polk's gracious manner and mentioned it to "Lean Jimmy," saying that they were pleased that Polk felt so much at home he did not mind to rest on the floor on a pallet. Lean Jimmy with his sense of humor replied that he understood that when and where James K. Polk thought there might be bedbugs he always slept on the floor. This remark turned the tide of Polk's popularity toward Lean Jimmy, who won the office he sought.

23. Letter written to his wife, when Jackson was Superior Court Judge as well as Major General, from the Tavern in Newport on the French Broad River.

Newport, Tennessee
March 22, 1803

My Love:

I am this far on my way to Knoxville from Jonesborough and being about to part with Colonel Christmas who has promised to call and deliver some garden seeds and this letter to you, I write, fully impressed with a belief that the letter and garden seeds will be handed to you.

These are a variety of seeds and as large quantities of each as I could obtain. If there should be any to spare, of any kind sent, I have said to Colonel Christmas that you would divide with him.

On the 15th instant, in Jonesborough, Mr. Rawlings' stable was set on fire. It

The McSween sisters' home, now the residence of Donald McSween

The Allen home at Wolf Creek, oldest in the County, 1737

The last visit Jackson made to the Parrottsville Inn was when he was on his way to be sworn in as President of the United States. On this particular trip he rode in a carriage drawn by four white horses. Some distance in front of the carriage, as required by an Old Tennessee law, rode a bugler on a white horse, who would call out, "Clear the way, the President of the United States is approaching." (Told to H. W. Huff by Sallie Brinkman, a music teacher in Parrottsville, who was reminded of the part her own ancestor had played at the Battle of Waterloo.)

The Wilson Inn passed from Major Wilson to Major Peter Fine through his marriage to Major Wilson's granddaughter. It now belongs to Everett Greer of Washington, D. C., who plans to restore it to its original state and preserve it in honor of the three Presidents who sought rest there, hoping it will eventually become a state and national shrine—housing relics of an age forever gone.

Another popular Inn was the Allen Inn, which is still standing on Wolf Creek. It was built in 1737, by the first Allen, who came from Rockingham County, Virginia, with his wife, and established his home in the wilderness.

ALLEN-INN—It is about 90 by 40 feet, with 14 rooms, of hewn logs, four large chimneys and a great porch. (It is now weatherboarded and ceiled.) The cabins in the yard add ten more rooms to this home, which was once used as a summer retreat for artists and musicians from all over the country. The boxwood garden on the east side of the home was designed by Emma Allen, daughter of Reuben, who used the Mount Vernon gardens as her model. Cypress from the swamps in Arkansas and English ivy make the place picturesque.[24]

Near Taylorsburg, the largest village in the county was another inn at one time, on the property now owned by Oscar Cate of Edwina, located between the present Edwina and Cosby sections.

---

and two more stables were burnt down, and four horses. With great exertion and the calmness of the night, the other buildings were saved.

During the distressing scene I was a great deal exposed, having nothing on but a shirt. I have caught a very bad cold, which settled on my lungs, occasioned a bad cough and pain in my breast.

It was with the utmost exertion, I saved my horse from the flames. Not until I made the third attempt, before I could force him into the passage. You may easily judge the anxiety by seeing the poor animals in danger.

I shall write you from Knoxville, and would write you more fully, but the Colonel has promised to call, from whom you can receive all the information that I could give.

I wish you to say to Mr. Goery that I wish my cotton planted between the 15th and 25th of April.

I hope the apple trees have been safely brought and planted. I have been afraid they received injury from frost, from the very severe frost that fell about that time. I hope it has been in his power to make your time more agreeable with the servants. I also hope that he has brought Aston to a perfect state of obedience.

I have not heard a single syllable from you since I left home. I hope you have enjoyed and are now enjoying health, and may health and happiness surround you until I have the pleasure of seeing you is the sincere wish of your affectionate husband.

ANDREW JACKSON.

Mrs. Rachel Jackson
(Copied from *Knoxville Journal*, April 22, 1922.)

24. Several generations have lived here. They were Reuben Allen, James Allen, David Allen; now Nell Allen Walker and her sons William Allen Cowan Walker and Ward. The post office of Wolf Creek, Tennessee, is kept in the Allen home. For several years it was known as Allendale, Tennessee, but soon after the Civil War the family had it changed back to Wolf Creek, Tennessee.

During the first session of the 22nd General Assembly of the State an act was passed naming the following men as Commissioners to incorporate Elizabethton, Sullivan, Jonesboro, Greeneville, Newport, Dandridge and New Market Turnpike Companies, and the following were named for Cocke County: Thomas Rogers, Alexander E. Smith, James Dawson, William C. Roadman, Samuel Haskins, John Stuart, John Tillett, R. W. Pulliam, N. L. Reese, William Robinson, David Harned, Abraham Fine, George W. Carter, Stephen Huff. They were "to open books for the purpose of receiving subscriptions to the amount of two hundred thousand dollars, to be applied to the purpose of making a McAdamized turnpike road from Elizabethton by the way of Jonesboro and Greeneville to Newport, or to some point on the Charleston and Cincinnati railroad, which may be situated nearer to Greeneville than Newport is situated." This was passed January 17, 1838.

In the first half of the 1800's, and even up to the Civil War, Cocke County was the gateway for a large traffic in horses, cattle, and hogs, from Tennessee to the Carolinas.

In the *Tennessee Gazetteer*, published in 1834 are the following lines: "It is estimated that five hundred head of hogs are driven annually from Cocke County to Southern markets."

Charles Lanman, one time private secretary of Daniel Webster, was a great traveler, and in 1848, reached the borders of Cocke County and in his *Letters from the Alleghany Mountains*, in a chapter "Down the French Broad,"[25] has this to say:

Judging of the whole, by a section, lying westward of Asheville, the French Broad must be considered one of the most beautiful rivers in this beautiful land. In depth it varies from five to fifteen feet, is quite clear, abounding in a great variety of plebean fish. Its shores are particularly wild and rocky, varying from one to four hundred feet in height, usually covered with vegetation. These present a most imposing appearance. With regard to botanical curiosities, it can safely be said that a more fruitful and interesting valley can no where be found in the union.

A turnpike road and an occasional tavern are on its banks, the road running directly along the water's edge, nearly the entire distance; and on account of the quantity of travel which passes over it, is kept in admirable repair. It is the principal thoroughfare between Tennessee and South Carolina, and an immense number of cattle, horses and hogs are annually driven over it to the seaboard markets. Over this road also quite a large amount of merchandise is constantly transported for merchants of the interior, so that

---

25. In riding down the French Broad, Lanman overtook a gentleman on horseback who also accompanied the traveler about twenty miles. During the conversation, Lanman was startled by an inquiry, in regard to the "latest news from China." It developed that the horseman was a dealer in ginseng, which found its principal market in China. "My friend described ginseng as a beautiful plant with one stem and some twenty leaves at the top, and growing to the height of eighteen inches," though only the roots were sent to market. "My companion told me that his sales amounted to about forty thousand dollars per annum, sold for about sixty cents per pound. What an idea! that the celestials are dependent on the United States for their celestial luxury, and that luxury a plant of the wilderness!"

mammoth wagons, with their eight and ten horses and their half civilized teamsters, are as plenty as blackberries and afford a virulentic variety of profanity to the stranger.

From the John Stevens and T. S. Gorman papers, one can understand why Tennessee was once known as "The Hog and Hominy State." On December 25, 1855, the hog sale of Andrew Ramsey amounted to two thousand dollars. On March 20, 1863, "Robert Allen received three thousand, eight hundred and fifty dollars in cash, also one note for two thousand, eight hundred thirteen dollars and eighty-six cents, out of the amount collected from Agnew Fisher & Co., for a lot of hogs sold them by Allen and Brooks, 1861. (Signed) John S. Stephens."

In Hawthorne's *American Note Books,* published in 1871 (page 195), are these descriptive lines of the business of hog driving:

"They are much more easily driven on rainy days than on fair ones. One of the pigs, a large one, particularly troublesome as to running off the road towards every object, and leading the drove. Thirteen miles is about a day's journey in the course of which the drovers have to travel about thirty miles. They have a dog who runs to and fro, indefatigably barking at those who struggle on the flanks of the line of march, then scampering to the other side and barking there and some time having quite an affair of barking and surly grunting with some refractory pig, who has found something to munch, and refuses to quit it. The pigs are fed on corn at their halts, (or stands along the way). The drove has some ultimate market and individuals are peddled out on the march, some die."

About 1880, it was customary for the farmers to feed their surplus corn to hogs, beginning about the 15 of August and finishing by the first of November. The hogs were then weighed and valued and made ready for the drive overland. It took about eighteen days to drive the one hundred and fifty miles to market the hogs. From Cocke, Greene, and Jefferson Counties, as many as twenty-five to forty droves of hogs, with between four and five hundred hogs, to the drove, went each year to South Carolina. Some droves were smaller, some larger, and would average about five thousand hogs to the county. A Newport citizen, Jesse W. D. Stokely, made five hog-driving journeys with his father, Charles Stokely, of Del Rio, and describes vividly these interesting trips.

There was no railway between Wolf Creek, Tennessee and Greeneville, South Carolina. Travel was by the Old State Coach, horseback and walking. The highways were kept up by Turnpike Companies. The drovers had to pay toll or tax on each head of hogs. I think it was a penny a head. They were driven from eight to ten miles per day. There were several people who kept drovers stands along the way and provided lodging and food for the drovers and pens and corn for the hogs. These pens for the hogs would consist of from one half to three acres of land. Often the sleeping quarters would be considerably crowded. I have spent the night where as many as ten droves of hogs were lotted and fed. This was about four thousand hogs, with one man to each hundred, making forty men, with a manager for each drove. A total of fifty men for whom beds and food must be prepared. The Stand Keepers would make about five beds down on the floor in each room with about three men to the bed. The menu for the meal would be plenty of milk, coffee, cornbread, biscuits, fresh meat, both pork and beef, cabbage, kraut, beans, potatoes and pies for dessert. It took a lot of food to feed fifty hungry men, to say nothing of the corn it took for the hogs.

These drovers of our County and adjoining counties were our most outstanding citizens. Men who owned the best farms. They were a very congenial group of men and formed very close friendships with each other during the years between 1877 and 1881. It took about thirty days to make the round trip. The following names are the Stand Keepers I knew personally during those years: Wash Allen, Wolf Creek, Tennessee, the Terminus of the East Tennessee-Virginia Railroad Company; Frank Lawson, on Shut-In Creek, N. C.; Henry Ottinger, Ferryman, four miles south of Hot Springs, N. C.; Thomas Garrett, across the French Broad River opposite Hot Springs, N. C.; Wash Farnsworth, (Colored) at the mouth of Big Laurel Creek; Mrs. Barnett, at Barnett Stand; Maj. W. W. Rollins, Marshall, N. C.; Capt. Alfred Alexander, Alexander, N. C.; Gen. Robert Vance, Vance, N. C.; Joseph Reed, Swananoah, N. C.; Press Patton, Skyland, N. C.; Dr. Fletcher, Fletcher, N. C.; McDowell Hotel, Hendersonville, N. C.; Col. W. S. Tabor, Flat Rock, N. C.; a Mr. Heart, Green River, N. C.; John Posey, Saluda Gap, S. C.; John Hightowner, Bayson Springs, S. C.; John Hodge, Saluda River, S. C.; a Mr. Montgomery, Greeneville, S. C.; Greeneville Hotel, Greeneville, S. C.; John Roseman, Anderson Road, S. C.; Col. Cager Williams, Anderson Road, S. C.; Jolly Pool, Anderson Road, S. C.; John Catlett, Anderson Court House, S. C.

It would take about ten days after reaching the market to sell and weigh the hogs. In order to market the corn that was raised on the farm it was necessary for the hogs to be driven to S. C., where the farmers could buy for themselves and for their tenants, merchandise needed at home.

The following names are only a few of the drovers that I knew personally and they were all from Cocke County: Alex. Stuart, Alex. Smith, W. R. Swaggerty, Wesley Davis, David Susong, George Susong, Jacob Susong, McCauley Susong, Charles Stokely, W. R. Stokely, David Stokely, Bryson Walls, George Walls, Duncan Easterly, Col. William Jack, Mark Jack, Sam Jack, William Sheffey, Joseph Huff, Andrew Steele, Asa Bayless, Job Bible, Robert Evans, Ralph Randolph.

An almost forgotten art was closely associated with the business of hograising. Many men were able to develop an artistic and highly musical call which invariably brought the hogs scampering to them in haste.

During the hog-driving days of the pioneers and into the Gay Nineties, the "Hog Drivers, Hog Drivers, Hog Drivers We Are!" singing game was enjoyed. Dating back to England, it was known as "The Three Dukes," but with a different tune.[26]

---

26. It is played after this fashion: a man and a girl are seated in the center of large circle. The girl is the man's daughter. Around the circle's edge two men march as though driving hogs. They begin the game by singing the first verse. The father sings the second, and so on alternately to the end of the game. Then the father gives the daughter to whomsoever he chooses in the audience surrounding the circle. He is supposed to give her to her "sweetheart." The hog driver to whom he gives the girl, then chooses another daughter to be seated by her father's side in the

Today, Newport is the meeting point of many important highways. U. S. 25, East, is the short line from Corbin, Kentucky, where 25 divides into East and West. At Newport these two divisions merge again into 25 and run to Asheville, North Carolina, and Augusta, Georgia, where it strikes U. S. 1. This is the short line from the Midwest to Jacksonville and the Florida and the East Coast. U. S. 25 runs West from Corbin, via Norris Dam, via Knoxville, Tennessee, to Newport, and jointly from Knoxville to Newport is U. S. 70, which comes from the far West, passing through Newport and thence on across to North Carolina to the Atlantic Coast—the Broadway of America.

Route 35 comes from Greeneville to Newport, via Parrottsville, and from Newport, thence to Sevierville and on to Knoxville. It commands a full view of the mountains the entire distance. This route with Tennessee 34 from Bristol have been promoted as short lines to the Great Smoky Mountains National Park from the Southwestern points of Virginia. The newly paved roads from Newport to Morristown and to Knoxville cut both time and distance from these points to Newport.

Route 75, which leads from Newport to the Great Smokies via Cosby, is one of the most scenic highways in East Tennessee, a distance of only fourteen miles to the Park Area, and is called the Governor Ben W. Hooper Highway.

Another beautiful entrance is by way of Yellow Spring Mountain Road. To take this route one leaves the Asheville Highway about three miles East of Newport, turning directly South at the Augusta Stephens

---

center of the circle. The couple then join the hog drivers and march with them after all say "whirley-burley" which means to reverse direction of marching. The song is sung over again until every man and maid has been called into the ring.

When the last daughter has been given away, all the men bow on bended knee to their brides while the father blesses them in an impressive manner. At the close of the blessing, each man kisses his bride, and the music of "haste, oh haste to the wedding" begins in a rapid, swinging, skipping step. All the couples make haste to the wedding by leaving the room entirely and the game is over.

HOG-DRIVERS SONG

Hog drivers, hog drivers, hog drivers we are
A courting your daughter so neat and so fair
Can we get lodging here oh here,
Can we get lodging here?

I have a pretty daughter who sits by my side,
But no hog-driver can have her for a bride
And you can't get lodging here oh here,
And you can't get lodging here.

You have a pretty daughter, tho ugly be yourself
We'll travel on farther and seek greater wealth
We don't want lodging here oh here,
And we don't want lodging here.

Hog driver, hog drivers, hog drivers you are
A courting my daughter so neat and so fair
So you can get lodging here oh here,
And you can get lodging here.

I have a pretty daughter who sits by my side
And Mr........(whomsoever he chooses) can have her for a bride
And you can get lodging here oh here,
And you can get lodging here.

place. This road gradually winds itself around Yellow Spring Mountain until it crosses at Rocky Top, thence through Humphrey's Gap and follows Big Creek, thence across Sol Messer Mountain, to the Roscoe Rollins Place, thence up Raven's Branch to the Davis Schoolhouse, where it follows up Big Creek, to Brown's Gap at the North Carolina-Tennessee State line where it is met by a similar road from the North Carolina side of the mountains. It was a WPA project, said to have been suggested by Frank Huff, who did not live to see it completed.

The Appalachian Trail, which is the world's longest one, running 2,050 miles from Mount Katahdin, Maine, to Mount Oglethorpe, Georgia, touching fourteen states, passes through the Great Smokies, Pisgah, Unaka and Cherokee National forests in Cocke County. Benton McKay conceived the idea of this magnificent continuous wilderness trail in 1921.[27]

The development of the Indian trails into the splendid highways of today has made the history of Cocke County an interesting and romantic one.

---

27. Guide books for this trail may be had by writing the Appalachian Trail Conference, 808-17th Street, Washington, D. C.

Early Settlers in Cocke County

Family Names

Some people set great store by their family names. They take pride in the fact that their ancestors were of Royal Blood, or that they came over in the Mayflower, or that they can trace back to some old Colonial Governor or President or family of wealth and distinction. This is a fine and splendid source of pride. It is indeed pardonable if it is not carried too far. We have to first come from somewhere before we can go anywhere and blood always tells, we are told. Our early families were more careful than we are about keeping the family bloodstream pure.

The Bible tells us that, "A good name is rather to be chosen than great riches and loving favor rather than silver and gold." And the greatest writer of all time said, "He who filches from me my good name robs me of that which not enriches him and makes me poor indeed." Thus we realize how wonderful it is to have been born with a good name.

To intelligent people names are always significant, interesting and often fascinating because of what they have come to symbolize.

We, of this day and time, have come to find out that beauty, romance, glamor, poetry, the fine arts, power, wealth, bravery, cowardice, poverty, various discoveries and inventions, robbers, liars, drunkards and all the sins of omission and commission are so entwined with names they seem to be part and parcel of these things.

Our family names handed down to us by our forebears and often our given names, become something sacred for us to protect and revere as the good deeds of many generations before us have clothed such names in glory. They are our most treasured and valued possessions.

Given names were the only ones people had at first but as the population increased it became necessary for the people to have specific and family designations. We note in Bible times such distinguishing appellations as, Joseph of Arimathea, Simeon, the son of Mary, Jonas, John the beloved, Judah of Galilee, Saul of Tarsus, Mary, the Mother of Jesus and Jesus of Nazareth.

Surnames were introduced to England from Normandy about the year one thousand, although the records show Saxon surnames prior to the Norman conquest. During the reign of Edward the V a law was passed making it compulsory for the outlaws in Ireland to adopt surnames. "They shall take unto them a surname, either of some town, or some color . . . of some art or science . . . or some office." As late as the beginning of the nineteenth century a similar decree compelled the Jews in Germany and Austria to add a German surname to their single names. Thus we see our surnames are not very old in world history.

English names often end in . . . son, ing, kin, from the Norse sonor ingr and kyn are of this type as are also the names prefixed with the Gaelic MAC, the Norman FITZ, the Welch, AP and the Irish, O literally means a descendant of . . . John's son became Johnson, William's son became Williamson or Wilson, Richard's son became Richardson, Neil's son became McNeils, Herbert's son became Fitzherbert, Hugh's son, became Fitzhugh, Thomas' son became Thomas or Thomason. Ap was dropped from many names. Reilly's son became O'Reilley and Conner's son O'Conner . . . etc. etc. etc.

From physical or personal characteristics came such names as Roger of small stature is now Rogerlittle (nicknames). Black Haired William became William Black and Blond John became John White.

Fox and Wolfe are of totemistic origin.

The common name of Smith has a significance known to few. It was the name given to the King's armorer. He was always an honored man in every court. By his skill and strength he made the armor in which men went to battle. Could that be a possible reason for so many SMITHS in the world? It was necessary for the Kings to have many Smiths to keep the wars progressing. Some claim that the first Smith was PHARAOH SMITHOSIS. Some claim the name came from Noah's son, Shem while others insist the name came from the Anglo-Saxon word SMITAN meaning one who strikes or smites with a hammer. Later it meant men who work in metals, as goldsmith, silversmith etc. In France it is known as Le Febre, in Italy, Fabbroni, in Scotland Mac Gowan, in Germany, Schmids, Russia, Skmittowski.

Another class of names is composed of surnames derived from and designating the place of residence of the bearer. Such names were introduced into England by the Normans who were known by the titles of their estates. They were names used with . . . de, dela, or del meaning of, or of the, hence the landowners often had de before the name like de Berri or Del after it like Of, Del eventually O'Dell.

The Saxon equivalent was the word . . . atte or . . . at the . . . John atte Brook, William atte Bourne and thus we have such names as At . . . well At . . . wood . . . At water, now the AT is left off generally.

Craft and trade names came later as . . . Webb and Webster, weavers of cloth, Wainright, a wagon builder, Baxter a baker, Miller, a mill-wright and Shepherd, a sheep herder.

Many names are difficult to classify because of corruptions of ancient spelling or forms of it thus disguising the names beyond recognition. Longfellow was Longueville, and Longshanks was Longchamps, Trouble-field was Tuberville, Wrinch, was Renshaw, Diggles was Douglas and Snooks was Seven Oaks.

No where in the world do we find so many different family names as in America. The English, Scotch, Irish and Welsh predominate.

Those of us able to trace our names back to sturdy ancestors have a right to be proud of our goodly heritage handed down by our honored family names. In the beginning it was only a word, a convenient label to distinguish one John from another. But now it has established itself as a part of the bearer's own individuality and as it passed to his children, his grandchildren and to their children, it became the symbol, of a family and all that family stood for from generation to generation. It became inseparably associated with the achievement, the tradition and the glory of the family. No wonder we cherish our good names. But we must not forget that we are of value ONLY in proportion to our ability to serve our generation, so regardless of whether our ancestors came over in the

Mayflower or met the boat when it arrived, or missed it entirely what now counts is what we can do to make the world a better place for those who are to carry our names on to the next generation.

The author has diligently endeavored to record the names of the families who came first to our County, by that I mean, by the year 1800. She repeatedly asked that such names be sent to her along with data of the arrival and descendants. If any have been left out it is the fault of those who should have sent in their names. With all early records destroyed by fire it has not been possible to find out the names of all our pioneering ancestors. Many, many families who came long after 1800 rendered valuable service in the establishment of our beloved home county. I have tried to list them among the NOTABLES. Their names were also requested through the county papers many times over, if they do not appear the author does not feel responsible for their omission.

A people who take no pride in the noble achievements of their ancestors are not likely to achieve anything to be worth remembering by their descendants. The people of Cocke County should look with pride upon the efforts put forth by those who have gone on before us, they were true pioneers who fought a good fight and carved out of the wilderness, for us, our wonderful county. We too, are pioneers, but of an entirely different type, pioneers none-the-less. Those of us now past fifty years of age have lived in the greatest era of all time, having passed from the "Horse and Buggy Days" to the limousine, from the narrow, rocky, muddy roads to highways as smooth as satin ribbons, from only clouds and stars above us, to the silver ships that Tennyson told us about one hundred years ago, from the tallow candle and lamps to the electric light, from all the primitive ways of life to the most modern ways of living.

In the early days of our county's history we had a very colorful MILITIA which drilled at the MUSTER FIELD in what is now OLD TOWN, or rather east of it. Many still living can locate the exact spot known as the Muster Field.

Colonel Joseph O'Neil, Colonel William Jack and Major William Robinson all belonged at the same time. They had very handsome uniforms for which they paid one hundred dollars each. General Salisbury's uniform was extremely striking. He wore an immense white plume in his headdress, it swept backward in graceful curves.

The drum major of this company was a mere boy, George Ogden, whose family had come from Boston. He was related to the French family of La Rue who had settled in the Dutch Bottoms and built the Hampton House with its thick walls of brick for protection from Indian attack.

(Information by Mrs. Jessie Orleans O'Neil Lee, great grand-daughter of Colonel Joseph O'Neil.)

Among the early settlers of Cocke County, there were a number of men of Scotch-Irish descent who possessed refinement and education, such as William Garrett, William Gilleland, William Lillard, John McNabb, William Jobe, Peter Fine, Abraham McKay, Samuel Jack and Colonel Alexander Smith, but the majority of the first settlers were roving adventurers, uneducated, and unpolished, whose highest aim and ambition was to obtain a fertile tract of land at the least expense. But along with this greed, they were daring and determined and valued their blood as a cheaper consideration for a rich tract of land than their money. Coupled with these attributes, their love of freedom, of country, of home, we cannot help admiring the character and valor of those who shared the glories of King's Mountain, and later under the leadership of "Old Hickory" at Talladega, at the Horseshoe, and finally upon the plains of near New Orleans, shed a more resplendent luster upon American arms. (McSween)

Fourteen years before Cocke County was known by its present name, it was settled on the "Chucky" river in the Northern part of the present boundaries. In 1784, many people settled in the Irish Bottoms. The daughter of George McNutt was the first white child born South of the French Broad River. The names of these first settlers were: Josiah, Benjamin and Alexander Roberts, John McNabb, Cornelius McGuin, Joseph and William Doherty. On the north side of the French Broad river were the Huff, the Ottinger, and the Boyer families. The north side of the river was called the Dutch Bottoms. One of the most active of these pioneers was John Gilliland who took part in organizing the State of Franklin and was a delegate to the Convention in 1785 to pass on the Constitution for the new state. He donated fifty acres of land for the laying out and building of a town on the French Broad River. He left a family of eight sons and several daughters.

Simeon O'Dell and his brother, Nehemiah, were the first to settle on Cosby Creek in the southern part of the County. They were both murdered by the Indians and scalped, and their guns carried away.

William Coleman cleared a plot of ground in the Fork of the Pigeon and French Broad Rivers and built one of the first cabins in the County, in the year 1763 or 4. This plot of ground was next to that of James Gilliland and formed the nucleus of the settlements of the valley of the two rivers.

The first settlement on the Big Pigeon River was made by Captain John McNabb at Wilton Springs. He procured a land warrant from the State of North Carolina in 1787. This warrant called for about 400 acres and included the Big Spring and the Indian town near it. He built a two-story house with portholes north of the site of the present one.

Captain John McNabb had two sons, George and John McNabb. To John he gave the upper part of the farm; to George, the lower part, the line running with the present lane from the Pigeon River, for it was the Indian boundary until that time. There were 800 acres instead of 400 when surveyed.

In 1793, the County Court of Jefferson County, of which Cocke County was then a part, appointed Peter Huff, Spencer Rice, John McNabb, William Lillard, Joseph Rutherford, Alexander Rogers, Thomas Christian and Henry Patton, a commission to lay off a road from the mouth of the Pigeon River up the south side of the French Broad to War Ford on the Pigeon River.

In 1797, when Cocke County was cut off from Jefferson County by Act of the General Assembly on October 9, the Commission appointed to locate the county seat and construct the needed buildings chose the site at Fine's Ferry on the French Broad River one and one half miles north of the present site of Newport.

Peter Fine was the first man to be given a license to run a ferry, which was the one at War Ford where Newport is now located. The Ford was opposite the home of the McSween sisters and is the site of the burial place of three Indians killed by John Sevier at or near the time of the last Indian battle fought in Tennessee which was about one mile below the present site of Newport on the Pigeon River. The property where the War Ford was located and the Indians are buried now, 1940 belongs to Everett Greer. Until the year 1884, the settlement around War Ford was known as "Clifton," named for John Clifton. Peter Fine also had a ferry on French Broad at Old Newport. Later, it was probably called the Cureton Ferry.

From July 2, 1791, to October 9, 1797, Cocke County was part of the territory that was ceded to the United States by the Cherokee Indians, by the Treaty of the Holston made by William Blount, Governor of the Territory South of the Ohio River, and the Cherokee Indians; Cocke, Sevier, and Hamblen all being cut off from Jefferson County and Jefferson County cut off from Greene County.

The burning of the original Court House destroyed valuable papers; the burning of the second courthouse destroyed many more, but records were kept by W. J. McSween, and much information gathered from these.

The McSween family was among the early settlers, coming from Moore County, North Carolina, and originally from the Isle of Skye, off the coast of Scotland. Murdock and his wife Margaret Jackson McSween settled south of Morrell Springs in 1820. They were Scotch Presbyterians and helped organize the first church of that faith. Morrell Springs was "entered" by Charles Morrell, a miller, and an influential pioneer who operated a cotton gin.

In the early 1800's, a large number of Pennsylvania Germans of "Dutch" made a community settlement in Cocke and Greene Counties, between the two county seats. It is said that as late as 1939, there were two hundred families in the community, 95 per cent of whom were landowners, whereas in the two counties as a whole, only about two-thirds were of the land-owning class. These families cultivate small farms, on which they raise most of their subsistence, and are "good livers," are thrifty, and are reputed to raise the best tobacco in the region. In large part, they maintain a community integrity though inter-marriages with families of other racial strains are not infrequent. (Judge Williams)

REUBEN ALLEN

Reuben Allen, the son of Ira and Anne Allen, was born in Shenandoah County, Virginia, and came to Cocke County, Tennessee, where he married Mary Jones (Polly), who was born April 2, 1788, on February 26, 1805. She was born in Greene County, and died November 13, 1864. He died November 7, 1825. Both are buried in the private Allen Cemetery, Wolf Creek, Cocke County. Records on file in The War Department, Washington, D. C., show that Reuben served in the War of 1812 from November 8, 1814 to May 16, 1815, as a private in Captain Joseph Hale's Company, Fourth Regiment (Bayle's) East Tennessee Militia. Prior to this he was listed as a lieutenant, April 5, 1798, in the records of Commissions of Officers in the Tennessee Militia of Cocke County. Their children (as listed in the Reuben Allen Bible, now the property of Mrs. Nelle Glenn Allen Walker, Wolf Creek) were: Rachel Allen, born November, 1805; James Allen, April 3, 1807; Margaret Allen, October 3, 1808; Eliza Allen, July 31, 1810; G. Washington Allen, April 11, 1812; Nancy Allen, October 1, 1813; Greene Allen, July 26, 1815; Cyntha Allen, June 28, 1817; Emaline Allen, May 2, 1820; William Allen, March 31, 1824.

Reuben Allen built the beautiful "Old Taveran" at Wolf Creek, and Abraham Lincoln, James K. Polk, Woodrow Wilson, and other notables have spent the night there.

THE ALLEN CLANS

By CORA MASSEY MIMS

There is some confusion, even in the minds of their descendants, as to the origin and number of several unrelated families in Cocke County. All agree that there were three principal groups. I have searched all available records, using also my own personal recollections, which reach back some 70 years, and it seems that these Allen clans may be classified as follows—Descendants of—

1—JACK ALLEN—One of two brothers who came to the Cosby section with the early settlers, and then passed on to Sevier County (afterward so called) where they built chimneys, leaving their names on the bricks: and there in Wear's valley they met Nancy and Milly Maddox, whom they probably married before returning to Cosby. When ready to settle down they built homes, not on Cosby Creek, but on Pigeon River—Jack at the mouth of Cosby Creek; and James a little farther up the river. Jack and Nancy reared a family of 11 or 12 children, and left documentary proof. He also left proof of his craftsmanship, of which much has been written.

It will be understood that "Jack" was the name by which John Allen was familiarly known throughout his lifetime and in local history. It is used in this record to distinguish him from other John Allens in his own family and in other Allen clans.

It is my best information that James Allen, his brother and his wife Milly Maddox had no children.

2—REUBEN ALLEN, came from the Shenandoah Valley of Va., previous to 1805, for in that year he married Mary Jones in Greene County, Tenn. Within a few years he secured some land, in what way we do not know, and established a home at the head of Grass Branch, which is the fine spring at the McSween place, flowing into Pigeon below the old Morell Mill. We do not know if he built this house, or if he lived in it, but we do know that in 1820, he sold this place to Murdock McSween, late of Moore County, N. C. Reuben died in 1825, and we find, a few years later, his family living at Wolf Creek, in a house said to have been built by the father of a 16 year old daughter, Fanny Hoss Wolf, who in 1827 had married James, a son of Jack Allen. So early do we find intermarriage in the Allen clans, and a duplication of names, since Reuben's oldest son was named James R. and might at this time have been head of the family. It seems that the Wolf family built only a part of the house at Wolf Creek. Colonial land grants place the acquisition of the place, and the probable building of the house as 1738. My information concerning this house and family comes from Mrs. Nell Allen Walker, a great granddaughter of Reuben, who with her family, still occupies the old house in which she was born, and where she has spent her entire life. Also some data from Mrs. Earl Mitchell of Knoxville, a great-great granddaughter of Reuben. Some has come from the McSween family directly related to my husband. I, myself, have a cherished personal memory of a night spent there when a child, including that of the "dog-trot" an open passage between the two sections of the house. Here the stairs went up to the second story and the room where I slept with my mother the night before we boarded "Old Buncombe" for Newport in 1879.

3—ISAAC ALLEN. It has been traditionally understood that this clan of Allens came from Culpepper County, Va., reaching Cocke County about the time Tennessee became a state—1796. Lists of early county officials at Old Newport, record the name of one Isaac Allen as the 2nd sheriff after statehood. John Allen is recorded as the 5th sheriff. There was no John born into the family of Jack Allen until 1812, and we find no record of a John in Reuben Allen's family during this period. So it seems apparent that these two Allen sheriffs were closely related, John being either brother or son of Isaac. However, there is no definite record of a *family* until we contact Sheriff John, who at some unknown date, had married Margaret, a daughter of Joseph Huff, one of the party of immigrants who had settled along the French Broad some 20 odd years earlier. Sheriff John Allen and his wife Margaret Huff Allen became the ancestors of a posterity confined rather closely for some generations to Cosby Creek, and their descendants are still numerous in that section.

And now I am on much surer ground, for Sheriff John Allen was the ancestor in direct line of my husband's grandmother Katherine Allen McSween. As an in-law of that family, I heard many tales of pioneer days, and their family life on Cosby Creek. The old John Allen home-site is now occupied by George Allen, a descendant of the 3rd generation. He is now, (1949) in his 80's.

In my younger married life I was taken to see great-aunt Elizabeth, a daughter-in-law of Sheriff John, then widowed, but still living in the old two-story log house. George, her son, was married in middle life, and afterwards built a new house, but the old one is still standing vacant, its front door riddled with bullet-holes, fired during the evil days of the Civil War. Isaac Allen II, oldest son of Sheriff John, married and also built a house on Cosby Creek. That house is now gone, but I remember its appearance some 40 years ago—a frame house with small rooms at either end of a long front porch. It was situated not far from the location of the present Cosby High School. Allen's Grove church stood on a nearby hill. A later building now stands on the same location. Here is a wonderful view up the Cosby Valley. In the Isaac Allen home there grew up a family of 10 children, 3 sons, and a brood of seven attractive daughters who all married good future citizens and scattered in various directions—some of them down Newport way.

THE BALL FAMILY

Long before 1800 the Ball family came from Ireland to Virginia. The first one was Alfred Ball. His son, Alfred Ball, Jr., came to Cocke County in 1800 and settled near Jefferson County line, but lived in Cocke County. His son, Alfred the III, was born here and he had eight brothers, Samuel, Isaac, John, Morgan, Joseph, Richard, Wm. and Euriah, sisters, *Jane Harrison, the mother of our beloved late Esquire John Harrison,* another sister who married a McMahan and Margaret Ball.

Sam, Ike, Alfred, John and Morgan Ball walked to Lexington, Ky., to join the Union Army. John Gorman was their captain.

Information by Wm. Morgan Ball of Knoxville and Wm. M. Ball's mother was Mary McNabb, a sister of Campbell McNabb, Elvira Stokely, Harriet Layman, Lizzie Gray, and Louise Frazier.

Senator Joseph Ball of Minnesota is a grandson of John Ball, the son of Alfred III.

JAMES AND THOMAS BOYDSTON

William Boydston (sometimes written Boilston or Boylston) was one of the earliest settlers in the County. James Boydston, a Tennessee Revolutionary soldier (McAllister's *Virginia Militia in the Revolutionary War,* p. 264.), was an older brother of William, and seemingly one of the two Boydstons who were in the battle of Point Pleasant, on the Ohio, October 18, 1774. James later moved from what became Cocke County to Rutherford County, North Carolina, where he had a grant of land in 1790. They served in defense of the frontier under Captain Daniel Smith, who was later Secretary of the Southwest Territory (William Blount, governor) and twice elected to the United States Senate from Tennessee. He took part in defending Castlewood, too. Later, Boydston moved to the lower part of Greene County, then North Carolina, that part of which was later Cocke County. Ramsey in his *Annals,* (page 190), and Williams in his *Tennessee During the Revolution,* gives an account of an Indian raid, in 1779, on his house, which was evidently fortified, in which four warriors were killed and a number wounded. The forayers were chased out of the settlements by a force under Captain (later Brigadier-General) George Doherty. Boydston served during the early part of the Revolutionary War as a Virginia militiaman, and later as such in the North Carolina (Tennessee part) forces under Colonel John Sevier. His name appeared on the tax list of Greene County in 1783, Greene then covering part of Cocke. A daughter, Priscilla, married Rev. Jacob Faubion, of French Huguenot descent, and they were the progenitors of a large family who lived in or near Old Newport.

THE BURNETTS

C. W. Beardsley, *English Surnames.* p. 454:
Nicknames from Peculiarities of Dress and Accoutrements.

An interesting peep into the minuter details of mediaeval life is given us in the case of names derived from costume and ensigncy, whether peaceful or warlike. The colour of the cloth of which the dress was composed seems to have furnished us with several surnames. For instance, our 'Burnets' would seem to be associated with the fabric of a brown mixture common at one period. Our great early poet, in describing Avarice, says—

> A mantle hung her faste by
> Upon a berch weak and small
> A burnette cote being there withall
> Furred with no minivere,
> But with a furre rough of hair.

[See *Century Dictionary,* 'burnet, burnette'.]

Henry Harrison, *Surnames of the United Kingdom* (1912), I. 59:

Dr. Edmund C. Burnett (with pipe) and his three brothers.

Burnet, Burnett—Of brown complexion (M.E. burnet = brown; O. Fr. brunet, brun = brown, and diminutive suffix.) [Gives one citation where Burnett = (probably) Burne-Head; O. E. burne, a brook.]

[The more commonly accepted explanation of the origin of the name BURNETT is that it is derived from Sir Roger Burnard, time of William the Conqueror.]

Although the Burnett family was not one of the very first families to arrive in Cocke County, it became one of the FIRST FAMILIES upon arrival.

Swan Pritchett Burnett was the first to come. He was born Oct. 24, 1779 son of Thomas and Elizabeth Littleberry Burnett, they lived near King's Mountain.

September the 19, 1801 Swan P. Burnett married Frances Bell, daughter of Thomas and Jane Montgomery Bell. She lived in Burke County, North Carolina. This couple made extensive purchases of land on the French Broad River near Asheville where they lived for some time before coming on down the river to Del Rio, where they purchased more land until they owned twelve hundred acres along this river. To this couple there came a full "baker's dozen" children and to each of the thirteen was willed a part of this wonderful river bottom land on September the 25, 1837 just before the death of Swan P. Burnett, December the 2, 1837.

Four of the above children married into the Stephen Huff family as follows: James Burnett to Caroline Huff, Jefferson Burnett to Mary Huff (First wife), Jesse Burnett to Evelyn Huff (first wife), Narcissa Burnett to Andrew C. Huff. Adaline Burnett to Jehu Stokely, the second Jehu Stokely, who was the grandson of Stephen Huff. (The first Stephen in Cocke County).

To complicate matters more in this kindship tangle . . . three daughters of Jehu the second and Adaline Burnett Stokely, married Susongs as follows: Mary Stokely to David Susong, Sue Stokely to George Susong, Lou Stokely to Jacob Susong. Thus it's easy to see what is meant by the saying when one is running for office in Cocke County, "If you can carry the first district, you can win because that is one big family who always vote together if at all possible."

THOMAS CHRISTIAN

Members of the noted Christian family resided in Cocke County at an early date, moving there from Montgomery County, Virginia, 1799, where on September 18, 1799, "Thomas Christian of the County of Cocke and State of Tennessee" executed a deed to land in Montgomery County. His brother-in-law, William Boylstone (sometimes written Boilstone) had removed yet earlier. William and Elizabeth Christian Boylston had a son Thomas, who married Elizabeth Gregg; also a son, Nathaniel, who married Dinah Rector Faubion. (According to Williams).

Notes from a genealogist of the Christian family say that Col. William Christian commanded the expedition of 1776 against the Cherokee Indians. One may infer that it was the reports by Christian men of the fruitful valley of the Forked Deer River that induced this later migration.

JAMES BAYARD CLARK

James Bayard Clark (1785-1853) settled in Cocke County, Tennessee, in 1810, married Elizabeth (Betsy) Daniel (1781-1848), of French

Huguenot descent. Their daughter, Lucindia Clark (August 31, 1812-November 25, 1887) married James Dawson, Jr. (1812-1857), the son of Jane Ketchen and James Dawson, Sr., a soldier of the American Revolution, who died in Anderson County on June 30, 1838. The Dawson family were descendants of English, French, and Welsh Kings, and of Oliver Cromwell. Many Cocke County families are of Royal Descent.

THE DAWSON FAMILY

The Dawson family came from Germany before 1800. They settled in the 3rd district area.

Dr. Abraham Dawson was one of the first members of the family born here. He spent his entire life in the present third district and was an efficient doctor.

Joseph Dawson gave his life for Cocke County while he was sheriff was killed in the mountains near State line, while on a moonshine raid.

Charles E. Dawson, a brother of "Sheriff Joe," as he was known, also became a sheriff many years after Joe's death.

This family along with five others in Cocke County are descendants of European royalty. They are, as follows: Stokely, Lovell, O'Dell, Vinson and Mrs. Polly Vance Britton Campbell through the Vance family. There may possibly be others unknown to the author.

CAPTAIN JOHN DENTON

Captain John Denton, who settled on the Big Pigeon River by 1785 and established Denton's Mill above William Whitson's Fort, was from Shenandoah County, Virginia. He was a direct descendant of the Puritan preacher, Reverend Richard Denton (1586-1662) of Wethersfield, Massachusetts, who removed to Hempstead, Queens County, Long Island, New York. Here his sons: Dr. Daniel, Nathaniel, Timothy, Richard and Samuel Denton were long active in the affairs of their day. His daughter, Sarah Denton, married William Thorne and was also connected with the Smith family. The Register of St. George's Church, Hempstead, abounds with Denton's and Combs records, although the family indicated a definite Quaker influence.

The first Shenandoah settlers were John, Jonas, and Abraham Denton. John Denton qualified as Captain of Foot in 1753, as did Samuel Odell. Under him was his son, Ensign John Denton, Jr. By 1767, the senior John Denton had died and his widow Sarah had married John Odell. She was given her dower of 139 acres on the north bank of the Shenandoah River, as well as the house and barn. The John Odells resided there until about 1773 when they removed to Washington County, North Carolina, upper French Broad River, Brush River, selling their land to Colonel John Tipton. Her Denton sons and their sons in turn resided near them. (The early writing of all names is often different to ours.)

John Denton, Jr., became Captain of the Militia by 1775, with Lt. Caleb Odell and Ensign William Odell. He lived on Passage Creek, near Caleb Odell in Powell's Fort, with his family of eleven. Soon after the 1783 census he removed to Big Pigeon in Cocke County, Tennessee, and located on the site that bears his name. Here he lived near his mother, Sarah Denton Odell, and his Denton kinsmen, Joseph, Isaac, James, Samuel, and Jonas Denton. Mourning Denton, one of the charter

Prof. R. P. Driskill and his students, May 16, 1902

members of Big Pigeon Church, was evidently his wife. (Data from Ann O'Dell, wife of Reverend Arthur Lee O'Dell.)

DRISKILL

The ancestors of the Driskill family came to Cocke County from Virginia before the year 1800. They were Irish pioneers and a very fine family.

The name in the Emerald Isle was O'Driskill, which indicated the fact that the family belonged to the landed gentry or yoemanry of Great Britain.

Joshua, Mildred, and Daniel Driskill settled in the Slate Creek section of Cocke County about fifteen miles from Newport.

Joshua married Sallie Jane Smith, a sister to the highly respected "UNCLE TOMMY SMITH," the Primitive Baptist preacher of early days, who lived to be one hundred six years of age and preached a sermon on his one hundredth birthday. Later than that date he preached at Friendship Church, three miles below White Pine in Jefferson County. The only person living in 1948 who has told me of hearing this sermon is Mrs. Lou Miller Robinson, who gave me the information.

Mildred Driskill married William Morris, Aug. 29, 1824. Her sister (or probably her brother's daughter) married Richard Holt. No one seems to be able to tell me her name or her relationship exactly to the above three.

The Driskill family has shown throughout its journey from pioneer days to the present that it has two outstanding traits, a religious inclination and a deep desire to avail themselves of every possible educational and cultural advantage. Much of this background is found in various documents, church records reflect the righteous endeavors of our forefathers, court records show their dealings with their fellow men, etc. etc.

From the Minutes of the Slate Creek Baptist Church, Jan. 22, 1818 to March 1876 are seventy two names. Ten of them are Driskills, John Jesse, Hannah, Milly (Mildred), Thomas, Joshua, Nancy, Sarah, Elizabeth and Moses. (Note the Bible names).

JACOB FAUBION

Histories of the Faubions and their relatives who settled in what is now Cocke and Greene Counties more than one and a half centuries ago are as old as the civilization in that section. Jacob Faubion came from Culpepper County, in the northern part of Virginia, and settled with his brother on land entered from the Government. They were French Huguenots. Their claim was filed about one mile west of Neddy's Mountain on Sinking Cane Creek, on land owned at present by Clint Mason and by Sam (Uncle Sam) Faubion. They camped about two hundred yards above the Mason home the first night they arrived. They erected first a blacksmith shop; next a mill; and then a log dwelling. The mill site can be seen just above the road where it crosses the creek.

When Jacob Faubion came he spoke very broken English. He did not speak his native language very often because he wanted his children to speak English. Only the names of two of them, John and William, are known. William married and built a house on the tract of land known as the Dave Susong place, but owned at present by the Gormans.

William followed his father's trade of blacksmithing, wagon making, and of millwright. He enlarged the business and employed several men. The Faubions then built the first mill on the French Broad River, known as the Faubion Mill; also the first bridge across the French Broad, just above where Bridgeport now stands. That is the source of its name.

When one of the other Faubions died, he was buried near where Sam Faubion lived. Thus started the Faubion graveyard, the first in that section. Upon William's death, his son John continued the business. Luther Jones, who died in the house in which the Reverend Charlie Huff now lives, learned his trade in the John Faubion shop.

John Faubion, William's brother, married a Miss Leah McKay, now spelled and pronounced McCoy. Ramsey's *Annals of Tennessee* tells that the McKays owned and kept a blockhouse, located seven miles from Cosby Creek, where they kept back the Indians who tried to slip in to kill the settlers. This was near where the Faubions settled. They had ten children: Henry, Barthema who married George McNabb; Diana, who married David Bible; Elinor who married James Smith; Didamy who married Noah St. John; (Abraham, Joseph, Moses, John no marriage record given) and Eliza, who married Jesse Glasscock.

The house John Faubion built is now owned by Sam Faubion. John's sons went west, except Harry or Henry, and located north of Kansas City, Missouri.

Barthema Faubion, who married George McNabb, lived near Bridgeport, and had five children: William; Emma who married Andrew Allen and had children, George and Elinor Allen; Jacob, whose children were Barthema and Margaret; Rachel who married Noah Holler and left descendants, Alton Holler and sister Sue; and Leah who never married.

Diana, who married David Bible, was born in her mother's fiftieth year. Her father lost his sight and had a personal servant, a Negro slave girl, Mary, who later lost her sight. Diana Bible had two children: Ellen Smith who married Robert McFarland Jones, and Lydia, who died at the age of fourteen years from a fall from a swing on the school grounds near Warrensburg.

Eliza who married Jesse Glasscock had a large family of children all living near Barboursville. Elinor, who married James Smith, had two girls, Ellen Stuart and Mary Keel. Their heirs live near Barboursville, too. Didamy married Noah St. John and lived in the state of Missouri.

Henry Faubion married Percilla Warren, who lived in Warrensburg, Greene County, Tennessee, and brought her to live in a house just above that of his father, near the Bethel Baptist Church. This is a part of the old Faubion place, now owned by James Freshour. Their house was built just above the falls on Cane Creek where another mill to saw lumber and grind grain was built eighty-five years ago, and stood until a few years ago. Henry had five children.

John Faubion, a wagoner and farmer, hauled supplies, especially salt, for the settlement from the coast of Virginia and from Baltimore and from South Carolina in a six-horse wagon. When General Jackson called for volunteers for his second army to put down the Indian uprising in the South and to finish the War of 1812, John Faubion left home for the muster field, at what is now Old Town, with his wagon of supplies, began the journey to join the General, with David Harned and John Cooper, who went as "foot soldiers." On their return home these men helped to break cane to feed the horses, which had almost starved to death during the siege of New Orleans. The foot soldiers arrived home first and fresh horses were sent to meet John Faubion somewhere in Alabama. David Harned died in Parrottsville at the home of his son Samuel, who married Laura Huff.

John Cooper married a Browning and was in the War of 1812. Both came from the same section in Virginia. The Coopers, like the Faubions, settled in the German settlement in Cocke County. They spoke excellent English. The Brownings spoke Alsatian, a mixture of German and French.

Abraham Faubion married twice, having ten children by the first marriage and two by the second. His first wife was Nettie Cooper, daughter of John Cooper. Their son, Henry Faubion, married Lula Horn of Clarksville, and had one daughter Alice, a teacher.

Sam Faubion never married. He taught school one week, farmed and kept books. He spent five years in the University. In his senior year he was Senior Lieutenant and Quartermaster. He was considered one of the best educated men in Cocke County.

Dora Faubion, Abe's fourth child, taught school several years, married a Mr. Spour, who owns an orchard in Oregon. She died a few years ago, at the age of sixty-eight, leaving a son and a daughter, both single.

Richard, the next child, married Anna Finney, daughter of Miller and Rachel Stevens Finney, president of Oberlin College and a noted revivalist.

The Faubions have a large number of relatives, not listed here, among them: Williams, Webb, Kelly, Maloney, Maloy, Spencer, De Busk, Mason, Sullivan. (Data compiled by Richard M. Faubion.)

THE FINE FAMILY

The Fine family were Holland Dutch. However, the name came from the word "fen," the name for low marshy lands, and is sometimes spelled "Fenn" or "Finn." These Fines were a part of a settlement in 1700 of Johannis Fine, who bought land at Hempstead, Long Island. Before the Revolutionary War, the Fine family was located in Shenandoah County near the Newman, Denton and Thomas families from Long Island, on the waters of the Shenandoah River near New Market. In the First Independent Company of Dunmore County of 1775, the Fine signatures included Thomas Fine, Sr., Peter Fine and Vinott Fine. In the Dunmore County Militia in 1775 under command of Captain Jacob Holeman were Andres Fine, John Fine, Peter Fine, Philip Fine and Winenot Fine. By the census of 1783, Thomas Fine was still residing there with four in family, near his sons, Vinott and John, but soon thereafter, John and Vinott Fine, joined their brother, Peter, who had married Patience McKay and removed to the French Broad River, near Fine's Ferry, which became an early landmark.

The father of these Fine brothers was Philip Peter Fine, Sr., of Maryland, 1764 to 1804, who served in the Virginia Army during the Revolutionary War. There was a daughter, Elizabeth. (Data furnished by Sam E. Leming, Waldron, Arkansas, who has a photostatic copy of land grants to this family in Virginia.)

John Fine also served in the Revolutionary War with Philip. In 1804, the latter moved into Frederick County, Virginia, just across the Potomac River, near the present site of Washington, D. C. There he married the widow Catheryne Parrott, who had two sons and two daughters. It is possible that these came with the Fine family to Cocke County.

Major Peter Fine represented the Big Pigeon Baptist Church in 1794, in the Holston Association and was the first, or one of the first, deacons of that Church after its organization in 1787. His daughter, Sally Fine, married Abraham Job, born in 1775, the son of David Job. (Same as Jobe.)

John Fine was born January 2, 1782 and died January 26, 1857. His wife, Nancy, was born on November 10, 1782, and died February 18, 1859. He came from Cocke County and helped organize the Baptist Church on Fork Creek, later called the Baptist Church on Sweetwater, the first Sunday in June, 1820. The members of the Church met at his home the first Saturday in August, 1821.

John had a grant, No. 686, from the State, dated, September 7, 1827. The present fair grounds are located on this tract of land. (Sweetwater, Tenn.)

The stage road from Philadelphia to Athens went by the Fine home, which was a "stand" and stopping place. Their children were John, Polly, Abraham, Sarah, Mahala, Minerva, Martha, and Nancy. (Lenoir's *History of Sweetwater Valley*, page 147, which conflicts some with other records.)

John Fine, son of Major Peter Fine, was in the War of 1812 and married Nancy Lee in 1800. She was the daughter of John and Agnes Jennings Lee. Their children were Peter Lee, Minerva, who married Jobe Taylor, John M., Sarah, and Elizabeth, who married Isaac Hill, all moved to Ashland, Oregon.

In 1833, Abraham Fine was made a Ruling Elder of the Pisgah Presbyterian Church of Newport, of which Mrs. Elizabeth Fine was a charter member in 1823.

The original family that came to Cocke County had also two other members, Wenden and Euphemeas Fine. Wenden died ten years before Cocke County was known as such, and nothing is known of what became of Euphemeas.

The entry of Peter Fine and wife, Patience McKay Fine, was opposite and above the first town of Newport, on the banks of the French Broad River, and included Fine's Ferry and the large island opposite the old homeplace of George I. Thomas, son of George and wife Katy (Lowery) Thomas. Peter Fine died here. He had several children who migrated to various sections of the country. One son, Abraham Fine, remained in Cocke County, where he became Elder in the Presbyterian Church, and also High Sheriff. While Sheriff he raided and broke up an organized band of counterfeiters that operated near Wolf Creek.

Captain John Fine located at what is now known as the Rutherford Farm on Sinking Creek, where he died.

Vinett Fine entered and located on the land known as the Swaggerty Farm and now owned by the Unaka Tannery and James A. T. Wood.

Colonel John Sevier attacked a party of Indians on Indian Creek in the summer of 1781. The place was near the County line, on the farm of William Phillips. Seventeen Indians were killed. Peter, John and Vinett participated in this battle. (This battleground was pointed out to W. R. Fine by his father, Isaac, a son of Vinett.)

In the spring of 1783, Colonel William Lillard and Major Peter Fine raised a company of thirty men and crossed the mountains to the Overhill town of Cowee and burned it because from this town had originated the aggressions upon the Big Pigeon and French Broad Rivers. Captain John and his brother Vinett Fine were members of the company. Such action antagonized the Indians who in the winter of 1783 began to steal horses and cattle from the Big Pigeon settlements.

Major Peter Fine and Captain John McNabb raided a company of men and followed the Indians across our mountains into North Carolina, where they killed one Indian and wounded another, but recovered the stolen horses. The Indians fired upon him, killing Vinett Fine, and wounding Thomas Holland, and a man by the name of Bingham. Because there was not time for grave-digging and apparently no safety in trying to escape with the body, the ice in the creek was broken and the body placed there. Before the men could return for it, the creek became flooded by a sudden change in temperature, the body was washed away and never recovered. To this day, the creek is known as Fine's Creek. (The "i" in Vinett pronounced as in "mine.")

Vinett Fine had several sons and daughters; Isaac, the father of W. R., who in 1857 married Nancy Wilson, granddaughter of Major William Wilson for whom Wilsonville was named. A daughter, Emma Fine Gray, became the mother of Jasper Gray. There were four other daughters and five sons. (Data from Jasper Gray.)

In the law office of William M. Crawford, of Newport, a descendant of the Fine Family, is the account book belonging to Major Peter Fine, in which he began keeping records in 1790. These are recorded in English pounds, shillings, pence. The birthdays of his twelve children are recorded as follows: Lidgard, September 2, 1775; Aron, July 5, 1777; Jonathan, May 22, 1779; John, January 2, 1782; David, August 12, 1783; Peter, September 18, 1786; Elizabeth, January 22, 1788; Abraham, March 24, 1789; Aron, June 7, 1792; Mariann, May 5, 1794; Rebecah, August 25, 1796; Pattey Tirevelan, September 10, 1799.

Peter's first wife, Rebecah, died September 7, 1802, aged 46 years. He married Ann Murrel, September 6, 1803. She died September 15, 1815, aged 67 years.

GILLETT FAMILY

Between 1850 and 1855 there lived in Cocke County, ten miles North of Newport, in the community now known as Fowler's Grove, a man by the name of John Gillett, who with his family and many slaves, constituted a full and complete community in industry and agriculture. They lived, wholly, fully and completely within themselves because they were self sustaining.

John Gillett owned a large tract of land, on which he grew all the farm products native to this section, including berries and fruits of all kinds. For meat for this family and its slaves, he raised, swine, sheep, cattle in great numbers, and chickens, geese, ducks, turkeys and guineas. For sweets he manufactured hundreds of pounds of maple sugar each year, barrels of cane molasses, and for most choice "sweetening" he kept innumerable stands of bees which were very productive because of the virgin timber everywhere and orchards and clover which afforded blossoms in abundance.

John Gillett grew cotton, flax and sheep for wool, from which was manufactured the family clothing, including the bed linens and other household linens, he also grew "tow" (which is part of the bark of the flax plant) also hemp, the bark of a much larger plant. From this product he made all cord and rope material needed with his machinery and household affairs.

For leather he tanned his own sheep and goat and cattle hides, from which was manufactured his own shoes for his family and for the numerous slaves. Some of the slaves were shoe and boot makers and worked constantly at this task. Others operated the machinery that converted the cotton and wool and flax into cloth much of which required constant attention and had to be done by hand. There was plenty of work for every slave to do and plenty of food and clothes for all. Would that such were true today in this age we call modern and enlightened.

John Gillett was a soldier in the Mexican War. While in Mexico he procured and brought home with him seeds of indigo and other plants that produce coloring matter. Under most difficult climatic conditions these seeds were planted and cultivated and for many years produced coloring matter for the wardrobes and household linens of this unusual family.

To secure the indigo color it was necessary to crush the root of the plant into a pulp and allow it to stand for twenty-four hours in cold water. Sometimes it required thirty-six hours before the roots could be removed from the water. The blue coloring matter "settled" in the bottom of the vessel that held the roots. This was dried and made into commercial indigo.

On this farm John Gillett had the equipment necessary for manufacturing hats. These were made for his entire family and the slaves, also for some of the neighbors. The "hatter" was a slave.

Some of the slaves that belonged to this good master were skilled mechanics and made all the farm implements and tools.

Some of the linens and coverlets made on this farm are now in the possession of the descendants of this family.

John Gillett buried his gold in his garden when he would accumulate a certain amount. Before he died he desired to find it if possible but had forgotten where he had placed it. He had his slaves dig up the entire garden and found it, or part of it. Within the last few years it has been reported that a considerable amount was found buried in a pot near this old residence. Cocke County seems famous for hidden treasures.

John Gillett had a brother-in-law (as many rich men have) but the brother-in-law was also rich and above all a Christian. That was his name. He lived on Clay Creek, near the Church of the same name, which is located on the old road to Morristown that we know as The Buffalo Trail. The widow of Lewis Bible now lives on the estate of Mr. Christian, the BACHELOR. This gentleman lived to be very old and accumulated a considerable fortune and many slaves. When he realized his end was near, he called together his slaves, both the men and the women, and related to them that it was through their labor that he had been able to accumulate his vast estate and in as much as he had no offspring, he thought it right and proper that they should receive his worldly possessions. He advised them that he had their certificates of freedom already executed, to be delivered to them at his death. His farm he had already "plotted" into many tracts, one for each slave, and he had seen fit to execute deeds in fee simple, a deed to each of his slaves to one tract of his land. This in appreciation of their life's labors.

At the death of Christian the slaves were duly declared free and each took possession of his part of the farm and "lived happily ever after." Many of these Negroes lived for many years on their little tracts of land given to them by their master. Others sold out and moved elsewhere because they thought other pastures might be greener.

Christian's metal box of silver and gold has never been known to have been found though it was diligently "Dug for" upon different occasions. It was probably buried at the foot of the rainbow, or if anyone found it they had sufficient means to journey into "the distance dim, where some limpid river ripples, beyond the rainbow's rim."

Information furnished by H. W. Huff, a descendant of John Gillett.

GILLILAND FAMILY

James E. Gilliland died in 1810. His wife, Susannah Gilliland, came from Lancaster, Pennsylvania, and settled in Rockinham County, Virginia, where she died in 1842, at the age of 92. Their children with year of birth if known, were: Jessie; Benjamin; William, 1771; Samuel, 1775; Henry, 1777; Nancy; Susannah; James E., Jr., 1783; Sheppard, 1786; Sarah, 1790; Elizabeth; and Tolly.

Alexander Gilliland had sons John, Robert, William and Thomas, and he was from Tryon County, North Carolina. John lived in 1783 at the mouth of Pigeon Creek and was a close friend of John Sevier.

James Gilliland of East Tennessee had a grandson, W. H. Huff, who lived at Newport. His mother was Sarah Gilliland and her mother a Miss Axley. Hugh Huff descends from this couple.

Abel Gilliland was of East Tennessee. One James Gilliland lived on the French Broad River and owned what was known as the Fork of Pigeon River, the finest farm in Cocke County, containing about 400 acres, which he sold to a Mr. Coleman before moving to Missouri. (Records in Land Grants State Archives, Book C. show that John Gilliland was granted land in Greene County, as early as 1796. He was also granted an island in Warford on the French Broad. He was a leader in the Zion Church. His wife was a sister of James Axley. They lived between the French Broad and Pigeon River in Cocke County, 1821.

HENRY GOUCHENOUR

Born in New Market, Va., 1825; died in Burnette County, Texas, 1869.

About 1848 some Virginia cattle buyers were passing through Dandridge, Tenn., and learned that they wanted an "outside" school teacher—upon their return to Virginia—they informed Henry Gouchenour of the fact and he proceeded immediately to go to Dandridge, Tenn. He secured the appointment as teacher and while there met and married Elizabeth Walker Cowan.

The following children were born to this marriage: Robert and Joel born Nov. 19, 1852; Charley G. born January 2, 1854; Blanche born April 10, 1856; Julia Emma born March 3, 1858; Hugh Henry born August 10, 1866, and Texie born November 29, 1869.

After his marriage Henry Gouchenour went into business at Parrottsville, Tenn. and with the firm of Lowry Eason & Co., of Greeneville, Tenn.

After a successful business at Parrottsville he formed a partnership with D. A. Mims and sold goods at "Old New Port" on the French Broad River which was then the County Seat until the Civil War. At the close of the war he rented the farm now known as the "Jake Susong" place. In 1869 he moved his family to Texas where he died that same year.

He was a man of high ideals, firm in his convictions and loved and respected by all who knew him.

His widow was married to M. A. Roadman in 1871 and to that marriage was born Ted Roadman, long a merchant of New Port, Tenn., who was also a newspaper editor. He died in 1936.

THE HOPKINS FAMILY

The 'hair-raising' stories of the Hopkins family of Cocke County would fill a large sized volume. The men of this family were known as, "The Fighting Hopkins Brothers."

Benjamin Parker Hopkins was the head of the family. He was born Dec. 4, 1808, in Sequatchie, Yancy County, North Carolina.

His Mother was Judith Cope Hopkins, his Father unknown in 1950.

About the time of the birth of Benjamin, Indians captured his Mother and for a long while the Mother and child were held captive. Finally a friendly Indian rowed them to safety.

The Father of Parker Hopkins went away to fight the Indians and was never seen again, there was a little girl Ruthie who in early womanhood married Captain John Edwards. In 1826 Benjamin Parker Hopkins was married in Jonesboro, Tennessee to Ruth Tinker. The ceremony was performed by Joseph Longmire.

Twelve sons and one daughter were born to this couple. They were, Abraham, William, Montgomery, Jasper, Jacob, Baxter, Benjamin (killed in war—prison) Israel, Horace, Anderson, Woodvil, Jack, Ance.

Ten of the sons joined the armies of the Civil War, Abraham, William and Montgomery (known as GUM) joined the federal army and the others joined the Confederate army. A deaf and dumb son and Little Benjamin, aged 12 stayed home with the sister and Mother.

In Dec. 1863, Abraham was sent to Cocke County from Knoxville to enlist men for the Union Army and to arrest deserters. While on the journey he was in a fight or skirmish where the Mt. Sterling Bridge now stands. Hopkins was wounded and died Dec. 16 1863 before receiving his Commission. His last words were, "I am glad to give my life for my country." "Gum," as Montgomery was called, was a member of Kirk's Regiment, and while passing through Cocke County, happened to 'run up on a bunch' of Confederate soldiers under Captain Mims. Gum shot a horse from under one of the soldiers. As the horse fell, the soldier threw up his hand as in salute to Gum, who recognized in him his own beloved brother, Jacob Hopkins, a Confederate Soldier. Gum quickly dismounted and hastened to the fallen horse and its rider, but Jacob would not permit him to tarry, lest the regiment overtake them. Gum gave his horse to his brother and darted off down the mountainside until the regiment had passed out of sight. Jacob, the Confederate, never once pretended to know who had shot his horse from under him, many of the regiment probably did not know he had met with such an accident, as he hastened on from the scene before the regiment overtook him. After several hours rest, the wounded horse 'came to' he had only a scalp wound and was 'addled.' He arose and wandered about as though in search for his rider or probably water. . . . Gum, who was still on Chestnut mountain hoping his brother would return alone and they could visit with each other, was glad to have his brother's horse and on it he rode away to George Kirk's camp which was on the right side of Highway 75 near the Tenn. and North Carolina line.

Along with the 8 Hopkins Brothers served, Jacob Wilde, Austin Gilbert, Nathan Davis, James Erby.

After the close of the Civil War, the Hopkins Brothers scattered to the four winds, each one of the 12 died in a different state. The girl died at 14 years of age.

The Famous Hopkins Millions on the West Coast in California belong to the Cocke County Hopkins Family. Their descendants in this County are Talitha Hopkins Clark (Mrs. R. P.) Lena Ford Parks, Bess Wilde, Dr. Hobart Ford and others.

THE HUFF FAMILY

John Huff and wife sailed in 1645 from Holland and settled in New Amsterdam (New York). They were of German descent, thrifty and lovers of the land. Their descendants journeyed to Pennsylvania where they were granted a tract of land. They dwelt upon it only a short time until they began to feel the urge to travel farther on into the new country, and we next find the family in the Shenandoah Valley of Virginia. Peter and Joseph Huff lived near Roanoke.

John, the son of Peter Huff, married the daughter of John Corder, whose wife was a Miss Sloat. Some of the family claim that Miss Sloat's name was Eleanor, while others insist that it was Mary and that she was known as Nell or Nellie. I note the family has kept the three names among their various families, probably according to their ideas of what the name was. Some of the present members of the family claim that it was the above John, son of Peter Huff who wed the Mary, Eleanor, or Nell Corder, be that as it may, we find this couple arriving in the French Broad River Valley near Del Rio and entering land October the 14, 1783. The GRANT for this land is one of the very earliest recorded, some claim the first in what is now Cocke County while others claim it is the second one. A copy of this grant may be found in the appendix.

To reach the French Broad Valley, John Huff and wife rode pack-horses, Peter Huff, a brother of John accompanied the couple and one child, Jennie Huff, daughter of John and wife. All the horses were heavily laden with household and personal needs.

The dates given me, claim that Peter Huff entered land October the 21, 1763. If this be true, he evidently had come twenty years previous to John and wife. His entry was six miles below OLD NEWPORT, on the French Broad River, opposite the mouth of the Big Pigeon.

Joe Huff entered land at Rankin, later sold it or rather exchanged it for a gun, which he felt he needed more in a wilderness country than he needed land. The farm is now valued at more than fifty thousand dollars.

John Huff and wife made a four acre clearing immediately after their arrival in the Del Rio area. The present Frank Huff home is located upon the land, but an older home, now belonging to Mrs. Hattie Huff McMahan and probably her sister, Judith Huff Runnion, is nearer to the site of the original home. John and wife dwelt in a cave near-by while they were building their huge log house and it was from this cave home or its environs, that their little son and daughter, Jennie were stolen by the Indians. (Page 864 Goodspeed's *History of Tennessee*) relates the incident and places the dates between 1783 and 85. The girl was scalped and left for dead, the boy was taken captive. The family pursued the Indians and found they had tomahawked the boy near War Ford (NEWPORT).

Little Jennie recovered and grew to womanhood and was then known as Jane Huff. She married Royal Stokely, the first to bear the name of Royal in America. He was the son of Jehu Stokely and wife Nancy Neal of South Carolina. This couple arrived in the Del Rio area about the same time the Huff family came, probably a few years later.

John Huff did not fail to make friends with the Indians by being friendly toward them. He was a peace loving man, and one who was devoted to his large family of a "baker's dozen" children whose names were as follows:

Jennie (Jane) born in Virginia, married Royal Stokely; Mary Elizabeth, married John Stokely; Nellie, married Elijah Sharp; Katie, married a Jester; Leonard, married a Chamberlan; Thomas, married Judith Nichols; Stephen, married Elizabeth Carson, first time, Eliza Spencer, second time; David, went to Texas. Peter, died at the age of sixteen years but had written a key to Pike's Arithmetic; Isaac, died in childhood and his grave was hidden from Indians. John, went west in early manhood as David did. Nathan, also joined his brothers in the "Westward Ho" idea. Joseph, married Susan Lillard, who belonged to the early family of that name so closely tied in with seven Presidents of the United States.

Stephen Huff and wife, Elizabeth Carson Huff, lived for many years in the old, old Huff home that stood until around 1900 when it was burned. Their children were: Andrew, who married Narcissa Burnett; John, who married Jane Huff; Robert, who went to Washington State; Tommy, Stephen, who married Nancy Sisk; Susan, who married Riley Brooks; Caroline, who married James Burnett; Mary, who married Jefferson Burnett; Eva, who married Jesse Burnett.

The descendants of the above family are many, among them, best known to me are, Tom, Steve, Lizzie, Jesse, Frank, Elizabeth, Mary Huff Clark, Annie, H. Williams, Eliza H. Gregg, Kate, John David, Mildred Boyle, Edd, Alex and their sisters, Mrs. T. S. Ellison, Mrs. Nell Woodward, and Miss Annie Huff. There are of course many whom I do not know and thus cannot name.

Descending from Peter Huff are Mrs. Lucinda Manning and those who are closely related to her.

An interesting story is told of Leonard Huff who took the cows to the pasture at dawn one morning and returned seven years later at sunset driving them home. He so thoroughly enjoyed himself among the Indians with whom he had lived the seven years that he was in no hurry to return and confided to his friends that he often climbed to the highest peaks of the surrounding mountains and gazed down upon his domain. He was most generous with the Indians, paying them well for his "board and keep," according to one of our most accurate historians of this part of the country.

The Huff family held on to their land entered by their thrifty and home-loving ancestors and many interesting and humorous stories have been handed down in this delightful family of substantial citizens.

One of the most beloved members of this family was Major James T. Huff of Bridgeport who clothed the name in glory and honor. He was a member of the 6th Battalion which later became part of the 60th N. C. Regiment. He was promoted to the rank of Major in December 1863. He lived a long and useful life.

THE INMAN FAMILY

By Mrs. May Inman Gray and Augusta Bradford
and Mrs. Ruth W. O'Dell

The descendants of Shadrach, Meshack and Abednego Inman.

The Inman family from early times was a religious family, and of English descent. The motto: "In Dominus Confidito." The family of Inman, Ionman, Ingman, are descendants of Edward the III of England, through John of Gaunt, Duke of Lancaster. This family raised a troop in the Royal cause under the Duke of New Castle and were at the fatal battle of Marston Moor, where several were slain. The others dispersed and the property was confiscated to Cromwell's party 1650-1652.

Their Coat of Arms is strongly Lancastrian and may have been granted them during the War of the Roses.

For five successive generations the Inman family lived at Bowthwaite Grange, Netherdale (or Nithisdale in Old English) County York, and intermarried with many of the principal families of that period.

The Inmans of Liverpool, the well known owners of the Inman line of Steamers, descended from the Inmans who lived at the Grange.

Wm. Inman, by his will 1614, divided to his sons, Robert and John, jointly, his land at Bouthwaite, lately leased to one John Chambers, to his eldest son, Robt. all the rest of his land and tenements at Bouthwaite. It is this Robert who is still known as "Bold Robin of Bouthwaite," being a man of uncommon stature and strength, he is credited with many strange and remarkable deeds, and the one by which he appears to have earned his sobriquet was the slaying of four men in his house at Bowthwaite. He had been collecting rents and came home, retired for the night. Thieves had secretly crept into the house and Bold Robin was aroused by the creaking of the old wooden floor. Hastily dressing, he encountered one of the thieves at the bedroom door. He at once threw him down the stairway, and the other three were also killed. No account is given of any trial or inquest. If there had been, Bold Robin would have been acquitted, the punishment for robbery was severe at that time. In the Civil Wars in England, Bold Robin 'sided' with Parliament against the King, also, his son, *Michael Inman*, a youth of eighteen years. Captain Anthony Beckwith was a son-in-law of Bold Robin. He was a Lieutenant in Parliament's service.

From the time of the death of Bold Robin, until the present century, Bowthwaite Grange has remained in the possession of his descendants.

Elizabeth, daughter of Frances Damebrock had married in 1756 to Michael Inman. She inherited Tudor House Beverly. This property remained in the possession of the Inmans nearly one hundred years. Christopher lived in this picturesque old Tudor House Beverly. By his will, Charles, the youngest took Harefield, Michael obtained the rest of the estate.

Most of these items are copied from Nidderdale and the Garden of the Nida. Miss Ethel Inman of the English family, think our American family are descendants of Christopher Inman. The family names are similar, also their characteristics and family resemblances.

Prior to Revolutionary war 1775, three Inman brothers, Shadrach, Meshach and Abednego, left their home in England, tradition claims, on account of a step-mother. They came to America, settled in Virginia, thence to N. C. afterwards to Tennessee. In 1767 these three brothers joined a party of hunters led by Daniel Boone, to explore the country west of the Cumberland Mountains. Meshach was killed by Indians near Nick Jack cave. Shadrach was wounded by a spear (this weapon is still in possession of his descendants). Abednego was wounded in the forehead by a tomahawk. He hid in a hollow tree where he lived nine days without food.

There were many Shadrach Inman's. The first was son of John and Henrietta Hardin Inman. He was an officer in the Revolutionary war, commissioned as Captain Jan. 5, 1774. Lt. May 7, 1777. He married Mary McPheeter, whose mother was Mary Jane McDowell, sister of Gov. John McDowell of N. Carolina. Shadrach Inman owned a valuable farm on Nolachucky River in Jefferson County Tennessee. He had many slaves, to his wife he willed, Nathan, Judah, Caswell, Lucy, Stephen, Matthew, Jennie, Sarah. To his grandsons in Cocke County he willed Simeon, Osborne, Jennie, Elias, Lettie, Toby, Susan, Nancy, Susannah, Alfred and Sarah. Jennie is mentioned three times.

The Mother of Shadrach, Meshach, and Abednego Inman requested that her name should be preserved through each generation (This must have given the family other ideas of the preservation of the three strange Bible names for men, because these three run through the family from start to finish). The first family had these names, Henrietta, Hardins, Hannah, Shadrach, Daniel, Ezekiel, Charles Thomas, John, Jeremiah, Sarah, Susannah, Rachel, Ann, Prudence, Margaret, and Elizabeth.

The second Shadrach Inman (in America) was Capt. of a Georgia Militia in Revolutionary times, was killed at the battle of Musgrove's Hill August 19, 1780.

Ramsey's "Annal's of Tennessee" give the following account of this particular battle. "The battle lasted one hour and one half. The Americans lay so closely behind their little breast work that the enemy entirely overshot them, killing only six or seven. Among whom, the loss of the brave Capt. Inman was particularly regretted. His stratagem of engaging and skirmishing with the enemy until the riflemen had time to throw up a hasty breastwork, his gallant conduct during the action and his desperate charge upon their retreat contributed much to the victory, and he died at the moment it was won."

Account of this battle is found in "King's Mountain and its Heroes," Rear Guard of the Revolution, also Wheeler's "History of N. V." pg. 57. The heirs of Shadrach Inman were given land in Georgia April 6, 1784 575 A County of Washington.

Shadrach Inman, Esquire, was made Capt. of a Company in Regiment of Militia in Greene County, North Carolina Jan. 5, 1887. R. Caswell, Gov. He had been made Lieutenant at Newbern, North Carolina in 1774.

THE JOBE FAMILY

The early history of the Jobe family is connected with Freehold, Monmouth County, New Jersey, where they were staunch Quakers. Some of their members moved to Cecil County, Maryland with members of the McKay family. Records in the Nottingham Monthly Meeting, Cecil County, show intentions to marry declared by the Jobe and McKay individuals.

By 1737 the Jobes and McKays seem to have established residences in the McKay-Hite Land Grant; yet in 1790 there were still Jobes in the West Nottingham Parrish: Daniel and Archibald.

The first Shenandoah County, Virginia, residents of the name were: Abraham, Joshua and Caleb Jobe. The first records of Augusta County show them in their established community with three of the McKay sons, March 18, 1746.

Road ordered from Caleb Jo's Mill down to Co. Line. . . James McKay, Moses McKay . . . William Hawkins, Zachary McKay, Joshua Job. . . 1746, May 12, Abraham Job apptd. Constable at Masaunting.

The family appears to have been established on the South Bank of the Shenandoah, and in the summer of 1750 both Caleb and Abraham were dead, leaving wills.

Caleb Job's will, June 4, 1750, named wife, Barbara with children, Samuel, Jacob, Nathan, Elizabeth with wife and Ephraim Leith, Executors Abraham Job, Moses McKay. By 1752, the widow married Ephraim Leith. The two sons were of age in 1750.

Abraham Job's will of July 25, 1750, Augusta County, named wife, Elizabeth, son, Elisha, trustee for widow, and after her widowhood equal executor with her other child; Rebecca, Isaac (infant), Phoebe, David (infant), Hannah, daughter Mary McKay and her son Isaac. She had married Moses McCoy (or McKay). The son Isaac was bound to James Brown, a hatter; David was to be bound to a saddler in West Nottingham. The widow, Elizabeth married 1753 Thomas Bragg. She could have been a Whitson. Later the son, Joseph Bragg, was in Colonel John Tipton's company of militia.

Elisha, a son by a former marriage, was appointed constable in place of his father, Abraham Job, in 1750. Mary married Moses McCoy, son of Robert McCoy, the land grantee. Their children were Isaac, born before 1750, who joined Baptists in 1771; Sarah M. Humes "disowned" by Crooked Run Meeting, for marrying contrary to Discipline; Jeremia, who in 1776 "gone out in marriage with a woman not of our Society"; Abraham, who "joined the Baptist disowned," April 11, 1771; Job, May 8, 1771, "disowned—neglected meeting and attended a marriage ceremony contrary to discipline;" Rachel, who married Leith, in 1778, "disowned—married contrary to discipline;" Moses, who in 1779 was also "disowned—neglected meeting and trained in Militia."

There are no records for Rebecca and Isaac, third and fourth children of Abraham and Elizabeth. Phoebe Job signed in 1760 as a witness for a marriage certificate at Crooked Run Monthly Meeting (Moore) with A. McKay and Jacob McKay; and again in November, 1760, she signed at Hopewell Monthly meeting for the marriage of her cousin, Andrew McCoy (eldest son of Robert McCoy, Jr., and Patience Job McKay) to Jane Ridgeway. There is no record for Hannah.

The seventh child, David Job, married Lezeanah. By 1774, he too had renounced the Quaker faith. He was enrolled in the early list of Captain John Tipton's Revolutionary War Roll (Romney List) with Jesse Job and Samuel O'Dell, the second. At this time he presented two wolf heads, which by law, gave compensation, two pounds ten shillings. In 1775, he lived near Samuel O'Dell in the Job family center. By 1783, he had removed to Cocke County and became one of the Charter members of the Big Pigeon Baptist Church in 1787. (Information from Ann, the wife of Rev. Arthur Lee O'Dell.)

David and Lezeanah Job had three children: Captain William; Abraham, born in 1775, who married Sally Fine, daughter of Peter Fine; and Joshua Job who married Ruth Tipton, the granddaughter of Colonel John Tipton.

Joshua and Ruth Tipton Job had sons: Enoch and Moses, who married outside the Quaker Church, 1770 and "were disowned for marrying by a hireling teacher."

JONES FAMILY

"Keeping up with the Joneses" has worked a hardship on many people in this country for hundreds of years and since I have been endeavoring to find out something about our various early families, I no longer wonder anymore about the significance of that old saying. I have found that the JONESES HAVE BEEN SOMETHING to keep up with in more ways than one. Everybody knows that the people who have the name of Jones are as numerous as the sands of the sea, indicating a prolific or virile family. That particular family characteristic has almost worked me to death just keeping in sight of them in my research trying to select the best known ones to mention in their most unusual and fascinating family story.

This family has not only been blest with great numbers, but with fine intelligence and with great wealth, a combination rarely found in one family. It seems that the Joneses had just about everything necessary to human happiness.

From Vol. IV. Makers of America, Page 266-272 is found authentic information relative to this family from which is quoted a few sentences. "The family of Jones traces back to a very early period. The name is of Welsh origin derived from the Christian name John. It was originally Johnhis (meaning John his son) was abbreviated to Johns and finally became JONES."

According to tradition, Roger Jones had borne a Captain's Commission in the Armies of Charles the II.

Captain Roger Jones was born about 1625. Came to Virginia at 35 with Lord Culpeper, as Captain of a sloop of war, for the suppression of unlawful trading. He married Dorothy Walker, daughter of John Walker, of Mansfield, in Nottinghamshire, England.

The children of Captain Roger and Dorothy Walker Jones were: Frederick, who settled in North Carolina, and Thomas, who settled in Gloucester County, Virginia.

Thomas Jones married, Feb. 14, 1725, Elizabeth Pratt, widow of William Pratt merchant, and eldest daughter of Dr. William Cocke and Elizabeth Catesby, sister of Catesby, the celebrated naturalist.

Colonel Thomas Jones gave his wife, as a marriage portion, eighty slaves, besides a large amount of valuable land and a number of houses and lots. He and his wife ranked among the leading people of Virginia. He seems to have been possessed of considerable money, as he patented several large tracts of land in different counties. He received one patent in 1713 of two thousand acres in King William County, again seven hundred and sixty-five acres in the same county. A patent was granted him by order of the council in 1716 for twenty-five thousand acres in Nansemond County. In 1719 an order for five thousand acres was granted him in Henrico County. And in 1726, six thousand acres in Hanover County. In 1731 he received another order for four thousand acres in Prince George County. No doubt he sold much of the land, dividing the balance into plantations which were cultivated by his slaves.

His principal crop was tobacco. The slaves were in the charge of overseers, and the tobacco was shipped annually to the cities of Liverpool, London, Glasgow, and other places. He made frequent trips to England, and on one of his visits in London, at the Virginia Coffee House, the favorite stopping place for Virginians in London, he received an invitation from Lady Margaret Culpepper to visit her at Leeds Castle. She was a daughter and co-heir of Seigneur Jean de Hesse, of the noble House of Hesse, in Germany, whose only child, Catherine, married Thomas Lord Fairfax, to whom she conveyed Leeds Castle in Kent. This invitation from Lady Culpeper indicates his social standing.

Two letters written by Thomas Jones from Williamsburg, Virginia, to his wife who was visiting in London, are still in existance. In one of them he gives a description of the Coat of Arms of Captain Roger Jones, his father, who had it emblazoned on his coach.

There seems to have been a great intimacy between the Jones and Culpeper families since, in his Will, Captain Roger Jones, makes the following statement: "I declare that a silver tankard in the possession of my said son Frederick is not mine, but belongs to my said son, Thomas, and was bought with money given him by Lady Culpeper."

In the History of the Jones family, the name of Frederick is of most frequent occurrence. Thomas had a brother and a son Frederick, and his brother Frederick, had a son Frederick. Therefore, it is reasonable to suppose, that Frederick Jones the founder of JONESVILLE, was ancestor of one of our Jones families in Cocke County. According to tradition, *Frederick Jones came from the eastern part of Virginia and settled in the western part of Washington County where he obtained grants of land to the amount of several thousand acres.* This was Washington County at that time.

"In 1792, when Lee County, Virginia was formed from Jefferson County, the county seat was named Jonesville, in honor of Frederick Jones on whose land the county buildings were laid out. Frederick Jones is said to have been the only one of the family to settle in that part of Virginia."

The parents of Frederick Jones, the founder of Jonesville, Virginia, were *Wylie Jones, (supposed to be the same Wylie who was Captain of 10th Virginia Regiment in War of 1812) and his wife, Mary Dickinson Jones.*

Samuel C. Jones, son of above Frederick and wife Mary Dickinson, was born Feb. 9, 1810 at Jonesville and died June 23, 1888. He was married in 1835 to Isabella Ann Wilson, in Sullivan County, Tennessee. She was the daughter of William and Mary Doyle Wilson.

Samuel Chandler Jones and wife Josephine Robinson Jones in 1880.

These were the parents of Samuel Chandler Jones Jr. and Ben D. Jones, who came early to Cocke County and became merchants. They had another brother John M. and a half brother Robert Jones, son of Sam C. and Eliza Shoemaker Jones, the second wife. These brothers came in 1859 to Cocke County, Robert, better known as Bob Jones, rode behind his brother John M. all the way from their home to Newport, or Gorman's Depot, as it was then known. He was only seven years of age but remembers it distinctly. He was the only one of the brothers living in 1940.

Sam Chandler Jones married Josephine Robinson, daughter of J. H. Robinson and they became the parents of John M., Rowena Jones Mc-Sween, and Eula Jones Holt.

Ben D. Jones wed Townzella Randolph, daughter of Judge J. H. Randolph and became the parents of James R., Robert, (deceased), William W. Jones, and Anna B. Jones Hooper, Janie May Jones Stokely, and Townzella Jones Fields.

The names of the ancestors of this family are extremely interesting and have been carefully traced back several hundred years into the dim and shadowy past of almost forgotten names, one of the prettiest of the women's names was Jane May, daughter of Joan May, which lends interest to our Janie May.

Robert Jones married Cenie Grantham, and their children were Robert, Jr., John K. and Sam C., Trilby, Eliza.

The Del Rio Jones family came originally from England where they were closely associated with the Earl of Granville. Cadwallader Jones was Gov. of Bahama Islands and father of Robin Jones, the first member of this family to come to America settled in Virginia, but in 1754 moved to Halifax, North Carolina, and his son, Robin, was agent for Lord Granville.

In 1756 he was appointed Attorney General for North Carolina, which post he held until 1766.

Robin Jones lived on an estate called, "The Castle." It was near Halifax. He was possessed of great wealth, educated his several sons at Eton. Wylie, a colonel in Revolution, graduated in 1758, after which he traveled extensively through Europe, returning to America in 1763. Russel and Robert Allen were other sons. Allen Jones became Brig. Gen. when Militia Districts were reorganized in 1776 at Mount Gallant, Northhampton. He married the daughter of Gen. Nathaniel Greene.

About this time the family moved from THE CASTLE to Halifax where they built a new home which they called . . . "THE GROVE," at which an incident took place that is delightfully remembered by the descendants of Robin Jones, who was not afraid to entertain strangers in his home, not that he might entertain an angel unawares but that he had a kind heart which he handed down to his posterity. The particular stranger who asked for lodging was John Paul, from Virginia, but who was born in Arbigland in Scotland, in 1747. At the time he called at "The Grove," he was traveling "incognito" because he had nonchalantly thrown a metal bucket at a sailor and unintentionally killed him. He sought refuge at the Jones home, which the family gladly gave. They fell in love with him and he became one of their number. (When I learned this I could better understand why the Del Rio Joneses were often referred to as the FIGHTING JONES they learned it from fighting John Paul)

Ben D. Jones and wife Townzella Randolph.

Bob Jones   Flint Ray

(Because many people want to have "PROOF" of all the legends told in families, I checked on this one, not for my benefit, but for those who are doubters and the following is what I found, sent to me by Honorable Sam K. Leming of Waldron, Arkansas, who is fast becoming a genealogist of some note so far as I am able to judge. Anyway he has sent me hundreds of dollars worth of authentic records from which I have received most valuable information of our people in Cocke County and elsewhere.)

"Captain John Paul was a Scotchman, who got into trouble on a ship and had to kill the Captain in self defense, but was an outlaw from Great Britain, came to Halifax, North Carolina for two weeks.

"Col. Wylie Jones was so impressed with him, he had him appointed Captain of a privateer. John Paul asked Col. Jones to lend him the use of his name to conceal his identity and in appreciation, Col. Wylie Jones adopted him."

Thus you see we behold the origin of JOHN PAUL JONES, the famous Fighting Father of our United States Navy.

On June the 27, 1776, Wylie Jones married Mary, the second daughter of Colonel Joseph Montfort, a descendant of Simon De Montfort, Earl of Leicester, who married Eleanor, the youngest sister of King Henry the third.

Robin Jones, the son of Wylie, was of a political mind like his father, and was elected to the North Carolina Legislature and to the *Continental Congress*. He is said to have been a great political force in North Carolina. He engineered and built powder plants and munitions factories and established a printing office in "furtherance" of the Colonies. He was made President of the Provincial Council of Safety at large.

Robin Jones and wife had seven children, left them all "well-fixed" with earthly possessions and good minds.

A grandson, Russel Jones, came from Buncombe County, North Carolina to Cocke County, Tennessee, in 1819. Settled at Big Creek . . . now Del Rio. With him, came his lovely wife, Sarah Hays Jones, daughter of Colonel Joseph Hays of Revolutionary fame. He was killed at Battle of Kings Mt. They reared a large family, eight sons and four daughters as follows:

Americus, who married Eliza Nichols; John, who married a Holland; Thomas, who married a Brooks; William, who chose a Davis for his wife; James, who wed another of the Nichols family; Charles, who wed a Justus, Jennie the daughter of Reuben; Marve, whose wife was a Woodson; Russel, who wed a Bell; Elvira, who became the wife of John H. Stokely; Evelyn, who wed Nathan H. Stokely; Frances, who married Jeremiah Elliott; Jane, who married Nelson Goodnough.

The above Americus and wife also had twelve children as follows:

John A. Jones who married Josephine Nease; Charles, who married a daughter of Charles Stokely; James, who married Ann Nichols; Marvel Mounteville Jones who married, Lena Stokely, daughter of Charles Jr. (son of John H.); Thomas, died in youth; Mary, who wed John Drummond, a photographer, who boarded with the family during the early days of the County's development. Matilda, who became the wife of Jack Bailey. Her daughter, Alice, wed a Jones ("Crit' Jones) and became the mother of three sons and each son became the father of a set of twins. One had two boys, one had two girls and the other a boy and

The Brides of the Jones Brothers. Ben D. and Sam C.
Standing—Miss Townzella Randolph, daughter of Judge James H. Randolph.
Seated—Miss Josephine Robinson, daughter of James H. Robinson.

a girl. Eliza Jones married William Harned and became the mother of our townsman Mack Harned. Sara Ann Jones married Andrew Huff. Her daughter, Lillian Waddell (Samuel C.), became the mother of Eulala who married Homer L. Livingstone and is now the mother of triplets whose names are Marilyn, Carolyn and William. Two or three of the family died in infancy. I mention the twins and triplets to prove the truth of my statement as to the virility of the family, the families of twelve might not be sufficient proof.

The descendants of the Jones families of Cocke County are too numerous to mention, the best known at the present time, are: . . . the late Judge Wylie Jones, of the District Court of Oklahoma. He had few equals as a lawyer and no superiors. He was the son of Marvel M. and Susan Woodson Jones.

The late Reverend C. O. Jones, of Oklahoma City, Oklahoma, the son of James and Ann Nichols Jones.

Honorable John T. Jones, was a son of Charles.

John A. Jones of Del Rio is Cocke County's Poet Laureate and a greatly beloved man. His poems are thoroughly enjoyed by all who have the privilege of reading them. He lives a quiet and peaceful life at his own home which he designed and helped to build. The years have been kind to him and no one dreams he is past 90 years, he is so active in both mind and body.

John A. wed Josephine Nease, daughter of Adam and Catherine Wilhoit Nease of Greene County or near the County line. This Jones family consists of two daughters and one son. Marjorie Jones Reeves, Bonnie Jones Burnett and Jennings all of whom are talented to a marked degree in the fine arts, each of the youngsters distinguished themselves in music at an early date in their lives and Marjorie has several beautiful paintings to her credit.

Among this Jones family's most cherished possessions is a very old violin brought over from the old world when the first Jones decided to seek his fortune in America. The violin is in a splendid state of preservation, was made in 1560 by D. Caspare de Salo in Brefcia. This is a little town in Italy.

Stradivari, the great violin maker was born in 1664, hence we see the Jones violin was made one hundred four years before Stradivari was born. It is of curly maple and has a solid back. It is worth a fortune, and this talented family fully appreciates and understands its value and cherishes it accordingly.

The interesting events in the lives of various members of the Jones family back and back into the remote past have been written in verse by John A. Jones.

A Bard Who Boasts His Blood

Why We Are Here

A lad from Wales went down to sea
On a British Man of War;
His heart was rife for a sailor's life,
He would be an English tar.

He'd be the Master of a ship
  And roam the seven seas;
He'd gather health, renown and wealth
  From every passing breeze.

He'd be an Admiral, serve his king,
  Make for himself a name;
To England's Fleet, by daring feat,
  He'd bring enduring fame.

He came to a land of uncrowned queens,
  Saluted the Union Jack,
Jumped overboard for one he adored,
  And vowed he would never go back.

He swam ashore resolved to wed
  And quit the rolling main;
He won success, with happiness,
  And proved a worthy swain.

History, now, recounts the act,
  Virginia was the scene,
Adown life's road these lovers strode,
  And Cupid walked between.

They lived mid scenes that tried men's souls;
  They stood the rigid test;
In spite of fate, they gave to state
  Its bravest and its best.

Their progeny have played their part
  In every field of thought;
In civil life, in stress and strife,
  They've counseled, served and wrought.

They helped to carve from wilderness,
  A nation truly great;
With pioneers and volunteers,
  They've added state to state.

They've counseled nation, state and church;
  The Congress, they've addressed;
In wagon trains they've crossed the plains
  To "The Winning of The West."

Mid the stirring scenes of seventy six,
  Their courage won applause;
For every man—rank partisan—
  Espoused his country's cause.

On many a bloody battle field,
　　By flaming cannons lighted,
They dared to stay in the thick of the fray
　　Till a country's wrongs were righted.

They saw a nation spring to arms
　　And, like Gibralter, stand;
They blessed the hour when British Power
　　Was swept from sea and land.

They built for peace, from Lakes to Gulf,
　　From Capes to Golden Strand;
They'd dared for right and won their fight
　　For home and native land.

A "Foster Son" won lasting fame
　　For victories on the sea;
An English Fleet had met defeat,
　　America Was Free.

The Congress had a medal struck
　　To witness his endeavor;
There'd fly at last from staff and mast
　　The "Stars And Stripes" forever.

The lad from Wales was Robert Jones,
　　Who shipped from British quay;
He risked his life to woo a wife—
　　That's why we are here today.

Across the earth our kindred sleep;
　　On state they have luster shed;
Wherever knight has died for right
　　They are bivouaced with the dead.

We weave for them a victor's wreath
　　And place it as love's token;
We say, farewell, sleep on, sleep well,
　　Until death's seal is broken.

　　　　　　Jno. A. Jones, Del Rio, Tennessee, Sept. 1, 1935
　　Read by Mrs. Marjorie Jones Reeves at the Jones reunion on the above date, Del Rio, Tennessee.

THE LEE FAMILY

　　The families of Fairfax, Washington and Lee settled in the county of Westmoreland, Virginia and their sons and daughters in many instances intermarried and named their children for the illustrious members of their families. A very striking and interesting example of this procedure is as follows:
　　Dr. Bushrod Washington Lee, the first, was named in honor of his maternal uncle, Judge Bushrod Washington, of the United States Supreme

Court (1798-1829.) At the christening of this child it was ordained that every second son of the following generations be so named. Dr. Bushrod Washington Lee was the first. His son the second, the nephew of Bushrod Washington Lee the second became the third and here it was thought the tradition was for the first time broken, much to the regret of the entire family. But to his surprise, O'Neil Lee, son of Jessie Orleans O'Neil Lee and Bushrod Washington Lee the third, sent to Nashville for his birth certificate at the age of thirty years and he discovered that his father had entered his name as Bushrod Washington Lee the fourth, as it had been ordained in the long ago that the name of the second son should be recorded. The Cocke County bearer of this family name, our Newport Attorney, O'Neil Lee, states that he hopes to carry on the tradition, in his second son, if and when, he has such, but that out of love and sincere affection for his maternal grandfather, Oscar O'Neil, he will continue to be known by his alias, O'NEIL LEE, as he has been known all his life. He has an older brother, Frederick Jefferson Lee. These two sons of B. W. Lee and wife received their scholastic educational advantages in California, where Frederick is now a Civil Engineer. He has one son, James Bradley Lee of San Diego, California. The second one is of course already named. Many of the young women of this family have adhered to the same tradition, which is said to have been started by George Washington who was asked to give the baby a name that he would be proud to carry.

THE LEMINGS FAMILY

In the settlement of Calvin Hoss, administrator of the estate of John Lamon, deceased, filed November 8, 1845, Washington County Court, there is provided support of the widow without mentioning her name, also: "The balance of the monies on hand, in the amount of $45.84 each, to be divided among eight heirs, Emannuel Lemons having received his portion."

It is presumed that this is the John Leming, son of Samuel who was born in Cocke County. Apparently Samuel Leming (Lemons or Lamon) did not move from Cocke County until after 1830 because the United State Census of Greene and Washington Counties for that year did not enumerate him. Therefore all his large family were born in Cocke County, as is shown by some pensions of the War of 1812 hereinafter. Their deeds involved land in the Nolachucky region. (Taylor's *Sullivan County History*.)

WILLIAM LILLARD

The story of the Lillard family, from which sprang several presidents[1] and other famous men of the United States sheds light upon the person-

---

1. James Madison, through James and Kesiah Bradley Lillard (parents of William of Cocke County) ; James Monroe, through Mildred Jones and Benjamin Lillard; William Henry Harrison, and his grandson, Benjamin Harrison, through Abraham and Jane Harrison Lillard; William Jennings Bryan, through Rachel Garrett and John L. Lillard, the parents of Nancy who married John Bryan (Their son Silas Bryan married Elizabeth Jennings, the parents of William Jennings.) ; Nathan Bedford Forrest, through Joshua, the son of Moses Lillard, VIII, and grandson of Benjamin and Elizabeth Lightfoot Lillard who married Miss Forrest, the only sister of Joseph Abraham Forrest, the father of the General; George Washington, through the Ball family of Susannah.

ality, political sagacity, and wealth of William Lillard, who might be deemed, "The Father of Cocke County," and for whom many people thought the County should have been named. He was the first member of the General Assembly who resided within the bounds of the County while it was still a part of Jefferson County. He introduced the bill to divide Jefferson and thereby create the County of Cocke, September 26, 1797. On October 9, 1797, the bill became a law. Lillard probably suggested that William Cocke be given the honor of the name of the new County.

For eighteen years William Lillard continued to serve the County as its State Representative, a longer period than anyone else has yet served in that office.

The Lillard family in America descends in direct line from a Welshman, Jasper Lillard, who spelled his name Lollard. He was also known as Moise (Moses) Lollard, and lived in France, on the Loire River, near Angers, from whence he operated a line of boats from Angers to Nantes and from Angers to Tours. His descendants continued this line for one hundred years. Jasper was also a vine grower of note.

The wife of Jasper Lollard was a Miss Isaacs, who gave up her religious belief to wed him, an avowed Huguenot. Their sons were Jean, Benjamin, Moise (Moses), Joseph, and David.

Soon after the Revocation of the Edict of Nantes, in 1687, Lollard smuggled his two sons, Jean and Benjamin, aged fifteen and seventeen years, out of France, down the River Loire, to the open sea, where they could reach a port to make negotiations to reach a free country. He did not wish them torn from him and nurtured in the Roman Catholic faith, or massacred.

Tradition says that Jean and Benjamin Lollard landed in Fredericksburg, Virginia, having come up the Rappahannock River, thence south to Richmond, and "took up" land on the James River. Determined to be thoroughly remolded to their new allegiance, the two brothers had their names changed to Lillart by special act of the House of Burgesses of Virginia. Soon after this, Benjamin was drowned in the James River, leaving Jean, from whom descended the family.

Somewhat later when Jean married Mildred Jones, he had his name, Jean, anglicized to John, and thence was known as John Lillard (1700).

At the death of Mildred Jones Lillard in 1720, John took his son, Benjamin, and moved to Prince William County, Virginia, where he married Martha Littlejohn. His son Benjamin, by first marriage, served in the French and Indian Wars and was at Fort Duquesne and with Virginia troops under Washington. He was also with Lord Dunsmore under Colonel Fleming, and later at Fort Pitt.

In 1724, Benjamin Lillard was married to Elizabeth Lightfoot, daughter of William Lightfoot, and sister of Philip Lightfoot, who married Mary Warner Lewis, only daughter of Charles and Lucy Talieferro Lewis. Elizabeth was also a first cousin to Light Horse Harry Lee of Revolutionary fame, who was the father of General Robert E. Lee and a relative of Francis Lightfoot Lee, signer of the Declaration of Independence.

Benjamin and Elizabeth Lightfoot Lillard lived in Culpepper County, Virginia, where their children were born as follows: James, 1725, married Kesia Bradley (parents of Colonel William Lillard); Thomas, 1726; John, 1737, married Susanna Ball, first and Anne Moore Thomas, second (John also served in Revolutionary War as Captain); William Lillard (no birthdate given); but named for his maternal grandfather, William Lightfoot, married Anne_____; Nancy married one Garrett; Elizabeth, married Lawrence Bradley; Sarah (Sally) married a Bradley; Benjamin Lillard married Frances Crow, first, and Elizabeth Hensley, second. He became a Captain in the Revolutionary War.

James Lillard[2] (called James II) and wife Jala Seal[3] removed from Culpepper County, Virginia, to Tennessee, in 1798. It is highly probable that they were induced to come "west" by Colonel William Lillard[4] who had evidently preceded them, and who seems to have been the Uncle of James III.

William Lillard was not only our first member of the General Assembly of Tennessee but also the first Colonel Commandant of the County, January 18, 1798. He was a captain of the militia in the days of the Southwest Territory, from Greene County, before Jefferson County was organized, and in the latter days after it was established. He was Colonel of a regiment (Second Regiment, Tennessee Volunteers) in command of General John Cocke (son of William) in the Creek War of 1813 and 14.

Colonel William Lillard married Rachel McKay Leith, daughter of Moses and Mary Job McKay, granddaughter of Abraham and Elizabeth Whitson Job, who were among the first Shenandoah County, Virginia, residents of the name.

Rachel McKay Leith Lillard was the sister of Lieutenant Colonel Abraham McKay, who with wife, Rachel O'Dell McKay, removed to Cocke County from Shenandoah County, Virginia, in 1783. She was the granddaughter of Robert McKay, Sr., the partner of Joist Heydt (Hite) who in 1731 secured from the Governor of Virginia an order for one hundred thousand acres of land in the lower Shenandoah valley, pro-

---

2. Sworn statement of James Lillard, III, verifies this:
I was borned March the 17, 1794, Culpepper County, Virginia, moved to Cocke County, Tennessee, 1798, to Smithland, Kentucky 1811, returned to Cocke County 1814, moved to Missouri Dec. 1817, returned to Rhea County 1825, married Polly Sandusky Feb. 1817. My father's name was James Lillard born in Culpepper County, Virginia 1752, married Jala Seal. My grandfather was James Lillard, who married Kesiah Bradley, my great grandfather was John Lillard who emigrated from England about 1700 with two other brothers. My father and Milly Lillard were brother and sister. I have two uncles, Austin and Ben. Signed, James Lillard.
3. James and Jala Seal Lillard had five sons and three daughters: Lewis; Mason; James III, who married Polly Sandusky; Sarah, who married a Taylor; John, who married Elizabeth Taylor; Jalea, who married a Taylor; William, who married Nancy Elder; and Polly, who married William Rogers.
4. Along with Colonel William and his brother James II came another brother, John Lillard, Sr., with his wife, Sarah Campbell, daughter of Elias Campbell. Their children were John, Jr., James, Abraham and Sarah, who married Alman Guinn and went to Rhea County. Abraham Lillard married Jane Harrison, a second cousin of President William Henry Harrison, and they moved to Polk County. Their father, John, Sr., had died at the Salt Wells in Virginia. Only John, Jr., and James of this family remained in the County and are the direct ancestors of the family now living here.
John Lillard, Jr., Cozby, married first Matilda Allen, and they had the following children: Matthew, Mark, Luke, John, Calvin, William, Russell, Mary, Matilda, Anderson, Elizabeth, "and perhaps three other children dying infants." His second marriage was to Susannah ————, from whom he had no children.

vided they would settle one hundred families on the land in two years. Both McKay and Hite[5] were from Pennsylvania.

It is evident that the Rachel McKay who married the Leith and was "disowned" by the Crooked Run Quaker Church is the same Rachel McKay, who later married William Lillard.[6]

Abraham McKay, a brother of Rachel McKay Leith[7] and the husband of Rachel O'Dell McKay, established his home three miles above Old Newport on the French Broad River, now the home of John and Hester Susong. He was Lieutenant-Colonel under Colonel William Lillard,[8] in a company of men organized to recover stock stolen by the Indians. His home became a fort after 1783.

---

5. Hite secured a group of Germans and Dutch—some Dutch Reformed and some Mennonites. McKay drew from his Quaker Association, the chief of which was the Jobe family, already connected by marriage. They were originally from Freehold, Monmouth County, New Jersey, though they were for a time within the bounds of the Nottingham Monthly Meeting, Cecil County, Maryland.

As business increased, the two proprietors took into the company a rich Scotch Quaker, Sir William Duff of King George County, Virginia, and his nephew, Robert Green, of Orange County, Virginia. The project failed because of the failure to secure the required number of settlers in the given time and because Lord Fairfax, of Virginia, also had a Grant claiming the Hite-McKay grant was within his bounds. Not until after 1795 was the case decided in favor of the Hite heirs. McKay withdrew from the company before 1752. He had a tract of seven thousand acres on Linville Creek, in what is now Rockingham County. In 1746 another twelve hundred acres was transferred to him. At his death in 1752, these lands descended to his four sons who kept it until 1768, when three hundred acres were sold to Tunis Van Pelt and six hundred acres, to Captain Abraham Lincoln, the forebear of President Abraham Lincoln. The Linnville Creek Baptist Church was built on that land in 1756, by the Reverend John Alderson. It had for its charter members, Samuel and Jonathan Newman, John and James Thomas, and John Harrison, who went all the way back to Oyster Bay, Long Island, to be baptized.

Joist Hite settled with his sons-in-law on the Opequon River, five miles south of Winchester, Frederick County, while Robert McKay chose the south bank of the Shenandoah River for his home, several miles above Riverton. Here was developed the Crooked Run Monthly Meeting, Quaker Faith, a part of Hopewell Monthly Meeting, nearer Winchester. Robert McKay, Jr., adhered to the Friends' Communion, as did all his brothers, except James McKay. Many of the third generation married out of the church and the Baptist revival of 1770 drew attention to the body.

The Church records show the independence of the Moses and Mary Job McKay family; as told in the Job records.

6. On page 50, LILLARD FAMILY, by Jacques Ephraim Stout Lillard, is a record mentioning William Lillard and wife, Rachel, and James Leith, son of said Rachel, all of Cocke County, Tennessee.

7. Some historians claim that the mother of Rachel McKay Leith Lillard was a McAlister. This seems to be in error according to above record. In addition to this proof, Jane Thomas O'Dell, at the age of ninety, often talked with the author of the relationship of the McKay, O'Dell, Whitson, Job, Leith, Lillard, and Faubion families. The same legend is also in the Lillard family, according to the present William Lillard of Newport.

Leah McKay married William Taylor who died in 1749. Later she married a Leith, which establishes the Leith-McKay relationship, twenty-nine years previous to Rachel's marriage to Leith. Rachel was a niece of Leah.

In Deed Book M, page 239, Shenandoah County, Virginia, is recorded "William Lillard and Rachel, his wife, and James Leith, son of said Rachel, all of Cocke County, deed to Isaac Hershberger, of Shenandoah County, Virginia, 568 acres of land in that county for two hundred pounds."

8. The roll of officers of the Second Regiment of East Tennessee Volunteers, commanded by Colonel Lillard, is as follows: William Lillard, colonel; William Snodgrass, lieutenant-colonel; William Bradley, first major; Isaac Allen, second major; Thomas Vandyke, surgeon; Thomas Nolen, adjutant; William Rutledge, quarter-

Houck's *History of Missouri* (page 261) gives the following sketch of William Lillard:

William Lillard, a member of the Convention from Cooper County, was born in Virginia and lived near Abington, Washington County, in that State. He was a Colonel in the Revolutionary War in command of Virginia troops and served under Washington and Lafayette and was also an officer in the War of 1812. He was a slave owner, and a man of considerable wealth. He first moved from Virginia to Jefferson County, Tennessee, about 1797 and represented that county in the Lower House of the Tennessee Legislature and subsequently represented Cocke County for eighteen years. He settled in Missouri Territory in what was then Cooper County (now Saline), in 1817, and was elected to the Constitutional Convention. He certainly was a man of magnetic influence, because Lillard (now LaFayette) County was named for him by those who knew him personally. In 1820 he was elected Representative of Cooper County to the first Legislature and in that year, Lillard County (now La-Fayette) was organized. He returned to Tennessee to live and entered land in the Hiwassee district probably about 1824, on account of ill health, due to malaria and died there about 1832.

His wife's name was Rachel McCoy, and he appears to have had three sons, Austin, John, Jeremiah and one daughter, Nancy, who married Joseph Allen, all of whom died in Tennessee, but a daughter of Nancy married Joseph Goodwin who settled near Springfield, Greene County, Missouri, most of whose descendants yet live there.[9]

THE McKAY FAMILY

Lieutenant Abraham McKay, with wife Rachel O'Dell, removed to Cocke County, Tennessee from Shenandoah County, Virginia, in 1783.

Sevier had negotiated two treaties by which the Cherokees had ceded to the State of Franklin all lands lying between the French Broad and the Little Tennessee Rivers. What is now Cocke County was then open to settlement.

By the 1783 census in Shenandoah County, Abraham McKay (or McCoy) had ten in family, with two blacks and lived near his brother, Jeremiah McKay, who had ten whites and one black. Nearby lived the widow of Samuel O'Dell and her sons, James and Jonathan O'Dell.

---

master; Arthur G. Armstrong, r. commissary; George Turnley, sergeant major; James Massengale, quartermaster sergeant; James Burrow, drum major; George Argenbright, captain; Thomas Sharp, captain; Zacheus Copeland, captain; Jacob Dyke, captain; George Keys, captain; Benjamin H. King, captain; James Lillard, captain; Robert Maloney, captain; Hugh Martin, captain; Robert McAlpin, captain; Thomas McCuiston, captain; Eilliam McLin, captain; John Netherton, captain; John Roper, captain; Abraham Gregg, ensign. (Tennessee State Archives)

9. The above historian did not seem to know the names of the other children given in old records as follows: Jeremiah married a Miss Jennings; Augustine married Loraida Taylor; James Lillard died in Tennessee with unknown descendants; William Lillard, Jr., born August 14, 1798, married Nancy Routh and died in Sweetwater Valley December 18, 1844; Rachel, John and Margaret Lillard, no record. (According to W. B. Lenoir HISTORY OF SWEETWATER VALLEY, a daughter, Louise, married Benjamin Routh, August 23, 1838.) The above Nancy, referred to by Houck (the daughter Nancy) married first a Sandusky at Abington, Virginia, who was in Cocke County in 1783, according to Ramsey. Nancy's second husband was Joseph Allen and her third was Absolem Coleman.

Abraham and Rachel O'Dell McKay lived on the French Broad River about three miles above Newport (Old Town). Soon after he established his new home, he became Lieutenant Colonel, under Colonel William Lillard in a company of men organized to recover the horses and cattle stolen from the new settlers on the French Broad and Big Pigeon Rivers. His place was maintained as a Fort after 1783 where the women and children could be kept in safety. William McCoy and William Whitson were sent as a committee asking that a Baptist Church be organized in the Shenandoah community now settled in Tennessee. He and his wife Rachel were among the charter members. He acted as the Clerk of the congregation until 1832, at which time, his son, Jeremiah, took over the duties. In turn, Jeremiah's son, Jeremiah McKay, also served.

Abraham and Rachel O'Dell McKay had eight children, of which the following five are known: Jeremiah, clerk of Big Pigeon Church, 1832 to 1845; Mary, born in 1780, married Benjamin O'Dell (born 1771), a son of Benjamin Odell and Mary Weaver Odell. Their children were Pebe, Nancy, Lewis, David, Job, Abraham, and Mary. Leah married John Faubion and their children were Henry, Barthema, Diana, Eleanor, Didamy, Abraham, Jacob, Moses, John, and Elizabeth Faubion. Abigail McKay married a Job, died in 1819 in Washington County and left a will. Her children were: Abraham, Sarah, Phebe, Joshua, Rebecca, and John. The fifth child on record was Elizabeth who married a Smith, from whom Cora Rorex descends. Mrs. Rorex was the first individual to contribute toward the publication of this book.

MCNABB

The McNabb story interests all lovers of history and I wish I could devote many pages to it because we have many of the family name in Cocke County.

The first ones came from Scotland, first pausing in the valley of Virginia where they took part in the activities of that day and place.

The multiplicity of John McNabb's has baffled the genealogists to such an extent that most of them have given up in despair. In this area which embraced part of N. C., Va. and Tenn., at that early date we know of the following JOHN McNabb's. . . . Highland John, Scottie John, Big Britches John, two Red John's, Captain John, Deaf John, Baptist John, Preacher John, Rough John, and Pretty John (The Ugliest one). The family always claimed they had no ugly folks until they began to marry into the Netherton family.

There were several Baptist McNabb's also. We have the record of Baptist, Samuel and John, who were full brothers and their half brothers David and James.

The home that Captain John McNabb built at what we know as Wilton Springs, served the double purpose of a home and a fort. It was made of hewn logs securely knotched down at the corners. The edges were "squared" between the logs was the "CHINKING" of limestone rocks and mortar. The floors were made of pine, cut with a whip-saw, and operated by hand. The nails used were made in his blacksmith shop. The house was one and one-half story high with portholes in the walls near the roof, they were cut so that the outside was a tiny opening but inside larger, sloping both ways so that the aim of the rifle might be directed in any direction. All outbuildings were placed so that they could be protected from the portholes.

In those days there was never a night without a Knight to stand guard. Captain John McNabb was the Knight of the Cosby and Wilton Springs area. He was the same Captain John who was with Vinet Fine when he was killed at Fine's Creek, N. C., and John and James Holland were wounded.

At the death of this first McNabb to come to our county he gave to his son, John the land east of the road leading to Gates store, to the Big Pigeon River. This son John reared a family of five sons, James, George, John, Felix and William, known as "Blacksmith Bill" McNabb. James became the father of Campbell McNabb.

To Captain John's son, George, he gave the land west of the roadway on which is located the Wilton Springs. This son George, had several children as follows: Malcolm, William 'Tanner Bill,' John (Deaf John), Alexander, Thomas. Daughters, Matilda, who married George I. Thomas, the son of George and Katy Lowery Thomas, the first of the name to come to the county. One of the daughters of George I. and Matilda McNabb Thomas, Jane, married Thomas O'Dell Sr. and thus became the grandmother of my children, Iris Ruth and Lynn Sheeley O'Dell.

The other daughter of George McNabb (First George) was Margaret who married John Baker.

Malcolm McNabb got the homeplace when his father died in 1857. He married a Miss Baker. Their children were: G. R. McNabb, Lt. R. A. McNabb, William and Samuel. The daughters, Jane, who married James McSween, Florence, who married B. A. Roberts, Kate, who married William Wood.

Malcolm was a merchant at Parrottsville with T. A. Faubion, he also ran a tannery. His splendid character and fine business ability crowned him with success in all his endeavors. He represented Cocke County in the Constitutional Convention of 1780. By his efforts in this Convention in withdrawing Cocke County from a 2/3 majority of the qualified voters of the county to remove a County Seat we were enabled to locate the Courthouse at Newport. He died June 21, 1898 and sleeps near his home on a high plateau, encircled by the fertile valleys of the Big Pigeon River. It is as picturesque and enchanting a spot as any in Bonnie Scotland, from whence his ancestors came and where many of them sleep. The variety and grandeur of the scenery cannot be described. From his grave can be seen the jagged peaks of the Great Smokies, deep gorges, cloud capped mountains, towering gray-green cliffs, rolling hills, green valleys. The singing waters of the creeks and the river lend an enchantment unsurpassed by the Vale of Cashmere. A lovely place to first behold the light of morn, as did Malcolm McNabb, Cocke County's Signer of our present Constitution of Tennessee, and a restful spot in which to sleep.

One of the most interesting stories of the McNabb Clan of Warriors is told of Enoch, son of James and Nancy Netherland McNabb. Enoch passed through all the battles of the Civil War until Chicamauga and in the midst of it, realizing that eight of his kinsmen McNabb had been killed, Enoch raised up and said, "Let me get one more Yankee" just then a bullet hit him and as he fell he exclaimed, "Eight McNabbs and all killed, now my head is shot off."

MIMS

Three brothers, John, Drury and William Mims, came from Wales about 1750 and settled in the Valley of Virginia. John went north. Drury and William reared families in Virginia.

The original Mims Farm of 4,700 acres is still in possession of some of their descendants. Some of their children settled in the Carolinas. A son, Drury I settled in Edgefield District, S. C. Two sons of William I, Drury II and William II fought under Francis Marion in the Revolutionary War. Drury the II was killed, leaving only one child, a daughter. At the close of the war of the Revolution William the II settled in Charleston District, S. C., and became a planter of wealth. He reared a family of five sons, William the III, Drury III, Albert, Alfred and Caswell. William the III and Drury the III married in S. C. Their children were daughters. Caswell died in S. C. unmarried. Albert and Alfred married in Tennessee. Their father, William the II having bought a farm in Greene County, one half mile below Easterly's ferry. He used this farm as a summer home and here the young man met the girls who became their wives. *Albert* married Elizabeth Evans and reared a family of several children. One daughter, Katherine, married a Bible, Almira married Thomas Christian, Godder, a son, married a Faubion. *Alfred*, born in 1800, married Margaret Easterly, born in 1807. She was the oldest daughter of Casper Easterly II whose grandfather, Conrad Easterly came from Germany and settled in Pennsylvania in 1740.

Alfred Mims I established a home known as the Fork Farm. He was active in community life but died when thirty-seven years old, being at the time a Colonel of the 12th regiment Tennessee Militia. He left a family of seven children. The oldest about twelve years of age. Their names were, Emilia, who married an Evans from S. C.; William the IV who died in California in 1851 unmarried; Jervis, who married Susan Woods and was the father of two children, Alfred II and Sallie; Drury Anderson Mims who married Margaret McSween and they became the parents of 12 children (our present Mims family in Cocke County); Mary who married William Smith, Aaron Lemuel who died unmarried; Moses Jasper who married Mary Hurley and settled at Leadvale. They became the parents of 12 children.

William Mims the III was the oldest son of Colonel Alfred and took much responsibility in the care of the family after his young father's death. His story is an interesting one. When 23 years of age he started out to make his way in the world. His first journey was to Winsboro, S. C. From there to Georgia where he assisted a slave merchant in selling a "drove" of negroes. William then went on down the Coosahatchie river to Appalachicola, Florida where he boarded a Gulf Schooner for New Orleans arriving in four days from Blakely. The great cholera epidemic was raging. He secured a position as Clerk in a wholesale store. After three weeks he became disgusted with the wickedness of the city and in April 1849 boarded a steamer, "The Uncle Sam" and made his way up the Mississippi to St. Louis in seven days. Here he changed boats for Independence Missouri, not far from Kansas City. Here the cholera plague was worse and he had an attack but recovered and remained a year teaching school. In May 1850 he started with a wagon train to California. Was five months on horseback over the Western trail. Reached Sacramento in the height of the Gold Rush, sick and discouraged, was in a hospital for weeks. The vice of the city appalled him. He secured employment in Feb. 1851, 25 miles out into the hills where in a few weeks his body succumbed and he died in March among strangers but with a message back to his mother of his steadfastness in the Christian faith.

Jervis Mims after his marriage settled in Morristown. After Federal troops occupied East Tennessee he was killed by Scouts who mistook him for his brother, Capt. A. L. Mims of the Co. E, Fifth Regiment, Tennessee Cavalry. Capt. Mims considered it a sacred duty to care for his brother's family and was faithful to this trust until death released him.

Drury IV (whom we knew as D. A. Mims) was seven years old when his father died. When he grew to manhood taught school for a while. Married in 1858 to Margaret Mc Sween. Conducted a mercantile business at Parrottsville and Newport for many years, later became connected with the Merchant and Planters Bank where he served as Cashier and later became the President of the Institution.

Aaron Lemuel Mims, born in 1834 became a student in East Tennessee University 1856 and 57 after which he taught for two years in S. C. Spent five years as student and instructor of Emory and Henry College. At the outbreak of the war of the Sixties enlisted in the Confederate Army, became a Lt. in Major Thomas S. Gorman's company, later became a Captain and served with distinction throughout the war. After which he taught school one year in Georgia, then became Principal of a Male Academy near Nashville. He conducted the school, Edgefield, for 12 years. Bought a farm at Antioch in 1880 where he lived until 1909 when he went to the home of his niece, Mrs. J. P. Thomas where he lived until his death in 1913. He was known throughout the state as a soldier, scholar, statesman, orator and Christian gentleman. He took much interest in political questions of the day and was twice nominated for Governor by the Populist Party and received a flattering vote. He was a forceful speaker on the lecture platform and a very devout man and the stay of the church in his own community. He cared for his mother until her death at the age of 92 years.

Moses Mims, born in 1835, was only two years old when his father, Colonel Alfred died. In 1857, Moses married Mary Hurley and established his home in Jefferson County. He was Station agent at Leadvale for 35 years, was active as a layman in the Church and prominent in Masonic circles, a most successful father in rearing his large family to be honorable men and women.

William Mims the II died in Greene County and was buried there at his summer home. His sons, Drury the III and William the III are buried in S. C., also Caswell, the unmarried one. Colonel Alfred was buried at Oven Creek Church yard in 1837 and 62 years later, the body of Margaret Easterly Mims was placed by his side.

The son of Jervis Mims was Alfred the II. Alfred the III lives at the present time (1951) in Newport, a bachelor.

The fourth son of Drury Anderson Mims was William the IV (W. O. Mims). Carl Mims son of C. B. and Lucia Rhea Mims is now (1951) cashier, Merchant and Planters Bank. The other son of C. B. Mims is Drury V. (Dr. Mims of the Mims Clinic). He has changed the spelling of the name.

THE O'DELLS

The O'Dells of the United States trace back to a common ancestor, William O'Dell of Concord, Massachusetts Bay Colony, their Puritan forefather who settled there in 1639. He came from the family seat in Bedfordshire, England, with a group of Puritan friends under the leadership of Reverend Peter Bukeley and Reverend John Jones. Theirs was the first inland settlement in Massachusetts. They purchased their land from the Indians, dealing with the ruler, Squaw Sachem.

In 1644, William O'Dell, with his two sons, William II and John, and his son-in-law, Samuel Morehouse, removed to Fairfield, Connecticut, where he died in 1676. (Will on record)

The sons of John were Samuel and John, Jr., who married Temperance Dickinson, daughter of the first President of Princeton University. They became the parents of Reverend Jonathan O'Dell.[10]

The family originally belonged to the Church of England, but later they joined other churches.

William II established his family on Long Island Sound, in what is now Westchester County, New York. He was known as one of the proprietors of Rye, a company organized to purchase lands from the Indians, to live on the lands and to dispose of them as a group. So successful was the venture that the company was increased from twelve to eighteen proprietors and two other purchases made, "Lame Will" and "White Plains." The final distribution of this project was not made to the O'Dell heirs until 1720. William married Sarah, daughter of Richard Vowels (1635-1697). Their children were: John, Samuel, Jonathan, Isaac, Stephen, Sarah, who married John Archer of Fordham, and Mary who married Matthew Valentine, from whom it is thought the Cocke County Valentines descend.

His eldest son, John O'Dell, received one-half of his father's property, and his sons and grandsons settled along the Hudson River in old Philipse Manor. They rendered valuable aid to General George Washington in his New York Campaign during the Revolutionary War, and from this son John descends Governor Benjamin O'Dell of New York.

The other half of William O'Dell's property was deeded to the younger sons. The southern O'Dells are related to Samuel, Isaac, and Stephen O'Dell. The Maine family descends from Reginald O'Dell; the Maryland family, from Thomas.

In 1730, the third generation of New York O'Dells became attracted to the Shenandoah Valley by land grants.[11] Samuel O'Dell settled South

10. Stilwell's NEW JERSEY HISTORICAL AND GENEALOGICAL MISCELLANEY contains the following: "Jonathan O'Dell, M.A., was appointed by the Society for propagating the gospel in foreign parts to succeed Mr. Campbell, as Missionary at Burlington, December 25, 1776, and arrived at Burlington, July 25, 1767, and was the next day regularly inducted into St. Ann's (now St. Mary's) Church, in said City of Burlington, by his excellency William Franklin, Esquire, Governor of the Province of New Jersey."
On page 82, "Married 1771, Reverend Jonathan O'Dell and Ann Decow, by me, William Thomason, at Trenton, may the 6."
11. Jacob Stover was the first Grantee, a German, from Pennsylvania. Following him was John Van Meter, a Dutchman from New York, who secured a Grant of 40,000 acres. This he sold to Baron Hans Jost Heydt (Jost Hite) who, though originally from Holland, had a Hudson River connection as well as a later one with

Branch, Shenandoah River, in 1744, and died in 1780; Caleb O'Dell settled Passage Creek and Powell's Fort in 1765, and died in 1798; John O'Dell settled North Branch, Shenandoah River in 1767.

Samuel O'Dell and his wife Elizabeth appear on the records in the Shenandoah Valley of Virginia as having settled on the Lord Fairfax tract of land on Passage Creek near Powell's Fort, the old Dunmore County in 1753, but previously Augusta County, and later Frederick County and during the Revolution changed to Shenandoah. Samuel was one of the first justices of Frederick County, when it was taken off Augusta County in 1749, and Captain of Militia in the French and Indian War under Lieutenant Colonel Lord Fairfax and Major John Hite, son of Joist Hite. He lived below Riverton among the McKays, Jobs, Whitsons on the south bank of the Shenandoah River, and died in Shenandoah County in 1780, leaving his property to his wife and three sons: James, Samuel and Jonathan.[12] Their children were: Jeremiah,[13] who married Leah Taylor, daughter of William Taylor and Leah McKay Taylor; Jonathan, who married Rachel McKay (or Whitson) and removed to Blount County, Tennessee; Benjamin, who married Mary Weaver, daughter of John George Weaver; Samuel, who married Elizabeth Job; James, who married Elizabeth Plumley, who died in Shenandoah County, 1807, leaving a will— their children were James, Abraham, Samuel, Jeremiah, John, Isaac, Jemima and Elizabeth; Rachel, who married Abraham McKay and moved to Cocke County, Tennessee; a daughter who married Alexander Mathes; Elizabeth, who married William Davis, son of John Davis.

Caleb O'Dell and wife Alice (a Newman-Thorne connection) arrived in Shenandoah County with Abraham Denton and Samuel Newman by 1755 and located on the North Branch of Shenandoah River. Before 1760, he had purchased land on Passage Creek. He lived here until 1778, one of the fifteen original justices of Shenandoah County, justice of the peace for Passage Creek Community and road overseer. In 1775, Caleb O'Dell was one of the signers for "The First Independent Company of Dunmore" and was one of a committee of eighteen to determine in 1775 war materials on hand. In 1778, Caleb O'Dell and his son, Isaac, sold their land on Passage Creek and he removed to Brush Creek in Washington-Greene County, Tennessee, of which Cocke County was then a part.

In 1872, he served on the first Grand Jury of Washington County which met in the log house of Charles Robertson. He purchased his land from Joseph Denton on Brush Creek and appears to have lived there until 1795, when his old friend, Colonel John Tipton witnessed for him in a sale of land. Caleb and Alice O'Dell had fourteen children in their family, one of whom, William, married Peggy Hobach and settled in Sullivan County, and was the forebear of Representative John Edd

---

Pennsylvania. Hite enlisted the aid of a New Jersey Quaker, Robert McKay, in his project, and they were able to increase their holdings to one hundred thousand acres, situated along the upper part of the Shenandoah River.

12. Page 119, Deed Book "B", Shenandoah County, Virginia, records a deed made by Samuel O'Dell and wife, Elizabeth, to Fergus Crawn (Crown) in 1774, witnessed by Elijah O'Dell, Charles Whitson and William Whitson. They signed their names to the deeds.

13. Jeremiah who wed Leah Taylor gives in his will to wife, Leah, and William Taylor, and to brothers, Benjamin, James, and Jonathan. Executors Brother Benjamin and William Taylor. Wit: Isaac and Abraham McKay, William Taylor.

O'Dell, who has been a member of the General Assembly of Tennessee and for two terms Speaker of the House, and is now the Secretary Attorney for the State Board of Claims; another, Catherine, married Jonathan Morrell in 1774; and Job, who lived on Brush Creek in 1792 and sold in 1795. Simon and Nehemiah were killed by the Indians in 1783.[14]

Abigail, daughter of Elijah and Ann O'Dell, married George Stephens.[15] John O'Dell[16] was married to Mrs. Sarah Denton, widow of Captain John Denton and the sister of Caleb O'Dell, in Shenandoah County, in 1767. She received her dower of 139 acres upon her marriage to John O'Dell. By 1772, they had removed to Tennessee and acquired land on Brush Creek, now in Greene County. Their children were: Jonas Denton, Captain John Denton, Jr., who came to Cocke County and established Denton Mill; Isaac, who died in 1795; Joseph, Brush Creek; Samuel, James. The children she bore John O'Dell when she became Sarah O'Dell Denton O'Dell were: William, Lewis, Uriah, and Reuben.

The three O'Dell families that ventured into the territory before it was known as Cocke County were Samuel, who married Elizabeth Job and died soon after his arrival; Isaac[17] O'Dell, who married Abigail Mansfield and later moved to Ray County, Missouri; and Benjamin O'Dell, who married Mary McKay. Samuel[18] was the son of Samuel and Elizabeth O'Dell of Shenandoah and a brother to Benjamin, Senior, who married the Weaver. This couple purchased land on Crosby (Cosby) Creek in 1783.

Jeremiah, son of Samuel, fought in the War of 1812 and was wounded on November 9, 1813. He is the Jeremiah O'Dell who went to Saline County, Missouri, and gave the fifteen acres on which to found the

---

14. Referred to in Ramsey's HISTORY and the two boys mentioned by Grannie Willhoit who lived in the fort at Wilton Springs.

15. The Stephens removed to Cocke County. This marriage probably accounts for the close tie that existed between "Aunt" Gustie Stephens, her brothers, and the O'Dell family.

16. The name was first known as de Wahul, according to extracts from the Bishop's transcript of the Registers of the Parishes of Bedford County, England, made by Frederick A. Blaydes, Esquire, Shenstone Lodge, Bedford. The de of course means among other things of, and CHAMBERS ENCYCLOPEDIA state that Odal or Udal rights (od, meaning property) are old Celtic rights to lands, still common in the Orkney and Shetland Islands. Other spellings are Wadhelle, Wahulle, Wodeul, Woodhull, and Wodell. Finally the W was left off and the name written as it is today. The name was always spelled with the small "d" in the early days. The present family use the apostrophe and a capital "D". Thomas O'Dell explained it this way: "Once it was Benjamin Odle, Abraham Odle, Tom Odle, Charlie, John, Jim, and George Odle, but Benjamin and Abraham, and Jim died, and year by year their names less mentioned. Then it was Tom Odle, Charlie Odle, and George Odle. Then Charlie married and I see it's now Charles A. O'Dell, next it will be George W. O'Dell, but I suppose it will always be old Tom Odle."

17. Ramsey, on page 279, "It continued to be necessary for two years to scout between Pigeon and French Broad Rivers. In that time Nehemiah and Simeon O'Dell were killed and scalped, and their guns taken." These were, of course, the sons of Isaac and Abigail Mansfield O'Dell.

18. A. P. Foster, TENNESSEE COUNTIES, records that Samuel O'Dell did not live long after establishing himself on Cosby Creek. His will, on file in Jefferson County, Book 1, page 45, gives his sons, Enoch, Solomon and Jeremiah, land on Cosby Creek to be divided at the death of his wife, Elizabeth, daughter, Sarah, daughter, Rachel. Exec. William Whitson and Enoch Job. Witnesses: John Denton, Isaac Odle, George Stevens. John Denton was named as guardian for Enoch, who later married Catherine Pryor in Greene County, and removed to Ray County, Missouri, by 1820.

County seat, Marshall. With him, Bartholomew Guin went from Cocke County to Missouri. His wife was Elizabeth Guggey. There is no record of Sarah, but Rachel is thought to have married Caleb O'Dell, son of Isaac, Sr., and removed to Ray County, Missouri, where she became one of the charter members of New Garden Church and died between 1824 and 1831.

Benjamin O'Dell, the first, son of Samuel O'Dell, the first, of Shenandoah County, Virginia, married prior to 1767, Mary Weaver, daughter of John George Weaver and sister of John Weaver. Her family founded the town of Weaverville, near Asheville, North Carolina. After his marriage, Benjamin lived in Powell's Fort, but removed to Washington County, Tennessee, where he acquired a land grant on Brush Creek with his O'Dell relatives. By 1790, he had removed to Buncombe County, North Carolina, where he owned land on both sides of the French Broad River. The 1800 census shows Benjamin there and in 1803, he was granted a deed to 250 acres on the French Broad River. He died about the year 1810. His children were: John, who by the 1800 census had a wife and six children under ten years; the second son, probably an infant. Benjamin O'Dell II was born August 11, 1771, in Shenandoah County, Virginia, the son of Benjamin I. In 1800, he married Mary McKay (August 18, 1780-1840), the daughter of Abraham and Rachel O'Dell McKay of the French Broad River, in Cocke County, her home being on the site of the present home of John and Hester Susong and at which she was probably born.

The family of Mary McKay O'Dell was deeply religious. Her father was one of the charter members of Big Pigeon Baptist Church and its first clerk. Benjamin O'Dell transferred his property interests from Buncombe to Haywood County soon after its organization in 1806, owning property on Richland Creek, Scott's Creek, and Waynesville. Benjamin O'Dell II was one of the first county judges for Haywood County. He was ordered "to view and say of erecting Iron Works in the County," was appointed to oversee matters pertaining to the moral welfare of the community, such as "baseborn-born-begotten children" and his last recorded task was "to oversee the election for Congressmen in June, 1819." He removed to Cocke County, where he was living in 1830. Further records were destroyed by fire.[19]

The eight children of Benjamin and Mary McKay O'Dell were: Phoebe, Nancy, Lewis, William who moved West before 1850, first to Central Illinois (a town there bears the name), thence to California. His son, William, born in Tennessee, died in Hood River Valley, Oregon, in 1891;[20]

19. Records copied from family Bible owned by his grandson, Thomas O'Dell and wife Ritta Jane Thomas O'Dell, by Ann, wife of the Reverend Arthur Lee O'Dell of St. Paul, in 1935: "Benjamin O'Dell departed this life on Thursday, the 28th of May, in 1840, in full confidence of a blessed resurrection. . ."
"Mary O'Dell, the consort of Benjamin O'Dell, departed this life on Wednesday, the 16th of January 1850 with a perfect knowledge that had the effect of smoothing all before her. In virtue she lived. In peace she died."
20. This William O'Dell crossed the plains in 1853 and located at Placerville, California, where he followed mining. Later he removed to Oregon where the town of O'Dell was named for him. His eldest son, Milton Delmar O'Dell married Mary E. McCoy, of Woodford County, Illinois.

David; Job; Abraham[21] (October 13, 1817-November 12, 1890); and Mary (March 26, 1820-September 12, 1858), who married John Malloy who went West with their two sons and expected to return for Mary after the birth of their third child.

Long a bachelor, Abraham, soon after 1850, journeyed West in search of his sister Mary's husband and her two sons, because youthful Mary was grieving her life away. No trace was found of John Malloy and the two little boys. After his return, he married Luvici Netherington (Netherton) daughter of James and Louie Thomas Netherton. "Louie" was the sister of George "I" Thomas, thus making her children and those of George "I's" first cousins. The children of Abraham and Luvici were double cousins to the children of Thomas O'Dell and wife Jane Thomas O'Dell. The father of Luvici, James Netherington, was the first Democratic sheriff of Cocke County.

Abraham and Luvici Netherton O'Dell purchased the old Cameron House, owned by Alex Stuart, in which no money was used, merely ten thousand dollars in personal notes held by Abraham O'Dell.[22] Their children were: Jacob, who married Lillie Robinson, affectionately known as "Lil." "Lil" later married a Finchem. Thomas and Frank O'Dell married the Boyer sisters and left families whose names are unknown to the author. Nannie Lou married a Huff. Mary died by her own hand in early womanhood. Ida married Hugh Woodson and died young, leaving two or three children, among them a son who distinguished himself in World War II.

The third child of Mary McKay O'Dell Malloy, Thomas, born January 4, 1852, was adopted by his grandparents and his name changed to Thomas O'Dell at the same session of the General Assembly when the name of James Brooks was changed. On February 5, 1874, Thomas O'Dell married Ritta Jane Thomas, daughter of George I. and Matilda McNabb Thomas and a granddaughter of George and Rita Campbell McNabb, also of George and Katie Lowery Thomas,[23] both of whom were full-blooded black Dutch, and could not speak English when they came to Cocke County.

Ritta Jane Thomas (April 5, 1850-April 23, 1940) was a member of the Newport Baptist Church. Their children were Elizabeth, James, John, George W., Charles A. O'Dell, and Rosa Hawk.

George William O'Dell died suddenly, November 5, 1944. Husband of Ruth W. O'Dell. Father of Iris O. Anderson and Lynn S. who married

---

21. The Minutes of the Pleasant Grove Baptist Church, Cocke County, record: "Abraham O'Dell recd. by experience July 28, 1840. Elizabeth O'Dell recd. 1841. 1842 John Wood, Elias Sisk, Polly Sisk recd. by experience. July 3, 1842 the Church met at Bro. John Weavers . . . Elias Sisk and Abraham O'Dell to be sent as delegates to Grassy Fork."

22. According to Bessie Tucker Justus, daughter of Alex Stuart.

23. Probably came with the Joist Hite German contingent from Pennsylvania and settled on the French Broad River about one mile East of the first Newport. The house they built is now the property of Esquire John Cogdill (originally Cogdale). Katie Lowery ran away across the fields to meet her bridegroom and did not have time to remove the beggar lice and Spanish needles before the ceremony was performed.

"Miss Ruth" and Prince John. When she taught in City Schools—1910 to 1920.

Hazel, daughter of Carl and Susan Slabberkorn.[24]   They have three daughters Susan Ruth, Rosalynn, and Iris Kaler.

Isaac O'Dell[25] and four of his sons removed to Missouri Territory, by way of Indiana. The eldest son, William, remained in Cocke County, and married Esther Netherington (Netherton). His son, William O'Dell II, was born about 1795 and married Margaret Wolf, born in Virginia in 1802.[26]   Their children were Job, born 1823, married Penelope (born 1826), and had children William and Margaret; Abraham, who moved to Texas; John, unmarried, went to California; Polly, born 1830, married Hartwell (probably Hartsell), and had children Isaac and Georgia; Isaac, born 1832, removed to Missouri; Henry, born 1835, died in Cocke County, married a Wolf who died in Texas at the age of 97. They had thirteen children—Jacob married a Pentland (Penland) and removed to Denton County Texas. Their third child, Nannie O'Dell, born 1884, married J. C. Pearce in 1902, and lives near Newport, the mother of a son Trent and a daughter, Elizabeth, both of whom are teachers in Cocke County.

Isaac O'Dell, the oldest one of the name was born in 1862, is still hale and hearty in 1950. Charles Abraham O'Dell, son of Thomas, Sr., and Jane T. O'Dell married Daisy Ailey, four sons James A., Joy, Vernon and Vergil.

MORELL

The advent of the Morell family in Cocke County is one of adventure, interest and intrigue and dates back to the year 1769, when a French youth became so imbued with a burning desire to seek his fortune in the

24. The parents of Carl were Maurielus and Josephine Kaler Slabberkorn of the Netherlands, who moved to Brazil where they had a coffee plantation. Carl was born in Rio de Janeiro. Susan Dykhuizen was born in Denmark and came to Holland, Michigan, in early womanhood. Slabberkorn means slab of cornbread; Dykhuizen, dyke-house. These two young Netherlanders met and married in Zeeland, Michigan.

25. The 1830 census of Ray County, Missouri, gives Isaac as being between 70 and 80 years of age and living with his son, Simon O'Dell.
Families of the four O'Dell brothers who moved to Missouri:
Isaac O'Dell—William married Mary O'Dell; Caleb married 1828, Jane O'Dell; Jane married 1830, Thomas Roe, Sr.; Simon married first Parilee Lewis—second, Sophia Tarwater; Rachel married William McKissack; James married Martha Crabtree; Susannah married first Elisha Riggs; Chaney married Benjamin Groves; Catherine married Jesse Riggs; Elizabeth married Samuel Burns; Isaac, unmarried.
Simon O'Dell—Evan married, 1825, Rhody Clark; Matilda married, 1825, Moses Hutchins; Mary married, 1825, William Hutchins; Job married, 1829, Elizabeth Roe; Thomas married 1832, Bet Clemmons; Samuel married, 1832, Polly Rowland; daughter; Reverend Isaac married, 1832, Eleanor Riggs; William married, 1840, Elizabeth Rippy; Joel married, 1843, Sally Adams; Oliver; with no record of the others of the sixteen children.
Caleb O'Dell—Edwin married, 1832, Letta Clevenger; Francis married Rachel Clevenger; Jane married, 1828, Caleb O'Dell; Isaac married 1828, Elizabeth Adams; John; Andrew married Sally Van Sickle; Abigail married David Pyhowin; son; Lourena; Elizabeth married Tom Clevenger; Sally married Joseph O'Dell; son.
Nehemiah O'Dell—William; James married, 1832, Polly Riggs; John married, 1837, Mary Shelton; Esther married, 1836, William W. Price; Nehemiah married Ann Elizabeth Covey; Joseph married Sally O'Dell; Mary married John Gentry; Simon married Elizabeth O'Dell; daughter; son.
26. The oldest graveyard in Cocke County is said to be six miles south of Newport on the original O'Dell farm on which Simeon lived, and the Doctor O'Dell who was one of the "seconds" in the Old Town Fight, mentioned elsewhere by W. J. McSween. It is now known as the Sheriff Will Allen farm.

new world, that he availed himself of the very first opportunity to do so, by making the opportunity himself. He learned that on a certain day, at a certain port, a vessel would "set sail" for America. He secreted himself in this West-bound boat and in due time landed on the shores of Virginia, where this adventuresome youth was punished for his "folly" by being "bound out" to a large landowner, that he might work out sufficient money to pay for his voyage. There was nothing else left for him to do but comply with the demand of the Captain of the ship, or so he thought, at the time. However, he soon discovered, to his delight, that the great landowner had a lovely daughter, and being French with a love and appreciation of the beautiful, he quite promptly fell in love with her and quickly decided that he was willing to not only be bound out to her father but to bind himself to her, "until death did them part." Time flies rapidly when a man is in love, and before he scarcely realized it, his passage money had been "worked out" and he was a free man, to take unto himself a wife and establish a home of his own in the new country. He married the planter's daughter and they lived happily ever afterwards, became the parents of three stalwart sons.

One of the sons, Charles M. Morell inherited his father's love of adventure, which carried him from his Virginia home to the "far West," beyond the Blue Ridge Mountains. He liked the Wilderness country beyond his beloved Mountains and decided to make his home among our Eternal Tennessee hills, and chose a most desirable location one mile South of our present Newport, at what is now known as The Morell Springs. Here, with his lovely wife, Eliza Coen Morell, a new home was established. A flour and grist mill was constructed and later a cotton gin and carding machine. These were the first, and therefore the only such industries in this part of our country, which of necessity drew a lucrative custom and rapidly enriched the owner.

To Charles M. and Eliza Coen Morell was born a son, Joseph Coen Morell, who lived his entire life on the good farm he inherited from his French father. The son took over the industries established by his parents and continued them for many years. When bolted flour became generally used he discontinued the flour mill.

The carding machine was sold to the Newport Mill Company where it was operated for a number of years.

Joseph C. Morell married Elizabeth Allen, daughter of Isaac Allen and reared our present Morell family. Lou, for many years was one of the county's leading teachers. Nora Morely Satterfield and Bertie Morell Huff all descendants of Chas. M. Morell, Jr. The original farm on which Charles Morell settled is still in the family and will always be, Home, Sweet Home" to this family. It is a wonderful thing for land to be handed down from father to son. Pot-rocks on the hill S.E. of the Spring indicate this once was the home of Indians. Charles M. Morell is now president of the City Milling Company, located on West Church Street, Newport, Tennessee (1940) where he is carrying out the traditions of his pioneering ancestors.

During the world war, a skirmish is said to have taken place at the Morell village which was named for the ancestors of this French family.

Oscar O'Neil

White Rock (now Mt. Camerer)

O'NEIL

The O'Neil family story, like that of most names beginning with 'O' is interspersed with interesting bits of family traditions intermingled with Shamrock and enlivened by Irish wit, for it was from the Emerald Isle the O'Neils came to America. They were said to be seven brothers. Generally it's only three brothers and one is made to wonder if "One flew East, one flew West, and one flew over the Cuckoo's nest." I find the records of only five of the seven brothers, however they claim that two went to Virginia. These records are in the accounts of the Comptrollers office, War of the Rebellion, in State Library of Raleigh, N. C.—In Vol. A, Book D, 1777 to 1783. Their names were Henry, Patrick, and Patrick Jr., Peter and Captain Peter O'Neil.

The two who came to Cocke County before 1816, had large families. Henry, Peggy, Betsy, Peter, Mary, Lucindy were the names of one family. The other brother's children were: Joseph, William, George W., Calvin, Harrison, Darius, Nancy and Maria. The mother of this last set was a Kitchen from Connecticut. From these descended the present ones of the name.

Colonel Joseph O'Neil was born March 4, 1804 and his wife (a first cousin), Nancy O'Neil, was born the same day. At the age of nineteen years they were wed. They were the parents of ten children. Pleasant, who married Mary Greene of Greene County; Marshall, who married, first, Elizabeth Susong, second, Malinda Hall; Angelina, who married John Thomason; Joseph, who married Mattie Ragan; Elizabeth, who married George Ogden; Margaret, who married Robert Henry; Nancy, who married her cousin, Dr. Oliver O'Neil; Jesse, who married Julia Sneed Lane first time, a Susong the second time; William, married Mahulda Mason . . . 9 children; James, married Orleans U. Mason, (sister to Mahulda) ten children, their names were: Oscar, William, Laura, Franklin, Andrew, Nannie, Alice, Margaret, Martha Jane and Ellen.

Oscar O'Neil, our townsman, with the fifty years of service as a member of the County Court, married Laura E. McClain, June 26, 1882, daughter of John Calvert and Ellen Gibson McClain. Ellen Gibson was a close relative of Henry R. Gibson. Oscar O'Neil and wife had but one child, Jessie Orleans Lee, to whom they gave every educational advantage in music and other arts. She wed B. W. Lee. They had two sons, Fred and O'Neil.

William O'Neil married Lucy Gray, they had one son, our present Gray O'Neil.

JOHN PARROTT

John Parrott, a Frenchman, son of Frederick Parrott, who came from Alsace-Lorraine, married Barbara Edwards, an English lady, living in America. There were five sons, all of whom served in the Revolutionary War. One of the five, John, entered several hundred acres of land in the Parrottsville section. Jacob, the son of John Parrott, built the first house in Parrottsville, for a tavern, in 1830, and is still extant, known as the Hale House. The tavern operated by Jacob Parrott was patterned after the houses built by the Virginia gentry and was located on the old stage road which led from Washington to the Southwest, connecting Jonesboro, the State Capital, with the National Capital.

George Parrott, another son of John, built his home near the tavern, but on the bank of Clear Creek; it was a two-story log and frame house. He spent much of his time with Tavern duties, connected with the Story Inn, sometimes called the Dry Fork Inn, located at what is now known as the Gillespie place.

Parrottsville, the third oldest town in the State, seven miles north of Newport on the Greeneville Road, was named for these first settlers.

JASPER PALMER

In the late 1700's, Jasper Palmer came to Cocke County from Virginia and "took up" 900 acres of land by grant—in the Parrottsville area—near the place later known as Givens.

His son, Wm., born in 1832, married Mary Jane Carmichael, born in 1830. Their daughter, Mary Palmer, married Joel Ernest Bowers, the parents of Chloe, Deema and Josephine Bowers. Chloe married, Wm. M. Crawford, and their daughters are Mary Elizabeth Simmons of Rome, Ga.; Martha Washington Ferguson, Morristown, and Josephine Bowers Baker, Jackson, Miss.

THE PECK FAMILY

The American family of Peck seems to have originated with four tall, unusual-looking brothers, all handsome, intelligent, large men, who came from Germany where they were known as Von Peck. Tradition relates that the four brothers decided to go to the "four corners" of the new country. On their way across the waters, they became so hungry that lots were drawn to decide which would be eaten first in case they did not find land by the next day. Fortunately, land was sighted the next morning. It is said that they carried themselves like kings. Their respective heights ranged from six feet three inches to six feet eight inches. Two of them became judges, one a doctor and the other an officer in the Revolutionary War.

Jacob Peck, one of the judges, came to Tennessee, and entered land in the Wolf Creek section of Cocke County. Each time a child was born into the family, more land would be entered in its name. Later one of the sons of this Judge Peck went to England and returned with a number of settlers who came to our County in the early days. The grandmother of the present Holland family is said to have been a member of that English Company. He was instrumental in getting the North Carolina Law repealed that gave the right to homestead instead of to buy land at the required price per acre (variously claimed at 10 pounds, 10 shillings, or ten cents per acre.)

Stories are told of the Pecks' highly developed sense of humor. One of the Judges Peck, who sat upon the Supreme Bench, was suddenly called home one day. When he returned and was questioned as to the trouble, he replied, "I just had to go home to measure my Pecks and I found I had a half bushel of them." Twins had arrived!

One of the four original brothers Peck had three sons and they too were tall, handsome, brilliant, well-dressed, and well-mannered. An artist was so struck with their appearance when he saw them walking along Canal Street, New Orleans, that he invited them to his studio for a portrait. The picture of these young men, William, Isham and Jacob

— 128 —

Peck, is now in the home of a member of the family in Jefferson City, Tennessee.

About the close of the Civil War, the Allen family at Wolf Creek sold much of their vast holdings to the Peck family. Dr. Isham Peck who was six feet and six inches tall, brought his third wife from Louisiana to the Wolf Creek Home of the Pecks. They had nine children, the youngest of whom was Robert Lee Peck, who for many years served as Chief Dispatcher of the Atlantic Coast Line Railroad, and who now lives in Sanford, Florida.

From pages 392 and 393 of Goodspeed's HISTORY OF TENNESSEE comes the following:

Jacob Peck, twelve years a judge of the Supreme Court of errors and appeals and at the time of his death, one of the oldest attorneys in the State was licensed to practice in 1808. He was a native of Virginia, but removed to Tennessee at a very early period of his life. A man of varied talents and extensive knowledge, his genius was of a high order. He had an exceptional fondness for painting and poetry and music, also took much delight in the study of zoology and mineralogy, in which science he was looked upon as an authority.

Adam Peck helped draft the Constitution of the State of Tennessee, and was a member of the first General Assembly. It is claimed that he built the first schoolhouse in Tennessee (Then North Carolina), the first grist mill, and that he also operated the first grocery store.

The descendants of this family suffered many tragedies. One of the three brothers was "sand-bagged" in St. Louis when he stepped across the street to purchase some fruit. Another took some powder for a headache, but was dead within a few minutes. Helen Peck, the eighteen year old daughter of Dr. Isham Peck, died suddenly at the Moravian School in Winston-Salem, North Carolina. The grief broke his heart and he was buried with the brother who took the headache powder. Another daughter, Ada Peck, six years of age, was practicing her music at their winter home in New Orleans, when she suddenly ran to her mother and said, "Mother, I'll never get to see the mountains again, and I'll never see 'Mammy Allen' again." (Referring to the wife of Reuben Allen.) Six weeks later, the child died suddenly with brain fever. Dr. Edd Peck, a son of Dr. Isham, the brother of Dr. Lee Peck, died by his own hand at Hot Springs. The Peck land that was entered by the first Peck that came to Tennessee had been given to Ada Peck. At her untimely death it was "heired" by her relatives. In 1936, Lewis and Lee Peck were the only ones living.

During the summer of 1935, a young forester from Connecticut kept coming to the Allen Home at Wolf Creek, irresistibly drawn to it. He was quite overcome and so were the Allens when he gave his name as Ralph Peck and was told the story of the other Pecks who had lived there before.

SANDUSKEY AND GORMAN

One of the first settlers, if not the first settler, in the Newport region was Emanuel Sandusky who is said to have come directly from Scotland, although his name in the Indian language means Cool Water. He was a Pole from Posen, Poland, and settled first in Washington County, in 1775 or 76, in the Jacob Brown settlement. Emanuel Sandusky and his wife moved to Newport, where their home was built on the site now occupied by the Cocke County Memorial Building. They had a son James and a daughter Mary (Polly), born in 1783. Sandusky (often written Seduskey) was a soldier under Sevier in the Revolutionary War.[27]

When their baby was three years of age she was stolen by the Indians. He searched diligently for her for miles in every direction. Whenever or wherever the Indians had a "swapping" of captive whites, Emanuel Sandusky was always present. After nine miserable years, he found a twelve year old girl, who he knew would be the correct age of Mary, purchased her, and took her home with him. The mother found a scar on the child's arm, the result of a burn, which identified her completely. However, Sandusky never gave up the habit of searching, probably hoping to find another child, or perhaps doubting that the one he found was really his own.

When Mary matured, she was courted by many, but she was won by John Gorman, who had come from Maryland, on his way to Louisiana and stopped to build a houseboat. They were married in the early 1800's. Their children were: George W. Gorman, born in 1802, Judith Gorman, John Gorman, Jr., Thomas Sandusky Gorman, David Gorman, Martha Gorman (born 1827), and Rose Gorman who died in early womanhood.

Emanuel Sandusky had seven sons and eight daughters, including Mary, thirteen of whom went with him to Missouri, after he sold his land to the son-in-law, John Gorman II. James Sandusky, the first to be buried in the Presbyterian Cemetery and his sister, Mary Sandusky Gorman, were the only Sandusky children left in Tennessee. John and Mary Gorman were the parents of eleven children. The four sons were: James, who went west and was buried in Brown County, Texas; David, who had fifteen children, nine of whom married in Cocke County before they journeyed to Missouri; John II, the father of Thomas Sandusky Gorman II (known as Pie Tom Gorman, because his mother was so fond of him she called him her "Little Pie."); Thomas Gorman, known as Major T. S., who married Delilah McGinty. The daughters of John and Mary Sandusky Gorman were: Rosa and Eliza who died young and were buried in the Presbyterian Cemetery; Desdemona Pulyan, Nancy Stancil, Mary Kingry, Martha De Arman and Judith Anderson, all of whom went west except Judith.

John Gorman, feeling that his days were numbered, divided his land among his children. The part located between the present City Mill and the W. D. McSween home near the Stokely Brothers Cannery, he gave to Thomas Sandusky Gorman; that between the Y. J. McMahan place and the Jack Farm (now owned by Stokely Brothers), to Judith and Martha Gorman; the present Y. J. McMahan holdings, to John Gorman, Jr. David sold the greater part of his property to his brother, Thomas S. Gorman, in order to follow his parents to Missouri. Thomas S. Gorman, sold a great part of his land to Murdock McSween, which is still in the hands of the McSween heirs. Later, Thomas S. Gorman bought Judith's land.[28] John

27. Land Grant No. 873, issued May 10, 1810, signed by Willie Blount, Governor, and Eli Scott, Register of East Tennessee, gave him land for his home.

28. The Old Presbyterian Cemetery is part of the land owned by David, who donated this spot to the County when his mother's brother James died. This appears to be one of the oldest cemeteries in the County. James Sandusky was the first white person buried in this spot.

Confederate Headquarters in Cocke County, known as Green Lawn when it was
the home of Alexander Smith, now owned by Allen Sisk.

The Masonic Hall

Gorman returned to Tennessee and died during the 1840's, and was buried in the Old Cemetery. Mary lived until 1853 and was placed beside her husband.

When the Civil War began, George W. Gorman cast his lot with the Yankees, and became Captain of Company "I," 2nd Tennessee Cavalry Volunteers. Thomas S. Gorman went into the Confederate Army and returned as Major Gorman. To him goes the honor of founding the town of Newport, and to David Gorman, a close second. These brothers gave generously of their river bottom lands to the Southern Railway, and the Depot was built on the line that ran between their holdings, and the place was known first as Gorman's Depot. The line is now marked by a small brass ring imbedded in the cement of the sidewalk in front of the Nelson and Bales Drug Store.

The land where the Masonic Hall now stands was donated by Major Gorman to be used forever for that purpose, or to revert to the Gorman heirs. The lot on which the Courthouse now stands was also given by Major Gorman, and also many of the streets and alleys.[29] He is said to have been the County's first bank, loaning money to all who needed it, ably assisted by Sam Jack and Swan P. Burnett.

Thomas S. Gorman married Delilah McGinty (sometimes spelled Mc-Guinty), born in South Carolina, the daughter of a rich cotton broker. He met her when she and her father tarried for a while en route west. Her father might have also settled here, but he feared to lose his daughter. Thomas S., after a while journeyed West in search of his sweetheart and returned with Delilah McGinty as his bride.[30] He died in 1876.

Four great-great-grandchildren of Emanuel Sandusky still living in Newport (1936) are George W. Gorman, George W. Pennell, Roy G. Pennell, and Sallie V. Pennell, (Sallie V. Pennell contributed much of this data in 1941.)

MAJOR WILLIAM CHESLEY ROADMAN

Major William Chesley Roadman, son of John Augustus Roadman and Elizabeth Lightfoot Roadman, was born in Williamsburg, Virginia October the 6, 1784.

---

29. In 1915, a few citizens, with the help of the Southern Railway and the Masonic Lodge, collected enough money to erect a monument to the memory of Major Thomas Sandusky Gorman in Union Cemetery, where his remains had been placed by order of the County Court, after thirty-seven years in a neglected spot. The inscription reads as follows:

To Major Thomas Gorman......1812-1876.

To Delilah M. Gorman........1819-1900.

To him: A faithful public official, a brave Confederate Soldier, a Christian Gentleman, a citizen whose wise generosity, helped build Church, County, Town, Lodge, Rail Road. Who had part and leadership in every good work. The sick he visited, the poor he relieved, the stranger he entertained, the oppressed he defended.

To her: Whose love and charity touched and blessed the lives of many, his constant companion and true helper, this monument is erected by Cocke County, the Southern Railway and Newport Lodge Number 234 A. F. and A. M.

Committee: Y. J. McMahan, R. C. Smith (Dr.), W. O. Mims, J. P. Headrick, G. W. Gorrell, and C. E. Dawson.

30. Although this union had no children, they reared Theresa Henry Headrick, who gave this information. The author liked to visit "Aunt Delilah Gorman" and saw her during her last illness and after her death.

Major Thomas Sandusky Gorman—Delilah McGinty Gorman

The T. S. Gorman Home

William Chesley Roadman was educated at William and Mary College.

After his marriage to Sarah (Sally) Muse Sanford, of Richmond, Virginia, which occurred November the 12, 1807, the couple came to Tennessee. They settled first at Jonesboro and later moved to Cocke County. Here Major Roadman acquired an estate of several thousand acres, which extended from the Oldtown bridge, on the French Broad River, to the Pigeon River on the West. He built a handsome home at Oldtown (Newport), designed after the style of his forebears homes in Virginia. Major Roadman did not devote his time exclusively to the cultivation of his broad acres. He engaged in the mercantile business at Oldtown and later became Postmaster. He became rich and influential and being a public spirited man, he did much for the welfare of his community.

During the war of 1812, he commanded a batallion of his countrymen, whose high purpose was to aid in the campaign against the British, at that time belaboring our Southern Coast, but the very day before they reached New Orleans, that great and decisive victory—The Battle of New Orleans—was won. After his return, Major Roadman was elected to the Legislature. He cared little for political preferment, but at the urgent insistence of his friends, he accepted the nomination and was elected Representative for Cocke and Sevier Counties in the Constitutional Convention of 1834, for the purpose of reframing and amending the State Constitution of Tennessee. Major Roadman also represented the First Congressional District of Tennessee in the National Convention which nominated Andrew Jackson for the Presidency of the United States.

Tradition has it that on Jackson's visits to Major Roadman, they found great pleasure in racing their blooded horses in the vicinity of the latter's home. (Some claim the race track was located on the site on which the business section of the present Newport is now located).

Major William Chesley Roadman died August the 28, 1849. The inscription on his vault in the old family burial ground is still clearly decipherable.

Ted Roadman's father, Marcus Aurelius Roadman was a brother to Julia Raleigh Roadman Smith. Several of Julia's children were older than Marcus Aurelius.

Ted's name was also Marcus Aurelius Roadman. He always wrote it M. A. Roadman but everyone called him Ted Roadman.

For years he was editor of a paper in the County. The last one he edited he called it the Newport Herald. He was also a merchant.

He married Nola Allen and to them were born three sons and one daughter, Dooley, Jimmie and John M. (called Mike) the girl was Dorothy and was seriously injured in a swimming pool when about grown. She died soon after the injury.

Dooley is a lawyer by profession, married the daughter of Caywood Mantooth the present postmaster and is employed in the post office. Jimmy in military service (air).

NAMES AND MILITARY RANK OF SONS OF GENERAL ALEXANDER EVANS SMITH AND WIFE, JULIA RALEIGH (ROADMAN) SMITH, NEWPORT, TENNESSEE, WHO SERVED IN THE WAR BETWEEN THE STATES.

(1) WILLIAM ROADMAN SMITH (80th Tennessee Infantry Regiment; later called *Mounted* Infantry). In the fall of 1862, he organized a company and was elected

Captain. This company was indentified with the 62nd Regiment C.S.A. Tennessee Infantry, which was commanded by Col. John A. Rowan, General John C. Vaughan's Brigade. In the spring of 1863, Captain Willaim Roadman Smith was promoted Major. He was captured at Strawberry Plains October 27, 1864, and was incarcerated in the Chattanooga Military Prison, Chattanooga, Tenn., where he began his prison diary on November 2nd. On November 19th, he with his fellow prisoners, started on a four day journey to Johnson Island Prison. Here his diary was resumed. Regardless of the hardships and suffering endured during this trying experience, his diaries show unwavering faith in God. Reduced almost to the point of starvation, he was finally released in April, 1864.

I have confirmed Major William Roadman Smith's military rank by Marcus J. Wright's "Tennessee in the War"—a compilation of names of officers, their rank, date of appointment, names of battles, dates, etc. etc. (war of 1861-1865). From family records, I know that he was in the Siege of Vicksburg.

(2) THOMAS LUCIUS SMITH. According to Maj. William Roadman Smith's family records, his brother, Thomas Lucius Smith, served one year in Branner's Battalion, at Mossy Creek. He was transferred to the 63rd Tennessee Infantry Regiment. C.S.A. He was promoted to the rank of lieutenant in the 62nd Infantry Regiment known also as the 80th Mounted Infantry. Thomas Lucius Smith fell mortally wounded during the siege of Vicksburg and died a month later. With him were Maj. William Roadman Smith and Theodore Melvin Smith, his younger brother.

(3) AUGUSTUS SMITH. Again referring to Maj. William Roadman Smith's records. his brother, Augustus, was a member of Osborn's Scouts. He was killed in line of duty by Federal troops, at Mossy Creek, or to be more accurate he died of a wound sustained the day before. My father, Theodore Melvin Smith was with him when he died, as were his wife and infant daughter, Nancy, who in after years became the wife of Selden Nelson, son of Judge T. A. R. Nelson, of Knoxville, Tenn.

(4) THEODORE MELVYN SMITH left his desk at the University of Tennessee, to enlist in the cause of his country, at the age of sixteen. *He was made Second Lieutenant in Company 1, 2d (Ashby's) Cavalry Regiment (formed from 4th and 5th Cavalry Battalions).* He served under Col. Henry Henry M. Ashby. Besides being at Mossy Creek, he fought in the Siege of Vicksburg, and other minor engagements.

I am relying upon Maj. Smith's records for the accuracy of the military records of Thomas Lucius Smith and Augustus Smith and upon verbal statements made by my father to me. I also know that his personal record, as outlined in item (4) is correct. Some of the rolls were lost or else were not made available to General Marcus J. Wright. In his list of Field Officers, Regiments and Battalions in the C. S. A., he does not include the names of officers lower in rank than that of Major.

My grandfather, Gen. Alexander Evans Smith, was appointed by Gov. Isham G. Harris, to provide ways and means to carry on the war. His title was General of the Militia and his appointment was made in 1861.

Major W. R. Smith was an alumnus of Washington College, as was his eldest brother Alexander DeWitt Smith, who died in 1860.

Thomas Lucius graduated at the University of North Carolina (Chapel Hill) cum laude and also completed the course in law at that well-known institution.

SARAH MUSE SANFORD ROADMAN

The old Roadman family Bible gives the date of birth of Sarah (Sally) Muse Sanford Roadman as of November 26, 1790.

The date of her marriage to Major William Chesley Roadman is shown as of November 12, 1807.

Sarah Muse (Sanford) Roadman was the daughter of Robert and Lucy Raleigh, (sometimes spelled Rawleigh) Sanford. According to tradition, these records were lost, this family lived in James City County, Virginia. It is claimed that the grandmother of Sarah Muse Sanford Roadman, Lucy Raleigh, by name, came from Richmond, Virginia. One of the old descendants told the writer that Sarah (or Sally, as she was popularly called) Muse (Sanford) was a very beautiful and accomplished woman. That she was well educated cannot be doubted. This inference comes from the beautiful penmanship, faultless composition and perfect spelling shown in letters, written by her to her daughter, at Salem College, (now in possession of the writer).

An item in the diary of Mary Pulliam, a descendant, is to the effect that "The Methodist Episcopalian" (a newspaper published in Knoxville, Tennessee at the time of her death) carried a very laudatory obituary notice, more than a column and a half long, eulogizing the life of Sarah Muse Sanford Roadman, full of the highest praise of her character in every relation of life.

She died November the 3, 1847, according to the Roadman family Bible and the inscription on her vault in the family cemetery at Oldtown:

(Born, married and died in the month of November).

The Raleigh, Muse and Sanford families were prominent in Virginia.

JULIA RALEIGH ROADMAN SMITH

"Born to Major William Chesley Roadman and Sally Muse Sanford Roadman, a daughter, Julia Raleigh Roadman Dec. 28, 1808.

Julia Raleigh Roadman was educated at Salem College, Winston-Salem, North Carolina. In addition to the regular course, prescribed by the curriculum, she studied music and art.

On August the 17, 1824 she was married to General Alexander Evans Smith, after which she became mistress of Green Lawn, a beautiful colonial home built by her husband's father, Alexander Smith, Sr., for his bride. (Mary De Witt Smith).

The home of Julia Raleigh Roadman Smith became the center of old fashioned hospitality, many friends of the Smith and Roadman families, whose names have gone down in history, enjoyed the lavish hospitality of the Smiths. Conspicuous among others were Judge T. A. R. Nelson, Judge McKinney and Hugh White of Knoxville, General Greene, United States Senator Josiah J. Evans of South Carolina, Judge David Campbell, U. S. Senator Joseph Anderson and Colonel Alexander Outlaw (the last four named kinsmen of the Smiths). And last but by no means least, ANDREW JACKSON and many socially prominent families from Virginia, South Carolina, North Carolina, Kentucky and Tennessee.

Julia Raleigh Roadman Smith came of aristocratic lineage. On the maternal side, her line of descent was from the Lightfoot, Lee and Corbin families of Virginia. These families intermarried with the first families of the commonwealth during that interesting period in which they lived and wrought, so that Julia Raleigh Roadman Smith had an enormous connection, represented by the best blood of the land.

On the paternal side of the house, little is known of the Roadman family by the surviving descendants for the reason that valuable records were lost. The late, lamented Dr. Tyler, son of President Tyler, who did so much for the preservation of Virginia records, established the fact that his kinsman, JOHN ROADMAN, by marriage through the Lightfoot family came to Virginia, from England, when quite a young man. He married Elizabeth Lightfoot. The Bruton Church records register the birth of a daughter and son, William Chesley Roadman. The baptism of certain slaves belonging to John Augustus and Elizabeth Lightfoot Roadman is also recorded.

In the "list of taxable articles," for Williamsburg, the number of horses, slaves, cattle, wheels, (meaning carriages or chaises) which belonged to John Augustus Roadman are given, Dr. Tyler also established the fact that John Augustus Roadman owned real estate in Williamsburg, all of which confirmed traditions handed down by older members of the family connection to the present generation of descendants.

John Roadman died while the children were yet small. The writer has done considerable research upon this line, but with small success and is of the opinion that John Augustus Roadman may have been the only Roadman who emigrated to Virginia.

His granddaughter, Julia Raleigh Roadman Smith was the mother of eleven children. Four sons of Julia Raleigh Roadman Smith and General Alexander Evans Smith fought in the War between the States. Three were officers. Two laid down their lives for their country. They were all college-bred men.

The Smith family intermarried with the Langhorne family of Lady Aster of Virginia, the David Brown Miller family of Western North Carolina, the Coffin family, the Hamilton, Jones and Rhea families of East Tennessee.

Julia Raleigh Roadman Smith died at Green Lawn. She rests beside her husband in sight of the home of so many joys and sorrows, which she had known so long. She died July 13, 1890 at the age of eighty two years."

COLONEL ALEXANDER SMITH, SR.

Colonel Alexander Smith, Sr., son of Peter L. and Nancy (Outlaw) Smith was born probably in Duplin County, North Carolina in the year 1766.

On March 30, 1803, he married Mary DeWitt, the daughter of Harris and Elizabeth (Brockington) DeWitt, of Darlington District, South Carolina.

Colonel Alexander Smith, Sr., was the grandson of John and Sarah (McRee) Smith. He was the great grandson of William McRee, Gentleman, who emigrated from County Down, Ireland, and settled in Duplin (then Northern New Hanover County) about the year 1739, (according to A. T. Outlaw, Genealogist).

William McRee was one of the first Justices and one of the first Vestrymen of the Episcopal church in that section.

The present generation of Smiths know little of their ancestor, John Smith (or Smyth, as the name appeared during his lifetime) on account of some of the records of the Smith family having been accidentally destroyed by fire. It is presumed, and upon excellent authority, that he married Sarah McRee probably in Ireland. By reference to certain Court Records, it is also natural to suppose that he was a man of substantial means, based upon the fact that these records show certain deeds of conveyance to lands in North Carolina, which were made by him.

In a family record written by Major William Smith, he states that "Peter and James Smith, brothers, emigrated from Scotland to America with their father about the middle of the seventeenth century and settled in the Tar and Neuse River region of the province of North Carolina near the town of New Bern." Peter and James were the sons of John Smith or Smyth. From Duplin County these sons moved to South Carolina and settled somewhere on the Pedee River.

The South Carolina Census shows that they were there in 1790. After a brief sojourn in the Palmetto State, James Smith returned to his former home in North Carolina and some years later died there.

Peter Smith disposed of his holdings in South Carolina and with his family moved to Tennessee and settled in Cocke County, near Newport.

On the maternal side of the house, Alexander Smith, was the grandson of Edward Outlaw III and Patience (Whitfield) Outlaw. The great-grandson of Edward Outlaw II, Gentleman and wife Anne Outlaw. He was also the great grandson of William Whitfield, Gentleman and Elizabeth (Goodman) Whitfield. His mother, *Nancy* (or Anne) *was the sister of Alexander Outlaw.* Alexander Outlaw married Penelope Smith, Peter Smith's sister. Three of their sons-in-law, viz: Senator Joseph Anderson, Judge David Campbell and Colonel Joseph Hamilton, together with their father-in-law became distinguished in the annals of Tennessee. They all served in the Revolution as did Peter, James and Alexander Smith and William Whitfield. Historians and genealogists are agreed that they belonged to "ancient and honorable families."

Alexander Smith enlisted in the Revolution at the age of fifteen. He served under General Greene and fought in the battles of Guilford and Eutaw Springs, was wounded in the last engagement.

In the Creek war he held the rank of Major and inspector-general. In the hard fought battle of the Horseshoe, a bullet whizzed through his whiskers. The writer possesses three letters from him, written to his wife, one, relating to the surrender of the Creeks and another relating to the impeachment of Cocke. He was a lifelong friend and admirer of his immortal leader, Andrew Jackson, who visited him in his home.

In his History of Western North Carolina, the author, John Preston Arthur, mentions Alexander Smith's appointment as one of the "Tennessee Commissioners to run and mark the boundary line from the Big Pigeon, at the Catalooche turnpike, Southwest to the Georgia line."

The Official Manual of the State of Tennessee also mentions an act passed by the General Assembly, at Murfreesboro, "September 17, 1821 confirming the boundary line between North Carolina and Tennessee, run by Alexander Smith, Isaac Allen and Simeon Perry, Commissioners for Tennessee and James Mebane, (according to Arthur), Montford Stokes and Robert Love for North Carolina.

In the year 1817, Colonel Alexander Smith, Sr., was appointed one of the Trustees for Anderson Academy. Anderson Academy was named for his distinguished kinsman, United States Senator Joseph Anderson.

Colonel Alexander Smith, Sr., was a man of considerable wealth and wielded an influence for good in the community in which he lived.

He died May 8, 1824 and was interred in the family burial ground at Green Lawn.

The above information on the names of those who ran the boundary between our State and North Carolina is information I have traveled to both Raleigh and Nashville to secure and failed to find same at each place and no one could tell me where it might be found. I am extremely grateful to Mrs. Walker for this bit of historical fact.

MARY DeWITT SMITH

"Mary (DeWitt) Smith, daughter of Harris and Elizabeth (Brockington) DeWitt and wife of Alexander Smith, was born in Darlington

District, South Carolina, October the 30, 1782. The granddaughter of Martin DeWitt I. Her father was a patriot of the Revolution. She came of an illustrious line of French ancestors.

Members of this family emigrated as early as the twelfth century to Holland where they played leading roles in the political, military, civic, social and religious life of that country. In reality, historians claim that they occupied the highest offices Holland had to bestow.

Others of this line settled in Brazil, Portugal and the West Indies, where they also occupied high official positions in the government of those countries.

Two outstanding examples of the American branch of the DeWitt family of Holland descent were Clinton DeWitt of New York, one time Governor of that State; U. S. Senator, several times Mayor of New York City, projector of the Erie Canal, writer and historian.

In the State of Tennessee, the late, lamented John Hibbett DeWitt, of the Court of Appeals, Nashville, president of the Tennessee Historical Society (for 13 years) and who occupied many other offices of trust and honor, was a shining example of the high ideals and lofty standards set by his distinguished forebears.

Martin DeWitt, who came to America about the middle of the seventeenth century, was the progenitor of the DeWitt families of South Carolina and Tennessee. He and six sons served his country in the Revolutionary War. Members of this family particularly Capt. William DeWitt, whose daughter, Dorothea married U. S. Senator Josiah J. Evans, a prominent Judge in South Carolina, were among the pioneers who took an active part in the development of the Cheraw District, on the Pedee.

Piety was an outstanding characteristic of the DeWitts as far back as the line can be traced, a fact often commented upon by historians. This family trait has been amply confirmed in the case of Mary DeWitt, through tradition and old letters written by members of the family with whom she came in contact. The influence of her lovely Christian womanhood was felt by all who knew her. She lived to be nearly eighty years of age. Died December 15, 1861. She sleeps beside her husband, Colonel Alexander Smith, in the old family burying ground at "Green Lawn," near Newport, Tennessee. (This home is now owned by Allen Sisk and has been known as the John M. Jones farm, the Stokely Susong farm, etc. It is near the City Park, once known as The Fair Grounds.)

Mary DeWitt Smith's great granddaughter, Mrs. Lucile Smith Walker, has in her possession photostatic copies of an unbroken record of the DeWitt line in Holland, which were taken from the Royal Library at the Hague. These photostatic copies are an exact reproduction of the De-Witt records as they appear on the library book. They are written in the Dutch of the twelfth century as it was spoken in Holland. The various coat of arms of the noble families, with whom the DeWitts intermarried, side by side with the DeWitt arms are shown. These records cover a period of three hundred and fifty years.

The information herewith given relative to the DeWitt family, Colonel Alexander Smith, General Alexander Smith, Sarah Muse Sanford Roadman, Major William Chesley Roadman, Julia Raleigh Roadman Smith and Mary DeWitt Smith has been contributed by Mrs. Mae Lucile Smith Walker. I am sure it will be greatly appreciated by the descendants of the above families, many of whom now reside in Cocke County.

THE STANBERRY FAMILY

From Washington County, Tennessee came John F. Stanberry the first of his name to settle in Cocke County. He lived at "Old Town" or the First Newport. He was twice wed, first when he was but sixteen years of age, to Maria Broyles on the 12 day of November, 1820. He was evidently a thrifty lad for he was able to post his own bond of twelve hundred dollars.

One year after his marriage, his young wife died at the birth of their son, Melchisedic Robinson Stanberry, the son died also. (Enough name to kill any baby).

Seventeen years passed before John F. Stanberry married again. The second time he chose for his bride Rachel Hoskins of Old Newport.

To this couple was born one son and two daughters. Samuel Hoskins Stanberry and seventeen years after his birth came one of the daughters, a year later the other one was born. They were Florence, who married J. P. Robinson and Louella, who first married Thomas Faubion, a nephew of "Aunt" Augusta Stephens and later Dr. Thornburg.

Samuel Hoskins Stanberry married Harriet Jane Clevenger who lived seven years only but bore him two sons, Doctor John F. Stanberry and Arthur Stanberry. Later, Samuel H. married Caroline Hale of Parrottsville. To them was born two children, one of whom grew to manhood and lives in California, Ralph Stanberry.

John Freeman Stanberry the II, who became Dr. Stanberry, was married to Ethel May Wood, September 24, 1902. To this union came two sons and one daughter; Samuel Hoskins, on July 28, 1903; John Freeman III on September 22, 1906; Mary Florence (Polly) June the 25, 1915.

One of the most successful and colorful of the members of the Medical Society was Doctor John Freeman Stanberry, son of Samuel Hoskins and Harriet Clevenger Stanberry, who graduated from the Lincoln Memorial College in 1896. This institution was located in Knoxville upon the site of the General Hospital property. He was probably inspired to become a Doctor from association with his uncle. After graduation, Doctor John F. as he was most always called, returned to his home in the Edwina section and began the practice of medicine. Like all doctors in those days he went horseback most of the time. It was the only way he could get to all the homes of his patients. His medicine and bandages and surgical instruments he carried in his "Saddle-Bags."

Dr. Stanberry was a man of most dynamic personality, always pleasing in manner and extremely buoyant and optimistic. His keen intelligence, his knowledge of psychology and how to apply it, his great vitality and zest and enthusiasm, made him one of the outstanding men of his time, not only in his own profession but of his generation. He had a large circle of patients and a larger circle of friends. His genial personality made him a great favorite everywhere. It is said that he never made an effort toward securing either friends or patients. Other Doctors were never jealous of him professionally. They all knew he didn't give a "continental" what they thought of him, therefore they thought well of him, he was refreshing to them, public spirited and always ready to render any service possible for the upbuilding of the County.

In the Medical Society meetings he always insisted that the members attend each meeting that they might learn from each other anything helpful in their profession or otherwise.

No other Doctor in Cocke County ever did more charity work than Dr. Stanberry. His love for humanity and all living things inspired him to render such service and to do so freely without hope of reward. He considered it part of his duty. Dr. Stanberry was quick-spoken, quick-motioned, he took a great interest in the game of polititcs and played it with a zest. His sense of humor was extremely well developed and his knowledge of subterfuge never failed to extricate him from any prank in which he chose to engage except once, and that was when he frightened his step-mother out of her wits with his human skeleton and she fell at his feet in a dead faint. He had not intended to frighten her, had just returned from college and was assembling his office equipment when she unexpectedly came upon him. She became his first patient, but she had been "patient" with him over a period of many years.

From his father, Dr. Stanberry inherited a good farm at Del Rio and added much to it by purchase. He preferred farming and stock raising to practicing medicine. His hobby was the breeding of fine hogs. The Duroc Jersey was his favorite. He exhibited them all over the United States. They won many prizes which brought him National Fame as a Breeder of Fine Hogs. Dr. Stanberry was a regular contributor to Stockman's Journals all over the Country. His favorite subject was the raising of pedigreed stock.

In 1910-11 and 12 he was continuously selling fine hogs to McKee Brothers of Versailles, Kentucky. For, "TENNESSEE PRIDE," he received one thousand dollars. This hog won the Grand Championship at the International Stock shows at Chicago. This distinction inspired him to continue his breeding of Duroc Jersey hogs, which he sold and shipped constantly to breeders in many states. They were all anxious to secure the stock of TENNESSEE PRIDE.

Horses were also a source of great delight to the Doctor. He kept the best that he could secure. His dogs ranked next to his hogs in his love for animals. They would follow him all over the place, they knew he loved them every one. The first airdale to make its appearance in Cocke County was brought in by Dr. Stanberry. He bought it from Dr. Toney in Colorado, paying him the unheard of price of $50. His neighbors thought that was the most terrible extravagance they could imagine. Dr. John didn't mind what anyone thought just so they kept it to themselves. It is said that he was equal to Andrew Jackson for fighting at the drop of his hat and dropping it himself. Because of this characteristic he was highly respected and never imposed upon. His red tie was sufficient warning probably.

In addition to the airdale, the finest pedigreed bulldog that could be found made its home at the doctor's house and at various times, collies, terriers, police dogs and greyhounds.

Dr. Freeman Stanberry the II, was truly a Southern gentleman, greatly beloved and greatly mourned. He died almost suddenly at his home at Edwina November the 27, 1922.

STOKELY

STOKELY

STOKELEY (English) Dweller at the Stoke-Lea, see STOKE, and Middle English *ley*. Old English *leah*.

STOCKLEY (English) Belonging to Stockley (13th-14th century Stockley (e, Stoklegh, etc.) ; or Dweller at the Tree-Stump or Trunk Lea. Old English Sto (c. Leah). Stockley and Stock, Calne, Wilts are referred to in the same Inq. ad q. Damn., A.D. 1445-8, as Stockley and Stocke.

(Harrison—Surnames of the United Kingdom, 1918).

STOCKLEY, STOKLEY, STOKELY. Local, "of Stokley." Two parishes in co. Devon, and a township in the parish of Brancepeth, in co. Durham, bear this name. Other smaller spots would probably bear it; v. Stock and Ley.

> Ralph de Stockleye, co. Suffolk, 1273 A.
> Pagan de Stockleye, co. Oxf., ibid.
> 1791 married - Phillip Stone and Temperance Stockley: St. Geo. Han. Sq. ii, 63.
> London, 2,0,0; Philadelphia, 8, 14, 3.

STOCK, STOCKS. Local, "at the stock," the stump, the trunk of a tree, post, &; from residence thereby; cf. Stubbs. A big, exposed tree-trunk, or clump of tree-trunks, would readily give a surname to one who lived close by.

(Charles Wareing Bardsley, Dictionary of English & Welsh Surnames, 1901.)

March the 23, 1938 I spent in this interesting section of our County and have recorded in Grace Moore Chapter my interview with Jehu Stokely of Nough, who is said to be well named and a direct descendant of the First Jehu Stokely who came to America.

If it is true that a young man's fancy turns to love in the springtime, it must be true that the fancy of an old man at such a season is oft wrapt in his memory of such experiences. At any rate Jehu Stokely was in a reminiscent state of mind on this particular spring day that I visited with him to see if I could find out what he knew of the traditions of the Stokely family.

The Stokely story glows, and glitters and sparkles from their earliest records on down to the present day and time, and runs along thusly, according to the information passed down from generation to generation.

Jehu Stokely the First, was born in Wales in 1747. He grew to manhood there and had been told from childhood of the wonderful deeds of his forefathers, one of whom was an Admiral by the name of Samuel G. Stokely, or was a member of the Admiral's fleet which destroyed the Spanish Armada. So pleased was the "Good Queen Bess" with the Seamanship of this Samuel G. Stokely that she made him a Baron. This gave to him the rank of nobility next below that of a viscount and above that of a Knight or baronet. Barons were originally the proprietors of land held in honorable service. Anyway, this young Jehu, the First, liked to think that his ancestor the Samuel G. Stokely was on hand when, "The Armada came to anchor off Calais to await the Duke of Parma and his Veterans. That he was present when "Queen Elizabeth had assembled her troops at Tilbury." When she, "clad in armor and mounted on a white horse, rode among them and made a speech which stirred their

W. B. Stokely home on Clifton Heights

James R. Stokely home on Clifton Heights

loyalty, 'Let tyrants fear,' she said, 'my strength and safety are in the loyal hearts of my people. I know I am a weak and feeble woman, but I have the heart of a KING OF ENGLAND'." (Niver's *History of England*, page 193.)

Queen Elizabeth not only made of Samuel G. Stokely a baron but she gave to him in marriage, her First Cousin. Henceforth from then on, in the Stokely bloodstream flowed ROYAL blood and from then on down the line to the present day, each family names a son "ROYAL" Stokely to keep ever fresh in the minds of the family the above story.

This First Jehu that grew to manhood in his native country of Wales very near the English line was a great lover of horses, so the story goes, and one day while riding with a friend, they came to a stream of rather deep water. Young Stokely's horse refused to ford the stream. The other horse walked bravely across. Its rider taunted young Stokely about his poor horsemanship which of course hurt his pride somewhat because he was proud of his ability to manage horses. After much patience and considerable coaxing of the animal, all to no avail, Young Jehu decided to break off a switch from an over-hanging bough near the water and with it persuade his stubborn charge into the stream. It worked admirably and he joined his laughing friend on the opposite bank and they rode on their way. However, someone reported him to the King for what was termed, "Malicious Trespassing" and for this act, Jehu Stokely was "BOUND TO THE SEA" for a period of SEVEN YEARS. This of course, enraged and humiliated the young man tremendously and he never forgave England for the punishment "meted out" to him. The more he thought about it, the madder he got, but he "bided" his time as best he could. During these seven years of his servitude he visited every known port in the world and became familiar with naval activities.

At the end of his SEVEN YEARS, Jehu Stokely landed in Charleston, South Carolina. As soon as he could be discharged from the English Navy, he cast his lot with one, JOHN PAUL JONES, who was commanding the American Vessel, Bon Homme Richard. This was Young Stokely's dream come true, this was his chance to show England what he thought of the treatment meted out to one of ROYAL BLOOD. It is quite easy to imagine how he enjoyed the attack of the much superior British Ship Serapis, off the Coast of England, where a terrible battle raged for hours. These vessels being so close that their cannon muzzles touched and when the American ship began to sink, Jones lashed the two ships together, and the fight went on more furiously than ever. The decks were scenes of fearful carnage, the British commander was forced to surrender and John Paul Jones and his men took possession of the British ship. I imagine that young Jehu thought that his ancestor Samuel G. Stokely had nothing much on him so far as seamanship was concerned, and that he wished the King of England could have witnessed the battle.

Young Jehu Stokely didn't feel that he had yet repaid England for his years of "servitude" on the sea. He enlisted next with the American soldiers in the Revolutionary War and became an ardent soldier in the Department of Heavy Artillery. At the Battle of Kings Mountain young Stokely was so thrilled with the "backwoods" fighters from the region of the Watauga in the over mountain country, that he made up his mind he would like to cast his lot among such brave people.

Sometimes after the close of the Revolutionary War, Jehu Stokely, with his young Irish wife, Nancy Neal, whom he had wed in Charleston, South Carolina, "set out" for the wilderness country, the Land of Promise, beyond the great mountains. It is not known exactly how long they were in finally reaching the Del Rio Valley, where they entered land. It is known that in 1802 Jehu Stokely bought from Captain Waddle a tract of land alongside that which he had entered, about three miles East of Del Rio. Here the home was established and three boys and five girls were born to Jehu and Nancy Neal Stokely. Here he died in 1816 and is buried on the farm now owned by James Burnett.

The children of this first Stokely family were as follows:

Susan Stokely who was born June 13, 1782, married Jehu Jester.

Royal Stokely who was born April 10, 1784, married Jane (Jennie) Huff.

John Stokely who was born Dec. 1, 1786, married Elizabeth Huff.

Thomas Stokely who was born 1789, Miss Axly, moved to Texas.

Nancy Stokely who was born Feb. 13, 1792, married Evan Fugate.

Polly Stokely who was born March 1794, married a Mr. Raines.

Sarah Stokely who was born 1797, married Daniel Smart.

Rhoda Stokely who was born 1802, married James Sawyer.

In another chapter I shall give the families of the above couples that those who are smart enough may figure their relationships, I cannot do so, it seems so complex and so interwoven that only a genealogist could unravel it.

John Huff Stokely, son of Royal and Jane Huff Stokely, father of William Stokely, grandfather of Jane Stokely, the mother of Grace Moore, therefore Grace's great-grandfather, had a most interesting life too, with something of the "intestinal fortitude" displayed by his own grandfather Jehu, according to the story given me by Jehu Stokely the son of John Huff Stokely, and brother of William.

Born Dec. 1, 1810, John Huff Stokely grew to manhood in the Del Rio valley of the French Broad River. In 1833 he decided he would like to visit his brother, Joseph, in Missouri. After reaching his brother's home he became enthused with the idea of enlisting with the Overland Merchant Brigades. The more he thought of doing so the more determined was his desires and he became a volunteer under Colonel William Bent. In this company were enlisted 208 volunteers who accompanied the 240 regulars of the Merchant Brigade as far as the Red River. They traveled over land with ox teams to draw the 108 wagons loaded with merchandise. The journey from St. Joseph Missouri, to Old Santa Fe, New Mexico and back to St. Joseph, the "Outpost" of that day and time, took many months and afforded opportunity for young John H. Stokely to make many friends, to see the country and to learn many valuable lessons that served him well throughout his life.

To feed these half a thousand men and their teams as they journeyed over the country was no small job. The "head-man" for providing the meat was none other than Christopher Carson, known as Kit Carson, who was born in Kentucky in 1809 and became one of the greatest Frontiersmen of America. He did most of the hunting for the Brigade and was often accompanied by John H. Stokely from the Tennessee mountains who was himself no mean marksman but a fit companion for the Kentucky youth of about the same age. They became warm friends.

— 142 —

Stokely Brothers

Left to right—Standing Jehu T. and George S. Seated—James R., William B. and John M.

As this great caravan slowly moved across the plains on its journey westward many pleasant evenings were spent in various contests along the way for amusement.

The members of this company had no fear of attack from Indians or robbers. They hauled along with them the first artillery that ever crossed the plains and hauled it a journey of 3000 miles and with it went the 240 Regulars to say nothing of the 208 Volunteers. They, therefore felt protected and enjoyed themselves in various ways as the teams rested. At one time they were opposed by hundreds of Indians, but after a fire of artillery the Indians fled and did not trouble them again.

Wrestling was quite a sport in those days and young John H. Stokely enjoyed it. On July 4, 1833 they decided to have a wrestling match to celebrate the day. Young Stokely, who weighed 196 pounds was chosen to wrestle with a Young Stepp who weighed 240 pounds. In the beginning of the wrestling the men were betting quite heavily on the heavier man but when Stokely began to throw Stepp "two best in three" (whatever that is) the tide turned and the betting went the other way.

The Buffalo herds along the way were "thick as flies" and furnished both food and fuel for the travelers, who ate the "jerked" or dried meat of the buffalo and used the dried chips for fire over which they cooked other food and made fires for warmth and light at night.

When they reached Santa Fe they loaded 4 of their wagons with silver and gold which was sewed "up" in Buffalo hides. They were six months on the return journey to St. Joseph, Missouri but never lost a dollar nor a man. The red bandana handkerchiefs they sold along the way for one dollar each.

As long as John H. Stokely lived he cherished the memory of his experience with the Overland Merchant Brigade and his friendship with Kit Carson, who was oft spoken of as, "The Pathfinder of the Plains." He later rendered valuable services in the territories and was brevetted Brigadier General Carson. He died in Colorado in 1868, a comparatively young man.

The first Stokely to arrive in Cocke County was Jehu and wife, Nancy Neal, of South Carolina.

The second Jehu Stokely in Cocke County was the son of John and Elizabeth Huff Stokely who was born March the 18, 1814, married Jane Adaline Burnett Dec. 1, 1836. She was born Feb. 14, 1820.

Jehu the 2nd died Feb. 25, 1885, Adaline died March 7, 1882. She was the daughter of Swan P. Burnett and wife Frances Bell Burnett.

Jehu II and wife, Adaline, had 6 children: Mary, married David Susong; Narcissa, married Joseph Carty; Jane Adaline, married Major James T. Huff; Susan Eleanor, married George W. Susong (These Susongs were brothers); Louisa Elizabeth, married Jacob Susong and the only son of Jehu the II and wife, Jane Adaline Burnett, was John Burnett Stokely who married Anna Rorex, sister of James Rorex. This couple became the parents of Stokely Brothers, famed the world over for their preservation of choice vegetables. These sons were: John M., W. B., James R. and George S. Another son, Jehu T. Stokely became a prominent attorney in Birmingham. All died suddenly in the very prime of life. Jehu T. lived the longest. His death came August 14, 1950. These

Beech-wood Hall, home of the first Roadman family, later the Jacob Susong home, originally belonged to William Garrett.

Col. Abraham McKay home sold to John Stokely who gave it to his daughter Eleanor Stokely Susong

five brothers had three sisters, who are still living in Newport. Anna Mae, Carrie Lou and Fanny Stokely Fisher, wife of Fred S. Fisher.

Jehu II and wife, parents of Stokely Brothers and their three sisters purchased the Abraham McKay (or McCoy) home on French Broad River in 1846, it is still standing and was very old at the time it was purchased, is now 1950, occupied by John Susong and two sisters, Mrs. Adaline Susong Smith and Hester Susong, grandson and granddaughters of Jehu II and wife, Adaline Burnett Stokely.

THE SUSONG FAMILY

This family name does not appear in the 1790 Virginia Census, it is not in the Pennsylvania Census for the same year, although it is claimed that a Susong family was in Virginia during the Revolutionary War Period.

In 1810 Washington County, Virginia Census lists Jacob Susong with four m. 9 F. in family.

In 1820 the Virginia Census seems to have either disappeared or was never taken.

The 1830 Greene County, Tennessee Census shows Andrew Susong Sr. with 6 m. and 3 F. in family. Other heads of Susong families listed in this census. Alexander with 3 m. 3 F. Elizabeth Susong with 4 F. and Andrew Jr. omitted.

1840 Census: In 7 Civil Districts of Greene County in 1840 we find Alfred Susong with 2 m. 3 F. John with 5 m. 8 F. Alex'r with 5 m. 5 F. Elizabeth with 3 m, 3 F. John, Jr., 1 m. 2 F.

Greene County for 1850, on page 215:

Nicholas Susong with Martha and 1 m. 2 F. William and Melvina with 3 F. Next House John Susong aged 60 with Charity 55 they had 1 m. (John) 8 F., names all listed in the 1850 Census. Andrew a young man is listed alone aged 23. Alfred and Sarah with 3 sons and 5 daughters.

Andrew and Susannah Susong listed on page 296 as born in Virginia. Their family became the ancestors of our Cocke County Susongs and are listed as follows. Their children all born in Tennessee.

Andrew Susong 67, Susannah Susong 51. Elizabeth 30, Mary 25, Nicholas 22, Alexander 19, George 15, Jacob 13, Anderson 11, Penelope 8.

In same 1850 Census of Greene County is Alexander Susong with 4 m. and 4 F.

In 1860 Census we find Andrew was still 67 but Susan was 60, Elizabeth 40, George 23, Catherine 25, Jacob 21, Anderson 19 and Penelope 16.

Another Andrew Susong appears on the 1860 census. He is listed with Sarah J. She is 31 and he is 44 and evidently the same Andrew listed alone or the one Andrew, Jr., of Elizabeth omitted. The children of Andrew and Sarah J. interested me; Margaret A. 6, William E. 4, John S. 3, Clark 2, Martha E. 6/12 and Nancy 17 and John Thompson 20.

(The next family is SAM THOMPSON, with wife and seven children and a John Thompson listed aged 20 in that family.)

After Sam Thompson House came John Susong with Charity ages 70 and 63, 1 m. 3 F. Wm. 43 and Levena 25 with a daughter 10, one 9 and Wesley eleven months.

By 1860 the family of Nicholas Susong seems to have increased considerably as the following listing would prove. 3 m. 4 F. Francis, Joseph, Margaret, Elbridge, Dorcas, Eliza, Harriett.

William Susong's family appears quite differently in the 1870 Census. Instead of Levena it is written Malvina for his wife's name. The Wesley has become Ersley, a girl, 11, Eliza E. is 20 and Lidy 7, Maria 5 and William 3.

In the 1870 enumeration Andrew Susong is listed as 76 and Susannah as 71. Elizabeth is 41 (only one year older than in 1860). In the same family group we find Russell, Penelope, Williams, Lavina 12, Frederick Fancher 16 (mulatto), Robert Fancher 9 (black), William A. Susong 27 (Trader in stock), Greene Susong 27 (black), Ary 25 and Fanny 7 (Ary black) and Fanny (mulatto).

Most of the Susong names listed gave Greeneville as Post Office, Midway was second largest number of names. 51 in first enumeration where names were given. 30 in second, 51 in third, about the same in the 1870 Census.

Cocke County, Tennessee, 1870 Census on page 10 shows the following of the name: George Susong, 36, farmer; Susan E., 26. Jacob A., 7/12, meaning of course, seven months of age.

On the same page is Stuart, Mary 38 (black) housekeeper; Stuart, Russel, 15 (black); Stuart, James, 11 (black); Stuart, Hannah, 10, (black); Stuart, Joseph E., 5 (black); Stuart, Carrie, 5 (black); Stuart, Eliza, 3 (black); Stuart, Mary, 1 (black).

This was a colored family who worked for us many years.

From the pen of Mrs. Adaline Susong Smith the daughter of the above George Susong is the following family history.

In a William & Mary College Quarterly in Vol. (?), Page 34, Virginia State Library, Richmond, I found that Andrew Susong enlisted in Col. Hartley's Regiment, Jan. 28(?), 1777 and he was a citizen of Virginia. His wife's name was Barbara and they lived in Berkely County. I rather think he was my ancestor.

"Andrew Susong, thought to be a native of Alsace-Lorraine is supposed to have enlisted in the Revolutionary Army, March 25, 1777, as a Private in Captain George Bush's Company, New Eleventh Pennsylvania Continental Line, 1777. (See page 650, Vol. 3, Pennsylvania Archives, Fifth Series.)

After the Revolution, he settled near Lexington, Virginia, thence came to Washington County, Va. and later to Greene County, Tennessee. He and his wife are buried at Susong Memorial Church near Greeneville, Tennessee.

Andrew Susong had three sons, Nicholas, Jacob and Andrew. Nicholas married Elizabeth McCaulay of Irish descent. He was born, 1764, died, July 1824. His wife was born, 1766, died, 1851. They are buried at Susong Memorial Church. They had two or three sons and several daughters.

Andrew, one of the sons was born Oct. 6, 1792, died Oct. 1, 1877. In 1818 he married Susannah Ball, a daughter of William Ball and his wife who was a Miss Chappelle (or Yeary) of Lee County, Virginia. (William Ball was of the Virginia family of Balls of which George Washington's mother was a member.)

James R. Stokely and wife, Janie Mae Jones

Mrs. Henrietta Cody Burnett, 1905
(seated).

Mrs. Adaline Susong Smith

Susannah Ball was born May 23, 1799, and died April 18, 1881. She and her husband are buried at Susong Memorial Church. They had thirteen children. Twin boys, John died in infancy. The sons: David, Nicholas, Alec, George, Jacob and Anderson. The daughters: Elizabeth, Katherine, Jane and Penelope. David, George and Jacob, purchased large farms in Cocke County, Tennessee where they lived until their deaths.

Mary Frances, Susan Eleanor and Louisa Elizabeth Stokely were daughters of John and Jane Adaline Burnett Stokely.

David Susong married Mary Francis Stokely. They had ten children. Jacob H. Susong married Louisa E. Stokely, they had two daughters, Sue and May. George W. Susong (born Feb. 2, 1835, died March 16, 1889), married Susan Eleanor Stokely (born April 7, 1844, died April 1, 1921). The marriage of George W. and Susan Eleanor Stokely took place on Oct. 15, 1868. They had seven children. Jacob A., Adaline, Georgia (Hickey), John, Elizabeth (Burnett), Katherine (Harvin) and Hester Susong.

My father purchased the William Carter farm in 1870. This is the farm now owned by Sea Allen in the Dutch Bottoms and called Allendale. My father, George W. Susong, lived there until his death in 1889."

From the pen of the Honorable J. A. Susong of Greeneville under date of March 27, 1940 comes the following information on the Susong family. It sheds light on this family which should be of interest to any member of it. "The Susong family, or its representatives, as you know, have generally been compelled to give more attention to the means of living, than to the meaning of life. However, I think there is no doubt that the grandfather of the older Susongs, Jake, George and Anderson, all of whom you know, came from Pennsylvania or Virginia, possibly from Pennsylvania through Virginia, and settled in Greene County. A kinsman of the same name stopped at Bristol. He had a number of sons, and some daughters, who lived and died in Greene County.

One of his sons, my grandfather, Andrew Susong, the father of George, Jake and Anderson, was, I understand, in Coffee's command in the Creek War, and saw service at the Battle of Horseshoe Bend, where the Creek power was broken and in War of 1812 under Jackson. He was Captain in the Militia, but all the Susong family, so far as I know, were among those who followed Johnson, Arnold, Brownlow and others, in adhering to the Union during the war. George Susong was in the Confederate Army.

Another branch of the family, also the descendants of another Nicholas Susong, son of John, not Andrew, settled, as you know, at Leadvale, and in the upper part of Hamblen County.

All the sons of my grandfather, Captain Andrew Susong, as he was called, David, Nicholas, Alex (who lived in Greene County and who was the father of A. G. Susong, now owner of what is known as the "FORK FARM"), George, Jacob, and Anderson, were all large land owners; as well as Joe and Elbert Susong, who more recently settled in Hamblen County, and in Cocke County, near Rankin. Alexander Susong, my uncle, owned large bodies of land in Cocke County, in the neighborhood of Salem.

David, George and Jacob Susong married respectively, Mary, Sue and Lou Stokely who were sisters of John B. Stokely, and aunts of the Stokely boys whom you know at Newport.

As above stated, my father, Nicholas, who died when quite a young man, a few years after the close of the Civil War, married Ellen Huff.

Alex Susong married Esther Gregg. Anderson married Frances Brown, of Greeneville, Tenn.

Of the later generations, you will know plenty, and my only request is that in dealing with them you do not make the shade any darker than is absolutely necessary."

The splendid sense of humor that J. A. Susong enjoys is well displayed in his last paragraph. He is a man of fine 'sense and judgment' as our mountain folk would term it. An attorney for the Southern Railway and a most able one. A landowner himself, highly respected and a man of affairs in his home county of Greene and in the State of Tennessee.

To Dr. Edmund C. Burnett I am indebted for the Susong Census. His wife being Elizabeth Susong, sister of Adaline Susong Smith who so graciously prepared the sketch of the family that follows the Census report. "Miss Addie" as her hundreds of pupils all over Cocke and Jefferson Counties, delight to speak of her, has had a most unusual and successful teaching career. No woman in our State has ever equaled her ability as a teacher. Her home is at White Pine. She was an A.B. graduate of the old Mary College, Winchester, Tenn.

THE WHITSON FAMILY

William Whitson, Jr., settled on the Big Pigeon River in Cocke County, Tennessee, in 1783, with his wife, Elizabeth. He was the son of William Whitson, Sr., who came to Shenandoah County, Virginia, about 1743, with a group from Westchester and Queens County, New York. The Whitson family center was in Oyster Bay, Long Island. Most of them settled near New Market along the South Bank of the Shenandoah River. However, William Whitson was near Thorne's Gap, in 1752, in the Blue Ridge, along the south bank of the Shenandoah River, with John Davis, Barnaby Eagen, Henry Netherington (Netherton) and Elisha Jobe, an older brother of David Jobe. The ford, leading from Thorne's Gap to Front Royal, was long known as Whitson's Ford.

In 1775, William Whitson had a large family. He was living near his son, William Whitson, Jr. Before 1783, William Whitson, Sr., removed to Washington County, Tennessee, where he died, leaving a Will. His estate fell to a younger son, Jesse Whitson and named daughters Susannah Eagen, Lydia McKay. Sons Joseph and Jesse were executors and witnesses were Henry Nelson, Jr., William Wood, and Reuben Rider.

There were thirteen children in the family: Joseph; Susannah, who married Barnaby Eagen, Jr.; George; Charles; John; Lydia, who married Jeremiah, son of Moses McKay; Leah, who married Jonah Denton in 1782; Jeremiah, who married Elizabeth Jobe in 1784; Jesse; James; William Whitson, Jr., who married Elizabeth and removed to Big Pigeon River in Cocke County; Ann, who married Isaac Denton; Lezeanan, who married David Jobe; Abraham married Sally Fine; Joshua married Ruth Tipton, granddaughter of Colonel John Tipton.

William Whitson, Jr.'s home became known as William Whitson's Fort, and was situated near the spring now known as Wilton. When plans were being developed for a Primitive Baptist Church for the new community established on the Big Pigeon, William Whitson, Jr., and Abraham McKay (or McCoy) were elected as a committee to meet with the Baptist

Association in Sullivan County, 1786. The next year the church was organized, and William Whitson and wife Elizabeth were charter members.

THE WOOD FAMILY

In the early days of Taylorsburg (Edwina), John Wood, of Irish descent, came from Shenandoah County, Virginia, riding a bay mare, with a few clothes tied to his saddle, and bearing a rifle, and accompanied by his dog. He married Fannie Grigsby of Grainger County and built his first home in Cocke County about one and one-half miles south of the present Ed Burnett home on the Big Pigeon, still standing, and in the hands of Carl Wood. The John Woods had eight sons and no daughters. Two of the sons married Padgett sisters; two, the Sisk sisters; two, the Gillette sisters; one, a Kelly, the first time, later, an Acton. One, Abraham, died unmarried. Later William's wife died and he married a sister to his brother, Grigsby's wife, Mary Gillette.

In 1830, John Wood built the house where his great grandson, Oscar Cate, lived. It was constructed of hewn logs, mortised together, weatherboarded and ceiled. The lumber was sawed with a "sash-saw," and the house was built by two men, Bell and Duncan, two stories high and about 60 by 20 feet, with four large rooms. The bricks for the great fireplaces were burned near the site. During the Civil War, this house was occupied by Gipson, the third son of John Wood, who had inherited this property as a reward for taking care of his aged father. The sons of Gipson Wood were James Wood, who served in Bragg's Army, and Toliver Wood, who served in the cavalry with Captain Hickey.

Sometime during the Civil War, a band of roving Union soldiers came to this home and attempted to rob the family, which consisted of five daughters, Phoebie, Elizabeth, Nancy, Fannie and Delanie, together with the "baby boy" John B, and their grandfather, "Virginia John" to distinguish him from the others. The girls protested and endeavored to protect their home against the robbers. Phoebie used an ax, Elizabeth held the door, and Nancy wielded a pitchfork. The other two girls comforted the aged man and the little boy. In this scramble, one soldier got his head fastened in the smokehouse door, where the hams and other meat hung. Finally, the soldiers agreed to leave the smokehouse alone if the girls would release the man. As soon as the soldiers left, the girls decided to cut a ham and enjoy it themselves, lest the men return in the night and carry the meat off. On the ground, they found two buttons from the soldiers' coats, cherished possessions of the family to this day.

This home is located on the old road between Big Pigeon and English Creek about six miles south of the present Newport. Over this road the pioneers often journeyed with their tax money to North Carolina. Many would spend the night with "Virginia John" Wood, who left more than five thousand acres of rich lands to his descendants, most of which he had bought.

The Wood family, as did all others, struggled to live during the reconstruction days, manufacturing their own clothes and household linens from raw materials. A white man by the name of Lewis was their shoemaker; and Dinah, a slave who lived her entire life with the family, was their cook. After the war, the five Wood girls did the work previously done by the slaves.

Cedar Croft, home of Col. James A. T. Wood

The John M. Stokely home now owned by Lyle C. Moore

"Virginia" John Wood was the great-grandfather of Ethel Wood Stanberry, daughter of Thornton Wood. John Wood had a son James Wood, who became the father of Esquire John, Tilman and William Wood. James liked Taylorsburg as did his father, and it is said that he changed the name from Taylorsburg to Sweetwater.

Esquire John, son of James Wood, lived until his death at the Edwina home. Tilman died unmarried and William and his wife Kate McNabb Wood had no children. Esquire John Wood wed Penelope Vinson and they had but one child, a son, Esquire James A. T. Wood, who married Ella McAndrew Shields, and lives in the colonial home on the Edwina road just above the tannery.

The Religious History of Cocke County

The Baptist Church

The Oldest Church in the County

Although it is said that the Baptist preachers went out with the pioneers into the wilderness Country to help establish the early settlements and usually found the Methodist preachers already established, this is scarcely true with Cocke County.

The first church in Cocke County was organized December 6, 1787, at the home of James English, located on the site of the present Ed Burnett home, at the mouth of English Creek just south of the Tannery. (This Church celebrated its 150th anniversary, December 4 and 5, 1937.)

On page 2D of the old Church Book is the following:

December 6, 1787. We the members of the Baptist Society on Big Pigeon River, being constituted of the principles contained in the Baptist Confession of Faith adopted at Philadelphia, the 25th day of September 1742, do with full and free consent of our minds, give up ourselves to each other and to act in all the discipline and ordinances of the Gospel as a Church of Jesus Christ, in witness hereof, we have hereunto set our names. Constituted by Eldership of Isaac Barton and Will Reno. Names: William Whitson, David Job, Abraham McKay, Elizabeth Whitson, Lezeanah Job, Rachel McKay (Rachel O'Dell McKay), Mourning Prior, Mourning Denton, Dorcas Job, Mary Whited. Received the same day by experience the following named gentlemen: James English, Nicholas Woodfin.

The first log building of this church stood on the East bank of the Big Pigeon River where the road from the French Broad settlement intersected with the Cosby road near the present home of Robert Clevenger. The second log house of this Primitive Baptist Church is located on Fine's Branch on the old public road from Newport to Cosby.

In the early days of Tennessee there were at least five Associations in the "Wilderness Country," known as follows: the Holston, in 1786; the French Broad Association, a few years later; Tennessee Association, 1802; Powell's Valley, 1818; Nolachucky Association, 1828.

Seven churches in the Constitution of the Holston Association, organized at Cherokee Meeting House in Washington County on Saturday before the fourth Sunday in October, 1786, ten years before Tennessee was admitted to the Union. The Washington County was of course in North Carolina, then, as was Cocke County. These churches were: Bent Creek, organized June 11, 1787, by Elders William Murphy and Tidence Lane; Cherokee Church, organized 1783; Lower French Broad, organized March 25, 1796 by Isaac Barton and Jonathan Mulkey; Buffalo Ridge Church,[1] organized in 1779 by Tidence Lane. No dates are given for the

---

1. Buffalo Ridge is the oldest church in Tennessee, organized three years after the signing of the Declaration of Independence.

organization of Kendrick's Creek, Beaver Creek, Greasy Cover, North Fork of Holston.

The Tennessee Association was organized December 25, 1802, at Beaver's Creek Meeting House. The French Broad Association was made up of the church from the Holston; the Powell's Valley, of twelve churches from the Tennessee Association; the Nolachucky Association, of churches from the Holston and Tennessee Association with Elder Thomas Hill, Moderator, and T. L. Hale, Clerk. They were: Bent Creek, June 11, 1785, by Elders William Murphy and Tidence Lane; Big Pigeon by Isaac Barton and William Reno, December 6, 1787; Warrensburg, 1787 by Isaac Barton; Bethel Church, South, 1803; Bethany, 1826; Blackwell's Branch, 1825; Robertson's Creek, 1813; Slate Creek, 1818. Prospect, Concord, Clay Creek, Gap Creek, County Line, Barton, and Mill Spring have no dates.

This church was said to have first been in the Holston Association, and in 1828 to have gone into the Nolachucky Association. Thomas Hale and Benjamin O'Dell were the messengers. Elder Thomas Hill was chosen as first moderator; Thomas L. Hale, clerk. Elder Hill was a member first of what was at that time known as "Forks of Little Pigeon Primitive Baptist Church," located where Sevierville now stands.

In July, 1801, the French Broad Church, where Dandridge now stands, appointed Duke Dimbraugh, a member of the Presbytery, to Fork of Little Pigeon, with Elder Richard Wood for the purpose of ordaining Thomas Hill to the ministry.

On December 25, Elder Hill represented the Forks of Little Pigeon Church at the organization of Tennessee Primitive Baptist Association. On August 4, 1803, Elder Hill was appointed by the Tennessee Association as messenger to the Holston Association. Later he appears on the minutes as a member of French Broad and Holston Churches. In 1820, he joined the Big Pigeon Church and at his death, March 1, 1845, was the pastor of the Bethany Church.[2]

During the time Big Pigeon Church was in the Nolachucky organization from 1828 to 1870 it was often represented in the Association by the following messengers: Elder Thomas Hill, John Huff, Lawson Sisk, Toliver Sisk, Elijah Breeden, and Brummit Bryant.

About the year 1835, Bethany Church moved to Cosby Creek, near the Pat Dennis home, later to Caton's Grove, then to McMillon, where it now stands. It was organized by Richard Wood and Daniel Laymon and John Driskill at the Large Meeting House in Jones Cove, the second Saturday in October, 1826. It was the Arm of the Bethel Church, on East Fork, of the Little Pigeon, which was organized in 1803 in December by Elders Richard Wood and Thomas Hill. Abraham Lillard was the clerk of the new Bethany Church.

The following interesting transaction is recorded on page 59 of Record Book, No. 2:

2. Page 227, Bethany Church Book, page 52, Little Pigeon Records.
The Articles of the Philadelphia Confession of 1742, upon which Big Pigeon Church was constituted, were first formulated and adopted by more than one hundred congregations of Baptists in London in 1689. The two articles were added by the Philadelphia Association.
Toliver Sisk was born in 1795 in Cocke County and joined Big Pigeon Primitive Baptist Church, December 5, 1829. He served as Clerk or Deacon until his death November 10, 1889.

We, the Primitive Baptists at Big Pigeon Church have sold the Meeting House lot to Elias Clevenger for sum of forty dollars and sold the house to Carson Clevenger for sum of ten dollars and the money received by Toliver Sisk and Brummit Bryant (Elder). The lot lying on the East Bank of Big Pigeon River, Cocke County, Tennessee, bounded as follows, South, by Carson Clevenger, East and North by Elias Clevenger, West, by Big Pigeon River.

Lot contained one acre; the deed was made March 6, 1877, to Elias Clevenger and signed by the members of the Church, to wit: Toliver Sisk, Lawson Sisk, Joab Blackwell, Sycha Blackwell, Margaret Runnion, Elizabeth Bryant, Jane Baxter, Bummit Bryant, William R. Blackwell, Clerk. The above sale was ninety years to the day from the date the Church was constituted December 6, 1787.

On January 16, 1858, the members of the old Butler Church who wished to be constituted into a Church met at the home of Nancy Huff, in accordance to appointment and after prayer, chose Humphrey Moant, Moderator; B. Bryant, Clerk. (Big Pigeon Record)

On June 6, 1789, (page 4 Book D) ... "William Whitson and Daniel Hill, Elders and Deacons. William Whitson, one of the constituted members. Daniel Hill joined April 4, 1889 by letter. May the 2, 1789, John Parker joined by letter. And on Aug. 8, 1789 was called to the office of Ruling Elder, and William Lillard appointed with him. May the 8, 1790, Peter Fine appointed Deacon.

About the year 1785 and 1786, at the settlement of French Broad and Big Pigeon Rivers in which settlements were found a few people distinguished by the name of Baptist. It pleased the Lord in the course of his divine providence to visit us by his ministers, namely, Jonathan Mulkey and William Reno, who labored in the word and doctrine among us. And there appeared to be that spirit of love and union as if we could dwell together in peace and love, under the consideration of which we requested two of the Brethern, namely, William Whitson and Abraham McKay to represent our circumstance to the Association held at Kendrick's Creek in the year 1786.

The request of the above petition was that they would appoint some of the brethern to inquire into our circumstances and our ripeness for constitution and if they found us fit, to administer the same. Which petition, the Association was pleased to grant us and appoint two of the ministering brethern to attend on us. And in December, 1787, met at Mr. James English home, on Big Pigeon River and after duly deliberating on the same were constituted on the principles adopted at Philadelphia in 1742. (Names given in beginning of this chapter.)

Sometime between 1787 and 1800 Bartlett and Scathy Clevenger joined by letter.

It is claimed that there is no other Primitive Baptist Church on Tennessee soil that can date her origin as far back as 1787 and successfully prove that she is in line and fellowship, both in doctrine and practice with the Old School Primitive Baptist in America.

Owing to the quaint habits, simplicity of dress, and of manner, this sect is sometimes characterized by the religionists of the present day as "religious fossils," and on account of their belief in original sin, election, predestination, and in the final perseverance of the saints, are sometimes known as "Hard Shells," and "Old Ironsides." (McSween)

An interesting item in Book C, page 30, Saturday, September 1, 1855. First: the church declares a non-fellowship in the Nonothing Order or Party (Know Nothing Party). Elder Thomas Smith, Mod. The Clerk, Jeremiah McKay.

The minutes would indicate that the Big Pigeon Church was with the Holston Association until 1825 and with the Nolachucky Association until 1870.

On page 134 of the oldest Record Book is the following: "N. B. January 1, 1859. The Church at Big Pigeon Church met and after preaching proceeded to business. First chose Brother B. Bryant, Moderator; T. Sisk, Clerk. Sometime in 1863 the War became so "troublesome" no more regular meetings were held until 1872, but on April the 13, 1872 . . . "We the Primitive Baptist Church of Jesus Christ, on Big Pigeon, at the house of Sister Sallie Roberts, after preaching by Brother Brummett Bryant proceeded to business. Received Brummett Bryant by declaration, called Presbytery to ordain Bryant. Appointed a meeting to be held at Brother Abe McKay's and after preaching removed to Elder Brother Thomas Smith and set as a Church. Brother Bryant to the ministry, and Brother Toliver Sisk, Deacon."

According to Deed Book No. 2, page 351, the Big Pigeon Church property was deeded to said Church by Willis Gray on April 1, 1878. Toliver Sisk, Trustee. The Click School House property was deeded by J. C. Morrell to Trustees Annias Bryant and John J. Click and Sam Baxter, December 26, 1877, (Book No. 2, page 282). This property was later deeded by trustee successors to Allen Hannon about 1920.

The minutes of this First Church in Cocke County, Tennessee, are in the library of Elder W. C. McMillan.

The eleventh Anniversary of the Nolachucky Association was held at Big Pigeon Meeting House in Cocke County on the Fourth Friday in September, 1838. An introductory sermon was preached by Elder William Anderson from Isaiah 3:10 and 11. They chose Elder Pleasant A. Witt, moderator, and Hughes W. Taylor, clerk. Letters from twenty-two churches were read and the following account taken: Bethel-South—Elder Elihu Millican, J. Cox, J. Howell, H. W. Taylor; County Line—Nathan Gray; Robertson Creek—Frances Walker, Thomas Arnot; Union—Vincent Reynolds; Concord, Elihu De Bush, N. Dunnagan, John Right, John Haun; Warrensburg—John Presterson, Thomas Stroud; Big Pigeon— Elder Thomas Hill, J. McKay, Toliver Sisk; Sulphur Springs—Abner Johnson; Black Oak Grove—Jacob Grubb, Edward Daniel, Isaac Hull; Buffalo Creek—John Callison, Thomas Dyer, H. W. Gilmore, James Dyer; Bethany—no letter, no delegate; New Prospect—Elihu Wester; Blackwell's Branch—Elder James Lacy, Moses Hodge, Reuben Groves; Hopewell—Elder David Lauderback, Margarter Sanders; Slate Creek—Simon Smith; Friendship—Elder Henry Randolph, Daniel Witt, George Crosby; Mill Springs—Daniel Murphy, William A. C. Newman, L. M. Newman; Long Creek—James Ellison; Dover—Ance Barton, Joseph Hale; Oakland —John R. Lockhart, Mannering Summers; French Broad—no letter, but their delegates were: Jesse Ammons, Luke L. Branson, George Peck, being present, were invited to seats, with the rest of the delegates, and as a manifestation of our fellowship with these bodies, the moderator, in behalf of the Association, gave the right hand of fellowship, appointed Brother

Thomas Lane to write to French Broad, and Elders Henry Randolph, Pleasant A. Witt, Brothers Jeremiah McKay, Nicholas Dunnagan, to bear the same; Elder Pleasant A. Witt to write to Holston; Elders P. A. Witt, William Anderson, David Lauderback, Thomas Hill, Brothers Abner Johnson, Nicholas Dunnagan, to bear the same.

The following excerpts are from the Minutes of Big Pigeon Church: On page 3 of Record Book D:

The fourth Saturday meeting, Sept., 1788, in session at the home of Abraham McKay on French Broad River, the following delegates were elected to attend the Holston Association, William Whitson, James English, Abraham, also Abraham McKay to prepare the Church letter to the Association. (The home of John and Hester Susong on the French Broad is on the site of the McKay Home.)

On February 28, 1789, at home of Samuel Job on Big Pigeon River. Elder William Reno preached. Jonas Cane received into the Church. Elder Reno, moderator; Abraham McKay, clerk. May the 2, 1789, John Parks received into the Church by letter and on August 8, 1789, called to office of Ruling Elder, also William Lillard was appointed with him. On May the 8, 1790 . . . (6 of Book D) Brother Peter Fine was appointed Deacon. October the 10, the following were appointed to the Holston Association: John Parker, John Netherton, John Mathes, Abraham McKay. January the 9, 1790, the Church sent William Keeler and Abraham McKay to petition Cove Creek Church for the ministerial help of Elder Jonathan Mulkey six months in the year. June 12, 1790, seven joined the Church, among them were the following: William Fox, Samuel Fares (by letter). Elder Jonathan Mulkey, Moderator, and Abraham McKay, clerk.

On June 11, 1791, the Church sent the following delegates to Holston Association: Joshua Kelly, Samuel Fares, Abraham McKay, Brothers Netherton and McKay appointed to write the letters.

March 10, 1792 (page 9 of Book C) . . . The Church sends Joshua Kelly, Samuel Fares and William Lillard to Bent Creek Church, respecting disorder in Little Beaver Creek Church. On May 10, 1792. . . . The above mentioned Committee returned from Bent Creek Church and reported. The Church declares non-fellowship at Little Beaver Creek, where Samuel McGee is member.

March 8, 1794 . . . Received a friendly letter from the Little Church at Little Pigeon (Sevierville) requesting us to look into the matter of their members who were living in the bounds of our Church to wit; Brother Jesse Isbell and wife and Vine Taylor. Upon investigation, this reports that Brother Jesse Isbol has gone to Caintuck (Kentucky). May the 10, 1794, committee appointed to see Vine Taylor, say that she has gone to Caintucky.

May the 10, 1794 . . . Church agrees to hold her meetings on French Broad River till times appear more safe in respect to the Indians. (Big Pigeon was the border line between the Indians and the White settlement for many years after the above date.)

June 7, 1794 (page 15 of Book C) . . . Motion whether it's agreeable to Gospel order for members to talk at large, in respect to matters done in the Church, as touching on fellowship, as also talking behind the back of any person they are aggrieved with, except be for information and that to be members of the Church . . . It's not agreeable, and members guilty of such behavior, are liable to be dealt with, as in other immoral conduct.

September 9, 1794 . . . The members appointed to look out a place suitable to build a meeting house, reported to the Church that they had found a place near Thomas Dillon on Big Pigeon River. It was further agreed that the meeting house be built by superscription and that Abraham McKay be appointed to draw the same as soon as convenience will admit.

This first church received with the white people many of the colored folk, and they were referred to only by their first names and as a man woman, or girl, of color, as Joe, a man of color; Luce, a black woman

April the 3, 1803 (page 39 D) . . . At this meeting the Church agreed that the brethern and members living up French Broad, about the mouth of the Big Creek (now Del Rio), become an Arm of this Church and that they have the liberty of holding monthly meetings among themselves and to receive members, provided that some of the members of this body be with them, with such help, as are legally qualified to administer ordinances. At this time, their deacon, William Lillard, reported he had hired a hand for Elder Kelly. The Church agreed to same.

September 28, 1821 (page 73, Book D). Benjamin O'Dell was ordained as Deacon by Elders Hill and Elijah. July the 5, 1823 (page 74, Book D) . . . Brother Abraham McKay resigned as Clerk, on account of old age and being feeble. He was succeeded by his son, Jeremiah McKay. Brother McKay has served this Church from its organization 1787, a period of thirty-six years, as Clerk.

September 4, 1830, William Huff and George Allen came forward and gave satisfaction; received Mikel (Michael) Branson by letter; the Church appointed Mikel Branson to the Nolachucky Association; John Driscol applied for a letter of dismission for himself and wife, Millie, which was granted.

The following names and dates they joined Church will interest their descendants:

April 4, 1789; May 2, 1789, John Netherton and wife, Elizabeth; on June 11, 1791, Peter Fine ordained Deacon; June 12, 1790, Samuel Fares, Elder. On the same date, William Fox was taken into Church by experience; by letter, William Vaughn, August 7, 1790; April 7, 1791, Joshua Kelly, Elder and on July 7, 1792, chosen as Pastor; April 7, 1781, James Nichols; December 6, 1787, Abram McKay, First Clerk served 36 years to July 5, 1823. Son Jeremiah McKay served as Clerk to June the 2, 1858; April 3, 1802, Jeremiah McKay joined Church by experience; December 6, 1787, James English; June 11, 1791, John Keeney by letter; January 7, 1792, Thomas and John Mantooth, each by letter; February 11, 1792, Joseph Hill; February 11, 1792, Jared Brickey and wife were labored to know why they had not joined the Church; Jared Rickey and wife were received into Church, May 12, 1792; May 12, 1792, Reuben Padgett; May, 1802, John Netherton; August 11, 1792, Michael Mitchell (ex); August 11, 1792, John Hird (ex); September 8, 1792, John Breeder by letter; September 5, 1795; John Mulkey by letter; January 2, 1796, Thomas Clevenger by letter; Reuben Allen by letter; April, 1796,

Reuben Hill; February 28, 1789, Samuel Hill and in 1790, Thomas Hill; February 3, 1797, Jonathan Davis; September 30, 1797, Philip Mulkey; November, 1800, Ezekiel Campbell; July, 1798, William Coleman, by experience; April 3, 1802, John Fine by experience; June, 1802, Abram McKay, Jr. by experience; May, 1802, Benjamin O'Dell by letter; June, 1802, Caleb O'Dell, by experience; July, 1802, Salander O'Dell, by experience; June, 1802, Martin Sisk by letter; June, 1802, Thomas S. Nelson; July, 1802, Peter Huff by letter; September, 1802, William Job, by experience; November 4, 1797, William Lane and wife, Elizabeth, by letter; 1803, Nathaniel Bowman; May 6, 1804, William Allen; September, 1809, Joseph Huff, Jr., by experience; April 6, Thomas Hicks, by letter; February 6, David Hicks, by letter; May 1, 1813, Hezekiah Randolph, from Hickory Creek Church, West Tennessee; April 1, 1814, Charlie Kelly; February 1, 1823, Anderson Vinson; October 1818, Jessie Lemons; June, 1824, John Driskill; August 5, 1826, Sam Miller; December 5, 1829, Toliver Sisk; April 5, 1851, Lawson Sisk; September 3, 1796, Joshua Clevenger.

Tidence Lane[3] was active in Cocke County in its early days. Ramsey's *History* states that the beginning of Baptist history in Tennessee was 1799 while Benedict's *General History of Baptists* places the date about 1780. Tidence Lane was the first pastor of Buffalo Ridge Church on Boone's Creek. He was the first Moderator of the first Association of

---

3. Tidence Lane was born in the Province of Maryland on August 31, 1724, the son of Richard and Sarah Lane and the grandson of Dutton Lane and Pretitia Tidings, or Tydings. He was named for his grandmother Tidings, but in the course of time the name became Tidence.

Tidence Lane's parents moved from Maryland to Virginia, thence to North Carolina, where he grew to manhood. His parents lived on the Yadkin River, not far from the home of Daniel Boone.

A Baptist preacher, Shubeal Stearns was having a successful meeting in North Carolina. Tidence Lane rode fifty miles on horseback to see the celebrated preacher. He tells his own experience.

When the fame of Mr. Stearn's preaching reached the Yadkin, where I lived, I felt a curiosity to go and hear him. Upon my arrival I saw a venerable man sitting under a peachtree with a book in his hand and the people gathering about him. He fixed his eyes upon me immediately, which made me feel in such a manner as I had never felt before. I turned to quit the place, but could not proceed far. I walked about, sometimes catching his eyes as I walked. My uneasiness increased and became intolerable. I went up to him, thinking that a salutation and shaking of hands would relieve me; but it happened otherwise. I began to think he had an evil eye and ought to be shunned. But shunning him I could no more effect than a bird can shun the rattlesnake when it fixes its eyes upon it. When he began to preach my perturbations increased, so that nature could no longer support them, and I sank to the ground.

William Bean built the first cabin in what is now Tennessee in 1769 near where Boone's Creek empties into the Watauga River, in Washington County. Tidence Lane is supposed to have come to the Western Settlements about 1777. He organized the "Buffalo Ridge" Baptist Church in 1778 or 1779. He was pastor of this church until 1784, when he sold his farm and moved to Jefferson County (now Hamblen County) near the present town of Whitesburg. There he and William Murphy organized the Bent Creek Baptist Church and Lane was pastor of this church for twenty-one years, resigning the year before his death in 1806. Tidence Lane was the first moderator of a Missionary Baptist Association in Tennessee, and at one time the family of General John Sevier attended his services.

Tidence Lane married at the age of nineteen and to this union nine children were born: seven sons and two daughters. Some of their descendants still live near Whites-

any denomination in the State of Tennessee, the old Holston Association at Cherokee Meeting House, in Washington County on Saturday before the fourth Sunday in October, 1786. David Benedict visited the valley of the Nolachucky in search for data in 1810 and stayed with Phillip Hale. The Tennessee Association was set off in 1803; and in 1828 the Nolachucky Association of fourteen churches was organized and covered the County.

In 1830 the East Tennessee Association was established "located wholly in the county of Cocke." The congregation at Mulberry Gap was rated first in membership originally. (Benedict obtained information after 1810 from Rev. Wm. C. Newell, whom he termed "in historical inquiries an expert man in full measure.") The earliest copy of the printed minutes of an association meeting in the County (Judge S. C. Williams) is in the C. M. McClung Collection, Knoxville: "Minutes of the Nolachucky Baptist Association held at Slate Creek Meeting House, Cocke County, E. T., on the fourth Friday in September, 1830, and following days."

Although the first divisions of the Baptist Church were earlier and in other parts of the country, the major division in Tennessee did not take place until between 1838 and 1840. This schism (Williams) was on the question of missions, operations led by Elder B. A. Witt, which resulted in the formation of a second Nolachucky Association.

Henry Randolph, an intelligent devout man, was one of the strongest of the Church's supporters. The following inscription is on his tombstone in the cemetery at Friendship, in Jefferson County:

Sacred to the memory of Elder Henry Randolph, Pastor of the Primitive Baptist Church at Friendship. Born July 4, 1778, died February 15, 1849.

He was able in the pulpit and gifted in prayer. He was firm in principle as he was in doctrine, and his voice and manner were impressive. He had a reputation for firmness, honesty and integrity of character. The following letter shows his manner of thinking and also gives some idea of the fight over missions in this section of Tennessee.

Jefferson County, East Tenn.
Nov. 2, 1839.

Very Dear Brethren in the Lord:—
I still continue to receive the correspondence from a number of precious brethren, through *The Primitive*, which revives my poor old heart to hear of so many valiant soldiers in the camps of King Jesus. And all appear to be so expert in handling the weapons of their warfare, the scriptures of truth, which was given by divine inspiration of God, and is profitable for doctrine, etc., that the word of

---

burg, where Tidence Lane is buried in an unmarked grave. (Data from ex-Mayor E. E. Patton, *Knoxville Journal*, June 18, 1944.)

Tidence Lane was the great-grandson of Major Samuel Lane, officer in King's service in the Province of Maryland, 1680. He was a brother of Dutton Lane, Virginia pioneer preacher who is mentioned by Semple and Taylor in their respective histories of Virginia Baptist ministers as a minister of prominence and influence. Tidence Lane was the father of Lieut. Isaac Lane, who under Col. John Sevier performed patriotic service at the Battle of King's Mountain, October 7, 1789.

God is the best word that I ever handled, to cut my way through the trials of the day, set up by men, and supported with money, which money, is the end of their row, and distress in the churches, the fruit that is produced from such conduct, without a thus said the Lord in his word.

Dear Brethern, I have had full proof of those wolves in sheep-skin for the last two years; for two years ago the Powell's Valley Association sent their delegates with a letter, informing the Nola-chucky Association that she would drop correspondence with us un-less we would protest against the institutions of the day which in-troduced the subject. At length it was laid over as a reference till last year; when the thing was revived, which was warmly debated on both sides. The Old School part standing to their old covenant, on which they were constituted, believing that the scriptures of the old and new Testaments are the word of God and the only rule of saving knowledge which they contended that the new school had departed from; and often requested them to bring forward their proof from the word of God which they failed to do. At last there was a motion made to lay it over one year longer, as a reference, which was carried by a majority of the Association requesting the Churches to send up their feelings and wishes relative to that matter, by their letters and delegates.

And now dear brethern, comes the hottest of the war in the Churches on the Mission question, for the missionaries and their friends, the go-betweeners, used all the industry they could, having a form of godliness but denying the power thereof, for this sort are they which creep into the houses, and lead captive silly women, laden with divers lusts. The dose commenced working last spring among the Churches that belong to the Nolachucky Association. On the fourth Friday in September last, we got rid of the anti-christian trash, the missionaries, and go-between men. For on the fourth Friday in September last, the Association met at Concord Meeting House Greene County and after several plans proposed how the Association should proceed, the following one was agreed to; that is that all the letters should be handed in; the old moderators and clerks still acting till the letters were read. They were separated as they were read. The new School Churches were laid to themselves and the old School to themselves. The Moderator being on the old School side, the new side requested their letters which were given up to them. They immediately nominated a moderator and clerk and violently rushed into the pulpit and commenced reading their letters over again in such disorder, that it was more like heathen than Christian. We insisted on the Clerk to stop reading, till we could come to order; but they paid no more regard to us than if we had been Hottentots or Turks. We then made a proclamation for the Old School Brethern to retire to the woods which opportunity they gladly embraced, and when we got to the woods we were separated from the trash and their benevolent institutions of money begging, and money-getting and soul saving plan which I call a money salvation. For if they ever get a dollar, its safe in their pocket. The Missionary beggars would rather get a dollar by begging than five dollars by hard work, for that would spoil his pretty, fair hands.

But to return to the woods, we there appointed our moderator and clerk and proceeded to business, as we formerly had done, only there was more of a oneness among the brethern in their deliberations than had been for several years.

Our Association was reduced to thirteen Churches and some of them very small, but I believe they are all of the pure stamp, or pure metal; for they have passed through the furnace of affliction and have come out of the fire well refined. And I hope we shall have peace for a while, till the Devil studies out some other plan that will take with the people, to go with the general atonement and all its kindred branches of doctrine; such as that of the spirit is striving with all mankind to make Christians, at protracted meetings, or anxious benches, as though God was no where else but there to convert their souls.

Brethern, it appears to me, that the blind are leading the blind, and they will all fall into the ditch together. They appear to compass sea and land to make proselytes, and when they are made, they are two-fold more a child of hell than themselves. It is said in second Thessalonians 2 ch., 7 verse, for the mystery of iniquity doth already work only he who now letteth will let until he be taken out of the way. And shall the wicked be revealed whom the Lord shall consume with the spirit of his mouth, and shall destroy with the brightness of his coming . . . 9th verse. Even him whose coming is after the working of Satan with all power and signs, and lying wonders, 10th verse—and with all deceivableness of unrighteousness in them that perish, because they received not the love of the truth, that they might be saved. 11th verse, and for this cause God shall send them strong delusion and they should believe it a lie. 12th verse that they all might be damned who believe not the truth, but had pleasure in unrighteousness.

Brethern, as soon as ever the separation took place in the Church, the Missionaries and their friends, the go-betweeners, (in the County started that which was spoken of the Lord, by the mouth of Elijah, the prophet, in First Kings 19th Chapter and 11 verse, "And he, God said, go forth and stand upon the mount before the Lord and behold, the Lord passed by, and a great and strong wind rent the mountains and brake in pieces the rocks before the Lord, but the Lord was not in the wind; and after the wind, an earthquake (12th verse), and after the earthquake, a fire; but the Lord was not in the fire; and after the fire, a still small voice."

Now brethern, for the life of me I cannot believe in those earthquakes, those winds and those fires; where exhorting, praying, and singing and whisperings are all carried on at the same time. It is a fox-fire and is calculated to please sinful nature. My opinion is, that it is the Devil's harvest, and if the Lord does not prevent and put a stop to this word of deception, that thousands will be sadly disappointed. For instead of reaching the fair climes of glory, they will land in darkness. "O Lord, prevent" is my prayer. But the scriptures must, and will be fulfilled, and it takes men enlightened by grace, to discern these things in this day of darkness when public opinion has become so fashionable among the people.

But the natural man receiveth not the things of the spirit of God, for they are foolishness unto him, neither can he know them, because they are spiritually discerned.

I must stop for the present. God bless you all.

Signed . . . Henry Randolph

The Baptists of the county were the hosts of a "Grand Council" of the Upper East Tennessee Association on August 25 and 26, 1843. Delegates from the mother Association, the Holston, and from the Nolachucky, Tennessee, and East Tennessee Associations met at Pleasant Grove Church[4] in Cocke County for the purpose of adjusting doctrinal differences that tended to retard the growth of the denomination. The chief matters for discussion were the old one: "Election" or "free salvation"; the other one that was proving difficult was missionary activity.

Rev. Rees Bayless, "the tall hickory of Cherokee" in Washington County, was chosen to serve as moderator. He was a strong man, deferred to by his brethren. "To his wise counsel and conservative bearing was due, largely, the harmonious action of the convention in the adoption, substantially, of the New Hampshire Confession of Faith and the passing of a resolution to cooperate in the work of missions." It may be truly said that this convention marked the beginning of a new era of vigor and fruitfulness. (Judge Williams.)

SLATE CREEK PRIMITIVE BAPTIST CHURCH

There is some difference of opinion as to the organization of the Slate Creek Primitive Baptist Church, but the minutes[5] from which most of this data is taken states that it was organized January 21, 22, 1818. This record, called "The Church Book," is enclosed in a handmade leather case seven by eight inches, with an overflap like an envelope to protect the outer edge. Leather strings tie the case. The beautiful penmanship, with its quaint spelling, is written with a quill-pen. The fly-leaf is dated March 5, 1818, signed by Simeon Smith three times, and by John Smith. Tommy Smith was moderator forty years and Moses Driscol clerk sixty years. Tommy Smith gave two acres of ground for the Slate Creek Meeting House, which was erected near the old Morristown road and a short distance from the present home of Dave Legg.

The membership of the Church, January 21, 1818, follows as recorded in the minutes:

Chas. Kelly, John Smith, Simeon Smith, Thomas Brezendine, John Driskill, Daniel Moore, Burrow Buckner, Joseph Wise, John Brezendine or (Broyendine?), Polly Smith, Joel Mason, Isaac

---

4. Pleasant Grove Minutes recorded and in State Library from 1838 to 1860 show the following surnames in that section, and some of these same names are familiar there today: Allen (25 times, each a different one), Bailey, Ballentine (Vallentine or Valentine), Baxter, Bridges, Bryant, Burke, Cameron (17), Clark, Clevenger, Click, Caffy, Davis, Denton, Fine, Fox, Frazure, Giles, Green (26), Hall, Harrison, Hartsell, Hightower, Holaway, Humberd, Jenkins, Kelly, Lemons, Lillard (12), Mantooth, Mathes, McGaha, McMahan (18), McMillan, McNabb (26), Morell, Murr, Netherton, O'Dell, Padgett, Philips, Prepwood, Quarles, Rains, Roberts, Rollens, Scroggins, Sims, Sisk, Smithpeters, Thomas, Vinson, Wood, Woody, Yarberry, Yett. The minutes also record that the members were admonished for whipping children unmercifully, for drunkenness, and for improper conversation.

5. Furnished author by Lennie Thomas Marshall.

Smith, Mildred Smith, Sarah Smith, Asa Holt, Susannah Holt, Joshua Driscol, Nancy Driscol, Elizabeth Alexander, William Smith, Susannah Smith, Daniel Buckner, Sarah Driskill, Hannah Driskill, Jesse Driskill, Lige Driskill, Lucy Alexander, Sarah Mason, Thomas Driscol, Elizabeth Williams, James Buckner, Sallie Mecazty or (Mecarty?), Mary Harmon, Elizabeth Jones, Pete Wise, Daniel Hurley, Nancy Martin, Rachel Philips, Patsy Brezendine, Betsy Freshour, John Prightsell or (Peightsell), Nancy Davice, Mary Carweles, Sally Smith, Lucy Kelly, James Williams, James Calfee, Sharrick Williams, Elijah Hill, Prithea Manning or Biltea, Debby Manning, Caty Smith, Catherine Gregory, Susanna Jester, Anna Kelly, Elizabeth Campbell, Agnes Hurley, Nathan Tery or Tizy, Patsy Fowler, Rhoda Ramsey, Lucy Moore, John Phillips, Rachel Phillips, Nancy Smith, Lucy Lofty.

From the State Library in Nashville, the following names together with those given are listed as having been members of Slate Creek Church as early as 1812. Only the surnames were listed, and the report states that the name of Driskill appeared ten times; Kelly, twelve times; and Smith, eighteen times. Others included Anderson, Boley, Boswell, Brady, Collen, Colour, Crumley, Dalton, Daason, Ellason, Fly, Hale, Henderson, Livingston, Manning, Miller, Talley, Whaley, Witt, Wood.

Their articles of faith are included in the following:

We do mutually consent and agree to embody ourselves together as a religious society to worship God through faith in Jesus Christ, depending on him alone for the salvation of our souls and the blessings add immunities of this life as it is contained in the scriptures of the old and the new testaments believing them to be the revealed mind and will of God, containing the precious and soul reviving doctrines justification by the imputed righteousness of Jesus Christ both active and passive, apprehended by faith, sanctification through God's grace and truth with the final perseverance of the saints in Grace and for a more full declaration of our principles in general as a distinct society, we refer to the confession of faith.

Saturday 15 of August 1820 Church met and after divine service[6] proceeded to business. First opened doors for reception of members.

Secondly took up the distress against Danile Moore. The Church laboring with him, there being no satisfaction granted, the Church excommunicated him.

Thirdly Catherine Moore applied for a letter of dismission which was granted.

Fourthly, whereas there has been report circulating through the country respecting Brother William Smith stealing and killing a sheep, he came forward and informed the church that he had a sheep killed through a mistake that was not his own and that he paid the owner thereof for the said sheep and cleared himself of the charge that was done through a mistake.

James Buckner was excluded for drinking too much spiritous liquors.

---

6. These notes also give interesting sidelights on the customs of the times.

Thomas Brizendine came forward and made confession that he had drunk too much spiritous liquors and had done several other things that was wrong. The Church forgave him.

Saturday the 27 of March 1821, the Church met and after divine service proceeded to business. First Brother Weitsell came forward and made confession that he got very angry and had struck a man and was very sorry for it. The Church forgave him. Brother Weitesville requested a letter of dismission which was granted.

Saturday 21 of April 1821—The Church met, after worship proceeded to business. First put Joshua Driskill under the censure of the Church for getting in a passion.

Saturday the 15 of September 1821 Took up the distress against Joel Mason and excommunicated him, the Church considers for taking unlawful intrust and for selling a cow to Brother Charles Kelly for a good milk cow and said cow proven in the church not to be such a cow as he said Mason represented her to be.

February 15, 1823, Church dismissed nine members for an arm on Clay Creek. On Saturday June 15, 1822, Charles Kelly, John and Simeon Smith and Daniel Hurley were named as delegates to attend Association to be held at Big Pigeon Meeting House on the 2nd Friday of August and following days.

February 1824, the 21 day, Saturday John Driskill came forward and confest that he had drunk too much and the Church forgave him. Nancy Driskill came forward and confest that she done wrong in talking about Brother John Driskill and the Church forgave her.

Saturday March 20, 1824 John Driskill and wife requested their letters which was granted.

Isaac Smith on this date agreed not to sell any more spiritous liquors.

Base-born child born to Anna Kelly, Church excommunicated her, but the man (as per usual) went "Scot free"—and was not even reprimanded. Joel Mason acknowledged he talked about Danile Hurley and was sorry for it. Church agreed to send for Brother Henry Randolph and Brother Joseph White to attend with us at our next meeting.

Saturday 18th of June 1825 Brother Simeon Smith and Brother Jesse Driskill were appointed as messengers to the Association. Brother Thomas Smith was agreed upon for ordination and Brethern Caleb Witt and Duke Kimbro, Joseph White, William Senters and Henry Randolph to meet at our next meeting as a Presbitery for that purpose.

Friday May 19, 1826 Susannah Smith came forward and confest that she was sorry for beating of Jonathan Ivirg and the Church forgave her. Jonathan Castilla, a missionary, came to Clay Creek and helped to organize Clay Creek Church.

March 17, 1828—Clay Creek Church received a letter arm of Long Creek for ministers to constitute the Church at Clay Creek which was granted. In 1829 this Church was represented in Nolachucky Primitive Baptist Association by Simeon Smith and Thomas Driscol. In 1830 by Elder Smith (Thomas) brother Simeon Smith, John Driscol and John Brozendine.

Feb. 22, 1829—Took up distress against Patsy Brazendine for mis-using the orphan children and striking her husband. Excluded her for the same. July the 11, 1835 Took up distress against Elizabeth Brazendine for stealing, repaired it to the next meeting. Second Saturday in August 1835 after altercating we believe it to be the truth and excommunicate her for same.

June 11, 1836 Zachariah Dalton and Sister Mary Dalton, his wife, received.

February 11, 1837 The Church met and after worship took up a case Joel Mason for having the slite of hand showed at his house and he acknowledged that he had done wrong and the Church forgave him. Brother Dalton came forward and acknowledged that he done wrong in going to see the slite of hand and the Church forgave him. Third took the case against Brother Thomas Kelly for absconding from us without a letter and excommunicated him for the same. Also Peter Wise for same offense. Simeon Smith also acknowledged to going to see the slite of hand and was forgiven.

Elizabeth Neddix by letter August 12 1837, the Church met at Slate Creek Meeting house to set in a Church way to do the things that is wanting in God's House.[7]

Zachariah Dalton and wife requested letter of dismission October 15, 1837. Moses Driskill and wife received into the Church by experience April 27, 1844.

Second Saturday July 8, 1871. First Moses Driskill appointed and the Church agreed to send for Brother P. A. Witt and Henry Randolph to ordain him. March 14, 1845 he was ordained by Elders Pleasant A. Witt and Thos. Smith. "Cister" Elizabeth Smith. Susanna Penny asked for letter of dismission July 10, 1850. Elder Cornelius Livingston and wife Nancy, June 13, 1868. David A. Livingston and wife Phebe and Caroline Gipson, Carter Talley, Harriet Hunter, John Miller, John Baly received into the Church.[8]

Second Saturday, July 8, 1871—First Moses Driskill appointed to cite Sister Mary H. Dawson to the next meeting in corce to show cause why she had not attended her regular meetings.

Second Saturday August the 12, 1871. We, the Primitive Baptist-Church of Christ at Slate Creek Meeting House convened together to do the things that is wanting to be done in God's House. After singin, prair, and preching, continued the business of the day. First called on Sister Mary H. Dawson to give her reason for not attending her Church Meeting. She being present, states to the Church that the Conduct of Cornelius Livingston, our pastor, is such that she didn't want to hear him preach and the reason I didn't was he tried to get me to commit adultry with him and refered to the scripture to prove that it was right and he tried to persuade me to leave my husband and run away with him. After hearing her defense, we,

---

7. This is the time of the division between the Old School (Primitive) and the New School (Missionary Baptist).

8. D. A. Livingston and wife Pheby came from Rutherford County, N. C. May 9, 1868, is the date of their Church letter from Bunkers Hill, signed by John W. Livingston, M. D. T. and I. P. Whisnant, Ch. L. K.

The "Arm Church" on the old Morristown road

Present home of Governor Ben W. Hooper

as a Church agree to relieve the sister of the charge of failing to attend her regular church meeting.[9]

The second Saturday in July 1873 Cornelius Livingston and wife, David Livingston and wife, Jesse Crumley and wife, and Caroline Gipson were all excluded for not attending their Church meeting.

In 1877 the Church had only twelve active members and ceased to function. They were: Thomas Smith, Simeon Smith, Joel Mason, Daniel Hurley, John Buckner, Sister Driskill, Moses Driskill, Elizabeth Miller, Elizabeth Smith, Sister Smith, Nancy Wallis and Elizabeth Camel (Campbell).

CLAY CREEK OR ARM CHURCH[10]

As there was no church building in the Clay Creek community until 1828, quite a number of Christian people organized Clay Creek Church, from the Concord Church in Greene County, which was established in 1823. Since it was an arm of that Church, it received the double name of Arm or Clay Creek Church. Thomas Christian gave the plot of ground on which the Church stands. The first building was constructed of logs and was thirty feet long and twenty feet wide, with a door in each end, and in the center of the building there was a hearth six feet square, upon which they built fires and around which they sat on wooden benches to worship.

Clay Creek was received into the Holston Association in 1828 and was dismissed from that Association in the same year. This Church was present at the organization of the Nolachucky Primitive Baptist Association at Bent Creek. With Joseph Manning as Messenger, the Church was represented in 1829, 1830, 1831, and 1832.

In September, 1832, an answer to complaint made to this Body by Big Creek,[11] Antioch and Slate Creek churches against the proceedings of Warrensburg, Clay Creek and Bethel South that "we send a committee of inquest whose duty it shall be to meet at Clay Creek Church-house on Sunday, October 30, 1832 and strive for a reconciliation, and report all necessary facts to our next Association. We also advise said churches to meet this committee on said occasion by delegates or otherwise."

In 1833 a call for report of committee was made. It said that a reconciliation was effected between the complaints of Warrensburg and Long Creek, and since that reconciliation that Long Creek had also effected a reconciliation with Bethel South. Also, Clay Creek Church was therefore losing her privilege from the Association because she had seceded from this Union.

In 1834, Big Creek and Long Creek asked if a Church had been excluded from the General Union, could the name of the ministers be published. An affirmative answer drew forth the hope that no minister would be offended for the public to know the name of his Church and the relation he bore to it. Also, the statement was made that these churches

9. The Scripture meant is in Acts 13:38-39; also Romans 7:4-6.
10. Story of Arm Church furnished by Mrs. Jessie Gregg Hazelwood.
11. It is said that the Baptist folk built their church on the rivers and creeks while the Methodist people chose the hilltops. One amusing story took place during a big revival meeting held at Big Creek. The baptizing was on a cold winter day, and the ice had to be broken for the services. A small, scrawny convert got cold feet, for when his turn came he shivered and shook, announcing, "Brethern and sister, I postpone mine until the May Meetin'." (According to Mrs. Duncan).

Baptist Church Building, 1937.

did withdraw from Clay Creek Church for seceding from the Union and that Ephraim Moore and Joseph Manning were members of that Church and claimed connection with the Party of Garrett Dewees. "This we believe to be a departure from the Faith."

In 1841, there were ninety-four members. One was excluded, six were dismissed, one was restored, nine were baptized, and two died. Joseph Manning was elected pastor and C. M. Hudson C. C.

During 1860 the present building was partly erected by James H. Hurley who had the brick burned and superintended the building, which was done by Dan Boyd and Will Dammern. The money was raised by subscription. It was not completed until after the close of the Civil War. John Thomas built the pulpit and made the benches.

First Baptist Church of Newport

On Tuesday, February 8, 1876, "A number of ministers and members of different Baptist Churches met for the purpose of taking into consideration the propriety of organizing a Baptist Church at, or near, the town of Newport." On Sunday, April 10, 1876, the Church perfected its organization, with twenty-eight charter members: Mr. and Mrs. N. S. Brooks, Mr. and Mrs. J. C. Morrell, Mr. and Mrs. John B. Stokely, Mr. and Mrs. William C. Brooks, James H. Randolph (who furnished the site for the Church), William F. Williams, Tipton C. McNabb, Mrs. Susan E. Susong, Mrs. Laura Clark, Miss Cassie Inman, Dr. and Mrs. L. W. Hooper, Mr. and Mrs. S. J. Campbell, Mr. and Mrs. J. G. Allen, Mr. and Mrs. Stephen S. Brooks, David S. Stokely, John W. Johnson, S. C. Jones, Jr., Mrs. Martha Inman, Miss Lou J. Susong, Miss Tennie Inman.

J. H. Randolph, Dr. Lemuel W. Hooper and John B. Stokely were the first Deacons of the Church; Sam C. Jones, its first Clerk; John B. Stokely, its first Treasurer; Rev. J. M. L. Burnett, its first Pastor.

The Church was organized in the Church Building of the Old Pisgah Church (Presbyterian) and stood across the street and several yards west of the present Cocke County Memorial Building. The old cemetery still marks the first site of Newport's first church of any denomination. The Baptists worshipped in this Church until the completion of their own building, a few services being held at the Old Town Court House.

The First Church Building was completed and dedicated on May 6, 1877, with Dr. C. A. Pope preaching the dedicatory sermon. This first building was elected on the site of the present one.

Soon after its organization, the Church petitioned the East Tennessee Baptist Association for membership in that body. The Association met that year at the Powder Spring Church in Sevier County, in September, 1876. John B. Stokely, Joseph C. Morrell, Lemuel W. Hooper, and Stephen S. Brooks were sent as delegates to this meeting, at which session the Church was admitted into the Association.

Preaching services were held once each month, on the Saturday before the first Sunday in each month. Soon services were held on the first Sunday as well.

As far as the Minutes show, Mrs. S. C. Baird was the first candidate to be baptized into the fellowship of the new Church, the baptism administered "at the Ford."

The East Tennessee Association held its annual meeting with the Newport Church in 1879. The minutes show that the Pastor's salary in 1881 was seventy-five dollars per year. In 1882 it was one hundred dollars, an

The Christian Church

The Methodist Episcopal Church

amount merely promised but not guaranteed. Rev. C. C. Brown became Pastor in January, 1883, but he served only four months, probably due to ill health.

A Women's Missionary Union was formed in 1882 and a Sunday School was organized on February 24, 1884. A Baptist Young People's Training Union was organized in 1912.

In 1886, the Church began to have two Sunday services each month and the Pastor's salary was set at three hundred dollars per year at this time. However, in 1888 the members were again meeting for only one Sunday a month and the preacher was receiving the sum of two hundred dollars per year.

Rev. J. C. Rockwell was the first resident Pastor of the Newport Church. Under his leadership the first parsonage was built on Woodlawn Avenue Dearly beloved by his congregation, he died during his services here. In 1900 Rev. J. M. Anderson adopted full time services for the Church at a salary of six hundred dollars per year, with a meeting each Sunday.

The present church building was completed in 1907, with Rev. B. R. Downer as pastor. The Sunday School annex, or Educational Building. was erected in 1929, with Rev. A. L. Crawley as Pastor.[12]

Among the pastors who have served this Church were: Rev. J. M. L. Burnett, 1876-1883; Rev. C. C. Brown, 1883-83; Rev. S. E. Jones, 1883-88; Rev. Jesse Baker, 1888-91; Rev. James C. Rockwell, 1891-93; Rev. W. C. McPherson, 1893-96; Rev. S. E. Jones (2nd term), 1896-1900; Rev. P. D. Mangum, 1909-10; Rev. J. W. O'Hara, 1910-19; Rev. A. L. Crawley, 1919-29; Rev. Mark Harris, 1929-34; Dr. Merrill Moore, 1934-41; Dr. J. P. Allen, 1941-43; Dr. W. E. Denham, 1944-46; Rev. Carl P. Daw, 1947-50.

The Tennessee Valley Authority numbered the Baptist Churches of Cocke County as thirty-eight, with 4,490 members, and property valued at $97,850. (Date unknown, presumably in the thirties.)

The Christian Church

The First Christian Church was organized in 1921 as a result of an evangelistic meeting conducted by Rev. C. L. Organ in a tent on the Court House lawn from June 18 to August 8, 1921.

The first house for the Christian congregation was built in one day on the present site by volunteer workers under the leadership of Rev. Arthur E. Simerly, and it was 32 by 48 feet. The first pastor, Rev. C. H. Stults, was followed by S. Marion Smith, both students in Johnson Bible College.

In 1928, the Church called Rev. Elliott who went to work at building a brick parsonage on Second Street and of building the handsome church now occupied by the congregation. It is of Roman architecture, brick-veneered, with beautiful windows, and costing twenty-five thousand dollars. Other preachers have been: Burton Doyle, E. L. Weinrich, R. M. Bell, R. M. Lappin and Allen Nance.

The Lutheran Church

The Lutheran Congregation was organized in 1845 by Rev. A. J. Fox. Prior to the organization, services were held in the home of Michael Ottinger, near where the Salem Lutheran Church now stands. Mr.

12. Data furnished by a member, Marjorie McMahan, in 1936.

The M. E. Church Building that stood where Dr. V. W. Montsinger's office is now located—(1950)

Ottinger went all the way to North Carolina in a two horse wagon to bring the Pastor into his community. The Congregation has had two buildings, the first of small frame construction was enlarged in 1873. For a long time a two-room schoolhouse was maintained across the road from the Church, and was known as Salem School.

The Church, a frame structure, erected in 1906 and seating 400, is of modern style architecture, with a cemetery adjacent. Twenty pastors have served the Salem Congregation during its hundred years of its life. In 1940, the baptized membership was 389. Of the 300 confirmed members, 86 bear the name of Ottinger. Other prominent names are Blazer, Bible, Eisenhour (Eisenhower), Hawk and Nease.

At first the religious services were held monthly, then every two weeks, now every Sunday.

Salem Church is located three miles East of Parrottsville about three hundred yards South of the highway, Rev. Davis, Pastor. This community dedicated a handsome new church recently. Each of its windows is in memory of a departed member. The Lutheran Church has recently erected a beautiful building in the town of Newport on Lincoln Avenue. Rev. L. L. Linebaugh is Pastor.

The Methodist Church

East Tennessee was the first section of the state to be penetrated by the circuit rider, and Jeremiah Lambert was the first Methodist circuit rider regularly appointed to a charge west of the Alleghany mountains, being sent to serve the Holston circuit in 1783. Then, there were sixty members in the Conference.[13]

Thomas Ware came from New Jersey, in 1789, the coldest winter the pioneers had known. He spent his efforts along the lower French Broad.[14]

Another of the early strong points of Methodism was the "County-line Church" on the road from Russellville to Rocky-Spring and on the line between Grainger and Hawkins counties. Here, too, was a camp ground known as "County line," and to the meetings held here the people flocked in wagons, with tents, from the South side of the French Broad, where many of them were converted.

Rev. R. W. Price in his *History of Holston Methodism* says that the first Methodist Church built in Cocke County was called O'Haver's Chapel located beside the road leading from Newport to Greeneville about nine miles from Old Newport. It was built of hewn logs and was near the home of John O'Haver who gave the land for the church site. There is reason to believe that the Church stood near an old cemetery on the land of the Gregg Susong Farm, near the Salem Post Office, that was called O'Haver Cemetery.

John A. Granade preached there and traveled the Green Circuit in 1802. Here the O'Havers, Easterly, Harneds, Swaggertys, Reeves and many others had membership.

13. The first Methodist conference beyond the mountains was held at Keyswood in 1788, the locality being recorded by Asbury in his journal as in Tennessee. Here the conversion and baptism of General William Russell, of Revolutionary fame, and his wife, known as Madam Russell, because of their prominence and social prestige, was a high light of the session. Madam Russell, the sister of Patrick Henry, became one of the saints of American Methodism.
14. *History of Methodism in Holston Conference*, by I. P. Martin.

John O'Haver later emigrated to the West. Jacob Easterly gave two sons to the ministry. Isaac, his eldest, who joined the Conference in about 1820 to 1822, married a Miss Mitchell in Sequatchie Valley, where he ultimately located. Christopher, the second son, went into a traveling connection, became a good preacher, married in Virginia, and located there. Samuel Harned was an intelligent, well-read layman from New Jersey who went as a guard for Bishop Asbury in one of his journeys through the wilderness.

"At the beginning of the eighteenth Century a great religious wave spread over Tennessee and the people of Old Newport caught the infection. The crowds that attended those early meetings were enormous; many slept in the open air, or under the trees; others slept in tents. This gave rise to camp meetings. It is said that these meetings were attended by a peculiar physical manifestation, popularly known as the "jerks." They were involuntary and irresistible. When under their influence, the sufferers would dance, or sing, or shout, sometimes they would sway from side to side, or throw the head backward or forward, leap or spring. Generally those under the influence, would at the end, fall upon the ground and remain rigid for hours, and sometimes whole multitudes would become dumb and fall prostrate. As the swoon passed away, the sufferers would weep piteously, moan and sob. After a while the gloom would lift, a smile of heavenly peace would radiate the countenance, and words of joy and rapture would break forth, and conversion always followed." (From an old record kept by Alonzo Dow.)

As the revival movement spread there was a great demand for preachers and places of worship, the congregations resorted to the woods, cleared the underbrush, cutting the saplings just high enough to enable those under the influence of the "jerks" to hold them. As an outgrowth, a camp ground was established near Old Newport (1820), somewhere close to the mouth of Clear Creek, on the north side of the French Broad River. It is said that at a series of revival meetings, held here, there were as many as eighty persons at the altar at one time.

Later this camp ground was moved to Parrottsville and at one series of meetings 250 persons were added to the Methodist Church. The principal tenters at these meetings were: Jacob Easterly, Jacob Faubion, William Garrett, Thomas Gray, Samuel Harned, James Gilleland, Abel Gilleland, Henry Potter, Jesse Reeves, Moses Faubion, James Holland, Jno. Holland, Reuben Allen, Baldwin Harle, George Parrot, and Thomas Fowler.

The first recorded visit made to Cocke County by a Methodist minister was in the year 1800 and 1801. About that date there came to the communities on the French Broad and the Big Pigeon Rivers John Adams Granade, a Methodist minister known as the "Wild Man." He was an eccentric individual, and at the same time preached a comparatively new and emotional doctrine, drawing large crowds. He created a sensation among the young settlers, some of whom claimed that he had mysterious power, with which he could work his listeners into a religious frenzy; others claimed that he was possessed of a devil. In 1801, he preached in the old courthouse in Old Newport, the first sermon ever preached in the town by a Methodist minister. On this occasion he was abused and grossly insulted by a ruffian shaking his fist in the preacher's face. William Garrett arrested the culprit and had him punished.

More than once, it is said that Bishop Asbury, also Bishop McKendrick preached at O'Haver's Chapel en route to appointments in North and South Carolina.[15]

Bishop Asbury stopped at the home of Jesse Reeves between Parrottsville and Paint Rock in 1801.

In 1800 there were four circuits with 1,141 members, 686 of which were colored. By 1802, there were 2981 members and East Tennessee had three circuits, Holston, Nolachucky and French Broad. At this time French Broad Circuit embraced the settlements on both sides of the French Broad River, and the membership totaled 648 whites and 14 colored. Rev. Louther Taylor was the circuit rider in 1802.

LORENZO DOW'S TRAVELS IN EAST TENNESSEE

Lorenzo Dow bequeathed to posterity a mental daguerreotype of himself in his many journals. He was greatly persecuted by the powers that were at the time, but Francis Asbury gave him a license to preach and soon he was on his way to Tennessee. His *Complete Works* are the source of the following quotations:

In crossing Saluda Mt., the way was narrow; whilst precipes were on one side, the other arose perpendicular; which rendered it dangerous traveling in the night, had not the mts. been on fire, which illuminated the heavens to my convenience.

February 14, 1804 I spoke in Buncomb to more than could get into the Presbyterian meeting house; and at night also and good I trust was done. The minister was not an A double L part man; but pious. Next day I rode 45 miles in company with Dr. Nelson; across dismal Alleghany Mts. by Warm Spring (Hot Spring, N. C.) and on the way a young man, a traveler, came in where I breakfasted gratis

---

15. Excerpts from Bishop Asbury's Journal:
   Tuesday, No. 2, 1802: We rode through New-Port, the capital of Cocke County, forded French Broad at Shine's Ferry, and came cold and without food for man or beast to John O'Haver's—but oh, the kindness of our open-hearted friends.
   Wednesday, 3. We laboured over the Ridge and Paint Mountain: I held on a while but grew afraid and dismounted and with the help of a pine-sapling worked my way down the steepest and roughest part. I could bless God for life and limbs. Eighteen miles this day contented us, and we stopped at William Nelson's Warm Springs. (Hot Springs). About thirty travelers having dropped in, I expounded the Scriptures to them.
   Bishop Francis Asbury in 1812 crossed the French Broad at Seehorn's Ferry, near Dandridge,
   and forded Pigeon River near its mouth on our way to James Gilliland; we came into our station stiff and cold.
   Sabbath, November 29, I preached and as also did Bishop McKendree.
   Monday, Dec. 1. Why should we climb over the desperate Paint Mountain when there is such a fine new road along the river. (This gives the approximate date of building of this road, about November, 1812.)
   We came by Nelson's (Warm) Springs.
   The previous year (1813) he preached at O'Haver's and ordained Joshua Witt as an elder. In 1814, he noted in his Journal:
   The work of God groweth in this neighborhood; there is a house of worship thirty-five by forty feet built on the bank of Pigeon River. ought this not to be in Holston Conference and unite with the circuits west of the Blue Ridge? This led to the organization of the Holston Conference.)

at an Inn and said that he had but 3/16 of a $ left, having been robbed of $71.20 on the way; and being far from home I gave him ½ of what I had with me.

He sold his horse, saddle, bridle, cloak and blanket, etc., for about ¾ of the value on credit (lost it forever) crossed the French Broad river in a canoe and set out for an appointment, hired a man to carry him five miles in hack for three shillings which left him but 1/16 of a $. The man with the two horses observed there was a nigh way

By which I could clamber the rocks and cut off some miles, so we parted; he having not gone 2/3 of the way, yet insisted on the full sum. I took to my feet the nigh way as fast as I could pull on, as intricate as it was and came to a horrid ledge of rocks on the bank of the river where there was no such thing as going around, and to clamber over would be at the risk of my life, as there was danger of slipping into the river; however, being unwilling to disappoint the people, I pulled off my shoes and with my handkerchief fastened them about my neck; and creeping upon my hands and feet with my fingers and toes in the cracks of the rocks, with difficulty I got safe over; and in about 4 miles I came to a house, and hired a woman to take me over the river in a canoe, for my remaining money and a pair of scissors, the latter of which was the chief object with her. So our extremities are other opportunities. Thus with difficulty I got to my appointment in Newport in time.

I had heard about a singularity called the jerks or jerking exercise which appeared first in Knoxville in August last (1803) to the great alarm of the people; which reports at first I considered vague and false. But at length, like the Queen of Sheba, I set out to go and see for myself; and sent over these appointments into this country accordingly.

When I arrived in sight of this town (Newport) I saw hundreds of people collected in little bodies and observing no place appointed for meeting, before I spoke to any, I got on a log and gave out a hymn which caused them to assemble around in solemn attentive silence. I observed several involuntary motions in the course of the meeting which I considered as a specimen of the jerks. I rode 7 miles behind a man across streams of water and held meeting in the evening and being 10 miles on my way (10 miles from old Newport, probably near Clevenger's Crossroads).

In the night I grew uneasy being 25 miles from my appointment for the next morning at 10 o'clock. I prevailed on a young man to attempt to carry me with horses until day, which he thought was impracticable, considering the darkness of the night and the thickness of the trees. Solitary shrieks were heard in these woods which he told me were said to be the cries of murdered persons. At day we parted, being still 17 miles from the spot and the ground covered with white frost. (Evidently not far from Chestnut Hill) I had not proceeded far, before I came to a stream of water from the springs of the mts. which made it dreadful cold. In my heated state I had to wade this stream 4 times in the course of about an hour; which I perceived so affected my body, that my strength began to fail. Fears began to arise that I must disappoint the people; till I observed some fresh tracks of horses which caused me to exert every nerve to overtake them; in hopes of aid on my journey, and soon I saw them on an eminence. I shouted for them to stop till I came up; they inquired what I wanted. I replied I had heard there was a meeting at Sevierville by a stranger and was going to it. They replied that they had heard that a crazy man was to hold forth there; and were going also; and perceiving that I was weary they invited me to ride, and soon our company was increased to 40 or 50 who fell in with us on the road from different plantations. At length I was interrogated whether I knew anything about the preacher. I replied, "I have heard a good deal about him" and have heard him preach, but that I had not great opinion of him, and thus the conversation continued, for some miles before they found me out, which caused some color and smiles in the company; thus I got on to the meeting. And after a cup of tea gratis, I began to speak to a vast audience and I observed about 30 to have the jerks, though they strove to keep still as they could these emotions were involuntary, and irresistible as any unprejudiced eye might discern. Lawyer Porter who had come a considerable distance got his heart touched under the word and being informed how I came to the meeting, voluntarily lent me a horse to ride near 100 miles and gave me a $ though he had never seen me before.

Hence to Maryville where I spoke to about 1500 and many appeared to feel the word, but about 50 felt the jerks.

On Sunday, February 19, he spoke in Knoxville, at the courthouse, the Governor being present. One hundred and fifty had the jerks. After the meeting he rode 18 miles to hold a night meeting at a settlement of Quakers, who said the Methodists and Presbyterians jerked from praying and singing too much, but that they (Quakers) were a "still peaceable people wherefor we do not have them." But twelve of them had them that night.

Dow's experience and various "tricks" would have rivaled those of many modern evangelists. They got him into all sorts of difficulties with those who were devoid of a sense of humor and with those who were jealous of his success.[16] (So it was then—even as now.)

---

16. He established "the mourners bench" or "anxious seat," (Reuben Holland said to Sallie Fox at one, "Jesus is right here. Lug him Sallie, lug him.") And also introduced protracted meetings throughout this section. It is said that Lorenzo Dow became weary of preaching to an unresponsive audience. While walking through the fields he heard a bugle blowing and found a little negro named Gabriel entertaining himself with the instrument. He took the boy with him to "meeting" to play for the congregation, and had him climb into a tree and hide, giving him thorough instructions to blow his trumpet whenever he came to certain words in his sermon. When his sermon failed to bring forth the penitents, Dow said, "All right, what if you were to hear Gabriel sound his mighty trumpet tonight, what would you do?" The Negro Gabriel sounded forth with all his power and the audience tumbled over each other to get to the first mourner's bench.

At another time, Dow is said to have heard of a man who called on another's wife, and he determined to break him from such a habit by letting the people know of these visits. One day the preacher called at this place and the Gabriel incident was discussed. Dow then asserted that he could actually "raise the devil," and would prove it in their midst if some one would furnish him with a match. An old barrel sat near apparently filled with cotton. He struck the match, set the cotton on fire and in a few moments out leaped the man who had called on the man's wife and had hidden in the barrel at the approach of other visitors.

From 1800 to 1812, Old Newport was visited and its congregation preached to by Moses Black, William Houston, Nathan Barns, Obediah Edge, Samuel Sellers, and the eccentric Irish preacher, George Ekin.

In 1812, a series of revival services in the old courthouse in Old Town resulted in the conversion of the most prominent citizens at that time, among them William Garrett and his wife, Thomas Gray, James Gilleland, and Wesley Harrison. At this time, the first Methodist Society in Cocke County, known as the Zion Methodist Church, was organized. William Garrett and wife, Colonel Thomas Gray and wife and two daughters, Wesley Harrison and wife, James Gilleland and wife, Abel Gilleland and wife, Richard Ellis, his wife and daughter, Lewis Anderson and wife, were members of the Society. Lewis Anderson who conducted a harness and saddle business in Old Newport, was a local Methodist minister and filled the pulpit at Old Newport from time to time for many years. He was said to have been an eloquent and forceful preacher, who solemnized all the marriages in and around Old Newport.

In 1814, the above-named members built a large frame church in the northwest part of Old Newport, on the high hill immediately back of the brick courthouse and on the north side of the road leading from the courthouse across the hill in the direction of the fork of the river. This was the first of its style in Cocke County, on the Nolachucky circuit, which at the time included the counties of Greene, Cocke, Jefferson, and Sevier. The land was donated by Abel Gilleland. William Garrett superintended the building of this meeting house, and furnished the lumber which was prepared at his own saw mill. Among the distinguished Methodist divines who filled the pulpit of the Zion Church were Bishops Asbury and McKendree, Thomas Stringfield, Jesse Cunnyngham, John Haynie, and John A. Granade.

On a road leading from Newport to Dandridge in the Turnley settlement, Pine Chapel (1811-12) became the outpost of Methodism South of the French Broad River. George Turnley headed the Society, which included the families of Lickliters, the Gigers, Gregorys, Dentons, Cowans, and McAndrews.

The growth of the Zion Methodist Episcopal Church was seriously retarded by some severe rulings of a Presiding Elder, Rev. James Axley, who would not allow a slaveholder to take any part in managing church affairs, not even to lead in prayer meetings. In 1816, the General Conference of the Church convened at Baltimore and authority was given to the several annual conference of the church to form their own regulations as to the buying and selling of slaves.[17]

On September 1820, John Haynie (later called Father Haynie) held the first camp meeting at Clear Creek and was assisted by George Elkin and Absalom Harris of North Carolina. John Rice and David B. Cummings were also Methodist preachers. A society was also established on the French Broad in the Holland neighborhood, and included John Holland, Sr., his sons, James, William, and Hugh; Reuben Allen and wife, with several children. John Fanshaw and family belonged to the Oven Creek Church. In 1823, a Society was established in Dutch Bottom in

---

17. Bishop Asbury died before the meeting of the General Conference in 1816, He had been a General Superintendent of the Church for about thirty-two years of the forty-four he had spent in America.

the house of Abraham Bocker. Newport Circuit was established in 1823 and the French Broad District became the Knoxville District in the same year. The presiding elders during this period were James Axley, Jesse Cunnyngham and John Tevis, John Nenninger and Thomas Stringfield. On November 27, 1824, the name French Broad District including eight circuits was restored to its former territory, which stretched from Maryville to Carter's Valley and across to Black Mountain, North Carolina. (Martin's *History of Methodism in Holston Conference*.)

Over a hundred years ago, an old log Methodist Church was built at Yellow Springs, and has until recently been used not only as a place of worship but as a public school building. The pioneers called the church Mount Pleasant, but when a family of bats was discovered some one said the church had become a bat harbor, and the church as well as the community as a whole has been called Bat Harbor. It was built of hand-hewn logs, with a huge fireplace of stone. Later, when it was moved a short distance to a better site donated by Mr. Greene Inman, the fireplace was replaced by a wood stove. The peg-leg benches have been exchanged for more comfortable ones, but the walls remain the same. Among those who had a part in the building were William Click, Jeff Click, a Mr. Sprouse, Greene Inman, and Joel A. Brooks. (Data from Betty Jo Winter)

Another Methodist society was established on Cosby Creek at the home of Samuel Broyles by William Garrett; another at the house of William Kelley, seven miles above Newport on the West side of Big Pigeon; also Garrett preached at the home of Maj. James Allen on English Creek; also, at house of Maj. James Ellis, six miles from Newport on Dandridge Road, at Wilsonville; too, at Jess Reeves' home twelve miles East of Newport, after the abandonment of O'Haver's. One Reeves, daughter married Robert H. Lee who became a preacher. Other preachers were William McMahon, A. J. Crawford, Thomas L. Douglass, W. B. Peck, W. P. Kendrick, Robert Paine who became a bishop, and Lewis Garrett, Jr. Thomas Stringfield and John Dever were presiding elders. Nigger Joseph, the slave of Francis J. Carter; Simon Boggers, slave; Thomas, a slave, also preached.

Meanwhile, the slavery question was separating the Church, and the Zion Meeting House became the property of the Methodist Episcopal Church, South. It was used as a place of worship by the Methodist people up to the beginning of the Civil War, and a few sermons were preached in it during and after the war. Some of the prominent members of the M. E. Church, South, were: William C. Roadman, Sr., his wife and daughter; L. D. Porter, his wife, daughter, and sister; John Cameron and wife, Mary Haskins, James Lawson and wife; Lucinda Clark, James R. Allen and wife; Rebeccah Clark, W. D. Rankin and daughters, Reverend Samuel Lotspeich[18] and wife, John P. Taylor and wife; Jacob P. Ragan and wife, Charity Cureton Ragan, Stephen Basinger and his wife, Jane Story Basinger.

18. About the year 1832, Samuel Lotspeich, a Methodist minister, moved to Cocke County, and purchased from William Garrett the farm on which J. H. Susong later resided. Reverend Lotspeich succeeded to a large patrimony, which gave him standing and influence in the community. Notwithstanding, his misfortunes fell thick and fast. First, three of his children while watching the laborers in the fields were forced by an electric storm to take shelter under a sycamore tree on the bank of a sluice of

Some of the pastors of this church were: William Garrett, George Eakin, John Bowman, Creed Fulton, William Milburn, James Mahoney.

Big Pigeon River. As they barely reached their place of supposed safety, an electric current struck the tree, instantly killing the smaller girl and boy, and greatly shocking the larger boy, Benjamin. This calamity was followed by the death of his wife. In the meantime, his oldest daughter, Barbara, married Elisha Moore, and they set up housekeeping in Jefferson County, just across the county line on the north bank of the French Broad River, opposite the Irish Bottom, in Cocke County. Reverend Lotspeich again married. A clash between his second daughter, Jane, and the stepmother, forced the former to live with her married sister.

Elisha Moore inherited a slave named Tom; and the four, himself, wife, sister-in-law, and Tom, composed the family. In June, 1853, the inhabitants along the banks of the French Broad were horrified to hear that Moore, his wife and sister-in-law were brutally murdered on the preceding Friday night, and that their bodies were then lying on the floor in a pool of blood, while Tom was missing. They were buried in the Leadvale cemetery.

By this time, an infuriated mob of armed men were scouring the country for the missing slave. A week later, he was captured, after being shot in the leg, in the middle of the Nolachucky river. He was taken immediately to the scene of his fiendish crime and was made by physical tortures to make the following confession to William Evans in the presence of D. A. Mims:

The house in which the bloody deed was committed had two rooms, one occupied at night by Moore, his wife and sister-in-law, the other by the slave. He stated that on the fatal night he procured an ax, ascended a flight of stairs to the loft, then descended a flight of stairs to his master's bedroom. He sat down at the foot of the stairs, laid the ax across his lap, and meditated over the crime he was about to commit. He thought of how good and kind his master had been to him. His heart failed him and without disturbing the sleepers he returned to his room and bed, where he tossed for about an hour. He thought over how he had bored gimlet holes through the partition that separated the rooms and through which he had watched Miss Lotspeich go to bed, night after night. His brutal courage returned, and he reentered his master's room, where he killed him and his wife before they discovered his identity. This aroused Miss Lotspeich, who began to scream, when he struck her upon the shoulder with the ax, knocked her down, outraged her person, and killed her. Barefooted, he left the house, crossed the French Broad River above the Ten Islands, crossed the Big Pigeon River just above its mouth, passed through the bottom lands of Colonel John Stuart, where he again crossed the French Broad River, where he got something to eat from Peter Kendrick. He again crossed the French Broad River, traveled down the same until he reached the Fork Farm, where he again crossed the river into the Huff bottoms. From this point he went to the house of James Still, a free Negro, in the bend of the Nolachucky River, where he was fed until he was captured.

Within a day or two, the slave was required to stand before the enraged father and brothers and sisters of his master. In accordance with the sentence they pronounced he was taken to a vise and tortured: First, all the bones of his hands and fingers were crushed; and when he was questioned as to the circumstances of the murder, he refused to tell. Thereupon other parts of his body were placed in the vise and smashed, when he stated the facts already mentioned. The only indication of any suffering was the clammy sweat on his brow.

Next, it was announced that he would be burned on the following Thursday at twelve o'clock. He was guarded in the room where he committed the murder and chained to the bloodstained floor. He stated during this time that he did not regret killing Miss Lotspeich, but he might not kill Mr. and Mrs. Moore, were it to be done over again, but was seemingly indifferent to their death. He gave no reason for killing them, but his whole confession disclosed that he was enamored of Miss Lotspeich. Although he was urged to prepare for the event, he seemed more inclined to deride the vengeance of God. On the appointed day, some six thousand people and one thousand slaves assembled. A pen was built around a small persimmon tree. A floor of green, unseasoned logs was laid within the pen, then it was filled around the edges with the richest pine obtainable. At the hour, the culprit was led to the center of the pen, he was handcuffed and chained to the tree, his arms extended above his shoulders and head. He even showed his captors how to bind him and laughed at the bystanders. Two relatives of the deceased stepped forward to light the

The last named had charge during the Civil War and for a few years afterwards.[19]

In 1941, the church boards of the M. E. and Southern Methodist Churches of Newport merged, Dr. L. H. Collum being the first pastor under the merger, with Rev. J. R. Chaney, of the First Methodist, and Rev. John L. Dean, of the Central Methodist were the pastors at this time. An architect, Allen Dryden of Kingsport, Tenn., chose the building of the Central Methodist Church as the new church home. The Committee of First Church included Dr. Fred M. Valentine, Chairman; Mrs. D. C. Williams, Viola Clark, L. B. Shults, H. A. Fancher. The Committee of Central Methodist Church had W. R. Neas, Chairman; Mrs. Ed Walker, Mrs. L. S. Reynolds, Charles Rhyne, Lacey Myers. The Committee on Resolutions included Charles T. Rhyne, Fred M. Valentine, M. O. Allen. Rev. Frank Porter, Rev. W. H. Ragan, Rev. Harrell Russell have pastored the church since its union. Rev. T. Paul Sims—1950.

The comparatively recent Tennessee Valley Authority figures gave the number of Methodist Churches in Cocke County as 22, with 1,087 members and property valued at $116,100. All other churches (not including the Baptist) numbered 23, with 1,298 members, and a $61,600 property value.

WITH THE METHODIST CIRCUIT RIDER ON THE SADDLE-BAG TRAIL IN TENNESSEE.

Contributed by Mrs. C. W. Turpin of Nashville, Tennessee.
(Mrs. Maud Turpin) Knoxville in 1950

This country is under a debt of gratitude to the Methodist circuit rider, the Methodist pioneer preacher whose movements westward kept pace with the movement of the frontier, who shared all the hardships in the life of the frontiersman, while at the same time ministering to that frontiersman's spiritual needs and seeing that his pressing material cares and the hard and grinding poverty of his life did not wholly extinguish the divine fire within his soul.

Facts of history bear out Roosevelt's appraisal of the influence of the circuit rider who followed the saddle-bag trail as civilization moved westward. For his coming into the Cumberland country has had a definite bearing upon the political life, the culture, education, social and religious life of the settlers of Tennessee and their descendants.

As one of the oldest western states, Tennessee early offered every inducement to the hardy settler to penetrate the wilderness beyond the Alleghanies. For here, nature had been lavish with her gifts. And these rich resources of fertile soil, mighty water power, kindly climate, coal-packed mountains, and abundant game, lured the adventurous pioneer to penetrate the dividing mountains and explore the fertile regions of the then, ultimate west.

---

first torch. The Reverend Lotspeich ignited the north corner of the pen, the brother of the deceased man lighted the opposite corner; then other relatives fired the other corners. A breeze fanned the flames into a sheet of fire, encircling the body of the doomed Negro. With one piteous yell, "God help me," his head fell upon his chest. (Story repeated to W. J. McSween by his old black mammy.)

19. Much of the preceding religious history came from the W. J. McSween article, in *Plain Talk*, December 22, 1933.

History does not give the exact date when Tennessee soil first offered sanctuary to the white settler. But it does reveal that when James Robertson first crossed the mountains in 1770, he found cut in the bark of a beech tree, in Boone's Creek Valley, between Jonesboro and Blountville, Daniel Boone's famous autograph: "D Boon cilled a bar Year 1760."

In the spring of 1772, the first civil government ever adopted west of the Alleghany mountains was planted by James Robertson and others on the banks of the Watauga River in East Tennessee.

To this inviting field, a steady stream of emigrants poured, and with them, came the Methodist Circuit Rider. That brave horseman of the wilderness followed the fortunes of the pioneers, sharing their hardships, comforting their sorrows, warning sinners, and striking terror to the lawless bullies who from time to time tried to break up the meeting or beat up the preacher.

The Circuit Rider was on hand at every frontier festivity. Log rollings, barn raising, husking bees, and other gatherings afforded him an opportunity to meet the people and preach the "word," for preaching did not wait upon formal meeting houses and church buildings in Tennessee. Wherever the wilderness people foregathered, there was the circuit rider, mingling with old and young, baptising babes, administering backwoods remedies, for doctors were scarce, and bringing to the settlement news of the outside world which he had learned as he rode his big Tennessee circuit.

He served individual and community needs in various ways. Sometimes it was to lance a "gum-boil" or pull a tooth, often he dispensed pills and powders to "puny" children and "drinlin" old flolks wracked with "misery." He faced with the settlers, the ever present danger from the Indians. And often he had to take the law into his own hands and administer justice with a heavy hand to rowdies. The muscular exhibition of applied Christianity frequently so excited the admiration of the offender that the encounter ended with the backwoods person having prayers with his erstwhile enemy and praying to such good advantage that a new convert was usually added to the "Society," as the Methodist congregations were called in that early day.

Circuit Rider was a natural and appropriate title for the first Methodist preachers in the New World. For the territory they were appointed to cover was called a circuit, and they literally rode it. No wheeled vehicle could penetrate the wilderness or ford the swollen streams. Rain or shine, hot or cold, the circuit rider went his way, until it became a common saying when weather was extremely unfavorable that, "Nobody but the crows and the Methodist Circuit Riders will be out today." Often night overtook him far from any human abode and he would pillow his tired head on his saddle, lying in the open until a new day dawned and he resumed his arduous, but never monotonous round.

East Tennessee was the first section of the state to be penetrated by the Circuit Rider, and Jeremiah Lambert was the first Methodist Circuit Rider regularly appointed to a charge west of the Alleghaney Mountains, being sent to serve the Holston Circuit in 1783. The first Methodist conference beyond the mountains was held at Keyswood in 1788, the locality being recorded by Asbury in his journal as Tennessee. Here the conversion and baptism of General William Russell, of Revolutionary fame and his wife, known as Madam Russell, because of their prominence and social prestige was a high light of this session. Madam Russell, who was a sister of Patrick Henry, became one of the saints of American Methodism.

To Benjamin Ogden, 22, a soldier of the Revolutionary War, belongs the honor of introducing Methodism into Middle Tennessee. The coming of the first circuit rider to Nashville occurred in 1787, when the town was only three years old. It is thrilling to imagine that scene when the young circuit rider, wearing the broad-brimmed hat and jeans characteristic of that day, rode on horseback, astride large and well filled saddle-bags, into the new settlement to begin his work in the rough building which was used at that time for a "courthouse, a free church and public meetings."

There was no organ or church choir, but the circuit rider found a congregation eager to hear the "word" and to join lustily in the singing as he "lined out" the hymns. Those early Tennesseans traveled long distances to hear their new circuit rider. Whole families came, down to the smallest children. Many of the young men and women came on foot carrying their shoes and stockings rolled up in a cotton handkerchief until they came near the meeting house, when they would turn aside, soon to appear in the congregation with feet arrayed as "neat as a pin."

The Methodists were the first to erect a church building in the growing city on the Cumberland. Of course it was not called a Church, but a Meeting House. It was a stone building erected in 1790. It stood on the public square and not far was the jail, with a whipping post and pillory hard by.

Referring to this meeting house in his daily Journal, Bishop Asbury wrote under the date of Oct. 19, 1800 that he met here a congregation of "not less than one thousand in and out of the stone church, which, if floored, ceiled and glazed, would be a grand church." It was here that James Robertson, founder of Nashville, and his wife Charlotte, were admitted to membership in the Methodist Society.

In the long list of circuit riders whose life and work shed luster on the Methodist movement in Tennessee, the name of Francis Asbury stands at the front. An Irish imigrant, he came to the New World in 1771 to be John Wesley's assistant on the big circuit designated simply as, "AMERICA."

Asbury had cast his lot with the colonies during the Revolutionary War and was a firm believer in the principles of Americanism. It was he who established the circuit system and kept the preachers on the move. The itinerant system he started has been the distinguished mark of Methodism from that day until now.

Up to 1783 all the preaching in America had been done in connection with the established Church of England. But complaint arose throughout America that their unordained preachers could not perform the offices of the Church, such as baptism, administration of the Holy Communion, marriage and burial rites. This situation irked the independent early Americans, who being no longer subject to the British Crown, saw no point in being under British rule ecclesiastically.

Asbury presented this case to Wesley, who ordained to the office of Bishop, one Thomas Coke and sent him to America to perform a similar office for Francis Asbury and set up an independent Church in America. But Asbury, sympathetic with the spirit of democracy rampant in

America, refused to assume the office of Bishop unless officially elected to that position by a popular vote of the preachers who had gathered that Christmas day 1784 at Lovely Lane Meeting House in the City of Baltimore. Thus he became the First American Bishop (Methodist) although not a native of this country. His election to episcopal office only increased Asbury's circuit riding efforts. Soon he became known as the "Prophet of the Long Road."

Asbury's trail led often to the big Holston and Cumberland circuits, which embraced the entire State of Tennessee and portions of neighboring states. Middle Tennessee especially, as a theater of early Methodist activity, was frequently visited by the horseback-riding Bishop; and this section of the State is the locale of many historic shrines of primitive Methodism, as planted by the circuit rider.

One of these shrines, Strothers Meeting House, where Asbury held the first Conference West of the Cumberland Mountains in 1802, has been removed from its original site in Sumner county and rebuilt on the campus of Scarritt College at Nashville. After being used as a place of worship for nearly sixty years, the old Meeting House passed into other hands, and for nearly seventy years it served as a corn-crib. However, the owner built a large barn over it to protect the logs from decay. In the removal to Nashville, a few years ago, the original logs were found to be in good repair. At the rear of the building a long window has been inserted, in a place the length and width of a log which was left open in the original building.

Another noted shrine connected with the circuit riding days of Bishop Asbury is Liberty Hill, twelve miles from Nashville, where a notable conference session was held in 1808. This was the home of the Rev. Green Hill, a local preacher, at whose former home in North Carolina, the first annual conference of the Methodist Episcopal Church in America was held in 1785. Liberty Hill is still standing and is in fair state of preservation.

Fountain Head Church in Sumner County, housed the first session of the Tennessee Conference in 1812, while the conference session held at the Bethlehem Church in Wilson County, near Lebanon, Tennessee, Oct. 20, 1815 is memorable as the last Conference attended by Bishop Asbury, who died March 1816.

Other centers of Methodist memory belonging to this region are the McKendree family burying ground in Sumner County near the town of Portland, and the residence of Bishop Joshua Soule, author of the constitution of American Methodism, who died in Nashville in 1867. All these shrines have been appropriately marked.

William McKendree was another Tennessee circuit rider who came into the office of Bishop by way of the saddle-bag trail. He was the first native American to become a Bishop of the Methodist Church. McKendree's activity began in Tennessee in 1801, a period that marked a new era in the West, for at this time the Camp Meetings began their unique and far reaching work.

McKendree was appointed presiding elder of the Western Conference, which embraced all of East and Middle Tennessee, Southwestern Virginia, Kentucky and a portion of Ohio. He was the first person in America to fill the office of presiding elder. He was later presiding elder of the Cumberland District, embracing nine circuits, one of which was in Missouri.

He had to travel a distance of 1,500 miles in order to cover his district. The last annual Conference McKendree attended was held at Lebanon, Tennessee, November 1834, and the last sermon he preached was in McKendree Church, Nashville, in the same month.

Peter Cartwright, a circuit rider who spent much of his ministerial life in the big district that included the state of Tennessee, was an eccentric person who gained notoriety on account of his ready humor, physical courage, and fighting propensities. It is related of him that while preaching during a conference session at Nashville, Tennessee, General Andrew Jackson entered the Church. The regular pastor who occupied the pulpit with Cartwright, flattered by the presence of so distinguished a person, pulled a Cartwright's coat and whispered, "That is General Jackson." Whereupon Cartwright replied audibly, "And who is General Jackson; if he don't get his soul converted, God will condemn him as quick as he would a Guinea Negro." Contrary to expectation, General Jackson, instead of horsewhipping the bold circuit rider, sought him out ot shake his hand, and invited him to have dinner with him at the Hermitage.

Cartwright served under both Asbury and McKendree, being ordained Elder by the latter at Liberty Hill, Tennessee, October 4, 1808. He prided himself on being a backwoods preacher and took delight in denouncing "citified" ways, fashion, and anything smacking of pretension.

Another noted character of those lively times who deserves mention because of his meteoric career in Tennessee, was Lorenzo Dow. "Crazy Dow," he was often called. He flourished about the year 1804. In spite of his rudeness, his fearless and powerful preaching endeared him to many. He preached often in Knoxville, Maryville, Sevierville and Nashville, wherever he could find a place, often renting a "grog-house" if he could do no better.

John Granade, variously known as the wild man, poet, preacher, was another unique character who became prominent in Tennessee during the circuit riding era. His special forte was describing the glories of Heaven so vividly that the enraptured listener would imagine himself to be walking the golden streets of the New Jerusalem; and he portrayed the torments of hell in a way to cause a sinner's hair to stand on end with terror. His colorful career was brief, lasting only three years.

The camp meetings which characterized the religious life of the frontier were the result of the zeal of the circuit rider. They were marked by dramatic scenes and emotionalism reached a high tide in a physical manifestation known as the "jerks." The scene of these meetings was usually the brush arbor, a rude shed covered with branches of trees. There was a dirt floor, spread with straw or sawdust. The rude backless benches were made of wood, usually with the bark left on. The shed was lighted by tallow candles fastened to posts. Blazing pine knots outside the shed cast weird, flickering shadows on men and women moving about in praying groups, or congregated around the "mourners' bench" at the front.

If the Methodist circuit rider gained fame as the Horseman of the Wilderness, no less will posterity remember him as Christianity's Troubador, for he found singing a powerful aid in his work. Called in derision, "those singing Methodists," their songs typed the gospel the circuit riders preached. Theology, doctrine, worship, repentance, hope, despair,

Presbyterian Church

happiness, the glories of heaven and the horrors of hell were all portrayed in the hymns and spirituals of that day.

Before the days of Meeting Houses it was customary for the circuit rider when he made a preaching appointment at the home of a settler to pass the word along for the "Blacks" to come early and have a "singing" before preaching began. They never forgot their duty to the colored people who were also doing their part to help conquer the wilderness.

No one ever accused a Methodist Circuit Rider of entering the ministry for material gain. Up until 1800 the salary of all preachers, Bishops and Circuit riders alike, was sixty dollars a year; then the amount was raised to eighty dollars and a number of years later to one hundred dollars, which munificent sum called from Bishop Asbury a solemn warning against the danger of the preachers becoming worldly minded. In the early days, as today, the preacher's salary was seldom paid in full.

The story of the rise and growth of Methodism in the wilderness of Tennessee is one of the most picturesque in American life. The coming of the Methodist Circuit rider into that far western land is a romance in the preaching of the gospel not excelled in the Christian era.

They did their work in a primitive way among a primitive people. They were men of heroic faith who feared neither privation nor suffering as they traveled the saddlebag trail through the trackless forests of Tennessee in a time that required the fearless courage, devotion and energy of youth for religious pioneering. Their work left as distinct marks upon the Christian world as those made by the Puritans.

In the van of the onward march of civilization they came—pioneers of the Cross and flaming evangels of light in the New Land!

The Presbyterian Church

Presbyterianism was later in Cocke County than in any other Tennessee County that adjoins it, and it never had a strong hold here. The County was within the bounds of, first, the Abingdon Presbytery from 1786; of Union Presbytery, Greeneville Presbytery and the Presbytery of French Broad, which was organized at Pisgah on November 11, 1825. Pisgah Church was established in 1809 by the Reverend Doctor Robert Hardin, and apparently revived at Newport in 1823 by the same minister.

From a very early date the settlements along the French Broad and Pigeon valleys were visited and preached to by Presbyterian ministers. Meetings were held in groves and private homes; and after a time, the old courthouse was used, and finally, Anderson Academy at old Newport. On August 16, 1823, the organization of Pisgah Church was perfected at Oldtown, with Reverend Isaac Anderson, D. D., the minister in charge and he preached from Psalms 48:12-14, which reads as follows:

Walk about Zion and go round about her; tell the towers thereof; mark ye well her bulwarks, consider her palaces, that ye may tell it to generations following. For this God is our God, forever and ever; he will be our guide even unto death.

The first ruling elders were Francis Baldridge, James Alexander, and Murdoch McSween. Among the twelve original members were Murdoch McSween and his wife, Margaret Jackson, Francis Haldridge and his wife, James Alexander and his wife, Mrs. Elizabeth Fine, Mrs. Alexander Smith and Mrs. Margaret Stuart.

The first Sunday School, organized in Cocke County by a Scotchman by the name of Caulder at some location on Big Creek, at an unknown date, might have been a Scotch Presbyterian one.[20]

Until 1837, all church meetings were held in Anderson Academy, one mile west of Oldtown. Dr. Robert Hardin had charge of the church until 1824; Rev. Gideon White, until 1830; Rev. William Minnis ˜and Nathaniel Hood until 1853.[21] About 1832, under the joint labors of these two men, sixty new members were received in a revival season.

About 1833, Abraham Fine was elected and ordained a Ruling Elder. Prior to that, G. W. Crookshanks held the same office. In 1835, R. B. DeWitt was elected Ruling Elder, and ordained by Rev. N. Hood. In 1836, John McSween, the Pisgah Presbyterian Church[22] was erected in Oldtown, and was used until 1860. It was a large frame building, on the South side of road leading from Newport to the old Muster field, and immediately in front of the house of Rev. Tillman Swaggerty, colored. Built on a steep slope, the rock underpinning at the east end entrance was five feet high. A colonial porch, the full length of the east end, was reached by flights of steps from either side. Daniel McSween, then a young architect, assisted in the planning and builting of this church. Among the influential citizens connected with the church at this time were General A. E. Smith, John Reynolds, Isaac R. Rogers, William H. DeWitt, Francis B. Howell, David Dobson, Alex S. Mathes, William Wilson, Daniel McSween, Harris DeWitt, Samuel McSween, Samuel Silson (Tilson?), Allen McLain, Alfred Cochron, Col. William Jack, Samuel Haskins. Among the women worshippers in the early years were: Elizabeth Ward, Sarah Ward, Louisa Haskins, Nancy McSween, Malvian Cochran, Mary Stuart, Julia P. Smith, Sarah Wilson, Harriet DeWitt, Mary Porter, Julia

---

20. Alexander Caulder owned some wonderful dishes that had belonged to his sister who was drowned in a shipwreck on the Ohio River after she had made a safe voyage with her brother across the Atlantic Ocean. The dishes were among the few things saved from the wreck. This old Scotchman cherished them so much that he did not part with them until age and hunger forced him to sell one at a time, for which he received five dollars. Jetta Boyer Lee tells the story of the "royal dishes" as related by Alexander Caulder.

Lord Gladstone and Lord Grant were East Indian merchants, the former the son of the grand old man of Scotland, William E. Gladstone, and often visited each other. Lady Grant's ladies Maid was a sister to Alexander Caulder. On one of these visits, Lady Grant told Lady Gladstone of the approaching wedding of her maid. Lady Gladstone, with a family of boys, had a set of dishes, a few pieces of which were broken. She gave this maid these dishes. Jetta Lee has one or more of these, Henry Penland bought some of them and also Dr. Richard Smith.

21. It is said that members of a prominent family were dismissed from church for looking through a window at some young people dancing.

22. An amusing incident is related by McSween, in connection with this church in 1841. When James K. Polk and James C. Jones (Lean Jimmy) were candidates for Governor of Tennessee at their Newport appointment, the Presbyterian Church was selected as the place for their discussion. An enormous crowd heard the debate, which was opened by Polk, and about the time of his preoration the underpinning at the east end of the house gave way. The building fell to the ground with a crash; the doors and windows were smashed to pieces. The terrified crowd, led by Lean Jimmy, rushed out of the doors and windows, leaving Polk standing alone in the pulpit. The crowd at once repaired to the Zion Church on the opposite hill, where Polk mounted the rostrum, and at once twitted Jones with cowardice for leaving the building. Jones retorted that the crowd was with him and would be with him on the Ides of November, which prophecy came true.

Langhorne, Elizabeth Jack, Mary Dobson, Mary Howell, Mary Fine, Hetty Jarnagin, Mary Jarnagin, Katherine Allen McSween, Delilah Gorman, Lucinda Dawson and Sarah Dawson.

Gen. Alexander Evans Smith was ordained Ruling Elder July 23, 1843, serving until his death, June 6, 1871. In 1850, Rev. W. E. Caldwell succeeded Reverend Minnis as Pastor. After one year, Rev. N. Hood again took charge. He was succeeded by Rev. Wm. H. Smith, known as "Uncle Harvey," who was pastor for twelve and a half years. Then the church remained vacant for two and one half years. The last members to worship at Oldtown were Uncle Harvey Smith and Mary Wilson Baer, known as "Grandma Baer." Both lived to an advanced age, Uncle Harvey having preached on his ninetieth birthday.

In 1858, a new house was built in what was the village of Clifton, near the residence of Tom S. Gorman, who later became Ruling Elder. It was a frame building, 32 by 52 feet, in a grove of stately oaks. The remains of many former citizens, among them William Jack, A. E. Smith, Abraham Fine, and H. H. Baer, rest in the old cemetery surrounding it. The Church was dedicated on August 27, 1859. The Pisgah congregation worshiped here until 1897, when they moved into their present building on McSween Avenue.

During the Civil War, the church was weakened, but a revival beginning on Friday before the first Sabbath in June, 1867, led by Rev. Harvey Smith and Rev. George A. Caldwell, resulted in the addition of thirty-five members. During the period from 1868 to 1871, the Rev. Harvey Smith again had charge of the church. During this time, T. S. Gorman, James H. Robinson, Samuel Henry were Ruling Elders. Samuel Wilson was also elected deacon.

In 1871, Rev. James H. Martin supplied and during this period John E. Williams and L. Melville Smith were ordained elders, while A. S. Fine and W. L. DeWitt were ordained deacons.

Following Rev. Martin, between the period of 1871 to 1897, Rev. A. C. Snoddy, John M. Rhea, J. P. Gammon, R. F. King, D. F. Smith, J. G. McFerrin and Sidney Doak served as pastors.

In 1876, William McSween and W. R. Smith were made Ruling Elders, and C. L. Peterson and W. H. Baer were ordained deacons.

In 1886, during the pastorate of J. G. McFerrin, J. H. Fagala was ordained Ruling Elder. In November, 1894, a congregational meeting considered the building of a new church. A committee of W. B. Robinson, J. H. Fagala, and W. G. Snoddy purchased the lot.

In 1896, W. H. Baer and DeWitt Smith were ordained Ruling Elders, and Dr. W. G. Snoddy and George W. Willis were made deacons. A building committee of J. R. Fagala, W. G. Snoddy and Barclay Leith was given the power to sell old building and apply funds on new structure. For about a year, the congregation worshipped over the building owned by G. F. Smith, known as Burnett & Baer Hall, and held some of their regular church services in the M. E. Church. In 1897, the cornerstone was laid, but it was dedicated in 1901 by Rev. Harvey Smith, using the same text used in the organization of the church in 1823. In 1898, the name of the church was changed from Pisgah to Newport Presbyterian, and Rev. H. H. Newman became pastor. In 1899, Rev. O. G. Jones took charge until 1900. Among the new members received at this time were Mrs.

Hiram Ruble (Lucile Robinson) and Mrs. Kyle (Nelle Young); also Mrs. Kenneth Runnion (Elsie Robinson). Professor Alexander Paxton was ordained as Ruling Elder. In 1901, Rev. J. R. McRee became pastor, serving until 1905.

Early in 1905, Rev. J. S. Black became pastor. During this period, George W. Willis, Dr. W. G. Snoddy, and Dr. R. C. Smith were ordained Ruling Elders; Messrs. George C. Duncan, Jno. M. Jones, W. D. McSween, H. C. Alexander, and Dr. E. G. E. Anderson, were ordained deacons. Doctor Black served for twelve years. Since his death, Rev. W. B. Doyle and Rev. O. G. Clinger have served the church. During these pastorates, N. L. Dennis, H. C. Alexander, Porter Barnett, Gordon Woodward, Hubert Anderson and W. L. Pickard have been ordained as Elders; H. C. Ruble, James Black, W. H. Masters, S. H. Rea, L. P. Robinson and James Morton, deacons.

The additional Sunday School rooms and kitchen were built in 1931, and just prior an organ was installed in memory of Dr. J. S. Black. About this time, Dr. N. L. Dennis, D. S., was called to the ministry. One other minister, Rev. Allen Maser has done mission work in the mountains. During the pastorate, Rev. O. G. Clinger, forty-six members were added to the church.

In 1926, Rev. D. C. Amick, D. D., took charge of the church. During this period a new manse was built and a large number of new members added. In 1931, a chapel was built at Mary Andrews Chapel. In 1932, the Newport Church took over the full supervision of the Presbyterian mission in Cocke County.[23] Dr. Amick and Dr. Charles C. Cowsert followed as pastors. Dr. Daniel A. Bowers is pastor in 1950.

The Quakers

In the first three decades of the 1800's there was a sprinkling of Quakers (Friends) in the County, but by no means as many as in Greene, Jefferson or Blount Counties. In 1834, they, joined by some Presbyterians and a few Methodists, petitioned the Tennessee Constitutional Convention of that year to incorporate in the Constitution a provision for the gradual emancipation of slaves. McGauhey, who represented Cocke and Greene in the Convention, supported the measure. Whether the Quakers were numerous enough to form a congregation or "meeting" is not now ascertainable. If not they were attached to meetings in Greene or Jefferson. (Judge Williams)

---

23. A large part of information furnished by Reverend Amick.

The Industrial Development of Cocke County

It is easy to understand why Cocke County was one of the earliest counties formed. When the early settlers stood upon the misty mountain tops and gazed down upon the fertile valleys that spread themselves between the three great rivers, it was love at first sight, and they settled in this land of promise. The majestic mountains protected them from the outside world and from the cold winds of winter, provided meat for food, and warm skins for clothing. The fertile valleys provided abundant crops of corn, wheat, and vegetables.

Through decades of groping experiment, Cocke County citizens evolved a tremendous success in the industrial development of their County's resources. This development of Cocke County began before the birth of the County, October 9, 1797. Its basic industry then and still is that of agriculture. No county in Tennessee has more productive soil. Thousands of acres of rich bottom lands, along the banks of the three streams that form the headwaters of the Tennessee River, make up much of the triangle of almost five hundred square miles, or 237,280 acres of its area. One-half of the County is mountains, and only 126,711 acres are in cultivation.

The first effort at the industrialization of Cocke County was made by the Birdseye Brothers, Ezekiel and Victory, assisted by Judge Jacob Peck, in the 1830's and 40's.

From various County and State reports, we find in 1830, 150 people lived in Newport. In 1851, Cocke County had 1295 dwellings, and the same number of families. The free population consisted of 3712 white males, 3790 white females, 37 colored males, 42 colored females—a total of 5781; the slave population, 619. In the next census Newport's population was 347; the County's, 14,308. In 1890, Newport had 1630 people.

The average assessed value of land in Cocke County in 1900 was $6.22 per acre; manufacturing establishments in the County, 73; capital employed $550,893; wages paid during 1900, $42,700; number of farms, 2,534; number of acres, 107,441; value of buildings, $109,570; value of livestock, $518,115; value of products not fed to stock, $737,800; amount paid for farm labor, $32,750; total value of land improvements except buildings $1,873,810. In 1913, the population was 19,399.[1]

Cocke County had a population of 20,722 in 1920 and an assessed valuation of taxable property in 1921 of $11,402,158. The number of farms was 2,800; railway mileage, 48. The staple products were corn, wheat, grass, livestock. Newport's population was 2,753. There were several churches and schools, two weekly newspapers, two banks, cotton and flour mills. It had the largest canning establishment in the South.[2] Its scholastic population was 6,652; number of high schools, 1; elemen-

1. *Handbook of Tennessee* by Thomas H. Paine, Commissioner of Agriculture.
2. Austin P. Foster, *Counties of Tennessee.*

tary schools, 86. Cocke County's population in 1930 was 21,775, of which number, 15,000 were engaged in agriculture. White people made up 98.1 per cent of the farm operators; 1,724 of number were full owners; 298, part owners; six, managers; with 1,266 tenants and 599 croppers. In the ninety-six counties in Tennessee, Cocke County took the following rank: 34th in the number of farms in 1935; 53rd in the value of farm products, 1935; 57th, in acreage for corn; 21st in tobacco, in 1934 (1,066,477 pounds); 60th in production of Irish potatoes in 1934; 79th, in sweet potatoes; 17th in wheat production; 7th in production of vegetables; 36th in cattle of all ages in 1930; 58th in swine, in 1935; 39th in sheep and lambs; 26th in colts under two years old; 27th in production of chickens in 1930; 41st in dairy products sold; 15th in forestry products sold. The average yield of corn for 1930 was 23.4 bushels per acre; the average of wheat, 9.4 bushels per acre in 1935.[3]

Cocke County's cultivated crops with acreages were: corn, 25,421; tobacco, 1,845; sweet corn, 1,500; Irish potatoes, 472; tomatoes, 219; cabbage, 209; sweet potatoes, 166; lima beans, 107; carrots, 50; asparagus, 50; beets, 42; watermelons, 31; turnip greens, 20; kidney beans; spinach, 10.

Of livestock, in 1930, there were 1,820 horses, 2,922 mules, 12,384 cattle, 9,216 hogs, and 116,726 chickens and other fowl. Cocke County produced then 1,804,886 gallons of milk and 398,665 pounds of butter. Her 1,914 farms produced 24,005 bushels apples; 493 bushels cherries; 7,073 bushels peaches; 594 bushels pears; 982 bushels plums and prunes; 18,142 pounds grapes; 105 pounds pecans; 6,566 quarts blackberries; 236 quarts raspberries; 7,285 quarts strawberries. She also had 2,834 hives of bees, producing 26,488 pounds of honey.

Cocke County's leading crops were corn 25,421 acres, producing 576,370 bushels; hay 11,824 acres, 13,434 bales, wheat 5,870 acres, 50,703 bushels; vegetables 2,568 acres, $167,002; Irish potatoes 472 acres; sweet potatoes 166 acres; tobacco, 1,845 acres, 1,608,280 pounds.

Forests cut for home and sale was $520,819; chickens and eggs produced, $240,470; other poultry, $139,000; dairy products, $318,846; cattle on farms, $509,780; hogs, $101,341.

In 1934, the County tax rate was $2.45 per $100; bonded indebtedness, $1,065,208; Newport tax rate, $2.50 per $100; bonded indebtedness, $264,432; county assessment valuation, $6,066,050; railroad and other utilities, $1,956,386; privately owned railroad cars, $37,383; personalty, $230,885; a total valuation of $8,290,704 and a total tax of $215,067.

Taxes were paid by the following industries: Southern Railway, Southeastern Express Company, Fruit Growers, Pullman Company, Union Tank Car Co., Postal Telegraph and Cable, Southern Bell Telephone & Telegraph Co., Tennessee Public Service, Western Union Telegraph Co., Skyline Stages, Inc., Etherton Transfer Co., Motor Express Co., Mathes Coach Line.

The area of the County is 458 square miles, with a population of 24,083 in 1940. The assessed value of property (1938) was $7,651,000; the tax rate (1938) was $2.52; per capita bonded debt (1937-8) $73.80; per capita expenditures (1937-39) $21.25; retail sales (1935), $1,924,000;

3. County Agent's Report in *Plain Talk*, January 22, 1937.

road mileage stage highway, 71.63 miles; value farm produce (1930) $4,141,000.

In 1944, the county assessment was approximately $7,500,000; rate, $2.60 per $100.[4]

The Coming of the Railroad

"In pioneer days the people hauled their goods in wagons from Richmond and Baltimore and Philadelphia. When they went after their supplies, they generally took loads of produce, the sale of which helped to reduce the expenses of the trips, which to Baltimore was said to be six or seven dollars.[5]

The same route was followed for twenty-five or thirty years. The merchandise retailed in East Tennessee is purchased chiefly in Philadelphia and New York, shipped to Baltimore and wagoned thence through the Valley of Virginia, a distance of 450 to 650 miles, or shipped from place of purchase to Richmond, thence boated up the James River to Lynchburg and thence wagoned a distance of from 200 to 400 miles.

The price of freight from New York to Baltimore and Richmond is about the same carriage by wagon from Baltimore to Knoxville, 500 miles is six dollars and fifty cents per hundred weight, being more than twenty two cents per ton, per mile.

Freight for boat loading from Richmond to Lynchburg is thirty cents per hundred and wagonage from there to Knoxville, distance 320 miles, is three dollars and fifty cents per hundred, making a difference of thirty percentum in favor of the Richmond and Lynchburg over the Baltimore and Valley Route.

A house in Jonesboro lost six hundred dollars in the expense of transporting their supplies this year in consequence of taking the Baltimore and Valley instead of the Richmond and Lynchburg."[6]

The first effort toward improving navigation in the Tennessee River basin was by the General Assembly of Tennessee on November 10, 1801, when an Act was passed incorporating the Nolichucky River Company, a joint stock company, whose capital should consist of 1,200 shares at ten dollars each. Such shares to be first offered to the citizens of Washington, Greene, and Jefferson Counties for a year before outsiders were privileged to subscribe. The subscription books of Washington County were to be kept by John McAlister at Jonesboro and by George Gillespie and Robert Love elsewhere in the County.

The object of this County was to improve the navigation of the Nolichucky River between the lower end of Benjamin Brown's island in the County of Washington and the confluence of the Nolichucky and the French Broad, by maintaining a clear channel, in every place not less than eighteen inches deep or twenty feet broad.

As compensation, the company was granted permission to erect three Custom Houses for the collection of tolls levied on all crafts, boats, rafts,

4. *Newport Times*, February 14, 1940.

5. Copied from Paul H. Fink, in "The Railroad comes to Jonesboro," a paper read to the East Tennessee Historical Society. See also F. A. Michaus "Travels to the West of the Allegheny Mountains." Also R. G. Thwaites "Travels West of the Alleghenies," pages 266-270.

6. According to William Rives in a letter from the *Railway Advocate*, Rogersville, Tennessee, August 20, 1831.

or floats passing by. The rates ranged from fifty cents to one dollar per ton, depending on the distance traversed.[7]

The Farmers Journal of Jonesboro on November 14, 1831, carried an article about meeting and discouraged the calling of Federal government for aid. Both the Tennessee and the Virginia Legislatures refused to subscribe for stock, which "threw cold water on the idea," and the hope of extending the railroad to Tennessee was abandoned. However, this did not kill the idea or lessen the need of the people for a way to ship their produce and to bring to them needed supplies.

Following rumors of the agitation for building of a railroad from the East into Tennessee, a charter was granted by the Legislature in the winter of 1831 to the Knoxville and Southern Railroad Company.[8]

The following September, a convention was called to meet at Asheville, North Carolina, to boost the plan. A dispatch from Knoxville, telling of the appointment of delegates appeared in the Jonesboro papers, but this road failed to materialize too.

In October, 1835, a meeting was held at Jonesboro, where six hundred citizens, mostly of Washington County, signed a memorial for presentation to the Legislature. This paper stressed the need for transportation facilities, showing the advantages other states were deriving from the Railroad and urged the Tennessee General Assembly to take suitable action to insure Tennessee's participation in this new prosperity.

These sturdy pioneers did not sit idly by and wait for the Assembly to do something about transportation, but they kept busy trying to get the rivers in shape for navigation by removing dams, and doing other constructive work. An allotment for this work was as follows: for the Holston, East of Knoxville, including North Fork, $24,500; for the Nolichucky, $12,000; for the French Broad, $11,500.[9]

At the same time an effort was being made for an improved "vehickle" road to connect with the proposed Charleston and Cincinnati Railroad. This was known as the Jonesboro, Greeneville and Newport Turnpike Company. The plan of this company was to authorize capital of $200,000 with which to construct a paved or graveled road from Elizabethton via Jonesboro and Greeneville to Newport, or to connect with the railroad at a nearer point. The extension from Jonesboro to Virginia by way of Blountville was also considered. The roadbed was to be not less than thirty feet wide, with toll gates each five miles, but this plan was terminated at the paper stage.

The first railroad survey made in Cocke County is said to have come in to Clifton (present Newport) by way of Caney Branch and Parrottsville section, parallel with the Old Stage Road to Washington. It is said that some construction work was done in the Caney Branch community, and it is the author's opinion that this survey must have been made by the James and New River Railroad Company, or the James and Tennessee River Railroad Company which met in Knoxville, June 27, 1841, and in Abington, August 25, 1841, with representatives from sixteen counties present. A commission of thirteen was appointed to correspond with counties in both Tennessee and Virginia relative to the construction of a railroad through this area.

7. Laws of State of Tennessee, page 297, Knoxville, Tennessee, 1801.
8. Private Acts of 1831.
9. Record from Minutes of Washington County Court, 1837.

Soon after this, the Hiwassee Railroad reorganized under the name of the East Tennessee and Georgia Railway and began construction of a road extending from Knoxville southward with connections farther South and West.

At the same time, the Virginia and Tennessee Railroad Company was at work, grading and placing rails from Lynchburg to Bristol, which, if and when completed, would leave but one hundred thirty miles across upper East Tennessee that would complete the connection by rail of the manufacturing centers of the North and East and the rural areas of the South and the West.

The people were eager to take advantage of this opportunity. In May, 1847, they held an enthusiastic meeting in Rogersville, Tennessee, where a "call" was issued for a general convention to meet in Greeneville, July 5, 1847. Between the above May and July dates, two meetings were held in the Jonesboro Courthouse where plans were discussed, statistics gathered and delegates chosen for the Greeneville Convention.

From ten Tennessee counties surrounding Greene came the delegates to the Greeneville convention. Three Virginia counties were represented. There were two distinct factions present, one that wanted all efforts concentrated on improving the navigation of Holston, Nolichucky and the French Broad Rivers, while the other faction was for railroad development. After three full days of discussion, a compromise was reached in the following resolution by Colonel Floyd.

Resolved that in the opinion of this Convention, $250,000 ought to be appropriated by our Legislature to be applied in the improvement of the Holston and French Broad Rivers, with a view to Steam Boat Navigation.

Resolved that in the opinion of the Convention, the interests of East Tennessee and Virginia require the construction of a railroad from Knoxville to Virginia (now in progress) through East Tennessee between Holston and Nolichucky Rivers so as to unite Alabama, South Carolina and Tennessee with Virginia and the North.[10]

Accordingly, two such bills were presented to the General Assembly. The Navigation Bill failed, but the Railroad Bill passed January 27, 1848. The railroad was approaching, but so far away that it took it practically twenty years to arrive in Cocke County. All agree on the date but different stories have been told as to its approach. It is the author's opinion that the two most convincing stories are true and that one has reference to the time when local people owned the road and the other refers to the time when the first train was brought in after the local people had sold their interests to the Cincinnati, Cumberland Gap and Charleston Railroad Company.

Mrs. Lou Miller Robinson relates that a number of local citizens organized a company to promote the construction of a railroad, and most of these became stockholders. The company elected Alexander Smith as the President of the Company. The first engineer was Thomas Swatts; the first fireman, Esau Mantooth, grandfather of Caywood Mantooth, the present postmaster. Captain Taylor of Near Morristown was superintendent, supervisor and conductor; Edd O. Tate was the first mail agent.

10. From 19th Annual Report of the President and Directors of the Stock Holders of the East Tennessee and Virginia Railroad, 1858, the address of Major John McGaughy.

Mrs. Robinson describes the celebration the day the train was to arrive in Clifton; the table for the picnic dinner sat where the depot now stands. It was in late summer when corn was in full "roasting ear" stage. People began to arrive in Clifton at the break of day to see the Iron Horse puff into the village. They lined up along the track on each side from the present depot to what is now the County Poor Farm, which was then the Major Robinson Home. The weary crowd was finally rewarded by the rumbling in the distance. A Negro man who had been a slave of the Robinsons heard a white woman remark as she saw the engine coming around the bend, "That lead horse must be awful tired, the way he is a puffing and a blowing." As the train came nearer, many of the Negroes and the whites became so frightened "they broke and ran with all their might, smack-dab across the cornfield" and knocked off more than wagon load of roasting ears in their flight to a nearby hillside. Rachel O'Dell told friends that she "rid her mare to see the train come in and the critter cavorted and cavorted so much she was scared she would be thrown onto the flat car." The train had a flat car and a coach on which and in which many people sat on their way to Clifton for the celebration.

Only two men were killed in the building of the railroad in Cocke County, and both fell from the Leadvale bridge, one drowning and the other breaking his neck.

"We the undersigned Stockholders in the Cincinnati, Cumberland Gap and Charleston Rail Road hereby constitute and appoint James R. Allen our attorney in fact to represent and vote the number of shares of stock set opposite our names in the meeting of stockholders to be holden at Morristown on the 15th May 1857:

Stockholders' Names	Shares	Stockholders' Names	Shares
J. R. Allen	25	Lemuel Watters	2
John Brown	10	Thos. J. Revis	2
John C. Clark	20	Neese Benjamin	2
F. D. Clark	20	John Carson	4
Wm. H. De Witt	12	L. D. Crage [Craige?]	8
Wm. Holland	8	M. A. Roadman	10
Samuel Lotspeech	20	Savid Susong	10
James Murray	4	Malcolm McNabb	10
Wm. McNabb	4	George L. Thomas	5
W. F. Morris	5	Alex. Stuart	14
L. D. Porter	5	A. Jones	5
Wm. R. Ray	20	D. R. Gorman	22
Andrew Ramsey	20	A. Hamiletton [?]	8
Stephen Huff	25	James Kilgore	4
Jehu Stokely	10	John Kenyon	2
Americus Jones	4	T. S. Gorman	40
Daniel Hedrick	2	D. Ward Stuart	10
D. D. Brooks	8	Jobe Parrott	10
N. W. Easterly	8	Rhote Allen	8
Thos. Chrest	4	James Hickey	10
Jas. Hurley	8		

On the back of this list is a notation, along with innumerable figuring. The notation is: "J. W. Patton and Compy, 4,500 shares. Vote to be cast by 3 largest stockholders Cocke, Jefferson and Grangers County."

[In copying all information I am careful to give the spelling as given, regardless of its letter arrangement.]

The local stockholders lost most all they had invested. The road went into the hands of a receivership composed of William and Robert McFarland, two attorneys who sold the company's interest to Cincinnati,

Cumberland Gap and Charleston Railroad Company, which was known as the C. C. C. Railroad Company and Robert McFarland Jones was appointed conductor.[11]

The second version comes from Mrs. Lillie Jones Duncan, daughter of Robert McFarland Jones, and the big difference in the stories is that the latter is placed at Christmas time.

"Old Beeswax," a correspondent to one of the county papers, said in his letter last week, "I'll bet there will be more people here on the 28th to see the oldest engine than were here to greet 'Old Buncombe' on its first visit to this place."[12]

As early as July 4, 1836, a Railroad Convention composed of delegates from all the Northern states, Maryland, the Southern states, met in Knoxville, Tennessee, and Robert T. Hayne of South Carolina was elected President. The Convention adopted measures for the construction of a road from Cincinnati or Louisville, to Cumberland Gap and up the French Broad River and on to Charleston. As this route was not satisfactory to the delegates from Georgia and the lower East Tennessee Counties, they went to work to secure a road by way of Augusta, Chattanooga, Athens, and thence to Knoxville. Later dirt was broken for this road at or near Athens and the road built which later connected with the East Tennessee, Virginia, which later became the East Tennessee, Virginia and Georgia Railroad, now the Southern.

When the road was finally started, it was financed by local capital, with General Smith the first president. After the road was completed, the company was reorganized and Colonel William McFarland was made President.

The history of Tennessee says, "On December 24, 1867, the Cincinnati, Cumberland Gap and Charleston Railroad was completed as far as Clifton, or the farm lands of Thomas S. and David Gorman, a depot site was secured and one was erected on the line between the Gorman Brothers farms. The town began to build up on both sides of the railroad between the hills and the river."

Just when the road became the property of the East Tennessee, Virginia and Georgia Company is not known, but a sketch of Robert McFarland Jones found in the *History of Tennessee* states that he began railroading as a brakeman at the age of seventeen years and worked his way to fireman, then engineer and later conductor and was the first conductor on the Morristown road, Western North Carolina branch of the East Tennessee, Virginia, Georgia Road, known as Buncombe.

In the springtime of 1868 a big celebration excursion (probably free) was run from Newport to Sulphur Springs near Morristown. Old Buncombe with a string of flat cars, with cross-ties for seats, came steaming up the lane of Colonel Jack's farm, which lead out to his mansion, where the woodpile was kept. At this point, the engine was "refueled" and then proceeded to the turntable, which stood near where the present Merchants and Planters Bank now stands. Here the train turned and was boarded by a large and enthusiastic crowd, most of whom were taking their first ride on a train.

---

11. Version of Mrs. Lou Miller Robinson.
12. Old Beeswax, 1929, the father of Otha Maddron, a clerk at the post office

During the years of 1867 and 68, Major McCauley as Chief Engineer had a most unusual crew; three of them were Roberts and all had Colonel before their names. They were Colonel Robert Clayton, Colonel Robert Coleman, Colonel Robert Jones, who with the help of their legal adviser, Colonel Thaddeus Coleman, surveyed and located the road. After the surveyors crew came the grading of the roadbed with Moses Heyden as general boss; John Dyerly was chief in laying the tracks; and Charles F. Askew built the bridges; a Mr. Gleason and Dennis Casey, with many others, constructed the stone piers. By 1869, the road was completed to Buffalo Rock, a point just beyond Wolf Creek. The train made one trip each day to Buffalo Rock and the traffic was transferred across the mountains by stage coach to Asheville, North Carolina. The little train returned to Morristown. The engine was a wood burner.

The conductor carried and distributed the mail and often stopped to pick up passengers. Children going to school were delighted to ride the engine. A Bill Thurman was the first engineer; John Thompson, the first fireman; and Captain Robert McFarland Jones, the first conductor. The last-named never liked to talk of his achievements and always said, "We" . . '. We built the road, we brought the first train into Newport." Jesse Stokely says that his father, the late Charles Stokely of the First District. with whom the surveyors and crew boarded while locating the road, con sidered him an outstanding character. He was known personally and loved by every family from Morristown to Wolf Creek. His tact and business ability enabled him to secure "rights of way" and depot sites as the pathway was hewn out of the wilderness for the "Iron Horse of Progress." He was always liberal in his praise of those who worked with him. He related many stories of camp life when he worked along the French Broad River and on Big Creek, where he took a plunge every morning, often breaking the ice to do so, in an effort to build up his resistance after a bad case of chills and fever, contracted in railroad construction work in Arkansas.[13]

From an old newspaper clipping, the author takes the following description of the engine, known as Old Buncombe.

Old Buncombe was an eight-wheel locomotive, built by the Rhode Island Locomotive works of Cincinnati, Cumberland Gap and Charleston Railroad Company. It was the only locomotive owned by this road. She made a round trip of eighty miles every day except Sundays, and for seven years without being in an accident. Her old engineer, Decatur Craig, said of her, "She presented a fine appearance, with brass shining like mirrors and iron and steel parts rubbed bright as nickle plate, the driving wheels painted a bright red, and the cab and pilot a dark green. She weighed about thirty tons, carried one hundred fifty pounds of steam and had cylinders fifteen by twenty inches. The boiler was of the wagon-top variety. When the C. C. C. R. R. began it belonged to Tennessee, so the locomotive was named after Governor Senter, the Chief Executive who lived near Morristown." (However, the engine was rarely called anything but Old Buncombe.)

In about ten years from the time the railroad was begun, it was sold to two individual owners, Jakes and McGhee who also owned other rail-

---

13. End of Mrs. Duncan's version.

road lines in Tennessee. Then Old Buncombe was exchanged for a smaller locomotive, called "The Fred Netherland." Her owners considered her too heavy for the C. C. & C. Railroad. Wood was used to fire the engine at first, but later Old Buncombe was changed so as to burn coal.

"Uncle Jordon Garrett," a respected citizen among the colored folk, related to *Plain Talk* many years ago his recollections of the crowds of people who came to see Old Buncombe and that in after years this engine became the property of Captain Gaddis who used it as a sawmill.

Old Beeswax stated in a letter to *Plain Talk* that Old Buncombe sawed many yards of lumber in the Cosby section, two of which were cut on his own lands. C. C. Culver was the fireman and G. A. Titus, the sawyer. It was next owned by William Swaggerty and later by Joe Whaley. Old Buncombe's capacity was twelve to fourteen thousand feet of lumber daily. It is said to be slowly rusting away in the Spruce Flats of Sevier County, probably unknown as Old Buncombe.

The author has in her possession many transfers and receipts relative to the railway, most of them signed, D. Ward Stuart, Agent. Some of them have the name East Tennessee, Virginia and Georgia R. R. Company; others, Cincinnati, Cumberland Gap and Charleston R. R. Co.

A note from the Secretary and Treasurer, G. W. Barnett, dated March 27, 1857, reads, "Received of T. S. Gorman, Collector for Cincinnati, Cumberland Gap and Charleston Railroad Co. on Stock collected in Cocke County, one thousand and eighty-eight dollars and 66 cents in receipts as shown in settlement on Books. Also 3 pr. ct. allowed on above credited him on individual stock."[14]

---

14. We do not properly appreciate the importance of the railroad to our County and State. We are prone to forget its pioneering efforts in providing transportation which made possible the rapid development of this country of ours and the part the railroad has played in building this Nation. Pioneering is still in progress in railroad circles. The constant progress being made in improving the world's safest, most dependable and economic transportation is a splendid example of modern pioneering.

Our railroads want and need more work to do, which will enable them to employ more men and women to thus help keep the railroads at the very peak of efficiency both for commercial business and for our National Defense.

In each and every emergency railroads have proved their dependability. Homes are warm, families fed and industries kept going because railroads have fought their way through the wilderness of doubt and they should be given equality with other forms of transportation in regulation, taxation and public policy in general. Railroads move instantly and rapidly to meet any challenge that confronts them, carrying food, fuel, shelter, medical supplies to stricken areas of floods and various disasters that different communities experience. Railroads have to be on constant guard to overcome winter difficulties, to deliver materials for our various industries and to carry the U. S. mail and the essential supplies upon which human life depends.

The railroads are the Nation's best customer, they spend a billion dollars each year for equipment, materials and other supplies necessary to their upkeep. They employ a million men and women whose wages of almost two billions of dollars per year stimulate local business everywhere. The progress of the railroad is but a continuous story of research in materials, appliances and methods of investment in plant and equipment to make their service better.

One year ago the railroads paid in taxes $355,766,000, a substantial contribution to the support of our public services and institutions. This is $974,701.37 per day.

The people of our country now use four "WAYS" of transportation: Waterway,

The Depot Force in 1920's—Left to right—George W. O'Dell, Clerk, H. M. Remine, Agent, Asa Wilson—Clerk Walter Remine, son of C. K. Remine. Back row—Clarence Rogers. In front of window, Mark Sisk.

Another . . . "Received of T. S. Gorman one hundred twenty-two dollars and seventy cents on account of 35 shares subscribed by him to the Cincinnati, Cumberland Gap and Charleston Railroad. July the 7th, 1858. Jr. Allen, Collection."

And: "I hereby constitute and appoint Thos. S. Gorman as my attorney to transfer on the Cincinnati Cumberland Gap and C. R. R. Co. Books the full amount of my stock in said road to James A. Rorex which amount is five hundred dollars. August 26, 1871. John Rorex.

In exquisite handwriting is the following: "Received December the 6th 1866 of James R. Allen, Agt. Transcripts of Two Indictments against George W. Carter Deed in favor of C. C. G. & C. R. R. Company for One hundred and fifty-three dollars and five cents rendered Oct. 6, 1858, and one other in favor George W. Croft for Two hundred and Six Dollars and Ninety five cents rendered June 19, 1858. This day filed in my office. M. A. Roadman C & M (Clerk and Master)".

"I this day assign my stock in the Newport Depot to Delilah Gorman received pay for the same this the 20 May 1878." Marshal Henrey.

The following letter from the Vice President of the East Tennessee, Virginia and Georgia Company[15] shows the struggle the company was having with the road at that time:

Knoxville, Tenn. April 26th, 1877.

Mr. T. S. Gorman,
Newport, Tenn.

Dear Sir
In Octo 1875 this company made you a payment on account of rent for Depot building at Newport. The receipt executed by you shows that the payment was not to be considered as an acknowledge-

---

airway, roadway, and railway. Of these four, the railroad is the only one that builds and maintains its "WAY" without aid of the money we all pay in taxes.

Railroads receive about one cent for hauling an average ton of freight one mile. Railroads would have to haul that ton of freight from the earth to the sun, a distance of ninety three millions of miles, to bring in enough money to pay the railroad tax for one day only. Out of each dollar that the railroads take in, they pay out more than nine cents of it in taxes. The annual cost of providing and maintaining the roadway takes twenty three and one half cents more. Out of each dollar taken in by the inland water carriers reporting to the Interstate Commerce Commission, two cents goes for taxes and NOTHING for channels, which are built and maintained by the public. Federal barge lines, Government owned and operated competitors of the railroads, do NOT pay taxes, and yet its channels are built and maintained by the public.

We should give our railroads a square deal, for that means a square deal for our already over-burdened tax-payers of this country. Thoughtful people who consider the National transportation problems today realize that the railroad provides the only general transportation service that moves over roadways maintained without expense to our TAX-PAYERS.

The Southern Railway Company, which operates through Cocke County, runs four passenger trains and about forty freight trains each twenty-four hours; pays hundreds and hundreds of dollars in tax and has a PAY ROLL of about thirty-eight thousand dollars per year, employing around sixty people in the county.

15. Tennessee Acts, 1869-79, p. 491. Sec. 113.

Be it further enacted that section 44 of an Act passed May 24, 1866, entitled an Act to Incorporate the Tennessee and Pacific Railroad Company and for other purposes, be so amended as to extend to New Market, Dandridge and New-

ment of obligation on the part of the company to be governed by any contract that you had with the former owners of C C G & C R R. It was then contemplated to arrange for the continued use of the Depot building on terms that this company could afford, or to abandon it. I am not certain whether or not Cap't Jaques or any other officer of this Company made any arrangement with you in regard to the use of the building after the time specified in the receipt. Please advise us fully as to your understanding or views in reference to this matter.

Since the C C G & C R R passed into the hands of the Company, we have not been able to make it pay expenses, and consequently we must arrange to get along without paying much if anything for the rent of Depot buildings.

Signed by C. M. McGhee, V. P.

The author cannot find the date of the transfer of the East Tennessee, Virginia and Georgia Railroad into the hands of "The Southern."[16]

It is impossible to estimate the value of the railroad to the development of industries in the County. Now the Southern Railway pays into Cocke County forty thousand dollars per year in taxes, with a yearly payroll of as much as $38,000, employing as many as sixty people in the County. It operates four passenger trains and about forty freight trains through the County each twenty-four hours. (1936-6 passengers daily)

Cocke County has around eighteen industries with products valued at thousands of dollars, employing 609 people, 26 per cent of whom are women; the total wages paid the workers in 1934 were $404,286. Newport had a population of 4000 within the waterworks area in 1930 and 7263 in 1950. It is the trading center for an area of 25,000 population, which includes most of Cocke County, a part of Jefferson County, Sevier County, in Tennessee; Madison County and Haywood Counties in North Carolina. Sixty per cent of Newport's shipping is done by railroad. Newport imports coal, cement, hardware, gasoline, drygoods, finished lumber, wheat and corn, cottonseed meal, tannic acid extract, fruit jars, sugar, citrus fruits, shoes, hides, and many other items. It exports canned vegetables, leather, flour, meal, lumber, hosiery, pigs, cattle, lambs, wool, poultry, eggs, and a few other products.[17]

The Lumber Industry

Forty per cent of Cocke County's total area is woodland. Therefore, lumber should probably be classed as her second most extensive industry.

---

port Turnpike Company by way of mouth of Sweetwater, up east bank of Pigeon River, via M. McNabb's and John Barker's Mill and cross said river at or near McKenney McMahan's thence up the west bank of said river to the mouth of Ground Hog Creek, thence to the top of Chestnut Mountain, to connect with Colotoochu Turnpike road at the most convenient point on said road and that Malcomb McNabb of Cocke Co. be, and he is hereby added to the Board of Commissioners for said road. Passed February 25, 1870.

16. According to Irving Stone in *Immortal Wife*, page 16, John Charles Fremont related his work in the survey to the proposed route of Louisville Cincinnati and Charleston R. R. and later as civilian assistant to Captain Williams of the U. S. Topographical Corps in surveying the Cherokee Country.

17. *Newport Times*, February 14, 1942.

Rhyne Lumber Company

Southern Railway Depot

It is doubtful if there is in the entire United States another area of like size containing such a variety of wood. The size and quality of her timber is sought after by consumers in this country and in Europe. Her commercial saw timber is oak, beech, cottonwood, aspen, ash, yellow poplar, hemlock, cypress, cedar, white, red and yellow pine.

A shipping point for lumber was established in 1870 at Big Creek (Del Rio) on land owned by Jesse and Jefferson Burnett.

In 1883, a Scottish Corporation, managed by A. A. Arthur, experts in floating timber, came to the County. They cut the logs in the mountains, hauled them to the Big Pigeon, which had been prepared for floating logs to Newport. "Booms" were placed in the river at different places and connected by huge chains. Sometimes they went straight across the river; other times, the chains went zig-zag connecting the great pens. When the "booms" were filled with logs they were opened and either taken from the river or allowed to float on down the stream to Knoxville. The first mill was at Newport, the second at Knoxville, but because of the swiftness of the Big Pigeon, the promoters soon discovered they could not stop enough of the logs at Newport. They abandoned the mill there and let all the logs float to Knoxville.

In 1901, Hart and Holloway came from West Virginia with the idea of making a success of the lumber industry in Cocke County. They were two years building the Tennessee and North Carolina Railway into the lumber territory. They went as far as Mount Sterling two miles south of the State line into North Carolina. Mr. Holloway was the president and John Hart, secretary. These men soon sold their interests to the James Estate of Pennsylvania, who operated the Mount Sterling or Cataloochia Lumber Company. In a short while, they transferred their holdings to William Whitmer and sons of Philadelphia, who called themselves the Pigeon River Lumber Company. After this the company became the Champion Lumber Company. Both companies claimed to have suffered heavy losses due to the ruggedness of the mountain section. Several years later, the Tennessee and North Carolina Rail Road, owned by Bell and Company and the Boice Hardwood Company, operated on a light scale. A motor bus was also placed on the railroad and made two daily trips to Crestmont with passengers and mail. This was discontinued, leaving the railroad bed.

Cocke County is said to have the largest lumber plant in East Tennessee. It was first organized in 1899 by George M. Speigle of Philadelphia, who came to purchase walnut and cherry lumber. From 1906 to 1926, it was known as the McCabe Lumber Company. For several years, Charles T. Rhyne owned a half interest in this company, which is known as the Rhyne Lumber Company, and handles all kinds of lumber and building material. It averages 250,000 board feet per month, employing fifteen men at $260 per week. By 1940 the company had expanded and Mr. Rhyne is now sole owner.

Flint Ray has quite an extensive lumber plant also, and ships much pulp wood from Del Rio. Bruce Helm owns and operates the Helm Lumber Company, which averages 7000 board feet per month.

During the early days of the County, mining went on in a small way. Prospectors sought silver, gold and barytes, but did not find the gold.

Office of the Chilhowee Extract Company

Plant of Chilhowee Extract Company

Counterfeiters spoiled silver mining and the Big Pigeon River proved a hiding place for much of the barytes, it is said.

Cocke County has had many kinds of industries, such as distilleries, "flax breaks," cotton mills, from the beginning, later a tannery and canning factory.

Distilleries in the County

It seems to the author that we should not object to the truth regardless of what it may be, yet she realizes that it is probably best to leave unwritten any objectionable chapters. However a word in defense of the pioneers who made our wines, brandy and liquors may not be amiss.

In the history of any pioneering people, one of the necessities of their existence, in the hard life they lived, was the preparation of various homemade remedies for the cold plague, snake-bites, accidents and any and all ailments common to people then as now. Doctors were "few and far between" and the only "PENICILLIN" available was their own home-made wines and liquors, which they thought no more of doing without than we think of using Stokely Brothers canned foods and juices.

In the early days of Cocke County, several government stills were operated. One was on the Will Gresham place at "Baltimore." Philip Nease owned the still, in the Salem section, most noted for its brandy, it was located near the present site of the Lutheran Church. Moses Nease ran another distillery, with brandy as a specialty, at, or on Long Creek. Another still was operated on the Thomas O'Dell Farm, on the spot where the old William McNabb log house now stands. The water was run in a trough of hewn logs from the spring to the still.

There was another still, run by Thomas Harper, on the road leading from Bridgeport, south to Wilton Spring. Thomas Harper's sons decided they would take the liquor in the stillhouse to old Newport on the French Broad River and hide it in the woods west of the town. It took them nearly all night to haul it with oxen and wagon, a distance of about four or five miles. After they left with the last load of barrels about three in the morning, they set fire to the stillhouse. Being government property, the officers sought the offenders; all but one escaped, and he served some time in prison.

Another government distillery was operated by Joe Hurley on his farm near the present site of Clay Creek Church and there was another at Edwina. Andy Ramsey operated a government distillery on the east bank of the Pigeon river, near the present home of Mrs. Cora Rorex on Rankin Road. It is claimed the first government distillery was established in the Cosby section by Jonathan Cozby.

A later distillery was the Poplar Log one, constructed in the summer of 1892, in the Carson Springs section, and began operation on August 11, 1892, under Government Survey 525, and later on 572 and 608.

In the early days, the settlers considered well-to-do hauled their surplus apples and peaches to the distillery to make their brandy and liquor, which they stored for winter colds and other ailments, the most feared of which was a kind of fever and chills, known as the "cold plague."

Cocke County's Government Distillery ran for many years under the supervision of Robert H. Jones known as Bob Jones. The gaugers at different times were George W. Johnson, James Drinnon, W. P. Bond, Peter Allen, C. G. Lyons. The Government required the gaugers to be changed each three months period. They received two dollars per day for their services and were permitted to "sample" the liquor.

The first distiller was J. C. Smith; foreman, W. P. Bishop. Oscar McNabb (colored) also helped. Mr. Jones attended to the managing, the buying of grain, and the shipping of the finished product.

For a long time, Cocke County held the doubtful reputation of being the worst illicit liquor manufacturing county in the United States, defrauding the government of one million dollars per year in taxes. However, that reputation is now waning, due probably to the fact that much of the area is in the Great Smoky Mountains National Park and to the assiduous work of the Alcohol Tax Unit. We vote dry.

Our First Tannery

The first Tannery in Cocke County was "set up" and operated by Butler Delozier, but owned by Aaron Bible. Later another one was operated in the Parrottsville area by Alexander McNabb and a tan-yard was conducted in Newport, on the banks of the Big Pigeon where the present Main Street merges into the River Road, opposite the home of W. D. McSween. The man who operated it was an expert tanner by the name of Crockett.

Aaron Bible, a Dutchman, was the son of George Bible, who came directly from Holland with his four sons, Moses, Aaron, Jacob and Ezra.

The first Tannery was built near the present site of the Over Mountain School house. In addition to the tannery, Aaron Bible conducted a shoe shop. He was an expert shoemaker which was a splendid trade for an owner of a tannery. He was also very "thrifty" and willing to work and before very long had quite "a start in life" and decided it was time to take unto himself a wife.

With this "thought in mind" he journeyed to the home of Reuben Justus, whose wife was Polly Stokely Justus, the daughter of Royal Stokely, the first. It was to their daughter Sarah that Aaron would pay court. When time came for him to ask her hand in marriage he devised a most unusual method of procedure. Young suitors generally dreaded this delicate task but not Aaron, the "well-to-do," he was sure of himself, mapped out his course and sailed into the sanctuary of Reuben Justus one Sunday morning and evidently found him reading his Bible as was often the custom of the early pioneers. At any rate, he said these words to Reuben, "Do you believe in giving the Bible justice, Reuben?" Justus being a God-fearing, upright man instantly replied in the affirmative, "Of course I do. Drat it all, I KNOW the Bible ought to have justice, what in the world makes you ask me such a question, Aaron?" He carefully scrutinized Aaron's face to see if he appeared to be alright. The young suiter, smiling, answered "I am glad you have such belief, confound it all, if you believe the Bible ought to have justice, give me Sarah." And Aaron Bible took Sarah Justus to wife and they lived happily ever afterwards in the good home he had prepared for her. They had more than fourteen hundred acres of land, much of which was rich in creek valleys and mountain coves to say nothing of the timber for the tannery and the thousand hills upon which his cattle grazed to produce the leather.

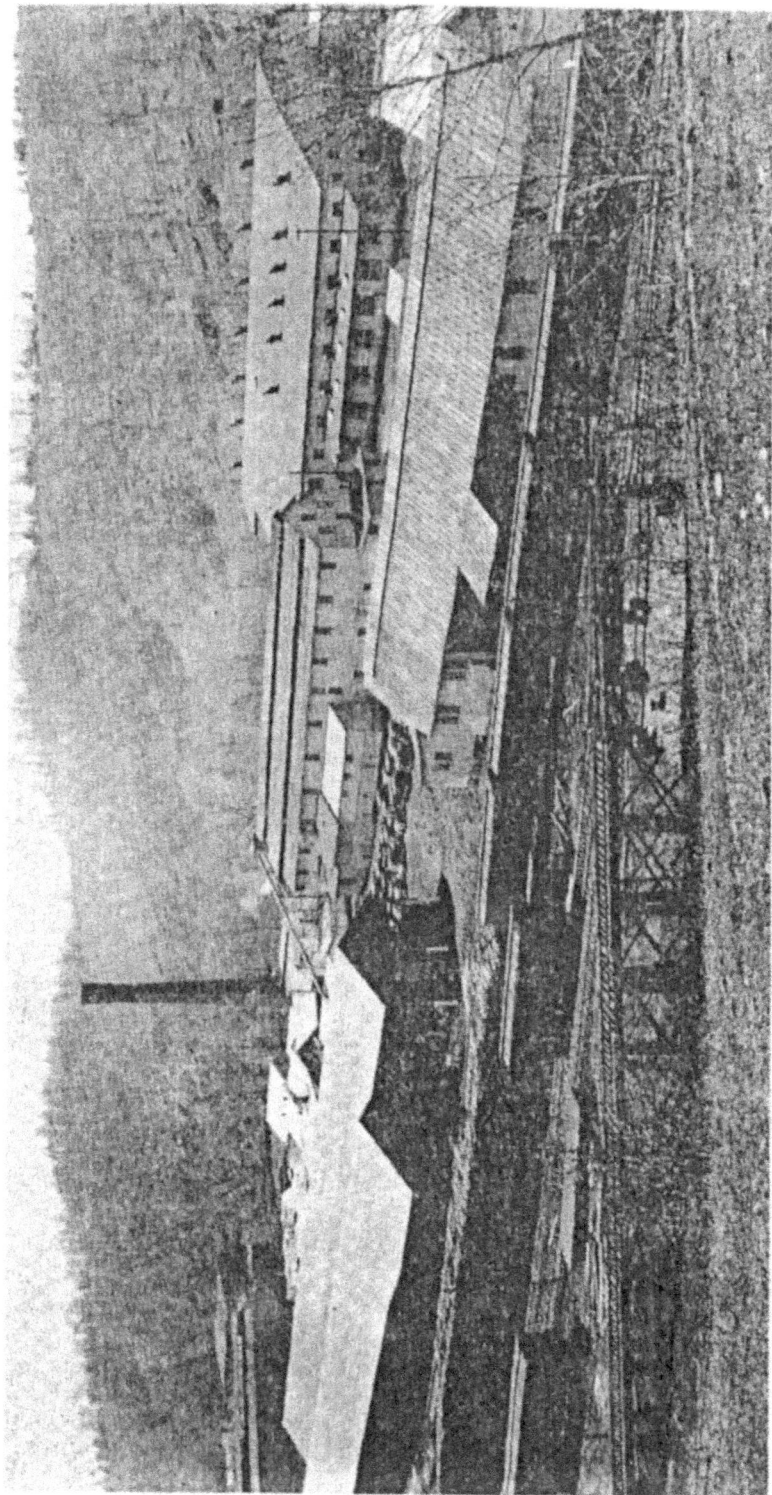

Unaka Tannery, Established by John W. Fisher.

On this mountain farm grew all sorts of fruit trees and berry plants native to this section. A great chestnut orchard of many acres was also a part of their domain. Innumerable stands of bees provided finest mountain honey for the table and to sell. Chickens, geese, turkeys, guineas, peacocks and all sorts of domestic fowls were all over the place furnishing eggs, feathers, meat and prosperity in general. Horses, sheep and hogs roamed the fields with the cattle.

The children of this couple came at seven year intervals. They were, Francis, a daughter, and two sons, Loyd and Leonard.

One of the sons published our first newspaper. He wrote his name Joseph L. Bible when he became editor. The other one became a photographer.

The girl married John Davis, who on Jan. 10, 1877 was murdered by Seth Bible. Later in life she married Barnett Smith, father of Ted Smith, who gave me this information verified by his wife, Chattie Stokely Smith Rainwater. The Bill of Indictment against Seth Bible is of such unusual "wording" that it is given in the Crime and Murder chapters.

The present tannery in the County was brought here through the efforts of C. F. Boyer. Mr. England, of the firm of England & Bryant, of Philadelphia, sent his son-in-law Charles S. Walton to Newport to look over the region to see if it would be a profitable investment. Mr. Boyer took Mr. Walton to Hall's Top to view the densely wooded regions, the site was chosen and the plant took the name of "The Unaka Tannery." The site was on the farm of William Swaggerty, one mile southeast of the Southern Depot at Newport and on the east bank of Big Pigeon.

The first buildings erected for the vats and tan yard were oblong frame structures about forty by one hundred fifty feet. The bleach houses and boiler and engine rooms were thirty by one hundred twenty feet, of frame construction and of sufficient capacity to prepare and tan about fifty hides per day. These buildings began to go up in the spring of 1893, and the chestnut, oak and hemlock trees began to come down. By the time the buildings were completed, the family of Philip and Fannie Fisher, long experience tanners, with their sons and their families, arrived from Bedford County, Pennsylvania. John W. Fisher, Superintendent of the plant, did not come the first year, but his twenty-year old unmarried brother, Jesse A. Fisher, became manager. The plant opened its doors for business, November 1, 1893. (Information by Jesse A. Fisher)

The first day, only fifteen hides were put to soak by Tommy Byars (a colored man always known as Uncle Tommy Bias). It gradually increased its capacity until four hundred hides were soaked each day, coming from packers all over the country, from Russia, India, and South America. The tanned leather was shipped to Philadelphia for sole and belt leather. Mr. John W. Fisher was the superintendent of a string of tanneries throughout this section for over thirty years.

It is now the A. C. Lawrence Leather Co., with home offices at Peabody, Massachusetts.

In 1903, the Chilhowee Company was organized by England and Bryan and is still in operation, but now owned by Mead Fibre Co. From 1903 to 1928, it was under the management of W. T. Buchanan. Since that time it has been managed by W. C. Ruble. This plant manufactures liquid chestnut extract for the tanning of leather. It uses thousands of cords of chestnut wood annually, and the extract is shipped in tank cars to tanneries throughout the United States. This plant is located south of the tannery, and many people think it is one huge plant. The office buildings are designated by Indian names.

The Old Way of "Blacksmithing"

By W. E. HAYES, (A Master Blacksmith)

My first knowledge of blacksmithing was more than ¾ century ago when I can first remember. There was a blacksmith shop near our home. It was in an old log building and I would go there every day and watch the old smith shoe the horses and make various tools. In those days they made all horseshoes and nails by hand. They also made plow-stocks and plow points, hoes, rakes, mattocks, picks, shovels, wagons and chains, etc. etc.

The blacksmith burned his own coal from pine wood which he cut into short blocks, split and stacked it into large mounds which he covered with leaves and dirt, leaving an opening in the center at which place he started the fire and when it was burning nicely he covered it with dirt. It would take about ten days for it to burn into coal. When cutting this wood the "richest" pieces were laid away to be used for making tar. Later he would burn what he called the tar kiln. This tar was used on the spindles of wagons.

The first wagons when I learned blacksmithing were called tarpole wagons. The axles were made of very tough wood. The smith would place small strips of iron on them and make small bands and place in the hub. The tar was used for grease.

Blacksmithing fifty years ago required much more study and skill than it does now, because he had to prepare all material for his finished product, the blacksmith had to know what to select, when to do so, and how to 'season' and fashion his various parts of any finished piece of work. The labor and skill required to build a wagon called for patience, time and long hours of toil. First the timber must be found in the woods, cut and split and carried to the shop where it was stacked a certain way until it had 'seasoned' which required a certain length of time. Then cut and 'shaped' and put together correctly.

The iron for this process of construction had to be secured. The smith would take small pieces and weld them together and make whatso-ever he needed. He was always most 'saving' with his precious iron. He would take the old worn out horse-shoes and weld them 'up' together with other pieces of iron and make them into new shoes and nails.

To make the trace chains and log chains it was necessary to weld together many small pieces and draw it out into bars then cut into short lengths and shape the lengths and place them together, one link at a time.

On rainy days when the farmers could not work in their fields they would bring their plows, hoes, axes and have them sharpened or new points put on the plows or a clevis to be made for a plow. Horses and mules would be to shoe on such days. Most blacksmiths kept some shoes made ready for just such occasions. In addition to his smithy duties the blacksmith had to serve as a kind of veterinarian. Often a horse or a mule would be brought in with a 'bad shaped' foot. The smith would have to trim the hoof a certain way and make a special shoe to bring the foot back to its proper 'shape'. Sometimes they would come in with a 'gravel' in the foot which would have to be extracted or cut out. Frequently, in our mountain country with the rocky roads we had long ago, a horse would get its hoof cracked. This had to be most carefully treated in order to save the horse's foot. The smith would trim the wall of the hoof very thin on each side of the crack along which he would sew a thin covering with small tongues on each side, the tongues inserted in the hoof. Next a special shoe with clips on it had to be made and put on the foot so that the clips could be closed around the hoof without the use of nails. Every three or four weeks this shoe had to be removed and the hoof trimmed and the shoe replaced. It required six months for the hoof to grow out enough to take off the plate and use a shoe with nails.

No horse was properly shod unless the blacksmith knew exactly how to trim the horse's hoof as well as how to put on the shoe. If the foot is not trimmed level, or the calk is too high or too low it places a strain on the ankle joint and causes swollen joints.

My first experience in 'shoeing' was on 'work-cattle' or oxen as you choose to call them. My father had a blacksmith shop along with his mill and he used work cattle for hauling logs and lumber. They would get very tender 'footed' walking constantly over the hundreds of rocks in the roadway. An old darkey worked as a blacksmith for my father, who decided one day that he would have the old Negro make some shoes for the oxen and see if that would not help the poor creatures to get over the rough roads. It worked well and I learned to make their shoes and to put them on with ease. Later however, father had them molded from malleable iron. The ox shoe is made in two parts because his hoof is 'forked'.

Hog-Rifle

When we speak of a 'Rifle' now days we think of a Winchester, a Springfield, or of a Martini-Henry Rifle. But in the 'olden days' we thought of a gun as a Hog-rifle, a Squirrel Rifle, which was one and the same gun. There was also what was known as the Flint-lock Rifle. The difference between the two guns is that the powder in the Flint-lock rifle is ignited by a flint, the Hog-Rifle by a cap. Many of these old rifles and also some muskets are still in good condition and often used today by our natives. The length of these guns varies between three and four feet not including the stock. They have what is well-considered the finest 'sight' or 'bead of any gun.

To load these guns is a very primitive process and rather slow it seems compared with present day methods. To begin with, most hunters carried with them a small pouch which they slung over the shoulder much as children carry their 'book-satchels' today. This pouch was generally made of some kind of leather or 'Tanned Hide'. In it, the hunter carried his 'patching', his caps and bullets along with the bullet molds which varied in size from one to two to three different sizes of bullets, different guns requiring the different sizes. A small 'charger' for measuring the powder. This was generally the tusk of a hog, was also kept in the 'shot-pouch'. There were two reasons why these pouches were made of the hide of an animal. First, of course, was the absolute necessity of KEEPING THE POWDER DRY. Second reason was the durability of thc leather pouches. If the hunter had no charger, he knew how to measure the required amount of powder into his hand. About a thimble full was sufficient for squirrel hunting, but for turkey or long range shooting it took more. The Hog-rifle has two triggers, one is pulled back, which is called 'springing the trigger', the hammer is pulled back to hold it in place, after this a very light touch on the other trigger fires the gun. After the powder has been poured into the gun a small cloth is placed over muzzle and ball placed on it and pressed in enough to admit carefully trimming off the cloth, after which it is moved on down to where the powder is by a 'ramrod' which is always carried with the gun and made of tough wood. The Cap is placed on the last thing before firing the gun.

The Flint-lock rifle is loaded the same way and the Musket much the same, except slugs of lead or shot may be used in the musket instead of bullets. Some of the Muskets used in the Civil War shot Ounce-balls known as "Minnie-Balls" a term that was probably derived from a 'MINION' which was a small cannon used in the seventeenth century. This name for the musket shots could have come from the word, 'MINNIE-SINGER' the soldiers might have considered the 'singing of the guns' as music of the 'Minnie-balls,' though a Minnie-singer sang only songs of love while the muskets sang the song of hate as is the tune of all wars. Minnie-singers were usually of high birth. They lived in Germany during the twelfth and thirteenth centuries.

The Hog-rifles were not expensive guns to shoot as the average cost of one-hundred shots is about fifteen cents.

Merchants

As these plants were developing within our County the merchants were reaping a rich reward by furnishing necessary equipment for the homes of the people. The earliest stores were those of Rankin and Pulliam, W. C. Roadman, D. A. Mims, B. D. Jones and Son, J. S. and D. G. Allen, and others.

The Journal of Rankin and Pulliam (property of Mrs. Lillie Robinson O'Dell Finchem) is a business ledger of 560 pages kept from May 15, 1837 to January 8, 1839 by one of these early firms. On May 14, 1839, $17,475.52 was recorded as the amount of credit business for one year.

From these records, one can easily form an idea of the character of the buying habits of certain citizens. John F. Stanberry, constantly bought building materials; George and Malcomb McNabb bought hats and paid five dollars each for them. Among those names appearing most frequently are: Aaron Baxter, Henry Jack, William C. Story, William Wood, Mark Brooks, Anthony Christian, John Mantooth, Esq., John Wood, Elias Sisk, James Gillian, Samuel Haskins, Alexander E. Smith. Lawson D. Franklin, who never failed to buy coffee, and a Mrs. Coleman who most always sent "Anthony" for ribbon, buttons, silk, and the like (it is easy to suppose that she must have been a dressmaker or a milliner.) The names of Major Anderson McMahan, Murdoch McSween, Charles Morrell, a Mrs. Womble, Loyd B. and Joseph Young, and Captain Allen Clevenger were also generous buyers. General A. E. Smith bought more of everything and more often than any other person. Lorenzo D. Porter ran him a close second. Others were Calvin McNabb, Thomas Mantooth, Esq., John and Isaac Boyer, Andrew and William Davis, also Colonel Peter I. Davis. The names of Captain Jonathan Allen, Dr. George W.

Porter, Dr. George Crookshanks, Noah Griffin, Reverend Nathaniel Hood, Pleasant North, George Parrott, Captain John Smith, and Joseph Youngblood appear many times. Also those of Berry Nichols, Robert Pulliam, Captain Robert Dennis, Majors John and Thomas Gorman, Captain Hartsell, Rev. Joseph Manning, Jacob Shults, David Harned, Daniel McSween, Dr. John M. Burnett, and Henry Faubion. Frequent customers were, Wright and Warren Brooks, William C. Burnett, James Burnett, Abraham McKay, Americus Jones, William McNabb, Joseph Wood, Abner Hicks, Major James Allen. Thomas Burnett, Frances Burnett, William Carter, William Gray, William Whitson, John Smith of Reverend Thomas, W. W. Bibee, Matthew Maxwell, Blackburn Sisk, Brummit Bryant, Francis Larrew, Royal Hall, George W. Hobarts, and Charles Morrell bought at intervals. Odd names on the ledger are Zachariah Stylers, Alfred Vanvacter, Leoney Chapman, Joseph Coontz, Joseph Fitch, Isaac Humbard, and Green Rose.[18]

The first store in the present Newport was opened by Thomas Evans, and it was soon followed by C. T. Peterson, Edward Clark, Roadman & Gorman.

In 1880, the business firms were Mims, J. G. Allen, Jones Brothers & Co., B. D. Jones, Clark & Robinson, J. S. Allen, William Crawford, V. T. Deaton, Brothers and Co., Burnett & Baer, S. A. Burnett, Robinson & Cody, Ramsey & Snoody, J. J. & Oscar O'Neil, J. S. Susong, John M. Davis, Case & Templin, T. M. Swanson, D. A. Mims, Ragain & Knisley, Hill & Connelly, Miss Sallie Anderson, J. H. Fagala, R. E. Mashby.

Old Mills

Mills were called Tub-mills because they were sometimes shaped like a tub. The process of converting grain into bread was long and tedious in the days of the pioneers, requiring much time and patience.

The mill was so constructed that "a turn of corn" could be placed in the mill at night and the mill "started" to grinding and next morning return and get the meal. The grinding made a terrible noise like a storm in its fury. It was all caused by the rock on top end of the shaft near the wheel.

To get flour was even more difficult than to get meal. It took much longer to cut the wheat with scythe by hand and spread it out on barn floor and thresh it with a "frail." This was a twisted pole of hickory wood which had been beaten by an axe until very soft. The pole was about the length of a broom with only the end of it beaten into the fibre-like substance. After the wheat was well threshed with the "frail," it was placed in a "fanmill" and turned by hand. This "concern" was made of wood, turned by a crank and was double geared. (I asked the old gentleman giving me this information how to spell "geared." Oh, he replied, "Just put it down without spelling it.") The fan-mill is screened and and blows out the chaff. After the fanning process, the wheat was next washed and spread out to dry, after which it was ground on the "burr" or rock then sifted by hand through a sifter made of muslin stretched over a hoop. It was called "a sarch." Long after the corn mills became complete they continued to "do" the wheat as above stated. Finally a process known as "bolting the flour by a hand reel." The

18. See also Appendix.

chests used for this were 5 and 10 feet sizes. The flour fell into the chest and was dipped up with a paddle by hand and placed into sacks, even as late as in the 70's. Most of these old mills derived their power from what is known as a "shot wheel." Occasionally there would be connected with the wheat and flour mills a "sash saw," which is something like a cross-cut saw, but straight on the teeth side, fastened in a sash or frame, propelled from a wheel below which sent the saw up and down. It is said that the sawyer could start the saw in the end of the log, in the early morning and go about his other work for half the day, return to the mill at noon, to find the saw most to the other end of the log. The plank was much more uniform in thickness, than work done much later by circular saw methods.

Cocke County being so abundantly supplied with creeks and rivers had many mills upon them. One of the oldest being the DeWitt Mill near Bridgeport. It was called The DeWitt Mill. Across the French Broad River at this old mill was a Covered Bridge which washed away before the Civil War days. The Mill was located near the old Brooks Mill a little ways East of the present Major James T. Huff Bridge at Bridgeport.

The Cane Mill served our people by being the means of grinding from the "sugar cane" a juice which was made into syrup known as sorghum molasses. When properly made from cane grown in a certain kind of soil, this syrup or molasses is quite delicious and of a beautiful color.

To grind the juice out of the cane, this mill was operated by a horse, hitched to a lever that had been fastened to the top of the mill which was never more than four or five feet high. It was very heavy and securely fastened to the ground by means of stakes. The two large iron rollers are near the top part of the mill, to which the lever is fastened. When the horse or oxen begins to walk around the lever turns the roller. The cane is fed by hand into these rollers, the juice runs through a cloth into a tub. Only three or four stalks of the stripped cane are placed into the roller at a time. The feeder must be careful not to allow his hands to get too near the moving rollers. The ground cane is thrown into the pathway for the horse to walk on, it soon becomes a soft road-bed, he gets very tired going round and round all day long. Sometimes they get dizzy and must be changed often. Others refuse to walk unless driven constantly. The very first cane mills were operated entirely by oxen, and juice boiled in kettles of 50 or 60 gallons capacity, placed in furnaces.

Later after the kettles came great flat boxes that held about 25 gallons, they were lined with sheet-iron and placed on a furnace about two feet high in which a hot wood fire was kept burning. It was not possible to make more than three runs a day the third one not coming off before nine or ten P.M. After the "box boiler" came the "evaporator," this arrangement placed the juice in sections and as it became nearer to molasses it ran into another section etc. until it was ready to come off the furnace. This arrangement makes much better molasses. All the different processes required constant attention to keep the proper heat and the boiling juice properly skimmed. In the early days the "skimmers" were made of the army canteens, each canteen divided into halves.

One man in a radius of ten miles had a cane mill. He would make the molasses or furnish the mill for all the people, charging fifty cents per day for the use of the mill. This was paid in molasses which were placed in kegs and barrels.

The "molasses makings" were gala occasions. Neighbors often helped with the tedious task. After all was finished, the very last "run" was allowed to boil until it would be candy when it was taken off the furnace and allowed to cool, when all hands were washed in the nearby stream and greased thoroughly with butter, and the "Candy Pulling" was in full swing. This work had to be completed before the first frost came in the early autumn.

The Cider Mills were extensively used in the olden days. When cider was fresh it was a delightful drink. When a few days old called hard cider. Later it became vinegar. It was made of apples and those not sour made the best. A favorite dessert was gingerbread made of molasses, flour, butter, and flavored with ginger and served with apple cider.

Another mill was that owned by R. A. (Rus) McNabb, who had bought it from John Baker about 1877. Later, in the 80's, he sold it to Will Denton.

The historical landmark of Captain John Denton is still known as the Denton Mill and is a combination of several mills owned and operated by Sam Raines. Wheat, corn and feed are ground in the mills, and a sawmill is also operated.

William Faubion attached a small cotton gin to his mill at Bridgeport. At one time, he built a flat boat, rigged with a paddle wheel in the rear end, which he attached to a blind horse in some way and sent this boat to New Orleans, loaded with flour and bacon, dried fruit, and feathers. The crew sold the boat at their destination, came back up the Mississippi and Tennessee rivers to Knoxville, and walked the remainder of the way home. Boating to New Orleans from French Broad, Nolichuckey and Holston rivers was a common sight in the early days. (Faubion.)

The Newport Mill Co. is one of the oldest mills now in operation. It began with the town of Newport and was first owned by David Gorman, brother of Thomas S. Gorman, who together with him owned the land upon which Newport now stands. At that time the present Newport was Clifton and Newport was on the French Broad River. David Gorman sold his mill to D. B. McMahan who had Thomas J. Russell for his miller. He was assisted by Uncle Sidney Oaks, colored. A saw mill was connected with the mill during the first years of its existence.

Later, the Newport Mill was owned by J. H. Randolph and son Rolph. The Randolphs tore away the old mill and were building a new one when they sold out to J. J. Denton, J. P. Robinson, B. D. Jones, J. G. Allen, A. R. Swann, and Elbert Early. They formed a partnership and rebuilt the mill into a first-class flour mill, with A. E. Sparks as manager, patronized by the citizens of the adjoining county. In 1890, the capacity of this mill was 225 barrels of flour, 1,500 bushels of corn meal, 50,000 pounds of brans, shorts and feed stuff daily.

In 1913, the Newport Mill Company was incorporated with a capital of $100,000. They increased their grinding capacity and the area of their floor space to approximately 200,000 square feet. The names of the flours they manufactured were Calla Lily, Silver Spray, Newport Queen, Little Elsie, Cotton Bloom, Olive Branch, and Harvest Moon. This flour was shipped throughout the Southland.

Stokely Bros. Cannery as seen from Clifton Heights with Hall's Top
in the distance.

The Newport Mill

For many years this enterprise enjoyed a splendid business, until various difficulties caused the mill to become idle. In February, 1935, it was again open for business under the name of Newport Co-operative Mills, Incorporated, owned and operated by the farmers of Cocke County and adjacent counties. It has an estimated business of $250,000 per year. This mill has an elevator capacity of 50,000 bushels of wheat and 24,000 bushels of corn, besides large warehouses for storing the finished product. The capacity of the flour mill is 350 barrels, 1000 bushels of corn meal, 40,000 of mill feed, and 10,000 pounds of scratch feed. It manufactures Nectar, Perfection, Calla Lily, So-Good, and Happy Day brands of flour.

In 1925, the Tennessee Public Service Company paid $100,000 for the light plant of the Newport Mill Co., which was then furnishing Newport its electricity. The value of this property was appraised for the town by Meese and Meese, Electrical Engineers of Charlotte, North Carolina, and found to be worth $24,608, with a replacable value of $37,000. The remaining $75,392 was paid for the agreement that they never again would generate power for sale.

The other Newport mill is known as the City Milling Company, locally owned, with J. E. Jones, first president; Barton Warren, first secretary and treasurer; Murray Stokely, vice-president of the stockholders. The other members were Charles Morrell, Estel Stokely (deceased), W. H. Gooch, superintendent. J. E. Jones moved away. Barton Warren and Murray Stokey long since deceased.

The capacity of this mill at its beginning in 1934 was one hundred thirty-five barrels of flour, 750 bushels meal, and ten tons of feed daily. For ten years its output has been about the same. It maintains a branch house in Asheville. Sixty per cent of its corn and thirty per cent of its wheat is locally bought.

Canneries

The world's largest canners of choice vegetables, the Stokely Brothers, have their home office in Newport. This industry was begun in Jefferson County in the spring of 1898 when two of the brothers had finished college and returned to their farms. Four of these brothers were interested in farming; the other one became a lawyer. Their first canning plant was small. They planted but sixty acres in tomatoes the first year. These brothers, John M., W. B., James R., and George S. Stokely learned the canning business by experience. Each success inspired them to try another vegetable. After their success with tomatoes, they tried sugar corn, although friends doubted the success of such an undertaking.

When Stokely Brothers first began to can vegetables their idea was to make a profit by growing vegetables and another by canning them. Later, they conceived the idea of doubling their farming profits by raising two crops on the same land in each year and at the same time maintaining and increasing the fertility of the soil. They also figured that by the same policy they ought to double, treble, or even quadruple their canning profits. Instead of having one canning season of six weeks on tomatoes, they have gradually developed about ten canning seasons. They have various methods of maintaining the fertility of their soils, the most natural and worthwhile of which is the feeding of their hundreds of cattle ensilage and cottonseed meal. The cattle are sold each autumn as beef on the Eastern markets, but hundreds are kept for stock purposes.

Stokely Brothers began under the firm name it still retains, Stokely Brothers & Co., with a capital of $3,900. On January 1, 1908, their capital was sixty thousand dollars. On January 15, 1917, the business of Stokely Brothers was incorporated with a capital stock of $200,000. James R. Stokely was made first president and treasurer; John M. Stokely, vice-president and secretary. They now have a capitalization of many millions of dollars, a marvelous showing for their forty years of business. All original owners deceased.

In 1933, it took 2,620 acres to supply Stokely Brothers with vegetables, seventy-five per cent of which were grown on their own lands. In addition to providing a ready market for farm products, this company has paid out thousands of dollars for such products and for salaries and wages, thus improving the living conditions for the hundreds of people employed by them.

The Indiana Packing Plants and Van Camp Company were taken over by Stokely Brothers and organized with the same officers: W. B. Stokely, Jr., president; John B. Stokely, son of John M., vice-president; Lyle Moore, vice-president and district manager for the Tennessee plants; J. B. Gregg, manager for the Newport plant. The company has many plants scattered over the United States.

The entire process of gathering, hauling and canning vegetables is from one to four hours. For example, green peas are canned at the rate of 330 cans per minute, twelve to fifteen hours per day, six weeks per year; tomatoes, two to three thousand bushels per day, four weeks per year.

It was not until 1935 that pork and beans were first canned at the Newport plant. The pork required the installation of electric refrigeration, which they added in connection with their modern dairy. Nothing in this vast enterprise is wasted, the peavines are placed in silos and pickled, then hauled out to the beef cattle. The sweet corn cobs are ground and placed with the husks in the silos and pickled for the beef cattle.

Recently, the Newport plant has arranged a "Dry-Pack" which enables them to proceed at all seasons of the year. The American Can Company formerly had a plant in Newport, and is now re-establishing it.

In January, 1941, the Company had 34 factories in fourteen states. In the year ending May 31, 1941, the Company's total sales were $21,510,000. During 1941 and 42, seventeen food preserving operations were added. The Company's preserving activities cover canning, bottling, freezing, dehydrating and barreling. During World War II, Stokely Brothers sold most of their output to the armed forces and government agencies.

The sales for the year ending May 31, 1942, totaled $342,113,000. Since then the company has established a production record exceeding that of any previous accomplishment. The company was awarded an "A" flag, August 8, 1944, the symbol of outstanding accomplishment by the government.

Orchards and Nurseries

Cocke County is well adapted to the growing of apples and berries, grapes, and other small fruit. The four principal orchards in this section are those of Ben W. Hooper, A. R. Swann, Elbert Carver, and

James R. Stokely. The Carver orchard of twenty acres is situated inside the limits of the Smoky Mountain Park and now belongs to the United States Government. The Swann orchard is located near the French Broad River not far from the A. R. Swann home in the edge of Jefferson County.

The Edgemont orchard, belongs to Ben W. Hooper, is located at the foothills of the English Mountains about two miles below Carson Springs. Its trees consist mainly of the Red Delicious, Golden Delicious, Stayman Winesap, and Red Winesap. James R. Stokely's orchard adjoins the Hooper orchard.

STOKELY ORCHARDS

In the early twenties a large apple orchard was set out by Former Governor Ben W. Hooper and his sons at the foot of the English Mountains in the Carson Springs section, six miles from Newport. In the thirties most of this orchard was purchased by Gov. Hooper's nephew, James R. Stokely, who has since added 1,500 of the latest improved varieties, and now the orchard has 3,500 trees occupying a full 100 acres on a choice plateau surrounded by the scenic English mountains. This section is ideal for apple-growing; the Southern latitude gives it the hot sun necessary for maximum growth and maturity while the mountain altitude gives it ample showers and clear cool nights necessary for highest color, flavor and finish.

Successful orchard culture, as one mountain wit has described it, is a "thirteen-months a year job." In January, February and March come pruning, fertilizing and replanting; in April, May and June come most of the spraying, without which all of the apples would be of "cow-pasture" quality, stunted by scab, worm or rot; in July and August come mowing and propping, a full crop requiring some thirty thousand props; September and October are the busiest months, with picking, grading, ring-packing, storing, trucking and selling the harvested fruit. November and December, according to Mr. Stokely, are the fastest selling months; when the weather turns freezing and hog-killing time is here, people want "plenty of fruit with their meat."

An average crop at the Stokely orchard is twelve to fifteen thousand bushels while a bumper one is twenty thousand. Half the trees are young ones, averaging ten years old, and will gain in productivity with the years; the remaining half, twenty-five year old trees, are still good for fifty more years of efficient apple-bearing if properly cared for. The varieties are those best adapted to this region of the country: Stayman (the most popular, cooking or eating), Red Delicious, Golden Delicious, Grimes Golden, Jonathan, King David, York, Rome Beauty, Old-fashioned Winesap (the last to ripen in October) and Early Redbird (the first to ripen in June). This East Tennessee mountain section produces not only the highest quality but the earliest maturing apple on the market, thus enabling the grower to get a two-weeks' jump on his Northern and Western competitors. It is truly "Fantastic Fruit from the Foothills of the Smokies.'

Mr. and Mrs. Stokely also have a well-known orchard near Asheville, N. C., which caters almost exclusively to the tourist and gift-package trade. Along with each 100 acres of apples in each state they possess an adjoining acreage of valuable timber, pasture and building land. This part of Mother Earth they are reserving for their young son "Dyke" to develop. Meanwhile, they are content with their apple-growing, occasional travel in the off-seasons, and books and music in their home of native stone in the mountains. Mrs. Stokely, the former Wilma Dykeman of Asheville, is also a writer, having had several stories published in national magazines.

The Valentine Nurseries, in the Cosby section, established in 1919, have the largest collection of Canadian Hemlock in the United States and they ship thousands of mountain ferns and other greenery weekly. In 1929, they shipped well over three million ferns.

Other Enterprises—1940

It would be impossible to describe, or even mention, all the many business enterprises that have come and gone through the years. However, Newport has several smaller manufacturing plants. The Fielden Manufacturing Company has thirty employees, manufacturing wash dresses for children and women, and wash trousers for men. The main office of the Dixie Hosiery Mills is also located here. Sam Rains has what is known as the Denton Mills at Denton. These Mills make altogether about three thousand pairs of hose daily. The Sevierville Hosiery Mills have merged with those of Newport, where the products are finished and shipped to the markets. Newport is the fifth shipping point in Tennessee.

Newport has one of the best equipped dry-cleaning establishments in East Tennessee. At first it was operated by Mr. and Mrs. Garfield Nease, who later sold it to Herbert Murray, and is known as the Newport Steam Laundry. The earlier laundries were the American Laundry and the Troy Laundry, around 1916.

These industries brought the need of banks to Newport. In 1888, the first bank in Cocke County was organized, with B. D. Jones as the first president; S. A. Burnett, first cashier; O. L. Burnett, first bookkeeper. It was known as the Newport Bank. A year later, the Merchants and Planters Bank was organized with W. B. Robinson, president; C. F. Boyer, cashier. These two banks consolidated into the Merchants and Planters Bank in 1891, with B. D. Jones, president; and C. F. Boyer, cashier. A year later, D. A. Mims became cashier. In 1938, the assets of this bank were $1,359,421.43.

The Appalachian Fair Association, organized in 1904 with John M. Johns, president, had much to do with encouraging the farmers to produce more and better products. The Fair Grounds have become a park.

Our County Fair has recently been reorganized and has just closed the most successful fair in its entire history. The following officials are responsible for its reorganization. Our horse shows are considered the best in the country.

Charlie Shipley, president; James A. T. Wood, vice-president; Jack Vinson, secretary; Howard Murrell, treasurer.

Directors: Gray O'Neil, Jim Maloy, Charles Runnion, Mrs. Lagretta Parrott, Guy E. Freshour, Mrs. Hugh Burnett, Robert Hickey, Artis Suggs, James A. T. Wood, Conrad Nease, Charles Ruble, Jr., Charles Rhyne, Sr., Robert Hill, Roy T. Campbell, Fred Chapman, Jack Shepherd, Lacy Myers, Mrs. C. E. Ottinger, Walter Layman, Glenn Chambers, Wade Butcher, Louise Netherton, Louise Seehorn, Mrs. A. H. Taylor, T. S. Ellison, Dewey Strange, Charles Seehorn, V. C. Adcock, Mrs. Joe Carpenter, Audrey Owens.

Vocational Teachers: Ralph Combs, Charlie Shipley, Edwin Lewis, Jack Vinson, Bruce Fox, Hershel Smith, Charles Snodderly, Mary Roe Ruble, Roy D. Brown, W. H. Proffitt, Robert Seay, E. G. Bryant, Ted Leatherwood, John Beeson, Howard Murrell, Ike Dawson, William Huff, M. G. Roberts, Delmar Baxter.

Extension Agents: Ruth Tate, Raymond Sutton, Hugh Russell, M. R. Brasher.

The Allen and Sellers monumental establishment did a flourishing business over a long period of time. George William Sellers, a native of Virginia, removed to Knoxville, in the early 80's, where he was connected with the Southern Monument Company, as sales manager. Later he removed to Newport, where he established in 1894 the pioneer monument firm name, G. W. Sellers & Sons. Its plant was located opposite the First Presbyterian Church on McSween Avenue, on property then owned by John Williams and later by the firm. As the business increased, some of the George W. Webb estate was leased. Later the plant moved to Church Street, where the Mims Hotel is now located. In 1909-19, the plant was discontinued because of the death of a member of the personnel and the ill health of the remaining members, but Edgar L. Sellers continued to design memorials for the firm he represents. The cornerstone of the First M. E. Church, South, was lettered and placed by this firm and dedicated by the church in 1909. The members of the firm were G. W. Sellers, John H. W. Sellers, and Edgar L. Sellers.

John C. Holder & Company established an undertaking and embalming business in the old post office building on Peck Avenue, in May, 1917. The firm consisted of John C. Holder and his father, C. C. Holder. Later they moved into the old post office building. In 1926, Hugh R. Holder bought the interest of C. C. Holder. They moved into their remodeled home on East Main Street in 1937. Later, John C. Holder bought the interest of Hugh R. Holder.

The Maloy-Suggs Funeral Home is a successor to Deaton-Willis establishment, and is now located next door to the city hall on Main Street.

On March 1, 1930, the Brown Funeral Corporation was organized with Tipton Brown as president; O. H. Fancher, vice-president; George R. Shepherd, secretary and treasurer; W. C. Sams, J. C. Lindsey, D. R. Large, James Hawk, directors. The interests of the various members of the corporation were acquired by Tipton Brown, and the Brown Funeral Home was dissolved. In March, 1936, the Brown Mutual Burial Association was organized, and now has 17,000 members. After the death of the young owner the business has been carried on by Mrs. Brown and other members of the firm.

It is impossible to measure the part that newspapers have played in the industrial development of the county. For this story see the chapter on Civic and Cultural Development of the County. Roads have also played an incredible part in this development. That story is told in another chapter.

Creed Boyer (Sheriff)

Joe Draper and bloodhounds

Captain R. A. Ragan of the Union Army.

Captain Thomas J. Gorman, Company H
of the Fourth Regiment of Tennessee Volunteers.

Cocke County, Tennessee's Hangings

Our terrible crimes of murder, our awful hangings, our tragic suicides, form several chapters of our history that everyone sincerely deplores and wishes our people had never written. But what has been done cannot be changed.

> "The Moving Finger writes; and having writ,
> Moves on; nor all your piety nor wit
> Shall lure it back to cancel half a line,
> Nor all your tears wash out a word of it."

The Rubiayat of Omar Khayyan

The first person hung in what is now Cocke County WAS A WOMAN, a kind old slave. She could not bear the idea of her little grandson being sold into slavery as she had been. Motherhood, the world over, revolts at such an idea.

As the little Negro child was being offered on the "Slave Block," she stood silently weeping in the great crowd, listened carefully to the "bidding" and when he was auctioned off she was heard to make the remark, "THAT MAN WILL NEVER GET HIM." Probably she had reasons for thinking he would not be a kind master, many were not. She loved her little grandson dearly, as only a grandmother can love a child. He was her only one and therefore doubly precious to her.

As quickly as possible, and as nonchalantly as though all was well with her, she stole the child away from the crowd and with him on her back plunged into the deep waters of the French Broad River at the ford, which was not so far from the Slave Block. The ford was about fifty yards west of the Old Town bridge over the French Broad.

In the old slave's desperate effort to escape with her grandchild, and in her excitement, it is probable that she stumbled, or the little fellow became quite frightened at the swirling waters, anyway, he fell from her back and was drowned.

Because she had made the remark at the time of the sale, and because the child had disappeared with her into the French Broad, those in authority decided she had purposely drowned him and for this she was hung. At the time of this event we were Greene County, North Carolina.

Between the years of 1874 and 1881, at the Musterfield two men were hung in Cocke County, Tennessee. The Sheriff who had charge of each execution was Honorable Creed Fulton Boyer. The Muster Field, where the soldiers of the early days had drilled and had been "mustered in" and "mustered out" of services, was the gathering place for all occasions during the early years of our development. It is located about one mile N.E. of our present Newport, but much nearer the Old Newport and S.E. of it.

Stephen Griffith (Some claim his name was Griffey, but most claim Griffith) was the first man to meet such a fate in Cocke County. He was convicted of a crime he went to his death protesting he did not commit. It is said that one of the men who testified against him, swore falsely.

It was customary for the Sheriff to ask the prisoner if he had anything he wished to say before the rope was placed about his neck. The
condemned man asked if he might sing his favorite song. The privilege
was granted. He sang, "Jesus Lover of My Soul, Let Me to Thy Bosom
Fly." He sang the four full stanzas as he stood in the wagon by the
dangling rope. Then he seated himself on his coffin and related in detail
the story of the experience that had brought him to such a tragic end,
and went to his death singing

> "There's a land that is fairer than day,
> And by faith we shall see it afar,
> For the Father waits over the way,
> To prepare us a dwelling place there.
> In that sweet bye and bye,
> We shall meet on that beautiful shore,
> In that sweet bye and bye,
> We shall meet on that beautiful shore."

This was November 15, 1874.

Sheriff Boyer and most of the people present were tremendously impressed with the innocence of the man. Just before the cap was placed on
the head of Stephen Griffith, Sheriff Boyer asked him why he did not
relate the story at his trial. To which he replied, "If I had told the
truth, my sentence would have been imprisonment and I prefer death to
going to the Penitentiary." Miss Linebarger of the Parrottsville section
of Cocke County stood near and heard the Sheriff ask the question and the
condemned man answered it as above. She also heard some of the
deputies state that if only they had known the truth of the matter they
would have treated the rope to a solution that would have caused it to
break with the slightest weight upon it and thus have spared his life. However, the rope did not break the culprit's neck, which seemed to
those present quite a singular co-incident in view of the circumstances
learned at the last moment. His last words were to Sheriff Boyer, "Let
me down easy."

Dan Potter, who stood near the hanging man, was asked to help in
the gruesome task by jerking the feet of the victim in an effort to break
his neck, but Stephen's neck did not break. He merely choked to death.
This fact further convinced the crowd that Griffith was innocent.

The immense throng of people at the Musterfield to witness the
"Hanging" on that autumn day, seemed somehow to thrill Dan Potter,
who made the remark that he wished he knew he would have the privilege
of dying before so great a throng of people. They had come from "far
and near" from all over East Tennessee and from Western Carolina.
Many had arrived the day before and camped on the grounds. They
came in ox carts, wagons, horseback and on mules and many came
"on foot."

A few years went by and Dan Potter's wish came true, as many of
our wishes do. It came about in this wise. . . .

Dan Potter was a very high tempered man. He worked in a blacksmith shop that was connected with the mill on the Big Pigeon River,
which at that time belonged to David B. McMahan, father of Y. J. Mc-
Mahan, who for so many years served Cocke County as one of its most

distinguished citizens, president, also cashier of the Merchant and Planters Bank.

Dave Mc, as he was called, owner of the mill and the blacksmith shop, was not pleased with some of Potter's work and probably told him so. This angered Potter terribly and from that day on he was constantly "whetting his knife" which he claimed was for the purpose of murdering Dave Mc the first time he "crossed his path" again. These threats distressed the McMahan family, except Dave, he paid no attention to them, he was a very large man and fully capable of taking care of himself under any and all circumstances, as most McMahan men are. However, this attitude of Dave did not lessen the danger that threatened him. His brother Willis was terribly distressed about it, and sought in many ways to heal the breach between the two. He would often drop in at the blacksmith shop and chat with Potter in a friendly fashion. Potter liked Willis McMahan better than he did his brother Dave, the owner of the mill and shop. The last time he called to visit with Potter was on a spring day in April 1878, almost at sunset. Potter was busy whetting his knife, which further distressed Willis Mc and he decided within his own mind that he would entice Potter away from the shop that he might avert a tragedy that seemed to be rapidly approaching. He felt that the friendship which had always existed between Potter and himself would in some way surely protect his brother Dave from Potter's wrath, his sharp knife and murderous intentions.

Willis Mc, being a kindly, friendly sort of man, persuaded Potter to go home with him, probably told him he had some good brandy, anything to get him away from his brother's mill until his fiery temper could cool a bit. Potter decided he would accept McMahan's invitation and together with his son Tom, a lad of 12 years, they walked peaceably away from the mill toward the western end of Newport.

The river and the mill were located then in the same place they now can be found, but the river was not then known as THE BLACK RIVER.

Dan Potter lived in a small two room house that stood just back of the Old Presbyterian Church that stood in the Western end of the present Newport. The church is no longer there but the graves that surrounded it are still the same and contain the dust of many of our pioneer citizens. Willis McMahan lived a bit farther toward the West on the road toward Sulphur Springs, which place is still known as The Old McMahan place.

When the two men and the little boy reached the Ben Jones barn lot, where the present handsome stone garage now stands, that was the property of the Jones heirs, Potter sent his little boy on home, (as he thought). But the boy was old enough to know that all was not well between the two men, he had probably heard his father's various "threats," anyway, he was afraid to pass through the graveyard in the twilight hour. He did not go all the way home, just walked a little in front of the men, constantly looking back to see if they were coming. He crouched in the shadow of the Church that he might not be discerned in the moonlight, and to his horror, he saw his father murder Willis McMahan. This of course added to the weird feeling he already had felt in approaching the cemetery and the fear that his father would come along and find him, he ran home with all his might and to bed, without a word to anyone, but was so upset he could not sleep, yet dared not be awake when his father came in. He was almost frightened out of his wits. He saw his father come in with blood on his hands, saw him wash them and "go back outside again." It was a terrible night for the lad, he was afraid to go to sleep, he dared not be awake when his father returned. The father was out and in the house constantly throughout the night. . . . why . . . he was constantly going and coming, we learn, from the dying man.

After Potter had stabbed McMahan several times, he cut his abdomen open, and left him for dead. Later he returned to see if any life was left in the body. He came several times and would carefully examine McMahan each time, and at each approach of the murderer, McMahan would hold his breath until Potter would go away. The last visit he made, he jerked his head back by holding him by the chin. McMahan was sure that this was when he was going to get his throat cut, "from ear to ear." But Potter seemed convinced that McMahan was "sure-nough" dead this time. He next dragged the body from near the Church where he had murdered him to the bridge that spanned the large gully that ran between what is now the Cocke County Memorial Building and the Gateway Garage. He placed the body under the bridge and threw the knife away toward the potato patch that was in the barnyard enclosure. Potter felt certain that it was useless to return to the body as he was dead and hidden for the time being, as he had left him with his intestines all out in the mud and he was not even breathing. The loss of blood was sufficient, in Potter's estimation, to insure McMahan's death. This was well past midnight. McMahan wondered what would happen next. He was afraid to call out to those who walked over the bridge, lest it might be Potter stalking around. A full thousand years seemed to drag by. It was SO dark by that time and McMahan felt life slipping away so rapidly. Finally, just before dawn, he heard hoofbeats coming from the direction of the Church, never before had they sounded like music to him. He knew Dan Potter would not be riding a horse, and he called out to the rider to please stop and bring him a drink of water. Elihu West was in a great hurry, he was going after the Doctor for his very sick wife. He recognized his neighbor's voice and told him his mission and that he would return in a few minutes with the water, he did not know the man was hurt until his return from the Doctor, when McMahan called again and told him he had been murdered and for him to go quickly and get water, and help and take him from under the bridge and to bring a doctor. Elihu West did not dismount but "spurred" his steed onward, notified his neighbors and delivered the medicine to the sick wife and got water to carry to the dying man, but his wife was prostrated with the idea of his leaving her lest he meet the same fate, but those he had informed hastened toward the bridge and by dawn quite a number had gathered there. A ladder from the Jones barn was utilized as a stretcher which was padded with hay and a quilt that had been quickly secured. The mud was washed from the man's face and hands and from his entrails. He was tenderly placed upon the improvised stretcher. By the time this was accomplished Dan Potter had joined the crowd, he rushed up quite excited and asked "Who in God's name has cut this poor man up like this?" He thought of course that Mc was dead, and that by such tactics he could establish for himself an alibi. Willis McMahan still knew enough to "play dead." (The McMahan's have always been noted for their good sense and quick thinking.) The voice and form of Sheriff

Boyer had not yet been recognized in the crowd and McMahan felt it wise to remain undisturbed until the arrival of the Sheriff.

The various men "took turns" at carrying McMahan to his brother Dave's home, which was much nearer to the bridge than his own home. All the way along to the home of Dave Mc, (which was opposite to what is now known as the Stokely-Shults Drug Store on main street of Newport,) Dan Potter kept repeating . . . "Who on earth could have committed such a crime" . . . using vile oaths each time.

By the time they reached their destination, young, fearless, brave, C. F. Boyer, the Sheriff, appeared on the scene, and as the men stepped down from the street, to the level of the house of Dave Mc, which was four steps lower than the street, Potter repeated his question to Sheriff Boyer. To his utter dismay, McMahan opened his eyes, raised his index finger, pointed it at Potter and said, "YOU, DAN POTTER, ARE THE MAN." Sheriff Boyer then and there arrested Potter on the steps to the house and took him straight to jail.

He placed him in a cell with Elbert Free, with whom he fought violently and constantly. Free bit pieces out of Potter's breast and spit them out before they could be separated, in fact, it looked as though they would "chew each other up" in spite of all that could be done. The Gingham dog and the Calico cat had nothing on Free and Potter.

Because of the rapidly approaching death of McMahan it was decided to have the preliminary hearing while he could testify. He died at 2:30 P.M. the second day after he was found under the bridge in the spring dawn of that April morn. He was about forty years of age. To this day it is not known why Potter killed Willis McMahan unless it was because of the grudge he held against Dave, the brother of Willis. "Greater love hath no man than this, that he give his life for his friend." Willis and Dave were great friends in addition to being brothers.

Just before the trial, Sheriff Boyer interviewed the twelve year old son of Potter and learned from the boy that his father came home late in the night with blood all over his hands. He also identified his father's knife that the officers had found in the potato patch, in the Ben Jones barn lot, where McMahan had told the men present at dawn at the bridge, where Potter had thrown it. He was able to indicate the direction in which Potter threw it.

Feeling ran terribly high in Cocke County, and for safe keeping, the McMahans insisted that Potter be placed in the Knox County jail. Dave McMahan was prosecuting the case, but Court did not convene until July. Potter's terrible conduct in the Newport jail also made it necessary for him to be transferred to the Knox County jail where he could be placed in a dungeon. Another prisoner was also in the dungeon. They crawled around in the dark until they found a way to escape by digging into the sewer line, through which they crawled the very short distance to the Tennessee river. For several minutes, they swam around in the river, during the dead hours of night, until they found a ferry boat, crossed the river and got away without being detected.

Sheriff Boyer received no word of the escape of the prisoners until seventy-two hours had passed. Probably the Knox County Sheriff knew nothing of the escape himself until that time and there was no telephone service.

On the morning of the third day after the prisoners had taken leave of the jail, Sheriff Boyer and many others "took the trail" at the Tennessee River, where the ferryboat had landed. They were all horseback, and most enthusiastic in the beginning of the "MAN HUNT." Sheriff Reeder of Knox County and several men joined the Cocke County party.

After about a week's intensive searching, the posse that began with Sheriff Boyer had about "quit him" and the chase was considered fruitless, but Sheriff Boyer was not easily discouraged. He continued alone and unaided, for another week. He rode and walked over every foot of the mountain sections of Cocke County. He did not take time to sleep longer than one or two hours at a time. Finally, while on one of our highest peaks, he saw Potter, some distance away, on another peak. Now that he had located him, his problem was to capture him. He knew that his task was a most dangerous one and that Potter would be well armed if it had been possible for him to secure arms. He also knew that he had to have a place to rest and sleep where he felt protected and that he had to have food. These questions were soon solved when Sheriff Boyer learned that the sister of Potter, Mrs. Will Freeman, lived in the mountains near the North Carolina and Tennessee State line.

To the Freeman home, Sheriff Boyer found his way and spoke to Will Freeman just as though he knew that Dan Potter would be there for food and a place to sleep that very night. Freeman was not willing to admit such a possibility, whereupon the Sheriff informed him that he knew he was harboring a dangerous criminal, and THAT HE HAD COME AFTER HIM AND WOULD TAKE HIM DEAD OR ALIVE and that if he would help him capture Potter that he would give him one hundred dollars in gold. Freeman was still reluctant, probably somewhat frightened with the thought of Potter's record, together with the knowledge of his relationship to him, (yet in some instances it has been known to be the fact that in-laws are not any too devoted, one to the other). Finally after considerable discussion, the Sheriff gave Freeman choice of going to jail for refusing to help him, or of helping with the arrest, at the same time warning Freeman, that if he tried any "funny work, or in any way what-so-ever gave his presence away" upon the approach of Potter, that HE WOULD JUST KILL HIM BEFORE HE HAD TO KILL POTTER, if it took such action to protect his own life. Freeman AGREED and the two shook hands, after which they made plans as to how to go about the difficult and dangerous task.

After two weeks constant searching, Sheriff Boyer was extremely weary and worn and exhausted for sleep. There was only one bed in the house. It was offered the Sheriff that he might relax, rest, and if possible sleep an hour or two, while waiting for Potter to come for food or sleep. Boyer was, of course extremely "leery" of going to sleep, but Freeman had agreed to sit up and listen for Potter and to come to the bed the moment he heard Potter "WHISTLE" from the mountain side. He was not to speak, but to pull or press on Boyer's arm, before he answered the criminal's signal by returning the whistle. Boyer listened more intently than Freeman for the whistle, but Freeman heard it and true to his agreement came to the bed, Boyer pretending to be sound asleep. Freeman pulled on his arm, but Boyer did not respond, just to give Freeman a chance to make sure of himself. The sheriff almost doubted Freeman, even if it were almost impossible for Freeman to do other than keep his agreement. Still Potter had a *first agreement* with his brother-in-law, to *let him know by whistle, if it were safe for him to come to the house,* and if he should not come down the mountain, Freeman was to remain silent and not answer the whistle. Probably the Sheriff's threat had much to do with his keeping his second agreement, anyway, he pulled the second time on Boyer's arm and much harder than before. The Sheriff raised his arm, neither spoke a word, lest the desparado was just out-side the door. Boyer arose from the bed, then Will Freeman opened the door of his mountain cabin and whistled into the darkness of the night. Boyer stood back of the door so that he would be protected from the man's vision should he be within "seeing distance" of the room, which was well lighted by the blaze from the great log fire on the hearth. Potter entered the open door, his hands were outstretched toward the fire. The night was bitter cold. Freeman closed the door securely. Sheriff Boyer commanded the criminal to raise his hands above his head, instead of holding them toward the fire. Potter instantly obeyed the command without turning around, realizing that he was securely trapped. He recognized the voice of Creed Boyer and said. . . . "I surrender Mr. Boyer" who, in turn, said, "You are my meat, Dan Potter."

It is "a thousand wonders" that Dan Potter did not attempt to murder Boyer before he got his hands tied behind his body. He might have thought that if he had attempted such a thing his sister and her husband would assist him, however, Dan Potter was well acquainted with Creed Boyer and knew how fearless he was and that he had a very keen mind, with a quick hand and a quicker eye. He stood there with his hands above his head, while the sheriff commanded Freeman to cut the cords from his ONE BED and tie Potter's hands behind him. It is not known if he tied Potter to his horse's bit or not, but it is known, *that alone and un-aided,* he walked this very dangerous criminal in front of him, all the way to Newport, on a dark night, a distance of 25 miles and *through the wildest mountain section of Cocke County.* IT WAS A MOST REMARK-ABLE FEAT, a most treacherous undertaking in view of the fact that Potter *had killed seven men in his short day.* He tried every way possible to find some means of escape, he kept suggesting to the sheriff, that he wanted to ride a while, to which Boyer replied, "Well, you can first walk a while, and I shall ride a while, then I shall ride a while, and you can walk awhile." Boyer had a most unusual sense of humor along with his fine intelligence. It was one of his most marked characteristics.

From the capture, to the trial of Potter he was kept in the Newport jail this time lest he might escape again.

The main witness against Potter at his trial was his son, Thomas Potter, aged about fourteen by the time of the trial. He swore same as at preliminary his father came home late the night of the murder and that his hands were bloody. He also identified the knife as being his father's. The boy's testimony had much to do with his conviction. It enraged the murderer and he swore he would kill his son.

When Potter was indicted and brought into Court for trial, he had not employed a lawyer, and advised the Court he was not able to employ one. In the meantime, General Pickle had been employed to prosecute Potter. The Court appointed Mr. Jerome Templeton to defend Potter, and he obtained permission of the Court for a private interview with his client. (George W. Pickle was an Attorney General and Reporter of Tennessee for sixteen years. He had practiced law in Newport in partnership with Jerome Templeton, with the firm name of Pickle and Templeton. This firm had dissolved while Potter was a fugitive from justice. However, the lawyers remained in Newport, each practicing alone.)

This arrangement was of course, not known to Potter, he thought they were still partners and when he learned that Templeton had been appointed to defend him and that Mr. Pickle was prosecuting him, he decided it must be some kind of a "frame up" that one member of a firm would not prosecute and the other defend. He became much enraged and when Templeton took him into a private room for the conference Potter accused Templeton of "double-crossing" him and drew from a secret hiding place a well whetted barlow knife with which he informed him he was going to "cut his throat" that it would make no difference if he killed one more man anyway. Templeton, being a cool headed man and devoid of fear, ignored Potter's threat, and very calmly invited him to be seated and discuss the matter as he wanted to know about the FRAME UP . . . etc. . . . The guard by that time had returned to the room and took the knife from Potter while Templeton explained that the firm of Pickle and Templeton were no longer partners and that he was to defend him.

The Supreme Court at Knoxville, Tennessee at its September term, 1880, affirmed the offense of murder in the first degree of which Potter had been convicted and ordered that the prisoner be kept in close confinement in Cocke County jail until Friday, the 12th day of November, 1880, and on the 12th day of November next, the said Sheriff of Cocke County, at some convenient place prepared for that purpose, within one mile of the county seat of said County, between the hours of ten o'clock A.M. and 2 o'clock P.M. shall hang the said, Daniel C. Potter by the neck until he is dead.

On the day previous to the hanging, the people began to arrive at the Muster Field. They came horseback, muleback, in ox carts, in wagons drawn by mules, and by horses; they came on foot. They were from all over the Eastern section of Tennessee and the Western section of North Carolina. Hundreds camped at the Muster Field the night of Nov. 11, 1880. It is said by those present, that never before, nor since, has Newport experienced such a drawing card. The Muster Field has, since that day, been known as, "The Potter Hanging Ground."

The gallows was erected with one post placed in the same hole that was used for Stephen Griffith's gallows, which consisted of two upright posts, set wide enough apart to drive a wagon through the space between them. A cross bar was placed on the top of the posts. To this crude structure the criminal was driven in a wagon, the rope placed around his neck and the wagon then driven from under him. Before the wagon was driven away a condemned man or woman was always given the privilege of saying whatsoever he felt inclined to say before his execution.

When Daniel C. Potter was asked if he had anything to say, he replied, "Yes, if I could only kill three more men the powers that be could cut me up and saw me in two, skin me, burn me, do anything to me that they might choose to do."

It is said by those who knew, that the three men Dan Potter wanted so much to kill were Sheriff Boyer, Major Thomas Gorman and his own son, Thomas Potter.

During the time that elapsed between the murder of Willis McMahan and the execution of his murderer, Daniel C. Potter, David McMahan, the owner of the mill, and brother of Willis, had died. It is said by those who heard it that on the morning of the execution Potter made the following terrible remark in the presence of many people: "I hope I will be hung in time to get to hell to eat dinner with Dave Mc." It is said that Dr. Hooper informed those listening that none of them would get any dinner that day, for Potter would kick all the pots over while he was hanging. This he evidently tried to do. When the sheriff placed the rope about his neck he jumped and kicked and plunged terribly and succeeded in getting the knot under his chin, thereby hoping to escape death, even though the law had taken its course. This ruse on Potter's part did not work with the sheriff, who deliberately had the team turned, which was an awful "undertaking" in that great crowd of people, finally it was accomplished and the wagon was driven back under the scaffold and the rope was rearranged on Potter's neck. The second time he was hung the knot went under his ear where it was supposed to have gone the first time. THIS DELAY, OF COURSE DELAYED HIS DEATH MANY MINUTES which enabled him to ENJOY a much LONGER period of DYING before the vast throng of people he had wished a few years previous he might have the privilege of dying before as had Stephen Griffith. It is said that considerably more than ten thousand people witnessed the gruesome ordeal, which was a much greater throng than were present at the Griffith execution.

> State of Tennessee
> Supreme Court at Knoxville
> September Term. . . . September 20, 1880.

Daniel C. Potter   In error   Murder
vs
The State

Comes the Att Genl. to prosecute for the State & the Plaintiff in error is brought to the Bar of the Court in the custody of its officer & appeared also by counsel;

And the Court being of opinion that there is no error in the record of the Court below.

It is therefore considered by the Court that the judgment of the Circuit Court of Cocke County, in this case, be and the same is affirmed; that for the offense of murder in the first degree of which he has been convicted, the said Plaintiff in error Daniel C. Potter is remanded to the custody of the Sheriff of Knox County, who is hereby commanded to convey or deliver the said Daniel C. Potter to the Sheriff of Cocke County, to be by him safely kept, in the jail of said Cocke County, in close confinement, until Friday the 12th day of November next; And on the said 12th day of November next, the said Sheriff of Cocke County, at some convenient place prepared for that purpose, within one mile of the County

Seat of said County, between the hours of 10 o'clock A.M. and 2 o'clock P.M. shall hang the said Daniel C. Potter by the neck until he is dead.

It is further ordered that the State recover of the Plaintiff in error the costs of this prosecution for which execution may issue; That the Clerk furnish to the Sheriff of Knox County a copy of this judgment to be delivered with the prisoner to the Sheriff of Cocke County to be and constitute his authority for the execution of this order to him, the said Sheriff of Cocke County.

Attached to above order the following. . . .

State of Tennessee

I, J. F. Deadrick, Clerk of the Supreme Court of said State at Knoxville, do hereby certify that the foregoing is a full and true copy of the JUDGMENT pronounced by said Court, in cause therein named, at its September term 1880, as the same appears of record in my office.

Given under my hand and the Seal of Said Court, at office in Knoxville, this 14th day of October 1880.

J. F. Deadrick, Clerk.

This Judgment written in a bold plain hand on legal cap paper folded in the center and again in the center on back of one side these words.

Copy of Judgment

Danl C. Potter In Error

vs

The State.

On other side in a beautiful hand, these words,

Came to hand Nov. 9th 1880.

Executed as commanded Nov. 12th 1880.

C. F. Boyer, Shff.

John W. Greene and Attorneys claim this to be a remarkable document with more volume in fewer words than commonly given in such instances.

This copy through the courtesy of Dr. H. S. Boyer and Mack Boyer, sons of Sheriff C. F. Boyer.

The School Teachers in 1894

Civic, Educational, and Social Development of Cocke County

The Newspapers

The development of any phase of Cocke County would be hard to separate from her newspaper history, but there would probably be no civic, educational, or social development, were it not for the press.

Cocke County has had numerous newspapers and many editors. The first paper was established at Big Creek (Del Rio) in 1875 by Joseph L. Bible, publisher, and John T. Jones, editor. It was a small sheet, 4 by 6 inches. Bible[1] distinguished himself by making his own press, for which he bought the type.

The EXCELSIOR STAR'S editor[2] was more or less poetic. One of the early issues carried this bit of verse:

What is more beautiful than the moon
Whether she rises late or whether she rises soon?

In 1876, Bible moved to Parrottsville and published THE REPORTER, and in 1877, he moved to Newport and continued his paper under the name of THE NEWPORT REPORTER.

The April 30, 1877, issue contained the following poem contributed by Mrs. Chattie Stokely Smith Rainwater, whose parents kept the poem 73 years.

TO-MORROW, AYA C. P.

One little word so often heard, how much from it we borrow
And build on air such castles fair for that bright day, To-morrow.
When cares oppress the troubled heart, and often when in sorrow
We hide a tear, suppress a fear and think upon To-morrow.
How very true and yet how few would willingly believe me,
Were I to say that happy day was made but to deceive me.
This day goes by altho we sigh, much from the next we borrow
But when today has passed away, where is our bright To-morrow?
It is not here to dry the tear, or yet to soothe the sorrow,
Why then do we trust in thee, untold, untried, To-morrow?

By the end of 1877, J. L. Bible had moved to Dandridge and there consolidated several papers into THE NEWPORT REPORTER, MADISON COUNTY NEWS, STUDENT'S MIRROR and THE DANDRIDGE WATCHMAN into THE WATCHMAN AND REPORTER, which he published until his death.

At a very early date, Taylor's HISTORIC SULLIVAN tells us that a Mr. Hoss moved from Sullivan County to Newport and established a news-

---

1. His father was an industrious person who tanned his own cattle hides and made them into shoes.

2. It is interesting to note that J. L. Bible, the editor of the first paper and J. L. Caton, the present editor, not only have two identical initials but both also introduce original verse into their columns.

The Normal, 1895, in front of the Courthouse

paper. Some claim his name was Calvin Hoss; others, Henry Hoss. No one knows the name of his paper, or the date of its publication.

In 1878, THE EASTERN STAR was published by A. J. Thomas and continued to 1883 under that name when it became THE EASTERN SENTINEL. A. J. Thomas was editor and Miss Mary E. Smith, publisher of this four-page, seven-column paper.

In 1884 (Taylor), THE STATE JOURNAL was edited by J. W. P. Massey, and in 1885, N. P. Phillips combined THE EASTERN STAR and THE STATE JOURNAL into THE STAR JOURNAL.

The year 1886 brought THE NEWPORT LEDGER, published by Rufus Christopher. About this date, Charles Huff and Hardin Kelly edited a paper at Parrottsville, followed by THE ARGOS or THE ARGUS, edited and published by Nimrod Parker.

On December 2, 1887, Jim Hood published the first issue of THE NEWPORT CITIZEN, four pages, 7 columns each, with an official directory, depot agent's report, county history, mail service, and sermon by DeWitt Talmadge.

This was followed by THE GAZETTE, editor unknown. THE TIMES, the first of several papers by that name, was owned and edited by F. H. Fagala, in 1889. In 1891, THE NEWPORT NEWS was published by Milton H. Bybee and edited by John T. Jones, the County's first editor.

In 1895, THE NEWPORT WEEKLY, was established and edited by Charles B. Haag, who came from Philadelphia, Pennsylvania, to Cocke County in the boom days. He became one of the promoters of its industrial development, married Hester Eliza Boyer, and lived in Newport many years. Soon after its establishment, Haag sold the paper to another Pennsylvanian, George W. Gardner, who edited the paper several years. He often claimed it was well-named, had great difficulty in keeping it alive, and finally let it die a natural death.

During THE NEWPORT WEEKLY'S existence, Newport had four other newspapers, THE NEWPORT TIMES, THE COCKE COUNTY REPUBLICAN, THE PLAIN TALK, and THE EAST TENNESSEE ODD FELLOW.

THE COCKE COUNTY REPUBLICAN was owned by a company of the following men: Alexander Ragan, C. F. Boyer, Henry Penland, Rufus Hickey, Walter Bibee. H. O. Lee was the manager and Walter W. Bibee, the publisher. This paper was later sold to Oscar L. Hicks.

In 1897, THE TIMES was edited by Henry H. Dukes.[3] In 1900, PLAIN TALK put in its appearance. It was established by Ex-Congressman W. C. Anderson at the time of his defeat by Walter P. Brownlow. Anderson, in conversation with Swann L. Burnett about his defeat said, "I would like to establish a newspaper and do some plain talking around here." Burnett replied, "Why don't you, and name your paper PLAIN TALK?" There is no other one by that name in the United States, although a magazine in Canada bore the name at the beginning of the present century.

In 1904, Frank Fagala sold THE TIMES to T. H. Campbell, who had long worked on the paper, as well as on the other four newspapers. Tom Campbell edited his TIMES several years and sold it to R. H. Sexton and John Holt who converted it into a Republican paper. Soon

---

3. In 1938, Dukes was employed on the MIAMI FLORIDA NEWS.

Plain Talk Office

R. P. Sulte, Editor—Hubert Greenway "Woody" (Woodrow) Lewis at the back.

after this transaction, Mrs. Campbell bought the PLAIN TALK from Bruce Susong, who owned and operated it. She hired her husband, Tom Campbell, who ably edited THE PLAIN TALK until February 15, 1926, when he sold it to R. P. Sulte, Sr., of Rockwood, Knoxville, and Virginia.

In 1906, THE NEWPORT TENNESSEAN was flourishing under its editor, O. L. Hicks. On January 4, 1906, the first issue of THE EAST TENNESSEE ODD FELLOW was entered at the Newport Post Office, a four-column four-page paper, 12 by 18 inches, bordered by the Odd Fellow links. This publication was edited first by Dr. J. F. Woodward and John H. W. Sellers and published by Walter W. Bibee. Later it was edited by Sellers. Bibee sold his printing press and T. H. Campbell published the paper for a year, after which George W. Gardner took over the publication, due to the illness of Campbell. The last issue of this paper was August, 1907.

By 1915, THE TIMES had again changed hands, edited by George W. Sheaff. The owners of the paper were: A. A. Cates, J. W. Kyker, J. A. Coggins, Watson Ford, Zeb Clevenger, John Harrison, Ben W. Hooper, O. L. McMahan and W. T. Fox.

Soon after this date Tom Campbell "bought back" THE TIMES from its stockholders and combined its equipment with that of his PLAIN TALK. Later, he purchased the Gardner equipment.

In 1917, THE NEWPORT HERALD was established and edited by M. A. Roadman (known as Ted Roadman). His wife, Nola Allen Roadman, ably assisted in its publication. Ted had previously edited THE PLAIN TALK a few years for the Anderson children (as Robert, Hubert, Bess, Julia, W. C., Jr. were called during the years they edited their father's PLAIN TALK).

The years 1920 and 21 saw the DIAMOND DUST and HOB-NAIL SPECIAL SHEETS edited by Urey K. Goodwin. His full grapevine service, such as that of September 24, 1921, amused the readers.

In 1928, Ted Roadman sold THE NEWPORT HERALD to R. P. Sulte, who kept it only a few months and disposed of it to Dick Edwards and George Likens, who, with O. A. Porter, published it a few months under the name of THE OPTIMIST.

After a few issues of THE OPTIMIST, the paper was sold to R. P. Sulte, who immediately sold it to George R. Shepherd, in March, 1932. Attorney Shepherd changed its name to THE COCKE COUNTY TRIBUNE, of which a Mr. Peake became editor. Later, Burnett Shepherd was editor. After a few years, it merged with the PLAIN TALK and became PLAIN TALK AND TRIBUNE, with R. P. Sulte, editor.

R. P. Sulte, who possessed a delightful personality, had long been an editor of various papers in Harriman, Rockwood, and Knoxville, before he came to Newport in 1926. He was versatile and had a highly-developed sense of humor, kept an open mind, and took an active part in the civic and religious activities in the town of Newport and in Cocke County. His editorials were widely-read and thoroughly enjoyed. He lived long enough to see the fruits of his labor and to realize that his was the best county paper in the state. He served as president of both the East Tennessee Press and the Tennessee Press Associations, and of the Newport Kiwanis Club. After his death, May 12, 1941, Woody Lewis became editor of PLAIN TALK AND TRIBUNE and served until February 26,

1942, when Attorney George R. Shepherd purchased from Mrs. Sulte, her husband's interest in the paper. When Mr. Shepherd became sole owner of the papers, the office force was reorganized and Joseph L. Caton of Knoxville became editor.

When Editor Tom Campbell sold PLAIN TALK and moved away February 15, 1926, to Lenoir City, he purchased a paper and edited it for almost four years. He then moved to Marshall, North Carolina, where he operated a paper for a few months; thence to Tazewell, where he managed THE PROGRESS for Harry Haynes a short while. Later, he worked in Jefferson City until he was called to Nashville, where he prepared political copy for Nashville and other state papers. Finally, his homesickness overcame him and he returned to Newport, where he reestablished THE NEWPORT TIMES, his first love, May 25, 1938, in which he states,

I have returned. I hope it will be my happy lot to dwell among, and to faithfully and profitably serve the people among whom I was reared and whom I learned to know and love. And when that service shall come to an end, and I have forever laid down the working tools of life, I want to be carried by loving hands to the open grave where I shall lay me down to sleep among the hills of Tennessee.

Cocke County welcomed T. H. Campbell home. He had become one of the best-known editors in Tennessee, outspoken and fearless, with the courage of his convictions, and had occupied a unique place among newspaper men.

On the editorial page of THE NEWPORT TIMES on its second birthday, May 29, 1940, Mr. Campbell said, "The TIMES editor came back to Newport to 'finish' and it is our hope we may leave an offspring in our chair. He is already being trained and understands we expect him to bat for us when the Great Umpire calls us out."

On April 11, 1941, Tom Campbell "laid down the working tools of life." THE NEWPORT TIMES was then edited by Steve Campbell, the first-born son of the Editor, until October 30, 1943, when the young editor had to answer his country's call for military duty. On this date, Judge George R. Shepherd bought THE NEWPORT TIMES from the Campbell family.

This takes the story of Cocke County's "Disseminators of Knowledge" almost through 1946, and now the combined papers are edited by J. L. Caton, a veteran newspaper man from Knoxville. Although Mr. Caton is a Democrat, he edited both the Republican and the Democrat papers for several years. At present, 1950, Jack Shepherd, son of Judge George R. Shepherd edits the PLAIN TALK and TRIBUNE, and Mr. Caton edits THE NEWPORT TIMES.

"SALUTE TO COCKE COUNTY"

By Mrs. J. H. Bell, of Cosby, Tennessee . . . February 26, 1940

Cradled in the arms of the Great Smoky Mountains, Cocke County boasts first of its healthful climate and scenic resources. Chain-like peaks embrace the county to the East and West, protecting it against storms and checking wintry blasts, giving the county a nature made air conditioning system which moderates the weather. In summer the lofty peaks catch prevailing winds and waft them down over the hills and valleys in the form of Sweet Zephyrs.

— 223 —

The county is unsurpassed in scenic resources. The unexplained mysterious blue haze, which gives the Smokies their name, enhances the beauty of the mountains.

The thriving city of Newport is the county seat and Northern Gateway to the Smoky Mountains National Park. From this center, roads, most of which are paved, branch out to Knoxville, Morristown, Asheville, Waynesville, Gatlinburg, and Sevierville. In addition, a network of farm-to-market roads gives the entire county excellent transportation facilities.

The major part of the population is engaged in farming, livestock, poultry and fruit raising, being the principal products. The soil is of high productivity, unexcelled for truck farming, very little soil erosion has damaged these farm lands.

Cocke county's industries include a large canning factory, a tannery, an extract company, several knitting, grain and feed mills and lumbering.

Educational facilities are excellent. There are three high schools, from which buses operate into the most remote districts.

Two beautiful rivers, The Pigeon and French Broad, and many smaller streams meander through the timbered regions of the county, giving the sportsmen an ideal area for hunting and fishing.

Last, but not least, Cocke County is the home of ex-Governor Ben W. Hooper and Ruth W. O'Dell, Tennessee's only woman legislator, and the world famous movie star, Grace Moore, was born here.

Early Amusements

Considerable revenue as well as pleasure was derived from hunting, in the early days. Among the familiar hunters were "Gray" John Sutton, "Peach-Eye" Jim Norton, Joe Campbell, Tom Barnes, and Samuel McGaha, who appeared at Old Newport to engage in the general muster clothed in red linsey hunting shirt, hanging loose over the belt, with buckskin moccasins, coonskin cap with tail dangling between the shoulders, with a cow horn for powder resting upon an otterskin shot pouch swinging around the body, and hunting knife fastened to shot pouch strap and flintlock rifle resting on shoulder.

One of the principal amusements was horse racing. The first horse racing ever done in the county was on the ground now the main street of the present town of Newport, and it is claimed that Andrew Jackson attended the races and engaged in the sport along with Colonel Alexander Smith, the Stuarts, the Jennings and the Neffs. In later years, the sport was followed by the Nethertons, Swaggerties, the Robinsons, the Sisks, and Stokelys.

The early settlers also took great interest in foot racing, jumping, and wrestling. There is a tradition that upon all public occasions, and particularly when the militia assembled, the fastest on foot, the fartherest jumper, and the best wrestler were awarded prizes. Even within the recollection of W. J. McSween, no man could equal William Campbell in a foot race and no one could withstand the knee lock of John H. Stokely in a wrestling match.

These settlers also tested their physical strength by the throwing of a stone, by wielding of an ax and a maul at a chopping and rail-splitting, and by the lifting of a handspike at a logrolling.

William Huff, the son of Joseph Huff, was said to have been the most powerful specimen of manhood ever reared in Cocke County, and always won the prize for strength. Sometimes when excitement was high and whiskey plentiful, the physical test was made by a fisticuff fight or pitched battle. To provoke a battle of this kind, it was only necessary for the party who desired to engage to jump up in the air, crack his heels together three times, and exclaim, "I am the best man in the county," or "I am much a man." Another kind of challenge was for the person who wanted to fight to step up by the side of the other pugilist and crow like a rooster and the fight would be on.

From an old letter dated, Newport, December 1, 1834, written by James H. Stuart, a student at Anderson Academy, to John McSween, a student of Maryville College, is taken the following: "Last week was Court week in our town and we had a time of it with your savage country folks, they cut all kinds of shines on Monday and Tuesday evenings, but after this they were as cool as you please. On Tuesday evening Major William Robinson whipped six of the bullies, which settled them. Court lasted from Monday morning until Saturday night, trying those savages. We will have them up at the next Court before old Scot (Judge Edward), and if he is drunk he will send some of them to the building."

The last pitched battle that was ever fought in Cocke County was in 1853, when Stephen Huff, Jr., a young man about nineteen years old challenged Phil Sutton, a man about twenty-four years of age. The two combatants were men of powerful build and strength, each claiming superiority to the other. The sequel, however, proved that Huff was the stronger and Sutton the most active. A formal challenge and acceptance passed between the parties and the time for the contest was fixed.

At the spring term of Circuit Court, 1853, the two met at Old Newport before something like 1500 people, among them the sheriff, justices of the peace, and other county officials. The battleground was at the old ferry, just above the Old Town bridge, and a ring was formed by driving stakes in the ground and stretching ropes. Sutton selected as his seconds Doctor Henry O'Dell, Dan Duncan, and Lawson Sutton; Huff selected as his, John J. Allen, or "Big Pot," as he was known, William Weaver, and Pleasant Lane. The seconds filed into the ring, taking the positions set apart for their respective combatants, and were immediately followed by Huff and Sutton, who were stripped to the waist, with their heads shaved closely with a razor and their scalps thoroughly greased with hog's lard. William Weaver kept them apart until everything was ready, and then he gave the command for the fight to begin. There was no sparring but the combatants rushed together like demons. Huff parried Sutton's first blow with his left arm, landing a terrific blow with his right on Sutton's jaw. Sutton recovered and returned the blow; then the blows by both came fast and thick, Huff gaining his advantage all the time. The Huff partisans, seeing his advantage, raised the whoop and yell for Huff. This caused O'Dell, contrary to the agreement among the seconds, to cry out for Sutton. This greatly encouraged Sutton, who closed in with Huff and threw him to the ground. He caught Huff by the throat, and some spectators thought that as he struck the ground he got hold of a rock and hit Huff with it. At this juncture, N. H. Stokely, seeing this act, cried, "Foul," cut the rope, and attempted to loosen the hold of Sutton upon Huff's throat, when he was instantly knocked down by Henry O'Dell.

Allen made a rush to rescue Huff, but was struck a stunning blow by Lawson Sutton. In a flash Allen recovered and returned the blow and then landed blows so fast upon Sutton that he never recovered himself. About this time, Tom Huff rushed into the ring waving a stick, but was faced by Henry O'Dell. Colonel William Jack advanced to the ring, and demanded that the combatants be separated, and this was done by Ash Woods. All eyes were centered upon two of the seconds, Allen and O'Dell, and it was momentarily expected that there would be a contest between those two men, for they had been selected on account of their superior physical strength. At that time, John Allen was twenty-three years old, six feet, three inches in height, weighing 210 pounds, strong, active, fearless, and determined. O'Dell was twenty-one years old, and of the same height and weight and with the same qualities as his opposing second. When O'Dell struck Stokely, Allen accepted the challenge and would have returned the blow had not Sutton prevented. Huff was never satisfied with the result of the battle, even after Sutton died. All the participants passed away before 1904, except Allen and O'Dell, who remained lifelong friends.[4]

In a letter written to Miss Willian Mims on January 15, 1924, J. H. Faubion, of Leander, Texas, told of watching fist fights in the early days from a horse-rack on a side street. One day when the "Melish" were in town and patriotism and John Barleycorn were at fever heat, two champions fought under that same rack. One fellow had the other's thumb in his mouth, and the other had his opponent's nose in his mouth. The jaws of the combatants were pried loose. In a short time the man whose nose was now bitten, no longer had one. The other man lost his thumb.

The people of that day were friendly and sociable, visiting or entertaining friends every Sunday. A wedding attracted much attention with its wedding dinner and "infair." Harvesting, house-raisings, corn-shuckings, and quiltings also were popular. Election and muster days brought out crowds and the man with a barrel of cider and a big basket of ginger cake.

Public hangings always drew huge numbers, and these came from the adjoining counties and from North Carolina as well, probably supplying the "thrills" that the movies do today. A famous one was that of Stephen Griffee (spelling according to Hugh Gouchenour), who was hanged for a crime he protested he did not commit on or about November 15, 1876. Dan Potter who helped in the gruesome task is said to have made the remark that he wished he knew he would have the privilege of dying before so great a throng of people. He got his wish on November 12, 1880, for a crowd estimated at ten thousand saw him hanged for the murder of Willis McMahan, one of the most ghastly deeds in the annals of Cocke County.[5]

---

4. Jasper Gray walked from his home in his crippled condition, a distance of seven miles, at the age of seventy, so that the author could benefit from the W. J. McSween articles in his old papers, from which much of the foregoing material is taken.

5. The author has an extensive and fascinating history of this murder found on page 210.

Education in Cocke County

The early settlers of Cocke County built Anderson Academy, named for Judge Joseph Anderson, one of the judges appointed for the Southwest territory and one of the first judges appointed for Tennessee as a State. While the Academy was not inside the Gilleland fifty-acre tract of land, it was considered one of the public buildings of the town of Old Newport. A lottery scheme was used to raise money to build this school. The Act passed by the General Assembly of Tennessee, September 13, 1806, provided that Isaac Leonard, Abraham McCoy (McKay), Peter Fine, Daniel McPhearson and William Lillard be the Trustees of Anderson Academy. The Act of October 17, 1811, provided that William Helm, Sr., Henry Stevens, William Garrett, John Shields and Charles T. Porter be appointed additional trustees. On October 28, 1813, the Legislature passed an act for a lottery for the benefit of the Academy, appointing William Garrett, Francis Jackson Carter, Charles T. Porter, John Shields, Thomas Fowler, Henry Stevens, and William Lillard trustees for the lottery. This lottery was to raise a sum, not exceeding five thousand dollars. By an Act of November 12, 1817, Colonel Alexander Smith, Francis J. Carter and Augustine Jenkins were appointed additional trustees.

From the lottery so authorized, the money was raised and the Academy was built between the years 1813 and 1815, one mile from Old Newport, on the top of the hill, fronting the house of William Garrett and on the left hand side of the road leading to the said house. J. H. Susong later lived at the Garrett house. The Academy stood a few yards up the hill and south of where the school house now stands. One of the first teachers here was Rudolph, of Virginia.

During the 1820's, Anderson Academy (according to Judge Williams) was a Presbyterian enterprise, Robert McAlpin, being one of the teachers. He had been a Captain in the War of 1812. Williams also states that the Academy was doubtless named in honor of Rev. Dr. Isaac Anderson, founder of Maryville College, who from 1812 preached throughout the region around Maryville. A remarkable product of the Academy was Joseph, a slave of Francis J. Carter, of Dutch Bottom, who sent him to Anderson Academy, where he stayed at the home of James Gilliland. Modest, humble, and of deep piety, he gained the confidence of the people and became a powerful Methodist preacher in the County. "His congregations were often large, and the intelligent of the County attended his ministry with interest and profit."

Other teachers were Nathan Hood, a Presbyterian preacher, Benjamin F. Boulden, and Montgomery Randoph. The last school was conducted in this Academy by D. V. Stokely in the year 1849 or 1850.

General A. E. Smith, Colonel William Jack, Alvy Jack, Alfred Cochran, D. Ward Stuart, George Stuart, W. A. Robinson, James H. Robinson, E. K. Robinson, James Swaggerty, Jr., Alexander Swaggerty, Colonel William C. Roadman, R. S. Roadman, M. A. Roadman, A. E. Smith, Jr., W. R. Smith, Lucius Smith and many others were educated or partly educated at the old Academy.

About the year 1836, Anderson Academy was the recipient of some six to eight thousand dollars due Cocke County from some of the surplus accumulated in the U. S. Treasury, allotted to Tennessee. The trustees loaned the money at interest, which was used to pay teachers. All young men and women of the county under certain ages had the right to attend the school free of charge.

The old Academy being some distance from town, the Legislature authorized its removal into the town of Newport, on January 26, 1848. The site for the building was on the hill opposite the old courthouse. A part of the money was appropriated for the construction of a building, the contract being let to John Seebolt, of Dandridge. By the first of the year 1850, the two-story brick building was ready for use. The lower story had one large and two small recitation rooms; the upper story was one large room. The building was surmounted by a large belfry, thirty feet high and fifty feet above the ground. Benjamin F. Boulden, James Davies, Reverend W. H. Smith, Pleasant Witt Anderson, Miss Rachel Waddell, and D. Ward Stuart taught in this new building.

J. H. Faubion tells of the early neighborhood schoolhouse, with the floor often just the earth, or split logs called puncheons. For seats, split logs with pins of wood for legs, and no back, sufficed. Usually a log was cut out of the wall for lighting and ventilation. Writing was taught on a shelf under the log window. In summer, pokeberries were used to make ink, and the teacher made pens from goose quills. The school, never more than three months, had only one teacher, even if a hundred pupils were in attendance. Often there were few books alike, and sometimes three or four would use the same book. On Fridays, the more advanced students had "to say speeches." His first teacher was James Manning, a son of Rev. Joseph Manning. Benjamin I. Boulden was feared and remembered as a great tobacco chewer. The last school Faubion attended was taught by Prof. Henry L. Davies, a real teacher, well educated, with the ability to make his ideas clear, but without the ability to enforce discipline. Like many others, he quit school permanently in 1861 to carry a musket.

At the beginning of the Civil War, Benjamin F. Boulden, a University of Virginia graduate, had charge of Anderson Academy. He was a classical scholar, a fine disciplinarian, and had a thorough knowledge of military tactics. When War came, he espoused the cause of the Confederacy and drilled his young men for military service, among them Captain Edd Allen and Captain A. L. Mims.[6]

One of the most beloved of the early teachers was William Maynard, who taught in the Old Presbyterian Church that stood in the west end of Newport. Pupils from various points in the County walked to this school. Isaac Haskins, a cripple, also taught in the early days, and William Walker. Robert Ragan taught about the time of the Civil War.

The commencement programs of the Parrottsville Seminary were attended by the young and older people from all over the County, surrounding counties, and Western North Carolina. They came in every available manner to the programs, which were always held in the springtime out in the open, where an enclosure had been made of brush (evergreen limbs, with roses and springtime blossoms intertwined). For seats,

6. Anderson Academy information from W. J. McSween articles.

slabs from the nearby mill were used by all who failed to bring their chairs.[7]

In 1875, Newport Academy was erected by Newport Lodge No. 234, F. & A. M., under the supervision of Prof. W. R. Manard. In 1885, a Baptist Seminary was opened under N. E. W. Stokely.

The Nawvacs, Christian missionaries, established a kind of industrial school in the old fifteenth district, about four miles South of Del Rio. All kinds of clothing, books, and literature were sent from churches throughout the country. Nearby citizens contributed toward a building fund, to which Joseph Draper gave fifty dollars, and his wife boarded two of the first teachers for four months without pay: Mariah Plantz and Hattie Myer. Later, William Nawvac lived four months in the Draper home.

7. C. B. Mims, copy of Commencement Program for Friday Night, June 4, 1880: Opening song, recitations and declamations; Howard Barnett, I Love the Summer; Cordelia Ailey, Make Childhood Sweet; Izora Shults, the Robin's Funeral; Julia Smith, Which is King?; Lucy Hale, Nobodies; Texie Goughenour, Composition; Music; Teddie Roadman, Perseverance; Bennie Hooper, The Barn Burner; Charlie Fagala, The Abbott's Will; Fannie Swaggerty, The Great Mistake; Samuel Gray, Just Obey; John M. Keener, Little Contrary; Lora Swaggerty, Both Ways; Lizzie Lewis, Composition; Belle Ragan, Composition; Carrie Smith, Time to Go to Bed; Griffin Byrd, Mother's Fool; Cora Lee Massey, Composition; Annie L. Smith, Composition; Ollie Mims, A Little Boy's Trouble; Maurice Langhorne, The Isle of Long Ago; Elen Hale, The Moneyless Man; Maggie Stuart, Answer to the Moneyless Man; Nannie David, Composition; Ella Gray, Composition; Thursie Henry, Composition; Music; Ella Fairfield, The Atlantic Cable; Texie Goughenour, Too Much of a Lady; Cora Lee Massey, Papa's Letters; A. M. Smith, All Quiet along the Potomac; William Smith, Moral Desolation; E. L. Mims, Composition; Archie Rhea, The Desperate Anault; Belle Ragan, Looking Back; Sallie Kidwell, Lips that Touch Wine; H. H. Gouhenour, Industry Necessary to Eloquence; Y. J. McMahan, Composition; Lucius Smith, Composition; George P. Mims, Composition; Augustus Smith, LaFayette's Visit; J. M. McMahan, Grandeur of the Universe; C. C. Davis, Tallurah; Leota Fairfield, Composition; Music; E. L. Mims, The Rivers of Time; A. J. Tucker, Anger and Love; Austin Hall, Religious Education; W. W. Lewis, National Prosperity; George P. Mims, My Mother, My Country, My God; J. W. Phillips, I Still Live; A. B. Smith, My Country, the Hero's Home; Y. J. McMahan, Soldiers Should Be Rewarded; Lucia Rhea, Composition.

Parrottsville School Program, May 29, 1897. Slavery of Intemperance, W. M. Brooks; Unjust National Acquisition, C. E. Burnett; Sparticus to the Gladiators, L. S. Brooks; Decision of Character, F. W. Bushong; The Rescued Pioneers, F. V. Carlisle; Results of Work, M. Dawson; Dignity of Human Nature, George Stuart; Reputation, Thomas N. Huff; Our Fallen Braves, J. W. Justus; America, G. E. Easterly; Opportunity for Work, P. Neas; Righteousness Exalted a Nation, I. N. Stuart; Education, S. H. Hudson; Essays; False Modesty, Minnie Bushong; Days that Are no More, Annie Smith; Reading, a Means of Intellectual Improvement, Jerusha E. Kess; Ruins of Time, Lizzie Justus; The True Goal of Ambition, Lizzie Huff; Our Departed Friends, Virginia Carlisle; Purity of Thought, Sue Justus; Trouble and its Remedy, Maggie Carlisle; Pleasures of Memory, Maggie Jones; Riches and Poverty, Ellen Ottinger; The Close of Life, Mariam Driskill; No Cross, No Crown, Selma La Rue; Memory's Mission, Dora Robeson; Life, Nannie Ray; Another Year, Nannie Robinson; No Night in Heaven, Lou Thomas.

Colonel O. C. King of Morristown delivered an address on Friday morning, May 30, 1897.

Parrottsville Program, Friday Evening, May 30, 1897. Declamations; Progress of Civilization, W. J. Jones; Motives to Intellectual Action in America, W. J. Parker; A Soul to Dare and A Will to Do, H. J. Robeson; My Country, The Hero's Home, J. A. Smith; The Moral Delinquency of the Times, S. H. Stuart; O, Man, Thou Pendulum, between a Sigh and A Tear, M. S. Wall; Orations: The Flight of Time, A. B. Hudson; Footprints on the Sands of Time, J. A. Burnett; False Standards of Respectability, C. A. Bushong; Night Brings out the Stars, T. L. Carty; Character, R. P., N. Y.

Cosby Academy

Edgemont School

About 1896, Mr. Nawvac married Miss Plantz. Immediately they decided to build a schoolhouse, to which his wife contributed $700. It was a two-story frame building and was used for a dwelling, a chapel, and a schoolhouse.

The Nawvacs remained in the mountains for four or five years and did much good. A son was born and when it died, they sold their building to the Presbyterian Church and went to China as Independent missionaries. After a few years they returned to their home in Wisconsin.

The Cosby Academy has an interesting background. During the early part of the twentieth century, prior to 1913, A. E. Brown, of Asheville, was Superintendent of the Mountain School System of the Baptist Home Missions Board. While speaking to the East Tennessee Association at Clay Creek, he expressed a wish for a school within the bounds of the Association. When the Association met at Newport the next year and authorized the establishment of such a school, the Home Board agreed to pay two thousand dollars, if the Association would raise four thousand. A board of trustees, with S. R. McSween, president, and John Weaver, secretary and treasurer, was appointed. Other members were Will Weaver, Harrison Wood, J. W. Padgett, Dr. J. H. Knight, A. A. Owens, W. R. McGaha, and Rev. J. W. O'Hara.

After the failure to agree on a site, Will Weaver found the beautiful one now occupied by the Cosby School, and the buildings were soon erected at a cost of eight thousand dollars. The Home Missions Board gave two thousand seven hundred dollars into the building cost and contributed hundreds of dollars toward teachers salaries. John and Will Weaver gave most of the lumber and J. W. Padgett gave five hundred dollars on the ten-acre site besides much labor on building construction. Other liberal donors were the ladies (including Miss Nannie Murray) of the various aid societies who helped furnish the dormitories, John Harrison, John W. Fisher, L. S. Allen, Y. J. McMahan, A. E. Roberts, Richard Templin, and A. A. Owens. The buildings were dedicated in July, 1914, and the school opened September 1, 1914, with an enrollment of 71 and the addition of 35 new pupils in the spring.

The first faculty consisted of Rev. L. C. Kinsey, principal; Miss Leta Huff, assistant in literary department and teacher of music; Miss Ada Mize, primary, and Mrs. L. C. Kinsey, matron. The first graduating class was composed of Mrs. Bess Kyker Williams, Mrs. Myrtle Shults Proffitt, and Miss Scottie Harrison.

Driskill; Strike for the Green Graves of Your Sires, God and Your Native Land, J. H. Burnett; The Onward Struggle, C. O. Jones; Dignity of Labor, J. A. Thomas; Life is What we Make it, J. P. Thomas; Essay; Looking Toward the Sunset, Cordie Ragan; Idle Dreams, Josie Ottinger; The Student's Hope, Sue Smith; Hope, Faith and Charity, Lizzie Burnett; The Influence of Music, Ida Bell; Never Alone, Lillie Richardson; I've Launched my Bark! Where is the Shore?, Addie Burnett; Hark! How the Bells of Memory Ring Tonight, Dosie Kenyon; The Dress is not the Man, Idella Easterly; The Brightest Sunshine Casts the Darkest Shadow, Flora Roadman; There's A Ripple in Every Stream, Barshie Stuart; My Pathway Lies Through a Valley Which I Seek to Adorn with Flowers, Mollie Carty; We Are Anxiously Waiting for the Golden Sometime, Ellen Ragan; The Fashions of the World Pass Away, Sallie Stuart; Our Literature, Carrie Burnett; The Dark and Golden Side, Maggie Kenyon (This program was printed by the *Newport Sentinel*, preserved by Paul LaRue and years later reprinted by another paper.)

The curriculum was made up of a twelve-year course, and it was planned to give one year of college work. The tuition for the first and second grades was one dollar per month; third and fourth grades, one dollar and fifty cents per month; seventh and eighth grades, two dollars per month; academic department, two dollars and fifty cents and three dollars for the month. Incidental fee for all was ten cents per month. All fees and board were to be paid at the end of each month.

For many years, over fifty per cent of the school graduates went to college. Over ninety per cent of the graduates had joined a church before leaving school. No student was allowed to graduate without having studied the Bible, with such teachers as Miss Addie Lowerie, who was with the school for fifteen years. Due to the depression, the trustees sold the property to the County, and the Academy is now operated as a county high school, with an enrollment of some 100 in the high school department and 125 in the grades.

The following citizens have served as principals of the Cosby School: L. C. Kimsey, P. S. (O?) Williams, W. A. Bowen, Robert Marshall, Professor Turner, L. R. Watson, T. S. Ellison.[8]

One of the most beautiful of the County's school buildings is Edgemont, which was constructed of native field stone and equipped with electricity, water, and furnace heat. It has bus transportation and was one of the first real consolidation projects in the County, merging Carson Springs (sometimes called Edgemont), the Wilsonville and Reidtown Schools. This idea began in 1926 and was completed by 1928. The cost is said to have been about seventeen thousand dollars, much of which was contributed by the State. The grounds were donated by Governor Ben W. Hooper, and the water was piped 6,800 feet, with a fall of 238 feet.

The students improved the grounds by cleaning off rocks and planting shrubbery and flowers. For more than a mile, the roadway from the school building toward Carson Springs has been planted in running roses by Mr. and Mrs. Ben W. Hooper, whose home is located at the end of the Mile of Roses.

A stone teacherage was furnished and an addition was begun, with the aid of funds from the Federal Government. This was to comprise a gymnasium, two classrooms with kitchen and dining room in the basement. This project was dropped when the County failed to meet its agreed part of the expense. The citizens in 1950 are hoping to see the work completed in 1951.

Edgemont is said to have the highest average attendance of any elementary school in the County, with an enrollment of more than 200 pupils, and the employment of six teachers.

One of the best-organized, best-equipped and most efficiently conducted grammar schools in Cocke County is the Sunset Gap School, under the Board of National Missions of the Presbyterian Church of the U. S. A., with Miss Sarah E. Cochrane as its executive. The land for this school was donated by Mrs. Betty Jane Hicks Williams, a noble mountain woman, known as Grandma Williams, who reared ten sons, many of whom live near the twelve-acre grounds of this school. Since its establishment, usually one-fourth of its enrollment has been made up of her grandchildren. In 1950 Miss Elizabeth Wright is executive.

8. Old newspapers and Mr. Watson.

Grammar School Teachers, School Year 1926-27. Front row left to right: Mary Susong, Grace Kunnion, Nannie Jones, Nina Wilson, Beulah Ottinger. Second row, left to right: Nelle Gray, Josephine Bowers, Katherine Smith, Frances Groddon, Myrtle Clark, Viola Clark. Back row, left to right: Mrs. Ruth W. O'Dell, Mrs. Eleanor Susong Little, Ella Hall, Mary Graham Robinson, Goldia Holder, Mrs. Reynolds, John C. Hammer.

The three frame buildings are large, well-painted, and the grounds are enclosed by a rustic pole fence. The main building is 99 by 56 feet, with eight rooms; the hospital is 29 by 54 feet, with seven rooms, with a sunny ward of 26 beds; the teacher's cottage is also well furnished. The nursery department in pink and blue has meant much to the mothers of that community.

The basement holds a "wash trough" made of rough boards, ten by four feet, and lined with zinc. Before lunch each day, each child is required to wash his hands with hot water and soap, and to dry them on paper towels. Each child is provided with a clean "nose rag" each morning, and this is discarded at the close of school. Special emphasis is placed on other health rules, such as innoculation and vaccination.

The girls are taught dressmaking and the boys manual training. All learn clay modeling. The school has twelve looms, a nice chapel, and a well-stocked library.

Sunset Gap School is the only one in the County with an executive that does not teach; that has a hospital and furnishes free medical and dental services; that makes a strong effort toward being a model school: that has a nursery; that teaches weaving; that selects its teachers for their spirit of service, their qualifications, and their ability to adapt themselves to their environment.

During the years from 1920 to 1923, the author served as the County Superintendent of Cocke County Public Schools. The following is a part of her report published in *Plain Talk*, November 10, 1921:

We have in the first district or Del Rio section, 19 schoolhouses, valued at $9,300; 24 teachers, drawing $1,705 per month. In the second district, Parrottsville section, there are 16 schoolhouses, valued at $17,100; 22 teachers drawing $1,780 per month. In the third district, Bybee section, there are 12 schoolhouses, valued at $22,425, 15 teachers, drawing $1,095 per month. In the fourth district, (Town section,) there are 16 schoolhouses, valued at $14,725; 20 teachers, drawing $1,030 per month. In the fifth district, Cosby section, there are 22 schoolhouses, valued at $25,500; 30 teachers, drawing $2,135 per month . . .

We have 8,127 children in Cocke County of school age. Of this number, 4,812 are now enrolled in our schools. The remainder of this number are over 17 years of age. The pro rata is $5.02 per child. The funds coming from the State hereafter are based entirely upon the daily attendance.

The Tennessee Valley Authority figures, probably in the 1930's gave the number of grade schools as 78; pupils, 5,490; teachers, 184. There were 3 white high schools and 1 colored high school, with 637 pupils, 22 teachers.

Societies, Bureaus, Clubs, and Associations

NEWPORT'S FIRST WOMAN'S CLUB

By Cora Massey Mims

"We the undersigned ladies agree to pay for the no. of seats annexed to our names for the purpose of supplying the School Room in the Masonic Hall at Newport Depot in Cocke County, Tennessee. Each seat to cost not more than two dollars and fifty cents. The mechanic will open his shop at Clifton for the putting up of the work and Each Ladie will order him to make the number she has subscribed all the cash to be paid when the seats are delivered. This 17 Dec. 1874.

Names of signers.

Delilah Gorman, Elizabeth Jack, Sarah Raines, Mattie Jones, Emma Hooper, M. J. Jones, Nancy McMahan, Martha Fairfield, Mattie B. Peterson, Laura Hale, Mary A. Baer, Pet L. Williams, Lizzie Loyd, Julia M. Fagalah, Elizabeth Click, Mary E. S. Rhea, Elizabeth Smith, Julia R. Smith, N. E. Smith, Julia R. Langhorne, Hattie E. Stuart, Lou E. Susong, J. M. Randolph, Laura A. Robinson, Sophia E. Bible, Elizabeth Ogden, M. J. Mims, M. K. Gorrell, N. E. McSween, C. M. McSween, Sarah Wilson, Mary Cureton, Pametra Perkins, Fannie Lewis, Josephine Morris, Liddie A. Swagerty, Beck Allen, Su Clevenger, Elizabeth Frazier, Laura A. Click, S. E. Susong. One illegible.

These 43 women subscribed a total of $177.00 supplying the school room with 70 seats. Each seat or desk accommodated two pupils.

The desks were stout and solid and graduated from small to large. Each desk had a table top for writing and an under compartment for books.

The name of the mechanic is not recorded but he did an honest job.

BEN W. HOOPER CAMP NUMBER 21, Department of Tennessee, United Spanish War Veterans, has the following members: Worley Acton, W. M. Balch, A. R. Blazer, Reuben J. Brown, Grant Burke, James M. Burke, Edom Cureton, James I. Green, Thomas Hall, Samuel Hensley, O. L. Hicks, John R. Holt, Ben W. Hooper, Joseph A. Lillard, William M. Lillard, Creed B. McMahan, Robert McNabb, David Owens, Creed Owens, George W. Pennell, Albert Stuart, John Taylor, Doctor F. Turner, John H. Webb.

O. L. Burnett, Pay Department U. S. Army, D. Conway, William R. Costner, Fermon Corn, Joseph Ellenburg, J. P. Fisher, Robert Fowler, James B. Freeman, Thomas McGaha, Charles R. Greene, Andrew Henderson, James Henderson, Chandler Jenkins, R. E. Jenkins, Samuel W. H. Large, Dock Large, Thomas McCaffey, Charles Pate, Isaac H. Price, Reuben Price, Joseph Price, R. S. Shelton, W. H. Shipe, Abijah Simmons, Sr., Abijah Simmons, Jr., J. H. Smart, Albert Stuart, Monroe Watson, Thomas Welch, J. R. Shoemaker, Russell Jenkins, Joseph Raines.

These soldiers fought in what was known as the Spanish American Philippine Insurrection, Chinese Rebellion.

THE AMERICAN LEGION Post 41 of Newport was organized February 28, 1921, with about sixty members. The officers were: Thurman Ailor, commander; E. S. Goepper, vice-commander; C. C. Ottinger, adjutant; J. B. Ruble, treasurer; the executive committee: E. M. Greer, Ernest Mims, Lyde Stokely, Hugh R. Holder, Dr. J. E. Hampton.

The majority of the members of this Post served with the Thirtieth Division overseas; a few served with the Eighty-first. The company, recruited by Thurman Ailor, a volunteer, with 161 Cocke County men, was first called Company E of the Second Tennessee Infantry. Later it became a part of the Fifty-first Depot Brigade, and finally was merged with the Thirtieth Division. The Company was commanded by Ailor the entire time of its services, from June 10, 1917, to the close of World War I, and returned to America April 11, after the Armistice was signed.

In 1939, this Post had more than 130 members and met in Memorial Building. In 1950 Oscar O'Neil Lee is commander.

THE AMERICAN LEGION AUXILIARY Unit No. 41 was organized at Newport, August 17, 1921, with a charter signed by L. Jere Cooper, Deputy Commander of the American Legion. Those most active in securing the organization were Mrs. G. F. Smith, Mrs. Jetta Lee, Mrs. D. S. Reed, Mrs. A. G. Neas, Mrs. Hugh Holder, Mrs. J. W. Ruble, Mrs. Jessie Stokely and Miss Mary Rowe Ruble. Mrs. G. F. Smith was chosen as acting president and became the first president of the Auxiliary; Miss Ruble, secretary; Mrs. Reed, vice-president and Mrs. Neas, treasurer. On March 2, 1922, the Auxiliary secured a permanent charter, and Mrs. G. F. Smith became first district chairman; Mrs. Fred Jones, president of the Auxiliary.

During 1921 to 1923, Mrs. Smith collected valuable records of ex-service men, which are preserved in the Memorial Building. In 1922, February, memorial trees were planted in memory of the twenty-seven gold star boys on the high school grounds, with suitable marble tablets inscribed with the soldier's name and record under the trees. By 1930, the Auxiliary membership increased to 101. *The History of the World War Veterans of Cocke County* by Mrs. Rutledge Smith of Nashville, was secured.

A BRASS BAND was organized in 1916 by Mr. Krino, and flourished several months. The author's late husband, George W. O'Dell, played the "Hellican" bass.

THE BUSINESS WOMEN'S CLUB of Newport was originally a part of the Women's Missionary Union of the Baptist Church, and was organized in the summer of 1923 by Miss Anna May Stokely, who became its first president. The charter members were Misses Anna May Stokely, Minnie Henry, Elizabeth Stokely, and Nell Hunter. Soon after the organization, the members withdrew from the Missionary Union and formed an independent organization.

The Club purchased a library, which in 1940 had several thousand books, with Miss Nannie Murray as librarian. A department and private reading room for children is also included. This club meets semi-monthly in the Cocke County Memorial Building, with more than thirty active members. Its main aim is "Better Women Citizens," Miss Lou Morell is Librarian now (1950).

THE CHORAL CLUB was organized April, 1937, under the sponsorship of the Kiwanis Club. The officers were E. I. Caraway, president; L. W. Morrow, director; Rosemary Driskill, pianist; Bernard Shults, secretary-treasurer; L. W. Morrow, E. I. Caraway, Rev. C. W. Taylor, Mesdames Irene Susong, C. W. Taylor, and L. W. Morrow, and Miss Rosemary Driskill, executive committee.

Singers from over the County were invited to join the Club and thirty responded. From time to time, the Choral Club has furnished the musical part of other programs and has given many concerts.

THE CLIFTON CHAPTER of the U. D. C. was organized by Mrs. J. W. Gillock, at the home of Mrs. Fred M. Greer, with the following officers, who served until October, 1927: president, Mrs. D. G. Allen; vice-president, Miss Annie Holland; recording secretary, Mrs. J. H. La-Rue; corresponding secretary, Mrs. W. J. Sanford; treasurer, Mrs. E. P. Bostwick; registrar, Mrs. J. W. Gillock; historian and flag custodian,

Mrs. Fred M. Greer; recorder of crosses, Mrs. Robert Walker; chaplain, Mrs. L. S. Allen. Soon after its organization, the roll call showed sixty-eight members. On October 10 to 12, 1934, Mrs. Fred M. Greer as president of the Tennessee Division presided at the 39th Annual Convention, in Columbia, Tennessee.

The Clifton Chapter (No. 1928) gave D. S. Sorrell, the only surviving Confederate soldier in Cocke County, a birthday celebration on August 6, 1939, at the Church in Nough. The old soldier carried home letters from President Franklin D. Roosevelt and Secretary of State, Cordell Hull. A gold-headed walking cane from Fred M. Greer was presented by John Ruble. Mrs. Francis Burnett Swann read an original poem, "To Our Veterans," and Bert Vincent, the Knoxville Sentinel stroller recorded the events. Mrs. Kate Mims Greer had charge of the program.

THE CLIFTON CLUB, named for Newport's first name, was probably the pioneer men's club, organized at some time in the Gay Nineties, with a membership of the younger business and professional men of the town and county. C. W. Perry was the first president, and was succeeded by P. T. Bauman. Other members were: M. A. Roadman, James R. Jones, Sanford and Oliver Burnett, John M. Jones, John Seehorn, W. D. Mc-Sween, Dr. E. G. E. Anderson, and many others.

This Club met over the W. B. Robinson Clothing Store on Main Street and frequently entertained for visiting young men and young ladies, especially around holiday seasons.

M. A. Roadman, one of its members tells of its demise:

My Club, the Clifton, was a social Club for young men and was organized with the agreement that no whiskey would be permitted in the Club Rooms. This rule was rigidly observed until one fateful day our ball club journeyed to Morristown to play a series of games with that city's teams. A great deal of money was bet on the games, one Newport man winning a $600 check from a Morristown citizen.

He goes on to tell of the special passenger car chartered for Newport people, of Newport's winning, of the boys smashing the windows in the coach, and of the gentleman winner of check announcing a celebration at the Clifton Club Rooms. Numerous members and non-members attended and there was never another formal meeting.

THE COCKE COUNTY FARMER'S ALLIANCE was organized at the Court House in Newport, November 17, 1888, by George Creamer, county organizer. Major Smith, S. R. McSween, and J. T. Miller were appointed committee on credentials; S. R. McSween, Tennessee secretary; J. T. Miller, president; William Sheffey, vice-president; J. M. Stuart, secretary; W. R. Swaggerty, treasurer; W. D. A. Byrd, chaplain; J. W. Lucas, lecturer; S. R. McSween, assistant lecturer; I. N. Winter, doorkeeper; H. O. Reams, assistant doorkeeper; Milburn Dawson, sergeant at arms; committee for the good of the order. W. R. Smith, chairman, George I. Thomas, and James Wood.

Other names on committees: O. M. Kelley, J. A. Blazer, and Harrison Wood, credentials; Newport delegates, J. C. Morrell, W. R. Smith; Edwina, I. C. Vinson, H. Wood, E. Fox, John McNabb; A. Dawson, James Keller; Salem, C. S. Parrott, T. Blazer, S. Eisenhour, R. G. Neas, A. D. Ottinger, P. M. Ottinger, Jonas Ottinger, Geo. Nease, J. T. Nease; Good Hope, W. D. A. Byrd and John C. Maloy; Point Pleasant, Andy Fowler and W. M. Fox; Brookside, J. W. Lucas, O. M. Kelley, E. Bible, J. T. Marshall; Rankins, C. B. McNabb, W. C. Spurgen; Executive Committee, Wm. Sheffey, chairman, O. M. Kelley and George Nease; nominating, J. C. Morrell, chairman, S. Eisenhour, Will Fox, John G. Maloy, Esq. McNabb. Resolution committee; C. B. McNabb, chairman, E. Bible, and Ezekiel Fox. The minutes ran for 67 pages, with various secretaries recording them. The most perfect writing was by J. D. Williams, Secretary, July 18, 1890. October 9, 1891, was the last meeting recorded, and the minutes were signed by J. A. Susong, secretary pro tem.

THE DINNER CLUB was organized on January 18, 1937, in a meeting presided over by Ashby Holland, with forty Masons present. Officers, elected for a term of only six months, were: Dr. Fred Valentine, president; Buford Harkins, first vice-president; Nathan Jones, second vice-president; R. Walter Smith, secretary-treasurer. This was a social club and met once each month, with wives, daughters, or sweethearts invited as special guests.

THE FARM BUREAU is an organization of farmers and their wives to ·learn how to conserve the soil, to grow more and better crops, to improve their homes, and to create more interest in agriculture. It has all day outings, in the summer. An important figure has been John Hampton, the bachelor farmer. In 1950 Joe Carpenter is president.

THE FOX HUNTERS ASSOCIATION (Cocke County) is a part of the Fox Hunters Association of East Tennessee, and has often been the host of the East Tennessee Association and of the Southeastern Fox Hunters, which embraces eight states. In 1950 known as The Smoky Mountain Fox Hunters Association.

The latter chose different locations for their chase—first, at Cedar Hill, in the edge of Jefferson County; second, at McNabb's Bluffs, near the Walters Bridge over French Broad River on the Morristown Highway in the Dutch Bottoms; third, on the Ed Burnett farm along Big Pigeon River, south of the Tannery and Extract plant. Donald McSween made color photographs of these activities. The local committee was Al Gresham, chairman; O. M. Watson, secretary; Tipton Brown; John Ruble; D. C. Williams.

THE KIWANIS CLUB was organized at Carson Springs Hotel, September 7, 1920, with its charter dated October 12, 1920. Its charter members numbered fifty and its first officers were: Dr. N. L. Dennis, president; Dr. L. S. Nease, vice-president; H. M. Remine, secretary; C. E. Ottinger, district trustee; directors, F. W. Parrott, John M. Jones, H. C. Ruble, W. R. Nease, W. J. Parks, Porter Barnett, Urey K. Goodwin.

It meets each Tuesday at noon in the dining room of the Methodist Church. In 1937 it sponsored the organization of the Choral Club.

THE MEDICAL SOCIETY of Cocke County was first organized in the year 1890.[9] Those who belonged then were: Doctors Joseph K. Gorrell, W. G. Snoddy, L. W. Hooper, R. C. Smith, Meriwether Lewis, Bell, Darius Neas of Parrotsville, John W. Ruble of Del Rio, and Caywood of Dandridge.

In 1907, the Society was re-organized, but failed to function. On October 13, 1913, a large number of physicians met in the City Hall and

9. Judge Williams gives among the Charter members of the Medical Society of Tennessee on its organization in 1830 Doctors George M. Porter and David C. Chamberlain from Cocke County.

organized the Cocke County Medical Society, and later with other County societies formed the Tennessee State Medical Association. Among its functions are the making effective of the opinions of the profession in scientific, legislative, public health, and social affairs.

Dr. R. C. Smith was elected president of the 1913 organization; Dr. C. E. Barnett, vice-president; Dr. David Seay, secretary. Among other members then were Doctors C. T. Burnett, John H. Knight, Adolphus J. Neas, John W. Ruble, Thomas, Holland, John F. Stanberry, Bingham.

THE PARENT-TEACHERS ASSOCIATION (data from Mrs. Cavott) was organized by the author, then superintendent of county schools, in the fall of 1920. She was elected president and Mrs. Rose Frawley (Mrs. P. F.), secretary. The Association purchased playground equipment and established a clinic for the treatment of trachoma in 1921. The next president was Mrs. Rose Frawley, followed by Mr. Frank Parrott.

In 1926, Mrs. W. J. Parks reorganized the Association and served as its president for two years. A curtain for chapel, a set of Compton's reference books for library, and lunch equipment were bought. She saw to it that the Association had membership in the National Association. When she moved to Asheville, the PTA was inactive until Mr. Radcliffe, principal of the Newport Grammar School was instrumental in having it reorganized, with Mrs. Carl West as president and Mrs. Marcus Fisher, vice-president. Mr. John Holder came to office in two months, and Mrs. Marcus Fisher became president. The school building and grounds were improved at this time. In April, 1935, Mrs. Longstreet Cavott was elected president, with new endeavors directed toward the buildings and grounds and the bringing of greater culture to the individual child and to the group by way of the American School of the Air.

The officers for 1937 and 38 were president, Mrs. Eugene Parrott; first vice-president, Mrs. James Murray; second vice-president, Mrs. Theodore Parrott; secretary, Miss Anna William; corresponding secretary, Mr. Charles Miller; treasurer, Prof. E. L. Radcliffe.

THE NEWPORT BALL CLUB was organized in 1939, and reorganized in 1944. Dr. Hobart Ford was head of it these five years. This group of local business and professional leaders assumed the responsibility of operating the ball club (The Canners) as a recreation park project.

The Newport Gun Club was organized in 1941 with weekly shooting matches held on the Gregg farm on Clear Creek. Some participants then were Clyde Correll, E. M. Babb, R. L. Scruggs, Geo. R. Shepherd, Horace Burnett, Ben Ray, Arlie Gray, Wilbur Hale, Dr. A. M. Mullen, Drew Ragan, Clarence Black, Don Holbert, Lawrence Gregg, H. A. Fields.

THE RIFLE CLUB was a revival of the old time "shooting-match" about 1936, and held its meetings on Thursday night, at the Gateway Garage. Officers were Dr. Fred Valentine, president; E. M. Babb, vice-president; Homer Vinson, secretary-treasurer; J. R. Denny, range officer. Among other members were C. D. Fisher, Joe Gregg, Oscar Allen, Woodrow Jones, P. T. Holt, Lawrence Gregg.

THE SERIA-SABIO CLUB,[10] the first literary club for married women (a few single ladies), was organized in 1906. The name is from the Spanish "would be wise." Its aim was not only self-improvement but

---

10. Information by Mrs. J. M. Masters in 1936.

civic improvement. The club colors were lavender and white and its flower, the white carnation (at first, the pansy).

Active members were: Mesdames J. M. Masters, W. C. Anderson, Hunley LaRue, George Duncan, C. B. Haag, Wilfred Masters, N. L. Mc-Sween, G. W. Willis, E. O. Wells, H. O. Lee, Will Helm, Sam McSween, and C. B. Mims; Misses May Early, Eva Fisher, Myrtle Mims, Grace Seaman, Ethel Snoddy, Jessie Willis, Honorary members were: Mesdames C. F. Boyer, J. A. Fisher, J. L. Robb, Sidney Seaman, and John W. Fisher.

Among its accomplishments were the furnishing of a room in the Grand View Tuberculosis Sanitarium for the use of their own members, or for any one not able to pay for one. It also provided a comfort kit. a Bible, and a hand-knitted sweater for each soldier boy in the first World War from the County. Mrs. George Duncan was War Mother and wrote letters to the boys in service; she also told them goodbye and greeted those who returned. This Club gave the returning soldiers a nucleus to start a recreation center for themselves. The entire floor (maple) of the auditorium of the Memorial Building was paid for by the Club. The Seria-Sabio Cook Book was a 101 page collection of practical and tested recipes.

THE SESAME CIRCLE was organized at the home of Mrs. Fred M. Greer, Friday, November 8, 1901, and perfected by Mrs. W. O. Mims. Its regular meeting time became Thursday afternoon from one to four, with the membership limited to seventeen. Each hostess had the privilege of providing any mode of entertainment she might consider "pleasurable" to her guests. Members brought light sewing or fancy work. Books were exchanged and discussed. Officers were president, Mrs. Bruce Robinson; vice-president, Mrs. B. D. Jones; secretary, Mrs. Fred Graddon. The following women were members in 1901: Mesdames H. N. Cate (Lillie Early), J. J. Denton (Lizzie Loyd), Fred S. Graddon (Ethel Campbell), Fred M. Greer (Kate Mims), B. W. Hooper (Anna B. Jones), Wiley H. Jones (Maud Miles), B. D. Jones (Ella Randolph), J. L. Manor (Ella Sykes), W. O. Mims (Cora Massey), J. F. Nease (Sallie Morris), W. B. Robinson (Louise Kyle), J. P. Robinson (Florence Stanberry), George F. Smith (Margaret Burnett), R. C. Smith (Josephine Robinson Jones), J. A. Susong (Irene Ayers), W. B. Stokely (Edith Estes), J. Stokely Susong (Lou Murray). When a member withdrew another name was suggested for membership. Mrs. W. D. McSween (Rowena Jones) became a member before the end of 1901.

THE SMOKY MOUNTAIN GOLF CLUB was organized several years ago and a golf course was located on the N. L. McSween farm east of Newport, near the Tannery railroad track. About twenty players generally qualify for the annual championship tournament.

THE TENNIS CLUB is one of Newport's most active ones. Among representative players have been: J. O. Cope, Van Shuping, Dr. David Kimberly, Charles Clifford McNabb, Jr., Fred Ottinger, Bud Stokely, Ben Cates, Carolyn Liebrock, Nancy Katherine Gregg, Marjorie Cates, Dorothy Jones Murray. When it was reorganized, the officers were: John C. Holder, president; Elizabeth Jones, vice-president; Bud Stokely, secre-tary, Everette McNabb, treasurer; J. O. Cope and Van Shuping, business managers.

THE TWENTIETH CENTURY MOTHERS' CLUB was organized about the time of the demise of the Sesame Circle, September, 1914. It entered the State Federation in 1916 and the General Federation in October, 1926. Its motto is: "It is not a question of how much we are to do—but of how it is to be done; it is not a question of doing more, but of doing better." The Club's colors are red and white, and the flower is the carnation. Its aim is to develop culture in the home, to promote education, civic improvement and public health, and to cooperate with the city, county and state government in every worth-while interest. The active membership is limited to seventy-five, elected by ballot. It has its own club rooms in the Masonic Temple, where it meets twice each month from September until May. The following women have served as president of this club to 1950: Mesdames W. J. Sanford, George Smith, W. O. Mims, D. Gray Allen, W. B. Stokely, J. R. Seehorn, J. A. Susong, F. W. Parrott, Oscar Klinger, L. S. Allen, W. D. McSween, F. S. Fisher, E. E. Northcutt, V. W. Montsinger, Fred Graddon, Charles Runnion, Horace Burnett, W. B. Harkins, Theo Parrott, L. S. Nease, J. Lacy Myers, Ben Teague, Miss Hester Susong, Mesdames S. E. Bales, J. B. Ruble, Clyde Driskill, Hugh Holder, Cam Porter, Edward Walker, Sr.

In 1938, the Garden Club Group of the Club was organized with Mrs. W. B. Stokely; vice-director, Mrs. Carty McSween; secretary, Mrs. Horace Burnett; treasurer, Mrs. A. H. Taylor. Its aim is "to stimulate knowledge and love of gardening among amateurs, to aid in protecting native trees, plants, and birds, and to encourage civic planting." The club is noted for its annual Flower Show.

THE YOUNG ARTISTS' CLUB meets twice a month, and is composed of musicians, for the most part. Some active members have been Ruth Duyck, Rosemary Ruth Driskill, Mary Stokely, Leta Helm, Viola Chaney, Anna Kate Shepherd, Buddy Nelson, Patsy Rhyne, and the daughters of Mrs. John Seehorn.

THE WINOOSKI CLUB was one of the earliest of the Women's Clubs, organized in Newport during the Gay Nineties, June, 1892, and entered the State Federation in 1901. The name is of Algonquin origin, meaning "Beautiful River" or "Stony River," for the "stonier" the river the more beautiful it usually is. Its aim was to promote self improvement along literary and musical lines and to promote better and happier social contacts. The Winooski Club met twice a month, had gold and green for its colors, and the holly for its flower. The following young ladies were the charter members of this organization (This includes the roll call of 1903 and 1904.): Anna B. Jones (Hooper), Rowena Jones (McSween), Jessie Willis (Borrow), Bessie Willis (Hurst), Nell Willis (LaRue), Stella Willis (Allen), June Early (Huff), May Early (Hendrix), Stella Belle (Reece), Rachel Malott (Fisher), Irene Ayers (Susong), Mattie Cureton (the music teacher), Jessie Susong (Harris), Dora Susong (Jones), Susan Paxton (daughter of professor), Jetta Boyer (Lee), Georgia Morris (Minter), Adaline Susong (Smith), Esther King Snoddy, May Susong (Andes), Sue Susong (Seehorn), Mabel Gleen McSween. Often the Clifton Club (gentlemen) would entertain the ladies of the Winooski Club, with dinners, parties, and dances.

The following is part of a paper prepared by May Frazier Leeper (Col.) as partial fulfilment of the requirements for the degree of Bachelor of Science.

Cocke County Money

Tanner School (Colored)

THE ESTABLISHMENT AND DEVELOPMENT OF NEGRO SCHOOLS OF COCKE COUNTY 1865 TO 1948
DEDICATION

I wish to dedicate this project
to Nora Seehorn Frazier my mother, for
her inspiration and encouragement.

Slowly the prejudice against Negro schools gave away; and slowly the people grew to build schoolhouses and to spare their children from the fields. In 1872 the State Teacher's Association prepared a bill asking for Negro schools, and this school law went in effect by legislation in March 1873. This section still continues to hold its prejudice and bit-terness toward Negroes but the faithful and true friends of education and to humanity stood fast, and usually they were called, "old Guards" to see that ignorance, prejudice and malice were erased so that the children of the slaves had their chance as world citizens.

Cocke was an early recipient of these educational advancements and advantages, before this bill was passed the friends of the Negro and mass education had started a school in Cocke County.[6]

THE HISTORY OF THE FIRST NEGRO SCHOOL OF NEWPORT

The following information was given to me by Mrs. Augusta Swagerty Foster who was a slave of old Colonel William Swagerty, and who lives in Newport, Tennessee. I quote: "The eighth of August, 1865 Mr. Swagerty rang the big dinner bell and called all of the slaves in front of the big house and told us that we were all free and that we would have to look out for ourselves and families now.

The following September, the first school in Cocke County opened near Clifton Heights. There were about forty to fifty children as I can remember. The first teacher was Mr. William Anderson who was white.

I remember that he would never use a hickory, but would thump our heads with his fingers.

The first school had three teachers which taught over a period of nine years. Aunt Augusta who is now ninety-six years of age has forgotten the name of the other teachers.[7]

This school was moved from the log cabin near Clifton Heights to the Zion Church I cannot say just how long the school was held in this building because the courthouse was destroyed by fire in 1884 and all the old records along with it. This record is approximately from 1897 to 1924.

Mr. John Swagerty one of the early teachers of the county gave this information. Later the school was moved to Jones' Hill where for years it accommodated all the children of Newport. The enrollment went from seventy to one hundred students. It was taught by one teacher, who was paid the handsome salary of eighteen to twenty-five dollars per month. The school at this time only ran for three months. Often the teacher paid the school commissioner ten dollars in order to get the school. This school was taught by Miss Jennette McLear, later Mr. Goodlow who

---

6 *Ibid.*
7 Mrs. Augusta Foster, A Slave, Newport, Tennessee, January 2, 1950. (Personal Interview).

moved from North Carolina. His son is now teaching in Dunbar High School in Washington, D. C. Some of the early teachers were: James Moss, Mrs. Josephine Thomas, Mrs. Parolee Rice, Mrs. Pearl Belle of Morristown, Tennessee, Mr. Arnold of Knoxville, Mr. Turner of Morristown, Monroe Senters of Knoxville, Tennessee.

In 1924 the new school was built through the political efforts of the Negroes. John M. Jones was running for Mayor and he promised if the Negroes would vote for him he would float a bond to build a brick schoolhouse. The following election every voting Negro came out to the election and Mr. Jones was elected by the largest majority vote ever polled for mayor in Newport.

The land for the school was purchased by J. W. Rice under false pretence because the man who owned the site would not sell it for a Negro school.

The ninth grade was added and taught by Mr. Leon Pope who was the first high school principal. The school was built particularly by the Rosenwald fund. Mr. O. H. Bernard, Hon. R. E. Clay came and made the necessary arrangements with the superintendent and board of education. More will be said about our county High School of which this was the beginning.[8]

GUM SPRINGS

Many of the descendants of Gum Springs and Newport derived from a Blackhawk Indian, Pinky Hunt, whose mother was an old squaw, named Sarah Hunt.

The story that has been handed down is that Sarah was old and sick. She was left in her tepee in the Gum Springs section to die. She pleaded that her boy be left with her, and her plea was granted.

The old woman died. The boy lived and grew into a man. There were no Indian maidens, so Pinky married a Mulatto girl named Vina Frazier. They had ten children, Ellen, who married Steve Swagerty; Sarah, who married Arnold Swagerty, Martha, who married Simon Cox, Annie, who married Jerry Foster, and Kate, who married Miller Matthews.

Pinky Hunt was granted one hundred acres of land. The tract lies on both sides of the present Morristown Highway. Pinky and Vina passed, this land goes to the children ten acres each. It is the children of these ten children, grandchildren, and great-grandchildren who live there now.[9]

The first schoolhouse in Gum Springs was an old two room log cabin, here the descendants of Pinky Hunt sent their children, for they too craved an education.

At the foot of the hill was a gum stump out of which bubbled crystal clear water. This spring furnished water for the community. Thus derived the name Gum Springs.

The first teacher was a Mr. Hardin (white) the next teacher was Miss Harriet Nelson who later became Mrs. Harriet Frazier. The enrollment was about thirty. The ABC's and the old Webster's Blue Back Spellers were the only materials used in the curriculum.

---

8 Mr. John Swagerty, "An early school teacher," Newport, Tennessee (Personal Interview) February 7, 1950.
9 Vincent Burt, "A Reporter" of the Knoxville News Sentinel.

This information was given to me by my mother, Mrs. Nora Frazier, who was one of the first students in that school.[10]

The following is a list of teachers who taught in this early school. Mrs. Smith Lee, Charles Pullen, Fair West, Miss Griffith, John Swagerty, Frances Nichols and Mrs. Manie Dawkins.

The school was later moved to the old William Jack farm on the Morristown road and from there to its present location.

In 1925 the county was able to build a modern school building with a kitchen and running water. This was made possible by the Rosenwald Fund. The school was then called the Rosenwald School.

The Superintendent at this time was Mrs. Ruth O'Dell who served from 1920-1924. It was through her efforts that this was accomplished. She improved the schools for both races. During her administration fourteen new schools were built and all the schools in the county were painted. Under her, all teachers were paid according to their certification. Also two extra months were added to the school year.

DUTCH BOTTOM SCHOOL

This was begun in the year 1875 the first school was started in an old house about the old Elex Clark home, and it was attended by parent and children. Mr. J. W. Rice said that he and his mother were in the same class and that she never learned to read anything except the Bible. Some of the old families were Ellis Clark, Calles, Roakes, Harrison, Alexander Clark, Taylors and Carmichael.

The first teacher was Mrs. Anna Brazelton, J. W. Rice, Mrs. Parolee Rice, and Mrs. Addie Taylor. This school was later changed to Grand View and in 1940 the Grand View school was consolidated with Rosenwald school at Gum Springs.

Most of the Negroes have left the Duttch Bottom Community because the Stokley factory has been brought to Newport and much of the fine farm land has been covered with water from the Douglas Dam.

THE DAWSON VALLEY SCHOOL

In the Forest Hill Community, in a little valley one-fourth mile off the Greeneville Highway almost hidden by trees, stands the little schoolhouse.

The building was erected by the citizens of that community. The nearest school was over three miles away and most of the children were too small to walk that distance.

The county was not willing to build another school at that time, but would give them a teacher if they had a building. Mr. William Dawson, Sr., Negro, gave the land. The men in the community gave their labor and material.

In October, 1916 the building was ready for use. A few crude benches were the only equipment in the school house. The building was unsealed. The first teacher was Miss Kate Swagerty who, with the help of parents and students went to work piling rocks, filling gullies, cutting branches, and making a playground.

Programs and pie suppers were given, until enough money was raised to buy the ceiling to finish the building. After a short time desk replaced the benches and equipment was added until it was a modern schoolroom.

---

10 Mrs. Nora Frazier, Newport Tennessee, Jan. 17, 1950, (Personal Interview).

The first day an enrollment of twenty-two children crowded the little school, all eager and willing to receive whatever the teacher had to offer. Miss Swagerty taught for ten years, Mrs. Parolee Rice several years, Rev. W. M. H. Stokley one year. Then in 1936 Dawson Valley was consolidated with Allen Chapel. The school was named for the late William Dawson who gave the site for the building and playground.[11]

ALLEN CHAPEL SCHOOL

The Allen Chapel School was built 46 years ago. It is located two miles from Parrotsville, Tennessee. The schoolhouse and the church are the center of the community.

The land was purchased from Mr. Ned Allen, there is two and a half acres on which the school was built. The first schoolhouse was made of logs. It was a very small schoolhouse and very inadequate. The children sat on benches and put their books on the floor. The first school teacher was Rev. J. M. Carson, he was from Johnson City, Tennessee. He taught for two years. The second teacher was Mrs. Knight from Knoxville. She taught for three years. The third teacher was Mr. Fayte Hamilton, who taught for six years. His home was in Allen's Chapel. The people were very proud of him. They asked him to contact the superintendent and school board about building a new schoolhouse. They consented and built a new schoolhouse where it is located today.

The new building was a weatherboarded building. The first teacher in the building was Miss Della Allen, who taught four years. The second teacher was Miss Frances Wilson. The third teacher was Irene Smith. The fourth teacher was Mrs. Mattie Reinhardt. The fifth teacher Miss Gladys Brabson. The sixth teacher was Miss Irene Smith. The seventh and the present teacher, Irene Stokley.[12]

OLD TOWN

A few of the early residents still live in the community, among them is a Mrs. Byers who has helped to make history both in our school and church. I obtained this information from her.

This data from 1883 to 1948, Old Town at one time the county seat is the oldest Negro schoolbuilding in the county. The other buildings were churches and houses not intended for school use. This school received children from Southern and Northern sections of the county.

The teachers and children were occasionally disturbed by Indian fights. Dr. Richardson was the first teacher, other early teachers following him were Andrew F. Fulton of Morristown College, he was sold with his mother on a block where the Morristown College now stands for $1400. Many cold wars were fought by the citizens of this community for this county school.

During this period there had been other schools throughout the county.

The following is a list of these schools:

1871 The Warford's School, teacher, Sam Warford
1872 Dento School, teacher, Steven Hudson
1878 Slab Town School, teacher, Eliza Bryant
1878 Allen Chapel School, teacher, Eliga Garrett

---

11 *Ibid.*
12 Mrs. Irene Stokley, Present teacher of Allen Chapel School, March 3, 1950, (Personal Interview).

Gradually these were closed and consolidated with other schools. So now there are only three elementary and one twelfth grade school in the county, namely: Old Town, Allen Chapel, Rosenwald and Tanner Training, the twelfth grade school.

These elementary schools are the nucleus for our twelfth grade school for when the children finish the eighth grade they are transported by bus to Tanner Training School. This school was named after Dudley S. Tanner who was then the agent for Negro Schools of East Tennessee.

From 1926 to 1931, Dr. Branch with Miss Young, Una Gorman, Lillie M. Mills and May Swagerty, worked hard to equip the new building. Later the principals were: Rochelle, Wright, Martin, Melford Miller, Nathaniel Crippens, Ragan Hudson, John Needam, these principals did a wonderful job of making this school into shape so that it would have a high school training and good rating.

This present building was inadequate for the housing of both the city elementary and high school children of the county; therefore, the Negroes petitioned the county court for an addition to the school. We met the county court in 1940, near election time and were promised ten thousand for the new building.

We waited three years for the fulfilment of this promise but nothing came of it. Then the state said we could no longer operate without a rating.

The Negro population once again met the county court, this time they were given some consideration. Before meeting the county court, the N.A.A.C.P. appointed a committee composed of Charley Brabson, Anna Lou Williams, May Swagerty and L. Swagerty who wrote the following petition and presented it to the citizens of the county to sign. It was first presented to the members of the county court to sign individually before the meeting in January. This was done in order not to lose their votes at the regular meeting. All members signed except one and he was ill at the time. The following is the petition:

To the Honorable Members of the County Court of Cocke County, Tennessee:

Gentlemen:

We, the undersigned citizens of Cocke County and patrons and friends of the school, do hereby petition the county court to provide the funds and erect a high schoolbuilding including a gymnasium for the training of our youth in high school subjects for the following reasons:

1. That the present building has never provided the necessary space which it takes to have an accredited four year high school.
2. That we have an enrollment now of forty-eight students taking high school courses, but they do not have the space and equipment comparable to approved high schools.
3. That the State may not continue to give credit to Tanner which does not meet the state requirements, such a notice has already been given Tanner.
4. That nine-tenths of the mothers and fathers of the children attending Tanner are unable to send their children away from Cocke County to a school to get a high school education, which could be and should be provided nearer home.
5. That to provide the necessary equipment and training for the Negro youth of the county, the court will have done something that will

"Uncle" Henry Boyd, Champion colored foxhunter

Mt. Guyot, from Tricorner Knob, the highest peak in Cocke County

reflect credit upon itself in opening the door of opportunity to itself to develop these youth into what we believe will be an asset rather than a liability to both races of the county and state.

Respectfully submitted,

Signed: Irene L. Cureton, Addie Cureton, Jerlyne Cureton, Leroy Robinson, Hubert Stokley, Kenneth Stokley, John Goodrum, Beatrice Goodrum, Sarah D. Jackson, Raymond Woods, Joseph Stokely, Letra Stokely, Lizzie Stokely, Anderson Williams, Earnest Stokely, Mack Olden, Augusta Olden, Sylvester Hamilton, Ted Rice, Bill Bryant, Samuel Robinson, James Bryant, Horace Woods, John Carr, Robert Stewart, Paul Posey, Arrie Linder, Harold Carr, Henry Mills, Maggie Robinson, Ida B. Thomas, May Swagerty, Bern Thomas, Anna Sue Thomas, Mamie Posey, Elizabeth Hannon, Roland Dykes, L. F. Swagerty, Anna Lou Williams, Clarence Thomas, Luther L. Dawson, Dorothy Elliott, Wm. Gilchrist, Andrew Thomas, Ben W. Hooper, O. L. Hicks, W. W. Jones, Hugh Gregg, Albert Stewart, D. R. Smith, N. F. Stokely, McKinley Breeden, Jonah Buckner, Benton Giles Bruce, Auctace Elliott, Bruce Gilchrist, Mary Stewart, Geo. R. Shephard, Katy Olden, O. B. McGaha, Author J. Gudger, Lillie M. Mills, Maggie Mills, Arlean Carr, Rev. E. C. Kennedy.

The new high school was erected in 1947. It has five fine class rooms and one large room used for the cafeteria, and it is modern in every respect.

AUTOBIOGRAPHY

I was born in Cocke County, Tennessee in 1899, in a little settlement called Gum Springs. I am the oldest of eleven children. When I was twelve my father died and my mother moved to Newport, Tennessee where she could find work.

I soon found my first job playing with and taking care of the Ben W. Hooper children. When he became governor of Tennessee, I made my first trip to Nashville, in the year of 1912.

In 1915 I was sent to Christianburg, Virginia to school. For two years I worked during the day and went to school at night. The work was very hard and I was young, so I did little more than work.

In 1917, I entered Morristown Normal and Industrial College in Morristown, Tennessee. Here I did my elementary and high school work. I finished high school in June, 1921 and started teaching in Cocke County, Tennessee. I have taught in this county, with the exception of six months ever since.

In 1924 I came to A and I State College and started my college work. I have attended this school at intervals since that time. I have been able to see many of the children I have taught grow into fine citizens, and I am now teaching their children.

If I have had a degree of success, I owe it to my mother for her untiring faith and courage. I shall ever be grateful to the faculties of A and I State College and Morristown Normal and Industrial College for the inspiration they gave me. I have been helped and encouraged by my many friends, among them are: Mrs. Mae G. Lawrence, Superintendent of New Jersey Home, Morristown, Tennessee and Miss Anna Mae Stokely of Newport, Tennessee.

I shall always be grateful to these and many other true friends.

Folklore

SADDLEBAGS—CARPET-BAGS, VALISE AND SATCHELS, ETC.

One of the most prized bags of my childhood memory was a beautiful 'carpet-bag.' In this was packed mine and my brother's night clothes and fresh suits for the next day when we would go to spend the night with some kith and kin at week-end visits which we often enjoyed. This bag was colorful with red and cream and brown predominating.

The Saddle-bags were also much used by our grandfather, the Methodist Circuit Rider. The sermons of John Wesley, for whom his own father was named were often carried in his saddle bags along with his well worn Bible and hymnal. One one side he carried his 'clean clothes' his quinine and medicine for 'heart-burn.' Many circuit-riders carried a pair of these bags which were thrown over the saddle. They were made of leather and were very durable and strong. Sometimes an extra 'satchel' or 'valise' was tied on to the back of the saddle if the preacher was to be away several days.

Later came the 'telescope' a rectangular shaped bag made in two parts like a 'suit-box' of the present day only much larger and held together with leather straps fastened all the way around. These bags would hold much or little as one's needs required. They were made of stiff cardboard, leather and imitation leather.

The various 'reticules' carried by the women of the pioneer days and later are well remembered by many people today. Especially the kind in which they carried 'tea-cakes' or dough-nuts to church to keep the children quiet while the preacher held forth with his one to two hour sermons. My mother was more modern, she never used tea-cakes to keep my brother and me quiet at such times but if we misbehaved she used peach-tree tea when we got home and she administered it freely and without sugar, burning hot. We always tried to sit beside some child whose mother had a bag of tea-cakes. My brother managed that.

Congressman William C. Anderson

Notables of Cocke County

The author found it impossible to learn every name that should be written upon Cocke County's roll of notables, because there are few records of the past, due in part to the many courthouse fires. Also, people are quickly forgotten in this complex civilization, if there is no written record. The following names have been sent in to the author by various citizens who had special reasons for doing so, although they did not always list them.

Repeated requests were made through the press and these were stressed by Editors Campbell and Sulte, who were intensely interested in the history of Cocke County and did much to encourage the research work necessary in preparing such data. The author deeply regrets any omission.

D. GRAY ALLEN and J. S. ALLEN, early merchants.

LOUIS SEAHORN ALLEN, owner of the Allendale Farm, noted for its blooded shorthorn cattle and cured hams, was a leader in the movement to establish the Great Smoky Mountains National Park; director of the Great Smoky Mountain Conservation Association; and director of numerous better roads and civic movement associations. He was formerly president of the Newport Millling Company, director of the Merchant and Planters Bank, a thirty-second degree Mason; a Shriner and Knight Templar. He served as deacon of the First Baptist Church, Newport, a number of years. He was formerly mayor of Newport and also chairman of the Cocke County Road Commission for several years. He was a graduate of the University of Virginia, where he was a member of Sigma Alpha Epsilon fraternity. He married Stella Willis, and they have one daughter, Miss Jane Allen, and one son, Jack Allen. Mr. Allen died at the age of sixty-nine.

NANNIE ALLEN, artist.

JUDGE PLEASANT WITT ANDERSON was the son of Highheel Jimmie Anderson and the grandson of Pleasant Witt; hence, Highheel Jimmie's wife must have been Witt's daughter. Judge Anderson was a brother of Dr. Samuel Anderson who married Julia Margaret Doak, and they became the parents of W. C., the Congressman, Miss Sallie, Miss Julia and Josephine Houston, known as Jodie. Other children were Mary Jane, Smith Pleasant, Joseph James, Alexander Eckles, and Samuel Doak Newman. Joseph Anderson, must have been the father or uncle of Highheel Jimmie and Isaac (the President of Maryville College.)

DR. SAMUEL ANDERSON, president of Carson and Newman College, 1851-1857.

WILLIAM COLEMAN ANDERSON was born at Tusculum, Greene County, near Greeneville, July 10, 1853. After attending a rural school, he entered Tusculum College and graduated in 1876. He studied law while serving as deputy county court clerk of Cocke County from 1877 to 78. He was admitted to the Newport bar in 1878 and began to practice law in Newport. He was a member of the lower house of the state legislature from 1881 to 83. He also served as a principal examiner for the General Land Office, Washington, D. C., 1889-92. He was promoted to chief of the Contest division of that office, February 1, 1892, and resigned the following August. In November of the same year he was made Chief of the General Land Office, but resigned to practice law in Newport. He was elected to Congress and served March 4, 1895, to March 3, 1897, but failed of re-election. He was founder and editor of *Plain Talk*, a weekly Newport newspaper. He died on September 8, 1902, and was buried in Union Cemetery, Newport.

CAPTAIN JOHN FLOYD ARROWOOD (Del Rio area) made a record in World War I second only to that of Alvin C. York. He was wined and dined over Europe, but forgotten at home. He was first American soldier decorated for bravery in World War I.

One of the most colorful citizens of Cocke County was ALEXANDER ALAN ARTHUR, a big, handsome, ruddy Scotchman, who greatly resembled his kinsman, Chester Alan Arthur, once President of the United States.

A. A. A., as he often signed himself, was born in 1845 in Glasgow, Scotland. After an interesting life of various business adventures he was sent to Newport as head of "The Scottish Lumber Company." He built our "Scottish Mansion," as it was called, in which he used many varieties of lumber. It is now the home of Hubert and Julia Anderson, whose father, W. C. Anderson, purchased it from A. A. A. about the time Mr. Arthur became interested in the development of Middlesboro, Ky. area where he was known as "Duke of Cumberland." An interesting story of his life is given by Robert L. Kincaid in his book, "The Wilderness Road."

Mr. Arthur's second wife is still living in Knoxville, 1950. She was Nellie Goodwin. His first wife was Mary Forest Brikenhead, who died in Boston, leaving two children.

Mr. Arthur had wonderful persuasive powers and was able to interest many organizations in his various developments during "The Gay Nineties."

HOOPER L. ATCHLEY, a soldier of World War I. Played many character parts in pictures. Died November, 1943, age 56. Buried at Reedtown in Phillips Cemetery, by the side of parents, P. S. and Elizabeth Atchley. Brother, J. Arthur Atchley, attorney in Knoxville.

NANCY PRESNELL BELL (Mrs. J. H.) of Cosby is the daughter of Mr. and Mrs. Grant Presnell and was born in Watauga County, North Carolina. She came with her parents to Cocke County in the gay nineties.

Mrs. Bell does feature writing and has also had several poems published in the Knoxville Journal and local papers and had two poems included in the 1941 Book of Modern Poetry.

Her salute to Cocke County appears in this volume and shows her love of her adopted home.

THOMAS BIBEE, private in the War for American Independence, was born in 1734, Goochland County, Virginia, and died in Cocke County, 1834, age one hundred years. He married in South Carolina, Wahnee, an Indian Princess of the Powhatan Tribe of Indians, a descendant of Pocahontas. They had one son, William Bibee.

AARON BIBLE, a Dutchman, was the son of George Bible, who came directly from Holland with his four sons, Moses, Aaron, Jacob, and Ezra.

EZEKIEL BIRDSEYE, Yankee in the County, was a most unusual personage who settled in Cocke County in the 1830's. He was a native of Connecticut, a man of intelligence and of some considerable means. An anti-slavery man, he endeavored to promote the Emancipation movement in this and adjoining counties, contacting leaders of like mind, such as Rev. Dr. R. R. McAnally and Rev. Robeson H. Lea, the latter of whom reported that in the adjoining County of Jefferson there was a manumission society with over 600 members. In Cocke County, there were doubtless many, but fewer than there were in Jefferson County. He mentions Tom C. Roadman and many other Newport men of the time. Birdseye conducted a correspondence with the celebrated abolitionist, Garrit Smith of New York State, and it is to the Smith Papers that we are indebted for Birdseye's letters, which shed much light on conditions in this county in the 1830's and 1840's. He and ex-Supreme Judge Jacob Peck, of Mossy Creek (now Jefferson City), were partners in land transactions in Cocke and Jefferson Counties, and in Western North Carolina. The two were also interested in the economic development of emigration from the North of men who would acquire landholdings from them.

In a letter to Garrit Smith of January, 1841, he said:

In my acquaintance with the South I have been induced to believe that improved communications between the North and South will contribute greatly to the overthrow of slavery. The South is in want of manufactures tools and implements of any kind. Agriculture is at a low stage. Most of the people here are willing to work and would hail with joy any manufacturing that would employ them at a low price.

He pointed out that a turnpike from Cincinnati through Cumberland Gap and Newport would reach Charlotte, N. C. Further: "steam railroad now extends to Raleigh," and with a turnpike from Raleigh through Newport to Knoxville, communication with the East would be much much facilitated.

Judge Peck and myself own very large tracts in this and adjoining counties on which we are anxious to establish improvements wholly excluding slavery. These lands are healthy and have great natural resources: Iron ore, waterpower, timber and rich mountain pasture grounds. We own French Broad for about 16 miles. That stream would make a fine place for a rolling mill or manufacturing town. . . A press might soon be established here and much be done to redeem the South which needs a practical example of the advantages of free labor.

Three years before the date of the above letter, Birdseye had written to Smith that "East Tennessee might be detached from the other part of the State of Tennessee and made a separate free State. I had hopes then that such might be the result. . . From my first arrival in this State I have endeavored to convince those with whom I became acquainted that such a decision would contribute to the well-being of East Tennessee. . . The movement is now (1841) popular in all East Tennessee. . . I attended the Internal Improvement Convention of East Tennessee of Knoxville. Not a single opponent appeared to oppose it in a discussion."

Much of the correspondence related to slavery, as was but natural. In Garrit Smith's home town in New York there lived a younger brother of Ezekiel, Victor Birdseye, also a native of Connecticut, and educated in Williams College, Massachusetts, where Ezekiel was probably educated. Victor twice represented his district in Congress, 1815-17 and 1841-43. He was an intimate friend and follower of Garrit Smith. The contact was established through Victor Birdseye. Ezekiel survived until the outbreak of the Civil War. It may not be doubted that he contributed materially to the building up of a sentiment which eventually made Cocke County a Unionist county.

The movement for a second State of Franklin, led by Andrew Johnson of Greeneville, a senator in the Tennessee legislature of 1841-43, is treated of in S. C. Williams' *History of the Lost State of Franklin* (second edition), pages 284-5. In that legislature, Cocke County was represented along with Greene County, by Samuel Milligan, later a Supreme Judge of Tennessee.

In the election of 1860, there being no Lincoln electors or ticket in Tennessee, we may assume that Birdseye supported John Bell of Tennessee, a candidate for the presidency on the Constitutional Union platform.[1]

DR. BLANCHE DOZIER BISHOP of Knoxville is a direct descendant of Col. Abraham McKay and deserves a special place of honor among Cocke County's Notables. She was born and reared in the Del Rio Area. Her husband, E. L. Bishop was long one of Knoxville's leading musicians.

JOHN BLANCHARD, minister and physician, a native of Cocke County, was the oldest son of John and Sarah Blanchard of South Carolina, and was born on March 30, 1821, on the French Broad River, ten miles from Paint Rock. He was of Welsh extraction.

On March 24, 1842, he was married to Miss Charlotte Justus by Elder Manning. In 1842, he was converted in a Methodist camp meeting at Parrottsville. Later he joined the church and was baptized by Elder Manning. He gave his days to hard work and his nights to the study of the scripture. In 1843, in the old brick meeting house at the mouth of Big Creek, Elder Blanchard preached his first sermon. On April 18, 1844, he went west, finally locating in Illinois. Two of his sons became ministers. At forty-three he took up the study of medicine and four years later graduated from the Eclectic College of Medicine, in 1869. He became a noted pioneer in education, temperance reforms, religion, and good citizenship. As a preacher, his style was quaint and effective. (Burnett)

BENJAMIN F. BOULDEN, a graduate of the University of Virginia, came to Cocke County about 1835 and taught his first school in the old Anderson Academy. Soon after he located in the County, he married Miss McKay, daughter of Abraham McKay, Jr. (granddaughter of Abraham McKay, Sr.). In 1846, Professor Boulden taught school at Parrottsville. Among his students were J. J. Burnett, J. M. L. Burnett, John Huff, Henry Coulter, three sons of Col. John E. Patton, Robert Huff, J. H. Clark, D. A. Mims, and David V. Stokely. He remained there until 1850, when he again taught at Newport for two or three years. During this time, his family lived one mile East of Newport on the Swaggerty

---

1. Judge Samuel C. Williams

farm, near the N. L. McSween residence. In 1857 or 58 he taught again at Parrottsville, and there had among his pupils, J. H. Faubion, Lieut. R. A. McNabb, George McNabb, George Rowe, James McLaughlen, J. V. Parrott, Jerome Shields.

Later, Professor Boulden moved his family to Sweetwater (Edwina) and lived near the James Netherton place. While here, he taught school at Pleasant Grove Meeting House and there he taught the Allens, Sisks, Clevengers, Taylors, McNabbs. In 1861, he returned to Newport to teach. His family consisted of his wife and five children: T. L., Wood, Martha, Tyler, and Jo Anne Boulden. T. L. became a second lieutenant, Co. C., 26th Tennessee. Wood became a Methodist minister of considerable note.

Captain George Stuart, who commanded Company C, 26th Tennessee Regiment, placed "Negro Bob" in the hands of Professor Boulden to be carried farther into Confederate lines. When he reached Atlanta, he sold Bob for $1500, partly paid in gold. With this money, he left Atlanta, went to his brother, Wood Boulden, a judge of a Virginia court, where he died without rejoining his family. The night after Bob was sold, he joined the Federal Army. After the war, a son of Judge Wood Boulden came to Newport and was taken by D. A. Mims to visit the old log school-house in which his scholarly and gifted uncle once taught or lived. (Data from W. O. Mims Scrapbook)

C. F. BOYER, clerk of the circuit court, was born in 1846, in Cocke County. He was the fourteenth of fifteen children of Isaac and Elizabeth Simms Boyer, natives of Virginia and South Carolina, respectively. Isaac Boyer, a farmer and a tanner, was a son of Jacob Boyer, a native of Virginia. C. F.'s parents settled in Cocke County about 1817 with their family. He enlisted in August, 1863, in Company A., Third Tennessee Mounted Infantry. He was appointed sergeant but declined the appointment. He served until December, 1864, when he was mustered out at Knoxville. He attended school two years at Parrottsville, and engaged in farming and merchandising until 1876. He was then elected sheriff of Cocke County, and was twice re-elected to the same office, serving in all six years. He was then elected circuit court clerk and was re-elected August, 1886. He became justice of the peace in 1869, and served about three years. He was married in 1872 to Miss Florence McNabb, a daughter of Alexander McNabb, a native of Monroe County, although he lived in Cocke County the most of his life. C. F. and Florence McNabb Boyer had seven children: Hester E., Henry S., Horace C., Jetta, George R., Creed Mc., and Franklin A. He was a Republican and a Master Mason. He owned a fine farm of three hundred acres, formerly owned by his grandfather, Padgett. While sheriff, Mr. Boyer hanged two men, the only ones ever hanged in Cocke County by law. He was many times Representative of Cocke County. (Goodspeed). Mr. Boyer's second wife, Anna Dennis Weaver bore him several sons and daughters. Otto, Maymie, Lucy, Jennie R., Burnett, Eula. Orlie and Homer Weaver were sons of the first marriage of Anna Dennis Boyer.

DANIEL BUCKNER was born in South Carolina, September 30, 1801, the son of a Henry Buckner, a personal friend and great admirer of Daniel Boone.

The family moved to Tennessee, settling in Cocke County, when he was quite a lad. Here in his fifteenth year, he was converted, walking twelve miles, to join the nearest Baptist Church, the old Lick Creek (now Warrensburg) Church, Greene County. He was baptized by Caleb Witt in the Nolachucky River.

In 1817, he was married to Miss Mary Hampton, of Cocke County, a granddaughter of Elder William Dodson of North Carolina, and a near relative of General Wade Hampton. They had three sons and two daughters. Dr. H. F. Buckner, the eldest son, was a missionary to the Creek Indians for thirty-five years, translating the Gospel of John into the Creek tongue and publishing a grammar of the Creek language. The second son, B. B., went through the Mexican War, but died in Mexico City, after peace was proclaimed. One son, R. C. Buckner was the founder of the Buckner Orphans' Home (Texas), also former editor and proprietor of the *Texas Baptist* and President of the Baptist General Convention of Texas. In all, the Buckner family had fifteen Baptist preachers. In the early 30's Daniel was appointed "missionary" by the State Convention, and was excluded from the Church for refusing to sever his connection with that body.

He was a man of powerful physical frame, six feet tall and weighing 250 pounds, with a powerful voice. He preached the gospel for more than 63 years and baptized 5,000 people, about 25 of whom became ministers. (Burnett)

BENJAMIN FRANKLIN BURNETT left Cocke County and went to Georgia, where he became a member of the Georgia Secession Convention in 1860, also of the Constitutional Convention of 1877 of Georgia. He returned often to visit in Cocke County.

DR. EDMUND CODY BURNETT was born in Henry County, Alabama, November 29, 1864, the son of Jesse Montreville Lafayette and Henrietta Sarah Cody Burnett.

At the age of three years, Edmund Burnett's memory began to record his childhood activities in Cocke County, where he lived on the ancestral estate on Big Creek, at what is now known as Del Rio, for he then started to school.

At the age of fifteen, he was sent to Mossy Creek College (now Carson-Newman College), where he received his A. B. degree in 1888, and the same degree at Brown University in 1890, followed by the Master of Arts in 1895 and the Doctor of Philosophy, in 1897. His thesis, *The Government of Federal Territories*, was published in the American Historical Association Report that year. Upon graduation here, he became successively assistant professor of mathematics and professor of Greek and modern languages at Carson-Newman; instructor in Greek and history, at Brown until 1899; English professor at Bethel College, 1899-1900; and professor of history at Mercer University, 1900-05. For a while, he served as treasurer of the Swann-Day Lumber Company, Clay County, Kentucky, with his brother-in-law, Colonel A. R. Swann. He was appointed a member of the Carnegie Institute historical research staff department in 1907, which position he held to his death.

His first duties in the research department was that of assembling and editing letters written by the delegates of the several states in the Revolutionary Congress, also the preparation of the American notes in the *American Historical Review*. The first volume, beginning with the Congress of 1774 and ending July 4, 1776, was published in 1921 under the title *Letters of Members of Continental Congress.* The eighth, and last of the series, was published in 1936.

His other publications include: Documents relating to Bourbon County, Georgia (Edited with introduction), *American Historical Review*, Volume XV., October, 1909, January, 1910; Note on American Negotiations for Commercial Treaties, *American Historical Review*, Vol. XVI, April, 1911; The Committee of the States *American Historical Association Annual Report*, 1913; Ciphers of the Revolutionary Period, *American Historical Review*, XXII, January, 1917; The Name, "United States of America," *American Historical Review*, XXXI, October, 1925; Edward Langworthy, *Georgia Historical Quarterly*, 1927; The Continental Congress and Agricultural Supplies, *Agriculture Historical*, July, 1928; Perquisites of the Presidents of the Continental Congress, *American Historical Review*, 1929; Washington and the Committee at Headquarters, *American Historical Annual Report*, 1932; Who was the Frist President of the U. S. (Carnegie Institute, 1932, and reprints in *Carnegie Magazine*, June, 1932); Our Union of States in the Making, *World Affairs*, September, 1935, (reprinted by the Carnegie Institute, 1935); Some Civil War Letters (Edited with introduction), *Georgia Historical ·Quarterly*, June, 1937; Letters of J. M. L. Burnett and others; Southern Statements and the Confederation, *North Carolina Historical Review;* The More Perfect Union: The Continental Congress seeks a Formula, *Catholic Historical Review*, April, 1938; The Catholic Signers of the Constitution: Daniel Carroll and Thomas Fitzsimons (Catholic University of America, 1938); About a dozen sketches in *Dictionary of American Biography* (eight volumes), 1921-1937, Carnegie Institute.

Dr. Burnett was awarded second prize of $400, the Loubat prize of Columbia University, for his book THE CONTINENTAL CONGRESS.

Dr. Burnett was married to Susan Elizabeth Susong of Bridgeport, Tennessee, October 9, 1914. They have four children.

He was a member of the American Historical Association, the Tennessee Historical Society, Phi Beta Kappa, and the Palaver and Cosmos Clubs.

His home was at Del Rio, Tennessee, and 1204 Newton Street, N. E., Washington, D. C.

Dr. Burnett died Jan. 9, 1949 in Washington.

FRANCES HODGSON BURNETT was born in England, in 1849, the daughter of Edwin Hodgson, a merchant, who died when he was 38 years old. William Bond (or Boond), a brother of Mrs. Hodgson, was a merchant in Knoxville, Tennessee. He brought his widowed sister and her family to America. They lived at New Market, but in 1866, they moved to Knoxville. The site of their home was on what is now the campus of Knoxville College (Negro). A marker was recently placed where the little house was destroyed by fire in 1900.

Frances Hodgson wrote her first story when she was sixteen years of age, and it was published in 1867 in *Godey's Lady's Book*. It is claimed that she sold blackberries to purchase stamps with which to mail her manuscripts. Her best-known work was *Little Lord Fauntleroy*.

In 1873, Frances Hodgson was married to Dr. Swan M. Burnett. They went to France to live that he might further his medical studies. While there a son, Lionel Burnett, was born, in Paris. When they returned to live in East Knoxville, Tennessee, the second son, Vivian, was born. It is said the family lived at two other places in Knoxville, also at Newport for a short time. Finally, they moved to Washington, D. C., where Doctor Burnett became an instructor in the medical school of Georgetown University. They were divorced in 1898. She married Stephen Townsend and left him. He married Margaret Brady of Washington.

Her son, Vivian, died in 1937, at 61. He was educated at Harvard and became reporter, writer, and editor of *McClure's Magazine*. His biography of his mother, *The Romantic Lady*, was published in *Scribner's*, in 1927, after her death in 1924, in Long Island, New York.

J. J. BURNETT, a farmer in the First District, was born February 7, 1824, in North Carolina, near Asheville. He was the eleventh of thirteen children of Swan P. and Frances Bell Burnett, natives of Virginia and North Carolina, respectively. He was the grandson of Thomas Burnett, a native of Virginia, who was killed by a Tory, about the time of the battle of King's Mountain, in which his brother Joseph was killed. He attended school at Holston College, Jefferson County, Tennessee. He was married February 10, 1853, to Miss Mary E. Huff, daughter of Stephen Huff, the son of John Huff, a native of Virginia. Their children were Jehu J., Stephen F., Jesse A., Frances E. C., Sissie Elizabeth J., and Cynthia A. Mary Burnett died about 1863. He was married a second time, October 10, 1867, to Miss Ester A. Lea, daughter of Alfred Lea, a native of Jefferson County. There were five children: Evalena, Henrietta M., Harriett C., Joseph J., and Swan A. Mr. Burnett was a member of the Missionary Baptist Church and a Democrat. (Goodspeed)

J. M. L. BURNETT was born in Buncombe County, North Carolina, near Asheville, September 14, 1829, the son of Swan P. and Frances Bell Burnett, and the youngest of thirteen children. His grandfather, Thomas Burnett, a Virginian by birth, was of Scotch descent. His mother, Jennie Montgomery Bell, of North Carolina, was part Irish. In 1835, the family left the old home and settled near the mouth of Big Creek (Del Rio), in Cocke County. At the age of thirteen, he was converted in a meeting held by Elders Manning and Ephraim Moore at Clay Creek Church and was baptized by Elder Manning. He preached his first sermon at Pleasant Grove Church on the banks of the Pigeon River, six miles from Newport.

On August 31, 1854, he was married to Evelyn Ann Huff, daughter of Stephen Huff. She died three years later, leaving a son and a daughter. On December 26, 1861, he was married to Miss H. S. Cody, daughter of Elder Edmund Cody, of Alabama. They had four sons and four daughters.

In 1859 and 1860, he was a fellow student of Dr. William H. Whitsitt in Union University, at Murfreesboro. Dr. J. M. Pendleton, one of the University professors made the statement, it is said, that J. M. L. Burnett and W. H. Whitsitt "were the finest, or among the finest linguists I have ever taught." Mr. Burnett had a special delight in reading the poet Burns. In 1871, he became an ordained pastor of the Fort Gaines Church, in Georgia. Elders Edmund Cody, Adiel Sherwood, and Dr. E. W. Warren constituted the ordaining council.

In 1867, with impaired health, he returned to his East Tennessee home, where he lived as a farmer-preacher the balance of his days. He declined calls to prominent pulpits and an offer of the chair of mathematics in a leading university. He served as pastor of his home church, Big Creek, Newport, Leadvale, Morristown, and others.

With Joseph Manning and Ephraim Moore, he was the principal founder of the East Tennessee Association, composed at first of four churches. He frequently was chosen as Moderator.

He had a good knowledge of Latin and Greek. He was a Fullerite in theology and Robert Hall was his model of diction and pulpit discourse. He was also gifted in conversation and in prayer.

He died August 1, 1883, leaving his widow and ten children, all of whom have made good. Dr. Edmund C. Burnett was one of these. (Burnett)

TOM CAMPBELL (deceased), editor and historian.

One of the most outstanding contributions made in 1950, to the religious and community life of Cocke County, has been made by Mr. JOE CARPENTER and wife, Mrs. Bernice Smith Carpenter of the Forest Hill Community. They have built a beautiful parsonage for the Forest Hill Church in memory of their only child, Edwin Carpenter, who gave his life in the Battle of the Bulge, in Belgium, World War II.

ARLIE BURKE CARTER, poet.

JERRY CARTER, of Del Rio, was the grandson of Wilbur Carter and Cynthia Burnett Carter and the son of Wilbur, Jr., and Blannie (Nannie) Carter. Dr. Wilbur was a Confederate soldier, who lost a leg in the Civil War. It is said that the doctors who amputated it hoped that the act would kill him.

Jerry was born at Del Rio, removed to Hendersonville, thence to Florida, where he ran for Governor, also for Senate. He was defeated by Senator Claude Pepper. Wilbur Carter taught his seven sons to become self-supporting at an early age.

THOMAS L. CARTY, prominent Knoxville attorney.

H. NELSON CATE, attorney.

JOSEPH L. CATON, editor, author, poet, and naturalist.

Promotion of BENJAMIN A. L. CLICK, son of Benjamin A. L. Click, Sr., of Newport, to the rank of major in the U. S. Air Force, has been announced at Tyndall Air Force base at Panama City, Florida, where he is stationed.

After arriving at Tyndall in October, 1949, Major Click was assigned as an instructor in the 3502nd Instrument Training Squadron. Entering service at Fort Oglethorpe, Ga., in September, 1941, he spent 30 months with the Fifth Air Force headquarters overseas during the war.

Major Click is married to the former Mary Lou Folschinsky of Burlington, Texas.

JAMES B. COGDILL, pastor of Mount Zion, a church constituted in 1853, for 22 years. He baptized 1,200 people into the Baptist Church, in the mountains of Cocke and Sevier Counties.

One of the most colorful characters who has lived in Cocke County recently was Sheriff GEORGE W. COLE who was born in Buncomb County, N. C. but served 8 years as Sheriff of Madison County before coming to Tennessee.

He was a lumberman and lived in the Del Rio area. He was "public spirited" and took great interest in county politics and knew how to play "em."

County officials 1937-1940. Standing, left to right; Isaac Black, Will Hampton, William Crawford, Wade Giles, George Hall (Recorder), Perry Valentine; seated, John Denton, Esq., and John Jenkins, Esq.

City Hall

Information given by Ethel S. Cole, wife of Harl J. Cole. She is the daughter of J. H. Franks and wife, Sallie Sorrell, and granddaughter of B. F. Sorrell, our last Confederate soldier.

ELLA V. COSTNER, nurse in World War I and World War II, with rank of lieutenant.

WILLIAM MANARD CRAWFORD is a practicing attorney of Newport. He is both a self-educated and self-made man, whose industry, close application and commendable ambition have brought him steadily to the fore. He was born November 23, 1889, in the city which is still his home, and his ancestors were among the earliest settlers of the State. A great-great-grandfather, Peter Fine, operated a trading post at old Newport before Tennessee was admitted to the Union and was one of the commissioners appointed to lay out the county seat at that place. A great-grandfather, Abraham Fine, born March 24, 1789, a son of Peter Fine, served as sheriff of Cocke County from 1838 to 1840.

The parents of William Manard Crawford were William Melvin and Mary M. (Killian) Crawford, both natives of Cocke County. The former was a son of Dr. Daniel Allen Crawford, a practicing physician, who was born in Greene County, Tennessee, but came to Cocke County as a young man to practice his profession, married Sarah A. Fine, daughter of Abraham Fine, and was prominently identified with the public affairs of the county until his death in 1859. William Melvin Crawford, the father of the subject of this sketch, was a school teacher in early manhood, a storekeeper later in life and died in 1916. Mary M. (Killian Crawford, the mother, died in 1905. They were the parents of two sons, the younger being Hugh D. Crawford, a farmer of Jefferson County.

The elder son, William M. Crawford, attended the public schools of Cocke County to the age of sixteen years, and then began work in a printing office, becoming in due time a journeyman printer and a member of the International Typographical Union. He was employed at his trade in various cities, and, while thus employed, educated himself in the law and was admitted to practice in 1915. For a time before receiving license to practice, he studied in the office of Judge Thurman Ailor, then a young lawyer in Newport and now one of· the justices of the Tennessee Court of Appeals.

Since his admission to the bar, Mr. Crawford has closely followed his profession and on various occasions has held public office, but has never been an office-seeker, preferring to devote his time and energy to the practice of his profession. Shortly after being admitted to the bar he became a member of the firm of Ailor, Carty & Crawford, composed of Thurman Ailor, Thomas L. Carty and himself. This arrangement continued until 1923, when this firm was dissolved by the removal of Mr. Ailor to Knoxville. Thereafter, he practiced his profession alone until 1927, when he joined a Knoxville firm headed by his former partner, Mr. Ailor, under the firm name of Ailor, Child & Crawford, the other member being George S. Child. This connection continued until 1931, when Mr. Crawford withdrew from this firm to form a partnership with Ex-Governor Ben W. Hooper for practice in Newport under the firm name of Hooper and Crawford. And in 1937, the business of this firm having grown to the extent of requiring another member to efficiently handle its business, Edward F. Hurd was invited to join the firm and did so, which now operates under the name of Hooper, Crawford & Hurd, and as such is one of the strongest and best known law firms in upper East Tennessee. Mr. Crawford is known as the county's best Chancery Court lawyer, in 1950.

(Biographical Sketch from "Tennessee Democracy," Vol. 4, Page 880)

LENNIE CRAWLEY, called the lightning artist.

ARDER (ARTHUR) DAVIS, a modern William Tell, lived in the early days of Cocke County. However, whenever he was drunk he always announced himself as William Tell and endeavored to prove his markmanship by shooting apples from the heads of his slaves. A rich man with many slaves, he lived near the Jones Bridge, on the Nolichucky River, on what is known as Buffalo Trail.

At all other times, Davis was kind to his slaves. At one of his swimming parties, his best slave was drowned. He sent for Thomas M. Jones, who lived five miles away, and the Negro was finally brought to life.

One day, exceedingly drunk, he staggered forth to do his William Tell stunt and could not find a Negro in sight. He asked his wife to pose with the apple on her head. Whether she had faith in her husband or was afraid of him, she complied with his request, and fell dead at the discharge of the gun.[2]

CAREY DENNIS, at present a major in the Army.

J. J. DENTON, a farmer near Newport, was born May 16, 1851, in Cocke County, the sixth of seven children of Jefferson and Charity Huff Denton, natives of Cocke County. Jefferson was the son of Thomas Denton, a native of England who at a very early date immigrated to America and settled at the mouth of Cosby Creek. Charity Denton was the daughter of John Huff, who formerly resided at the present site of St. Louis, Missouri. J. J. Denton engaged in the grocery business when nineteen years old. He was married in 1876 to Lizzie Lloyd, daughter of G. W. Lloyd, a tanner and native of Cocke County who later moved to Texas. They had four children, George, James, Loyd and Dixie Denton.

DR. WASHINGTON J. DEWITT, physician and surgeon of South Carolina, brought to Old Newport by his father, Harris DeWitt. Educated at Greeneville College, he read medicine under Dr. Fore on Nolachucky, moved to Paris, Tennessee, in 1822, to Texas, in 1842. (This is family of the late Judge John H. DeWitt of Tennessee Court of Appeals and President of Tennessee Historical Society.)

LORENZO DOW, an eccentric individual, was born October 16, 1777, in Coventry, Connecticut, the son of Humphrey B. and Tabitha Dow. He died February 12, 1834, at Georgetown, New York.

Consumptive in appearance, Dow dressed plainly when young, but in later years he wore long hair and a flowing beard, which made him one of the most picturesque preachers of his time.

An educated man and an extensive traveler, here and in Europe, his wife Peggy was his constant companion until her death in 1820. He attacked the ruling vices with caustic rebukes, biting sarcasm and strong mother wit. He always kept his appointments to the hour, although he often made them 12 to 18 months in advance.

---

2. Data from Lillie Jones Duncan.

His sayings were handed down from generation to generation, and babies all over the country were named for him.[3]

JOSEPH B. DRAPER was born in Asheville, North Carolina, on May 10, 1862, of Scotch-Irish and French ancestry, the great grandson of Israel and Jane Baird, and the grandson of Samuel and Margaret Anne Baird. Thomas Draper, Jr., was known as Little Tom, the Fiddler. The Drapers were from Virginia and one of those, Charles, invented a loom; and Edward, a telescope. Tom, the Fiddler, in his travels stopped at the Inn and married Margaret Ann, the schoolteacher daughter of the innkeeper Baird, who traveled with her husband with his magic lantern show until her baby was born. She named him Joseph Beeden for her two brothers. J. B. Draper was born and reared at his mother's Uncle, James Baird's home. He was a doctor in Asheville, and the boy spent much time with Jane Baird Weaver, his great aunt, the wife of Rev. Mont Weaver, a Methodist preacher, for whom Weaverville, North Carolina, was named. In 1885, Joseph started out to "cure" tobacco for a living. Swann Huff, in search of an experienced tobacco curer, found young Joe Draper and took him to the Del Rio section.

The home of Swann Huff was near that of Jack Penland who had thirteen children: Harriet, Jane, Dora, Sarah, Julia, Alice and Eunis (twins), Victoria, James, Thomas, Henry, Stevenson, Wesley. J. B. Draper married Alice, one of the twins, who became the mother of thirteen children: Ervin, Ashley, Evert, Chesley, James, Solomon, Jesse, Eunis, Bonnie, Ada, Lee, Lucile and Margaret Ann. Eight of these lived to maturity.

Joe Draper's first bloodhound "Brock" never lost a track in four years. His first experience was trailing three boys who had robbed a second-hand clothing store operated in the mountain section by missionaries by the name of Nawvac (sometimes Nawk). Brock took the trail and found the culprits in eight hours.

The second two bloodhounds were Jack and Francis, from the Rookwood Kennels at Lexington, Kentucky. Their first job was "tracking" Dolphus Jeans and Swann Greene for taking a goose from the farm of Joshua Foreman. The sleeping youngsters were found beside the tied goose.

Joe Draper charged from ten to thirty dollars for the services of his dogs and the "chase" took him into Greene, Sevier, Hamblen, Jefferson, as well as Cocke County, also to Madison County, North Carolina. He owned in his lifetime around seventy dogs, fifty of which he trained himself.

Joe Draper was elected constable at Bridgeport six times, then deputy sheriff for four years, and Deputy U. S. Marshall two years. His first wife, Alice Penland Draper, died in 1916, and he married twice afterward. He died on June 10, 1945, at the age of 83.

KENNETH WITT DRISKILL was born April 8, 1912, the son of Richard P. and Sallie Parrott Driskill of Newport, Tennessee. He graduated as the valedictorian of his high school class and an accomplished pianist. He entered the University of Tennessee in 1929. In 1931, he joined the cavalry; then, attended West Point Preparatory

---

3. See also Chapter on Religion for account of his travels in Cocke County.

Lt. Kenneth Driskill

Lt. Mitchell McMahan

Cocke County Memorial Building honoring Country's veterans of all wars.

School, 1931-1932, at Fort McPherson. He entered the U. S. M. A. at West Point, from which he graduated in 1937. Then he was changed to the 31st Infantry, where he was a member of M. Company, which included men six feet in height, or taller. Soon after graduation, Lieutenant Driskill was sent to the Philippines on Foreign Service, where he spent two years. He married Laura Owen Walton, daughter of Major and Mrs. Charles Manley Walton on March 11, 1939, at the Cathedral of St. Mary and St. John, Manila, P. I.

On April 2, 1940, Lt. Driskill and his bride returned to the States, and were stationed at Fort Benning, Georgia, where he was transferred to the 29th Infantry. Early on the morning of August 30, 1941, he was found dead of gunshot. He was a member of the Methodist Episcopal Church. He is buried in Union Cemetery, Newport. He was one of the most brilliant and best loved young men of Cocke County, our only West Point graduate.

RICHARD PLEASANT NEW YEAR DRISKILL, of Irish descent and originally O'Driskill of the landed gentry, was born January 1, 1859, in a log cabin near, or on, the Drewry Dawson Farm. In 1867, the Driskills moved to Fowler's Grover where they, all but Richard, went to school. Due to the difficulties of the reconstruction period of the South, Professor Driskill could neither read nor write when he was 21 years of age. George R. Stuart, teacher of the Parrottsville School, persuaded Richard to enter school, where he "shacked," doing his own cooking.

Driskill made remarkable progress and finished the course quickly. He then attended Emory and Henry College, where he graduated with honors. He taught his first school at Brier Thicket, immediately after finishing school at Parrotsville. He taught for many years here, where he instructed, inspired and governed the school. He served as County Superintendent for a number of years. At the time of his sudden death, October 23, 1915, he was head of the City Schools of Newport. It is said that at least three thousand citizens paid their last respects to him as he lay in state in the Tabernacle near the Court House, on October 25, most of them being his former students. His marriage to Sallie Parrott of Parrottsville, December 27, 1897, was blest with four sons and two daughters: Thomas, Clyde, Richard, Kenneth, Annie Rowe, and Rosemary Ruth. The boundless energy of this great teacher spent itself in a worth-while life of inspiration.

COL. WILSON L. DUGGAN, SR. Attorney in the early 30's. Representative in general assembly for twelve years. Family was from Massachusetts, having originally lived in Norstrom, England. The first Duggan, Robert, entered and obtained grants for the land which still belongs to his descendants.

HON. W. L. DUGGAN, JR. Both representative and senator.

LILLIE E. JONES DUNCAN, on November 28, 1875, was born to Robert McFarland Jones and wife Ellen S. Jones. They lived in her maternal grandparents home on Little Chucky Creek, in Greene County, near Warrensburg, Tennessee. In the veins of this newborn babe flowed the blood of a mixed ancestry of French Huguenot, Scotch, English and Holland Dutch. One of her grandmothers was the first girl white child born in Tennessee; this family being closely connected with the early history of East Tennessee.

At the age of three and one half years, life and death presented itself to this little girl by presenting her with a brother and by robbing her of her mother on the day the boy was nine days old.

Together these children grew to maturity, the girl always feeling keenly the responsibility of the care of her brother. They had a happy childhood, roaming the woodlands, climbing trees, grooming and riding the horses, going to school in the little country schoolhouse of Gum Springs in that section of country.

The grandmother of Lillie Jones gave her much valuable training in the art of gentle and gracious living both religiously and domestically.

Her father, with great love and tenderness for his motherless children endeavored to take the place of both father and mother, often taking his children with him to work that he might have the pleasure of their company and that he might impart to them his knowledge of nature, God's wisdom and man's weakness. Robert McFarland Jones was a wonderful father to his children, they idolized him in childhood, reverenced him in old age. He provided abundantly for them giving them every advantage possible that they might develop into worthwhile citizens. He brought them up in the way they should come and they have not departed from his teaching. His memory is a great benediction to each of them.

After completing the course taught in the country school near her home, Lillie E. Jones was sent to Morristown High School and later to the Rogersville Synodical College. A college maintained and owned by the Synod of the Southern Branch of the Presbyterian Church. From this school she graduated in 1894, became a teacher in the Greene County Schools.

In 1897, George C. Duncan, senior partner of the hardware firm of Duncan and Greer in Newport, brought Lillie E. Jones Duncan to our town as his bride and here she has lived since that time and has been an important factor in the upbuilding of our town and county. She came to us quite familiar with the early development of Cocke County and this entire section as related to her by her father who was connected with the surveying and building of the Old Buncombe Railroad, the first railroad in Cocke County. Robert McFarland Jones brought the first train into Newport over the Old Buncombe Railroad.

It was not until 1919 that the idea of the wonderful garden we now enjoy as High Oaks Tulip Gardens was begun. If a serious illness had not forced Mrs. Duncan outdoors she might never have conceived the idea of this development. She had no idea at that time that she would live to complete her vision and make a garden of such supreme beauty and magnitude as the outstanding High Oaks Gardens have become. However, each year found her carefully and artistically beautifying another barren place, thereby giving more work to more people who were in need of employment, a charity, she to this day continues. Supervising, instructing, working herself alongside those who help her until she has developed and expanded the small hillside garden of 1919 to ten acres of fragrant loveliness which is located in the very heart of our town and is the center of interest and civic pride. A living monument, to a living woman, a source of continuous beauty the year around, a resting place for all who love and appreciate beauty, a source of inspiration to all who have the ability to think.

High Oaks Hall, famous for its beautiful gardens, is the home of Lillie Jones Duncan

The Dave Gorman home, later known as the Randolph home.

Each springtime for many years, these gardens have been thrown open to the public. Thousands of visitors from most every State in the Union and from SEVEN foreign countries have wended their way through High Oaks Tulip Gardens. Many have gathered ideas and inspiration for their own homes and gardens, stories and pictures of this masterpiece of artistic landscaping have appeared in many magazines throughout the country.

Mrs. Duncan does not confine her activities to her wonderful gardens but since the death of her father has carried on the affairs of the R. M. Jones estate. Rents and looks after several farms in Cocke County. She is greatly loved and highly respected by all her tenants and by the servants she employs in her home and gardens. She is considered by most people to be the most public spirited citizen of Newport.

The small apartment business in Newport was originated here by Mrs. Duncan. She has maintained for several years eleven apartments, five of which are electrically furnished and equipped so that they can be lived in by strangers coming into the town with only a suitcase.

Mrs. Duncan is a personage in her own right, a kind and considerate woman who believes devoutly in the Supreme Ruler of all things, has faith in humanity and in the future of Cocke County and East Tennessee. She has endeavored to pass on to the younger generation this spirit and to impart to them her love of beauty and cleanliness of character that has ruled her life.

Newport and Cocke County owe to Lillie E. Jones Duncan a debt of gratitude for creating within its midst such a garden that attracts to itself the thousands of visitors that come annually with the birds, the bees, the butterflies and the blossoms of springtime. She is immortalized in the blooming of her flowers.

MRS. SUSAN FRAWLEY EISELE. Received 1936 prize as best (Blue Earth, Minnesota) County newspaper correspondent in the nation. Writes with a penny pencil. Daughter of Mrs. Rose Frawley, who was born and bred in Switzerland, and who came to Newport when a young matron. The first Catholic Church in Cocke County was established there through Mrs. Frawley's efforts and on her property.

DR. EVERETT M. ELLISON, a native of Cocke County, received his high school education in the County, attended the University of Chattanooga, and received his degree in medicine from George Washington University. He began his general practice there and followed it for thirty years, until his death in Mexico, where he was vacationing, at the age of sixty.

Dr. Ellison married Fannie Mae Huff, the second time. There were three daughters by his first marriage: Elizabeth, Margaret, and Nancy. Dr. Ellison's first wife was Alberta Hunt.

Dr. Ellison was prominent in church and civic life in the nation's capital, and was active in the Round Table, having served as international president of that organization. Being an uncompromising dry, he took an active stand in the defense of prohibition. He held his residence in Cocke County and voted by mail in every election.

He was buried in the family cemetery at Parrottsville.

J. H. FAGALA, first resident photographer, was located where our present laundry now stands, the birthplace of *Newport Times*. Son, Frank

Fagala was its editor, 1899. Later, *Plain Talk and Tribune* was housed on same lot in present building.

ELIZABETH SHINE FARRAGUT, the mother of America's first and greatest Admiral of our Navy, David Glasgow Farragut, lived in Cocke County. She was Elizabeth Shine, daughter of John and Eleanor McIver Shine, of Shine's Ferry, on the French Broad River. Major George Farragut, father of the Admiral, frequently passed by way of the ferry in going to and from North Carolina on business missions for Governor William Blount of the Southwest Territory and probably met and courted Elizabeth in his journeyings (According to Judge William's "George Farragut," in East Tennessee Historical Society publication.)[4]

On the blank leaf of an old Bible, now in possession of the Admiral's family, there is the following record:

My Son,—Your Father, George Farragut, was born in the island of Minorca, in the Mediterranean in 1755, the 29th of September in Ciudadella, came to America in March 1776.

Your Mother, Elizabeth Shine, was born in North Carolina, Dobbs County, near Kinnston, on the Neuse River, in 1765 on the 7th of June. Her father, John Shine; Mother, Ellenor McIver.

COL. J. H. FAUBION. Texas legislator and great lover of his Tennessee home.

MRS. JENNIE ST. CLAIR CARSON FELKNOR. One of Newport's beloved teachers. Buried in St. Paul cemetery near Lowland on old Morristown road.

ABRAHAM FINE. Early pioneer sheriff.

JOHN W. FISHER was born July 15, 1855, in Clearville, Pennsylvania, and was educated in the public schools and Williamsport Seminary. His manner of address was so effective that it is said he could have been a minister. He began his business career and finished his apprenticeship in Philadelphia. In May, 1894, he moved with his wife and children: Verne, Arthur J., Eva May, and Frederick S., to Newport, as first superintendent of Unaka Tannery. They lived in what was known as the Bridge House, which was remodeled and named "Bide-A-While," where they lived for thirty-four years. He became one of the most honored and influential men in the community. He was a member of the Board of Trustees of Grant University (now Tennessee Wesleyan). Later, he became an active member of the County School Board. His versatility gave him a place in the field of invention. For years, he operated a gas and oil plant in Buffalo, New York. Such conveniences as drinking fountains and lighting arrangements in the public buildings were gifts of Mr. Fisher. One of his last philanthropic efforts was his use of sixty thousand dollars of his own money when he assumed the office of president of the First National Bank, which was thus enabled to overcome the threat of failure for a while.

The author endeavored to express her appreciation of his life when she became state representative by her first official act, naming the new state highway bridge near his home, The John W. Fisher Bridge.

---

4. Some historians are inclined to believe that she was born in Cocke County. It is said that John Shine operated a ferry near Old Newport, but it was evidently the Peter Fine Ferry and Shine probably operated it after Fine's death.

ISAAC FRANKLIN, SR. Slave trader and stage coach driver, operating from New Orleans to Alexandria, Virginia.

LAWSON D. FRANKLIN is said to have been the first millionaire of Tennessee. He was the son of Isaac Franklin, Sr. The family lived in a large house with a stairway leading up from the outside. Up this stairway, young Franklin led his white stallion to the roof. However, the horse refused to come down. Finally, they tied his feet together and dragged him down the stairway.

When Lawson D. and his brother, Robert, were riding together in a buggy between Leadvale and Jefferson City, their team became frightened and ran away, killing Robert. After this tragedy, Lawson D. indulged in no more pranks. He became a stage coach driver and married Elizabeth Rogers, from the Irish Bottoms. Her people opposed the marriage, but he told them they would see the time he would own all they had. He drove his stage coach to Mississippi and Louisiana, and saved enough money to make good his prediction.

DOCTOR FOWLER, author of an arithmetic, is buried in Parrottsville, 1840.

DR. ARTHUR FOX, a well-known Baptist evangelist, is a native of Cocke County. He returns each spring to his mother's grave and preaches. His son, Rev. Paul Fox, was graduated from the seminary in Louisville with the Ph. M. degree. He is also a graduate from Mars Hill College, and took his B. A. from Carson-Newman College.

His daughter, Miss Sarah Fox, is also a graduate of Mars Hill College, with her B. A. degree from Meredith College, North Carolina. She went in 1937 as a missionary to Jerusalem, Palestine.

WILLIAM GARRETT, one of the earliest lawyers of the County, was born in Orange County, North Carolina, son of Lewis Garrett, on December 10, 1774. As a young man he removed to Cocke County and began to practice law. He married Betsy, the daughter of Thomas Gray.

William Garrett became attorney-general of his circuit, and afterwards served as circuit court clerk for a generation and as county court clerk from 1798 to 1828. He amassed a considerable estate.

In 1813, he, as contractor, descended the rivers to New Orleans with eight boats loaded with supplies for the United States Navy. About this time he was converted and joined the Methodist Church, of which his wife and her father were also members. Later he became a local preacher and was ordained a deacon. The growth of Methodism in this and surrounding counties was due to Garrett and his wife, Betsy Gray Garrett. His activities as a preacher reached Washington County on the east and Mc-Minn County on the west. "Perhaps no local preacher of his day performed more labor or accomplished more for his church than he."[5]

The Garrett home was one of unbounded hospitality. Among those entertained there were five Methodist bishops, Asbury, Whatcoat, McKendree, George, and Roberts. Among others who have lived on this homesite, long known as Beechwood Hall, were the Roadmans, the Susongs, and the Seehorns.

Gray Garrett, the son of William and Betsy Gray Garrett, while practicing law at Dandridge, represented Jefferson County in the General As-

5. *East Tennessee Methodism.*

sembly, and was district-attorney, 1837-1843. He was also a member of the Constitutional Convention of 1834, from Claiborne, Jefferson, and adjoining counties.

Another son, William Garrett, Jr., moved to Alabama, where he was in public life for many years. He wrote interesting accounts of "The First and Early Methodist Churches in Cocke County."[6]

WILLIAM GARRETT, JR., was born May 6, 1809, at Newport, the son of William and Elizabeth Chilley (Gray) Garrett, the former a Methodist minister, a trader and a farmer; grandson of Lewis Garrett, and of Thomas Gray, of Surrey County, Virginia.[7]

Colonel Garrett was forced to leave school in his eleventh year due to financial reverses which came upon his father. Until he was twenty-one years of age, he assisted on the farm, and spent much of his time in keeping the records of his father, who was for thirty-three years clerk of the county court of Cocke County. In 1833, he moved to Alabama and settled in Benton, now Calhoun County; engaged in merchandising first at Alexandria and later at White Plains; fought in the Creek War; was elected assistant clerk of the house of representatives in 1837 under Gideon B. Frierson, clerk; was elected clerk of the same body in 1838, 1839, and 1840; resigned the clerkship in 1840 on being elected secretary of the state of Alabama, and held the latter position without opposition for ten years; was again re-elected secretary of state in 1849 after the seat of government was removed to Montgomery; declined re-election in 1852 to retire to his plantation in Coosa County; was elected to the house of representatives in 1853, and unanimously chosen speaker of that body; was nominated for the senate in 1859 by the Democratic party of Coosa County, and was defeated by forty-seven votes in a vote of two thousand three hundred three; was elected a delegate to the Democratic national convention at Charleston, S. C., as a representative of the Douglas wing of the Democratic party of Alabama; was elected to the state senate from Coosa County in 1863 for a term of four years, defeating Captain Leander Bryan of Wetumpka, and served until the legislature was dissolved by the close of the war; was appointed provisional secretary of state, July, 1865, by Lewis El Parson, provisional civil governor of the state; resigned that position and was elected to the state senate in October, 1865; served as

---

6. McFerrin's *Methodism in Tennessee*, Vol. 2, pages 483-500.
7. Thomas Gray, in 1865, was a representative from Dobbs County, North Carolina, in the colonial assembly of that state in 1768, and was retained as representative for Dobbs and Dublin Counties until the Revolution, was an intense patriot during the War of Independence, a member of the bar of North Carolina for many years, moved to Jefferson County, Tennessee, in 1796, and was appointed by President Washington United States District Attorney for the new state of Tennessee in 1797; great-grandson of William Garret; great-great-grandson of Thomas Garrett; great-great-great-grandson of William Garrett, a Quaker, who came to America from England in 1684, with his brothers, John and Thomas, and settled in Darby Township, near Philadelphia, where he died in 1724. The Garretts are of Saxon origin; in the sixth century quite a contingent of them went over from England and helped subdue the Danes. Again a number of them came to England with William, the Conqueror. Members of the family have been ennobled and knighted by the English royalty in church and state for centuries past, and they were accorded the coat of arms which is still in use by the family in England. Sir William Garrett was lord mayor of London in 1551, and one William Garrett was first chairman of the original Virginia Colony Company. John Garrett was raised from knighthood to the baronetcy of Lanier by James I.

chairman of the senate committee on finance and taxation; retired to private life after being disqualified to hold office under the reconstruction acts; was a member of the state constitutional convention of 1875; was a Democrat and a Methodist; wrote and published during the later years of his life, "Public Men of Alabama," 1872, the original manuscript of which, together with his entire correspondence and papers, was burned soon after his death.

William Garrett died August 24, 1876, on his plantation near Nixburg, Coosa County, and was buried in the yard.[8]

GEO. W. GORREL studied law in the office of Pickle, Turner and Jones. Admitted to the bar in August, 1890, and was associated in practice with Judge Jno. K. Shields. In 1890, he was appointed to the United States Commissionership by Judge Jackson. He was a delegate to every Democratic state convention for years.

JASPER GRAY. Historian, farmer, teacher.

THOMAS GRAY came from North Carolina to Cocke County about the same time as did William Garrett. He was a prominent lawyer, was admitted to the bar in the Southwest Territory and licensed by Governor William Blount to practice in the courts of the Territory, January 7, 1796, probably the date of his and Garrett's arrival in the County.

Soon after his arrival, Thomas Gray was appointed by the President of the United States, George Washington, United States District Attorney for East Tennessee. He was either a Revolutionary War hero or the son of one.

A paragraph from *Niles Register* of Philadelphia, under date of August 12, 1826, proves that he could easily have been old enough to have served in the Revolutionary War, about 30 years old in 1776.

> The bar of Tennessee has produced a rather singular instance of longevity and industry. Col. Gray of Cocke County has been a practicing attorney for sixty-five years. But a few days ago he delivered his valedictory speech in the Court House before Judge Edward Scott, and it is said to have been distinguished by great animation and a perfect recollection of the facts of the case. He is now upwards of eighty years of age.

ESQUIRE JOE GREEN of Hartford was known as the Mountain Prince. His famous "Pig Decision" brought him much publicity. Two men were claiming the same three pigs. They took the matter to the magistrate's court. Esquire Green decided he would take the pigs himself, but after adjournment, he gave each man a pig and kept one for himself. His son McKinley Green is an attorney in Johnson City.

J. L. HARRIS, a pioneer worker and missionary, was the son of James Harris, born in Lincoln County, North Carolina, July 23, 1827. In 1853, he married Miss Sarah Jane Spangler of his native state. He preached his first sermon in the old brick meeting house at the mouth of Big Creek, now Del Rio. In September, 1918, he died at the age of 90. During his ministerial life he baptized 1,000 persons and married 800 couples. He was father of our present David M. Harris.

WILLIAM HOMER HARRIS, "The Smilin' Cowboy." Radio entertainer. Homer Harris was born May 18, 1909 at New Prospect, near Hartford. Son of David M. and Deborah Laws Harris.

---

8. Probation of will in Courthouse, Rockford, Coosa County, Alabama.

Homer Harris as he played to the U. S. Troops in England 1944.

From earliest childhood Homer has been interested in music and kept the idea uppermost in his mind. Through his school years he was constantly 'strumming' his guitar and singing.

After passing through Cocke County Schools and attending Cosby Academy he went to Knoxville to Draughon's Business College and after finishing the course there he got a job in Cincinnati, Ohio where he got his first opportunity to take part in an orchestra entertaining in the hotel dining rooms.

Next he went to Dallas, Texas where he worked in the State Fair as entertainer, alternating with the same kind of work for Montgomery Ward at Muskogee, Oklahoma, after this experience he went to Los Angeles, California where he was a night club entertainer and tourist guide. Dude Ranches and Palm Springs seemed to interest him greatly, and Hollywood beckoned, but he had to give up the call and go to war on May 20, 1942. Bob Hope discovered him in London and he was soon singing in hospitals in England, France, Germany and Belgium. After 38 months of such service the war was over and young Harris returned to his native East Tennessee where he has since been employed by Radio Station WNOX, Knoxville.

"Prima" his horse is the joy of his life. He is looking forward to "settling down" on his "Little Ranch" near Bishop, California. He hopes Leap Year will present him a musically inclined partner that they may "live happily ever afterwards." He says it's like Heaven to live in California.

J. P. HENDRICK, large property holder, contractor and builder, an ardent Republican.

ROBERT HICKEY, SR., attorney and southern gentleman of the old school.

O. L. HICKS, Sheriff, magistrate, Spanish War veteran, Editor.

REV. NATHANIEL HOOD. Early teacher, Presbyterian preacher, Revolutionary War soldier. Married Isabella W. Edgar. Their son, Dr. S. P. Hood, of Knoxville, a Confederate veteran.

DR. S. P. HOOD, son of Rev. Nathaniel and Isabella W. Edgar Hood, was born November 9, 1834, at Newport. He married in 1857, Margaret ·Goodwin, of Grainger County. They had six children.

L. W. HOOPER, M. D., was born February 4, 1839, in North Carolina, the youngest of fourteen children born to John and Margaret Ledbetter Hooper, natives of Georgia and South Carolina, respectively, and of German-English and English origin. His grandfather, Absalom Hooper, was a blacksmith, highly respected among the Indians, who called him "Steke Santone," i. e. "Little Keg," referring to his small stature. He spent seven years in the Revolution, part of the time as cannoneer at Charleston, S. C., and received two wounds, one in the knee which made him a cripple for life. Margaret Hooper's father was also a soldier in the War for Independence. Both grandfathers were the first settlers of western North Carolina, and were only permitted to stay among the Cherokees by their being blacksmiths.

When twenty years of age, L. W. Hooper came to Dandridge, Tennessee. He received a good academic education, and read medicine with Dr. J. C. Cawood, of Dandridge. He then graduated from Bellevue Medical College, of New York, and began his successful career as a physician at

Ben W. Hooper when he was Governor of Tennessee

The home of Dr. Lemuel W. Hooper

Newport. Doctor Hooper earned money to educate himself by his own efforts. On April 21, 1870, he married Sarah E., a daughter of William Norton, a native of North Carolina. Both were members of the Missionary Baptist Church, in which he was a deacon from the time the Newport church was organized. He was a Republican and a Master Mason.

HON. BEN W. HOOPER was born October 13, 1870, in a cabin, now the site of the Methodist parsonage, overlooking Newport. At a tender age, he went to St. John's orphanage, Knoxville, from which his father, Dr. Lemuel Hooper took him at the age of nineteen years. He was admitted to the bar in 1894.

The Republican party of Cocke County nominated him to represent the county in the Lower House of the General Assembly, when he was 21 years of age, the youngest person so honored in the county. He served in the legislature of 1893-95 with Cordell Hull and Joseph W. Byrns. To this position, Hooper was reelected two years later.

In 1898, at the beginning of the Spanish-America War, Hooper was commissioned Captain, and he raised a company of men from Cocke and Johnson Counties, which saw active service in Porto Rico. Captain Hooper served until March 15, 1899, when his Regiment of the 6th United States Volunteer Infantry, was mustered out.

Captain Hooper then resumed the practice of law in Newport and subsequently served approximately four years as Assistant United States Attorney for the Eastern District of Tennessee.

On September 25, 1901, Miss Anna B. Jones, daughter of Ben D. and Townzella Randolph Jones, became the bride of Attorney Hooper.

To this union were born three sons and three daughters, Ben Jones, Randolph, and Lemuel; Anna B., Janella and Newell, all of whom grew to maturity. Automobile accidents claimed the lives of Ben Jones and Randolph within four years of each other.

In August, 1910, Attorney Hooper was nominated by the Republican party as its candidate for Governor of Tennessee. His opponent in this convention was Alfred A. Taylor. The following September, he was also endorsed by the Independent Democratic Convention and was elected November 8, 1910.

His opponent was Governor Malcolm R. Patterson, who withdrew from the race, and Robert L. Taylor, United States Senator, who was nominated by the Democratic organization. The campaign was Senator Bob Taylor's first defeat in state politics. Thus, Governor Hooper won the distinction of defeating both of the famous Taylor brothers in the same year. Two years later, Governor Hooper was re-elected over Benton McMillan, who had twice been Governor of the state and had served twenty years in Congress. The principal issues in both campaigns was the enforcement of the prohibition law and the stamping out of its nullification in the large cities of the State.

Governor Hooper did not allow political or personal costs to prevent his carrying out campaign pledges. McGee's History of Tennessee gives the following summary of his administration:

1. Appropriations for pensions of soldiers of the Civil War and widows of such soldiers, pensions increased.

2. Appropriations for public schools have been increased, and a compulsory school attendance law passed.

3. The Agricultural Department has been strengthened and the Immigration Bureau added.

4. The prison system has been improved by the parole and the indeterminate sentence law, and the purchase of 2,312 acres of land adjoining the farm of the main prison, thus giving more room for out-of-door work for prisoners.

5. A reformatory for bad or unfortunate boys has been established.

6. The Health Department has been made more efficient by the vital statistics law and the pure food and drug act.

7. Labor laws have been enacted limiting and regulating the labor of women and children, creating a Department of Workshop and Factory Inspection and a Workman's Compensation Commission, and making various provisions for the health and safety of laborers.

8. A Banking Department has been established for the examination and regulation of state banks.

9. The office of State Auditor has been created for the purpose of having all public accounts of the state and all expenditures of state funds examined by experts in accounting.

10. A law has been passed requiring banks that receive the state's money on deposit to pay interest on that money as long as they keep it.

Governor Hooper's most outstanding legislation was probably that of prohibition enforcement. The Nuisance Bill gave ten citizens the privilege of going into court and closing any place that sold liquor, as a public nuisance. The Jug Bill made it unlawful to ship liquor inside the State, or for a person to receive more than one gallon at a time, from outside the State.

Early in Governor Hooper's first term, he was offered the United States senatorship to succeed Robert L. Taylor, by his political opposition in the legislature, but spurned the offer to turn the state government over to his opposition and deprive his supporters of the fruits of their victory at the polls.

In 1916, Governor Hooper was nominated by the Republican Party without opposition for the United States senatorship, but was defeated by Kenneth D. McKellar. Eighteen years later, in 1934, he was again nominated without opposition for the same honor and was again defeated by Senator McKellar.

In 1921, Warren G. Harding, President of the United States, appointed Governor Hooper as one of the members of the United States Railroad Labor Board. This Board was composed of three groups, one representing the public, one representing the railroads, and the other representing railroad employees.

Governor Hooper served five years on this Board, during four of which he was Chairman. In October, 1921, he prevented the great strike of all train-service employees, on all the railroads in the United States. Governor Hooper went alone into the convention of the officials of the Railroad Brotherhoods, convened in the Masonic Temple, in Chicago, to call the strike, and by an appeal to reason, induced three of the four brotherhoods to call off the strike, already voted by employees.

Those who are acquainted with his work on this Board have always given him credit for acting judicially and impartially in his decision between the railroads and their employees. He wrote a great number of strong opinions upholding the right of railroad employees to organize and to function in such organizations in their dealings with the railroads. At the same time, he exerted all his influence and power to prevent strikes and the consequent disorganization of business and commerce.

"Intestinal fortitude" has carried ex-Governor Hooper through financial reverses, political defeats, tragedies, and disasters. Among them were the sudden deaths of two of his sons, the burning of his home with its collection of valuable books.

Ex-Governor Hooper, with the vigor and appearance of a much younger man, now lives quietly in his home at the foot of the English Mountain, with his family. His official integrity has never been questioned.

HAZEL HORTON, daughter of Jesse and Jessie M. Gregg Horton decided to become a lawyer when she "grew up." She went to Washington, D. C. to practice where she married Senator Louis Goldstein from Colvert County, Maryland. Senator Goldstein is still a member of the Maryland Senate, 1950.

BOBBIE and BILLY HOWELL, former residents of Newport, now of Knoxville, are ballet dancers in New York City.

CAPT. A. C. HUFF was born in 1819, in Cocke County, the son of Stephen and Elizabeth Carson Huff, his mother being a daughter of Andrew Carson, an early settler. Cap. Huff's great-grandfather, John Corder, and grandfather, John Huff (both of Virginia) were pioneer settlers of Greene, now Cocke, County. Stephen Huff, of German and English descent, was born in a fort, in 1796, which was built for the protection from the Indians. The fort was later converted into a dwelling, where Stephen died at the age of seventy-three. Capt. A. C. Huff married, at the age of twenty, Narcissa, a daughter of Swan P. Burnett. They had twelve children. His wife died in 1880. In 1863, Capt. Huff commanded Company B, second North Carolina Infantry, Federal, and was mustered out in March, 1865. In 1883, he married Mrs. J. R. Shackelford, of Lexington, Georgia, a daughter of William and Elizabeth A. Latimer. He served as a justice for two terms; once by election, and once appointed by Governor Brownlow. He was a member of the Missionary Baptist Church, a strong Union man, and always voted the Republican ticket. (Goodspeed)

ANNIE LAURIE HUFF, poet, Parrottsville. Associate Professor of English, Austin Peay State College. Poem on Philander P. Claxton, president of school, brought favorable comment.

ELIZABETH HUFF, poet.

MAJOR JAMES T. HUFF, Confederate soldier, was born near Del Rio, June 3, 1839. When the Civil War began he was a student in

John W. Fisher

Major James T. Huff and Grandson
Jimmy Huff Clark.

John A. Jones—Poet laureate

Mae Justus

Mossy Creek College. He left school to enlist in the Confederate Army, serving as a private until summer of 1862, when he became Captain of a company organized near his home. He was promoted to the office of Major in December 1863. After the close of the War, he built up one of the largest estates in Cocke County. In August, 1869, he married Jane Stokely. They reared a large family, Frank S., Jesse, Annie, Laura, Mary, Elizabeth, and Josephine. The Huff Home was located at Bridgeport. They secured their water from a spring fifteen or twenty feet in the French Broad River, well-protected from the river water with a wall, a small bridge led to it. A field near the home was cleared in the shape of a broad axe and the shape is still discernible from the highway. Major Huff died September 24, 1919. His great heart and kindly spirit endeared him to every Cocke County citizen.

DR. WILLIAM HUNT, one of the earlier physicians, was born in Washington Co., near Johnson City, in 1810. He graduated at Transylvania University in 1839 and settled and practiced in Cocke County until 1854 when he removed to Cleveland, Tennessee.

COL. WILLIAM JACK, farmer and stock dealer, was born in 1817, in the Irish Bottoms, opposite the mouth of the Chucky River, on the French Broad River, the fourth of seven children of Samuel and Nancy Rogers Jack. The latter was a daughter of Alexander Rogers, a native of Ireland. Samuel Jack was native of Pennsylvania, of English stock. In 1842, he married Elizabeth, (died May 14, 1864) a daughter of Richard DeWitt, of South Carolina, who fought under General Jackson in the Indian Wars. Their children were Samuel W., Harriet E. (married Captain George Stewart), Rowena (married S. W. Cromer), Marcus D., Julia (married John Young), William, and Charles. Elizabeth died May 14, 1864. He was a Democrat, a Master Mason, and in doctrine, Presbyterian. (Goodspeed)

WILLIAM ANDREW JOHNSON, 87 year old ex-slave of President Andrew Johnson died in Knoxville, Tennessee, at the George Maloney Home, May 18, 1843. He visited President Franklin D. Roosevelt at the White House in 1937 and was presented with a silver-headed walking cane. His mother, Dollay and her brother Sam, were bought as slaves by Andrew Johnson near Parrottsville. She was only fourteen then. Her youngest son, William, was only one of her children born in Greeneville. After the Civil War, William and his mother lived in the tailorshop, where they baked and sold pies. William was seventeen when President Johnson died. He cooked for many years at Weaver's Restaurant in Knoxville.

BEN DICKERSON JONES. Early merchant and promoter of industrial development.

BOB JONES. Government distiller.

REV. C. O. JONES. Oklahoma City evangelist.

JOHN AMERICUS JONES, *poet laureate of Cocke County*, is a direct descendant of Eleanor, the sister of Henry VIII, and a member of the Jones family that sheltered John Paul, who later became the head of the United States Navy, and was known as John Paul Jones.

REPS JONES enlisted November 9, 1861, in Company F, 43rd Tennessee, in Roane County, Tennessee. He was promoted to First Lieutenant, May 22, 1863, and was captured at Vicksburg, Mississippi, July 4, 1863, where he was paroled on July 9, 1863.[9] He married Mary McClung Pate.

NATHAN JONES, internal revenue tax collector.

ROBERT McFARLAND JONES, father of Lillie Jones Duncan, was born in Jefferson County (now Hamblen), October 28, 1847, the son of Thomas M. and Lavenia McFarland Jones. Thomas M. was born in Cocke County, in 1816, the son of Daniel Jones of Virginia, who emigrated to Cocke County in the early days of its history and entered land, as a pioneer. He served in the War of 1812. He moved to Jefferson County, in 1845, but moved back to Cocke County. Lavenia McFarland Jones was born in Spring Vale, Jefferson County, the daughter of Robert McFarland and a granddaughter of Robert McFarland, a native of Scotland and who was the first sheriff of Jefferson County. She was a sister to the Robert McFarland who served as supreme judge of Tennessee. She died April 17, 1850.

Robert McFarland Jones began railroading at the age of seventeen as brakeman, and worked at various places as fireman, engineer, conductor. He became the first conductor on the Morristown Road (Western North Carolina Branch of the East Tennessee, Virginia and Georgia Railway (Buncombe). He quit railroading April, 1873.

W. B. JONES settled in Cocke County, and married Mary Jarnagin of Granger County. He was the father of Reps Jones.

WYLIE JONES. Attorney. Moved to Oklahoma. Married Miss Maud Jones, a music teacher. Their daughter, Minnie Aletha, is an English teacher in Hollywood.

ALLEN D. JUSTUS, formerly of Newport, died in New York City, at the age of 58, year (1946). Before leaving Newport fifteen years ago, he was principal of the city school, and as a prominent member of the American Legion took an active part in the erection of the Newport's Memorial Building. At the time of his death he was connected with the Internal Revenue Department of New York City. Misses May and Emma Justus are his sisters, and Hal his brother.

EMMA JUSTUS. Poet, long with Red Cross in Knoxville.

Home Again

Take me back—let me go
Over upland and low'
Through a wood and meadow night;
In a brook let me see
Blue sky around me
And clouds float lazily by.

---

9. U. D. C. Files.

Take me back—let me feel
Loving arms while I kneel
At evening beside my bed;
Then a "Tuck-me-in-tight"
Once again, a "Good-night,"
And Heaven in whispers o'erhead.

Take me back fleeting day,
Someone's waiting for me—
At the gate—I see her sweet smile;
And listening I hear
Her voice—like a prayer—
As we walk in the evening awhile.

Home again—has a part
Evermore in my heart,
Where memories in solitude wait;
A halo of love
Seems to fall from above
To greet me there by the gate.

—EMMA LAURA JUSTUS

MAY JUSTUS, teacher and author of juvenile literature, was born near Del Rio, but later moved with her parents to a small mountain farm near Bridgeport and Bat Harbor. Her father was a teacher who died soon after the removal; her mother, Margaret Brooks Justus, a descendant of Samuel Doak, who assumed the entire burden of rearing the children. May Justus finished grammar school and studied at home. At sixteen years of age she took the teacher's examination and was certified to teach school in Cocke County. When she had saved enough money she went to high school in North Carolina, where she received her diploma in five months, and has been teaching since, in Summerfield School near Monteagle. The many books she has written are widely read.

In the meantime, she studied in Haywood Institute in Clyde, North Carolina, Northwestern University, and the University of Tennessee. Early in life, she wrote religious poetry. Later she contributed to the *Youth's Companion*. After teaching in the Kentucky mountains, she began writing stories of mountain life for children, which Doubleday Doran & Company published. *Peter Pocket*, her first book, was written in 1927. Other books are *Betty Lou of Big Lay Mountain, The Other Side of the Mountain*, and *Honey Jane*, published in 1935, the Junior Literary Guild's book for December of that year. *Gabby Gaffer* and *Gabby Gaffer's New Shoes* are fairy tales out of print now. A book of child's verse is now ready for the publishers. She has also been working on school readers for the State of California, in which State her *Gabby Gaffer's New Shoes* won the Julia Ellsworth prize.[10]

O. M. KELLEY, farmer, was born in 1846, in Greene County, the fifth of seven children of Wylie and Eliza (Kelley) Kelley, natives of

---

10. Data from Elizabeth Huff.

Kentucky and Greene County, respectively, the former serving as justice of that location for many years in both Greene and Cocke Counties, and both of English Irish stock. In 1866, O. M. married E. C. Susong, a daughter of John Susong, a native of Greene County. Their children were Effie J., Williard E., Carrie R., Lee H., Jennie E., George S., Essie V., and an infant. He was a Democrat, and he and his wife were Presbyterians, in which church he was a ruling elder for many years. He moved to Cocke County in 1875.

JAMES M. KYKER raised the largest family and bought a hundred dollar bond for each of "my 21 children" during the First World War. He requested that his grave be concreted and the top then concreted over leaving all space inside a vacuum, for he could not bear the idea of dirt being thrown in his face, for he said he had had enough flung at him in this world. His request was carried out.

RICHARD KNIGHT established a church in the Grassy Fork area.

M. A. LANGHORNE, Tacoma, Washington.

W. W. LANGHORNE, attorney at law, was born January 23, 1841, in Smithfield, Virginia, the eldest of nine children of Maurice and Louisa Drew Langhorne, natives of Portsmouth and Smithfield, Virginia, respectively. Maurice was a minister in the Protestant Methodist Church. W. W. received a good academic and college education, and studied law under Robert Whitfield, at Smithfield, and under Taswell Taylor, of Norfolk, and was admitted to the bar in 1866, at Lynchburg. He enlisted April 19, 1861, in Company F., Sixth Virginia Infantry, and served until May, 1864, when he was disabled. After recovering, he served in different capacities until his capture at the fall of Richmond, when he was carried to Point Lookout, where he was retained until June 22, 1865. After his release, he came to Newport and taught the first school ever held there. He married October 8, 1868, Julia R. Smith, a daughter of A. E. Smith, native of Cocke County. Their children were Morris A., Willie D., Julia E., and Lillian R. (Goodspeed)

A LaRUE is supposed to have buried $40,000 on the A. C. Hampton farm in the Dutch Bottoms, near a walnut stump, according to an old slave's story. The Ogdens, descendants of the LaRues, tried to find the treasure.

J. C. LaRUE, merchant and farmer, was born October 3, 1824, in Knox County, and came to Cocke County, when twelve years old. He was the third of seven children of Francis and Nancy A. Young LaRue, natives of Knox County. The father was a Whig and a soldier in the War of 1812. The LaRues were of French and the Youngs of English origin. Up to his 28th year, J. C. was the main support of his father. In 1861, he married Margaret J. Parrott, a daughter of Samuel Parrott, a son of George Parrott, for whom the village was named. Their children were Samuel B., Selma A., Frank D., Fannie K., James H., Charles W., Horace L., Hugh F., and an infant. The third and fourth, and the seventh and eighth were twins. His wife was a Methodist, and he was a Master Mason and a Republican. He was constable four years, and county clerk for the same length of time. (Goodspeed)

WASHINGTON, Sept. 13—EDWARD B. LAWSON, a native of Newport, Tenn., but a legal resident of this city for many years, is serving now as the United States Minister to Iceland, with headquarters in Reyjavik.

Mr. Lawson was born Sept. 25, 1895, and took his B. S. degree in the Foreign Service School of Georgetown University here in 1942. He got his master's the following year.

He served with the U. S. Expeditionary Force in 1918-19, and on his return to civilian life after World War I, joined the Commerce Department's Bureau of Foreign and Domestic Commerce, serving until 1927.

Between 1927 and 1930, Mr. Lawson was assistant trade commissioner at Johannesburg, South Africa, and for the following five years served as trade commissioner there. He was our trade commissioner in London from 1935 through 1937. In August of 1937, he was appointed commercial attache to our embassy at Praha. While there he also served as our delegate to the 25th session of the International Institute of Statistics meeting at Praha in 1938.

On July 1, 1939, Mr. Lawson became a foreign service officer, Class 5, and was detailed temporarily to the Department of State, though assigned to the Commerce Department.

On Jan. 11, 1940, he was named commercial attache at Managua, Nicaragua. Three years later he had advanced to Class 4 in the Foreign Service. He was transferred to Ankara early in 1944, and in the following spring was advanced to Class 2 in the Foreign Service. In September of 1945, Mr. Lawson was appointed counsellor of our embassy at Ankara, in charge of economic affairs.

By the spring of 1947, he had advanced to Class 1 in the Foreign Service and was named the following year as counsellor of the embassy for economic affairs at Mexico City.

It was from that post that he was promoted to Minister to Iceland.

—Copied from a Knoxville newspaper.

GUNDA LEWIS. Head of Lewis Scouts.

MERIWETHER LEWIS, the father of Dr. Meriwether Lewis of Newport, was a native of Buckingham County, Virginia, born September 11, 1802, and died November 25, 1882, at Newport.

Professor Lewis, a graduate of Hampden-Sydney College, did post-graduate work at Union Theological Seminary. He was admitted to the bar in 1822 and practiced his profession in Buckingham County and Prince Edward for a number of years, before he began teaching. He spent practically all of the last fifty years of his life teaching and preparing young men for college. He was president of Mars Hill College from 1866 to 1873.

He married December 15, 1827, Amanda M. Cosby, the daughter of Dabney and Frances Tapp Cosby, of Buckingham County, Virginia. Their children, who grew to maturity were James Kent, killed at Gettysburg; Dabney, who went through the War and died in 1873; Dr. Meriwether Lewis, the youngest, of Newport; Fanny, who taught with her father, Marie and Ella Vernon, also teachers of art and music. Dabney Cosby, the father of Amanda Cosby, was the son of Zachary Cosby, a Minute Man of the Revolution, who married Susan Dabney, the daughter of Captain James Dabney, in whose regiment he afterwards served in the Revolutionary War.

Professor Meriwether Lewis was the son of Edward (?) and Mary Freeland Lewis, the daughter of William Mace Freeland and Elizabeth Pendleton Freeland of "The Meadow" on the James. The parents died when the children were young and their father's sister, Anne, wife of Col. Robert Biscoe of "Peaceful Retreat," Upper Powhatan County, reared them. The children were Meriwether, Robert Barbour, William Mace, Maria Ann, Jane I., Eliza G., and Pamela. Robert became a teacher and William Mace, a lawyer. They were both in the Mexican War.

The remains of Meriwether Lewis, Sr., were laid to rest in the Presbyterian Churchyard, at Newport, November 27, 1882: He was the middle of five generations of Meriwethers, leaving a son and a grandson bearing the same family name. He was married sixty-one years and a member of the Presbyterian Church for fifty-five years.

(Data by M. Liston Lewis, his grandson, Carnegie Library, Nashville.)

1. The following shows the relationship between the Cocke County Meriwether Lewises and Meriwether Lewis, explorer:

Jane Meriwether, daughter of Nicholas (2) Meriwether and wife, Elizabeth Crawford, married Col. Robert Lewis of Belvoir, grandfather of Meriwether Lewis, the explorer.

Jane Meriwether, daughter of David, and granddaughter of Nicholas (1) Meriwether, married David Cosby. She was the first cousin of the wife of Col. Robert Lewis of Belvoir.

Lucy Meriwether, daughter of Thomas and Elizabeth Thornton Meriwether, was the mother of Meriwether Lewis, the explorer. Lucy was the niece of the above Jane, wife of Col. Robert of Belvoir.

DR. MERIWETHER LEWIS of Newport was born at Halifax Courthouse, Virginia, July 26, 1848, and died December 15, 1890, the son of Professor Meriwether Lewis and Amanda Cosby Lewis, of Buckingham Courthouse, Virginia, and related to the explorer of that name. He was a cadet at the Hillsboro Military Academy, Hillsboro, N. C., in 1865, and did duty in the last months of the War, but was never under fire. His father was a lawyer and later a college professor. He was also President of Mars Hill College, North Carolina, just after the Civil War.

In 1867, young Meriwether Lewis began the study of medicine under Dr. Oscar M. Lewis (not a relative) and entered Louisville Medical College in 1868, graduating there in 1872. In the same year he began the practice of medicine at Lenoir City, Tennessee, in partnership with Dr. B. B. Lenoir.

In 1874, the parents and sisters of Dr. Lewis came to Newport, where they taught a select school, also, music and art. He finally settled in Newport, where his practice extended over a period of nearly eleven years, 1879 to 1890. Doctors W. G. Snoddy, R. C. Smith, L. W. Hooper, and Archibald Rhea were his contemporaries, but he was most intimately associated with Doctor Snoddy. He never had a day's vacation during this time. The year of his passing he was offered the Chair of Anatomy at the Louisville Medical College.

Dr. Lewis was a Master Mason and was always athirst for knowledge, having obtained his Master's degree after he began the practice of medicine. He was well versed in Latin, read French well, and contributed various articles to medical journals, such as THE NASHVILLE JOURNAL OF MEDICINE AND SURGERY.

Doctor Lewis was married to Miss Rebecca Jennie Gentry, January 2, 1876, the daughter of John Wesley and Nancy Alexander Gentry, of Blount County, at Lenoir City, Tennessee. (Contributed by son, Meriwether Liston Lewis, Carnegie Library, Nashville.)

A McCOY was the first, or one of the first blacksmiths in the County. His specialty was magic rings, which he made for Joe Frady, a magician

Congressional Medal of Honor
Winner, Sgt. Charles McGaha and his grandmother McGaha.

of considerable note. Frady used these rings, made in the Del Rio section, at his appearances in the Charleston Exposition in 1902, and they were carried on his European trips many times. He used five rings in his tricks.

MASTER SERGEANT CHARLES L. McGAHA of Cosby, thirty two years of age is Cocke County's Congressional Medal Winner, the highest honor the Country can bestow upon its soldiers.

Sergeant McGaha was born and reared in the Cosby section of Cocke County in his present home. The McGaha family have been Cosby residents for more than four generations. English, Irish and Scotch blood courses their veins.

Sergeant McGaha received his medal of honor for courageous and distinguished action on Luzon when his Superior officers became casualties of the Japs. He wears two service stripes, he is ready for his third one, seven gold over-seas bars representing forty-two months continuous service over-seas; American defense ribbon; one star; Asiatic-Pacific Campaign Ribbon with four battle stars; American Theatre Ribbon; Good Conduct Medal; Victory Medal; Purple Heart with one cluster and is waiting on orders for two more; Bronze Star for gallantry in action; Infantry Badge and Congressional Medal of Honor.

His mother, Mrs. Laura McGaha and his grandmother, Mrs. Jane McGaha and other members of his family accompanied him to Washington, D. C. March 25, 1946 where President Truman presented the Medal on March 27.

Newport Post 41 sponsored an appropriate reception and celebration for the County's most distinguished Soldier Son on March 30, 1946. Governor Jim McCord and other officials of Tennessee and the United States were present. Donald McSween, Adjutant of Post 41 was Master of Ceremonies. Three other Congressional Medal winners were present for the celebration. They were Sgt. Raymond H. Cooley, Paul B. Huff and Charles H. Coolidge.

Colonel Henry X. La Raia, recruiting officer for East Tennessee and Colonel Joy T. Wrean, representing General of 4th service command were also present. From Colonel La Raia we learned that in World War two, Cocke County ranks highest in Tennessee Counties, in ratio of Volunteers. This is of course in proportion to its size and population.

ANDREW J. McMAHAN, noted for his brilliant mind, the youngest person to serve as superintendent of county schools, being 21 years of age at the time.

Supt. T. & N. C. Railway at the time of his accidental death while riding over the route.

Left widow, Glennie Roberts McMahan, three daughters and one son, Marjorie, Florence, Glennie Kate and Stanley McMahan.

MANSFIELD McMAHAN. World traveler and journalist. Stories in *Plain Talk.*

MARJORIE McMAHAN. Teacher and writer.

Y. J. McMAHAN. Banker and justice of the peace for many years.

ALEXANDER McNABB, son of George McNabb, brought the first lamp to Cocke County, in 1851. It is of glass, six inches high, to the end of the two wickholders, and made of brass with a little chain attached which holds a kind of thimble with which to extinguish the light. The fluid burned was called gas and resembled kerosene. The lamp, resembling an old-fashioned dinner bell, was such a curiosity that people took their children to see the bright light. Bought in Cleveland, Tennessee, it is the link between the time of the tallow candle and the oil lamp, and is now in the possession of Mrs. Jetta Boyer Lee, granddaughter of Alexander McNabb.

MALCOLM McNABB. Signer of the Constitution.

DONALD McSWEEN, son of the late W. D. McSween, attorney, and wife Rowena Jones McSween, graduate of the University of Tennessee, where he was editor of the *Orange and White* and appeared in *Who's Who Among Students in American Universities and Colleges*. He also attended Cumberland University at Lebanon. For some time he had a position in the Title Section of the Land Acquisition Department of the TVA. He is the fourth generation of the McSween family to practice law in Newport. His hobby is his stamp collection, illustrating every form of service to, from, and within the United States, and first day covers. The total number in his collection probably exceeds three thousand or twenty-two volumes mounted.

KENNETH McSWEEN is a graduate of Westminister Choir College at Princeton, New York, with the degree of Bachelor of Music, of class of 1939. He is accomplished in piano, organ, voice, and conducting.

MABEL McSWEEN. Poet and teacher. Poems honored Otto Boyer, Kiffin Rockwell, Burnett Smith, and Robert Africa, who gave their lives in World War 1.

JUDGE W. D. McSWEEN was born in 1876 and died June 21, 1945. He was one of the leading attorneys for more than forty years and a member of the law firm of McSween and Myers. Prior to his appointment as Judge of the Second Judicial Circuit of this State, he was senior member of the law firm of McSween and Shepherd. He was a graduate of Washington & Lee University, from which he took his law degree in 1898.

He was past-president of local Chamber of Commerce and also of the Kiwanis Club, former president of Merchants & Planters Bank, and a deacon in the Presbyterian Church. He was a 32nd degree Mason and a Shriner. In 1925, he was appointed to the Court of Appeals by Gov. Peay—but resigned. He was married to Miss Rowena Jones, who died in 1927. They had one son, Donald, who was assistant Area Director with the War Manpower Commission, at his father's death.

W. J. McSWEEN, attorney at Newport, was born May 3, 1848, in Cocke County, the youngest of five children of William and Catherine Allen McSween, natives of North Carolina and Cocke County respectively. William McSween came to Cocke County in 1820, when ten years old. He was clerk of the county court, circuit court clerk of Cocke County for twenty years, clerk and master of chancery court for about ten years, and represented Cocke County in the Legislature of 1840 and 41. W. J.'s grandfather was Murdock McSween, a native of North Carolina. and Murdock's father was a native of Scotland, who after the battle of Colloden, came to America under the protection of Flora McDonald.

W. J. McSween attended Emory and Henry College, during 1866-68. then graduated in 1871 from the law department at Cumberland University, beginning to practice law immediately in Newport. He was married in November, 1876, to Miss Florence Kidwell, a niece of Judge William McFarland and a daughter of William Kidwell, of North Carolina, who came with his father to Cocke County in 1820. Their three children were William K., Mabel, and Lillian. Mr. and Mrs. McSween were members of the Presbyterian Church. He was a Master Mason and a stanch Democrat, representing Cocke County in the Legislatures of 1885 and 86, being elected in a Republican county. (Goodspeed)

According to ex-Governor Hooper, he was a vigorous, fiery man, powerful before a jury and an accomplished trial lawyer. He was also a man of generous impulses. He enjoyed birddogs, fox hounds, and shotguns. Although he differed with the ex-Governor in politics, he supported him in his race for governor, an evidence of his broadness of mind and generosity of spirit.

JOSEPH MANNING was born in Cocke County near the French Broad River, September 22, 1806, and in his nineteenth year was married to Lucinda Huff by Joseph White. The second Saturday in October, 1828, he and his wife joined the Clay Creek Church. A year later he was ordained deacon. In June, 1831, he was granted liberty to exhort in the Long Creek and Clay Creek churches. In May, 1833, Manning and Moore were ordained to the ministry. Elders Manning and Moore were joint and alternating pastors of this new church for several years, and Manning singly for a long term of service. The longest of any record in the county.

On August 12, 1833, Elders Manning, Moore, and Henry Hunt organized the Big Creek Church at the mouth of Big Creek on the French Broad River and May 19, 1938, Manning and Moore, aided by Elder Garrett Dewees, organized the Pleasant Grover Church, six miles from Newport on the Pigeon River, with Elder Manning as its first pastor. He was also one of the leaders of the East Tennessee Association. He was pastor at Concord, Greene County, 23 years; Dandridge, Jefferson County, 14 years; Sevierville, Sevier County, 6 years; French Broad, in Cocke County, 21 years; Pleasant Grove, Cocke County, 40 years; Big Creek, Del Rio, nominally, till his death, September 10, 1883, a period of 50 years. He and his yoke-fellow, Ephraim Moore, bore the brunt of battle over a large part of East Tennessee in the Antinomian and anti-mission controversy of the 30's and 40's. He received little pecuniary compensation during this crisis. In his preaching, Elder Manning emphasized the doctrines of grace, the atonement, the priesthood of Christ, and justification by faith, and was strictly a New Testament preacher, also a gifted singer. (Burnett)

REV. L. H. MASSEY. Brookport, N. J.

WILEY P. MASSEY. Schoolman in Texas. Close relative of Mrs. Cora Massey Mims.

DR. JAMES M. MASTERS and wife and sons came to Newport in the "Gay Nineties." Mrs. Masters was a Conner. They purchased the Grand View Hotel and converted it into a T.B. Sanatorium which Dr. Masters successfully conducted until his death. He kept his patients here from late spring to early autumn when he moved them to Florida.

Dr. and Mrs. Masters were greatly beloved by all who knew them. Their sons were: Sherman, Wilfred, Charles, James, Herbert and Quincy. Only one of them, Herbert, still resides in Newport in 1950, only three are living; Sherman in Oklahoma, Wilfred in Florida.

Grandview Hotel of the early days later Mr. Master's Sanitarium. Shortly before it was destroyed by fire became the Cherokee Hotel.

Hotel Rhea-Mims

ANDREW MILLER, according to his daughter, Mrs. Lou Miller Robinson, had the first threshing machine in the county. It was built by Chrisley Witt at Witt's foundry. He threshed his own crop of wheat and then moved the machine to the Major William Robinson farm. (Chrisley Witt's father was the early Primitive Baptist preacher whose name often appears in the minutes of that church.)

CORA MASSEY MIMS (Mrs. W. O.). Historian.

D. A. MIMS. Merchant, Banker, Southern Gentleman.

W. O. MIMS, attorney, took his A. B. at Emory and Henry and his B. L. at Cumberland University.

GRACE MOORE, the daughter of Colonel Richard M. and Tess (Jane) Stokely Moore, was born in the home of her maternal grandparents, William and Emma Huff Stokely, on December 5, 1901. This home stood on the West bank of Big Creek between Del Rio and Nough, sometimes known as Slabtown. Other brothers and sisters that followed were: Herbert, who died when he was about ten years old: Martin, in Texas; the twins, Emily and Estel, who died when he was six or eight; Jim, Richard, Jr., (who died in 1944), another girl who died at two or three years of age.

When Grace was very small, her parents moved to Jellico, Tennessee, where she grew to young womanhood and began singing in the choir of the Baptist Church. For a time she seriously considered becoming a missionary to foreign fields. Although stage careers were frowned upon, Grace determined to become a great singer like Mary Garden.

While Grace was in school at Ward-Belmont, Nashville, Mary Garden gave a concert in the City. The words that Miss Garden gave her were Grace's incentive to attend the Wilson-Green School of Music in the Nation's Capital. At the end of her first concert, she was chosen to sing in public concert with Giovanni Martinelli, celebrated tenor of the Metropolitan Grand Opera Company. Press notices were so flattering that she took "French leave" of the School and went to New York, accompanied by a fellow student, Blanche Le Garde.

Miss Moore's first job seems to have been at the Black Cat Cafe. Next, she went with a touring company through the West. The company was left stranded by their manager in the Dakotas, from which it was rescued by the Actors Equity Association. Her first appearance on Broadway was a featured singing role in "Hitchy Koo," produced by Charles Dillingham, and starred by Raymond Hitchcock and Julia Sanderson. Jerome Kern wrote the music and she finally sang "Moon of Love" taking the Star's role, when that lady became ill.

At this time she was meeting many noted people, among them Conde Nast, Ethel Barrymore, Marie Tempest, Ina Claire, Alma Gluck, Geraldine Farrar, Enrico Caruso, and Antonio Scotti.

At one time, Miss Moore lost her voice from overstrain with the chance of recovering it only if she maintained a six months' complete silence. After this terrible experience, she spent a year in Paris, where she shared an apartment with Neysa McMein, the sculptor. Here she met Irving Berlin, to whom she had been recommended by Robert Benchley. He offered her the leading role in "The Music Box Revue of 1924." At the end of her first season, she was given an audition by the Metropolitan, but was told that her voice was not yet ready. She continued in the "Music Box Revue" in 1925 and 26. Otto Kahn then told

Grace Moore at her Debut—February 7, 1928—With her parents—Colonel
Richard M. Moore and wife "Tessie" Jane Stokely Moore
in New York—Met. Theatre.

her that she would never become an opera singer. She wagered one hundred dollars with him that in two years time she would make her debut at the Metropolitan.

Grace returned to Paris where everything seemed so bleak that she soon lost confidence in herself. She wrote Mary Garden for advice, and Miss Garden cabled and commanded that she live in her own apartment in Monte Carlo, prescribing a course of study and instructing her own accompanist to help her.

After eighteen months of intensive study in Paris, she was granted another interview by Otto Kahn before Gatti Casazza, the managing director of the Metropolitan. She received her first contract with the Metropolitan Grand Opera Company, with the comparatively small salary of fifty dollars per week. On February 7, 1928, when she made her debut in "La Boheme," a special Grace Moore train went from Tennessee carrying her friends and relatives, to see and hear her sing.

For three successive seasons, she continued with the Metropolitan, singing in "Faust," "Romeo et Juliette," "Manon," "Carmen," "Pagliacci," and "Tales of Hoffman." On her European tour she sang "Romeo et Juliette" in Liege; "Manon," in Bordeaux; and "Louise," "Manon" and "La Boheme," in Paris at the Opera Comique. Her favorite opera was "Louise."

When she returned from Europe, the Metro-Goldwyn-Mayer Company signed her to play in "New Moon" on condition that she lose fifteen pounds. For some reason, the picture did not click. Her second picture, "Madame du Barry" was better. She made a tremendous success in "One Night of Love." Her award of the gold metal of the Society of Arts and Sciences was given her for this performance. Other pictures were "Louise" and "Love Me Forever." After Miss Moore's picture, "I'll Take Romance," she rejoined the Chicago Metropolitan Opera Company, where she made her debut in the title role of Massenet's opera, "Manon."

At a command performance for their majesties, the King and Queen of England, "La Boheme" in London's Covent Garden, she took thirteen curtain calls. She was also decorated with the Chevalier Legion of Honor in France, in 1939.

Miss Moore married Valentin Parera, artist, actor, and writer of Madrid, Spain, July 15, 1931 at Cannes, France, a marriage singularly successful. Their American home was Fairway Acres, Sandy Hook, Connecticut; and their French home was between Cannes and Grasse.

Miss Moore enjoyed radio, screen, and opera success, shared by her husband. In 1944, Doubleday, Doran & Company published her own story of her life, You're Only Human Once. Her hobbies were white furs, perfume, her people, her husband, and the Tennessee mountains. Her death at the peak of her career brought sorrow to the whole world.

On January 25, 1947, in Copenhagen, Denmark, at the K. B. Hallen Concert Hall, Grace Moore gave her last concert to a packed house of more than four thousand souls. She closed her concert with "Chiri-Beri-Bin" the song she helped to make famous in the beginning of her musical career.

At the hotel d'Angleterre she told a newspaper man that she had told him all her past and that only the future was left for her and to another reporter of a Copenhagen newspaper, Berlingske Tidende, she said, "It is wonderful to live and sing. It is a great thing to feel that one is able to

Grace Moore (a favorite pose)

help other people with one's voice. I want to play in a new opera where the heroine does not die in the last scene or go mad. That is why I love Charpentier's "Louise." The girl is alive when the curtain falls and it is wonderful to be alive isn't it?"

Almost no sooner made than granted, was this earnest wish of Tennessee's beloved Grace Moore. Her transition to the choir invisible was so quickly made that she is probably playing the role she wanted to play in a new opera where the heroine would never die. She chose well because her dynamic spirit, charged and supercharged with personal magnetism was not created to die. She lived the abundant life, scaled the heights because she was so vibrant with life eternal. Many there be who claim that the only way to die is by accident and instantly so that death is robbed of its horror. Although Grace Moore's dramatic life has had a tragic ending she has been spared the greatest of all tragedies, that of old age and loneliness and the knowledge of being forgotten. She made her exit at the very zenith of her career when all the world still loved and admired her.

Her love for her husband and mother was ever uppermost in her life and the last thoughtful act she performed was to send to each a cable before she boarded the airplane in which she perished.

Grace Moore had just finished her memoirs and in referring to the fact said, "Many people write their memoirs when they are old and forgotten. But I wanted to write mine while I am still on top and feel that I can give people something through my singing and not only just by memories . . ."

At the time of her death Grace Moore was still under contract to the Metropolitan Opera, but had been singing abroad so that she could be near her husband, Valentin Parera, a Spanish actor, who was ill at their home in Mougins, France. She had left her Connecticut home with Congresswoman Clara Booth Luce.

Copenhagen loved Grace Moore and proved it when King Christian conferred upon her the "Ingenio del arti" medal, Denmark's highest artistic decoration. She had also been made a Chevalier of France's Legion of Honor and had sung a command performance before British Royalty in Covent Garden.

The whole world loved Grace Moore and received her with open arms from the time of her debut on February 7, 1928 at the Metropolitan Opera House in New York City to the day of her death in Copenhagan, Denmark on January the 26, 1947.

In opera she was known for her four roles in Mimi, Tosca, Manon and Louise.

She will be remembered in the pictures of, "I'll Take Romance," "When You're In Love," "One Night of Love" and in "Love Me Forever."

She had a voice that made people listen and a personality that made people love her because her heart was overflowing with love of her home, her people, her native land, particularly, the Tennessee mountain country. She once said that she belonged to the masses and she proved it by singing to the masses wherever she found them assembled and they wanted her to sing. She sang in bull rings, on busses, in parks, at horse

Grace Moore in "Love Me Forever"

shows, at weddings or wherever folks wanted to hear her sing. She made good will tours and entertained the fighting men at her own expense during the world war. Grace Moore was the Southland's idea of a prima donna. She was of the south, southy, and that was something the world liked about her.

Only a few times in the history of the world have so many people in the various "walks of life" been shocked and grieved as on Sunday afternoon, January 26, 1947, when the news of her death flashed around the world over radio. The time was 2:30 in Copenhagen, Denmark, and 9:30 A.M. Eastern Standard time. The Royal Dutch Airliner which she had just boarded crashed and exploded on the snow-covered Kastrup Airport as it took off for Stockholm. All the 22 passengers aboard were instantly killed. With Grace were two French passengers, her accompanist, Jean Loup Peltier and M. Malbac.

Prince Gustav Adolf, forty years of age and second in line for succession to Swedish throne, was among the passengers. The fifty-four-year-old pilot of the ill-fated plane was W. J. Geysendorffer, the oldest pilot and one of the best of the Royal Dutch Airlines.

Funeral services for Grace Moore were held in Copenhagen, Denmark; Cannes, France where the people gave thousands of dollars to Cannes charities in memory of the "FRENCH GIRL FROM TENNESSEE." In Paris, France impressive and very beautiful services were held and in the Riverside Church in New York City and at last, in Chattanooga, Tennessee in the First Baptist Church, conducted by the pastor, Dr. John A. Huff.

Valentin Parera, the devoted husband of Miss Moore brought her body home to rest in the shadow of the mountains she so dearly loved. When he arrived with many of their New York friends he found from six to ten thousand people waiting in Chattanooga to pay homage to the departed prima donna, and to extend to him and to her beloved mother and brothers and sisters, heartfelt sympathy.

The friends from New York were: Dorothy Kirsten of the Metropolitan Opera, Emily Coleman, music editor of *Newsweek* magazine, Frederick Schang, head of music department of the Metropolitan Opera Company, Jean Dalrymple, Miss Moore's former public relations counsel, Helen Ruth Matthews, former secretary, and Van Truex, a New York artist. Congressman Estes Kefauver came from Washington, D. C.

Miss Moore's immediate family in waiting were: her mother, Mrs. R. L. Moore. Her sister, Mrs. Thomas L. Mahan of Chattanooga. Brothers, Richard L. and James Moore of Chattanooga and Martin Moore of Highland Park, Illinois.

The impressive service conducted by Dr. Huff on Sunday afternoon February 23, 1947 will never be forgotten by anyone present. Dorothy Kirsten sang, "Ave Maria" and members of the American Legion stood as an Honor Guard on each side of the flower laden casket.

Grace Moore was buried in Forest Hills cemetery under the brooding summit of Lookout Mountain while the winter winds moaned a farewell requiem through the mournful pines. She was placed beside the grave of her father, Colonel Richard L. Moore who also had a sudden transition on November 27, 1944.

Thousands of friends witnessed the burial and as they silently stole away from the sacred resting place of the dead they did so with misty eyes and with a prayer in their hearts hoping that the warm southern sun would always shine kindly there and that the gentle southern zephyrs would blow softly there in summer and in autumn time and that the green sod covering her grave would never die but keep ever fresh and green like all who knew and loved her will keep in our hearts her memory. And as long as musical records last her golden voice will often reverberate through the homes of her loved ones in her beloved Tennessee mountains.

LYLE S. MOORE, an official of Stokely Brothers Canning Company and Colonel on former Governor Gordon Browning's staff.

W. F. MORRIS, farmer and owner of timber and mineral land, was born October 15, 1825, in Cocke County, the eldest of five children of William and Mildred Driskell Morris. His father came from South Carolina; his mother, Cocke County. James and Martha Morris, his paternal grandparents, were natives of South Carolina, and of Welsh origin. The Driskells were of Irish ancestry and were originally O'Driskill.

In 1866, he married Elizabeth Josephine Montgomery, of Greenville, South Carolina, a daughter of Chevis C. Montgomery, who died in 1882. Their children were Bertie, Maggie A., Lillie Pauline, and Katie Maudine. He and his wife were members of the Missionary Baptist Church. He was a Democrat and a Master Mason. In 1853-54, he represented Cocke County in the Legislature; in 1860, he was census taker for the County. (Goodspeed)

JONATHAN MULKEY was born October 18, 1752 and died September 5, 1826, after having been a minister for fifty years. He was a Virginian of Welsh descent. Mulkey was a leader in the Holston Association for many years and for seven years its Moderator.

SARAH MARY MARGERY ROSA MURPHY was born in 1834 in Stratford-on-Avon, in the Shakespeare house, the granddaughter of the Earl of Sherrott, Colchester, England, and second cousin to Queen Victoria. She was educated in England and Ireland and acquired her musical training in a Berlin Conservatory. She came to America with her mother in girlhood, arriving in Charleston, South Carolina, after a two-months voyage in a sailing vessel. Here in 1857, she married Charles O'Brien, a native of Cork, Ireland.

They lived in a home of luxury until the war brought financial ruin. They are said to have left Charleston with nothing but their children and a trunk of Confederate money, and lived at Laurens, South Carolina, for some time. They came to Del Rio in a wagon about 1872, where the youngest child was born. They lived near the Cave church, where she lost her husband. Later she lived on the Morell farm. She taught school in Newport at the Academy and also had private music pupils. She had several daughters: Mary, later Mrs. George Rankin; Annie, Mrs. J. B. Jones; Margaret, Mrs. C. B. McNabb; and Lizzie, Mrs. James Robeson. Her sons were John, Richard, and Albert O'Brien (still living in 1940). She died at the age of eighty-three years, at the home of her daughter, Mrs. Jones, in St. Augustine, Florida. (Data from a former student of hers, Mrs. W. O. Mims, *Newport Times*, October 2, 1940).

JOHN A. MURRELL, leader of a band of counterfeiters, who plied their trade in the fifties, on the top of Middle Fork Knob, with activities reaching from Virginia to Missouri, and from New York and Philadelphia to New Orleans. The stamp they used was called "Old Sook," and the money they made was freely circulated in Georgia. It is claimed that they dug their silver from nearby mines, one of which was thought to have been the Buck Track Silver Mine, so named because of a deer track found in the rock near the entrance. They were captured in 1854, John Huff and Royal Stokely II, engaged in the capture. After the molds used were taken from the river at Edwina, they were placed in the vault of the Merchants and Planters Bank. It is said that Murrell once killed a man on horseback because he thought he had money. He found only twenty-five cents and remarked that anyone who carried no more than that ought to be killed.

LORD NAPIER of London, England, and his wife with their children, Anna, Beatrice, Eliza, Francis, and Robert, lived for a time in Cocke County, on Fork Farm, which he bought from General Alexander Smith.

One Napier boy, Francis, the handsomest of the children, often visited his neighbors and was always anxious to find an ear of red corn. The family not only had a governess, called Miss Miya, but also a shepherd, for Lord Napier planned to raise sheep, his hobby.

It is said that the family brought with them barrels of dishes, silverware, the most exquisite linens, and much farm machinery. Lord Napier bought up all available stock, for he did everything on a magnificent scale, but his creditors began to push him. It is thought that he notified his relatives in London, for Mrs. Napier's sister arrived with sufficient gold to purchase the properties, but she did not feel the property worth it.

Suddenly the Napiers left, taking only a small part of their magnificent "layout," of silverware. It is claimed that his brother in London died and he was next in rank; hence, the swift departure. The property was sold by the creditors; General Smith took back his farm. For a long time, various families kept table linen and silverware from the sales which were held at the George and Alex Stuart home and the Petersons. (The Will Helms, Mrs. Lillie Robinson O'Dell Finchem, etc.) Among the effects were life-sized portraits of the Napiers in full dinner attire.

DARIUS NEAS, M. D., was born January 5, 1849, in Greene County, the tenth of eleven children of Philip and Elizabeth Bowers Neas, natives of Greene County, and of German descent. The former died March 2, 1873; the latter in April, 1880. The paternal grandfather, John Neas, Jr., of Greene County, was the son of John Neas, Sr., and a farmer.

Darius graduated at Mosheim College, Greene County, May, 1873, and then taught at Parrottsville and at Caney Branch, also reading medicine at the same time. In 1877, he graduated from the medical department of Vanderbilt University; and in 1878, the University of Nashville. He practiced at Parrottsville. On April 7, 1881, he married Ida M., daughter of B. F. Bell, of Greene County, now Cocke County. Their children were Vernie E., U. Roy, and Brent. He and his wife were Lutherans, and he was a Republican. (Goodspeed and Ida Bell Nease Nelson.)

SUELLA BURNETT NEASE. Musician, both instrumental and voice. Teacher.

JOHN NEFF (Sometimes called Nave)

About the time Cocke County was created, John Neff owned all the land from the Sinking Creek bridge to the top of English Mountain, securing it by entry. Later he sold it to William McSween, the son of Murdock McSween.

John Neff's hobby was brick-making, and his home was built where the "Gorman Home" now stands. One day, he drove his spirited team of horses to Morrell Mill, on Morrell Spring, south of Newport. When they became frightened and ran away they were directed to a huge tree, where one went to the right and the other to the left. This stopped them, and probably saved his life. He was so thankful that his dying request was that he be buried beneath it with a brick tomb over him. His family built a temporary frame structure over him and left. Years later, when the dilapidated tomb was brought to the attention of neighbors, they wrote a son in Missouri who had a mason construct the vault, which is one half mile west of Newport. near the Bridge, about fifteen feet wide and 7 feet in height.

MARSHAL MICHEL NEY may have been one of the Cocke County teachers between 1835 and 1845. He was a unique character who figured in French history and as a youth of eighteen joined the Regiment of the Colonel General, later known as the Fourth Hussars. Young Ney, whose military genius ranked with that of Napoleon Bonaparte, became world-renowned for the part he played in the French Revolution.

Marshal Ney was ordered executed by Louis XVIII on December 7, 1815. It is said that he was enabled to make his escape by the aid of friends of a secret order, assisted by the Duke of Wellington, and that he came directly to America with Paschal Luciana and others who landed at Charleston, South Carolina, only fifty-two days after the date of the supposed execution. Young Ney was known as Peter Stewart Ney and became a kind of wanderer through the Carolinas to Virginia. He taught school in various places, never remaining long at any one place. It is said that he always kept one of the pupils seated near a window overlooking the approach to the school to notify him of any visitor. Those who visited him spoke in a language unknown to the children.

This gentleman is known to have taught at Cleveland, North Carolina and at Statesville, and that he boarded with Colonel Houston. It is said that when he read of the death of Napoleon he fainted and fell to the floor of the schoolroom. The boys poured cold water on his face. He dismissed the pupils and was not able to teach again for several days. He tried to commit suicide and when reproved for this act, said that with the death of Napoleon his last hope had vanished. He was never again to have a happy moment, and his wanderings became more pronounced. When French officers called he would move again as though he wished to evade them, but many recognized him. For his ransom, it is said that Napoleon was willing to pay the sum of three million (francs?).[11]

NICHOLS PINCKNEY. (colored). With thrift and hard work he bought one hundred acres of land, near Gum Springs. Paid one dollar per acre.

JOHN O'HAVER. Methodist pioneer worker for whom O'Haver's Chapel named.

OSCAR O'NEIL. Squire Oscar O'Neil, Justice of the Peace in Cocke County for over fifty years, was a descendant of the Revolutionary soldier Darius O'Neil who was born in Culpeper County Virginia, May 18, 1764 and came to Cocke County with his family in 1781.

---

11. Data from James R. Jones.

W. J. Parks, president of Tenn.-North Carolina R. R. in its heyday, pictured with son Jack.

Frances Allison Pless on diving board at pool in City Park

M. OTTINGER, a bachelor, is said to have dug up $40,000 in gold and turned it into the government when President Roosevelt called for all gold.

PAUL OTTINGER graduated from Tusculum College, with the distinction of Magna Cum Laude and as valedictorian of his class. During his college years he was vice-president and president of the honor society, treasurer of his class and the Y. M. C. A., varsity debater and debate manager, a member of the President's Council and Polity Club as well as president of his dormitory. He took second place in extemporaneous speaking at the Applachian Forensic Tournament, was co-winner of the Smoky Mountain Forensic Tournament, and a delegate to the National Phi Kappa Delta convention at Topeka, Kansas. He was also elected to membership in *Who's Who In American Colleges and Universities.* He earned his way through college. His major subjects were history and English, and his minor field, economics.

Newport has had many splendid mayors, but none ever surpassed the executive ability of HON. W. J. PARKS, the political astuteness of DR. LOYD NEASE who served several terms, and the popularity of our present genial mayor, DR. CHARLES W. RUBLE, JR.

ANNIE BALCH PARROTT (Mrs. Frank). Historian and church worker.

CAPTAIN JAMES PEARCE was born March 24, 1748, a resident of Washington County, North Carolina, later known as Greene County. He raised a company of volunteers under Colonel John Sevier in 1799. He marched to the French Broad River. He raised another company of volunteers in the spring of 1780, and marched against the Indians to Beaver Creek. In the fall, he and his company, under Colonel Sevier, marched to King's Mountain. He was later ordered by Colonel Sevier to guard the frontiers along the French Broad River.

Captain James Pearce was married in 1771 to Margaret Dungan in Frederick County, Maryland. They lived in Berkeley County, Virginia. She was born February 4, 1755, the daughter of Jeremiah Dungan who moved into Washington County, 1779. Their children were: George, Elizabeth, John, Mary, Sarah, Rebeccah, Margaret, Solomon, James, Orpha, Jeremiah, Thomas, and Charlotte. (The name is variously spelled Pierce, Pearse, Pearce, Purse.)

Captain Pearce died April 1, 1833, in Sevier County and his widow died February 20, 1837, at the home of her son-in-law, Thomas Gibson.

SARAH ELIZABETH PEARCE. Poet, teacher, historian.

JUDGE JACOB L. PECK. Landowner. Member of State Supreme Court.

GERTRUDE PENLAND. News writer, daughter of James R. Penland.

JAMES ROYAL PENLAND was born on a farm near Del Rio, Tennessee, July 6, 1856, the son of John Jackson Penland and Ellen Justus Penland. He attended the public schools of Cocke County, later going to Weaverville College, in Weaverville, N. C., and to Grant University, in Athens, Tennessee, where he graduated in 1880.

He studied law in the offices of Pickle & Turner in Sevierville, Tennessee, and was admitted to the bar, in 1884, becoming a member of the partnership. A short time later, the firm was dissolved when the senior members moved to Knoxville, and Mr. Penland continued to practice his profession in Sevierville and throughout East Tennessee.

He served his district for three terms in the State Senate, from 1888 to 1894. He was presidential elector from the Second Congressional District for the Republican ticket in the second McKinley campaign, 1900 and again in 1904. He was appointed Assistant United States District Attorney for the Eastern District of Tennessee in November, 1904, and in 1906 was appointed United States District Attorney, succeeding Will D. Wright. In February, 1913, he was elected Republican member of the State Board of Elections for a term of six years. Upon his appointment as District Attorney he had moved to Knoxville, and when he returned to private practice he remained there.

He was married to Sallie Stuart of Parrottsville, October 21, 1885. There were five children: Gertrude, Dean Stuart (Mrs. Arthur Rodgers), LaVerne (Mrs. Penn W. Worden), Clifford, Herman.

Mr. Penland was a lifelong member of the Methodist Church, and for many years served on the Board of Trustees of Trinity Methodist Church, Knoxville. He was a Scottish Rite Mason. He died July 17, 1918.

ROBERT PENLAND. A Revolutionary soldier who lived in Fine Creek settlement.

GENERAL G. W. PICKLE (Pickel). Attorney.

VERNON C. RADER, chemist, is said to have been born in Cocke County in the early 1800's and in the area we now know as Hartford. Went to California, probably in the Gold-Rush days, returned only once, according to Maurice V. Samuels of California, who furnished the above information. If Vernon C. Rader's identity could be established and we could find proof that he was born in Cocke County a most interesting scientific discovery would be proved to the satisfaction of those interested in a discovery made by Vernon C. Rader. The loss of our early records has handicapped all who have tried to do research work in Cocke County. If only his name written in an old book or signed to any sort of document or manuscript could be found the investigators would accept it as proof that he once dwelt among us and that he is not an imaginary character as some doubters have claimed he must have been.

JAMES H. RANDOLPH, lawyer, was born October 19, 1825, in Jefferson County, Tennessee, the son of James M. Randolph, a native of Jefferson County, and the grandson of Henry Randolph of Roanoke, Virginia, a pioneer of the same county. Welsh, German and Indian blood flows in the Randolph veins.

When two years old his father died, and his mother then moved to Grainger County, where he received his boyhood education. His mother removed to New Market, Tennessee, where he and his only brother entered Holston College, and obtained their education. Shortly after this he read law by himself and was admitted to the bar, being examined by Judge Robert M. Anderson and Chancellor Thomas L. Williams, and began the practice of law at Newport, Tennessee.

He was elected to the Legislature in 1857-61 and to the State Senate in 1865-66. He bitterly opposed the secession of the State. He was elected circuit judge in 1870, over James M. Meek, and Walter R. Evans, and re-elected in 1872 over J. P. Swan, resigned at the end of seven years to become a Republican candidate for Congress, to which he was elected. He was identified with the remonetization of the silver dollar, making greenbacks equal to gold, repealing of the bankrupt law, and the repeal of laws unfavorable to the widows of soldiers, and making laws favoring them.

In 1848, he married M. J. Robinson, a daughter of Major William Robinson, formerly of Kentucky. Their children were William, H. M., Rolfe M., and Townsella.

Between 1870 and 1871, Judge Randolph moved from Old Newport to his farm which adjoined Alva Jack and James Robinson, his brother-in-law.

In the early 1880's, the Newport Mills became his property. The Judge also owned a packing house and much real estate.

Judge Randolph died in Newport, August 22, 1900, and was interred in Union Cemetery. (Goodspeed and others)

ROLFE MONTGOMERY RANDOLPH, the son of Judge James Henry Randolph, was a real estate operator in his day and developed for his brother-in-law, the late Ben D. Jones, the Jones-Randolph Addition, known as Jones Hill, in Newport. Union Cemetery was made possible largely by his efforts. In early years he dealt in fine horses and cattle, and in later years he became an auctioneer and salesman of both real estate and merchandise. He was a handsome, kindly, and useful citizen.[13]

A. W. RHEA, M. D., was born in 1838, in Blountville, Sullivan County, Tennessee, the eldest of four children of Joseph S. and Sarah F. Williams Rhea, natives of Sullivan and Carter Counties, respectively. He was the grandson of Samuel and Nancy Braiden Rhea, natives of Scotland, and of Archibald Williams, a native of Carter County, Tennessee.

When small he was taken by his parents to Watauga Bend, in Washington County. He attended the academy at Jonesboro, and also Washington College for some time. He studied medicine with Dr. Carson, of Jonesboro, and received his medical education at the University of Virginia. He began the practice of medicine at Newport.

He was surgeon during the Civil War for the Sixty-Second Tennessee Confederate States Army serving during the war. He was married in 1861 to Miss Mary E., daughter of General A. E. Smith, natives of Tennessee. They had two children: Lucia M. and Archie W. He was a Democrat in politics. His home stood on the present Lyle Moore residential site. (Goodspeed)

MARCUS AURELIUS ROADMAN was known as Ted, although he signed his name M. A. Roadman. His father, also Marcus Aurelius, was a brother of Julia Raleigh Roadman Smith. For years he was the editor of some County paper, the last one being called the *Newport Herald*. He was also a merchant. He married Nola Allen, and they had four children: Dooley, Jimmie, John M. (Mike), and Dorothy, who died from an injury in a swimming pool when about grown. Dooley, a lawyer, married the daughter of Caywood Mantooth, present postmaster, and is now with the United States Post Office Department. Jimmie is in the military service (air).

GENE ROBINSON (Wrote as Jack Archer). Reporter. Humorous articles for Newport papers during World War I.

DR. FRANK PIERCE ROBINSON, formerly a resident of Cocke County who named Del Rio for Del Rio, Texas, died this year (1946) at the age of 84. Dr. Robinson was an alumnus of the University of Tennessee and was widely known for a bitters prescription he gave his Del Rio

Kiffin Rockwell

The Baptist Parsonage where Kiffin Rockwell was born

patients. He was later general agent for the Short Line Railway Association. He was a Major of the 60th U. S. Volunteers in the Spanish-American War and served as first chief surgeon of the national home for disabled volunteer soldiers, now the Mountain Home Facility, at Johnson City. His wife, Ella Moore Robinson and a son, F. P. Robinson, Jr., preceded him in death. Other children are Miss Swannie Robinson, Mrs. L. C. Willis, of Greeneville, and Mrs. Carl B. Lyle of Rogersville. Doctor Robinson was widely known as a physician and as a former candidate for Congress. His home is on the Andrew Johnson Road, near Greeneville.

REV. VENTREE ROBINSON (Mammy Robinson—colored). Born in Dalton, Georgia. Lived thirty-four years in Cocke County. Held revivals from Tampa to Baltimore. Radio speaker. Meetings attended by thousands of white and colored. Died October 14, 1942.

W. B. ROBINSON. Merchant, financier.

LOUISE KYLE ROBINSON (Mrs. W. B.), a flower lover, an authority on birds, and of unusual intelligence. She had one of the most interesting collection of pitchers in Tennessee, from every country in the world, and from every state in the Union. They are of pottery, porcelain, china, glass, copper, brass, tin, shells, cornstalks, stamps, and of all colors. At one time, there were more than one thousand in her collection. She gave hundreds to Grace Moore; her most beautiful ones, to her daughters; and many to Jennie Ruth Boyer Robinson, her daughter-in-law. Her article "Our Feathered Friends," was widely read.

KIFFIN YATES ROCKWELL was born September 20, 1892, at the Baptist parsonage, on Woodlawn Avenue, Newport, the son of James Chester Rockwell, a North Carolina poet and writer, and Loula Ayers Rockwell, a teacher, and now a doctor in Asheville.

Kiffin spent much of his childhood on his maternal grandfather's plantation in Marion County, South Carolina; the remainder, in Newport. He was educated in the Asheville High School, Virginia Military Institute, Washington and Lee University. He received an Annapolis appointment, but resigned after a few months at Werntz' Preparatory School for the United States Naval Academy.

On August 3, 1914, Kiffin, together with his brother, Paul Ayers Rockwell, and the late Edgar J. Bouligny (cousin to General P. T. Beauregard), of New Orleans, were the first American citizens to offer their services to France against Germany in the World War I. On August 7, 1914, they embarked for France on the S. S. St. Paul and enlisted in the Foreign Legion immediately upon arrival in Paris.

Assigned to the Second Regiment of the Foreign Legion, they underwent a month's training at Toulouse before going to the front the beginning of October, 1914. The fall and winter were spent in the trenches along the Aisne River, and around Rheims in the Champagne sector. They were transferred to the First Regiment of the Legion on March 15, 1915, were moved North of Arras, and took part in the attack against Vimy Ridge, May 9, 1915.

While charging Neuville St. Vaast with the bayonet, Kiffin was shot through the thigh with a machine bullet. Upon leaving the hospital, he found himself unfit for the long marches made by the Legion, and was transferred to the French Army Aviation Corps. He trained at Camp Avord, and received his flying brevet in November, 1915. During the winter of 1915 and 16, he was on duty at LeBourget Field, as a member of the Paris Air Guard.

Kiffin Rockwell was one of the four founders of the LaFayette Escadrille was ordered to Verdun, where Kiffin destroyed another German plane on May 24, and was painfully wounded in the face by an explosive German bullet. He refused to enter the hospital and continued to fight. He was given another citation in French Army orders, and another Palm was added to his Croix de Guerre ribbon. The Escadrille remained here throughout the summer. During the month of July, his official record shows that he engaged in more air battles than any other pilot in French aviation.

Early in September, the LaFayette Escadrille was ordered back to the Alsace sector. The pilots were given new Spad aeroplanes. Kiffin took his Spad over the lines for a tryout, early on the morning of September 23, 1916. Just inside the French lines, he sighted a huge German two-seater observation plane. He dived to attack it, but a German bullet tore a great hole in his chest. His plane fell just within the French lines, where his broken body was dragged from the wreckage. They found that his wrist watch had stopped at 9:50 o'clock.

Kiffin Rockwell was buried at Luxeuil-les-Bains (Haute-Saone), where he was given a funeral worthy of a General. The inhabitants of the town have placed a handsome bronze memorial over the grave.

Kiffin Rockwell's decorations and medals included the Legion of Honor, Military Medal, Croix de Guerre with four palms and a silver star, the Croix de Combatant, the Verdun Medal, the French Victory Medal, French World War Medal, French Volunteer's Medal, Wounded Soldier's Star, the United Daughters of the Confederacy Medal of Honor, and many others. The Asheville, North Carolina Legion Post was named for him, as was the Post of the Veterans of Foreign Wars at Newport, Tennessee. Aviation fields in France and the United States were named for him. His name is engraved on the walls of the Panthenon in Paris, the Monument of the American Volunteers who died for France, Place des Etats-Unis, Paris, the LaFayette Escadrille Memorial Monument, and elsewhere. His Sigma Phi Epsilon fraternity brothers at Washington and Lee University placed a bronze tablet to his memory, in the Robert E. Lee Memorial Chapel, at Lexington, Virginia. Many poems were written to his memory, including ones by Edgar Lee Masters and Paul Mowrer. His *World War Letters* were published in book form in 1925 by Doubleday Page. Kiffin Yates Rockwell was the first Southerner to fall in World War I.

LT. COL. PAUL A. ROCKWELL, son of James C. and Loula A. Rockwell, and brother to Kiffin Rockwell, has served in his fourth war, his first, however, with the United States Army. During World War I, he enlisted in the French Foreign Legion. Following the war, when France was involved in the fight against the Riffian chieftain, Abdi-El-Krim, in North Africa, Rockwell again enlisted in the French Foreign Legion, this time in the flying service. He flew with the French in Morocco, later making his home in Paris for several years. In September, 1939, he again offered his services to France and served with the French until the country was overrun by the Germans. He returned to Asheville in the winter of 1940. He was given a commission as major in the United

States Army in May, 1942, and entered active service shortly thereafter. Some months later, he was promoted to Lieutenant Colonel.

Lt. Col. Rockwell holds membership in a number of honor societies and clubs in the United States and France, among his honors the Knight of the Legion of Honor of France. He is a leading authority on the history of the American service in the Foreign Legion and in the La-Fayette Escadrille. His family, Mrs. Rockwell and two sons, Kiffin Yates Rockwell, II, and William Kenneth Rockwell, and a daughter, Mrs. V. Jordan Brown (formerly Loula Rockwell), reside in Asheville, North Carolina.

CAPTAIN D. K. ROWE, as he was known, spent many years of his life in Cocke County and reared an honorable family in our midst. He was the son of John and Nellie Dodson Rowe and was born Feb. 29, 1840, in Carter County, where he grew to manhood, and joined the Union Army Company K, 10th Tennessee Cavalry under General Thomas.

After the war was over, Captain Rowe continued his studies in Washington College and became a teacher. He taught the sons of Nat Taylor in Happy Valley and for several years, he taught in that area of Tennessee. When Bob and Alf Taylor each became Governor of the State, each made him a Colonel on the Governor's staff, an honor he greatly appreciated.

In 1872, Captain Rowe married Mary Frances Elizabeth Burnett, of Del Rio. She was the daughter of James M. and Caroline Huff Burnett, and the granddaughter of Swan P. Burnett and wife on her paternal side, and of Stephen Huff and wife on her maternal side. The children of this couple were: John Burnett Rowe, William Stephen, Jesse T., James H., Swan E., Horace and Nellie Rowe.

In speaking of his mother, Burnett Rowe paid her a wonderful tribute as follows. . . .

"She gave up a home of plenty and cast her lot with an Ex. Soldier of the Civil War, a school teacher by profession, and although she found some thorns in her pathway, she never looked backward with regret. She met all barriers bravely and without complaint, like the heroine she was. She believed that the blessedness of life depended far more on its interests than upon its comforts. She knew life was hedged about with pain and pleasure, too strange for deep sorrow, too unfathomable for great joy. She was a born philosopher, with a strong mind which she retained until her very last days. Under the stress of threatened danger, she remained cool and calculative through the process of reasoning."

GEORGE SAMPLES Cocke County's Legless World War Veteran volunteered in May, 1917, joining Captain Thurman Ailor's company of Volunteers which formed here, they became part of Headquarters Company, 120th Infantry and went to Europe. The group saw action in Belgium and France. During the attack on the Hindenburg Line on Sept. 29, 1918, George Samples fell with what was thought to be fatal injuries. Mike Crino, a well known musician of our County was with the ambulance crew found Samples with both his legs badly mangled. Crino rushed him to the hospital where they were removed.

At the time of the death of Samples, July 3, 1938, he had undergone seventeen major operations. Yet, in spite of all this he refused to become an invalid, he learned to drive a car and did taxi service just to have something to do. He attended all State Legion Conventions and several

National ones where he was always given a big hand in the parades where he rode in his wheel chair and over each wheel were signs which read . . . "I did my part."

George Samples left his widow, Edwyn Robinson Samples and one daughter, Carol, his mother and several other relatives to mourn his passing.

JACOB L. SHULTS prides himself on being the ugliest man in the County. Also, together with his father, he has lived under the administration of every Governor that Tennessee has had from June, 1796 to 1950. Mr. Shults has served the County in various capacities from teacher, board of education member to direct representative in the General Assembly of the State.

He writes for the local papers under the name of Razorback. His sense of humor is highly developed. It was the author's privilege one Sunday to attend a "singin" in the Cosby section where Shults lives. Both were candidates for the Legislature. He was asked by the singing master to select any hymn he would like to have them sing. He chose, "I'll Go Sweeping through the Pearly Gates." The crowd realized the significance of his choice and when it was finished the same courtesy was extended the writer who chose "When the Roll is Called up Yonder I'll be There," and she was!

G. G. SIMS, son of Elliott and Joanna Sims, was born September 10, 1813. His father was a native of South Carolina, and George was brought up as a millwright. On November 4, 1833, Sims was married to Miss Mary Fine, a daughter of Abraham Fine, of Cocke County. They had three sons and four daughters. On December 28, 1843, he was baptized. and licensed to preach on April, 1846, and was further liberated in May, 1847, and was ordained by Antioch Church, Jefferson County, November 8, 1847. He did the most of his preaching in Sevier, Jefferson, Blount. and Cocke Counties. His name appears frequently in the Minutes of the Tennessee, the Nolachucky and East Tennessee Associations as "Correspondent," "Messenger," or "Visitor."

The late MARK SISK, who married Mollie Swanson and was a brother of Will Sisk was the first man to sell gasoline in Cocke County. He was the agent for the Standard Oil Company.

In the "Gay Nineties," the agent at our depot called Mr. Sisk to tell him that a five gallon drum of gasoline had arrived and to please come after it immediately. When Mr. Sisk arrived there was no one to deliver the drum to him. The agent and his helpers had fled and were hiding under the bridge back of the depot. They called to Mr. Sisk to be very careful lest "the stuff blow up." The news of this strange fluid had spread up and down "Front Street" and all the merchants were inside looking out expecting to see Mr. Sisk blown to bits.

The gasoline was taken to Mr. Carl Babb on "Back Street" where he had a shop located where Myers Chevrolet Company is now, opposite to the Rhea-Mims Hotel. Mr. Babb had acquired a gasoline engine which was the wonder of the century but useless without the gasoline. Mark Sisk soon became known as "The Oil Man," and his letters were often thus addressed.

His brother, Will, is still living and was ninety, November 11, 1950.

Information by Louzelle Sisk Babb, daughter of Mr. Sisk, and daughter-in-law of Mr. Babb.

Mary Ann Sklar

Little MARY ANN SKLAR, daughter of Mr. and Mrs. Eddie Sklar, was born in Newport, Tennessee January 12, 1942.

In the sixth year of her life, Mary Ann began her musical career by learning to play the accordion. Her teacher was Tony Musco, of Knoxville. Now, at eight years of age this child is a well known star in the world of entertainment. She first appeared on Horace Heidt's show, Original Youth Opportunity and has also played on the Dick Contino shows in Nashville. She has won in both beauty and personality contests for children.

Mary Ann is in great demand as an entertainer and has appeared on the programs of many and various State conventions. Recently in Chicago she represented TENNESSEE on the program of the International Lion's Club Convention.

Within the last two years Mary Ann has played on eighteen radio stations and one television program. She is now, 1950, a well known professional entertainer.

Several American Legion Posts and the Kerbela Shrine Club of Knoxville have designated Mary Ann Sklar as "SWEETHEART" of their organizations, and the Knoxville Boat Club chose her as their MASCOT the first year of her life. Her parents are charter members of this club.

MR. AND MRS. EDDIE SKLAR came to Cocke County in 1932 from their home in Nashville. They are both professional speedboat drivers and have participated in nationally known boat races for many years. All of their boats bear the name of "Mary Ann," for Mrs. Sklar, who was Mary Cooksey of Nashville. Their boats are designated Mary Ann I, II, III, etc. Mr. and Mrs. Sklar are known as "Mary and Eddie," at the various races they attend.

ADALINE SUSONG SMITH. Daughter of George and Eleanor Stokely Susong, an outstanding teacher who is teaching in 1946 at White Pine High School, and is past 75.

The Headquarters for the soldiers of the Confederate Army in the years from 1861 to 1865 was the home of GENERAL ALEXANDER E. SMITH, who lived and died on the estate which was handed down to him by his Father, Colonel Alexander Smith.

From a letter in the files of the Tennessee Historical Society relating to old citizens of Cocke County, and written to Dr. J. G. M. Ramsey in 1874 by a Mr. Garrett of Bradford, Alabama, I find these interesting lines.

"Among early settlers in Cocke County mentioned—First Colonel Alexander Smith, who settled on the North side of the Big Pigeon and owned a large body of land, extending from the War Ford down some two miles. He possessed a large degree of energy as his success testified. He became wealthy and died in 1824, a man of great substance of character and property. He was a lad in the days of the Revolution and took an active part in assisting the Whigs, giving information, hiding out stock and taking part in the skirmishes of that day. In one of these he received a sabre cut upon the head that was a mark of honor while he lived. In the Creek Indian War of 1813 he was a Major, and bore himself with marked bravery and coolness in every engagement in which he participated. This was especially the case at the battle of "Horseshoe," where he led his command gallantly in the charge upon the enemy's works. His devotion to agricultural pursuits, with the gains which rewarded his well directed industry and energy diverted his mind from public pursuits, and he was never so much in his element as when riding over the large plantation and viewing his heavy harvest of grain, his fine large fat cattle and hogs and in looking to his stables of horses. He grew quite corpulent in his latter days. He was a useful, public spirited citizen, exerted a large influence upon the public mind of the Country around, and in his death was much regretted. His large property descended to his widow and only son, the late General Alexander E. Smith, who lived and died on the patrimonial estate; filling many offices of trust, particularly that of Representative in the General Assembly from the Counties of Cocke and Sevier. General Smith filled the measure of a good citizen in the attributes of intelligence, public spirit and a generous affluent hospitality. He died in 1872."[12]

One day during the Civil War, Union Soldiers were sent to Green Lawn with strict orders to burn to the ground the home of General Alexander E. Smith because within its protective walls of brick had been "harbored" Confederate Soldiers. If there is one thing a soldier endeavors to do it is to carry out the orders of his Superiors. These Union Soldiers seized upon the quickest method whereby they might set the house on fire and at the same time frighten away the inmates. They set fire to the fragile lace curtains that adorned the windows in this home of great wealth. They had not for a moment, the faintest idea of the bravery and brains of General Smith's daughter, Mary, who rushed to the flaming curtains and snatched them from the windows and threw them outside with a fearlessness that won the admiration of the soldiers. They stood aghast admiring the bravery of this young woman and listened to these words that fell from her lips, "If you YANKEES burn this house our dear Grand-Father, Colonel Alexander Smith built for his home and handed down to us, our Confederate Soldiers will be here next week and no UNION HOME will be left standing in this County". The soldiers went away as though they were considering the wisdom of their course. To say the least they had set fire to the house it was supposed to burn to the ground as the orders were given.

Major George W. Gorman, who was a Union man, rode his horse to death that very night in order to get the order "to burn" rescinded. He had to ride to Knoxville. Horses took the places of our present modes of transportation, radios, telephones and telegraph wires. I'm wondering where Major Thomas Gorman, the Confederate Major was that particular night. Probably he sent his brother Major George upon this errand. For the Civil War was a purely franticidal strife.

In this grand old home at Green Lawn there was a vanishing stairway and many secret openings where various commodities were hidden. Under the house was a large room for the storage of supplies such as corn and wheat and potatoes and barrels of molasses, wines and what-so-ever would keep there.

Over the dining room was a place about half story high in which was hung all the meat, a vast quantity of it. The only means of entrance was through a small transom over the dining room door where a secret opening went into this "loft". In order to get into the meat house a small Negro slave was lifted to the transom and went in and out after meat when needed. He also hung the meat. His name was Simm Smith.

---

12. Mae Lucile Smith Walker.

I have never learned where the money was kept, it was probably invested in slaves, in land, in cattle and horses and hogs as General Smith's father had done before him.

After the awful war between the states was ended and General Smith returned to his home he found he had only ONE COW and ONE JENNY left of all his stock of fat cattle and hogs and horses.

The only slave he could find was LITTLE SIMM who had hidden under the Ash-hopper to keep from being driven away from his home. He grew to manhood and many living now remember him. He was one of the good old fashioned kind of darkies the South loved.

ALEXANDER DEWITT SMITH, brother of Major W. R. Smith, an alumnus of Washington College, died in 1860.

AUGUST SMITH, according to Major W. R. Smith's records of his brother, was a member of Osborn's Scouts. He was killed at Mossy Creek, or rather died of a wound sustained the day before. Theodore Melvin Smith, also his wife and infant daughter, Nancy, were with him when he died. In after years, Nancy became the wife of Selden Nelson, son of Judge T. A. R. Nelson, of Knoxville.[13]

GEORGE FARRAR SMITH was born to George Farrar Smith, Sr., and Judith Metcalf Smith, 92 years ago (1950). His ancestors came from Exeter, England, and settled first in South Carolina; later, this George F. Smith came to Tennessee, settling on Chuckey, thence to Columbia. His mother was descended from Letitia Martin of Martinsville, Martin County, Virginia, and her husband Barnett Metcalf, who lived in Fayettville, but had another plantation at Huntsville, with one hundred slaves on each. Barnett Metcalf's brother Charles was knighted by Queen Victoria and became Governor General of Canada. Another went to India and became Governor General of Jamaica.

George Farrar Smith was educated in Bingham Military School, Vanderbilt University, and a Philadelphia College of Pharmacy and Science, from which he graduated in 1880. He served as captain on the Brigadier General's Staff when the coal miners were giving trouble at Jellico and Coal Creek and the National Guard was called out. Margaret Burnett went to Mary Sharp College at Winchester, where she met Captain Smith, who married her. When his drugstore at Winchester burned, he decided to move to Newport and for many years owned and operated Smith's Drug Store. George F. Smith was twice elected Mayor of Newport in the early 1900's.

Eight children were born to the Smith-Burnett union, the eldest Burnett lost his life in World War I. His mother saw to it that a tree was planted on Cocke County High School grounds in memory of each soldier who did not return from this war.

THEODORE MELVIN SMITH left his desk at the University of Tennessee to enlist in the cause of his country, at the age of sixteen. He was made Second Lieutenant in Company I, Second Cavalry Regiment (formed from the Fourth and Fifth Cavalry Battalions), under Colonel Henry M. Ashvy. Besides being at Mossy Creek, he fought in the Siege of Vicksburg and in minor engagements.

THOMAS SMITH (Uncle Tommy Smith), a preacher of the "old school" type in Cocke County, lived to be 102 years and two months old.

13. *Ibid.*

He preached his last sermon on his 100th birthday at the old Slate Creek Church, near Parrottsville. His text was Judges 15:14, 15, 16, the record of Samson's feat of slaying "heaps" of the Philistines with the "jawbone of an ass." He was a member of the Slate Creek Church for many years, and representative of this church along with others in Holston Association as far back as 1818. Slate Creek was one of the churches dismissed from Holston to form the Nolachucky organization (Bent Creek, 1828) by her "messengers Thomas Smith and Simon Smith." For the next ten years, he was regularly appointed messenger to the Nolachucky. In 1837, he preached the introductory sermon. (Burnett)

THOMAS LUCIUS SMITH, according to Major W. R. Smith's family records, of his brother, served one year in Branner's Battalion, at Mossy Creek. He was transferred to the 63rd Tennessee Infantry Regiment, C. S. A. He was promoted to the rank of lieutenant in the 62nd Infantry Regiment known also as the 80th Mounted Infantry. He fell mortally wounded during the Siege of Vicksburg and died a month later. His brothers, William Roadman and Theodore Melvin, were with him. He graduated from the University of North Carolina, cum laude, and also completed the course of law at that institution.[14]

WILLIAM ROADMAN SMITH, of the 80th Tennessee Infantry Regiment, later called the Mounted Infantry, was a son of General A. E. Smith. In the fall of 1862, he organized a company and was elected Captain. This company was identified with the 62nd Regiment, C. A. A., Tennessee Infantry, which was commanded by Col. John A. Rowan, General John C. Vaughan's Brigade. In the spring of 1863, Captain Roadman was promoted to Major. He was captured at Strawberry Plains, October 27, 1864, and was put in the Chattanooga Military Prison, Chattanooga, where he began his prison diary on November 2. On November 19, he and his fellow prisoners started on a four-day journey to Johnson Island Prison. Here his diary was resumed. Throughout his trying experience, his diaries show unwavering faith in God. Reduced almost to the point of starvation, he was finally released in April 1865. He was an alumnus of Washington College.[15]

Cocke County has a real Santa Claus who for 34 years has served various cities at the Christmas season. Robert Ripley once said: "Believe it or not there is a real Santa Claus." His white hair and beard, his blue eyes and pink skin delight all children everywhere to say nothing of his kindly smile. He lives on Cosby, R. 3. His name is C. E. SPRIGGS.

DR. JOHN F. STANBERRY. Beloved doctor and nationally known Duroc Jersey hog fancier and breeder.

JOHN F. STANBERRY, Jr. Radio expert—short-wave, Oklahoma City. First amateur operator in fifth district of six states to contact Felix Best of the Byrd expedition in 1940. Now employed by Government. Speaker in NCA convention for foreign representatives, 1946.

A. M. STOKELY, a farmer in First District, was born in 1850, in Cocke County, the sixth of thirteen children of Nathan Huff and Evaline Jones Stokely, natives of Cocke County. The father was justice of the

14. *Ibid.*
15. *Ibid.*

peace for several years, a trustee of Cocke County, and a successful farmer. He was the grandson of Royal and Jane Huff Stokely.

He was married in 1881 to Miss Katie Jackson Murray, a daughter of J. C. Murray, of Greene County, but a resident of Cocke County many years. They had three children: Jessie May, Hattie Evaline, and Marvel Murray Jones. He was elected trustee of Cocke County in 1878, and was re-elected in 1880. Both Mr. and Mrs. Stokely were members of the Missionary Baptist Church, and Mr. Stokely was a Democrat. (Goodspeed)

BEN D. STOKELY. Artist with camera. Moving pictures taken all over the world. World traveler, stamp collector. Marine in World War II.

BUD STOKELY graduated from the University of Missouri, School of Journalism, where he worked as correspondent for the International News Service, furnishing services for five Missouri dailies. In World War II.

CHARLES STOKELY, SR., farmer and stock dealer, was born June 19, 1821, on a farm in Cocke County, the seventh of ten children of Royal and Jane Huff Stokely, both of English and English Dutch descent, respectively. The father was a justice for twenty-one years, and the mother, a native of Virginia, who came to Cocke County when eighteen months old. The paternal grandfather, Jehu, a native of England, was a sailor for seven years, and in 1747, settled in Charleston, South Carolina, and afterward lived in North Carolina and in Cocke County. The maternal grandfather. John Huff, from Roanoke County, Virginia, came to Cocke County about 1785. About 1850, he married Sarah, daughter of John Black, of South Carolina. Their children were Mary J., Sarah E., Thomas, Rhoda E., Susan C., Royal J., Nancy A., Steven D., John B., James, Jesse, W. D., Cora B., Lilla. He and his wife were members of the Missionary Baptist Church, of which he was some time deacon. He was a Democrat. (Goodspeed)

MURRAY MARVIN STOKELY received his degree from the School of Electrical Engineering, Clemson (S. C.) College. While there he was a member of Tau Beta Pi, national honorary engineering scholastic fraternity; the Tiger Brotherhood, local honorary fellowship organization; the American Society of Electrical Engineering, and the Y. M. C. A. council. He held the military rank of Major. He is the son of Mrs. Emma Stokely.

WILMA DYKEMAN STOKELY. Writer, radio speaker, wife of James R. Stokely, Jr.

CAPTAIN DAVID STUARD, a near relative of Ensign John Stuard who in 1757 was one of the two who escaped from the massacre of Fort Loudon.

In 1800, Capt. David Stuard, a surveyor, assisted in locating original entries for land in East Tennessee and was one of the surveyors and commissioners that established the state line between Tennessee and North Carolina. He came into Cocke County with the Jacks, McNutts, Wards and Rogers, all of whom settled in the Irish Bottoms. There were three Ward brothers and two sisters; one married Capt. Stuard, the other married Samuel Jack. David Ward is a descendant of Cirus Ward, one of the three Ward brothers.

CAPT. M. E. STYLL, an extensive dealer in real estate. In 1891 was associated with B. D. Jones in developing the western end of the town. Eighty acres were sold off as lots.

ROBERT P. SULTE, late editor and owner of *Plain Talk* and *Tribune*, whose friendly spirit encouraged all who knew him.

GEORGE W. SUSONG, farmer and stock dealer, was born February 2, 1835, in Greene County, Tennessee, the ninth of thirteen children of Andrew and Susa Ball Susong, natives of Lee County, Virginia, the former an old resident of Washington County, Virginia, and a soldier of the War of 1812, and the latter a daughter of William Ball. His grandfather, Nicholas Susong, with his brothers, Jacob and Andrew, came to America with General LaFayette during the Revolution, and fought with the General. The brothers first settled in Virginia and afterward near Bristol. In 1867, George W. settled in the "Fork of Pigeon," and in 1868, he married Eleanor, a daughter of Jehu Stokely and wife (nee Burnett) natives of Cocke County. The former, the son of John Stokely, Sr., died February 26, 1885. The children were Jacob A., Jamry J., Addie, Georgiana, John B. S., Susan E., Louisa K., and Hester C. His wife was a Baptist; he was a Democrat and a Master Mason. After 1870, he owned the Carter Farm, in the Dutch Bottoms. (Goodspeed)

JAMES SWAGGERTY was a moneymaking man, a trapper of muskrats and mink. Each Sunday he would count his money in the loft of his home. He kept saving until he was able to buy one thousand acres of land from Colonel Joseph O'Neil, but sold four hundred acres of it to the Newport Development Company, which sold it to the Tannery Company, which still owns it. To each of his children: James, Margaret, Abigail, William R., David, Florence, George, and Alexander, he gave five thousand dollars.

W. R. SWAGERTY (Swaggerty), farmer and stock dealer at Newport, was born August 3, 1842, in Newport, the sixth of ten children of James and Nancy Clark Swagerty, natives of Cocke County, of German descent. He was a grandson of James Swagerty (1773-1868), an early settler and native of Virginia, for many years justice of the peace. His first wife, Delilah, died March 21, 1844, aged about seventy-one years. He was married again on November 22, 1844, to Nancy H. Johnson. W. R.'s father, James Swagerty, Jr., was born in 1800 and died in 1885. W. R. enlisted June, 1861, in Company C., Second Tennessee Infantry, C. S. A., and served until 1864, when after the Battle of Missionary Ridge. he was captured and kept as a prisoner of war in Sevierville jail until the close of·the war. He was wounded at the battles of Murfreesboro and Chattanooga. He was married in December, 1866, to Miss Lydia Allen, a daughter of James Allen, a native of Cocke County, a farmer, who served in the Mexican War. W. R. and Lydia Allen Swagerty had six children: Lora Anna, Fannie Dale, James M., Nannie Laura, Hattie Murray, and Eunice. He was elected justice of the peace in 1882, and was a Democrat and a Master Mason. (Goodspeed)

FRANCES BURNETT SWANN, poet.

From page 76 of Francis Burnett Swann's Book of Poems, I copy. by permission, a few lines on her father and on page 77 a few lines from the poem on her mother. These lines are typical of the majority of parents in Del Rio.

MY FATHER

(The Rev. Jesse M. L. Burnett)
His life was short as given the span
Of years allotted unto man;
Yet, greatly lived, full and complete
In all that makes life rich and sweet.
A noble presence, a scholar's mind,
A tender heart, ways, loving kind;
A great soul, given in ministry;
Loved and revered as few can be.

MY MOTHER

(Sarah Henrietta Cody Burnett)
This be my song of one who gave
Her daily life, young lives to save,
Who to her children gave her best
And blessing them, by them was blest.
Who gives of strength and thought and time
To homely service, makes sublime
The daily round, in love and pride
"The common task" is glorified.
Amid ancestral scenes we grew
Deep rooted in the home we knew.
Through all our youth in love and pride
There still those long wrought ties abide.

Cocke County has had a most unusual notable in the person of MRS. JUANITA BREEDEN TEMPLIN, daughter of Mr. and Mrs. James Breeden and the first wife of Forrest Templin.

This ambitious young woman began her business career in 1937, as one of the youngest in the state. She began with a very modest capital of only $1,200 and by wise management built it up to $35,000 in the ten years she operated her "Modern Miss Shoppe For Lovely Things to Wear."

Thus a mountain girl born with a love of the beautiful and a courage to struggle toward expressing it in a profitable way became an inspiration to other young people "to strike out on their own" and make for themselves a place in the business world.

DR. PAUL W. TRANSOU was Newport's first resident chiropractor. A native of Winston-Salem, N. C., he lived here many years (and the women claimed he was the handsomest man in the whole world).

MAE SMITH WALKER, granddaughter of Gen. A. E. Smith, daughter of Theodore Melvin Smith, business woman, club woman, newspaper correspondent, magazine editor, naturalist, genealogist.

THOMAS WARE was in Holston two years, 1787-1789. He was admitted in 1784 at the historic Christmas Conference. His was the longest ministerial career of any of the early preachers in Holston. For some time before his death, on March 11, 1842, he was the oldest Methodist preacher in America. He was born in Greenwich County, New Jersey, December 19, 1758. He volunteered to come to Holston with John Tunnell and Micajah Tracey in 1787. He served among the new settlers on the lower Holston and French Broad Rivers and shared with them the dangers and hardships of the frontier; was with John Tunnell when Mrs. Elizabeth Russell and her husband were converted; and was a member of the first conference west of the Blue Ridge, at Keywood, Virginia, in May, 1788. He was circuit rider, station preacher, presiding elder, missionary to Jamacia. Elected in 1812 one of the Book Stewards and served four years. He was one of the great men of his day.[16]

DR. OSCAR WATSON, son of County Agent, O. M. Watson, received his degree of Doctor of Medicine from the University of Tennessee. He interned at Saint Joseph's Infirmary, Fort Worth, Texas. He is a graduate of Cocke County Central High School, and operated the Burnett farm at Del Rio before entering the University.

JOHN WEAVER. School teacher, surveyor, historian, politician, foxhunter, postmaster, Santa Rosa, Texas, authority on Cocke County history.

COCKE COUNTY'S DOCTORS AND LAWYERS IN 1950

Doctors: Harry J. Lemmon, Fred Valentine, Glenn Shults, Drew Mims, R. W. Smith, J. E. Hampton, Charles Ruble, Jr., W. E. McGaha, Loyd Nease, Huff (Cosby), Dennis Branch (colored).

Dentists: Hobart Ford, C. A. Redmond, A. M. Mullen, V. W. Montsinger, Sr., V. W. Montsinger, Jr.

Lawyers: Ben W. Hooper, William M. Crawford, Edward Hurd, George R. Shepherd (Judge), Elmer C. Greer, John C. Porter, Oscar O'Neil Lee, Donald McSween, Carty McSween, M. O. Allen, Fred W. Parrott.

---

16. Martin's *History of Methodism in Holston Conference*, 1944.

Citations

"LIEUTENANT L. S. NEASE 307th Infantry at Mervel on the 8th of September 1918 attended wounded throughout the day without rest for over 24 hours, with utter disregard of personal danger from shell fire, both high and explosive gas."

OTIS PAUL BAILEY was a member of the company receiving the following citation. "I Company, 60th Infantry, Nov. 5, 1918. Place, near Clery les Petit. At a critical time when our forces were held up in crossing the Meuse, near Clery les Petit, Nov. 5, 1918, the foregoing named officers and men, all of I Company, 60th Infantry, displayed extraordinary courage and heroism in advancing over a lightly constructed pontoon bridge in the face of heavy enemy machine gun and artillery fire. Lieutenant O. K. Morrison and 80 men succeeded in crossing the canal, east of the river, and at dawn advanced, in the face of terrific rifle and machine gun fire, without awaiting orders, against a vastly superior force of the enemy then in position on hill 260. The portion of the company under Captain E. C. Allsworth swam the canal under heavy fire after the bridge had been destroyed, joined the attack, advanced about a kilometer, killed many of the enemy and captured three officers and one hundred men" By Command of Brigadier General Castner.

BURNETT SMITH enlisted from Walter Reed Hospital, Washington, in the medical dept. of the U. S. Army in 1917. He was a druggist. Sailed for France in May 1918 after a training course at Fort Oglethorpe. Burnett was attached to Evacuation Hospital number 8, which unit arrived in France at the beginning of Chateau-Thierry drive and was stationed at Juilly. During the two months this unit was stationed at Juilly, they handled six thousand soldiers who were wounded. During the Argonne drive this hospital was stationed near Verdun.

The book, "STRETCHERS," by Frederick Pottle, a member of hospital number 8, gives a detailed account of the activities of this hospital. It was written as a memorial to Burnett Smith and nine other men who gave their lives in service.

CAPTAIN JOHN FLOYD ARROWWOOD son of Mark Arrowwood was the first American boy decorated for bravery. He went over with the first division. Displayed the greatest of bravery in the face of battle. At Belleau Wood he participated in a skirmish in which a number of sharpshooters were stationed in trees "mowing down" the Americans. Arrowwood silenced the guns by killing the leader of the German company and capturing fourteen of the sharpshooters. General Pershing decorated Arrowwood with the Croix de Guerre. European papers were full of the story of this brave mountain man from Cocke County, Tennessee.

KIFFIN YATES ROCKWELL received many citations four of which are signed by Joffre, two by R. Nivelle, two by Louis Barthou, and two by Rollet. I like the following one best of all.

"Kiffin Yates Rockwell, Sergent-pilot with Escadrille n. 124; enlisted for the duration of the war. Having entered the aviation de chasse, he revealed himself immediately to be a pilot of the very first order. of admirable daring and bravery. He never hesitates to attack an enemy, no matter what may be the number of adversaries he encounters, usually obliging the enemy, by the skill and sharpness of his attack, to abandon the struggle. He destroyed two enemy machines. Has rendered the most valuable services to the aviation de chasse of the army by unsparing efforts during four months at Verdun."

Signed . . . . R. Nivelle.

Many others of our native sons have citations but I am able to secure only these for the records herein given.

From the Source of Records of Great War, I find the following words:

FIRST LIEUTENANT WILLIAM W. JONES: rendered patriotic services to the National cause during the Great War.

Entered United States Army May 12, 1917 at Fort Oglethorpe Georgia as private Infantry. Commissioned Second Lieutenant Infantry Aug. 14, 1917.

Received orders for overseas duty and arrived in France Sept. 24, 1917. Assigned with British Army for five weeks. Physical and Bayonet training. Assigned to 26th Infantry and fought with them through the following engagements: Aisne-Marne, Ansauville, Cantigny, Luneville, Montdidier-Noyon, Seicheprey, Somme Offensive, Soissons, St. Mihiel, and Defensive Sectors of Alsace and Lorraine. Was wounded near Verdun October 18, 1918. Confined in Red Cross Hospital number 1. Neuelly-sur-Seine, seven months. Discharged from service June 24, 1919 as First Lieutenant Infantry. Received Regimental citation and Croix de Guerre.

THOMAS WEAVER DANIELS was awarded the Purple Heart. He was the son of James Daniels and wife, Nora Solsbee Daniels, of Del Rio.

This young man was a volunteer and at the time of his death Nov. 8, 1942, belonged to Company G. 60th Combat Team and was in French Morocco, Africa. His Lt. Willard H. Barnwell wrote the parents of Thomas Weaver Daniels that he fought most valiantly and that no man could have done more. He was in his "teens".

War Records of Former Cocke County Soldiers Secured From Washington

L. S. Allen, always on the lookout for old historical matters and articles, recently wrote the war department in Washington for the records of some of his relatives who served in the Confederate army during the Civil war. He received an immediate answer and the correspondence is here printed. Many of the older people of the county will be interested in reading same.—Ed.

Newport, Tenn., July 14th, 1931.

Adj. Gen. Chas. H. Bridges,
War Department,
Washington, D. C.

Dear Sir:

Any information you can give me in regard to the following parties will be much appreciated: Capt. Edwin Allen (my great uncle), Co. C, 26th Tenn. Reg.; Lewis Allen, his son, same company; Wm. Allen (my uncle), same company; Andrew Allen (my uncle), same company. All of the above from Cocke County, Tenn.

Thanking you very kindly for any information you will give me, I am

Most cordially yours,

L. S. ALLEN.

Washington, July 21, 1931.

Mr. L. S. Allen,
Newport, Tenn.

The records show that Edwin Allen was appointed Captain of Company C, 26th Regiment Tennessee Infantry, Confederate States Army, June 27, 1861, and enrolled for duty at Camp Cumings, near Knoxville, aged 43 years.

He was killed at the Battle of Murfreesboro, December 31, 1862.

The records show that Lewis Allen, private, Company C, 26th Regiment Tennessee Infantry, Confederate States Army, enlisted June 27, 1861, at Camp Cumings, Knoxville, Tennessee age 21 years.

He was captured at Fort Donelson, February 16, 1862, and died at Camp Morton, Indiana, July 7, 1862.

The records show that W. W. Allen, also shown as William W. Allen, private, Company C. 26th Regiment Tennessee Infantry, Confederate States Army, enlisted October 18, 1862, at Taylorsburg, Tenn., age 26 years.

Company muster roll for May 1 to August 31, 1864, last on file, shows him absent, captured at Resaca, by the enemy, May 15, 1864.

Union records show that he was captured at Resaca, Georgia, May 16, 1864, sent to Military Prison, Louisville, Ky., forwarded to Military Prison at Alton, Illinois, May 23, 1864, transferred to Camp Douglas, Ill., August 23, 1864, where was paroled and transferred to Point Lookout. Mr., for exchange, March 23, 1865, but he died there, April 25, 1865, cause of death shown as inflamation of the lungs. He was wounded in action at the battle of Murfreesboro, Jan. 2, 1863.

The name of Andrew Allen has not been found on the rolls on file in this office of Company C, 26th Regiment Tennessee Infantry, Confederate States Army, which cover the period in part, from December 21, 1861, to August 31, 1864.

The records show, however that one A. M. Allen, private, Company C, that organization, enlisted October 18, 1862, at Taylorsburg, age 32 years.

He was killed in action at Murfreesboro, January 2, 1863.

C. H. BRIDGES.
Major General.

The Aftermath of Christmas Day 1855

Christmas Day 1855 must have been an unusual celebration of that particular day according to the record found in the papers of one of Cocke County's 'moneyed' men.

Twenty-five notes made to I. B. Young, dated Dec. 25, 1855 and sixteen notes made to Lawson D. Franklin and a number to T. S. Gorman all of the same date and for sums ranging from five to twelve dollars were placed for collection the following June 11, 1856 and July of the same year. Sheriff B. Bryant collected $111.71 and Deputy Sheriff A. J. Gillett, collected $97.

Lawson D. Franklin was one of the first millionaires in East Tennessee, according to some of the oldest citizens. The story of the Franklin Brothers is a fascinating one.

Cocke County issued script at that time, probably earlier and also later, this dollar bill is evidence of the fact.

It is of interest to know that there was once a registration law in the county. The commissioner on July 31, 1869 was G. W. Loyd, who signed the registration certificate of John Stevens (Stephens).

On this same Christmas Day 1855, the "hog-sale" of one man, Andrew Ramsey, amount to two thousand dollars. J. B. Casheler bought them. (Suitable name indeed) There is no evidence that Ramsey loaned any of it.

Indians

If Cocke County has, at present any thoroughbred Indians they have not made themselves known to me. We have only a few families of Indian descent who have given me permission to mention their names.

Ann Bibee Mitchel of Knoxville was born in Cocke County and descends in direct line from the Indian Princess, Wahanee who married Thomas Bibee in 1760 in Goochland County, Virginia. Bibee was born on March the first day, 1734.

William Bibee of the above couple became the father of William Walker Bibee, born August the 10, 1837. He married Sophia Elizabeth Ogden in 1860. W. W. Bibee died on his birthday in 1898. The children of this couple were, Milton H. known as "MILT," W. Walter, known as "WALT," George P., Mary, James, known as "JIM," Marvin and Lena Bibee.

Milton Bibee married Luella Allen. They had six children. Ann Allen was the firstborn and gave me the information on this family.

Walter married Ellen Free, James married Teulon Ottinger and Lena married Lawson Madron.

Ann Bibee Mitchel (widow of Earl Mitchel) lives in Knoxville and takes much interest in all historical and patriotic organizations.

Another woman who married a Cocke County man is descended in direct line from the Iriquois Tribe. Her grandmother was a YOYO who married George Shaffer and bore him eighteen children. Nine of them born in Bellville, West Virginia. Mary Riel is the granddaughter of John Riel, originally, O'Riel, an officer in the Union Army and also a granddaughter of George Shaffer (known to us as Shaver) who was an officer in the Confederate Army. A heritage like unto the author's.

Mary Riel came to Cocke County in 1930 to wed one of our splendid young men, Earl Templin. All of her life she has been interested in children of delinquent parents and has cared for more than twenty-five such unfortunate boys and girls. Earl and Mary live in Akron, Ohio, where they have a business of their own. He is a brother of our townsman, Forest Templin. They are the sons of Richard Templin.

The Templin family came to our County while it was yet Jefferson. With them came the Webb, Licklighter, McAndrew, Gregory and several other families. They settled near the present Alfred Swann farms and their first place of worship was known as Pine's Chapel.

These families were English and Scotch people. The first Templin to arrive married a Webb. The first McAndrew (Joseph) married Susannah Lucretia Gregory, the daughter of George W. and Susannah Few Gregory. Their lands bordered the south bank of the French Broad River from "Old Town" to the Beaver Dams it is claimed by descendants of these families.

There are those now alive who claim the Baxter and Campbell families were with this group of arrivals in America and that the Baxters brought along a small trunk full of money which was then as now, guarded with great care. The little trunk was preserved through many generations of this family. Pride of ancestry is strongly marked in the Baxter family which proves they have had a splendid history.

Otha Baxter who has the Newport Motor Court and also an apple orchard on the Sevier County line remembers having heard of the "MONEY TRUNK" in the original family. His orchard of three thousand trees producing ten thousand bushels of Stark's varieties of apples should soon fill a money chest to say nothing of his motor court.

The heroic lives lived by our immediate ancestors in the East Tennessee Mountains have never been properly appreciated because no one ever took the time and trouble to relate the many interesting experiences through which they passed. Most of them lived and died, unknown, unhonored and unsung.

As we of this generation look back upon their bravery, their courage and industry we realize that they were indeed the BUILDERS OF AN EMPIRE and that they fought and bled and died for much bigger things than crowns. They fought for and won higher seats than thrones. They made this country what it has become because they had a vision and were seekers of the truth, "Ye shall know the truth and the truth shall make you free." They were seeking freedom to worship God as they chose. Each little church in the valley, and on the hilltop, with its spire pointing Heavenward should remind us, more than it does, of the lives of those who have gone on before us. Our ancestors dared the unchartered seas and somehow were able to make their own charts. Most of them had for a compass a great FAITH in GOD which enabled them to pass ever onward with courage. Each generation has carried on what was so nobly begun by those who had "marked the way," and blazed the trail. Each generation has added its own particular contribution, until now our horseless carriages with belted wheels, our winding trails of steel, our satin ribboned highways of glossy smoothness, our harnessed waterways, and our trackless airways have altogether shared in their contribution to our present civilization.

So young, though, are we in this country, that our very own homes stand upon the land our Dreaming Ancestors "ENTERED" when it was new and fertile. Many of those homes are still standing, precious reminders of the lives of those who lived in them. Many of our cherished possessions were fashioned by their hands. We are just beginning to realize and appreciate our priceless heritage.

Our today is what yesterday has made it and all admit that it is a wonderful day in which to live. Our tomorrow is going to be only what we of today make it. It is a wonderful thing to realize that we are the descendants of the trail blazers, the courageous FEW, who dared to do what seemed impossible but were willing to face danger, death and destruction, in this mountain wilderness of primitive beauty, that their posterity might have homes of peace and plenty, free from the dangers that were theirs and their own forefathers. Since the beginning, the dreamers have been earth's conquerers. "No vision and you perish, no ideal and you are lost. A heart must cherish some hope at any cost, some dream to cling to, a rainbow in the sky, some melody to sing to some service that is high," said the poet of old, and truly did he describe our pioneering ancestors of East Tennessee.

One of the finest traits of character the early settlers had in common was their desire and ability to establish permanent homes. They encouraged their children to do likewise because they knew that the future of this country depended upon the class of people who have permanent homes of their own.

Too many people these days are on wheels, roving over the country with no certain place to call home. The army of those who live in trailers and automobiles is growing larger from year to year. Towns and cities are filled with people who are constantly moving from one apartment to another to satisfy their wanderlust. It is becoming a rare thing in many localities to find people upon their own land to the second and third generation. Cocke County has many families representing the fifth generation still on the land.

People who are constantly on the move are never bulwarks of State or Nation. Generally they pay no taxes, seldom rear large families, nor support civic organizations of any kind, to say nothing of promoting churches and schools. Instead, they are evading every possible responsibility. It is an indication that our civilization is showing a tendency toward one of history's periodical declines which has always plunged the world in darkness retarding the race for a long period of time. To counteract this tendency, stories of those who settled this country to establish homes should be of interest and help encourage our people to remember the example set before them by their fathers. We must be made to see that we have our duties of citizenship in this wonderful country handed down to us by our earliest ancestors and preserved whole and One by our immediate grandparents.

As we of this day and time look back over the years we realize how rich our people were in many ways. They enjoyed sweet contentment of which the poets still sing. They owned their own homes and were free from debt and worry. They extracted their subsistence from their own soil which gave them a feeling of independence and security unknown to many of their descendants who must depend upon jobs with machinery. Wintertime brought rest and leisure which enabled them to cultivate their minds, or work with their hands. They owed nothing they could not pay. They had faith in God and each other. They were not too proud to work. They felt it a disgrace not to do so. They were smart enough to keep their desires and incomes together. They knew how to enjoy what they had. They knew how to be good neighbors and always willing to lend a helping hand in time of need or sorrow. They were steadfast as "Our Eternal Hills." They were not without gaiety and fun. They celebrated their holidays. They had various forms of amusement, clean and wholesome.

Their love of romance oft displayed itself in their tragic ballads, such as "Fair Ellen" and "Lord Thomas," and mournful "Barbara Allen" and others equally as "lonesome and pathetic." The age old songs our Hill Folks sang have at last identified us with Tudor England and Stuarts, a historical corroboration which proves that romance is ever deathless.

We of this particular mountain section of Tennessee have oft noticed how we have been held in derision, by sensational scribblers in magazines or over the radio. This is sufficient proof that such writers do not know the difference between highlanders, crackers and clay-eaters and common white trash, that even the slaves of the ante-bellum days frowned upon and were able to easily differentiate between them.

Our people of the East Tennessee Mountains are, as a rule, families who dwell together in peace and harmony, with ideals and dreams, with desires for advancement that would serve as excellent patterns, for those who are prone to make fun of them. Generally speaking, our Highlanders are now the Modern Puritans, compared with many of the people of other sections of our country, many of whom seem to think that we are all moonshiners, boot leggers, roughnecks, with horns, and otherwise uncouth and extremely ignorant.

Of course, as in all society, we admit that we have a few degenerate strains of idle, lazy, good-for-nothing, ne'er-do-wells, but as a rule, we have fewer of that class than other sections of the country. Our people as a whole do not approve child marriages, even though we once had one, wife-beaters and wife-plowers are the exception and not the rule. Other states have unfortunate occurrences the same as we have had.

Visitors from the cities and the vast open spaces are prone to wonder why we do not get out of these hills and mountains. Not only do they wonder, they often come right out boldly and ask us why we do not do so and frequently the disdain that shows their feeling of superiority amuses us. My answer to such a question has always been, "Because I have better sense than to leave the home and the faith of my fathers, besides, where would I go to find greater opportunities?" Those who have been so foolish as to leave the enchantment of our everlasting hills do not stay in peace and contentment in their new homes because the longing to return overcomes the hill-born. It has never been explained nor understood why this is true. To wander amid the hills in the dewy morn or at twilight is to feel their solitude, we are lost in flat countries. Our great altitude seems very essential to the welfare of our eagle hearts, and no one leaves but to return.

To these staunch and heroic characters, no monuments have been erected, no tablets inscribed, no poems sung, yet the women of Sparta never exhibited greater heroism and self sacrifice, nor the Caesars and Napoleons displayed more courage and bravery than our own mountaineers, who lived and moved and had their beings in the shadows of the Great Smoky Mountains of East Tennessee. When I think of them and the experiences through which they passed I long for the gift of eloquence that I might properly sing their praises. The times in which they lived were indeed trying years filled with adventure, dangers, hardships and privation—that those of us who have descended, to the present day have not experienced. But we have dangers and hardships of a different nature and it is yet to be seen if we are to solve our difficulties as well as those who went before us met their problems. They lived and died unknown, unhonored and unsung, but are no less deserving because there was no one to make known their various deeds of valor.

It is an established fact that the mountains of East Tennessee have filled the armies of the Republic in every War. It is said that they "turned the tide" of the Revolution when they marched to King's Mountain. They sent into the Union Army of the Civil War more men than any other Section of equal population. The first and second Congressional Districts of Tennessee alone gave more soldiers into the Union Army than any other state of equal population. These sturdy pioneers did not enter the services under the inspiration of martial music and flying colors. Instead, they had to find their way at night across rugged mountains, through hostile forces and many of them were killed before they reached their destination. Thousands of them became footsore, tired and hungry, scratched by briars and thorns as they traveled to join the army of their choice. Very few of them left slaves to care for and work for their families. In the fertile coves and valleys and on the steep mountainsides, their wives, daughters and mothers toiled early and late that they might wrench from the soil a meager subsistence for themselves and families, while their sons and husbands, brothers and sweethearts fought for the cause they thought to be just.

The very name, VOLUNTEER STATE, heralds to the world, the courage and undaunted faith of Tennesseans in times of need or in any great crisis. Tennessee's prompt and great response to the call of Country in time of War has never been surpassed and in all probability never been equalled by any other state. Our men have never waited to be drafted. They have been patriotic enough to VOLUNTEER. Hence the name VOLUNTEER State. This is perhaps due to the fact that in their veins flows the purest Anglo-Saxon blood that can anywhere be found. For sheer achievement, Tennesseans can always be depended upon to, "DO THEMSELVES PROUDLY." It is said that as the breed ran in 1806, a Tennessean could go anywhere, anytime, and do anything. It's therefore no matter for wonder that the fixed opinion a genuine native of the Volunteer State is, *that they have no superior, if indeed an equal.* Those who were born and bred in the mountain section of the State refuse to bow the knee to any man to this day. This feeling has been handed down probably from our proud old freedom loving Anglo-Saxon forefathers.

All who read know something of the lives of our outstanding heroes and heroines such as John Sevier, our first Governor, known as Nolichucky Jack and his first wife, Sarah Hawkins, second wife, Bonnie Kate Sherrill. The thrilling story of Davy Crockett and his many loves. His marriage license hangs in our Dandridge Court House. The greatest lover and love-story of the State is found in Andrew Jackson and his beloved Rachel, whom he wed twice and for whom he would fight at the drop of a hat and drop it himself. Our Greeneville Tailor, who became a President and our James K. Polk and wife whose wonderful home is still preserved, are examples of our thrifty citizenship. These and dozens of others have been heralded in song and story, but the simple folk of the mountain section have been little known and less understood. It is only in recent years that they have been appreciated and that our wild and rugged "Land of High Horizons," has become known to the outside world. Its mysticism and beauty attracts thousands monthly and as they learn our quaint mountain ways and customs and discover that to the Cherokees, whose ancestral home is our Great Smoky Mountains, every river bend, gray-green cliff, towering peak and winding trail had its own romantic significance. Every dashing stream and turbulent river where the shining trout gleamed, and every clear and placid pool in whose clear depths is exquisitely mirrored this gorgeous "Land O' the Sky," held for the Noble Cherokee, a legend of mystic beauty. Every ridge, cave and waterfall had its story handed down from generation to generation. The entire region that lies majestically above the clouds became to them the climax of sublimity, strength and inspiration. How could they feel otherwise in such primitive and rugged beauty as beheld in "THE LAND OF MISTY BLUE HILLS." In every direction one beholds the handiwork of the Master Artist. 'Tis here the yard length ferns grow in great profusion. 'Tis here the glossy beauty of the galax leaves oft carpet the earth "for miles around." Over the dead logs and on the great gray limestone rocks cling luxuriant moss of the softest texture, with marvelous colorings from green to gold. Dainty oxalis and fragrant juniper berries, with their spicy taste and brilliant color grow in great abundance.

The trailing arbutis with its fragrant pink-white blossoms also adorns the moss covered rocks and old decaying logs. In such places we also find the tiny, glossy, waxy white blossom of the evergreen pipsissewa. Its fragrance is unforgetable. A thousand or more other mountain flowers perfume the air with their sweetness and brighten the foilage of the landscape with their various rich colorings. The snowy beauty of the millions of dogwood trees in spring proclaim to the mountain folk that it is time to plant their Indian corn. The tender blush of the Judas tree here and there heralds the approach of springtime even before the dogwood begins to show its snowy blossoms. Each of these trees has had woven about it a scriptural legend. The Judas, or redbud, being thought of as the one on which Judas hanged himself when he betrayed his Lord, hence its name. The dogwood being the tree chosen from which the cross was fashioned because its wood was firm and strong. Ever afterwards these trees grew bent and twisted and unsuitable for either purpose for which they were said to have been used. Each spring the Judas tree bursts with blushing shame and the dogwood's bloom in the form of a cross, two long and two short petals. In the center of the outer edge of each petal are nailprints, brownish red with rust, while in the very center of the blossom is the crown of thorns.

Over all this mountain region of mystic beauty, floated then, as now, an indescribable silvery-blue veil of smoky mist. The breath of the Great Spirit that brooded and watched, with love over all and endowing them with a sense of security and peace as the evening twilight settled down upon this mountain perfection. Is it any wonder then that the Indian's God is nature? And that all that takes place in nature is but a manifestation of a Supreme Being's control of the universe. Is it any wonder that to such manifestations he prays and chants? Praying to the sun for heat, that he may not feel the cold, and that the snow may melt so that his flocks may have water and grass. It is easy to understand why the Indian beheld with awe the storms, floods, and the earthquakes because to him such indicated the anger of the Great Spirit. The spiritual life of the Cherokees was closely allied with the phenomena of nature. Probably his Pale-face Brother would be better off in many ways, if he too, walked with his head in the clouds and his feet in the shadows, and as he walked listened for and heard the silent voices all about him. If we did so and OBEYED, we too might become mystic and close to the earth and its fullness thereof. And incidentally we might know more of and understand better the spiritual forces all about us. The Indian's natural vision is so very much more enchanting than ours. He lets beauty fill his soul with color, line, and melody. He never forgets that from the tree comes much of his food and his bow and arrow, from the flint his arrowhead, from the beast of the mountain side, comes his sinewed string, his meat, and moccasins. He realizes that all his needs are supplied from the physical things about him, for which he constantly remembers to THANK the Great Spirit. At each DAWN he stands entranced, facing the East in perfect adoration, with his prayer in his heart and on his lips. Again at sunset he watches the day slip away with another prayer, as he stands with his face toward the West, silent, reverential, trustful, always ending his prayer with "All is well."

MY TENNESSEE

By FRANCES BURNETT SWANN

Page 47 in GARDEN PATHS

(*Permission granted by Mrs. Swann*)

To lift mine eyes unto the hills

So steadfast and serene;

To feel new strength and hope flow in

From every peaceful scene

For this I pray, day after day,

Away from Tennessee.

'Tis here at rest beneath the sod

My own beloved lie;

And there at last I'll lay me down

Under the same blue sky

My heart at rest, within thy breast,

Beloved Tennessee.

The day in 1937 the General Assembly and Governor of Tennessee gave to the Author the title . . . "LADY O'DELL" . . . *an honor never given to any other woman member of the Assembly.* Mrs. O'Dell served through seven sessions of the Legislature, *five of them a voting member and two of them a paid member.* She was elected TWICE to the *General Assembly, the only woman elected more than once. Three of the sessions she attended were Extraordinary Sessions* but *gave her the same experience she would have received in a regular session.* Her major legislation *was the enactment of Tennessee's Marriage Laws* WHICH SHE SPONSORED and EVENTUALLY PASSED after TREMENDOUS EFFORT and by the *help* of our *present Governor, Gordon W. Browning.*

Box 85
Edgemont Road
NEWPORT, TENNESSEE

APPENDIX

GRANT FROM THE STATE OF NORTH CAROLINA TO JOHN HUFF, 1788

State of North Carolina, Number 646

To All to Whom These Presents Shall Come Greeting:

Know ye that we for an in consideration of the sum of ten pounds for every hundred acres hereby granted, paid into our treasury, by John Huff, have given and granted, and by these presents do give and grant unto the said John Huff, a tract of land containing four hundred acres, lying and being in our County of Greene, lying on the North side of French Broad River; beginning at a stake, thence West, two hundred and nineteen poles, to a buckeye on the bank of said river; thence down the different meanders, three hundred and eighty poles to an elm on the bank of the river; thence East two hundred and nineteen poles, to a stake, thence South, fourteen degrees East, three hundred and forty-two poles to the beginning as by the plat hereunto annexed doth appear, togeth with all woods, waters, mines, minerals, hereditaments and appurtenances, to the said land belonging or appertaining.

To hold to the said John Huff, his heirs and assigns forever, yielding and paying to us such sums of money yearly or otherwise as our General Assembly from time to time may direct, provided always, that the said John Huff shall cause this GRANT to be registered in the Register's office of our said County of Greene within twelve months from the date hereof, otherwise, the same shall be void and of none effect.

In testimony whereof we have caused these our Letters to be made patent and our Great Seal to be hereunto affixed. Witness Samuel Johnson, Esquire, our Governor Captain General and Commander in Chief, at Fourfield the eleventh day of July in the thirteenth year of our Lord one thousand seven hundred and eighty-eight.

By his Excell'ys Com'd Samuel Johnson, W. Williams, D. Sec. State of Tennessee

Register's Office

Greene County

I, S. D. Thacker, Register of Deeds for the State and County aforesaid, do hereby certify that the foregoing is a true, correct and perfect copy of the Grant executed by the State of North Carolina to John Huff, under date of July 11, 1788, as the same appears of record in my office, in Book No. 3, page 35, at Greeneville, Tennessee.

Given under my hand, at office in Greeneville, Tennessee, this March 12, 1917.

S. D. Thacker . . . Register.

OUTLAW INDENTURE

THIS INDENTURE made this fifth day of June in the year of our Lord one thousand seven hundred and ninety nine between Alexander Outlaw, Attorney at Law of Jefferson County and State of Tennessee of the one part and William Garrett, Attorney at Law of the County of Cocke and State, aforesaid of the other part Witnesseth, That the said Alexander Outlaw for and in consideration of the sum of Four Hundred Dollars to him and in hand paid, the receipt whereof is hereby acknowledged, hath bargained and sold, and by these presents, doth, bargain, grant, sell, alien, cutoff, and confirm, unto the said William Garrett, his heirs and assigns, forever, all his right, title, property, interest, claim and demand of, in, and to a tract of parcel of Land, lying and being in the County of Cocke and State aforesaid, in the forks of French Broad and big Pigeon Rivers, it being part of the land the property of John Gilliland, deceased, and transferred by will to Priscilla Welch, alias Priscilla Gilliland, daughter, and one of the legal devisees of the said John Gilliland, deceased, and since transferred by Deed from the said Priscilla Welch, alias Priscilla Gilliland, to the said Alexander Outlaw, and supposed to contain One Hundred acres, be the same more or less, to be laid off and described in manner and form, as directed by the last Will and Testament of the said John Gilliland, deceased, which said tract, or parcel of Land, I do by these presents, sell, convey and confirm, unto the said William Garrett, his heirs and assigns forever, all my right, title, property interest, claim and demands, of, in and to the Estate of the said John Gilliland, deceased.

In witness whereof the said Alexander Outlaw hath hereunto set his hand and affixed his seal the day and year above written.

A. S. Outlaw (Seal)

Signed sealed and delivered in
the presence of us
Abe S. Outlaw
James Tremble
State of Tennessee,
Personally appeared before me Archibald Roane one of the Judges of the Supreme Court of Law and Quity the within named Alexander Outlaw, and acknowledged the within to be his act and Deed for the purposes therein contained and mentioned.

Given under my hand and seal this 29th day of September, 1799.

Archibald Roane   (Seal)

Let it be registered.

Archibald Roane   (Seal)

October 28th, 1799
Then was the within Deed Registered in my office in Ledger A Folio 224, by me.

R. W. Carson, Regr.

THE SANDUSKY* GRANT, Number 873

STATE OF TENNESSEE

All to whom these presents come GREETINGS:

In persuance of an Act of the General Assembly passed on the twentieth day of November, 1809, State of Tennessee, unto Emanuel Seduskey (Sandusky) of land containing 97 Acres and Roods (which means forty square poles) lying in the County of Cocke, in the District South of French Broad and Holston and Pigeon River.

There being due and chargeable on said land, $97.75, the interest due thereon. On river bank corner to Seduskey's and running with same South, 12½ West, 195 Poles to saplin, then East 79 Poles, to a small bush in a sink, with a line of a survey made for Isaac Leonard. North ten, East to a post oak, John Hood corner, then with his line, North 16 Poles to a chestnut 35 Poles to the beginning. (Much of the Grant is dim, but the above is what can be discerned.)
Wiley Blount signed as Governor. W. D. Blount, Secretary
Grant of Tennessee for Land in Cocke County.
(Courtesy of Sewanee Hedrick, daughter of J. P. and Theresa Henry Hedrick.)

CHARTERS, GRANTS, DEEDS, WILLS

The first Charter granted by an English Sovereign to an English Subject was by Queen Elizabeth to Sir Humphrey Gilbert to any lands he might discover in North America. Its date was around June the 11, 1578 and it was to be of perpetual efficacy, provided the plantation should be established within six years (Page 164, Goodspeed's HISTORY).

The Second Grant was by Queen Elizabeth to Sir Walter Raleigh and dated March 26, 1584. It was similar in provision to that granted Sir Humphrey Gilbert. Sir Walter Raleigh's patent included what is now TENNESSEE. And this grant was named "VIRGINIA" by the Virgin Queen herself.

*Emanuel Sedusky is listed as a Revolutionary Soldier in Mrs. Penelope J. Allen's Book on Revolutionary Soldiers. In Cocke County Regiments commissioned, he is listed as a member of a regiment of Cavalry, 2nd Brigade, July 13, 1807. (Cornet) and James Seduskey is also listed (Cornet) in Cavalry regiment, Hamilton District, December 22, 1798.

From page 65. . . . . One hundred years in the Cumberland Mountains, by Hogue and by his permission I copied the following interesting Grant from King Charles the first.

"In 1647, King Charles I. of England granted all the land lying between the 29th and 36, 30 parallels of latitude and between the "Southern Virginia Seas on the East and as far as The Southern Seas on the West" to Edward, Earl of Clarendon, George, Duke of Albemarle, William, Earl of Craven, John, Lord Berkley, Anthony, Lord Ashley, Sir George Carterett, Sir Colleton and Sir William Berkley.

Twenty one years later, in 1668, George, Anthony, William, Sir George Carterett, Sir John Colleton and Sir William Berkley conveyed the boundary to the Governor of the Territory. They reserved to themselves one half of all the gold and silver on the lands.

This Grant covered Tennessee to the parallel of 36, 30 which passes through our State almost at the Northern State line which means that our County and all that border it and the others across the state of the same latitude were included in this Grant. Most of the grants began, "By the grace of God, I, (King or Queen as the case demanded) of Great Britain, France and Ireland, Defender of the Faith" etc. etc.

The many North Carolina Grants (which meant Tennessee at that time) were oft recorded in Sullivan County and are now in land office, Nashville, Tenn.

Grant number 34 is to. . . . . John Sevier and Richard Carswell and includes the islands in the French Broad River that the "WAR PATH" leads through. November the first day 1786.

Grant number 43 in Book B is to William Ausley (or Ansley), Price Creek, in Greene County and includes both sides of the "WAR PATH." Nov. 1, 1786.

Grant number 266, Book B, To James Hubbard at the UPPER WAR FORD on Dumplin Creek Sept. 27, 1787.

Grant 487, to Thomas Stockton, includes the Indian Old Field on the French Broad River, opposite the mouth of Little Pigeon, Sept. 20, 1787. Richard Carswell Governor.

EXCERPTS FROM THE RANKIN AND PULLIAM JOURNAL

The first day of the Journal is Monday, May 15, 1837, and the first name recorded is that of Alexander E. Smith pr. Alexander, who bought ½ pound of salts for 12½c and one paper of pins for 12½c; second, Captain Allen Clevenger pr. Howard, 2 ounces indigo and madder at 20c each; third, William Robinson bought one pair of suspenders for 80c; Samuel Haskins sent by Stanberry for one skein of silk, 6c; William Huff (French Broad), indigo and madder, $1.25; Loyd B., one vial of Bateman's Drops, 13c.

On the next day, Lorenzo D. Porter bought one half pound of tobacco, 37½c per pound and two dressed buckskins for seating, $3 each. On May 17, Edom Kendrick. pr. L. D. Porter bought 1¼ yards of linsey and 2 skeins of cord silk, 88c. William Jack bought a pattern for pants of striped drill for $4, also 3 yards of white drill, 62c, and a spool of thread for 12c. Edom Kendrick, by Mrs. Story, ¾ yards of Irish linen and one bunch of tape, 63c; Joseph Youngblood, one pair of shoes, per. R. Justice, $1.38; Reuben Justice, a thimble, a pair of shoes, indigo and madder, shirting, a comb, 2 pounds of tobacco, $4.02; Joseph O'Neil, 2 oz. each of indigo and madder, 40c; Charles Inman, by Nancy Welch, 2½ yards of cambrick for 56c, ¼ yard of gingham, 37c and 2½ yards of edging at 12½c per yard; Mrs. Coleman, by Nancy, ¼ yard green silk, 1 yard pink silk, 2 skeins silk, 12c worth of wire, a total of $1.37; one beaded reticule per S. Huff's daughter, $2. The same page carries the name of Enoch Netherton pr. Mrs. Mantooth, 4 yards of calico, 31¼c per yard and 2 sealskin caps at $1. each; Malcomb McNabb, 1 pair saddlebags, $4, ¼ pound of powder, 2 pounds of sugar, and a coffee mill, all $2.46; John Gilliland, pr. Thomas Bryant, one pound of powder, 50c.

On Thursday, May 18, William Robinson bought a silk pocket handkerchief for $1.25; James Swaggerty, Jr., pr. lad (or lady) 10 yards pink gingham and 2 pairs cotton hose, $3.96, 1 yard calico 25c, 1 pair shell side combs, 75c and one sealskin cap, 87c; Stephen Huff, one beaded reticule, $2; Joseph Manning, one coffee mill, $2, one razor, $1, one knife, 87c, one tuck comb, 12¾c, two knives, $1.25.

On Friday May 19, William C. Roadman bought ¼ dozen saws for $2.38; Caleb Isenhour, one fine pocket knife, $1.25; Samuel Wilson, one white hat at $6 and one pair pumps at $1.50; Joseph Pagett pr. William Gilliland one ounce indigo, 3 red, 12, 58c; William DeWitt, 3½ yards bleach domestic, pr. daughter, 88c; Ezekiel Fox, pr. son, coffee, $1, tobacco, 37; William Wilson, one fine knife, per Alfred Cochran,

75c; George Rodgers, 2½ yards linen, 63c, patter for pants and trimmings casimere, $6; Lawson D. Franklin, 1 spool of thread, 8c; James McMahan, 3 yards brown jeans, $1, 2½ yards bleach domestic, 25c, and 1 pair shoes, $1.25.

On Saturday, May 20, Alexander E. Smith, cash, $1, 1 fine bonnet, $3.50, 7 yards calico at 42c and 2 yards of gingham at 37c, $3.09; 4 yards bleach shirting, $1, 1 pair yellow cotton hose, 75c, 3 yards shirting, $1.12, all came to $10.32; Lerments M. Bennett, one gunlock $1.50 and one box of caps, 25c.

On Monday, May 22, Abraham McCoy bought 3¼ yards stripe drill at 75c, $2.44, one fine knife at $1.25, one fine casimere vest and trimmings at $4.50, one vest and trimmings at $1, one cotton handkerchief, 25c; David O'Dell, balance on pants, 13c; John Allen of John, two weeding hoes, $1, coffee pot, 50c, 2 yards Vest ends, 25c, 1½ yards Rouen Casimere at 25c, 3 yards of shirting at 12c, 1 dozen buttons at 6¼; 1 yard calico at 37c, 1 vest pattern, at $1.25, 1 yard lining, 21c, total of $4.65; John Harrison of Reuben, 2½ yards calico and 1 yard of calico, 67½, 1/2 yard cambrick at 37c, 1½ yards lace at 12c, sugar 50c, lead 6¼c, 1 comb 25c and 1 pair gum elastic garters 25c; James Allen, son of John, three kinds of calico, two kinds of combs, 4 tin cups, 1 yard Bobinett, 3 yards lace, 1 pasteboard, 1 fine hat $5 and 1 umbrella $1.25, sugar and coffee $2. He had 8 pounds of feathers which gave him a credit of $2.67 on the same bill. The remainder of the bill for $22.69 is by James Allen, son of Hiram, 3 yards casimere at $1.25, 1 skein of silk and 1½ yards of ribbon which came to 38c, 1 vest and trimmings $1.62, coffee and sugar ($1.83), 1 knife 50c, 7 yards calico and one box hooks and eyes, $2.93.

On May 23, 1837, Alexander E. Smith, pr. daughter, ½ yard pink check gingham, 19c; William DeWitt, pr. daughter, 1¼ yards apron check, 31c; Joseph Hickey, 6 yards brown domestic 22c, $1.35; 3 yards brown linen at 25c and ½ pound pepper at 25c, 88c, 1 cotton handkerchief 25c, 1 blunch leading lines 13c.

On Wednesday, May 24, Thomas Gorman purchased $34.10 worth of goods: 1 pair stirrup irons $1.50, 1 slate 50c, paper 37½c and ½ pound of lead, 44c, 3¼ yards blue cloth and trimmings, $30, ¼ yard more of same blue cloth for vest $2.25.

On Thursday, May 25, 1837, William Morris bought 1 spike gimblet 19c, 1 white wool hat at $1.25, 3 yards of shirting at 25c, $2, 6½ yards casimere at 25c, 4 yards calico at 25c, all $2.63, ribbon and blind bridle, $1.44.

On Friday, May 26, Richard DeWitt bought one pair of small boots for $3.50 and two pairs of small shoes at 87c per pair; Captain John Davis, indigo and madder, $2.50, powder and brimstone 42c, one hammer 38c.

On Monday, May 29, Alexander E. Smith bought one shell comb for $4; Rachel O'Dell, one dollars worth of calico; Daniel McSween, 6 yards of domestic and 1 yard Irish linen for $1.12, a vest pattern for $2.50, ½ dozen pearl buttons 25c, 1 skein silk and 1 punch of tape with 1½ yards lining for 31c. On May 30, Major Anderson McMahan bought a pair of shoes for $1.87 and one wagon whip for $1.

On May 31, Holcomb Lovell bought 7 yards of calico and flints, $2.69; Alexander E. Smith, per your mother, different kinds of cloth, a yellow bandanna for $1.25, and 1 nutmeg per Sarah, total of $16.49; John F. Stanberry, a pocketbook, 50c Bartlett Sisk, ounce indigo for 40c. The next day John F. Stanberry bought himself a pair of Morocco boots for $4.75; Lorenzo D. Porter, a bottle of black varnish for 38c.

On June 10, Murdoch McSween purchased a Rogers hat per William for $5; on June 13, Thomas Mooneyham, a pair of shoes per the stage driver; on June 14, Andrew Ramsey, per lady, purchased $25.65 worth of supplies and she paid 38c on the bill: William Morrell per grandson, a vial of castor oil for 13c.

On July 3, 1837, Thomas D. Arnold bought one yard of ribbon for 17c; July 4, Mrs. Neff, mother of Isaac, 1 handkerchief, 1 marion dress, $3.42, 1 yard lining and 3 yards calico, 81½c, 4 yards calico and 7 yards domestic, $2.75; 7 yards calico at 25c and pepper 26½c, $2.07½; Malcomb McNabb and George McNabb each bought a Rogers hat $5; George W. Kelly, brother of Jonathan, a pocket knife 87½. On July 8, John Wood (Red Head), Green Inman, Samuel Ogden, Pleasant Loyd made purchases, along with many others.

On July 11, William Huff, per lady, made a bill of $57.23 and Samuel Lotspeich, per daughter, bought 2 yards ribbon at 30c per yard. William Wilson, the Major, generally sent one of his forty slaves to purchase for him, Alfred more than the others; Thomas I, or "J" Henderson came often and also William Ellison and Henry Runnyon; on July 17, Sevier McMahan bought a round-a-bout for $1.50. The next day, William Hale decided he wanted one too.

On July 22, John Stanberry purchased a padlock for 13c and on July 24, 13c worth of nails. On July 24, Robert Bell bought himself a pair of "red flannels" which took three yards of cloth and cost $1.13; July 27, Allen Hightower, a pair of cotton cards for 88c; July 29, Joseph Youngblood bought a pair of shoes for $1.75; July 31, Thomas Burnett purchased brown linen and nails, $6.10; John Stokely, a small oven and lid, also a pot for $2.25, 6 pounds of sugar, 11 yards shirting, both amounting to $2, and six cents worth of camphor.

On March 6, 1838, Dr. John M. Burnett bought a pair of ready-made pants for $10, also a fine razor strap, for $1.25. John Lewis (Buncombe), Robert Dennis, James C. Holland, Abraham, John and James Allen, William Cureton and Permento M. Bennett were also in the store at this time.

On April 2, 1838, Jeremiah McKay bought a whip for $1.12. On April 7, Mrs. Elizabeth Burnett bought 2 bales cotton at $2.25 each, indigo and madder $1, 1 pair shoes $1.75, 10 yards fine bleach sheeting, a total of $10.59; James M. Burnett, bottle of snuff, 37c; Mrs. Frances Burnett, one fine bonnet and ½ yard of lining, $6.25.

On Friday, April 13, Mrs. McNabb (of George) bought two remnants of calico for $1.75, 2¼ yards of check at 25c each, three pasteboards at 75c, one yard of cambrick and twenty yards of domestic. On April 16, James Burke bought a hat for $5 and Royal Stokely 2 bales of spun cotton for $4. On Saturday, May 7, 1838, William and Richard DeWitt came to the store. Also Jacob Shults, Esq., purchased a bill of $12.91½. He gave the merchants $5 in cash and 118½ pounds of feathers, which gave him a credit of $6.18½. On May 12, Jeremiah McKay, Isaiah Butler and Abraham McKay visited the store and Abraham bought 100 fish hooks for 50c. June 5, Charles Morrell bought castor oil, 50c paregoric 12c and 1 gross paper 25c and a paper of pins for 6c. June 11, Thomas Mantooth, Esq., bought 30¾ yards domestic at 12c, $3.84.

On June 21, Anthony Christian bought a cradling scythe for $2. June 23, William Kelly, Esquire, purchased coffee and cotton for $1; Mark Brooks, a thimble for six cents and Matthew Brooks by David, powder and lead, 33½c, a dozen needles and a dozen fishhooks; Levi Boyer of Jonathan, a silk handkerchief, 75c; Allen Clevenger, a cradling scythe for $1.75; on July 21, Allen Hightower bought a hat for Philip Jefferson for $3; August 4, Captain Joseph Young purchased a girth for 25c, one pair of shoes for $1.50, and 25c worth of tobacco.

On August 6, William Webb, paid balance on spun cotton, $1.75; August 8, Joseph Williams, Esq., one patent axe, $2.50; David Harned, one wool hat for James H. Davis, $1; August 9, 1838, Captain James H. Davis, one calico dress, $2.50; Dr. George Porter, one bottle castor oil, 62½c, I vial laudanum 12½c; Lewis Boyer, ½ pound pepper 25c and ½ pound copperas 9c. On August 11, 1838, Thomas A. R. Nelson (a Jonesboro lawyer) purchased a pair of suspenders for 50c; Eli Hollinsworth, one dozen coffin screws for 18c; Colonel Peter Davis, 2½ ounces indigo; Samuel and Davis McSween each purchased 15 1/3 yards of shirting, $2.86 for each gentleman; Colonel Gray Garrett, a silver pencil for $1.50 and part of a bottle of snuff for 25c; R. J. McKinney bought himself a vest pattern for $2.45, also a silk handkerchief for $1; Dr. J. F. H. Porter paid four dollars on his account.

On August 13, Jephtha Wood bought a pair of shoes and socks for $1.87½; Stephen Caton, 1 bale spun cotton $2; 3½ yards cotton cloth $2.62½. On October 16, 1838, cash paid first investment Charleston and Cincinnati Railroad for 10 shares bank stock, $125; Doctor N. Jarnigan also visited store. Lewis Boyer bought leather often. George Easterly and George Parrott bought large bills from the firm. William King and Company must have been a firm near by as their name appears occasionally. Sally and Lucinda Gooch brought feathers to the store. On December 3, Richard Cureton bought a cotton handkerchief and William Cureton purchased four skeins of silk.

OUR SOLDIERS OF ALL WARS

It is not possible to secure the names of all the soldiers of this county who have enlisted in the armies of the different wars. The author hopes that her effort will serve as an incentive toward a more complete roll of those who have volunteered their services when their country called.

REVOLUTIONARY WAR SOLDIERS WHO OBTAINED PENSIONS* IN COCKE COUNTY, TENNESSEE

William Boydston, private, annual allowance $46.66. Received $116.65; in Virginia militia; enrolled as a pensioner June 13, 1833, age 81 years.

---

*Compiled by Selden Nelson, published in *Knoxville News-Sentinel*, June, 1910.

William Bragg, pt., annual allowance $20.00, received $60.00, in Virginia militia, enrolled as a pensioner, Oct. 18, 1833, age 69 years.

Joseph Burk, pt., annual allowance $20.00, received $60.00, in North Carolina militia, enrolled as a pensioner, June 18, 1834, age 72 years.

Thomas Bibee, private, annual allowance $56.66. received_____in Virginia line of service March 31, 1834, age 100 years.

William Coleman, private, annual allowance, $20.00, received $60.00, in North Carolina line of service, enrolled December 20, 1833, age 72 years.

John Campbell, private, annual allowance $21.55, received $46.65, in Virginia line of service, enrolled as a pensioner December 8, 1833, age 69 years.

William Davis, 2d, private, annual allowance, $60.00, received $180.00, in the Virginia militia, enrolled as a pensioner, August 26, 1833, age 72 years.

John Fogat, private, annual allowance $23.33, received $69.99, in Virginia line of service, enrolled as a pensioner, June 13, 1833, age 71 years.

John Henry, private, annual allowance $36.66, received $109.00, in Virginia line of service, enrolled as a pensioner October 18, 1833, age 81 years.

William Lofty, private, annual allowance $20.00, received $60.00, in North Carolina line of service, enrolled as a pensioner, May 16, 1834, age 72 years.

James Milliken, private, annual allowance, $81.66, received $244.98, in South Carolina line of service, enrolled as a pensioner, June 8, 1834, age 89 years.

Samuel Martin, private, annual allowance, $81.66, received $244.98, in South Carolina line of service, enrolled as a pensioner, June 8, 1934, age 89 years.

Thomas Palmer, private, annual allowance $40.00, received $140, in Virginia militia, enrolled as a pensioner, August 3, 1833, age 73 years.

James Potter, private, annual allowance $40.00, received $100, in Virginia state troops, enrolled as a pensioner, December 20, 1833, age 75 years.

Lewis Sawyer, private, annual allowance $40.00, received $100, in North Carolina militia, enrolled as a pensioner, August 16, 1833, age 87 years.

William Smallwood, private, annual allowance, $20.00, in Pennsylvania line of service, enrolled as pensioner, June 7, 1833, age 74 years.

Allen Sarrett, private, annual allowance $40.00, received $120, in South Carolina line of service, enrolled as a pensioner June 13, 1833, age 71 years.

Barlett Sisk, private, annual allowance $30.00, received $90, in North Carolina line of service, enrolled as a pensioner, September 18, 1833, age 75 years.

Peter Wise, private, annual allowance $30.00, received $90.00, in Pennsylvania line of service, enrolled as a pensioner, April 18, 1833, age 81 years.

Samuel Yates, private, annual allowance $30.00, received $90, in Pennsylvania line of service, enrolled as a pensioner, August 20, 1833, age 77 years.

According to Judge Williams, the following Revolutionary soldiers (with ages) were living in Cocke County in 1840: William Bragg, 75; Peter Wise, 89; Darius O'Neil, 76; Bartlett Sisk, 79; Samuel Yeats, 85; Joseph Burke, 75; Henry Click (son), 59; Allen Saratt, 77.

Virginia Revolutionary soldiers who removed to Cocke County: William Boydston, William Bragg (son), William Davis, Thomas Palmer.

Another list gives Pleasant Bibee, enlisted 1788, in Capt. Kendall's Co., 60 years, in 1818, Virginia regiment.

Record of Commissions of Officers in the Tenn. Militia 1813. Compiled by Mrs. John Trotwood Moore, March, 1949. Tenn. Historical Journal.

Derrett, John H., Lt. Reg. of Cavalry 8th Regiment, Feb. 11, 1813.

Fine, L., Capt., 8th Reg., Feb. 11, 1813.

Goan, Shadrick, Lt. 8th Reg., Feb. 11, 1813.

Hill, Jesse, Lt. 8th Reg., Aug. 31, 1813.

Irwin, Joseph, Junr., Capt. 8th Reg., Aug. 31, 1813.

Jack, Samuel, Capt. 8th Reg., Aug. 31, 1813.

Jackson, Robt., Capt. 8th Reg. Feb. 11, 1813.

McMillan, Capt. 8th Reg., Aug. 31, 1813.

Nave, Henry, Ensign 8th Reg., Aug. 31, 1813.

Nelson, John, Lt. 8th Reg., Nov. 8, 1813.

Sisk, Elias, Ensign 8th Reg., Aug. 31, 1813.

White, John, Cornet Reg. of Cavalry, 8th Reg., Feb. 11, 1813.

White, Wm., Capt. Reg. of Cavalry, 8th Reg., Feb. 11, 1813.

Record of Commissions of Officers in the Tenn. Militia, 1812. Mrs. John Trotwood Moore, March, 1948.

Dunn, Wm., Ensign 8th Reg., July 24, 1812.

Easterly, Jacob, Ensign 8th Reg. July 24, 1812.
Gilliland, Wm., Lt. 8th Reg., July 24, 1812.
Irvin, Joseph, Ensign 8th Reg. July 24, 1812.
Jackson, John, Lt. 8th Reg. July 24, 1812.
Jackson, Robt., Capt. 8th Reg., Oct. 8, 1812.
Maughan, James, Capt. 8th Reg., July 24, 1812.

The record in Second Commission Book, Page 219, mentions most of the above as being commissioned only during good behavior.

James Boydston is named as a Tennessee Revolutionary soldier. He was an older brother of Wm. Boydston. He seemingly was one of two Boydstons who were in the Battle of Mt. Pleasant on the Ohio, Oct. 10, 1774. James later moved from what became Cocke Co. to Rutherford Co., N. C. where he had a grant of land, 1790.

Thomas Boydston married Elizabeth Newport. (Sufficient proof of Newport family living here in the early days as history claims.)

Samuel Boydston is twice listed as Revo. soldier, son of James, frequently the James Boydston is on tax list of Greene Co. in 1783. Greene then a part of Cocke County.

COCKE COUNTY REGIMENTS OF MILITIA COMMISSIONED OFFICERS* (1788-1801)

Adams, Williams	Captain	April 12, 1798
Allen, Isaac	Captain	June 16, 1800
Allen, Reuben	Lieutenant	April 5, 1798
Bragg, William	Ensign	December 11, 1798
Campbell, William	Captain	December 11, 1798
Clark, Thomas	Lieutenant	April 5, 1798
Clevengher, Richard	Ensign	April 12, 1798
Cooper, Joel	Lieutenant	April 5, 1798
Croslin, Samuel	Ensign	December 11, 1798
Denton, John	Captain	December 11, 1798
Fine, Ledgerd	Lieutenant in cavalry regiment, Hamilton District	December 22, 1798
Fine, Peter	1st Major	January 11, 1798
Harle, Baldwin	1st Major in cavalry regiment, Hamilton District, vice Charles McClung, resigned	October 10, 1800
Henry, George	Ensign	April 5, 1798
Holland, Thomas	Captain	April 3, 1800
Hutchans, Smith	Captain	April 5, 1798
Inman, Daniel	Lieutenant	December 3, 1798
Inman, John	Captain	December 11, 1798
Jones, Thomas	Captain in cavalry regiment, Hamilton District	December 22, 1798
Jack, William	Captain	July 8, 1800
Lammons, Samuel	Captain	April 3, 1800
Lillard, James	2nd Major	January 18, 1798
Lillard, John	Captain	April 5, 1798
Lillard, William	Lieutenant-Colonel Commandant	January 18, 1798

REGIMENTS—PAGE 392

McGlolen, John	Captain	April 5, 1798
McMullin, Samuel	Captain	April 5, 1798
McPherson, Henry	Ensign	April 5, 1798
McPherson, Joseph	Ensign	April 3, 1798
Matthews, Obadiah	Lieutenant	December 11, 1798
Maybary, Frederick	Lieutenant	April 5, 1798
Mitchell, Nathaniel	Lieutenant	April 3, 1798
Neely, William Washington	Lieutenant	June 16, 1800
Ogdon, John	Lieutenant	April 5, 1798
Rector, John	Captain	April 5, 1798
Scott, William	Ensign	April 5, 1798
Seduskey, James	Cornet in cavalry regiment, Hamilton District	December 22, 1798
Snelson, James	Lieutenant	July 8, 1800

Snodgrass, James	Ensign	July 8, 1800
Stinnet, William	Ensign	June 16, 1800
Styers, Henry	Ensign	April 5, 1798
Williams, Thomas	Lieutenant	June 16, 1800
Yoacham, Solomon	Lieutenant	April 12, 1798

*Compiled by Mrs. John Trotwood Moore, in *Tennessee Historical Quarterly* March, 1942

COCKE COUNTY REGIMENTS OF OFFICERS IN THE TENNESSEE MILITIA, 1808*

Barnett, William	Ensign Volunteer Rifle Company 8th regiment	September 28, 1808
Drenon, Robert	Lieutenant 8th regiment	September 28, 1808
Guinn, Bartholomew	Captain 8th regiment	September 28, 1808
Jennings, Thomas	Ensign 8th regiment	September 28, 1808
Jones, William D.	Lieutenant Volunteer Rifle Company 8th regiment	September 28, 1808
Lamb, John	Captain 8th regiment	September 28, 1808
McClennehan, Joshua	Lieutenant 8th regiment	October 5, 1808
Mitchell, Thomas	Captain Volunteer Rifle Company 8th regiment	September 28, 1808
Neel, David	Ensign 8th regiment	October 5, 1808
Odell, Nehemiah	Ensign 8th regiment	September 28, 1808
Penell (Perrel), George	Ensign 8th regiment	September 28, 1808
Sutton, Joseph	Captain 8th regiment	September 28, 1808

*Compiled by Mrs. John Trotwood Moore, in *Tennessee Historical Quarterly*, March, 1944

COCKE COUNTY REGIMENTS OF OFFICERS IN THE TENNESSEE MILITIA, 1809*

Bigham, Josiah	Ensign 8th regiment	October 2, 1809
Campbell, David	Captain 8th regiment	October 2, 1809
Ginnings, James	Ensign 8th regiment	October 2, 1809
Ginnings, Thomas	Lieutenant 8th regiment	October 2, 1809
Jones, Branch	Captain 8th regiment	February 11, 1809
Kenny, Thomas	Captain 8th regiment	October 2, 1809
Lillard, John, Junr.	Lieutenant 8th regiment	October 2, 1809
McPherson, Bartlett	Lieutenant Volunteer Rifle Company 8th regiment	March 28, 1809
Mcrary, Benjamin	Ensign 8th regiment	October 2, 1809
Smith, Elias	Ensign 8th regiment	February 11, 1809
Solomon, James	Lieutenant 8th regiment	February 11, 1809

*Compiled by Mrs. John Trotwood Moore, in *Tennessee Historical Quarterly*, September, 1944

COCKE COUNTY REGIMENTS OF OFFICERS IN THE TENNESSEE MILITIA, 1809, 1810*

Hern, Stephen B. W.	Ensign Rifle Company 8th regiment	August 29, 1810
Matthews, John	Cornet regiment of cavalry 2nd brigade	October 15, 1810
Rector, Presly	Lieutenant Volunteer Rifle Company 8th regiment	February 20, 1810
Smith, Alexander	First Major 8th regiment	May 1810
Snodgrass, James	Lieutenant regiment of cavalry 2nd brigade	March 14, 1810

*Compiled by Mrs. John Trotwood Moore, in *Tennessee Historical Quarterly*, September, 1945

COCKE COUNTY REGIMENT*

Allen, James	Captain 8th regiment	April 9, 1811
Allen, James	Lieutenant 8th regiment	October 4, 1811
Campbell, Russell	Lieutenant Light Infantry Company 8th regiment	April 9, 1811
Coleman, Benjamin	Ensign 8th regiment	April 9, 1811
Cunningham, David	Captain 8th regiment	February 5, 1811
Fugan, Evan	Lieutenant 8th regiment	October 4, 1811
Grant, Richard	Lieutenant 8th regiment	February 5, 1811
Goodsey, Burley	Ensign 8th regiment	October 4, 1811
Gregg, John	Ensign 8th regiment	October 4, 1811
Gregg, Samuel	Captain 8th regiment	February 5, 1811
Hutson, John	Ensign 8th regiment	October 4, 1811
Jackson, Robert	Lieutenant in Volunteer Rifle Company 8th regiment	April 9, 1811
Jennings, James	Lieutenant 8th regiment	April 9, 1811
Jennings, Williams	Ensign 8th regiment	April 9, 1811
Jones, Daniel	Ensign 8th regiment	October 16, 1811
Lillard, James	Captain Light Infantry Company 8th regiment	April 9, 1811
Marberry, Leonard	Ensign 8th regiment	February 5, 1811
Marberry, Leonard	Captain 8th regiment	October 4, 1811
Milligan, Alexander	Lieutenant 8th regiment	February 5, 1811
Moon, William	Lieutenant 8th regiment	April 9, 1811
Morgan, Evan	Ensign 8th regiment	October 4, 1811
Ode, Nehemiah	Ensign 8th regiment	May 8, 1811
Potter, William	Ensign 8th regiment	February 5, 1811
Potter, Wilson	Lieutenant 8th regiment	October 4, 1811
Strain, James	Lieutenant 8th regiment	February 5, 1811
Ward, David	Captain 8th regiment	April 9, 1811

*Compiled by Mrs. John Trotwood Moore, in *Tennessee Historical Quarterly*, March, 1946

COCKE COUNTY COMMISSIONS

Derrett, John H.	Lieutenant 8th regiment of cavalry	February 11, 1813
Fine, L.	Captain 8th regiment	February 11, 1813
Goan, Shadrick	Lieutenant 8th regiment	February 11, 1813
Hill, Jesse	Lieutenant 8th regiment	August 31, 1813
Irwin, Joseph Junr.	Captain 8th regiment	August 31, 1813
Jack, Samuel	Captain 8th regiment	August 31, 1813
Jackson, Robert	Captain 8th regiment	February 11, 1818
McMillan, Daniel	Captain 8th regiment	August 31, 1813
Nave, Henry	Ensign 8th regiment	August 31, 1813
Nelson, John	Lieutenant 8th regiment	November 8, 1813
Sisk, Elias	Ensign 8th regiment	August 31, 1813
White, John	Cornet regiment of cavalry 8th regiment	February 11, 1813
White, William	Captain regiment of cavalry 8th regiment	February 11, 1813

Compiled by Mrs. John Trotwood Moore, March, 1949.

WAR OF 1812

In 1811-12, as the wars with Great Britain and the Creek Indians approached, the status of Cocke County in the structure of the Tennessee Militia was:

In the First Division under the command of Major General John Cocke of Grainger County.

In the Second Brigade under Brigadier General George Doherty of Jefferson County.

Cocke County's Regiment was the Eighth and was commanded by Colonel William Lillard.

CONFEDERATE SOLDIERS FROM COCKE COUNTY

Since the author has found it impossible to gather a complete list of these men, she has thought it best to use the lists of each contributor as given, although there seems to be duplications.

FROM W. O. MIMS' SCRAPBOOK

Company "F" Fifth Regiment,
Tennessee Cavalry, C. S. A.,
Organized November 22, 1861
Commissioned Officers of First
Organization

Thomas Gorman, Captain, wounded and retired.

McKinney McMahan, First Lieutenant, retired . . . over age.

John Baker, Second Lieut., retired . . . over age.

A. Lemuel Mims . . . Third Lieut.

Re-Organization of Confederate Army

A. L. Mims, Captain
G. W. Harper, First Lieut.
R. A. McNabb, Second Lieut.
A. R. DeWitt, Third Lieut.

Non-Commissioned Officers

William Bryant, First Sergt.
F. G. Lewis, Second Sergt.
James Fox, Third Sergt.
B. W. D. Gorrell, Fourth Sergt.
B. F. Hopkins, Fifth Sergt.
George Evans, First Corporal
W. N. Penland, Second Corporal
T. W. Davis, Third Corporal
John Allen, Fourth Corporal
Garland Harper, Bugler
Albert Duncan, Assistant Bugler
Joel Lewis, Farrier (one who shoes horses, a veterinary surgeon) C. S. Jones, blacksmith

Privates

Wilson Allen
A. W. Andes
Daniel Bassett
W. N. Bassett
James B. Black
John Boling
George Brooks
W. N. Burke
George W. Carter
Jesse Clanton
John Clevenger
G. W. Clark
W. F. Coley
Robert Cogdill
Grantham Davis
Zebalon Davis
John A. Denton
William Denton, Jr.
James P. Duncan
Joseph Edwards
A. W. Evans
William Fine
A. J. Fox
Isaac Fox
Perryan Giles

George Gorrell
William Gorrell
Tillman Gray
Samuel Hance
John W. Hall
John Harper
Mark Harper
T. D. A. Harper
William Harper
John S. Headrick
James Henry
Marshal Henry
Baxter Hopkins
Jacob Hopkins
Jasper Hopkins
L. A. Hopkins
Stephen Huff
Robert Huff
Wiley Jones
Thomas W. Leatherhood
Rufus Lewis
John Lewis
J. N. B. Leoins
George Mathes
Jonas Mathes
Samuel Gann
Nathaniel Giles
Malcolm McMahan
Sanders McMahan
James W. McMurry
D. L. Porter
Gilbert Raines
Hiram Raines
Isaac Raines
James Raines
John Raines
Joel Raines, Jr.
Joel Raines, Sr.
Thomas Raines
Bethual Samples
James Samples
Ezekiel Scroggins, (retired)
John F. Seahorn
Addison Sisk
William Sisk
J. R. Smith
N. A. Smith
James Stafford
David Stokely, Jr.
Samuel Tinker
James Warren
W. T. Weaver
Eli Whitson
James Whitson
Stephen Whitson
Grit McMahan
R. A. McMahan
William Whitson
G. W. Williams
Joel Williams
John Williams
William Wilson
Jefferson Woody
Toliver Woods

As rapidly as companies were organized they were "Lettered." The above company was given the letter "F" and assigned to the 5th Tennessee Cavalry, Colonel G. W. McKenzie, commanding. Said Regiment was assigned to Colonel Ashby's Brigade, Wharton's Division, General Joseph Wheeler's corps, "Army of Tennessee" General Joseph F. Johnston commanding and surrendered at Charlotte, North Carolina, May 3, 1865, at which time Capt. A. L. Mims was acting as Major of said Regiment, and R. A. McNabb, commanding said Company "F."

Their pay roll was made at Funnel Hill, Georgia, April 30, 1864. Companies D. G. and H. constituted the 3rd squadron, R. A. McNabb, 2nd Lt., commanding Co. F and also 3rd squadron.

Colonel Thomas Weaver, father of Mrs. Mildred Weaver Burnett (Mrs. Joe J.) had in his Regiment one hundred men from Cocke County. He was of Hood's Division, and Lt. Colonel in command at Chicamauga.

GOODSPEED

Soldiers in Company "C," 26th Infantry from Cocke County Edward Allen, Capt. A. C. Hickey, First Lt. J. W. McNabb and A. H. Swaggerty, Second Lts. Company E 5th Tennessee Cavalry of Hancock County lists Thomas S. Gorman, Captain. Company F, A. L. Mims, Captain.

COMPILED BY J. W. D. STOKELY

Some of these were members of Capt. Edwin Allen's Company, others Maj. James T. Huff's Company, while a few others given at random and from memory.

Edwin Allen, Captain, J. S. Allen, Joseph Ables, Vanny Bolch, Stephen Brooks, David Brooks, Royal Brooks, Nathan Brooks, Tom Brooks, Luke Brooks, Burrell Brooks, Allen Brooks, Wright Brooks, Jefferson Burnett, James P. Burnett, Rev. J. M. L. Burnett, David Boyer, Brummit Bryant, George Brotherton, Austin Branch, John Davis, Arthur Davis, R. Ellis, Jr., Tilman Faubion, Jack Fox, Jesse Fox, Calvin Fox, Ezekiel Fox, Vinson Fine, William Franks, Samuel Jack, Alvin Jack, R. M. Jones, William Jones, M. M. Jones, R. A. Justus, William Kendrick, Jack Lewis, John Messer, D. A. Mims, Mose Mims, Geneix Mims, Andy Miller, Fowler Morris, James Morris, Thomas Moore, Joseph Morrell, James Owen, L. D. Penland, James Roberts, William Robinson, Lt. James Robinson, Mar. W. R. Smith, Melvin Smith, Alexander Smith, D. S. Sorrells, Ira Sisk, Samuel Stansberry, Charles Stokely, Sr., Charles Stokely, Jr., Royal Stokely, Joseph Stokely, William R. Stokely, Jr., Elisha Stokely, William Strange, George Stuart, James Stuart, George Suson, W. R. Swaggerty, David Templin, Burwell Thomas, George I. Thomas, A. S. Winneford, Seehorn Allen, Jacob Thomas, John McNabb, Joe Brown, S. J. Campbell.

Grundy Lewis Scouts   Joseph Morrell and Seehorn Allen Jenkins Scouts.

Big Texas and Little Texas (probably the Texas Rangers).

George Netherton who died in prison.

James McMahan, Ephraim Cate, James Wood, Robert Rollins, George Cate, Thomas Cate, Howard Clarke, W. W. Blanchard, John H. Stokely, M. M. Jones, Henry Fox, Jacob Henderson, Joseph Costner (Joseph Wilson), James Hannah, Will Whitson.

Muster Roll of Company "I" of the Second Tennessee Cavalry of Volunteers Lt. Colonel W. F. Prosser, George W. Hutsell, Major. These were Union soldiers.

Captain of Company "I" George W. Gorman, appointed by Governor of Tenn.

First Lieut. Company "I" George W. Webb, appointed by Governor of Tenn.

Second Lieut. Company "I" Andrew J. Webb, appointed by Governor of Tenn.

First Sgts.: John Gorman, Elliot S. Newcomb, William R. McCarter, William E. Mason, Anderson H. Rainwater, Nathaniel A. Harrison, James Harrison.

Corporals: William T. Buchanan, Crocket Newcomb, William M. Moon, John Ball, Madison H. Smallwood, James H. Rinehard, William Reneau.

Bevrage Branum, the wagoner; William Vollentine, the saddler; Henry Vollentine the blacksmith (one roll gives him as brigade wagoner).

Privates: James Branum, Benjamin Benson, William Branum, Lewis Breeden, Marcel Breeden, Matthew Breeden, Alfred Ball, Morgan Ball, James R. Ball, William R. Burchfield, Jesse Case, James Clabber, John Denton, Wilson D. Fox, John Fox, Carroll Fox, Allen Gann, James Gorman, Pleasant Hurst, William Hurst, Andrew Hurst, Emanuel Hurst, Isaiah Hurst, Tilman Hurst, Russell Harrison, William B. Harrison, Arthur James, William James, Rufus Jones, Fowler Jenkins, Abraham Jenkins, Duggan Jenkins, Adam Keeler, Abraham Keener, Isaac King, Perry Loveday, Redman Mapels, Samuel Mapels, Wilson Mapels, James Mapels, Samuel McGaha, John McCoig, James Miller, Claiborne Miller, Rufus Patterson, Jeremiah Phillips,

John Rinehard, John Rainwater, George W. Shellton, Samuel Shrader, James M. Teague, William Thomas, Augustus Taylor, Robert Vollentine, Abraham Webb, Sebron Goforth, William Croft, Eli Coffee, Daniel Francis, Calvin Hance, Tennessee Loveday, John Patterson, Ellis Patterson, Thomas Pruett, Manon Rollens, Elias Wingwood, Samuel Williams.

Additional names found in another roll: Beveredge Branum, Abraham Birditte, George W. Birditte, Meal Breeden, Billy Ball, Wesley Moris, John McMahan, James H. Rinehart, James Strange, James Tirly, Alissah Blaylock, 1st Lieut., Abraham Mapels, William Compton, Hasten Poe, Sergt., Jacob H. Flinn, Sergt., James Broadrick, Sergt., William Flinn, Corporal, Samuel Ball, Jr., Samuel Ball, Sr., Isaac Ball, Marion Branum, Joseph Francis, William Francis, Joseph R. Hance, Wesley Inman, John McCarter, Josiah McCarter, Evans Mason, William Smith, John Smith, John Griffin, Nathan Griffin, Brumint Rose.

This Company enlisted September 22, 1862 for a period of three years, and were mustered out of service January, 1863, the 26th, at Murfreesboro by John H. Young, a Captain.

LIST BY MRS. T. E. SATTERFIELD

Joseph Coen Morell, John Morell, John T. Allen, David Stokely, James H. Ponder, Lieut. James Nelson, Thomas B. Huff, Capt. John M. Hickey, James H. Robinson, Andrew Miller, James Seahorne Allen, Reuben Allen Justus, Lieut. John M. Jones, William Russell Stokely, Samuel K. Smith, Lieut. McKinney McMahan, Capt. James Morris, Vinson Fine, William Denton, Murray Vinson, Alexander Smith, Isaac Stephens, George W. Susong, Irwin Reams, Capt. Lemuel Mims, Charles Holland, Charles Fisher Askew, Maj. James T. Huff, A. B. Hedrick, T. N. Harper, Abraham Faubion, W. H. Hedrick, D. S. Sorrell, Joseph Huff, Maj. Tom Gorman, Leonard Huff, M. M. Jones, J. R. Knisley, M. M. Jones, Robt. B. Neely, W. M. Pack, James Allen, Allen Brooks, T. D. A. Harper, William Bryant, Lon Morell, Willis Gray, Charlie Mason.

An additional one is Caswell McNabb, a Captain.

UNION SOLDIERS (Goodspeed)

Company E was from Cocke County and Greene County and was commanded by First Lieutenant Lemuel Bible for the greater part of the time.

Company D was from Cocke, Grainger and Green Counties. Thomas H. Reeve, first captain; Gaines Lawson and R. S. Lane, later captains.

Company K mainly from Cocke County, James H. Kinser, captain; Robert A. Rogers, first lieutenant; Alexander Rogers 2nd lieutenant. No company was recruited entirely from any one county, but the counties from which came the greatest number of men are as follows:

Company H Cocke County, Moses Wiley, captain when mustered out.

Company K from Cocke and surrounding counties, J. M. Hendrickson, captain; J. R. Shults, first lieutenant; P. M. Lissenby, 2nd lieutenant.

Company I 2nd Tennessee Cavalry, George W. Gorman, captain; George W. Webb, first lieutenant; Andrew Jackson Webb, 2nd lieutenant. This company was organized at Cumberland Gap, September, 1862.

It is said that more Federal soldiers went from the first and 2nd districts of Tennessee than from any other state in the Union. (Compiled by Brownlow.)

FEDERAL SOLDIERS OF COCKE COUNTY IN CIVIL WAR

Calvin Adkins, Arnold Ailey, William Allen, John Archer, Matthew Bacon, Elbert Bible, Ezra Bible, Jonathan Bible, Lemuel Bible, Preston Bible, John Bird, John Black, Reuben Black, Solomon Black, Ironeas Blazer, Philip Blazer, Tillman Blazer, Matthew Boleypaw, Creed Fulton Boyer, Henry Brown, Levi Buckner, Jasper Butler, Charles Adam Campbell, William Campbell, William H. Campbell, William Canuph, Joseph Carlisle, J. Frank Case, Jesse Case, Joseph Case, Isaac Cates, O. P. Chambers, Ellis Clarke, William Clarke, Isaac Clevenger, Peter H. Cline, W. P. Conken, Nathan Davis, Abraham Dawson, Alexander Dawson, Cudge Dawson, David Dawson, Dewey Dawson, Thomas Denton, B. Frank Driskill, John Ealy, Joseph Edwards, Elbert Ellis, Richard Ellis, John F. Ellison, James Erby, William Evans, Hiram T. Fancher, Levi L. Fancher, Andrew Fancher, Alexander Fowler, Whig Fowler, Carter Fox, Robert Fox, Andrew Franklin, Joshua Franks, Austin Frazier, John Frazier, Alexander Freshour, George Freshour, John Giles, William Giles, James Gilliland, John Gray, Joseph Greene, Joseph S. Greene, William Greene, John Gregg, Isaac Grindstaff, Levin Gwin (Goin), James Hale, John Hale, Archibald Hall, Henry Hall, James Hammond, Charles

Hance, Samuel Harned, William Harned, Ezekiel Harris, Harvey Hayes, William Henderson, E. G. Hensley, John Heritage, David Hicks, Joel Hicks, Ervin Holbert, John Holder, Joseph Holdway, Howard Holt, James Holt, Obediah Holt, Dr. Lemuel W. Hooper, George House, Capt. Andrew C. Huff, Frank Hensley, Greene Inman, Joseph Inman, James Jarnigan, Austin Jenkins, Calvin Jenkins, Toliver Jenkins, Thomas Johnston, W. C. Johnston, John Jones, Russell Jones, Wiley Jones, W. Duggan Justus, Jack Kelley, Frank Kelley, Capt. Kinser (Jas.?), David Knight, Alfred Knisley, Jacob Kyker, M. L. Kyker, John Lane, Matthew Lauderdale, Asa Layman, Preston Layman, Griff Lewis, W. M. Love, John Lovell, Greene Loyd, John Maddron, _____ McAlister, _____ McAnnally, Giles McGaha. Henderson McGaha, James B. McMahan, James B. Mahan, William McMahan, Henderson McMillan, Alexander McNabb, Campbell McNabb, Lemuel McNabb, Henry McSween (colored), William Miller, James Mooneyham, Dempsey Moore, William Moore, Abner Morgan, James Morrow, Allen Myers, Adam Nease, John T. Nease, Powell Nease, Thomas Nease, Benjamin Nolen, Adam Ottinger, Alfred Ottinger, Calvin Ottinger, Christopher Ottinger, Ironius Ottinger, Jacob Ottinger, James Ottinger, Michael Ottinger, Peter Ottinger, Frank Ouzey, James Overholt, J. F. Owenby, James Owens, John Ownsby, Byrd Palmer, Charles S. Parrott, Andrew Peters, Frank Peters, John Peters, C. T. Peterson, William Phillips, J. D. Pierce, Matthew Rader, Capt. Robert A. Ragan, 1st Lieut. Alexander Ragan, Isaac Raines, A. H. Rainwater, J. W. Rainwater, Eli Ramsey, James Randolph, E. S. Redwine, Elihu Redwine, Joseph Redwine, Frank Reece, Reuben Reece, Thomas Reece, Andrew Renner, Brummit Rose, Joseph Rutherford, James Samples, _____ Sane, Calvin Sartin, Andred Sawyer, George Scruggs, Samuel Sexton, George Shults, John R. Shults, M. D. Shults, M. S. Sisk, Eli Smelcer, Ephraim Smelcer, Newton Smelcer, B. F. Smith, John D. Smith, John K. Smith, John Smith (colored), Samuel Smith, Andrew J. Sneed, A. Sprouse, Philip Stiles, Carter Sutton, J. Mitchell Sutton, Harrison Swagerty (colored), John Swagerty (colored), Tillman Swagerty (colored), L. B. Talley, Gus Taylor, William Tritt, Reuben Underwood, D. C. Walden, James I. Waters, _____ Webb, James Whitehead, Lawson Whitehead. J. M. Wilds, J. B. Williams, William Williams, Eli Williamson, Joseph Williamson, Marshall Wilson, Jacob Winters, James Wise, Sirom Wise, Andrew Wood, Jeptha Wood, William Wood, F. M. Wright, Mecajah York, Levi York.

(Compiled by Mrs. Jetta Lee, and published in *Newport Times*, Sept. 21, 1938.)

SPANISH-AMERICAN WAR SOLDIERS*

Sixth Regiment U. S. V. Immunes Company C. Officers.
Captain, Ben W. Hooper
First Lieut., John F. Fuller, Silver Lake
Second Lieut., Alvin Barton, Knoxville
Sergeants
First, Hudson B. Anderson, Newport
Q. M., Reese B. Godwin, Newport
Lewis E. Mock, Silver Lake
William H. Blalock, Canton, N. C.
J. C. Donnelly, Mountain City, Tenn.
George F. Robinson, Laurel Bloomery, Tenn.
Corporals
William F. Cureton, Newport
John M. Payne, Osborne, Tenn.
David F. Britton, Greeneville, Tenn.
Thomas M. Acton, English
Allen M. Stout, Essex, Tenn.
Andrew F. Venable, Laurel Bloomery, Tenn.
Gus C. Winter, Salem
Lewis W. Cass, Johnson City
Edom Cureton, (Company Cook) Newport

Musicians
Perry B. Givens, Narrows, Va.
J. F. Hale, Rogersville, Tenn.
Artificer
William H. J. Eastridge, Dowell, Tenn.
Wagoner
Abijah Simmons, Nailon, Tenn.
Regimental Field and Staff
Colonel, Laurence D. Tyson
Lieut. Colonel, Andrew S. Rowan
Senior Major, Paul E. Divine
Surgeon Major, Frank P. Robinson
Assist. Surgeon, First Lieut. Z. D. Massey
Assist. Surgeon, First Lieut., John W. Cox
Chaplain, Captain John T. Phillips
Regimental Adjutant, J. Baird French
Regimental Q. M., First Lieut. Frank E. Murphy
Sergeant Major, Sam M. Henderson
Quarter Master Sergeant, William P. Bradshaw
Hospital Steward, Jos. B. Spencer
Hospital Steward, Henry M. Cass
Hospital Steward, Bruce M. Montgomery

*Copied by author from Soldier's Memorial, Memorial Building of Cocke County.

Principal Musicians, John J. McDonald and John Loge, Jr.
Privates

William M. Balch, Parrottsville, Tenn.
Dollie Campbell, Help, Tenn.
Morgan Clevenger, Newport, Tenn.
Darius Gregg, Newport, Tenn.
David Gregg, Newport, Tenn.
Ebb Green, Newport, Tenn.
Isaac W. Grindstaff, Newport, Tenn.
Benjamin Hammonds, Newport, Tenn.
William C. Harris, Newport, Tenn.
James H. Holt, Parrottsville, Tenn.
Richard Holt, Bybee, Tenn.
William A. Holt, Parrottsville, Tenn.
William J. Holt, Newport, Tenn.

McKinney Hurst, Newport, Tenn.
Albert Jones, Del Rio, Tenn.
James A. Linebarger, Caney Branch
Samuel A. Parrott, Parrottsville, Tenn.
George W. Pennell, Newport, Tenn.
Jacob Phillips, Caney Branch
Albert Stuart, Newport, Tenn.
Rufus Stuart, Newport, Tenn.
Right B. West, Eng.
Second Lieut. John Q. Tilson, resigned Sept. 20, 1898
Q. M. Sergt. Oscar L. Hicks, English, Discharged
Harrison Shults, Costner, Tenn.
George W. Samples, Newport, Tenn.

The men of this Company were enrolled in Cocke and Johnson Counties. Mustered into service at Camp Wilder, Knoxville, Tennessee, July 9, 1898. Left for Camp George H. Thomas, Chicamauga Park, Georgia, July 31, reaching destination same day. Retained at Camp Thomas until Oct. 6, 1898, when they left for New York to embark for Porto Rico on Oct. 9, on board the U. S. Transport Mississippi, arriving at San Juan, Porto Rico Oct. 15, *being the first United States Troops landed there.*

Left San Juan Oct. 17 by rail for Arecibo, Porto Rico where they went into barracks; left Arecibo on U. S. Transport Chester, Feb. 12, 1899, disembarked at Savannah, Georgia Feb. 17, where they went into Camp Onward to be mustered out.

COCKE COUNTY BOYS IN WORLD WAR I*

NEWPORT, TENNESSEE
Allen, James (dec'd)
Archer, Willie
Allen, Mel
Archer, Jack
Anderson, W. C.
Ailor, Thurman
Allen, Roscoe R.
Allen, Ben
Allen, Obie
Amick, Rev. D. C.
Barnett, Fred
Bowman, Wm.
Butler, Oscar S.
Bryant, William M.
Ball, W. A.
Bradley, W. A.
Bradley, W. P.
Buckner, W. H.
Bishop, Frank
Bowers, Mack
Baxter, Lawrence
Breeden, Leonard (dec'd)
Burke, Clifford
Bell, William
Barnes, C. A.
Barnes, William A.
Barnes, Walter C.
Black, Everett
Black, Howard
Breeden, Ruben J.
Burnett, Ulius S.
Black, Jesse B.
Burnett, Wm. B.

Burnett, Horace
Bryant, Liston
Bostwick, Elmer
Blazer, Grove L.
Burke, Arthur
Bynum, Ben (col.) (dec'd)
Brown, Chas. B.
Balch, Fred
Clar, Oliver L.
Combs, Horace
Crino, Michael
Cooper, Hormer
Clark, James
Clevenger, Probe
Clevenger, J. Mack
Combs, Claude
Clevenger, Forrest
Cureton, Bayless (col.)
Clevenger, Leonard
Clevenger, Allen
Clevenger, Luther
Cureton, Darius
Clevenger, T. C.
Cline, Ernest A.
Carty, Joe
Carty, Bruce
Caton, Herman L.
Coker, Homer
Campbell, Roy T.
Caughron, Harrison
Clark, Wesley
Dodson, Homer
Dennis, Bruce
Driskill, Thomas M.

Dunn, Otto
Davis, Luther
Epley, Bruce
Epley, Chas.
Evans, Ceaser
Evans, John T.
Epley, Ben
Evans, Edgar
Fox, Alvin W.
Franks, W. C. (dec'd)
Fine, Bruce
Foster, Chas. W.
Foster, Walter
Freshour, Guy E.
Freshour, Edd
Frazier, Leonard
Franklin, Lawson (dec'd)
Fine, Alton
Fancher, Hobart O.
Fancher, Herman W.
Ford, Dr. Hobart
Fisher, Art J.
Frazier, Rufus (col.)
Greer, Everett
Greer, Elmer C.
Gregg, Kenneth
Gregg, Estel
Grindstaff, Aden C.
Gregg, Dock
Gregg, Claude
Green, Swan L.
Gregg, James
Gregory, Wm. S.
Gregg, Melvin
Gudger, Wm. (col.)

*Incomplete list prepared by local American Legion post under supervision of Commander J. Carty McSween, in *Newport Plain Talk*, November 11, 1930.

Goeper, Edd
Gorman, Fred M.
Gardner, Leonard M.
Gregg, Hugh
Grooms, Noah
Green, Ralph
Gentry, A. J.
Gentry, C. W.
Holland, Leon
Holt, Herman
Holder, Hugh C.
Holder, John C.
Hixon, Claude
Holt, Bonnie L.
Hill, Robert
Hicks, Arthur
Hurst, Mitch
Harper, Neil
Harper, J. Mac
Hill, James
Hicks, Ernest
Hall, Willie (dec'd)
Howard, Henry
Holland, Robert
Hill, Roscoe
Hill, George
Hall, J. Massey
Hightower, Ernest
Harvey, James
Howard, Carson
Hurst, Marion B.
Hall, Frank
Hall, Earl
Hampton, Dr. J. E.
Hill, Jno.
Harkins, William B.
Howell, Frank Jr. (col.)
Holt, Herbert
Hedrick, Worth
Holt, R. B.
Haney, Sam (col.)
Hance, Hunley
Hartsell, Claude H.
Hartsell, Edward
Henry Thomas J.
Hicks, C. Beech
Hicks, Oscar
Howard, Henry
Hammer, Prof. J. C.
Harris, Bernard
Harrison, Earl
Harris, Rev. Mark
Hance, Wm.
Hall, Milburn
Harvey, Zenas
Hamilton, Sol (col.)
  (dec'd)
Henry, Lee
Holt, Willie (dec'd)
Hicks, Caleb
Haynes, Charles
Inman, James
Jones, B. L.
Jones, Charles
Jones, Lawrey

Jones, W. W.
Jones, Fred B. (dec'd)
Justus, Allen D.
Justus, Martin
Jones, Sam H.
Jenkins, Scott
Kropff, John C.
Keisler, Guy (dec'd)
Knisley, Clyde
Kyker, Robert B.
Kendrick, Creed (col.)
Layman, Walter
Lane, Robert
Lane, Bruce
Lee, Hugh
Ledford, Oscar
Lillard, Hubert A.
Lee, Omar
Lowe, Harry
Lindsey, Tip
Lindsey, Pat
Lemmons, Dr. H. J.
Long, Ballard E.
Lee, Marvin
Moss, Burl
Mantooth, L. E.
Miller, Mark J.
Morefield, Robert
Moore, Hobart
Moore, Phillip (dec'd)
Mantooth, Leonard
Medlin, Oscar
Myers, J. Lacy
Murr, Oscar
Mims, Ernest
Masters, Herbert F.
Maddron, J. L. O.
Mayfield, Luther
Moore, Brenice A.
Moore, Charlie D.
Morrison, J. Archie
Murray, Morris
Mantooth, Roy
Morrow, James
McGaha, Charles (dec'd)
McGaha, Sam (dec'd)
McCurry, Arch
McMahan, William
McMahan, Hugh
McNabb, Charles
McMahan, Noah
McMahan, Richard
McSween, J. C.
McCravy, T. (col.)
  (dec'd)
McGaha, Dr. W. E.
McMahan, James Howard
McNabb, Lemuel A.
McCroskey, Charles J.
McGaha, Samuel R.
McMahan, George B.
McNabb, J. Ruby
McMahan, Chas. (dec'd)
Nease, Dr. L. S.
Neas, Orville A.

Norris, Charles A.
Norris, Turner J.
Norris, Henry
Ottinger, Robert
O'Neil, Doll
Ottinger, Reuben
Ownby, Walter
O'Dell, Fred
O'Dell, Henry
Ownby, Carris A.
Ottinger, Clayton
Price, Chas.
Pitts, Porter M.
Price, Grant
Parks, Mathew
Parrott, Robert R.
Parrott, C. E.
Proffitt, Walter E.
  (dec'd)
Penland, Willis
Petree, Claude
Proffitt, Horace
Phillipps, Wm.
Reed, Dan (dec'd)
Reneau, Dan
Rollan, Hollis
Rice, Richard
Raines, Horace
Rhinehart, Mitchell
Ramsey, Hawkum
Ramsey, Galleon
Ramsey, Lawrence
Rice, Edgar
Reece, Lucius
Rea, Silas
Robinson, Herbert F.
Robinson, Lindsey P.
Ramsey, Lee
Ruble, John B.
Ruble, Greer
Rich, Richard
Rich, Paul V. (dec'd)
Runnion, Charles
Runnion, W. J.
Ramsey, Garfield
Rollins, Hollis J.
Rhea, William B.
Russell, William
Ray, Ed.
Ray, _____
Rector, George
Rader, Don (dec'd)
Robeson, Oscar L.
Reese, Chas.
Reese, Lester
Robinson, Eugene
Smith, Bart (col.)
Sparks, Cletus
Samples, Bartley
Stokely, Edward (dec'd)
Shults, Ottis
Seay, Thomas
Shoemaker, Lem
Sisk, Campbell
Steward, Sam (col.)

Stokely, Alex
Samples, James
Samples, George
Smith, G. A.
Sparks, C. D.
Stokely, Arthur A.
Smith, Talley
Smith, Evan Otey
Stanberry, Eugene
Shults, Joseph
Stokely, J. Lyde
Stokely, Melvin
Sutton, Isaac
Steward, Charlie
Shults, Dallas C.
Sprouse, Jesse (dec'd)
Sprouse, Frank
Sample, William D.
Strange, Luther D.
Swagerty, Luther, (col.)
Taylor, Frank
Taylor, Herbert
Turner, R. H.
Taylor, Loss
Taylor, Anderson (col.)
Taylor, Ben
Thornton, Willett
Thompson, James
Vest, Will (dec'd)
Walker, Roy
Wilson, Roy
Wheeler, Roy
Williamson, William
Webb, Rufus
Welch, Vernon
Williamson, Robert M.
Williams, Alf (dec'd)
Webb, Milford
Willis, Walter
Wood, Bernie
Wood, Clay
Wood, George
Wood, Carl
West, Earl
Webb, Sam
West, Howard A.
White, Thad
Williamson, Creed
Williams, Add
Wood, Fred
Walker, Edd (E. K.)
Walker, F. C.
Wright, George R.
Williams, Hubert E.
Whipple, Robert B.
Williams, Gather
Weaver, Wm. Homer
Watson, Oscar R.
Wilson, S. S.
Wood, John H.
Williams, Luther
Wilson, Hugh E.
PARROTTSVILLE,
  TENNESSEE
Amos, Jesse

Bailey, Henry
Bailey, Carl
Balch, Claude
Barger, Crawford
Carr, Henry (col.)
Critselous, Lamon H.
Cagle, Joe
Cline, Hurley
Collins, Mike
Cashen, Henry
Collins, Willis
Cashen, Harvey
Dykes, Loyd (col.)
Dawson, J. D.
Dawson, Max K.
Dunn, Lafayette
Eisenhower, Wayne
Eisenhower, Fred
Fowler, Bede
Fox, Thomas B.
Fox, Elmer
Fowler, Walter
Gregg, Minnis
Gorman, Carl
Keller, Charles L.
LaFollette, Leonard
Maloy, Eli
Mason, Gus
Mooneyham, Houston
McMillan, Ted
McNeeley, Swann (col.)
McCreaken, Clyde
Neas, T. G.
Neas, Loyd E.
Neas, Joe N.
Neas, Zora B.
Ottinger, Robert (dec'd)
Ottinger, Lon
Ottinger, Herman (dec'd)
Ottinger, Erwin
Ottinger, Melvin E.
Ottinger, W. B.
Phillips, Joe
Rader, Milas
Rader, D. D.
Smith, Harry
Sane, Robert
Sane, Ben F.
Stepp, Burnett
Smith, Hobart
Smith, Roy
Sane, Andrew
Stewart, Edd
Stepp, W. C.
Stevenson, James
Stephenson, Jesse
Smith, William Roy
Stephens, Ike
Trentham, James (dec'd)
Talley, Lawrence (dec'd)
Winters, Sibley
Winters, Robert (dec'd)
White, Burn (col.)
COSBY, TENNESSEE
Allen, Bartley

Allen, Vernie
Benson, John
Baxter, Jasper
Bryant, William
Bryant, Jethro
Butler, Bruce C. (dec'd)
Ball, J. V.
Bryant, J. C.
Black, William
Bryant, Charlie
Baxter, Scott
Baxter, W. C.
Breeden, Bruce
Ball, Lawson (dec'd)
Campbell, Wilse (dec'd)
Campbell, C. F.
Costner, I. A.
Campbell, Oscar
Carver, Bruce
Carver, Peter
Campbell, Joe
Caldwell, William T.
Costner, Rufus C.
Campbell, Curtis
Crawley, Joseph
Dennis, Gar
Dorsey, W. B.
Dorsey, Luther
Dennis, Fayette
Dorsey, Mansfield
Denton, Bud
Davis, Floyd
Edmonds, Esley
Enlow, Curtis
Erby, Cecil
Frye, George
Fowler, John
Fowler, Joe
Giles, John
Giles, George D.
Hannah, Orville
Huff, Doctor
Hartsell, McKinley
Hartsell, W. O.
Hance, Willie E.
Harrell, Joe I. (dec'd)
Harrell, W. Chan
Hooper, Johnson
Huff, Lawrence V.
Henry, G. T.
Jenkins, DeLozier H.
Jenkins, Samuel H.
Jenkins, Stanley
Johnson, S. C.
Large, Allen
Large, Walter
Large, Thad
Lindsey, Jethro
Lindsey, F. A.
Lane, C. H.
Lane, J. O.
Lavmon, Bruce
Mann, Hobart M.
Maddron, Hobart
Mathes, Eli

McKinney, Burnett
McGaha, Albert
McGaha, H.
McGaha, John D.
McGaha, Ray
McGaha, Russell
McGaha, L. B.
McCarter, Leonard
McCarter, William (dec'd)
McMahan, Isaac A.
McCarter, Charles
Norris, Beecher
Parks, Matha
Proffitt, Gus
Proffitt, Creed H.
Perryman, Oliver
Proffitt, Raymond
Proffitt, David H.
Proffitt, David L. (dec'd)
Proffitt, Walter
Phillips, Olin (dec'd)
Ramsey, Berry
Ramsey, Steward
Rollen, Vander C.
Stinnett, Clyde
Smith, Hobart
Smith, Thomas
Smith, Robert
Smallwood, James O.
Shults, Harris
Shelton, Walter B.
Shults, Isaac
Smith, Dallas S.
Smith, William H.
Stinnett, Clyde R.
Shults, Dallas M.
Templin, Earl
Valentine, Bruce C.
Valentine, Oscar
Valentine, Scott
Valentine, Milburn
Webb, Jesse
Webb, Wilson
Webb, Chancy
Webb, Dugan
Williamson, Add (dec'd)
Webb, P. M.
Wilson, George L.
Williams, Mark
Williams, Fred
Williams, Wardan
Williams, J. B.
Williams, Earn
Williams, Luther
Williams, James C.
Wilson, S. C.
BOOMER, TENNESSEE
Russell, Willis
Rathbone, Fayette
Self, Walter
HARTFORD,
  TENNESSEE
Brown, Charles
Baxter, W. N.
Ball, Ben

Banks, Loyd
Ball, Jesse
Barnes, Harrison
Clark, Wesley
Cagle, Joe
Coggins, Milas
Caldwell, Andrew
Duckett, Ben.
Ford, Rufus L.
Ford, Robert
Green, James M. (dec'd)
Gray, Isaac (dec'd)
Green, Lewis
Grooms, Ance
Green, Walter
Green, Ben A.
Green, Hobert
Grooms, Tommy
Hill, Joe S.
Hill, Joe R.
Hensley, Jesse
Johnson, Jesse
James, Arthur
James, Willie (dec'd)
Johnson, Robert
Miller, Dallas
Messer, William
McGaha, William
McMahan, Ralph
McMahan, John W.
Parton, Reuben
Rollins, Roscoe
Rose, Joe
Smith, Luther
Vess, Wm. N.
Valentine, A. H.
Williams, Chas.
Wild, Wm. G.
Wild, Bartley
BYBEE, TENNESSEE
Arms, Henry
Arrowood, John C.
Butler, Arthur
Bradley, Richard
Buckner, Walter
Brown, James E.
Chamberlain, Leon J.
Dawson, Charles J.
Dawson, Oscar
Fox, Luther
Fox, LaFollette
Fowler, Estle C.
Freeman, A. L.
Holt, Preston G.
Holt, Andrew
Holt, Herbert
Holt, Dan
Hayes, G. W.
Holdway, Dewey
Holt, Burgett W.
Holt, Walter
Holdway, Dave
Hayes, Ike
Knipp, George W.
Knight, Claude

Knight, Connie
Lewis, James
Lingo, Mack
Moyer, Bob
Moore, James Emett
Moore, Phillip (dec'd)
Padgett, Hobert
Padgett, Richard
Ragan, Dennis
Stephenson, Matt
Sneed, Lon
Sexton, John
Tuner, L. W.
Toby, Burnett
Turner, Hubert
Turner, W. F.
Turner, Robert
Thomas, Bruce (dec'd)
Thomas Ben H.
Wise, Donald
Yarbrough, Claude
Yarbrough, Floyd
DANDRIDGE,
  TENNESSEE
Bush, Alger
Cody, M. C.
Cody, A. W.
Edmonds, Mitchell
Gray, Lee
Lewis, James
Rhinehart, John L.
Rainwater, Ben
Strange, Wm. M.
Taylor, Wm. R.
Williamson, Creed
WOLF CREEK,
  TENNESSEE
Franklin, G. H.
Franklin, A. J.
McFeatures, Carter
  (dec'd)
McFeatures, Charles
Parker, Robert
Shelton, Bulow
WHITE PINE,
  TENNESSEE
Shaver, Hobert
BRIDGEPORT,
  TENNESSEE
Brooks, Lawrence D.
Brooks, Homer D.
Brooks, Roy
Gorrell, John
Harper, Fred
Shell, Landon
Suggs, Estil
Wiley, John C.
Wiley, George L. (dec'd)
BROWNS, TENNESSEE
Brown, Henderson
Brown, Clay
McFall, Norman
Phillips, Ben
Phillips, Jno. R.
Wilson, John, Jr.

RANKIN, TENNESSEE
Harper, Bert
Lewis, Elijah
Parker, David
Parker, Claude
Sexton, John
Stuart, Aurelius
Tompkins, James
Whitlock, Walter
DEL RIO, TENNESSEE
Askew, Roy
Ball, Worley
Bible, Bernie
Burgein, Chas.
Brown, Chas.
Barnett, L. B.
Clark, Mark
Church, Henry
Chandler, Bart
Cogdill, Cal
Click, Noah
Cogdill, Frank R.
Cutshall, Joe D. (dec'd)
Cutshall, James M.
   (dec'd)
Deniston, J. C.
Douglass, J. C.

Evans, Mark
Fowler, Hugh E.
Fowler, Roy
Fox, Charles W.
Fox, Berry
Fowler, Cartha
Fowler, T. W.
Finney, James Joseph
Green, Walter
Green, J. R.
Green, Isaac R.
Goodnough, Wayne
Gibbs, J. J.
Hess, Marve
Harris, Loney
Haney, James T.
Hall, Isaac
Holt, Joe
Holt, Chas. J.
Harris, T. D.
Jones, Loney
Jones, Loyd
Jones, Wm. G.
Jones, Swann
Jackson, Loyd (col.)
Kreemer, W. F.
Kelley, Thomas

Kerby, Thomas
Kelley, George
Kilgore, Loyd
Laws, Osborn Riley
Mooneyham, Spurgeon
Massey, Dug
Marrow, Jesse
Moore, Charlie
Moore, John
Norwood, James H.
Norwood, Rufus N.
Nichols, Claude N.
Presnell, Pless
Pack, Nathan
Pack, Jesse A.
Roberts, Robert A.
Roberts, Joe D. (dec'd)
Stinnett, Garfield
Smith, Chan
Self, Loyd
Suttles, F. C.
Self, Chas. W.
Stokely, Joe
Turner, Walter
Turner, Frank E.
Turner, Carl (dec'd)
Woody, Nathan L.

LOST LIVES IN WORLD WAR I

Allen, Obie
Archer, Sam
Austin, William
Barnett, Fred
Baxter, John
Boyer, Otto
Clark, George Rankin
Ellison, Ernest N.
Fish, William McKinley

Free, Charles G.
Gillespie, Guy
Hall, William
Holdway, Ben
Holt, Hobert M.
Johnson, Robert
Lee, Marvin
McFeatures, Carter
Maloy, Robert

Nolen, Edward
Ottinger, Herman B.
Reese, Luther
Rockwell, Kiffin Yates
Smith, Burnett
Sprouse, Jesse
Talley, Lawrence M.
Trantham, James C.
Turner, Reuben Henry

COCKE COUNTY SOLDIERS WHO GAVE LIVES IN WORLD WAR II*

Oliver F. Baxter
Eston A. Baxter
Hal H. Baxter
Joseph A. Brown
Swannie H. Burke
James D. Butler
Oliver R. Butler
Albert M. Campbell
Hugh M. Campbell
Cleve H. Carver
Darium R. Cody
Kenneth O. Crowe
Luther L. Cureton
Tom W. Daniels
Richard W. Dover
William S. Foster

Elmer J. Giles
Milburn B. Hall
J. C. Hawk
Hollis J. Holt
Ivan F. Holt
Roy A. Johnson
Manyard Lackey
Troy W. Laws
Y. J. Leatherwood
Clifford Lewis
Luther S. McGaha
C. C. McIntosh
James F. McMillon
Lloyd R. McNabb
Albert M. Olsakovsky
Jess W. O'Neil

John W. Ottinger
Glenn H. Pearce
Lester Phillips
Samuel E. Phillips
Bill Ramsey
Walter I. Ramsey
Isaac N. Reece
J. D. Shelton
Arthur Shults
J. D. Smelcer
Charles M. Siggs
Glenn E. Tweed
William R. Waller
David A. Williams

*Official compilation of the War Department in *The Knoxville Journal*, June 28, 1946

Pvt. Rome Huston Hance, son of Rev. and Mrs. Hugh Hance was the first Cocke County soldier to fall in the Korean War, Aug. 18, 1950.

ESCAPE FROM EAST TENNESSEE TO THE FEDERAL LINES

By Captain R. A. Ragan, Published in 1910 Contributed by his daughter

Mrs. Clinton L. Dooley, Sequoyah Hills

Knoxville, Tennessee

The information in this chapter has been gleaned from the above story and is full of interest to all Cocke County people descended from this family of Ragan.

In 1845 Allen Ragan and wife, Jacob Ragan and Charity Cureton Ragan came to Cocke County from Greene County, there they had lived on the banks of the Nola Chucky River, here they settled on the banks of the French Broad River. There were six children in this family, they were Robert Allen, Alexander, Laura, Creed, Mary and James Ragan.

In 1860 R. A. was elected Lieutenant Colonel of the Militia and in the fall of 1861 was in the employ of Frank Clark who fattened hogs and drove them each year to the South Carolina markets. R. A. went with Clark to drive the hogs but became ill with "yellow jaunders" jaundice and had to remain in Spartanburg until he became well. He was astounded to find there excitement, rebellion, and Confederate Flags everywhere. The Negroes were 'frightened out of their wits' two of whom he had seen hung for burning houses which had been 'set on fire' by white men.

As soon as Ragan was able he decided he had better return to East Tennessee where there was no war. His fast saddle horse carried him away from South Carolina in a hurry. He experienced a feeling of great relief when he reached the top of the Blue Ridge Mountains. From this great height he looked to his 'right' and beheld the Holston and Watauga Rivers flowing through East Tennessee's peaceful valleys, next he saw the beautiful Nola Chucky where he was born and as he journeyed along the French Broad came into view and almost before he could realize his good fortune he was home to Newport on the Big Pigeon.

In 1861 Tennessee voted against secession by a majority of 68,000 but on May 7, 1861 a Military League, offensive and defensive, was entered into between Commissioners appointed by Governor Harris on the part of Tennessee and Commissioners appointed by the Confederate Government and ratified by the General Assembly of the State, became a part of the Confederate States to all intents and purposes although an Act was passed on June the 8th for people to decide the question of separation and representation in the Confederate Congress or no such representation. (Page 7)

The most prominent Union Leaders at that time in this section were, Andrew Johnson, Thomas A. R. Nelson, W. B. Carter, C. F. Trigg, N. G. Taylor, Oliver P. Temple, R. R. Butler, William G. Brownlow, John Baxter, and Andrew J. Fletcher.

R. A. Ragan was a School Teacher at the time the Legislature had exempted from service all teachers, black-smiths and millers. However, the law was soon repealed and every man from 18 to 45 had to join the CONFEDERATE ARMY or be conscripted. Robert Ragan did not know of the repeal and had not joined the army. He was arrested in the school house by Confederate soldiers but given the privilege of going by his home two miles away to see his wife as he had requested. He was not allowed to have a private conversation with her. She was a Neas and as brave a Union Woman as her husband was a Union man. She watched the soldiers drive her husband along across the fields, making him lay down and up the fences on the way until they came to the home of Henry Kilgore, the conscript officer. Kilgore registered Ragan's name on the Conscript Rolls which enraged him 'to the core' but he dared not express himself. Next day he was taken to Knoxville by three men arriving there at two o'clock in the morning. They placed him in a stockade with about 300 ragged men who had declared themselves for the Union. When Robert Ragan entered the stockade the men exclaimed, "There is another Lincolnite."

These men seemed half starved, many were half naked, having lost their apparel in the woods trying to make their escape to the Union lines, some were hatless and shoeless. When 'daylight' came with it came a wagon of old poor beef which the driver threw over the stockade on the ground. Some of the soldiers, or men rather, threw pieces of it against the wall to see if it would stick but it was too poor.

Jacob Ragan, the father of Robert was a relative of John H. Ragan, Post Master General of the Southern Confederacy, telegraphed to Richmond that his son was under arrest that he had committed no crime and that he was a school-teacher. The authorities at Richmond immediately wired Leadbeater, the commanding officer to release Ragan. However he had scarcely been released until word came that he would again be arrested at which 'news' he disappeared for many months trying to get to the Federal lines. Finally he heard of a man in Greene County who would pilot men to the Federal lines. Joseph Smith of Parrottsville accompanied him to Greene County for a few days stay. They hid in a straw stack on the banks of the Nola Chucky. They were fed by an old lady, Minerva Hale who was a strong Union sympathizer. Joseph Smith left Robert Ragan in the straw stack and he never saw him again. Ragan was impressed that he should not try to get to Kentucky with the PILOT, he returned to his home in Cocke County in the night. All the men who went with the pilot, William Worthington, were captured except two, and the pilot they escaped by jumping into Lick Creek, a small but deep stream. They sank into the water as though they had drowned. The others were taken to Vicksburg and placed in the Confederate Army, Joseph Smith was shot in the foot and died of blood poison, the other men were never heard of again.

For several days Robert Ragan stayed with his Uncle who lived between the Big Pigeon and the French Broad Rivers he stayed upstairs all the time while there and soon decided he had better be on his way again. He next went to his Father's home three miles from Newport on the Greeneville Road. During the second day of his stay at 2 o'clock in the afternoon he got word of a regiment of Rebel Soldiers crossing the French Broad River at Newport (Oldtown) he felt they would search the house for any Union sympathizers, he knew not what to do as a Rebel family lived in sight of the house and would see him if he left in the afternoon. His mother suggested that he put on his sister Laura's dress and sun-bonnet and cross the road, this he did just before the soldiers arrived, many of them stopped at the house. Robert watched the regiment pass from his hiding place near the barn.

This was the first Rebel Regiment he had seen and it made him more anxious to get to the Yankee lines. That night he went to Neddy's Mountain which was nearer his home and remained there until such a time as he could get to Kentucky. He received word to meet a pilot at a school house on a certain day, on the Nola Chucky in Greene County. It was that day that Chris Ottinger and John Eisenhour, two Union men were killed. May 6, 1863 he was on his way to the above mentioned place. He had reached the home of his wife's father about sunset. Mr. Nease looked out the door toward the road and saw the lane filled with soldiers and called quickly to his son-in-law who was in the house preparing for bed, he ran out barefooted, bareheaded and without his coat, jumped a high fence on south side of the house passed the loom house, jumped another high fence keeping the house between the soldiers and his flight until he was out of sight, sat down in a brier thicket to try to concentrate on what was best to do next and felt something stinging his foot and upon examination found he had cut the ball of his foot to the bone when he leaped the high fence and landed on a limestone rock. This discovery maddened him and he felt like he was ready to fight the whole Confederate army. He crept back to the house. From the kitchen window a light burned he could see the soldiers seated at the table, about 20 of them. He crawled along on 'allfours' until he reached the 'big-house' door and entered. The men had stacked their arms in the sitting room and left their accoutrements on the floor, there was no light in this room, he knocked lightly on the stairway and his sister-in-law came in astounded to find him there. He sent her to tell his wife to come outside and meet him in the garden but the soldiers were watching the family too closely for the message to be carried. Ragan wanted to pick up the guns and shoot two or three of the men but he knew if he did so all the family might be murdered and the house burned, for such is war. Instead of obeying his impulse he remained in the garden until the men had left the house after which he went in and dressed his wounded foot as best he could, he bound well and over this placed the top part of an old shoe to protect it and journeyed on with his haversack full of eats on his way to the school house to meet the boys.

Men from 'all parts' were making their way to this particular place on the North side of the Nola Chucky. Alfred Timmins was shot while crossing the road on his way to enlist with the Union forces. The ball came out through his right eye. He fell to the ground but after a while regained consciousness and made his way to the river which he crossed to the camp. Those present dressed his wound and he continued on to Kentucky with them. 420 men gathered for this journey.

Because of the terrible condition of his foot it was not possible for Robert Ragan to join the throng. He was afraid to return to his home knowing if he should be caught he would be hung to the first limb or shot, his foot was giving him so much trouble he could not travel very rapidly not more than two or three miles per night, sleeping in barns in the daytime buried deep in the hay wondering if those who came to feed their stock would pierce his brain with the pitch-fork. Finally by the third night he had reached the barn of Philip Easterly who was his wife's Uncle and lived but one and one half miles from Ragan's home. For six or more weeks after he reached his home he had to stay out in the woods in the daytime and in the barns at night but his wife would come and dress the foot two or three times each day it was in a terrible condition and he thought amputation would be necessary.

July 1863 came and with it information that George Kirk would meet some men in Greene County to take them to Kentucky. Robert Ragan made up his mind that he would not be prevented from making this journey if he had to crawl. About one hundred men gathered at the appointed place, crossed Waldron Ridge, the Watauga, Cumberland, Holston and Powell Rivers under very great 'hardship.' When they finally reached Camp Dick Robinson in Kentucky they found many East Tennessee men who had made their way through the mountains. Colonel Felix A. Reeve was organizing the Eighth Tennessee Regiment of Infantry. Ragan volunteered to return to Cocke County and recruit a Company. With his brother, Alexander Ragan, Iranious Isenhour, James Kinser and James Ward they started for East Tennessee. It was a perilous journey. "James Ward could not see a wink at night." This was not known until we had passed the Cumberland Mountains so they had to lead him most of the way as they had to do their traveling at nighttime. When they reached the home of Benjamin F. Nease, the father of Emeline Nease Ragan, wife of Robert Allen Ragan, they found that the Confederate soldiers had visited him and informed him that if he did not reveal the hiding place of his money that they would hang him. This he refused to do and was hanged in a nearby blacksmith shop but before he had became unconscious his daughter appeared and told them where the money was hidden whereupon they let him down but he was so weak he could not stand. Ragan remained at the home of his father-in-law and sent for his own father to come to see him there at a certain place in the woods. He came and gladly returned with the message that a 'PILOT' would be 'on hands' at a certain place on the farm of Benjamin F. Nease on a certain date and those who wished to join the Union forces should meet him there. On the appointed day the men began to appear one, two and three at a time. The roads and bridges were all guarded by Confederate Soldiers which made the journey through the woods and streams most treacherous either way it was undertaken. No one had any idea of the identity of the 'PILOT' who did not make himself known until about one hundred men had assembled. When a pilot was captured it meant certain death for him either by rope or gun.

The women had prepared warm clothes and food for the men. Many had cut up their last blanket to make warm underwear for their husbands. The men had 'rubbed up' their old rifles until they looked like army ones and as they reached the Nola Chucky River a terrible storm was raging and when the lightning flashed they could see it run along the barrels of the old guns. Each man had been instructed before leaving the Nease farm to not speak above his breath and if possible not to break a stick underfoot on the long journey. Reuben Easterly kept the Ferry. He was a staunch Union man. Robert Ragan asked him to 'ferry over 120 Union men' and although the river was 'up' terribly, he got them safely over to the other side. It required two trips to get the men all over the river when Ragan asked Easterly how much he charged for such service in the middle of the darkest night imaginable and in a terrific storm he replied . . . "Nothing, and I wish you a safe journey to the PROMISED LAND."

"After crossing the Chucky River we were to journey into the Chucky Knobs where we were to meet several other Union men," the story runs, and there they found fifteen men waiting for them, among them Judge Randolph of Cocke County. Several of the men's wives had prepared rations and haversacks for this dangerous journey. The hour for leaving this place was eight o'clock at night, by which time their little company had increased considerably. They traveled fifteen miles that night and next day they laid in the woods along the banks of the Watauga River which they crossed as soon as night came. Some in a canoe, others swimming over. By day break they had come to the Holston River, as the men would cross it they would find a place to rest and sleep until the others had followed them. An old canoe was used by those who could not swim. It was most midnight before the last ones crossed when they all got themselves together and marched onward toward their destination. After they had traveled something like a half mile they heard a man 'howling' at the top of his voice. Ragan sent two of the boys back in great haste to find out what the trouble might be. They found they had left JIMMIE JONES who was asleep on the bank of the river. He dreamed that the 'rebels were after him' and it 'woke him UP' whereupon he began screaming or howling like a lost dog. The men were afraid the Rebels WOULD HEAR him and capture the entire company.

Next after this they crossed Bays and Clinch Mountains, both of which were quite steep and rugged. Then came the Clinch River which was also a dangerous crossing. Next came Powell's Mountain, Waldon Ridge and Wild Cat Mountain. The nights were so dark the men marched in single file through these many narrow paths, Robert Ragan leading, the one back of him holding to his coat-tail and so on down the line. No man was allowed to speak 'above his breath.' Those that would fall would sometimes be dragged along several feet but never speak or murmur. All night long they marched until they were weary and worn when dawn came. They rested in the woods near Powell's River which was considered a very dangerous part of the country. Powell's Valley was next to be crossed after the river and these places were well guarded by Confederate men who were determined that no one should pass going to the Federal lines.

The night being so dark we lost our trail. Ragan knew that in this neighborhood was an old man named Walker who had befriended him on his previous journey through this particular section. After wandering about through the woods for hours he found what he thought was the old man's log hut and eventually got him to come to him by knocking on a rail some distance from the house. He approached slowly and asked Ragan what his trouble was and after learning that they were lost Walker assured him that such had oft been the case in this particular section of country and that he would go and get the men and bring them safely to his cabin. The Confederate soldiers were traveling up and down the road so that it was necessary to avoid roads. In two hours time, Walker returned with the lost company. They were hungry and weary but there was nothing for them to eat at the humble home of Walker except some Irish potatoes in the ground and some apples on the trees, the 'REBELS' had taken everything the old man had except his potatoes and apples. He went to work and dug the potatoes about two bushels of them, gathered an equal measure of apples and cooked them in old buckets. Ragan got his men in line as soon as 'DINNER WAS READY' and as the potatoes and apples were passed the men took them out with their hands, many of them burning them in their eagerness to eat of the 'delicious and inviting repast.' By the time this meal was served it was about two o'clock in the afternoon. They tried to sleep until night when they had to cross the 'DEAD-LINE.'

Two men were detailed to keep the others from snoring because it was only three hundred yards to the roadway where the Confederate Soldiers were riding back and forth constantly in search of escaping men to the Union lines.

When night came it was time to cross the 'DEADLINE' into Powell's Valley. Many had been killed at this place within the ten days previous to Ragan's Crossing. Walker had provided the men with a guide. He was placed in the 'lead' and all the men were following quietly and in good faith. After about a mile Ragan became suspicious as he had crossed this point before and felt he was being taken too far West. He placed the guide under arrest and returned to the starting point and picked up the proper trail. The man had not intentionally misled them he was bewildered and frightened and the night was very dark. Finally at three o'clock in the morning the men had reached the dreaded place where so many had lost their lives and their bodies were still to be seen on either side of the roadway. The men from Cocke County stood in the dark woods in *single file*, 130 of them. They could hear in the distance the rattle of sabers and the galloping of the rebel cavalry. They stood motionless and silent as death. The dust from the horses' hoofs settled on their shoulders. They felt they were about to cross the 'Valley of the shadow of death.'

As soon as the Cavalry would pass out of sight the Union men were sent across the four hundred yard wide valley, twenty five of them at a time. After this perilous crossing of the Dead Line we were soon to the top of Cumberland Mountain to what is known as Bailes Meadow, a name and place familiar to every 'pilot' man who had crossed the mountain, states Robert Ragan. Many of the men were almost naked and quite a number were barefooted from the rough traveling they had been forced to do through the mountains to reach their destination in safety. On page 34 of Mr. Ragan's story I find this interesting paragraph, which I shall give in full for those who now live in Cocke County and are the lineal descendants of this brave and brilliant man who had the courage of his convictions and was not afraid to express himself.

"James H. Randolph of Newport, Tennessee was with us. I was sorry for him as well as the others. His shoes were entirely worn out and his feet were bleeding. I can remember the circumstances as though it were but a few days ago. He looked at me and said, 'Bob, when we get back to Tennessee we will give them H— and rub it in.' He was mad, worn out, and nearly starved to death, but we were out of danger and began to realize that we were free once more."

Upon reaching Camp Dick Robinson in Kentucky the men found that Colonel Reeve had his regiment about made up. *The men from Cocke County were organized into Company K which about completed the regiment.* After the boys were fed and had time to rest, wash and shave, their new uniforms were ready, they were about the happiest set of men one could imagine.

The army was preparing to march into East Tennessee which pleased these new soldiers very much indeed because for two long years they had been endeavoring to get into the Federal lines and had often been chased by the Confederates from one place to another and many of their wives severely punished because they refused to divulge the whereabouts of their scouting husbands. Robert Ragan states that when he got on his uniform with its straps on the shoulders and his sword hanging by his side he doubts if General Grant or General Sherman ever felt as 'BIG' as he felt in that new Officer's uniform.

The first of August 1863 they were ordered to be ready to march at any time. They reached East Tennessee below Knoxville the last of August. They passed between Bean Station and the city of Knoxville. They camped at Bull's Gap a few days. While there Ragan asked Colonel Reeve for a detail of six men to go across the country about eighteen miles to visit his home and find out if any 'REBELS' were lurking around in the neighborhood. When they reached to within a mile of Parrottsville they sent a Union Woman to the town to find an old colored man by the name of DAVE ROADMAN and tell him to come to a woodland just above the village of Parrottsville. About ten o'clock in the night the old man came to the appointed place. From him they learned that Henry Kilgore, the gentleman who had conscripted Ragan, Tillman Faubion and Cass Turner were in the town, that Kilgore was at home and the other two men across the street at Faubion's house. Into the town of Parrottsville the Union Soldiers went. George Freshour was a Sergeant in Ragan's Company, one other man and Ragan surrounded Kilgore's house, the other three men went to the Faubion House and captured Faubion and Cass Turner. Sergeant Freshour went to the front door of Kilgore's home and knocked, while Ragan stood at the back door and the third man at another door. Someone opened the door for Freshour but informed him that Kilgore was not there. Freshour insisted that Kilgore must be in the house. He went in and searched for him under beds and all about where he thought a man could hide, finally finding him in the kitchen crouched behind some barrels. They brought him out and took him across to the place where the other two prisoners were and immediately started with them down Clear Creek.

"Henry Kilgore was a conscript officer during the beginning of the Civil War and furnished Leadbeater's Command, which was stationed at Parrottsville, with all the information he could obtain as to where the Union men kept their corn, wheat, bacon and bee gum."

"Tillman Faubion was a nice man, but a strong rebel sympathizer."

Cass Turner lived between Sevierville and Newport, in Cocke County. He was a conscript officer. Both Kilgore and Turner were terrors to the Country.

Freshour walked behind Kilgore and insisted upon Ragan giving him permission to kill him. Turner was a short fat man and could not walk the 'foot-logs' along the way. He would slide across on his stomach. He weighted about 200 pounds.

About ten miles from Parrottsville was the home of a Mrs. Bible whose husband had been captured by the Rebel soldiers and carried away to Tuscaloosa where he died. Freshour asked her if she had any money. She replied there was a beehive in the barn that the soldiers had not found. Freshour took from this hive a pound of soft honey placed it in Kilgore's tall white 'plug' hat and made him wear it. The honey ran down his face, eyes and ears. "The cause of the Seageant's little act of pleasantry was the fact that Kilgore had sent rebels to Freshour's father's house, and they took all of his bee-hives, wheat, corn and bacon—in fact, all he had. The rebel now had an opportunity to taste the 'sweets of adversity'."

After Captain Ragan and Sergeant Freshour 'piloted' these three men to Knoxville and turned them over to the authorities they returned to their command at Bull's Gap.

Captain Ragan gives many interesting and amusing incidents in his story of the escape from East Tennessee to the Federal lines and many details of different battles in which he fought. He also pays a splendid tribute to "The noble patriotic women in East Tennessee, whose untold sufferings would fill a volume and who should have their names and deeds recorded so that generations yet to come might honor them and reverence their memory." What brave, loving mothers, wives and sisters of East Tennessee, who faced the tempests of hatred and persecution during the Civil War; whose willing hands were always ready to minister to the suffering and distressed who carried food to the hunted and perishing Union men who wore the homespun wrought by their own hands, who through waiting years never faltered in love and faith and duty to friend or to country.

"The deeds of the loyal men of East Tennessee, could they have been told individually in all their thrilling details and sufferings while they were living, would rival in patriotic interest the stories of Robert Bruce, William Wallace or the brave Leonidas who with his three hundred Spartans held the pass at Thermopylae against the hosts of Persian aggressors."

THE CIVIL WAR STORY OF ROBERT RAGAN

The following men served as pilots for the Union men in this section who were in sympathy with the Union and wanted to join that army: Daniel Ellis, James Lane, A. C. Fondron, James Kinser, and David Fry. James Lane was killed at the foot of Cumberland Mountain in Powell's valley, while conveying men to Kentucky. Robert Allen Ragan lived longer than any of the other men who served as 'PILOT.'

One of his most interesting stories of that day and time is Old Uncle David's prayer which was delivered by an old colored man before the Union men crossed the Holston River. He lived in a little log cabin on a farm. Was an old fashioned preacher and of course a strong Union man. The prayer is as follows:

"O Lawd God A'mighty! We is yo' chil'n and 'spects you to hea' us without delay, cayse we all is in right smart of a hurry. Dese yer gemmen has run'd away from de Seceshers and dere 'omes and wants to get to de Norf. Dey hasn't got any time to wait. Ef it is 'cordin to de destination of great Hebben to help 'em, it'll be 'bout necessary fo' de help to come right soon. De hounds and de rebels is on dere track. Take de smell out ov de dog's noses, O Lawd! and let Gypshum darkness come ober de eyesights ob de rebels. Confound 'em, O Lawd! De is cruel, and makes haste to shed blood. De long has pressed de black man and groun' him in de dust, and now I reck'n dey spects dat dey am a gwin' to serve de loyal men de same way. Hep dese gemmen in time ob trouble and lead 'em through all danger on to de udder side of Jo'dan dry shod! An' raise de radiance ob you face on all de loyal men what's shut up in de Souf! Send some Moses, O Lawd to guide 'em fru de Red Sea of Flickshun into de Promis' Land! Send some great Gen'ral ob de Norf wid his comp'ny sweepin' down fru dese parts to scare de rebels till dey flee like Midians and slew dereselves to sabe dere lives! O Lawd, bless de Gen'rals of de Norf! O Lawd, bless de Kunnels, O Lawd, bless de Capt'ins! O Lawd, bless der loyal men makin' dere way to de Promis' Land! O Lawd, Everlastin." Amen.

"This prayer, offered in a full and fervent voice, seemed to cover our case exactly and we could join in the 'AMEN.' We then crossed the Holston River, but not dry shod."

It is not generally known that about four hundred Union sympathizers in the Knob Section of our County refused to go into the Confederate Army. They were made up of farmers, mechanics and blacksmiths. On one of the high hills in the Knob country these men constructed breastworks. They sawed off gum tree logs about the length of a cannon, bored holes in the logs large enough to load with tin cans full of large bullets and pieces of iron. From wagon tires they made iron bands to fit around the log cannons to prevent them from exploding when fired. It was said they could fire these wooden guns with accuracy.

The Confederates heard of these preparations and sent Leadbeater with his command to Parrottsville for the purpose of 'looking after these men.' With a large force he went into the knob country and captured one hundred of these men and brought them to Parrotsville where the army was in camp. They placed the men in a large one-story frame school house and placed a heavy guard around the prison. They kept them there for some time and treated them terribly. Hamilton

Yett, a strong Confederate came into the camp and said he wanted "To look at the Animals." Such an expression enraged the prisoners, Peter Reece picked up a piece of a brick from the fireplace and threw it at Yett fracturing his skull. The soldiers took Reece out and hung him to a tree close to the prison, where he hung for three days. His wife and other women came and took the body down and hauled it away, no man being allowed to assist them.

It is said that William Denton, who owned the Denton Mill above Edwina was considered one of the bravest of the County's Civil War soldiers. He is given credit of performing a feat equal to that of Alvin C. York of the World War according to tradition handed down by the citizens of his neighborhood. The story told is that some where above the present mill-site along the Big Pigeon River he captured an entire company of Union soldiers who had deserted and formed a company. They lived in the fastness of the mountains and would come down upon the citizens in the valley of the river and rob them of their food. This went on for some time, until William Denton decided that the 'bushwhackers' as they were called had robbed and plundered long enough. He enlisted some neighbors and together they went after the deserters captured and disposed of them according to the military tactics of that day.

From Thomas De Arnold Byrd of Florence, Texas comes the following story of the death of his grandfather, Mark Fox, as told to him by his mother:

"In 1862 or 3 a company of Rebel soldiers made a raid down the Newport road. Near where Seldon Hill lived a mountaineer took a shot at them wounding their doctor in the arm. That made them mad. As they continued on down the road and just West of Haskews Chapel (Chestnut Hill), and old negro, Finley Patterson lived, he saw them coming and took leg-bail and saved his hide. At Bird's Cross Roads went South 2 or 3 hundred yards, to where Mark Bird, my grandfather's brother lived. (Your mother will know the place). They shot him and set his house on fire. In the meantime, grandfather Fox had started to Chestnut Hill to get some news of the war. After the killing of Uncle Mark, the Rebs went on down the road. Uncle Joe Shrader saw them and hid in a large brush pile, on top of the hill near where Aunt Edna Fox lived. The Rebs and Grandfather met opposite Uncle Joe who could see and hear all they said and all they did. They began to curse and abuse grandfather for being a Union. He gave them a bawling out, then the commanding officer gave orders to shoot him and all other men that they saw. After the Rebs had gone on Uncle Joe went on home and sent some of his children to tell mother and sisters. They took a horse and sled and went after him. Their only brother was a prisoner of war. All other Union had to hide out regardless of age."

"In your story on the Birds and Foxes you have all the information I could give you with this correction. E. S. Early bought the mill in 1879 from grandfather, who died July 5, 1889 age 94 years."

This reference is to the Blowing Cave Mill. And it was this grandfather Bird who was the gentleman for whom Bird's Cross Roads was named. He was one of the first county officials of Sevier County and served many years as its Trustee, also as Justice of the Peace and was the first postmaster at Bird's Cross Roads and continued to serve until his death. His name was John Bird. He was a soldier in the war of 1812.

The following letter came in a dainty envelope 2½ inches wide and 4 inches long. State of Georgia, Walker County, Headquarters, Detachment 2nd Tennessee Calvary On the Field, June the 23, 1864.
Dear Wife :-

It is with pleasure that I embrace the present opportunity of dropping you a few lines which will inform you that I am well, hoping when this letter comes to hand it will find you and the children enjoying the same blessing.

I am in the best of health and the boys under my command are in good health. I have forty-two men with me. I guarded a drove of beef cattle through from Nashville. We are herding our cattle now seven or eight miles South of Chattanooga. I was in Chattanooga today. It is very likely that I will stay here for several days. I have a fine camp. We are living well. Had dew berry pies for supper. The boys are all busily engaged cooking. We will have coffee, hard tack and bacon to finish our supper.

A Cocke County Seal

Wounded men are coming in every day. There is more hard fighting now than there has been since the war commenced. We are losing a great many men, but we are gaining ground every day.

I was twelve days on the road from Nashville to Chattanooga.

I want you to write me as soon as you get this letter. Give me all of the general news. I would love to see you and the children. Change the Baby's name to Mary U. instead of Mary L. Her name is Mary Ulysses. I will have to close for want of paper and candle and lay me down to sleep and think of you and my darling Babes at home. Remaining your Husband until·death, Good Night. G. W. Webb to Mary Webb and Gregory and Mary U. Webb.

Under date of April 30, 1865 Mary (Polly) Shrader Webb wrote to her husband Captain George W. Webb as follows this excerpt from her letter in my possession.

"I will inform you of the times in this country. The Rebels are still in Cocke County and occasionally down in our country. It is the Lewis Scout. Captain Buckner from N. C. was with them. They had about 60 men. They killed Wm. Allen who lived on the Ma Kisic farm on Pigeon and Wm. Hurst. The last raid they made down here about two weeks ago they killed several men in Cocke County.

There is a large force of Federal men in Asheville, N. C. now and it is thought they will clean the Rebels out of the country before very long. Signed—Mary Webb.

This was my grandmother's report to my grandfather Webb. I have many interesting letters each wrote to the other 1861 to 1865.

COCKE COUNTY OFFICIALS

It is impossible to secure the names and dates of service for all the officials who have served Cocke County. The several Courthouse fires destroyed all records kept in them at the time. From the private papers of Major Thomas Sandusky Gorman, a few such names and dates have been taken, such as signatures to notes, bonds, etc.

Major Gorman seems to have been equal to a bank in handling money for the people. Older citizens claim that Major Gorman, William Jack and Jehu Stokely were the financial wizards of their time. D. K. Gorman was also a "moneyed" man. From one of his letters dated April 4, 1874, he states that he deposited one thousand dollars in cash with his merchant, as a reserve fund for a trip he wanted to take with his wife to Tennessee, "but the merchant went broke."

Major Gorman took many newspapers, the most important of which are as follows from receipts found among his papers: *The Knoxville Tribune* (with the word "Tribune" marked out and "Register" written over it), dated May 12, 1849, and signed by John Miller McKee; May 12, 1850, *The Columbian and Great West*, signed by John P. Taylor; May 16, 1860, *The Knoxville Whig*, signed W. G. Brownlow, per Kenshe; Dec. 1, 1984, *Union American Weekly*, signed by Grigsby, Agt.; March 28, 1878, *The Morristown Gazette*, signed by John E. Helms. These publications were all two dollars per year.

The following names and dates give evidence of those interested in the affairs of Cocke County during the life of Major T. S. Gorman. They were justices of the peace: L. D. Porter, April 23, 1842; W. W. Bibee, November 4, 1844; W. P. Gillett, May 21, 1846; Stephen Basinger, June 15, 1855; Charles Kelly, April 4, 1856; T. S. Gorman, 1857; Anderson Fox, March 8, 1858; C. Brockway, February 5, 1866; W. B. Allison, January 12, 1877; William Robinson, May 14, 1842; Daniel Stephens, July 30, 1845; Giles Joyner, April 3, 1854; George I. Thomas, October 18, 1855; Joseph Rutherford, April 8, 1856; William Cureton, July 19, 1858; S. (Sol) McGinty, January 21, 1860; L. M. Gregg, February 5, 1866. (The names of various sheriffs, county court clerks and postmasters found in the Gorman papers appear in the regular lists of such officials.)

MEMBERS OF GENERAL ASSEMBLY FROM COCKE COUNTY

William Lillard, 1797-1809; Alexander Smith, 1811-1813; William Lillard, 1813-1817 (a total of 18 years); Isaac Allen, 1817-1823; George Stuart, 1825-1827; Isaac Allen, 1827-1829; Alexander E. Smith, 1831-35; Alexander Milliken, 1835-37; William Ogden, 1837-39; William McSween, 1839-41; Alfred Lea, 1841-43; Wilson Duggan, 1843-51 (During the '43 session Grainger was represented by John Cocke, Sr., son of William, and during the '45 session, Anderson and Campbell Counties were represented by William G. McAdoo); W. F. Morris, 1851-53; W. A. Campbell, 1855-57; J. H. Randolph, 1857-59; T. S. Gorman, 1859-61; J. H. Randolph, 1861-63. This was the 34th General Assembly.

Sheriff R. Walter Smith

From 1865-67, the General Assembly had no number but was known as the Brownlow Legislature and Cocke County's representative was S. H. Inman (evidently Shadrach, as each Inman family at that time carried the three Biblical names of Shadrach, Meshack and Abednego, as requested by the mother of the first three sons to carry the names). Sevier County, at this time, and also Knox were represented by Charles Inman.

The 1867-69 General Assembly resumed the number and was known as the 35th Session. S. H. Inman again represented Cocke County. A. Ragan (probably Alexander), 1869-71; Isaac Allen, 1871-73; A. Ragan, 1873-75; S. A. Burnett, 1875-77; W. L. Duggan (Wilson), 1877-1881 (From 1881-83, he was Senator.); W. C. Anderson, 1881-83; S. A. Burnett, 1883-85; W. J. McSween, 1885-87; P. B. Huff, 1887-89; William Moore, 1889-91; R. L. Hickey, 1891-93 (James R. Penland, a native son, was Senator, but lived in Sevier County.); Ben W. Hooper, 1893-95; (J. R. Penland, Senator.); Ben W. Hooper, 1895-97; J. D. Williams, 1897-99; M. G. Walker, 1899-1901; D. C. Waters, 1901-1903; A. Hampton, 1903-5 (H. N. Cate was Senator.); J. W. McMahan, 1905-7; John R. Brooks, 1907-9 (Election contested by Hickey); John R. Brooks, 1909-11; F. W. Parrott, 1911-13; C. F. Boyer, 1913-15; O. L. McMahan, 1915-17; Joe J. Burnett, 1917-19; C. F. Boyer, 1919-23; Oscar W. Easterly, 1923-25; C. F. Boyer, 1925-27 (Dr. Paul Shields was Senator.); John Mantooth, 1927-29; F. W. Parrott, 1929-31; Jacob L. Shults, 1931-33; (O. L. McMahan was senator from the 4th Senatorial District, living at Morristown.); John J. Hampton, 1933-35; Jeter S. Ray, 1935-37; Ruth W. O'Dell, 1937-39; Ruth W. O'Dell, 1939-41; F. W. Parrott, 1941-43; James A. T. Wood, 1943-45; Aubry Bryant, 1945-47. Rep. West—47 to 49.

Senators listed from 1796 to 1869 have no addresses given other than the district. The following appear to be Cocke County men: Gray Garrett, 1827-29; B. F. Bell, 1853-55; D. V. Stokely, 1859-61; Lewis F. Self, 1869-71 (Postmaster at Wilton Springs in 1857.); M. A. Driskill, 1879-81; W. L. Duggan, 1881-83 (A law partner of W. J. McSween but later moved to Sevier County.); James R. Penland, 1891-93; H. N. Cate (Newport), 1903-5; Dr. J. A. P. Shields (Hartford), 1925-27. Dr. R. W. Smith—1945-47.

The first Senator before the region became known as Cocke County was George Doherty with Alexander Outlaw and Adam Peck as Representative. This was in 1796 at the first General Assembly of the new state of Tennessee. In 1797, Adam Peck and William Lillard were the representatives and James Roddy, the Senator.

But as early as 1789, John Ellison, then of the Cocke County part of Greene County, represented the latter county in the House of Commons of North Carolina, and sat in the North Carolina Convention, which ratified the Federal Constitution in 1789. To William Lillard goes the honor of being Cocke County's first representative and of rendering the longest service. Eighteen years.

Not more than five or six have been Democrats: James A. T. Wood; R. L. Hickey; Jeter S. Ray; T. S. Gorman; W. J. McSween; probably, P. B. Huff, M. G. Walker, Alex Smith, and William Lillard.

POST OFFICES, POSTMASTERS, SALARIES

From Dr. Edmund C. Burnett's historical letter in the *Newport Times*, under date of February 21, 1940, the following Post Office data is taken:

The earliest Guide found was for 1803 when Newport was the only post office in Cocke County, and it remained the sole one until Parrottsville was set up in the thirties. It is found first in the Guide for 1836, but no list has been found for the period 1832-36. In 1853, Bridgeport and Cato appear (no list for 1852 has been found): in 1855, Wilsonville; in 1857, Taylorsburgh; and in 1859, Hackletooth and Wolf Creek. Cosby first appears in 1862 (the Guides for 1860-61 are missing); Jonesville, in 1862, was the name used for a few years for that locality, later to be named Big Creek (now Del Rio). Cosby, Jonesville, Taylorsburgh, Wilton Springs, and Wolf Creek remain in the lists down to 1867, but with no postmasters named. In 1868, these had disappeared, and the only post offices in the County were Newport, Parrotsville and Wilsonville.

In 1870 seven post offices are listed, with the salaries of the postmasters: Big Creek, $12; Bridgeport, $12; Gorman's Depot, $12; Newport, $200; Parrottsville, $46; Rankin's Depot, $12; Riverside, $12. Wilsonville is missing, the business no doubt having been taken over by Gorman's Depot.

From Boyd's Post Office Directory (as it was then called), comes the list of April 1, 1873, naming the post office, the postmaster and the salary: Big Creek, Stephen A. Burnett, $61; Bridgeport, Davidson Sprouse, $20; Cosby, Joseph M. Ragan,

A Cocke County Seal

$30; Gorman's Depot (c. h. meaning Court House), Charles T. Peterson, $280; Newport, William Cureton, $12; Ogdensville (Wilsonville), Jesse J. O'Neil, $3; Parrotsville, James C. La Rue (spelled Larne), $54; Rankin's Depot, Andy Ramsey, $99; River Side, G. W. Allen, $41; Wilton Springs, Malcolm McNabb, $12.

The postmasters are named first in the Guide for 1811; some of the later Guides do not name them. Below is the record so far as Dr. Burnett could find it:

NEWPORT—Augustine Jenkins, 1811-19; William C. Roadman, 1822-46; John F. Stanberry, 1850-; John P. Taylor, 1851-53; David W. Stuart, 1854-59 (Mr. Stuart signed his name D. Ward Stuart on local receipts. John P. Taylor served next according to T. S. Gorman papers.); Henry H. Baer, 1865-68.

PARROTTSVILLE—William B. Hutson, 1836-37; Samuel W. Hughes, 1842-; James Kilgore, 1846-; Joseph H. Davis, 1850-51; Malcolm McNabb, 1853-57; T. A. Faubion, 1850-; Nat W. Faubion, 1865-67; James C. La Rue, 1868.

WILSONVILLE—Henry H. Baer, 1850-59; David F. Gorman, 1865-67; W. W. Bibee, 1868.

BRIDGEPORT—Edward McMahan, 1853-69; William H. DeWitt, 1859-.

CATO—Andrew C. Huff, 1853-55; Jacob Weaver, 1867-; John Huff, 1859.

WILTON SPRINGS—George McNabb, 1855-; Lewis F. Self, 1857; David B. Britton, 1859.

HACKLETOOTH—Jacob Shults, 1859.

WOLF CREEK—Green Allen, 1859.

Cosby first made its appearance in the 1862 Guide (Guides for 60-61 missing). During the sixties Cosby lost its official status and, says Dr. Burnett, "It is a wonder some other place in the state did not seize upon the name . . . but the name remained unappropriated, and in 1870 Cosby took its place once more among the post offices of the County; henceforth to stride across the pages of history, the name a household word, wherever two or three were gathered behind the barn."

DEL RIO POST OFFICE

On July 15, 1869, the Big Creek post office was established in Cocke County, with Stephen A. Burnett as postmaster. Its name was changed to Del Rio, June 7, 1888. Mr. Burnett's salary was twelve dollars. It received its first mail service six times a week on Railroad Route No. 10,270, running from Warm Spring, North Carolina. The Cincinnati, Cumberland Gap and Charleston Railroad Company were contractors for this service. Domestic money order business was established on January 2, 1900, and international money order service, on March 15, 1939. Rural delivery service was established on February 2, 1903, with one carrier at six hundred dollars per year.

The following list prepared by the office of the First Assistant Postmaster General, shows all postmasters of record who have served at the post office, with dates of appointment: Stephen A. Burnett, July 15, 1869; Swan L. Burnett, January 7, 1875; Marvel N. Stokely, March 9, 1886; Marvel N. Stokely, June 7, 1888; Swan L. Burnett, February 26, 1889; James H. Burnett, June 10, 1890; Marvel N. Stokely, July 14, 1893; Nathan A. Huff, June 15, 1897; John W. Justus, December 29, 1902; Nathan F. Stokely, May 23, 1914; Louella Jones, February 27, 1917; Miss J. Myrtle Cole, December 14, 1921 (she became Mrs. Horner, July 1, 1929.); Miss Nannie F. Jones, January 26, 1934 (Miss Nannie F. Jones, who was still postmaster, 1950, contributed this data.)

CIRCUIT COURT CLERKS

William Garrett; Henry K. Stephens, 1810: Alexander Outlaw; Daniel C. Chamberlain; William D. Rankin, 1830-44; William McSween, 1844-56; D. A. Crawford, 1856-59; Isaac Allen, 1859-60; H. H. Baer, 1860-70; William Campbell, 1870-72; H. H. Baer, 1872-74; John F. Stanberry, 1874-82; C. F. Boyer, 1882-1890; Owen Harrison, 1890-94; Joseph Dawson, 1894-98; W. H. Bybee, 1898-1902 (Owen Harrison served out Bybee's unexpired term.); O. L. Hicks, 1902-10 (J. L. Shults served out Hicks' unexpired term.); Clyde McMahan, 1910 to 1914; C. H. Lovell, 1914-18; David L. Holt, 1918-34; Creed Rollins, 1934 (Death terminated his service.); Perry A. Valentine, 1945 (Death terminated his service.); Iliff McMahan still serving in 1950.

CLERKS AND MASTERS

David Stuart, 1856-58; W. C. Smith, 1861 (Probably served for McSween.); William McSween, 1858-64; M. A. Roadman, 1864-76; John D. Smith, 1877-88; John R. Shults, 1888-98; John Stuart, 1898-1906; Haynes O. Lee, 1906-7; S. A. Burnett,

1907-10; A. A. Cates, 1910-34; R. P. Clark, 1934-46. Since 1946 the office has been held by Viola Clark. Still serving 1950.

COUNTY COURT CLERKS

William Garrett, 1798-1831; George M. Porter, 1831-36; William J. McSween, 1836-38; D. F. Evans, 1839; John F. Stanberry, 1839-41; Royal Hall, 1841-2; John F. Stanberry, 1842-44; John Gorman, 1844-48; Allen McMahan, 1848-50; Royal Hall, 1850; Allen McMahan, 1851-52; V. A. Harrison, 1852-54; A. Jones, 1854-56; L. D. Porter, 1856-57; W. B. Harrison, 1857-60; D. Ward Stuart, 1860-62; Gorman, 1863; H. H. Baer, 1863; James C. LaRue, 1864-66; John Justice, 1866; William H. Wood, 1866-68; P. W. Anderson (Pleasant Witt), 1868-74; William H. Penland, 1874-82; John T. Jones, 1882-90; W. H. Penland, 1890-98; Rufus Hickey, 1898-1910; John Holt, 1910-1918; Perry A. Valentine, 1918-26; Walter C. Cureton, 1926-30; Frank W. Parrott, 1930-34; Robert Parrott; Frank W. Parrott, 2 terms followed to 1950. Donald Cody elected in 1950.

On April 1, 1863, Samuel McGinty was chairman of the County Court. J. H. Robinson's term as Chairman expired on January 1, 1891.

REGISTERS OF DEEDS

Alexander Anderson; Alexander Milliken; John H. Penland; William H. Wood; John Cameron, 1846; John P. Taylor, 1849; Thomas Bell; John P. Taylor, 1853; Charles Brockway; Addison Ragan, 1868-70; William Cureton, 1870-78; Abraham Weaver, 1878-82; Samuel Cureton, 1882-1890; Allen Bryant, 1890-98; Burnett Rowe, 1898-1902; Felix Shults, 1902-10; T. D. Haun, 1910-22; U. G. Burke, 1922-30; Mrs. Arlie Burke Carter, 1930-34; George Hall, 1936-Feb. 6, 1940 (When automobile accident ended Hall's term); Neil Harper, Feb. 20, 1940-Sept. 1, 1940 (Being one-half of term and elected by the Court); Orphas Bryant (Elected in regular 1940 election to fill unexpired term of Hall and re-elected for four year term in 1942, to end Sept. 1, 1946.) Neil Harper next served a term or two followed by Jack Rollins to 1950.

SHERIFFS OF COCKE COUNTY

William Jobe; Thomas Mitchell; Isaac Allen; James Jennings; Benjamin Coleman; John Allen; Abraham Fine, 1838-40; James R. Allen, 1842-44; Thomas S. Gorman, 1852-54; William Johnson; B. Bryant, 1854-55; R. C. Ottinger, 1856-; T. S. Gorman, 1856-58; John D. Smith, 1858-60; James Netherton, 1860-62; T. S. Gorman, 1863-; James Netherton, 1865-; John D. Smith, 1866-68; David Sprouse, 1868-72; James Netherton, 1872-74; John Bible, 1874-76; C. F. Boyer, 1876-82; John A. Balch, 1882-84; J. I. Waters, 1884-90; William Allen, 1890-92; John F. Nease, 1892-94; Isaac Cates, 1894-98; J. S. Dawson, 1898-99; A. C. Hampton, (coroner, acted a short period after death of Sheriff Dawson.); John F. Nease, 1899-1904; C. F. Boyer, 1904-1908; W. B. Hartsell, 1908-10; C. E. Dawson, 1910-14; Flint Ray, 1914-18; John Holt, 1918-24; G. C. Duncan (coroner, served almost one year during Holt's term in office.); O. L. Hicks, 1924-28; Mack Harper, 1928-30; O. L. Hicks, 1930-32; R. Walter Smith (Doctor), 1932-38; Charles D. Fisher, 1938-44; Charles S. Runnion, 1944-46; Charles D. Fisher, 1946 to 1950 when Dr. R. W. Smith was elected sheriff.

SUPERINTENDENTS OF COUNTY SCHOOLS

J. Calvin Smallwood; Washington Boyer; Robert B. Hickey; W. J. Hatley; J. M. Thomas; Frank W. Parrott; Andrew J. McMahan, 1900-06; Richard P. Driskill, 1906-12; Oscar L. McMahan, 1912-20; Roy T. Campbell (served out McMahan's unexpired term.); Mrs. Ruth W. O'Dell, 1920-23 (Part of unexpired term and one full term.); Roy T. Campbell, 1923-32; Patrick C. Williams, 1932-36; Wayne Waters, 1936-40; Roy T. Campbell, 1940-42; Deck Williams, 1942-44; Mrs. Lagretta Cureton Parrott, 1944-1948—still serving in 1950.

TAX ASSESSORS

J. K. P. Baxter, 1888-92; John Easterly, 1892-94; David McMahan, 1908-19; James A. Coggins, 1920; Wade Giles, 1920-32; Isaac C. Black, 1932-44 (Died in office); Cleo Jones, 1944-46; Cleo Jones; John Riley Holt, 1946-1950.

TRUSTEES

William Coleman; Joseph H. Green; Isaac Smith; John Allen; James Dawson; William Robinson; Sanders McMahan; John Cameron, 1855-6; Robert Ragan; J.

A Cocke County Seal

Wood; Joel Wrenn; John Hale; Henry Penland; M. A. Driskill (spelled Driscoll), 1878-80; A. M. Stokely (spelled Stockeley), 1880-84; B. A. Proffitt, 1884-88; John F. Nease, 1888-92; J. M. Stuart, 1892-96; W. H. Bear, 1896-98; J. C. Easterly, 1898-1904; Nathan Huff, 1904-10; R. H. Sexton, 1910-16; C. D. Balch, 1916-18; B. H. Teague, 1918-22; J. Windfield Kyker, 1922-30; William H. Hampton, 1930-32; Frank W. Parrott, 1932-36; William H. Hampton, 1936-44; William Ottinger, 1944-46; Victor Webb, 1946-48. Serving in 1950.

GARRETT LETTER
(From Tennessee State Archives)

Bradford, Coosa Co., Ala., 1st Dec. 1874

Doct. J. G. M. Ramsey,
Knoxville, Tenn.

Dear Sir:

I proceed to give you information as far as in my power of the pioneers of Cocke County, regretting my inability to afford much. The County was in its organization come ten or twelve years old when I was born, so that many of the pioneers had passed away by death, and removed to the west and north west, to the new States opening up there, before I had reached an age and acquaintance to know many. Of those mentioned in the first volume of your Annals, as Commissioners to locate the Seat of Justice, I knew personally but one, Major Peter Fine. He was one of the first settlers and defenders of the settlements made south of French Broad river. He was for many years Chairman of the County Court, and controlled and gave direction pretty much to the public business of the County—Possessing integrity and decision of character he was well fitted for the times in which he lived. His settlement was directly opposite New Port, on the north side of the river and embraced the Ferry at that place, where he died in 1826, at an advanced age, greatly respected and was interred in his own burying ground by a large concourse of his fellow Citizens. He had several sons, who mostly emigrated to the West. Abraham the youngest lived and died in Cocke County—He was a brave soldier in the war with the Creek Indians in 1813, and returned home with a good character for gallantry in action. He filled many offices with faithfulness and credit, especially that of Sheriff. He was a man of fine character, a worthy member of the Presbyterian Church, and died many years ago leaving a good name to his descendants.

WILLIAM JOB. (Jobe) Another of the Commissioners with Major Fine was elected the first Sheriff of Cocke County, an office that he held and discharged the duties of faithfully for many years. His name was the synonym of integrity.

WILLIAM COLEMAN—who settled on the South side of Big Pigeon a few miles above its mouth was another one of the pioneers. He was if I mistake not, the first County Treasurer of Trustee, holding the office for a great many years—and lived to a great age.

COL. JOHN McNABB, who seems from your annals to have settled first in the Watauga Country, and to have been actively engaged as a soldier in the stirring times of the Revolution, was an early settler on Big Pigeon, opposite the mouth of Causbie (Cosby) Creek and owned a large body of land in the bend of the river. He had seen much of military life in the early times—and if I mistake not was elected the first Colonel of Militia in the County. For many years he exerted a large and beneficial influence in his community and County, assisted by his wife, an intelligent lady—who tho much afflicted in the latter years of her life, presented a lively, cheerful disposition. They both died in the communion of the Methodist Church and their descendants to the third and fourth generations, many of them still reside in that Country.

COLO. WILLIAM LILLARD was an early settler on Causbie's Creek and had no little participation in the measures of defense against the Indian attacks of those days. He possessed strong points of character and was a man of some mark in frontier settlements. He was the first Representative elected from Cocke County and continued to occupy that position for many years. At the opening of the Missouri Territory he removed to it and was elected a member of the Convention that formed the first constitution of that State. He afterwards returned to East Tennessee on a visit and I saw him as the guest of my father—of medium height, he was heavy set and a frame for endurance and strength. He still carried a fresh cheerful face.

ALEXANDER OUTLAW was the first clerk of the Circuit Court appointed. He was a son of Colo. Outlaw, an early settler on Nolachucky river who participated in the early settlement and organization of the State. The "big bend of Chucky" below & opposite the mouth of Bent Creek, was known in the early days as "Outlaws bend" and the Outlaw residence as "Soldiers Rest" (But you have the history of the Outlaw family I suppose.) Mr. Outlaw did not hold the Clerkship a great while and the duties were mostly discharged by a young lawyer Henry K. Stephens, who succeeded to the office and held it for several years when he resigned and went to the North West.

WILLIAM GARRETT was the first Clerk of the County Court, and held it until 1831. He came from Kentutcky whither his parents emigrated when he was quite young, in one of the companies that followed Daniel Boone, and he grew up amid the Fort life hardships and exposures of the period from 1776 to the defeat of the Indians by General Wayne, which put a stop to their hostilities. Self-educated he first taught school in Kentucky, and in the meantime studied law, which he practiced for many years with industry and energy leading to success; a part of the time as prosecuting attorney for the State in his district. He was associated at the bar, in personal friendship with the prominent lawyers of that day in East Tennessee; Such as Judge William Cocke, Jenkins Whiteside, Joseph Anderson, Joseph Hamilton and many others. His clerical abilities were of a high order, and his hand writing was clear, plain and regular. This resulted in a good degree from the use of the bark of the Buck Eye, upon which he learned to write. The process was obtained by pulling off the bark in pieces, laying it out to dry and afterwards using it. He married Miss Chilley Gray, a daughter of Colonel Thomas Gray, and about the year 1810, he left the bar to engage in other pursuits. He settled on the North side of Big Pigeon—adjoining and below the plantation of Colo. Smith. Mr. Garrett, was possessed of much energy and enterprise of character. At the commencement of the war of 1812, he made a contract with the Government of the United States, thro General Helm, an agent of the Navy, for delivering in New Orleans of a large quantity of Navy stores, such as Cordage, pickled pork and beef, and whiskey. Eight large flat boats were necessary to convey this material down the river, one of which sunk with the cargo in the Mississippi River inflicting no little loss and damage; returning from N. O. in the Spring of 1814 he traveled the whole distance to his home near New Port, passing through the Chickasaw Nation by the trail route—rested at home a few days and thence to Washington City on horseback, without a shower of rain upon him from New Orleans to Washington. In 1839 Mr. Garrett, then in Nashville, was elected Recorder of the City, an office that he held by successive elections for twelve years, when voluntarily retired on account of age and infirmity. (For further notice of Mr. Garrett see McFerrins *History of Methodism in Tennessee* but particularly the Appendix, by his son William Garrett.)

Mr. Garrett, reared a family of six sons—from whom went into the practice of the law—Gray Garrett, the eldest, took decided position in his profession, and was for a quarter of a century connected with law and politics in East Tennessee. In 1834 he was a member of the Convention that made the Constitution of that year. Afterwards he was Attorney General for the Circuit in which he resided. A premature deafness embarrassed the latter years of his practice—and in 1847 resulted in paralysis, of which he died one year after, leaving but one son, Henry A. Garrett, now a successful lawyer in Dadeville, Alabama.

The second son of Mr. Garrett, Henry, settled in Dresden, Tennessee, in the practice of law in 1827, where he prosecuted his profession successfully until 1835, he removed to Mississippi, married and settled in Adams County in planting, where he died in 1844. William Garrett the third son (not a lawyer) settled in Alabama. (See *Reminiscences of Public Men In Alabama*, pages 145-151.)

LEWIS A. GARRETT, the fourth son settled in Tazewell, Tennessee, a lawyer, and afterwards retiring from the practice, after a successful prosecution of the profession for 18 years settled in Grainger County, near Bean's Station on the Judge Jake place where he prosecuted the business of farming with energy and success until the war between the States came on. In this a true Southern man he was subjected alternately to the ravages of the Federal and Confederate soldiers which ruined him pecuniarily. He died of paralysis of the lungs in 1871.

PHINEHAS GARRETT, another son settled in Nashville where close attention to business and industry brought him success in popularity and office—he was filling a lucrative office to which he had been elected by the people, when the war commenced and when Andrew Johnson as Military Governor of Tennessee, assumed the control of Tennessee, refusing to take the required oath he was of course ostracized

A Cocke County Seal

and greatly injured, but nothing of this sort could break down his patriotic devotion to the South. He died in 1872 from the result of a fall.

THOMAS GRAY GARRETT, the youngest son of Mr. Garrett, settled in Alabama in 1841 as a lawyer, and was twice elected solicitor of the 9th Judicial Circuit—His success guaranteed a good fortune in his profession when he married a lady of large property and returned to planting.

Among early settlers in Cocke County may be mentioned 1ST. COLO. ALEXAN-DER SMITH who settled on the north side of Big Pigeon and owned a large body of land extending from the War Ford down some two miles. He possessed a rare degree of energy as his success testified. He became wealthy and died in 1824, a man of great substance of character and property. He was a lad in the days of the revolution and took an active part in the skirmishes of that day. In one of these he received a sabre cut upon the head that was a mark of honor while he lived. In the Creek Indian War of 1813 he was a major and bore himself with marked bravery and coolness in every engagement in which he participated. This was especially the case at the battle of the "Horse Shoe," where he led his command gallantly in the charge upon the enemy's works. He (his) devotion to agricultural pursuits, with the gains which rewarded his well directed industry and energy diverted his mind from public pursuits, and he was never so much in his element when riding over his large planta-tion and viewing his heavy harvest of grain, his fine large fat cattle and in looking to his stables of horses. He grew quite corpulent in his latter days. He was a use-ful, public citizen, exterted a large influence upon the public mind of the Country around and in his death was much regretted. His large property descended to his widow and only son the late General Alexander E. Smith, who lived and died on the patrimonial estate; filling many offices of trust, particularly that of Representative in the General Assembly from the Counties of Cocke and Sevier, and as an Elector. General Smith filled the measure of a good citizen in the attributes of intelligence, public spirit and generous affluent hospitality. He died in 1872.

2nd. JOHN SHIELDS was an early settler in the practice of law. Without being brilliant or eloquent, he devoted himself assiduously and faithfully to the interests committed to him professionally and had success until age and infirmity retired him to his home on Nolachucky. He raised several daughters, intelligent, industrious and domestic in their tastes, as were most of the ladies of that day. One of these ladies married Chester Jernagin, another married George Stuart, another his brother John, merchant of large property and influence, the former elected in 1825 a representative in the Legislature. Another married Gen'l Tilghman A. Howard, who was senator in 1827; afterwards removed to Indiana, and in 1838 was elected to Congress from the Bloomington district, and was defeated for Governor in 1840. In 1842 President Tyler appointed him Minister to Texas to advance the cause of annexation and he died soon after entering upon his duties. And another married Doctor Samuel Shields, who settled at Blains Cross Roads—Mr. Shields lived some years after re-tiring from the bar, highly esteemed for his probity of character.

3rd. MAJOR WILLIAM LENNARD settled at the Warford, and was an active and useful citizen. A merchant of good business qualities and had his standing and elements of character prospects of a good future in preferment, but his life was cut short by a hurt received in a fall from a horse.

PAUL McDERMOTT settled on the south side of Nolachucky river in Cocke County. His wife was a daughter of Colo. Outlaw. Mr. McDermott was drowned in French Broad river. He left one son Wm. P. H. McDermott, who afterwards married and settled in the Tellico Country.

The Inmans were early settlers on Nolachucky where there was for many years a large connection of the name. John Inman was for a long time chairman of the County Court.

4th. COLO. THOMAS GRAY settled between French Broad and Big Pigeon in 1795. A lawyer from North Carolina. He was appointed by President Washington, United States Attorney for the district of Tennessee. His life was long and eventful, full of action and vicissitude. He was licensed to practice law in Virginia (of which State he was a native) in 1764 by Judge Whythe and Randolph. In 1765 he was appointed and commissioned council for the Crown in Lundenburg County, Va. His commission signed by Lord Fauquier, Colonial Secretary. Afterwards he removed to North Carolina and settled in Newbern. He took an active part in the early move-ments of the patriots of that State and was successively a delegate to the Congress of that State from Duplin and Johnston Counties and was elected as Wheelers *History of North Carolina* shows—to a general Congress to derive action and effective measures of resistance. He had acquired a good property which was taken from him and destroyed by Lord Cornwallis in his memorable march through that State, reducing him to comparative poverty. From this however he recovered partially in after years. He was for sixty years a practitioner at the law and made his last speech before Judge Edward Scott in the Court House in New Port in 1825, at the age of 85 years. He died in September 1829 at the age of 89 years. Colo. Gray possessed many strong points of character and filled a large place in society and at the bar. He was tall and slender but with a strong constitution and great endurance, which carried him through life with a large amount of physical and mental vigor. A son of his, Alexander Gray, was among the first Judges of the Supreme Court of Missouri, having settled in St. Louis in the initial stage of that State. Colo. Gray's only lineal descendants are through his daughter, Mrs. Garrett, who married William Garrett, whose family has been noticed.

W. GARRETT

The Cherokees were most difficult to subdue of their great love of country and their delight in war and glory (if such it might be termed). They would oft creep about the remote settlements committing theft and murder.

In March 1781 Col. John Sevier gathered together 130 men and marched with them against the middle settlements of the Cherokees taking by surprise the town on the headwaters of the Little Tennessee River. Fifty warriors were slain and fifty women and children taken prisoners. Twenty towns were burned and crops destroyed. During the summer of the year a band of Cherokees invaded the settlements then forming on Indian Creek (and after the above who can blame them). General Sevier with one hundred men marched from Washington County (meaning this very area) crossed the Nollichucky, proceeded to near the present town of Newport on the French Broad River (Old Town) crossed the river, and also the Big Pigeon, at War Ford (The present Newport) and unexpectedly fell upon the trail of the Indians, surrounded their camp, and by sudden fire killed seventeen of them. The others escaped. This camp was on Indian Creek some claim it's English Creek now.

In the spring of 1782 settlements were formed South of the French Broad River. (Which of course was Indian Ground) Of this intrusion the Cherokees complained and Governor Martin of North Carolina wrote to Colonel Sevier in reference thereto asking him to prevent the encroachments complained of, and to warn the intruders off the lands reserved to the Indians, and if they did not move off according to warning he was to go forth with a body of militia and pull down every cabin and drive them off, "laying aside every consideration of their entreaties to the contrary." The Indians could well see that the white people kept steadily encroaching upon their hunting grounds and reservations. They felt that TREATY LINES WERE FEEBLE barriers against the expansive force of the settlements.

Chief Raven thought that if a wall, strong as the Chinese Wall could be built to the skies, it would not be out of power of the white people to pass it. (Our RAVEN'S BRANCH was named for this Chief some claim). The Chiefs felt there was no remedy but war. (Does not our so called present civilization seem to think the same thing?)

That the reader may know of the exact location of these Indian Hunting Grounds it is of interest to give the boundary which was fixed in May 1783 by the Legislature of North Carolina as follows:

"Beginning on the line which divides this State from Virginia at a point due North of Cloud's Creek, running thence West to the MISSISSIPPI, thence down the Mississippi to the 35 degree of North latitude, thence due East until it strikes the Appalachian Mountains, thence with the mountains to the ridge that divides the waters of the French Broad River and the waters of the Nollichucky River; and with that ridge until it strikes the line described in the Act of 1778, commonly called Brown's line; and with that line and those several watercourses to the beginning."

There was reserved, however, a tract of land for THE CHEROKEE HUNTING GROUNDS as follows: "Beginning at the Tennessee River where the Southern boundary of North Carolina intersects the same near the Chicamauga Towns; thence up the middle of the Tennessee and Holston Rivers to the middle of the FRENCH BROAD RIVER, which lines are not to include any islands in said river to the mouth of BIG PIGEON RIVER thence up the same to the head thereof; thence along the dividing ridge between the waters of Pigeon River and Tuskejah River to the Southern Boundary of this State." Thus we see that all of Cocke County South of French Broad and Big Pigeon was the Hunting Grounds of the Cherokees, and by special reservation as such.

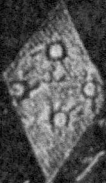

A Cocke County Seal

On page 87 of Goodspeed's *History* we find that Governor Sevier if possible to maintain peace between his State and the Indians appointed commissioners to negotiate another Treaty with the Cherokees. The Commissioners appointed were, William Cocke, Alexander Outlaw, Samuel Wear, Henry Conway and Thomas Ingle. Negotiations were begun at Chota Ford July 31, 1786 (During State of Franklin Period) and concluded Aug. 3, 1786. The Chiefs who concluded the negotiations were Old Tassel and Hanging Maw.

The proposition made to the Indians was that the Cherokees would give up the murderers among them, return the stolen horses and permit the whites to settle on the NORTH SIDE of the Tennessee and Holston Rivers, as they intended to do at any rate. The whites would live at peace with them and be friends and brothers.

The land claimed in this Treaty was the Island in the Tennessee River at the mouth of the Holston, and from the head of the island to the dividing ridge between Holston and Little River and Tennessee to the Blue Ridge and the lands sold to them by North Carolina on the North side of the Tennessee River. These terms were agreed to and the Treaty signed by Old Tassel and Hanging Maw, the Chiefs.

During the existence of the State of Franklin the Cherokees were quiet, having a wholesome dread of the courage and ability of Governor Sevier, but with the fall of the Franklin Government they renewed their hostilities.

From Page 93 Goodspeed's *History Tennessee* we find that in the year 1786 Congress appointed Commissioners to treat with the Cherokees and other Southern Tribes. These Commissioners say in their report to Richard Henry Lee, President of Congress, "That there are some few people settled on the Indian lands whom we are to remove, AND THOSE IN THE FORK OF FRENCH BROAD AND HOLSTON BEING NUMEROUS, the Indians agree to refer their particular situation to congress and to abide by their decision." Although these persons had settled contrary to Treaty stipulations entered into by Virginia and North Carolina in 1777, yet they were too numerous to order off, hence the necessity of obtaining the consent of the Cherokees to refer the matter to Congress. The same report furnishes an estimate of the number of warriors of the nations of Indians living South of the Tennessee and in reach of the advanced settlements which was as follows: Cherokees, 2,000; Creeks, 5,400; Chicasaws, 800; Choctaws, 6,000 . . . . total number of warriors 14,200 besides the remnants of the Shawnees, Uchees and other tribes.

That this great number of Indian warriors were not able to crush out the white settlers in Tennessee at that time is most remarkable. They could easily have had the help of the Northern Tribes and yet they did not undertake it. The courage and determination of our first settlers had become well known to the Indians.

For the sake of the children who read this story I must add here that the race of red men who have the earliest claim to the territory now embraced in Tennessee boundaries are said to have been the Iriquois or Confederacy of Six Nations. However, it was for the most part unoccupied by them says Goodspeed's *History*. The Achalaques had a kind of secondary claim to this region.

In Schoolcrafts great work on Indian Races of North America is a map showing the location of the various Indian Tribes in the year sixteen hundred, which if authentic proves that the Archalaques then occupied most of Tennessee, east of Tennessee River and also small portions of Georgia, Alabama, and a considerable portion of Kentucky. The ancient Archalaques were the same tribe or Nation as the Cherokees. They have no 'L' in their language and hence substituted the letter 'R', therefore in a manner similar to that in which the modern Chinaman substitutes 'L' for 'R' by a few other slight changes the name Cherokee is easily obtained. Of course it 'stands to all reason' that our beautiful word APPALACHIAN probably came from the ancient Archalaques.

The Noble Cherokees, as we often hear them called by those who understood and loved them as they were in their native state, had many fine and splendid qualities and we should know something of them as they were, not as we drove them to become by our own hostile and deceptive attitude toward them.

They had a profound faith that we would do well to emulate. They saw beauty in everything about them. They were poetic and great home-lovers. They worshipped the Great Spirit which we have almost forgotten how to worship. They had sincere veneration for the relics of The Mound Builders, the origin of which, they knew nothing, (even as we) but they considered them the vestiges of an ancient and numerous race and one much farther advanced in the arts of civilization than themselves.

We have several mounds in this section of Tennessee. On the French Broad River about a mile above the mouth of Nollichucky is a mound thirty feet high with very old trees on the top of it. On the North bank of the Holston River five miles above the mouth of French Broad are six mounds on one half acre of ground. They are irregularly scattered. The bases are from ten to thirty feet in diameter. The largest is ten feet high. Near these mounds on a bluff one hundred feet high, are painted in red colors the figures of the sun, moon, birds, fishes, etc. Most of the mounds have been opened and interesting contents discovered such as pottery ware, flint stones, shells and skeletons, etc.

North of Rankin on the East side of the French Broad River is a mound about 25 feet in height. It is elsewhere described.

In the Dutch Bottoms, on the L. S. Allen farm, once the Carter place and the George Susong farm, are seven mounds in a row that appear to be set apart and not connected with the nearby hills and knobs. Many have thought they might have been constructed by the ancient Mound-builders. They are beautiful and never fail to interest travelers.

Data compiled from Biographical Appendix, Knox Co., Tenn. (Goodspeed) p. 978.

TENNESSEE ACTS—1847-48

CHAPTER LXXXVII

An Act to authorize the Trustees of Anderson Academy in Cocke County to remove the Academy to Newport, the county seat.

Section I. Be it enacted by the General Assembly of the State of Tennessee:

That the Trustees of Anderson Academy in Cocke County are hereby authorized to remove the Academy to Newport or to within one mile of that place;

Provided, they can procure a good right and title to an eligible site, convenient to good water, upon which to erect said Academy.

Section 2. Be it enacted, that so soon as the Trustees obtain a right and title, to a suitable site, they may proceed to remove said Academy from its present location, and are authorized to use a portion of the Academy fund for that purpose.

F. BUCHANAN,
Speaker of the House of Representatives.
J. M. ANDERSON,
Speaker of the Senate.

Passed Jan. 26, 1848.

REPORT—COMMITTEES

27 CONGRESS—2ND SESSION

Serial No. 408, U. of T. Library.

27th Cong. 2nd Sess. House of Reps. Report No. 408 (Abstracted)

GEORGE AND REUBEN ALLEN

March 8, 1842. Read and laid upon the table.

Mr. Turney, from the Committee on Private Land Claims submitted the following:

Report: The Committee on Private Land Claims to whom was referred a bill for the relief of George and Reuben Allen, report, etc., etc.

A Bill to confirm to George and Reuben Allen the title of certain lands heretofore purchased by them of John B. Chandernah, etc.

Lands—from the Indians.

(Goodspeed)

COCKE COUNTY, TENNESSEE

Began to be settled in 1783, along the "Chucky."

Several persons located in a fertile section since known as the "Irish Bottom." Among the earliest settlers was George McNutt, whose daughter was the first white child born south of the French Broad. Others who located in that neighborhood were: Josiah Rogers, Benjamin Rogers, Alexander Rogers, John McNabb, Cornelius McGuinn, Joseph Doherty, William Doherty and others.

A settlement was made north of the French Broad by a colony of Pennsylvania Germans, among whom were the Huffs, Boyers, and Ottingers. This vicinity then took the name of the "Dutch Bottom."

Peter Fine was licensed to keep the first ferry in the county, he settled on the river opposite the old town of Newport.

In 1783 John Gilliland made a crop of corn at the mouth of Big Pigeon, and a year or two later brought his family to the place where he continued to reside

A Cocke County Seal

until his death about 1798. He left a large family, eight of whom were sons. He took an active part in organizing the State of Franklin, and was one of the delegates elected to the convention of 1785 to pass upon the Constitution of the new State.

William Lillard was the first representative of the county in the Legislature from Cocke County. He lived on the river below Old Newport.

TENNESSEE ACTS—1792-1803
CHAPTER LXIII—p. 294

An act to authorize the County Court to lay an additional county tax for certain purposes therein mentioned. (Passed Oct. 29, 1801.)

Whereas the prison of Cocke County has been destroyed by fire:

Be it enacted by the General Assembly of the State of Tennessee that the County Court be and is hereby authorized and empowered to lay an additional tax not exceeding two years, for the purpose of building a prison, and to discharge the arrearages due for building the court-house, not exceeding 12½ cents on each white poll, 25 cents on each black poll, 12½ cents on each 100 acres of land, $1.00 on each stud horse for covering mares, 25 cents on each town lot to be collected by the Sheriff, accounted for, and paid into the hands of the commissioners appointed for said county, for the purpose aforesaid.

TENNESSEE ACTS 1847-8
CHAPTER CLII

Sec. 4. Be it enacted, that it shall and may be lawful for the County Court of Cocke County, at its April or July term to appoint seven commissioners to lay off an additional Civil District, on the head waters of Cosby's Creek in said county.

Passed Feb. 5, 1848.

TENNESSEE ACTS 1792-1803
CHAPTER XIII. p. 168

An Act to add part of Greene County to the county of Cocke. (Passed Jan, 2, 1799)

Sec. 1. Be it enacted by the General Assembly of the State of Tennessee, that from and after the passing of this act, the line that divides the county of Greene from the county of Cocke shall begin at the corner of Green and Jefferson Counties, on Nolichucky River at the end of Bay's Mountain, from thence up Nolichucky river to the mouth of Oven Creek from thence a direct line to Major Gragg's so as to leave his plantation in Greene County from thence a direct line to the Painted Rock on French Broad River, below Warm Springs, from thence south to the Cocke County line, and all that part lying south of the said line shall be a part of Cocke County.

Sec. 2. Be it enacted, that the Sheriff of Greene County shall have the same power and lawful authority to collect and receive all his arrearages of taxes and executions in that part of Cocke County, that was formerly part of Greene County in the same manner as if this act had never been passed.

CHAPTER LIII. p. 290

An Act to appoint a commissioner to run the line between the counties of Greene and Cocke. (Passed Oct. 29, 1801.)

Sec. 1. Be it enacted by the General Assembly of the State of Tennessee, that David Stuart, be, and is hereby appointed a Commissioner to run the line between the counties of Greene and Cocke agreeably to an Act, entitled "An Act to add a part of Greene County to the county of Cocke," passed at Knoxville the second day of January 1799.

Sec. 2. Be it enacted, that Thomas Holland be, and is hereby appointed to attend with said David Stuart, to mark the line between the counties aforesaid.

Page 290.

Sec. 3. Be it enacted, that David Stuart shall received $2 per day for running, and Thomas Holland $1 per day for marking said line, to be paid by the treasurer of Cocke County, and their receipts shall be sufficient vouchers in the hands of the treasurer in the settlement of his accounts.

Sec. 4. Be it enacted, that the said David Stuart shall take an oath before some justice of the peace in Greene County that he will justly and truly run the aforesaid line accordingly to law.

CHAPTER IX. p. 126

An Act supplementary to an Act, entitled "An Act to divide the county of Jefferson into two separate and distinct counties (Passed Oct. 11, 1797.)

Where as by an Act of the general assembly passed this sessions, entitled "An Act to divide the Co. of Jefferson, into two separate and distinct counties" no provision is made directing at what place the citizens of the new county of Cocke shall vote, for representatives to congress at the ensuing election, to be held on the second Thursday and the day following of October in instant, to remedy which,

Be it enacted by the general assembly of the State of Tennessee, that the electors of the sd county of Cocke shall be entitled to vote for a representative to congress at the said ensuing election, on the second Thursday and day following to Oct. instant, at the courthouse of the county of Jefferson in the same manner as heretofore used, any thing in the said Act to the contrary notwithstanding.

JOURNAL OF THE HOUSE OF REPRESENTATIVES

P. 100. 2nd Sess. 6th Gen. Assem. held at Knoxville, Mon. 28 July 1806, Sat. Sept. 13, 1806.

The following persons were appointed Justices of the Peace:

Cocke County: Henry Stephens, John Netherton and James Wood.

Jefferson County: John Parrot, Wm. Griffin and Hugh Kirkpatrick.

Knox County: Wm. Minett, Senior, Harris Gammon, John Miller, Thomas Read and Beriah Frazier.

1st Sess. 7th General Assembly of the State of Tenn. Began at Kingston, on Mon. the 21st day of Sept., and continued by adjournment to Knoxville, on Wed. the 23rd 1807.

WHEN KINGSTON WAS A CAPITAL FOR A DAY

At a meeting of the General Assembly of the State of Tenn. on Mon. the 21st day of Sept. 1807 at the town of Kingston, the following members appeared, produced their credentials, were qualified and took their seats.

From the County of:

Blount: Mr. Jas. Scott.
Carter: Mr. Alexander Doran
Claiborne: Mr. John Vanbibber
Cocke: William Lillard
Davidson, Mr. Thomas Wmson
Grainger: Mr. Jno Cocke
Greene: Mr. Robert Guin
Hawkins: Mr. Wm. Young and Mr. Wm. Bradley
Jackson, Overton and White: Mr. Jno Crawford and Mr. Henry I. A. Hill.
Jefferson: Mr. Christpher Haynes
Knox: Mr. Jas. Trimble and Mr. Thos. Dardis
Montgomery and Stewart: Mr. Willie Blount
Roane and Anderson: Mr. John Kirby
Robertson and Dickon: Mr. Anderson Cheatham
Rutherford: Mr. Jos. Dickson
Sevier: Mr. Jno Cannon
Smith: Mr. Joel Dyer
Sullivan: Mr. John Tipton
Sumner: Mr. Samuel P. Black and Mr. James Cryer
Washington: Mr. Wm. Mitchell
Williamson: Mr. Chapman White
Wilson: Mr. Robert Edwards.

1825-1900 UNION CEMETERY p. 1197

Hon. J. H. Randolph, lawyer, born Oct. 19, 1825, Jefferson County, Tenn. In 1848 married M. J. Robinson, a daughter of Major William Robinson of Ky.

Issue: William H. M. Randolph, Rolfe M. Randolph, Townsella Randolph.

James M. Randolph, his father, a native of Jefferson County, Tenn., was the son of Henry Randolph of Roanoke, Virginia, who was a pioneer of Jefferson County, Tenn.

CHAPTER LXXVIII. p. 43

An Act for the benefit of Wm. Vinson. Be it enacted by the Gen. Ass. of the St. of 10, that the Treasurer of East Tenn., be, and he is hereby authorized and directed to pay to Wm. Vinson of Cocke Co. the sum of $18.00 out of any money in the treasury not otherwise appropriated in full compensation for a gun lost by said Wm. Vinson, in the public service during the late war with the Creek Indians.

F. W. Huling,
Speaker of the H. of Rep.
D. Burford,
Speaker of the Senate

Passed Nov. 7, 1833.

TENN. ACTS PRIVATE

1833 - 1st Sess. 20th Genl. Assembly of the State of Tenn. 1833. p. 174

CHAPTER CCC.

An Act to repeal the Act incorporating the inhabitants of the town of Newport.
Be it enacted by the General Assembly of the St. of Tenn. that the Act heretofore passed incorporating the inhabitants of the town of Newport, in the County of Cocke, be, and the same is hereby repealed.

F. W. Huling,
Speaker of the House of Representatives
D. Burford,
Speaker of the Senate

Passed Nov. 30, 1833.

CHAPT. CLXXXVI. p. 99

An Act to divorce Calloway Allen from his wife Sarah.
Be it enacted by the Gen. Ass. of the St. of Tenn. that the bonds of matrimony heretofore entered into, and now existing, between Calloway Allen, of the County of Cocke and his wife, Sarah Allen, be, and the same is hereby, dissolved.

F. W. Huling,
Speaker of the House of Rep.
D. Burford,
Speaker of the Senate

Passed Nov. 25, 1833.

TENNESSEE ACTS 1837-38

CHAPTER CCXXXIX. p. 348

1st Sess. - 22 Gen. Assembly of State of Tenn.

An Act to incorporate the Elizabethton, Sullivan, Jonesboro, Greeneville, Newport, Dandridge and New Market Turnpike Companies.

Commissioners Appointed—Section 1. Be it enacted by the General Assembly of the State of Tennessee, that, William B. Carter, Benjamin Brewer, David Nelson, James J. Tipton, Alfred W. Taylor, Samuel W. Williams, John O'Brien, Robert Reeve, William Stover and William Gott of Carter County—

John Blair, Elijah Embree, Nathan Gammon, Samuel B. Cunningham, John Bayless, Seth J. W. Luckey, Matthew Stephenson, Ebenezer Barkley, Frederick Davatt, Ebenezer Mothers, William Carmichael, Joseph Duncan, Samuel Greer, John Ryland, A. W. Brabson, William Mathes and George Tilford, of the County of Washington—

George Jones, Richard M. Woods, William M. Lowry, John Dickson, William Dickson, William K. Vance, John McGaughey, Thomas D. Arnold, David Johnson, Andrew Johnson, M. G. Fillers, Joseph A. Earnest, George W. Foute, Alfred Russell, Alexander Henderson, James Broyles, James Moore and Valentine Sevier of the County of Greene and—

Thomas Rogers, Alexander E. Smith, James Dawson, William C. Roadmon, Samuel Haskins, John Stuart, John Gillett, R. W. Pullium, N. L. Reese, William Robinson, David Harned, Abraham Fine, George W. Carter and Stephen Huff of the County of Cocke, are hereby appointed commissioners to open books for the purpose of receivinig subscriptions to the amount of two hundred thousand dollars, to be applied to the purpose of making a McAdamized turnpike road from Elizabethton by way of Jonesborough and Greeneville to Newport, or to some point on the Charleston and Cincinnati railroad which may be situated nearer to Greeneville than Newport is situated, etc., etc., etc. Passed Jan. 17, 1838.

TENNESSEE ACTS 1847-48

CHAPTER CLXIX. p. 272

An Act to amend an Act entitled an Act to authorize Benjamin Parker Hopkins and William Tinker of the Co. of Cocke to open a turnpike road and for other purposes.
Section 1. Be it enacted by the General Assembly of the State of Tenn.:

That Benjamin Parker Hopkins and William Tinker of the County of Cocke shall have the further time of two years from and after the passage of this Act to open and complete said road, etc.

Passed Feb. 4, 1848.

TENNESSEE ACTS 1792-1803

Lib. No. 345.12 p. 207. 1-5. Sess. 1

CHAPT. XXXIX

An Act authorising the County Court of pleas and Quarter Sessions of the County of Cocke, to open a certain road therein mentioned. (Passed Oct. 26, 1799.)

Whereas a road from or near the town of Newport in the County of Cocke, to cross the mountains by the way of the old fields of Big Pigeon, into the state of Georgia, would not only be of considerable advantage to the inhabitants of said county, but would be of great convenience to persons passing from this state to the state of Georgia and South Carolina. etc.

TENNESSEE, GREENE COUNTY COURT MINUTES, 1817-1819

U. of T. Library

Library No. 976.89 g. 795. p. 44.

Reuben Allen, overseer of the road from the ford of the river near George Farnsworth to the road leading from Wilson's ford to Fine's Ferry.

CHAPT. LVII p. 30.

An Act to authorize Wm. P. Gillet to open a turnpike road.

WM. P. GILLET, MAY OPEN ROAD

Sect. 1. Be it enacted by the Gen. Ass. of the St. of 10, that Wm. P. Gillet is hereby authorized to open a turnpike rd commencing at Newport in the Co. of Cocke, and running up the so. side of French B. River to Holland's ferry which road, when the situation of the ground will permit, shall be cut 18 ft. wide clear of stumps and other obstructions and where sd. road has to be cause wayed it shall, if the ground will permit be 12 ft. wide and if there should be any creek or creeks that require it there shall be good sufficient and substantial bridges built over them, etc, etc.

Passed Nov. 1, 1833.

CHAPTER LXXVIII p. 122.

An Act to authorize Stephen Huff, Peter F. Kendrick and William Robison of the County of Cocke to open a Turnpike Road in said County and for other purposes. etc.

Sec. 8. Be it enacted that this charter is hereby given to said Stephen Huff, Peter F. Kendrick and William Robison, their heirs and assigns for the term of 30 years.

Sec. 12. Be it enacted, that John P. Long, William Cumming and Jeremiah Fryer, shall be appointed Commissioners of the aforesaid road. etc., etc., etc.

etc. said com. shall proceed to license said proprietor to keep a toll gate on said road which license shall be under their hands and seals, and thereupon said proprietor may proceed to erect a toll gate on said road and shall be entitled to receive the following rates of toll, to wit, on all wagons, loaded, drawn by four or more horses, mules or oxen, fifty cents. Not loaded twenty five cents for each carriage of burthen drawn by two horses, mules or oxen, twenty five cents; for each four wheel pleasure carriage, sixty cents; for each two wheel ditto, thirty cents; for each man and horse, or mule, ten cents; for each loose or led horse or mule not in a drove, five cents; for each head of horses or mules in a drove, four cents; for each head of cattle, or sheep, two cents; for each head of hogs, one cent that may travel over the same. etc., etc. Passed Jan. 18, 1848.

TENNESSEE ACTS 1847-8

p. 214—CHAPT. CXXXII

An Act to alter and change the times of holding the Circuit Courts in the Counties of Cocke and Sevier, and for other purposes.

Section 1—Be it enacted by the General Assembly of the State of Tenn.—That hereafter the Circuit Courts for the County of Cocke shall commence and be held on the third Monday of March, July and Nov., etc. Provided, the first terms of said court in the year one thousand eight hundred and forty-eight, shall be held at the times heretofore prescribed by law.

Sec. 2—Be it enacted, That hereafter the citizens of the Counties of Greene, Jefferson, and Cocke, may file their bills in Chancery in the Chancery Court at Greeneville in the County of Greene, or in the Chancery Court at Dandridge in the County of Jefferson, as they may choose provided that nothing in this Act shall in any wise repeal the second section passed Jan. 30, 1844. Chapter 201, etc.

Passed Feb. 4, 1848.

The balladry, which our Anglo-Saxon forebears brought into the wilderness, West of the Alleghenies, has remained unchanged in its primitive charm and beauty. Ballads are a birthright of our mountain people and it is a splendid thing that we are now endeavoring to preserve them. Never until recently have they been printed, but sung down from generation to generation, 'by word of mouth,' each generation adding to or taking away as suited their fancy but careful never to destroy the sentiment of the theme, careful to preserve its charm and beauty.

Our original ballads came from the Elizabethton period. They are filled with romance, their word beauty is often exquisite, they are generally sung to rhythmic melody that is oft repeated over and over. 'A ballad is always a dancing song,' so say our mountaineers. How wonderful it is for us to realize that our ancestors have been able to come down through the years singing, singing, singing, dancing and swinging, a free and happy people. Recently at two o'clock in the morning 1 was awakened by a singer on his way. I breathed a prayer of thanksgiving that 1 lived in a place where people had that much freedom. He was plaintively singing "Barbara Allen." No one has yet been able to take from our people these lovely old songs of their hearts. There is nothing more interesting to a person who has any desire to know about the 'days that are no more,' than the study of old, old folklore. These delightful old folk-ways that persist in spite of this modern age of skepticism. Yet, it's necessary to be a bit skeptical to believe in folklore, by that I mean skeptical of materialism, which is nothing more or less than the belief that nothing exists except what can be apprehended through the senses. We have to admit that many of the old charms and remedies really did work but how, we know not. Even though it has been almost 200 years since the Scotch Irish settled in our mountains, we can even yet detect, from a few surviving customs, a clear and distinct identification of our Anglo-Saxon blood, which is now considered the purest in the United States. Few writers have been able to record our mountain dialect in its true form, for lack of knowledge of the people, their customs and traditions back of them, this has heretofore been impossible, (thanks to our isolation probably).

The desire for rhythmic action and the enjoyment of singing never dies, although passive recreation has pushed such desires to the background. We are rapidly becoming a generation of button pushers and dial twisters, seldom experiencing the joy and exhilaration of the games our forefathers knew and enjoyed. In addition to the pleasure derived from such, the exercise in playing was most beneficial. It is in our mountain sections that we find the singing games and the true American Folk-dances which we are trying to revive throughout the country. Our Singing games invite wider participation than the square dance because they carry an appeal free from suspicion of any evil motives. Generally they are not quite so strenuous and can be enjoyed by the middle-aged and the old without fear of becoming conscience stricken. Some have felt inclined to try to believe that the dance should not be indulged in by Church members, yet they saw no harm in doing the Century old. "Jolly is the Miller," "Skip to Ma Lou, My Darling," "Hog Drivers," "Limber Jim" and many other Singing games that were played at all the "PLAY-PARTIES" of our people. They thoroughly enjoyed the music, the mingling, in neighborly fashion, of folk of the neighborhoods, in various sections. These games, together with the singing, afforded a pleasure, wholesome and enjoyable. Although these singing games were molded after the folk dances of other countries, especially those of England, they have become distinctly American, due to having developed in an entirely different environment. Our early settlers adopted them to the conditions of their early life, often recomposing them accordingly. We have discovered that those found in Indiana, Missouri, Arkansas, Oklahoma, Texas and TENNESSEE are VERY similar and in many cases the same. "Lord Thomas and Fair Elender" seems to have become a great favorite. It is now traced back to the time of Chaucer. My Great Grandmother, Sarah Catheryne Byrd Francis, sang it to me while I sat and cried. . . . Part of it was recorded in Geographic Magazine, Page 240 for August 1936, as the favorite of the Smokies. It is sung in a mournful manner but not more so than Barbara Allen, which is much more familiar to all.

The early families of this County not only made their own clothes from the cotton, wool, and flax, but they had to devise means whereby they could keep them clean. Cleanliness is said to be next to Godliness. Probably, we, of this generation and time, find it easier to be cleanly than to be Godly, while our ancestors found it easier to be Godly, but they were both it seems.

Every home had its 'ash-hopper,' not so far from the kitchen doorway. This was made of boards and resembled the letter x when finished. The bottom of the top side was filled with corn cobs for about a half foot, this supplied the drainage or place for the lye to run out. On the cobs, the ashes were poured, only hickory wood ashes were used by the careful housewife. When the hopper was full of ashes water was poured over them in great quantities to thoroughly wet them. After they were wet, only about two or three gallons per day were poured on for a certain number of days, or as long as the lye came out sufficiently strong.

In a kettle was placed the old meat trimmings, the 'cracklens' from the lard and any discarded old meat bones, etc., and the lye poured over it all. This was constantly stirred until the lye dissolved the meat scraps after which the proper amount of water was added and boiled until it 'flaked' when poured from a cup or generally a 'gourd.' To test it was to use a feather and if it took the down from the quill it was too strong and more water was added. It then had to boil until it would 'flake.' Some would boil it until it was very thick and they could then slice it when it got cold. Soap-making was almost the same method used to make jelly. It was quite an art to get either just right.

To make hominy the same kind of lye was used as to make soap. Because our people raised so many hogs and made so much hominy we were known as "The hog and hominy State." To raise corn and feed it to the hogs was more profitable than to sell the corn in the bushel.

The soap made from the process just given was called Lye-soap. It was very strong and hard on the hands. To prevent this many used a 'battling block and paddle' to get the clothes free from soil. The block was always of the whitest wood obtainable, generally white oak. The paddle was made like a boat paddle only much stronger and shorter. The clothes were first wet and placed on the block, then the soap poured on and the battling began. They were turned over several times and beaten until clean, then thrown in a great iron pot with the soap still in them and boiled for about 30 minutes. When thought to be cleaned they were lifted from the boiling suds with the paddle and thrown into a running stream if possible that had been 'backed up' for such purposes. After a few minutes in the clear, running water the clothes were wrung by hand and thrown into a tub of indigo water where they were quickly washed through and placed 'on the pailings' to dry. They were always 'white as snow' by this process.

After the weekly washing was on the 'pailings,' the kitchen and porches were scrubbed with the boiling lye soapsuds from the pot. A broom for scrubbing was made of hickory sapling with one end split into thin, narrow splits, only enough of the sapling left to turn the splits back down over and tie to hold in place, then the end of it cut off so as not to be in way of the scrub-broom. White sand was sprinkled freely on the floor during the scrubbing and after the floors had been gone over with these suds and broom they were rinsed with clear water and a light broom made of 'broom corn.' When the floors were dry they were clean and beautiful. If it was not possible to have a hickory scrub-broom one was made of shucks which 'answered the purpose.' The chairs were treated to the same cleaning process as the floors.

All kinds of 'butter' was made in great brass kettles placed in a furnace out in th- backyard. These furnaces were made of rocks and mud and the kettle placed in them. Apple butter, peach butter, jam and marmalade were made this way. The 'stirrir' was about six feet long and used constantly to keep the 'butter' from sticking on the bottom. Pumpkin butter was the last kind made each year. Limbertwig apples were used if possible for apple butter.

The cultivation of the cotton, flax and wool was as interesting as its 'conversion' into cloth for household and clothing needs.

Our first settlers found little time for idle dreaming and next to no time at all for mischief. Their survival in this new country necessitated not only eternal vigilance but constant work. The changing of the raw material they had to first produce, into food and raiment required much skill, patient toil and a knowledge that few of their descendants possess. Most of us would starve to death or be forced to join the nudist colonies if we were to find ourselves in a mountain wilderness with only our hands, an axe and a few seeds.

In the early days most of the industrious families raised cotton, flax and sheep, from which they manufactured their own household linens and clothing. The seed from the cotton was picked out by hand, even long after the cotton gin was invented. This furnished employment for the children and if they were unable to get the cotton all picked by the time it was needed by the Mother, a 'Cotton picking' was had and all the neighbors came in and finished the job after which a 'frolic' was enjoyed and all the games and square dances furnished the entertainment along with the fiddlers and banjo pickers who furnished the 'mountain music.'

The cotton was then 'carded' and ready for its various uses.

The sheep were allowed to wear their woolly coats until warm weather when it was taken from their backs by hand, this process was known as a 'sheep shearing' when the neighbors again assisted each other. They were all 'good neighbors' in those far away days. After the wool was taken from the sheep it had to be washed and then the various burs and 'spanish needles' and 'beggar lice' picked out of it after it had dried thoroughly. This was known as 'a wool picking' and was gladly attended by all the neighbors, just as they helped each other harvest their crops and gather in their winter wood, etc., etc. Even helped each other with 'the Hog-killing' in the autumn time and the 'molasses making' etc. When the wool was dry and picked, it was ready for the 'artist' with the 'Cards' or 'wool-comb' as more modern women call the 'cards.' To card and spin wool and weave it into cloth after coloring it was indeed an art and one most of our grandmothers and all our great-grandmothers knew quite well. The coverlids, bed spreads and blankets and beautiful flaxen material handed down to us furnish abundant proof of such knowledge. The spinning wheels and looms and the dainty little flax wheels are now greatly cherished by us all.

The preparation of the flax seems to have required an entirely different process than that necessary to get the cotton and wool ready for use. The flax was first passed through a 'Flax Break' which broke the bark into small pieces, so that it could be 'scutched.' The flax break was made of wood and similar to a comb, or 'cards' of the cotton and wool requirement. After the flax break was used the flax was next spread out on a scaffold in the rain and allowed to stay there until the wood decomposed. Next came the 'scutching' process, which was to place it on a smooth block or stake driven into the ground and beat it with a paddle until the bark was all off the flax. It was then passed through a flax wheel, fed into it by hand from a staff that stood over the wheel. After the spool was filled it next went on to a reel which measured it. After a certain number of turns the reel would 'pop' which indicated a certain number of yards. After this process it was ready for the loom.

The 'refuse' from the 'scutching' was saved for the purpose of 'caulking' boats. It was known as 'toe' and was placed in the 'joints' of the bottom of the boat. It was always put in from the bottom side of the boat. In those days boats played a most important part in the 'traveling' of our people and until as late as the 70's, flat boats sailed our rivers. They were 16 by 18 feet wide and 75 or 80 feet long and carried from one thousand to eighteen hundred bushels of grain. Various other products were, of course, likewise transported.

(From The Flax, Boat and Mill Information given me by Newman Anderson, direct descendant of Samuel Doak.)

National Park Service historians conducted their studies in the Eastern Sections of Blount, Sevier and Cocke Counties of Tennessee and in the Western portions of Haywood and Swain counties of North Carolina.

Knoxville News-Sentinel, Feb. 8, 1938, under heading, "Quaint Speech Vanishing in Smokies, Study Shows."

"Youths discarding lingual heritage of Scotland and England. It is becoming more like that in the lowlands." This was the report of Joseph S. Hall, youthful linguist of the graduate school of Columbia University, after investigating in the Great Smoky Mountains National Park. The National Park Service and Civilian Conservation Corps co-operated with him in the study.

This lingual heritage of our mountain people had survived with freshness and vigor and I for one, hate to see it become lost or merged with the "plantation" type. It has always been such a delight to hear the fine old expressions of our ancestors as: "wust" for worst; "larn" for learn; "afeard" for afraid; "afeard" is still in general use throughout England, Scotland and Ireland and was a feature of approved literary speech during the time of Queen Elizabeth. "Fotch" and "cotch" for fetch and catch has been most commonly used. "Year" for ear. Only a few days ago I was coming home through a "driving" sleet storm, met a lad at the City Mill who spoke so cordially and remarked so casually that his "YEARS" were about to freeze off and that he would be all right if it were not for his "years." I could not refrain from pausing and saying to him these words, "Son, that is my trouble, too." I thought to myself as I journeyed on how much I would give to exchange ages with him. Our ancestors pronounced "year" to rhyme with "pear," they said "thar" for there, "whar" for where, and "bar" for bear, "engern" for onion.

Even in my late day I have heard our natives say, "hearin" and "hyerd" for heard, "guarden" for garden, "gwine" for going, "crick" for creek, "yander" for yonder, "becayse" for because, "crap" for crop, "ain't" for are not, "haint" for am not, "hant" for haunt, "yit" for yet, "chimbley" for chimney, "finent" and "fernent" for opposite, "climb" and "clumb" for climb and climbed, "cheer" for chair, "instid" for instead, "kiver" for cover, "kittle" for kettle, "gal" for girl, "led" for lid, "shore" for sure, "yaller" for yellow, "rid" for rode, "fit" for fight, "scart" for scared, "mout" for might, "larnen" for learning, "jist" for just, "sich" for such, "taters" for potatoes, "maters' for tomatoes, "warnuts" for walnuts, "sallet" for salad, "obleged" for obliged.

It is also a noticeable fact that our mountain people seldom pronounce words that end in "g" correctly. They fail to sound the "g" saying "goin" for going, "comin" for coming, "mornin" for morning, "rainin" for raining, "singin" for singing.

The quaint sayings of our people are also interesting such as. . . . "Bran-fire new," "tip-top" for perfect, "out-landish" for ridiculous, "reckoned" for supposed, "lowed as how" and "knowed-as how" for supposed or thought, "chock-full" for full, "infernal mad" for indignant, "all sorts" for various kinds, "a leetle better" for better, "Old Nick" for the Devil, "knocked his trotters from under him" meaning to place another ill at ease. "Noah's fresh" for rain, "ticklish business" referring to questionable morals, "confounded or consarned mad" meaning highly indignant, "tarnation mad" mad as it is possible to get, "barking up the wrong tree" mistaken identity, "plague-take-it" for vexation, "goosey" for foolish, "doless" for good for nothin' folk, "he needs grit in his craw" (or gizzard) when referring to a backward person, "little shaver" for little child generally meaning a boy, "little chunk of a gal" for a little girl, often they were spoken of as "fillies." When parents would become vexed with their offspring I have heard them say "you need a good brushing," when my grandfather would say that to my brother when we were children I wondered why he would say that for when I saw nothing on his clothes and oft I'd get the clothes brush and hand to him. Sometimes he would say, "I'll dust you off therectly," meaning he would spank him in a moment. These expressions puzzled me for years. "Licking" was also used to designate a whipping. "Larping" was often used to express the superlative degree in food as "this pie is larping." "Pretty as a speckled pup under a red wagon," "pretty as blue shoes with red strings." When referring to a cowardly person he was termed, "yaller," referring to foul odors, one said, "it smells like Kyarn" (carrion). A sunny day in winter was called a weather-breeder. "Mark my word" for remember what I am saying, etc.

INDIAN NAMES

In order that our boys and girls who read this story may get some idea of the beautiful way in which our Indians have identified themselves with our country I am giving a few of their lovely names and their meanings.

Adahi	In the woods	(Cherokee)
Ahaluna	Lookout place	(Cherokee)
Akwenasa	My home	(Cherokee)
Amaiyulti	Near the water	(Cherokee)
Alaska	Peninsula	
Alleghany	Beautiful river	(Algonquin)
Amicaloa	Tumbling water	(Cherokee)
Anamosa	White fawn	
Apalachee	On the other side	(Creek)
Apalachicola	People on the other side	(Creek)
Ayeliyu-adahi	Heart of the woods	(Cherokee)
Biloxi	A turtle	(Choctaw)
Canadawa	Running through the hemlocks	
Canastota	Lone pine tree	

Chattanooga	Hawk's nest, colored rocks	(Creek)
Chehawhaw	Where otters live	(Cherokee)
Cherokee	Cave people	(Choctaw)
Chickamauga	A group of Cherokees	
Chicago	A large and lovely place	(Chippewa)
Connecticut	Long tidal river	(Mohican)
Dakota	Friends, allies	(Sioux)
Erie	The wild cat	(Huron)
Etiwaw	Pine tree	
Gatiyi	Dance house	(Cherokee)
Hiawatha	River maker	(Mohawk)
Idaho	Light of the mountains	
Illinois	The men	(Algonquin)
Inagei	In the wilderness	(Cherokee)
Iowa	Sleepy ones	(Sioux)
Juniata	They stay long	(Iroquois)
Kalamazoo	The otter trail	
Kansas	People of the wind	(Sioux)
Kentucky	Land of tomorrow	(Iroquois)
Manhattan	Island, place of drunkenness	(Algonquin)
Massachusetts	Near the great hills	(Algonquin)
Merrimac	Sturgeon, swift water	
Mexico	Habitation of the God of war	(Aztec)
Miami	Very large	
Michigan	Large lake	
Milwaukee	Good earth	(Chippewa)
Minnehaha	Laughing water	(Sioux)
Minnesota	Cloudy water, sky tinted water	(Sioux)
Mississippi	Gathering of all the waters	(Algonquin)˙
Missouri	Muddy water	
Moccasin	Indian shoe	(Algonquin)
Mohawk	Eaters of live meat	(Iroquois)
Mondamon	The Great Spirit	
Muscogee	A swamp	
Mystic	Great tidal river	(Algonquin)
Nantahala	Noon sun	(Cherokee)
Narragansett	People of the point	(Algonquin)
Natchez	Hurrying man	(Choctaw)
Navaho		
Navajo	Knife whetting people	
Nebraska	Wide river	
Neenah	Water	
Niagara	At the neck	(Iroquois)
Nokomis	Grandmother	(Chippewa)
Ohio	Beautiful river	(Iroquois)
Okaloosa	Black water	(Choctaw)
Oklahoma	Red people	(Choctaw)
Omaha	Up stream, going against the wind	
Oneida	Granite people	(Iroquois)
Ontario	Beautiful lake	
Oceola	Medicine drink or rising sun	
Oscaloosa	Wife, if a Chief	
Ottawa	Traders	
Paducah	A Chief	
Panama	Named for a Chief	
Pariola	Cotton	
Pasadena	Crown of the valley	
Penobscott	Rocky place	(Algonquin)
Pensacola	Rowboat people	
Peoria	Carriers, packers	(Algonquin)
Pocahontas	Playful or stream between two hills	
Pontiac	A Chief	
Potomac	Counsel fire, place of burning pine	
Poughkeepsie	Safe harbor	(Algonquin)

Powhatan	At the falls	
Quantico	Place of dancing	
Rappahannock	Quick rising water	
Roanoke	Shells used for money	
Saginaw	River mouth	(Chippewa)
Sandusky	Cool water	(Huron)
Saratoga	Alkali waters	(Mohawk)
Savannah	The Shawnee Indians	(Creek)
Schenectady	Beyond the plains	(Mohawk)
Seattle	Named for a Chief	
Seminole	Runaways	
Senatobia	My white sycamore	(Choctaw)
Shasta	A Chief	
Shawnee	Southerners	(Algonquin)
Shenandoah	Sprucy stream	
Sing Sing	Place of stones	
Sioux	Enemies, snake	
Spokane	Children of the sun	
Susquehanna	Beautiful smooth water	
Suwanee	Echo	(Creek)
Tacoma	Mountain of God	
Tallahassee	Old town	(Seminole)
Tallahatchie	Rocky river	(Choctaw)
Tallapoosa	Stranger, newcomer	(Creek)
Tallula	A bell	(Choctaw)
Talohoah	Ever singing	(Choctaw)
Tamarac	A larch tree	(Algonquin)
Tampa	Near to it	(Creek)
Tecumseh	A panther, Chief	(Shawnee)
Tennessee	Meaning unknown. It is a Cherokee word for River with the big bend, and is claimed by some to mean 'Long Lost' which is quite an appropriate meaning for the river. The white people will henceforth think of it as meaning "Land Of Beauty," recently decided upon as most appropriate by our nomenclators.	
Texas	Friend	
Ticonderoga	Noisy waters	(Algonquin)
Tippecanoe	Great clearing or Buffalo fish.	
Tomahawk	Hatchet, weapon	(Algonquin)
Tombigbee	Box or coffin makers	(Choctaw)
Topeka	Indian potato	
Tuscon	Black Creek	
Tugalo	Forks of a stream	(Cherokee)
Tulsa	Dancing ground	(Creek)
Tupelo	A shouting	(Choctaw)
Tuscahoma	Red warrior	(Choctaw)
Tuscaloosa	Black warrior	(Choctaw)
Tuskegee	Warriors	(Creek)
Utah	Meaning unknown	
Wabash	Gleaming white	
Waco	A heron	(Creek)
Wahoo	An elm or an egg	(Creek)
Walla Walla	Rapid stream	
Wampum	Shell money	
Wichita	White man	
Wigwam	Lodge	
Winona	First born daughter	
Wisconsin	Holes in river bank in which birds nest	
Wyoming	Large plains	
Yazoo	To blow on a horn	(Choctaw)
Yolo	Thick with rushes	

(Probably our YALU is a combination of the above two words. It is a place where the rushes are thick and also a place where the trains blow when coming toward the East.)

Yosemite ....Grizzly bear
Yukon ....The river
Yuma ....Son of the Captain
Chilhowee ....In Cherokee—means all fine—so says Chief Standing Deer
                      in a letter to me March 3-38.
Unaka ....Means white man

Many people think that 'Eureka' is an Indian name but it is not given in my dictionary of Indian names. On page 946 of Volume 2 of The new Teachers and Pupils Cyclopaedia it is given as a word now used to signify an expression of triumph at the time of making a discovery. It means, "I have found it."

Our lovely Cherokee names like Cheoah, Chilhowee, Hiwassee, Nantahala, Ocoee, Oostanaula, Santeetlah, Swannannoa, Tallulah and Unaka and many, many others are as liquid as our limpid streams, as softly molded as the gentle outline of the mountains they identify. How interesting it would be to learn all of our euphonious Indian names.

The following excerpts from Ramsey's "Annals" should be of interest to our Cocke County people.

In the introduction, on page 2 are these words, "No section of the United States has furnished more of interesting and attractive incident, than is presented from a review of the first exploration and settlement of Tennessee."

Page 8—"With what zeal should we of the present day cherish a grateful and hallowed remembrance of the wisdom, patriotism and enterprise, which have bequeathed to us such a country, and endowed it with the 'patrimonial blessings of wise institutions of liberty and religion.' How keen should be our regret that we know so little of those who have done so much for us."

Page 26—"It is known that the Cherokees do not pronounce the letter 'r' and call themselves—'Chelakees',"

Page 33, Foot-note.—

"Thus Queen Elizabeth executed the first patent from the English Sovereign for any lands within the territory of the United States to Sir Walter Raleigh. Its date is March 25, 1584. The present State of Tennessee is within the boundaries but nearly two centuries elapsed before that part of the queen's grant was settled."

Page 35 and 36—

"March 24, 1663 Charles II granted to Edward, Earl of Clarendon, Monk, Lord Craven, Lord Ashley Cooper, Sir John Colleton, Lord John Berkeley, Sir William Berkeley, Sir George Carteret, all the country from the Atlantic to the Pacific Ocean, included between the 31 and 36 parallels of latitude, and constituted them its proprietors and immediate sovereigns."

"In June 1665 the proprietaries secured by a second patent an enlargement of their powers, as to include all the country between the parallels of 36 degrees 30 minutes and 29 degrees North latitude, embracing all the territory of North Carolina, South Carolina, Georgia, Tennessee, Alabama, Mississippi, Louisiana, Arkansas, part of Florida and Missouri, much of Texas, New Mexico and California. The part of the Northern boundary extending from top of the Alleghany mountains to East Bank of Tennessee River was the line of separation between Virginia and Tennessee, and Kentucky and Tennessee."

Pages 39 and 40—"Thus 180 years after the discovery of America, 130 years after DeSota crossed the western limit, (part of which is thought to be Tennessee) did Marquett and Joliet, coast along and discover the Western boundary of Tennessee. Thus 100 years after Queen Elizabeth had signed the patent to Sir Walter Raleigh, did La Salle claim for his Monarch, Louis XIV, the rich domain with the illimitable and magnificent resources of the Great Mississippi Valley."

In volume 2 page 362 Summary Historical and Political, of British settlements are these words, "Early in his administration, Colonel Alexander Spotswood, Lieutenant Governor of Virginia was the first who passed the Apalachian Mountains or Great Blue Hills, the gentlemen, his attendants, were called, 'Knights of the Horseshoe,' having discovered a horse pass."

"As early as 1693, Twenty Chiefs of the Cherokees waited upon Governor Smith and solicited protection of his Government against Esaw and Congaree, (Coosaw Indians who had lately invoded their country and taken prisoners, Page 43)."

Page 45—"By prior discovery, if not by conquest, or occupancy, France claimed the whole valley of the Mississippi. Louisiana stretched to the head springs of the Alleghany and the Monongahela, of the Kenhawa and the Tennessee. Half a mile from the head of the Southern branch of the Savannah river Herbert's spring, which flows to the Mississippi. Strangers who drank of it would say they had tasted of French waters."

"This remark of Adair may probably explain the English name of the principal tributary of the Holston. Traders and hunters from Carolina in exploring the country and passing from the head waters of Broad River of Carolina, and falling upon those of the stream with which they inosculate West of the mountains, would hear of the French claims as Adair did, and call it, most naturally, French Broad."

Page 49—"The Cherokee Indians marked out a path from Augusta to their Nation, so that horsemen could then ride from Savannah to all the Indian Nations."

Page 60—"In all their border conflicts, in their wild adventures into the wilderness, in their frequent invasions of neighboring tribes, in their glorious participation in the struggle for Independence and Freedom, in all wars with Europeans or American enemies, the Sons of Tennessee, have every where achieved success, triumph, victory, conquest and glory."

Page 63—"A voyage in a canoe, from the source of the Hogohegee to the Wabash, required for its performance, in their figurative language (Indian) 'two paddles, two warriors, three moons.'

"The Hogohegee was the Holston River sometimes spelled Holstein and named for a man by the same name who is said to have discovered it.

"The Wabash was the Ohio River and the Cherokee River was the present Tennessee river. It is interesting to note the Mississippi was spelled Mitchisipi.

"This particular section in which we live was once a part of the land that be-longed to the Six Nations. On page 74 of Ramsey's Annals we read—"The territory of which we are speaking was claimed, though not occupied, by the Confederacy of the Six Nations. These were called by the early French Historians, Iriquois, by the English, Mohawks.

"In 1762 these tribes conquered the Illinois and Shawanee Indians, the latter of whom were also incorporated with them. To these conquests they added, in 1685, that of the Miamis, and about the same time carried their victorious arms westward to the Mississippi, and Southward, to what is Georgia. In 1711 they incorporated with them the Tuscaroras, when expelled from North Carolina. Governor Pownal, in his "Administration of the British Colonies," says that these tribes carried their arms as far south as Carolina and as far west as the Mississippi. A vast country, twelve hundred miles in length and six hundred miles in breadth, where they destroyed whole nations, of whom, there are no accounts remaining among the English; and, continues the same writer, the rights of these tribes to the hunting lands on the Ohio may be fairly proved by their conquets over the Shawanees, Delawares, etc., as they stood possessed thereof at the peace of Ryswick in 1697.

"In further confirmation of this Indian title, Butler adds, "It must be mentioned that Lewis Evans represents in his map of the Middle Colonies of Great Britian the country on the South-easterly side of the Ohio River, as the boundary lands of the Six Nations. In the analysis to his map he expressly says that the Shawneese, who were once a most considerable Nation have been subdued by the Confederates and their country has since become their property.

"At a celebrated Treaty, held more than a century since, at Lancaster, the statement made by the delegates in attendance from the Six Nations to Dr. Franklin, was, 'that all the world knows that we conquered all the nations back of the great mountains; we conquered the nations residing there, and the land, if the Virginians ever get a good right to it, it must be by us'. These Indian claims are solemnly appealed to in a diplomatic memorial, addressed by the British ministry to the Duke Mirepoix, on the part of France, June 7, 1755. 'It is a certain truth,' states the memorial, 'that these lands have belonged to the Confederacy, and as they have not been given up or made over to the English, belong still to the same Indian Nations.'

"The Court of Great Britain maintained, in this negotiation, that the Confederates were, by origin or right of conquest, the lawful proprietors of the river Ohio and the Territory in question.

"In support of this ancient, aboriginal title, Butler adds the further testimony of Dr. Mitchell's map of North America, made with the documents of the Colonial office before him. In this map the same as the one by which the boundaries in the Treaty of Paris, in 1783, were adjusted, the Doctor observes, 'that the Six Nations have extended their territories ever since the year 1672, when they subdued and were incorporated with the ancient Shawaneese, the native proprietors of these countries.' This, he adds, is confirmed by their own claims and possessions in 1742, which include all the bounds as laid down in the map, and none have even thought fit to dispute them.

"Such was the aboriginal title to the greater part of Tennessee in 1767, when white settlers approached its eastern boundary. On the 6th of May of this year a deputation of the Six Nations presented to the Superintendent of Indian affairs a formal remonstrance against the continued encroachments of the whites upon their lands. The subject was immediately considered by the royal government; and near the close of the summer, orders were issued to Sir William Johnson, the Superintendent of Northern Indian Affairs, instructing him to convene the Chiefs, Warriors and sachems of the tribes most interested."

"On October 24, 1767 3,200 Indians of 17 tribes convened and on November 5 a Treaty of Limits and a deed of cession to the King of England, were signed. This was at Fort Stanwix, which is the present Utica, New York. In this Treaty the Indians aver, "they are the true absolute proprietors of the lands thus ceded, and that for the considerations mentioned, we have continued the line South to the Cherokee or Hogohegee Rivers, because the same is, and we declare it to be, our true bounds with the Southern Indians and that we have an undoubted right to the Country as far South as that River.

"The cession thus made by the Six Nations, of the country North East of the Tennessee River, is the first deed from any of the aboriginal tribes for any territory within the boundaries of Tennessee.

"Some other tribes claimed that the Six Nations had no right to an exclusive claim to these lands because they were the common hunting grounds of the Cherokees and the Chickasaws also.

"There is no mention of any delegates from the Southern tribes attending this great meeting at Fort Stanwix. However, it is claimed that some visiting Cherokees were present, says Haywood, and that upon arrival, they immediately tendered to the Indians of the Six Nations, the skins of the animals they had killed enroute for their support, saying, 'They are yours, we killed them after we passed the Big River.' (Meaning the Cherokee or Tennessee River.) This was also proof of their acquiescence in the validity of the claim of the Six Nations. These claimed the soil, not as its aboriginal owners but by right of conquest, and tradition concurs in admitting their right to that extent. But the Cherokees had long exercised the privilege of hunting upon these lands, therefore regarded with jealousy and dissatisfaction, the approach of the white settlements." Page 76.

Who is there among us today who can honestly blame the Indians for their love of their native land and their desire to cling to it at any cost?

On Page 80—"In the map accompanying Adair's book, the river from the head of the Holston to the confluence of the Tennessee and Ohio is called Cherake. The Cumberland is called Old Shauvanon or River of the Shawnees. The Hiwassee is called Euphasee. Tennase, is the stream now known as Little Tennessee."

On Page 81—"Cherokees, Adair says of the Cherokees, their National name is derived from Chee-ra- fire which is their reputed lower heaven, and hence they call their magi, Cheera- tahge, men possessed of divine fire."

Page 83—"They, the Cherokees were the mountaineers of aboriginal America, and like all other mountaineers, adored their country and held on to and defended it with a heroic devotion, a patriotic constancy, and an unyielding tenacity, which cannot be too much admired or eulogized."

Page 83—"Currahe is only a corruption of Cherokee. It means the mountains of the Cherokees."

Page 96—"May the time never come, when the self-sacrificing toil and daring hardihood of the pioneers of Tennessee will be forgotten or undervalued by their posterity."

Page 103—"The misgoverned Province of North Carolina sent forth most of the emigrants to Watauga. The poor came in search of Independence, others to repair their broken fortunes, the aspiring, to attain respectability unattainable in the country of their nativity. Others came prompted by the noble ambition of forming a new community, of laying broad and deep the foundation of government and of acquiring, under it, distinction and consequence for themselves and their children."

On page 123—"In South Carolina, Judge Drayton, in a charge to a Grand Jury said, in speaking of liberty, "English people cannot be taxed, nay, cannot be bound by any law, unless by their consent, expressed by themselves, or by the Representatives of their own election."

On page 133—"Felix Walker, Thomas Gomley, William Tatham and John Sevier all served in that office. (Clerk of Watauga Association Council of five members selected by the thirteen.) Lewis Boyer was the Attorney."

On pages 134, 135, 136, 137 and 138 is recorded a petition to the Provincial Council of North Carolina from the inhabitants of Washington District, including the River Wataugah, Nolachuckie etc. begging the Council to annex them as they had found out they did not belong to Virginia and finding themselves on the Frontiers and being apprehensive that, for want of proper legislature, "we might become a shelter for such as endeavored to defraud their creditors, considering also the necessity of recording Deeds and Wills" . . . etc., etc. A wonderful document from beginning to end. John Carter served as Chairman of the Committee that prepared the document. 113 men signed it. The names familiar in this particular locality are. . . . Boyer, Greer, Morris (Gideon and Shadrack) David Hickey, Brown, Robinson (John), Clark (William), Isaac Wilson, John Moore, John Davis, Frederick Vaughn, Oldham Hightower, Jarret Williams, Ossa Rose. This document is without date but it was received August 22, 1776.

Sixty years later the grandson of John Carter the Chairman of the above Committee, Honorable W. B. Carter from the same Watauga locality was president of the convention that formed the present Constitution for Tennessee.

"It is thought that John Sevier must have known George Washington before he came to Watauga is why he suggested the name of Washington District. Anyway, be that as it may, we became the first section of country to honor him.

"No record is found of the General Assembly of North Carolina taking action upon this petition. It is supposed that they invited the Watauga Association to send its delegates to the Provincial Congress at Halifax November 12, 1776. This Congress continued in session to December 18, 1776. A Bill of Rights and a State Constitution were adopted. Charles Robertson, John Carter, John Haile and John Sevier were among the delegates from Washington District, Watauga Settlement.

"In that part of the Declaration of Rights adopted by the Congress, specifying the limits of the State is the proviso, "That it shall not be so construed as to prevent the establishment of one or more governments westward of this State, by consent of the Legislature. It is thought this provision was SUGGESTED by the young Legislators from Watauga."

"The Franks" were the men from Franklin.

On page 143 of the Annals is an interesting bit of information.

"Boyd and Doggett who had been sent out by Virginia traveling on the path that Greer left (meaning Andrew Greer one of first Watauga Settlers), were met by Indians near a creek, were killed by them and their bodies thrown into the water." The Creek is in what is now Sevier County and has ever since been known as Boyd's Creek. A watch and other articles were afterwards found in the creek. The watch had Boyd's name engraved on the case. He was a Scotchman.

"Page 175—"The General Assembly of North Carolina in November 1777 formed Washington District into a COUNTY of the same name, assigning to it the whole of the present State of Tennessee."

"At the same session of the General Assembly provision was made for opening a LAND OFFICE in Washington County at the rate of forty shillings per one hundred acres, with the liberal permission to each head of a family to take up 640 Acres himself, 100 Acres for his wife and the same for each of his children."

On Page 270—"Danbury Feb. 11, 1782.

"Governor Alexander Martin, To Colonel John Sevier:

"Sir: I am distressed with the repeated complaints of the Indians respecting the daily intrusions of our people on their lands beyond the French Broad River. I beg you, sir, to prevent the injuries these savages justly complain of, who are constantly imploring the protection of the state and appealing to its justice in vain. By interposing your influence on these, our unruly citizens, I think will have sufficient weight, without going into extremities disgraceful to them and disagreeable to the State. You will, therefore, please to warn these intruders off the lands reserved for the Indians by the late Act of the Assembly, that they remove immediately, at least by the middle of March, otherwise they will be drove off. If you find them still refractory at the above time, you will draw forth a body of your militia on horseback, and pull down their cabins, and drive them off, laying aside every consideration of their entreaties to the contrary. You will please to give me the earliest information of your proceedings. The Indian goods are not yet arrived from Philadelphia, through the inclemency of the late season; as soon as they will be in the State, I shall send them to the Great Island and hold a Treaty with the Cherokees."

"The Cherokees of the upper towns continued to complain and remonstrate."

Page 271—"A Talk to Colonel Joseph Martin, by the Old Tassel, in Chota, the 25 of September 1782 in favor of the whole nation. For his Excellency, the Governor of North Carolina. Present, all the Chiefs of the friendly towns and a number of young men.

"Brother: I am now going to speak to you. I hope you will listen to me. A string. I intended to come this fall and see you, but there was such confusion in our country, I thought it best for me to stay at home and send my Talks by our friend Colonel Martin, who promises to deliver them safe to you.

"We are a poor distressed people, that is, in great trouble, and we hope our elder brother will take pity on us and do us justice. Your people from Nollichucky are daily pushing us out of one of our lands. We have no place to hunt on. Your people have built houses within one day's walk of our towns. We don't want to quarrel with our elder brother; we, therefore, hope our elder brother will not take our lands from us, that the Great Man above gave us. He made you and He made us; we are all his children, and we hope our elder brother will take pity on us, and not take our lands from us that our Father gave us, because he is stronger than we are. We are the first people that ever lived on this land; it is ours, and why will our elder brother take it from us? It is true, sometime past, the people over the great water persuaded some of our young men to do some mischief to our elder brother, which our principal men were sorry for. But you, our elder brothers come to our towns and took satisfaction, and then sent for us to come and treat with you, which we did. Then our elder brother promised to have the line run between us agreeable to the first treaty, and all that should be found over the line should be moved off. But it is not done yet. We have done nothing to offend our elder brother since the last treaty, and why should our elder brother want to quarrel with us? We have sent to the Governor of Virginia on the same subject. We hope that between you both, you will take pity on your younger brother, and send Colonel Sevier, who is a good man, to have all your people moved off our land. I should say a great deal more, but our friend, Colonel Martin, knows all our grievances, and he can inform you. A string."

On Page 277—"In 1784 at the August term of Court in Jefferson County, a road was laid out from the mouth of Bent Creek to the mouth of Dumplin (now Sevier) Also from the County line, South of Chucky and where the War Path crosses the same, the nearest and best way to the War Ford on the Pigeon." (Now Cocke County).

Page 278—"The Indians, late in the year (1783) commenced hostilities, by stealing horses and cattle and retreating across the Pigeon into the Mountains in what is now Cocke County. Major Peter Fine raised a few men and pursued them. After killing one Indian and wounding another, and regaining the stolen property, they began their return and encamped. They were fired upon in the night by the savages, who had followed their tracks. Vinet Fine, a brother of the Major was killed and Thomas Holland and Mr. Bingham were wounded. After the departure of the Indians, who hung around the camp till morning, the white men broke a hole in the ice and put the body of V. Fine in the Creek, which has ever since been called Fine's Creek. The wounded men were brought in safely and recovered.

"It continued to be necessary for two years, to keep out scouts between Pigeon and French Broad. In this time Nehemiah and Simeon O'Dell were killed, scalped, and their guns taken. A boy ten years old, named Nelson, was killed and his horse taken several miles up Pigeon. McCoy (Mc Kay) Fort was built on the French Broad three miles above Newport. (Near where the rock falls are located not far from the present home of Frank Huff) Whitson's on Pigeon ten miles above Newport where Mc Nabb since lived (Wilton Springs) Wood's five miles below. These were all guarded several years."

Page 280—"The settlements upon the French Broad and its tributaries extended rapidly. This induced a renewal of hostilities on the border settlements. Major Fine and Colonel Lillard raised a company of thirty men and penetrated through the mountains to the overhill town of Cowee and burned it.

"When the early settlers heard of North Carolina ceding the Over-Mountain Counties of North Carolina to the Federal Government they realized that for two years time lawlessness would reign if they didn't do something to prevent it, as Congress had two years to decide whether to accept these counties or not."

On page 285 are these words; "The opinion became general with the entire population that the sacred duty devolved upon themselves to devise means to draw upon their own resources, and by a manly self reliance, to extricate the inhabitants of the ceded territory from the unexpected difficulties by which they were suddenly surrounded. Self protection is the first law of nature. Salus populi suprema lex."

On page 286—"In this dilemma it was proposed that in each Captain's Company two Representatives of the people should be elected, who should assemble, as committees, in their respective Counties, to deliberate upon the State of Public Affairs and recommend some general plan of action suited to the emergency. These Committees for Washington, Sullivan and Greene Counties, met and recommended the election of Deputies from each of the Counties, to assemble in Convention at Jonesboro with power to adopt such measures as they should deem advisable.

"The election of the deputies to the Convention was held and resulted in the choice for Washington County, of John Sevier, Charles Robertson, William Purphey, Joseph Wilson, John Irvin, Samuel Houston, William Trimble, William Cox, Landon Carter, Hugh Henry, Christopher Taylor, John Chisol, Samuel Doak, William Campbell, Benjamin Holland, John Bean, Samuel Williams and Richard White.

"For County of Sullivan, Joseph Martin, Gilbert Christian, William Cocke, John Manifee, William Wallace, John Hall, Samuel Wilson, Stockley Donelson, William Evans.

"For County of Greene, Daniel Kennedy, Alexander Outlaw, Joseph Gist, Samuel Weir, Asahel Rawlings, Joseph Ballard, John Manghon, John Murphy, David Campbell, Archibald Stone, Abraham Denton, Charles Robinson and Elisha Baker.

"Davidson County sent no delegates, probably none were elected.

"These deputies met on August the 23, 1784, at Jonesboro. John Sevier was made President and Landon Carter Secretary of the Convention.

"The committee on Public Affairs: William Cocke, Alexander Outlaw, Landen Carter, William Campbell, John Manifee, Joseph Martin, Charles Robinson, Samuel Houston, Gilbert Christian, Daniel Kennedy and Joseph Wilson.

"This committee decided that the 'Convention had a right to adopt and prescribe such relations as the particular exigencies of the time and the public good may require; that one or more persons ought to be sent to represent our situation in the Congress of the United States, and this Convention has just right and authority to prescribe a regular mode for his support.'

"This report was received and adopted by the convention. The question was taken 'On motion by Mr. Cocke, whether for or against forming ourselves into a separate and distinct state, independent of the State of North Carolina, at this time.' It was carried in the affirmative.

"28 voted for the measure and 15 voted against it."

On Page 290—"The deputies then took into consideration the propriety of having a new Convention called to form a Constitution, and give a name to the Independent State. They decided that each County should elect five members to the Convention. The same number that had been elected in 1776 to form the Constitution of North Carolina. They fixed the time and the place of the meeting to be at Jonesboro on 16th of September and then adjourned. However the Convention did not meet until November and broke up in great confusion. The members had not harmonized upon the details of the plan of association.

"The General Assembly of North Carolina was in session at Newbern and repealed the act for ceding her Western Territory to Congress. They also formed a Judicial district of the four western Counties and appointed an assistant Judge and an Attorney General for the Superior Court, which was directed to be held at Jonesboro. They also formed the militia of Washington District into a Brigade and appointed Colonel John Sevier the Brigadier General."

Page 291. 2nd January 1785.

"Dear Colonel:- I have just received certain information from Colonel Martin that the first thing the Assembly of North Carolina did was to repeal the Cession Bill and to form this part of the Country into a separate District by the name of Washington District, which I have the honor to command as General. I conclude this step will satisfy the people with the Old State, and we shall pursue no further measures as to a new State. David Campbell, Esquire is appointed one of our Judges. I would write to you officially, but my commission is not yet come to hand.

I am, dr. Colo. with esteem, yr. mt. obdt.

Colo. Kennedy.   JOHN SEVIER."

Stokely Land Grant, copied from the original by Dolly Masters.

"John Sevier begged the people of the four Western Counties of North Carolina to decline further action in respect to a new government. The people were insistent and persistant and determined and held an election to select deputies from each County to attend the Convention. They were elected as follows: From Washington County—John Sevier, William Cocke, John Tipton, Thomas Stewart and Rev. Samuel Houston.

"For Sullivan County: David Looney, Richard Gammon, Moses Looney, William Cage, and John Long.

"For Greene County: James Reese, Daniel Kennedy, John Newman, James Roddye, and Joseph Hardin.

"This number being less than half the number the Convention previously elected and chosen by the Counties and not by the Captains companies and represented larger bodies of their fellow citizens, were less trammeled by local prejudices and instructions. Their action less restricted, their deliberations freer and more enlightened. In this body as now composed was considerable ability and some experience. They met at Jonesboro and appointed John Sevier President and F. A. Ramsey, secretary."

Page 292—"The Convention being organized and ready for business, the Rev. Samuel Houston, one of the deputies from Washington County arose and addressed the Convention on the importance of their meeting, showing that they were about to lay the foundation on which was to be placed, not only their own welfare and interest but perhaps, those of their posterity for ages to come; and adding that, under such interesting and solemn circumstances, they should look to Heaven and offer prayer for counsel and direction from infinite wisdom.

"The President immediately designated Mr. Houston and he offered up a solemn and appropriate prayer, in which all seemed to unite.

"A form of a Constitution under which the New Government should be put in motion was submitted and agreed to, subject to ratification, modification or rejection of a future Convention directed to be chosen by the people, and to meet on Nov. 14, 1785 at Greeneville. Ample time was thus given to examine the merits and defects of the new organization and by discussinig them in detail, to harmonize conflicting opinions.

"In due time the election was held and members of the legislature chosen for the new state. It is thought they were composed of about the same members who had constituted the two previous conventions. It is known that Landon Carter was the Speaker, Thomas Talbot, the Clerk of the Senate and William Cage Speaker, and Thomas Chapman, Clerk of the House of Commons. John Sevier was chosen Governor.

"David Campbell elected Judge of the Superior Court, Joshua Gist and John Anderson Assistant Judges. The First Session of the Legislature of Franklin terminated on March 31, 1785 after the passage of more than a dozen measures or Acts such as establishing a seat of learning, a militia, providing for a State Seal, dividing Sullivan County, directing a method of electing members dividing Greene County into three Counties, Sevier, Caswell and Greene, establishing the value of gold and silver coins, (foreign) fixing salaries tax rates etc etc. . . .

The salaries received are of interest and are recorded on page 296. "Governor, 200 pounds annually, Attorney-General 25 pounds for each Court he attended. Secretary of State, 25 pounds annually and his fees of office. Judge of Superior Court, 150 pounds per year. Assistant Judges, 25 pounds for each Court. Treasurer, 40 pounds annually; each member of the Council of State, six shillings per day, when in actual service."

In the law levying the tax for government support was the following clause: "Be it enacted, That it shall and maybe lawful for the aforesaid land tax, and all free polls, to be paid in the following manner: Good flax linen, ten hundred at three shillings and six pence per yard; nine hundred, at three shillings; eight hundred, two shillings and nine pence; seven hundred, two shillings and six pence; six hundred, two shillings; tow linen, one shilling and nine pence; linsey, three shillings; and woolen and cotton linsy, three shillings and six pence per yard; good clean beaver skin, six shillings; cased otter skins, six shillings; uncased ditto, five shillings; raccoon and fox skins, one shilling and three pence; woolen cloth, at ten shillings per yard; bacon, well cured six pence per pound; good clean tallow, six pence per pound; good clean beeswax, one shilling per pound; good distilled rye whiskey, at two shillings and six pence per gallon; good peach or apple brandy, at three shillings per gallon; good country made sugar, at one shilling per pound;

deer skins, the pattern, six shillings; good neat and well managed tobacco, fit to be prized, that may pass inspection, the hundred, fifteen shillings, and so on in proportion for a greater or less quantity."

"In the forming period of society, when the pastoral and agricultural have not been merged into the commercial and manufacturing stages, where the simple wants of a new community confine its exchanges to the bartering of one commodity, or product for another, there can be little use for MONEY. There is does not constitute wealth, and is scarcely the representative of it. On the frontier, he is the wealthiest man who owns the largest amount of wild lands, while thousands of acres around him are vacant and unappropriated; or who has money to lend, which no one near him wishes or needs to borrow; but he whose guns and traps furnish the most peltries, who owns the largest flocks and herds, and whose cribs and barns are the fullest, and whose household fabrics are the most abundant. In a new settlement, these are wealth and constitute its standard."

Pages 364, 365, 366, 367 and 368 are interesting letters of General Shelby and Governor Caswell of North Carolina relative to the counties of Washington, Sullivan, Greene and Hawkins endeavoring to establish a government of their own. It is said that nothing yet had occurred in transactions between the Franklin and North Carolina States so well calculated to heal the breach as the letter of Governor Caswell and the action of the North Carolina Legislature communicated in it.

On Page 376—There is a reference to the Elholm District which embraced all the territory of the State of Franklin below Washington County, viz; Greene, Caswell and Sevier Counties. Washington District at this time probably embraced Washington, Sullivan, Spencer and Wayne Counties. (Mero District embraced the three Western Counties Davidson, Sumner and Tennessee County at a later date when these counties were formed).

From the various bits of information that I have been able to find I am of the opinion that we were once known as Caswell County in the District of Elholm, before we became Jefferson County in the Territory South of the River Ohio.

One of John Sevier's most ardent admirers was a foreigner, Caesar Augustus George Elholm, he was either a Frenchman or a Polander, a member of Pulaski's Legion at the seige of Savannah where he performed a feat that was most unusual. John Sevier sent Major Elhom on many important missions to Georgia whereupon the Legislature of Georgia Feb. 3, 1787 authorized the Governor to draw a warrant on the Treasury in favor of Major Elholm for the sum of fifty pounds. (Three names are often found among Welchmen).

Page 377 is reference to Thomas Napier as follows. . . . "Resolved, That the application be made to the Governor and Council by William Downs and Thomas Napier, Esquires, Commissioners, or either of them, for their direction and approbation, to have ten tracts of land, containing ten thousand acres each, to be laid out in the bend of Tennessee, for public use."

On Page 433—"In 1783 the General Assembly of North Carolina designated the boundaries of the Cherokee hunting grounds, making the Holston, the French Broad and the Big Pigeon Rivers a part of these boundaries.

Sevier and Caswell Counties alone maintained their allegiance to the new state of Franklin and adhered to Governor Sevier and his fortunes.

Page 434—The land embraced within the limits of Sevier County of State of Franklin, had not been acquired by treaty or otherwise under North Carolina laws, The inhabitants according to the N. C. laws were violating them and trespassers on Indian lands (after the State of Franklin ceased to exist) Measures were at once adopted to frame a temporary form of government suited to the exigencies of the occasion. The nine Articles on page 435 resemble the Articles of the Watauga Association. This Government continued until after the County became the Territory South of the River Ohio.

Page 397—Governor Sevier's Circular to the Military of Franklin.

28th November, 1787.

"Major Elholm is just now returned from Georgia with expresses from the Governor of that State, requiring an aid of fifteen hundred men from the State of Franklin, to co-operate with them against the Creek Indians, under the following conditions, to wit:

All that will serve one campaign, till a peace is made, shall receive as follows

A Colonel, one thousand two hundred Acres;

A Lieutenant Colonel, one thousand, one hundred;

A Major, one thousand;

A Captain, nine hundred;

A First Lieutenant, eight hundred;

A Second Lieutenant, seven hundred and fifty;

Non-commissioned officers, seven hundred;

Privates, well armed and accoutred, six hundred and forty;

Any general officer, called into the service, to have the following proportions:

A Major General, fifteen hundred Acres

A Brigadier-General, fourteen hundred Acres

The bend of the Tennessee is reserved for the troops of Franklin, which is a desirable spot, and will be of great importance to this State. We are to have an additional bounty of fifty acres, on every one hundred acres, in lieu of rations, and all other claims against the State of Georgia, which make our proportion of lands amount to half as much more as what is above allotted. A private man's share, if he finds himself, amounts to nine hundred and sixty acres, and officers in proportion."

Page 402—A Franklin Land Grant or Warrant.

"State of Franklin, Caswell County.
Number 17, April 20, 1787.
To the Surveyor of said County, Greeting:

Whereas, James Ruddle hath paid into the Entry-Taker's Office of this County, ten shillings, for one hundred acres of land in said County; you are hereby required to receive his location for the same, and to lay off and survey the above quantity of land, and make return thereof to the Secretary's office, agreeable to law.

Given under my hand, at office, this 20th day September, 1787.

JOHN SEEHORN, E.T.
(Entry Taker)"

(This name I have noticed in a place or two it is spelled Zanhaun.)

Page 413—Captain John Zanhaun, Caswell County, Franklin State.
"Favored per James Sevier.

"It would require two or three days for the Governor's message to reach Captain Zanhaun's residence; fully as many to notify to the militia the purport of the dispatch, and to assemble them together; and as many more to reach the Governor's headquarters, ten miles above Jonesboro."

Page 592—is the interesting record of Doctor James Cozby's defense of his home a few miles east of Knoxville. The Dr. kept his plot of ground near the house free of all undergrowth so that he could easily detect the approach of an Indian.

The evening of April 22, 1794, the domestic animals gave their usual 'tokens of the presence of Indians' the wise old Indian fighter quickly observed the approach of 20 warriors who hid themselves in the fence corners and in the woods near his clearing. Immediately the Doctor barricaded his doorways and extinguished all fires, primed his two guns afresh and prepared to defend his castle and his family. He had a wife and several children but only one of them could shoot.

This did not discourage the Doctor, who well understood the value of stratagem and he was an accomplished strategist as later he demonstrated in his rescue of John Sevier who was being tried for treason in Morganton, North Carolina.

In this defense of his family he displayed a skill and bravery that always seemed to set him apart from his fellows. From the portholes in different parts of the house he would keep constant vigil and when a form would come into the range of his keen vision he would give loud commands as though he had a whole platoon of soldiers that he was directing or commanding. It worked. The Indians went away in the direction of a neighbor's cabin. Next morning the family of William Casteel were all dead except one who was scalped and left for dead, but before burial she showed signs of life and Dr. Cozby dressed her wounds, she did not recover for two years. The remainder of the family of six were buried in one grave.

Page 648 we find— "Schedule of the aggregate amount of each description of persons, taken agreeably to "An act providing for the enumeration of the inhabitants of the Territory of the United States of America South of the River Ohio;" passed July 11, 1795.
Jefferson County of course includes Cocke County up until Cocke is formed.

	Free white males 16 years and upwards including heads of families	Free white males under 16 years.	Free white females including heads of families.	All other free persons.	Slaves	Total	Yeas	Nays
Jefferson County	1,706	2,225	3,021	112	776	7,840	714	316
Hawkins County	2,663	3,279	4,767	147	2,472	13,331	1,651	531
Greene County	1,567	2,203	3,350	52	466	7,638	560	495
Knox County	2,721	2,723	3,664	100	2,365	11,573	1,100	128
Washington County	2,013	2,578	4,311	225	978	10,105	873	145
Sullivan County	1,803	2,340	3,499	38	777	8,457	715	125
Sevier County	628	1,045	1,503	273	129	3,578	261	55
Blount County	585	817	1,231	00	183	2,816	476	16
Davidson County	728	695	1,192	6	992	3,613	96	517
Sumner County	1,382	1,595	2,316	1	1,076	6,370	00	00
Tennessee County	380	444	700	19	398	1,941	58	231
	16,179	19,944	29,554	973	10,613	77,262	6,504	2,562

"I, William Blount, Governor in and over the territory of the United States of America South of the River Ohio, do certify that this schedule is made in conformity with the schedules of the Sheriffs of the respective Counties in the said Territory, and that the schedules of the said Sheriffs are lodged in my office.

"Given under my hand at Knoxville, November 28, 1795.

WILLIAM BLOUNT."

On page 658 it is recorded that George Doherty was the first Senator from Jefferson County (of which Cocke was then a part) and Alexander Outlaw and Adam Peck the first Representatives in the First Assembly after we became Tennessee.

Page 674—William Blount and William Cocke our First United States Senators.

Page 689—the record of the formation of COCKE COUNTY. The Assembly convened at Knoxville Sept. 18, 1797 and on October 9, 1797 Jefferson County was divided and the County of Cocke laid off. Seven Commissioners appointed to select a place for Court House.

ALLEN FAMILY
From a John Weaver Letter to P. T.

"I have thought that many people might be interested to know who made the brick, who built the house, and what became of the brick in the old courthouse that was once the Temple of Justice for Cocke County.

"The brick was hauled to Newport and put into the house in Eastport where Solon Nease had his store.

"That building was built by colored people for a lodge room. Mr. T. D. A. Harper, who was the grandfather of your sheriff, told me that those bricks were made and the courthouse was built by John Allen, commonly known as Jack Allen.

"My father who knew a good deal about the early history of Cocke County, also told me the same thing.

"Mr. Harper married a granddaughter of Jack Allen, and my father also married a granddaughter.

"I don't suppose there is any public record of this fact that he built the house as all of the early records of Cocke County were burned. I suppose this information came down to these men by tradition, but I don't think there is any question about the truthfulness of it.

"It is certain that Jack Allen was a brick mason. In several of the early land grants and warrants issued to him and others that I have examined, he is referred to as John Allen, the "brick layer."

"I believe that he burned the first brick and was the best "brick-layer" that Cocke County ever had, judging from the brick structures and chimneys on Cosby and in the English Creek Country that he built many of these old chimneys, now more than 100 years old, are as good as when they were built.

"He built the chimney at the old homeplace where your scribe was raised and recently sold before coming to the West. That chimney has stood for more than 100 years, all the while subjected to the hottest fires during the winter season and never had any protection in the back, and is now burned away in the back very little. Anyone examining that chimney will readily conclude that to the one building that chimney, brick laying was not only an art but a science as well.

"Jack Allen settled near the mouth of Cosby Creek and burned the brick and built the house that stood there so many years ago.

"Jack Allen was a man of unusual attainment and education for his time. I get this from having read his writing and papers. I have read his will disposing of his property. It is a very interesting document, well worded and written in a beautiful handwriting. I think L. S. Allen has it.

"There are more people in Cocke Co. and elsewhere today, who could trace back to Jack Allen as one of their ancestors, than could trace to any other man who ever lived in Cocke County. Many of them perhaps don't know that they are the descendants of this man. I think it would be a very safe bet that there are living today at least 25,000 people who have Jack Allen as one of their ancestors. This statement at first thought might seem like a wild exaggerated guess. Of course it is a guess, however, but is not an exaggerated one and is more likely to be under than to be over the number if one will only figure for a moment.

"There were 11 children, that I know, and I think there were 12. All these 11 married and had rather large families but one.

— 367 —

"Capt. Ed Allen, one of the sons, was a Captain in the Confederate Army, was killed in the battle of Murfreesboro. He had only one son, Lewis, who died in a hospital at Memphis or Vicksburg.

"There were 3 other sons, Russel, James and John (Short Finger), each of them had rather large families, and 7 girls.

"Two of them married Sisks; two married McMahans; one married Abraham Denton; one married Wm. Allen, and one married Isaac Weaver.

"Count 5 generations and count an average of 5 to family and you have more than 30,000. But many of these have reached into 6th and 7th generation and are scattered into perhaps every state in the nation.

"Capt. Ed Allen organized and became the Captain of the First Company out of Cocke County into the Confederate Army. This company was made up of Cocke County men, and became Co. C. in the 26th Tenn. Regiment. Austin Hickery was made 1st Lt., Alex Swagerty, 2nd Lt., and Allen Clevenger, 3rd Lt.

"Capt. Allen was killed in the battle of Murfreesboro and the company was re-organized with Geo. Stuart, Capt., James H. Faubion, Orderly Sergeant. This Co. took part in all the battles of M. Tenn., Chickamauga, Missionary Ridge, Dalton, Altoona, New Hope Church, Kenesaw Mountain and Atlanta, and with Hood back at Franklin and Nashville."

THE ANNALS OF HAYWOOD COUNTY NORTH CAROLINA

By W. C. ALLEN

On page 17 of this book we find that there was once a great river in what is now Western North Carolina and that it ran between the Great Smoky and the Blue Ridge mountains and that during all those long, prehistoric periods this wonderful river disappeared or was "DEVOURED," so the author tells us by a pack of piratical wolves that we now know as, The Big Pigeon, The French Broad, The Watauga, the Hiwassee, the Little Tennessee and the Nollichucky Rivers.

In the remotest geological period, the source of the Big Pigeon was once at or near Waterville, or rather where Waterville, N. C. now is. In the course of ages, the stream has cut its way backward through mountain gorges, on through Cattaloochee, Fine's Creek, Crabtree and Iron Duff until it reached the banks of the GREAT RIVER near where Clyde is now located and by continuous erosion and pressure, the river bank gave way, and a large volume of water turned from its course from the ancient river into the Big Pigeon and followed the bed of that stream, widening and deepening it as it is today. The same result happened when the French Broad tapped it near Asheville and reduced it to the volume of Mud Creek and Hominy Creek.

The source of Hominy Creek is now about half a mile from the bed of the Big Pigeon and is slowly and gradually cutting its way backward toward the Pigeon with the inevitable result finally that in the natural order of events, the Big Pigeon River will yield to the pirate raids of Hominy Creek, be diverted at Canton from its course and made to flow down Hominy Valley into the French Broad, at or near Asheville instead of near Newport, Tennessee as at present. When this happens, a million years hence, from a geological standpoint, the city of Canton, N. C. which now seems safe astride the Big Pigeon River will become the prey of whirling waters and will again be at the bottom of the resurrected river which will come to life by the junction of the Big Pigeon with Hominy Creek. In that event, the ancient river being restored, will have its revenge upon the Big Pigeon which assisted in its destruction millions of years before.

On page 24 of the above mentioned book by W. C. Allen are these words, "The Pigeon River, as it winds its way among the verdant hills as if seeking an outlet from its pent up condition traverses the county from South to North and empties into the French Broad just beyond the Tennessee line. It forms as beautiful a valley as can be found in the whole world."

"The name Pigeon River was once changed to "Buford" in honor of the President of the Rail Road Company but that name did not seem to be fitting, for it never became generally known by it, this means the town of Canton which for ninety years was known as Pigeon River." Page 175 above Book.

The following interesting data was sent to me by Honorable Sam K. Leming of Waldron, Ark. He sends it for two reasons, first he is interested in the Story of Cocke County and wishes to help in its writing by contributiong anything of in-

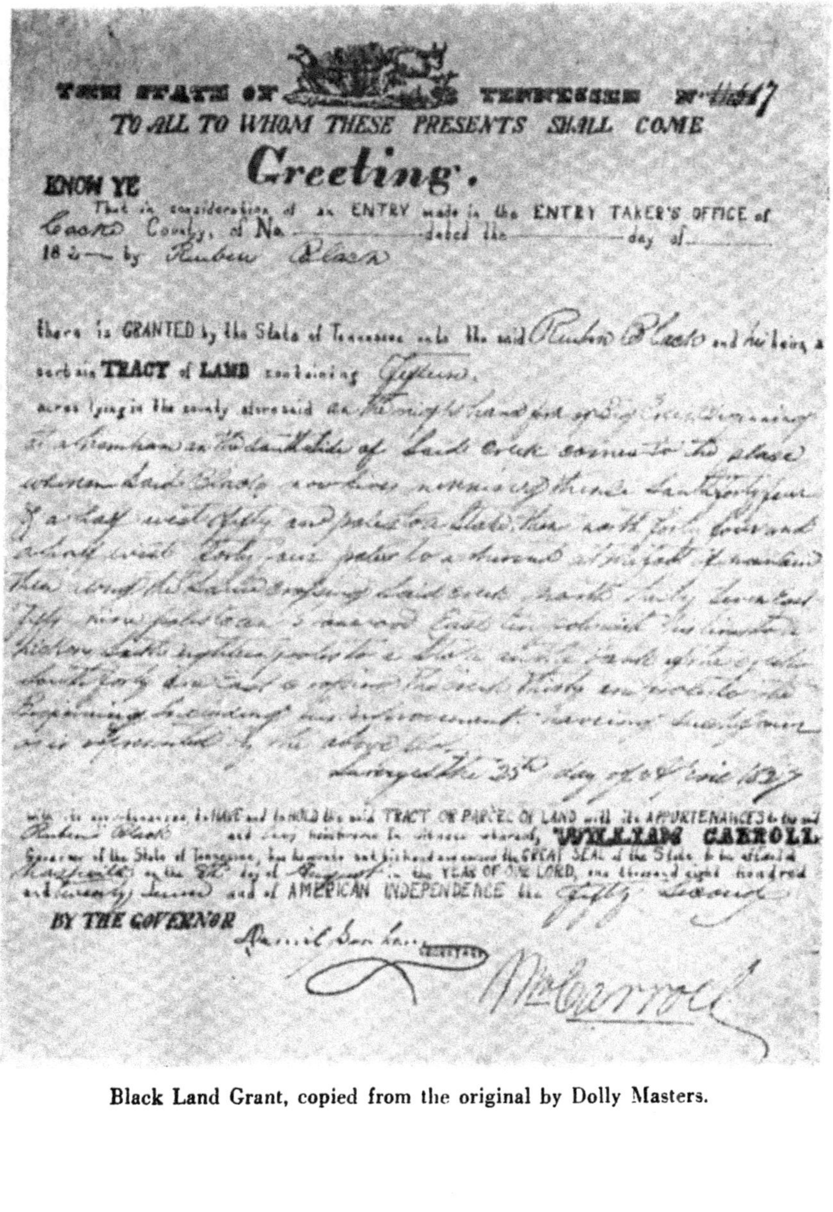

THE STATE OF TENNESSEE №

TO ALL TO WHOM THESE PRESENTS SHALL COME

Greeting.

KNOW YE

That in consideration of an ENTRY made in the ENTRY TAKER'S OFFICE of _____ County, of No _____ dated the _____ day of _____ 182__ by Reuben Black

There is GRANTED by the State of Tennessee unto the said Reuben Black and his heirs a certain TRACT of LAND containing Fifteen

acres lying in the county aforesaid *[handwritten text largely illegible]*

Given the 25th day of April 1827

with its appurtenances, to HAVE and to HOLD the said TRACT OR PARCEL OF LAND with its APPURTENANCES to the said Reuben Black and his heirs in witness whereof, **WILLIAM CARROLL** Governor of the State of Tennessee, has hereunto set his hand and caused the GREAT SEAL of the State to be affixed at Nashville, on the 2nd day of August, in the YEAR OF OUR LORD, one thousand eight hundred and twenty-seven and of AMERICAN INDEPENDENCE the Fifty second

BY THE GOVERNOR

Black Land Grant, copied from the original by Dolly Masters.

terest that he is able to secure. Second he wishes to find out all that he can of his grandmother who was Sarah Mitchell, the wife of his great grandfather Leming, (Lamon, Lemmons, Layman etc. spelling).

Tennessee Genealogical Records by Mrs. Edythe R. Whitely, Nashville, Tennessee copied from records in Archives Division, State of Tennessee as follows:

Vol. 6 page 12. Cocke County.

Deed from William Small to Alexander Outlaw, 218 acres land, Aug. 6, 1800. William Small of Cocke County, Tennessee to Alexander Outlaw of Jefferson County Tennessee, land whereon said Small now lives and William Thornton formerly lived on Big Pigeon River adjoining said Thornton and John Nave, William Bells Grant. Witnessed by Paul McDermott, Chas. T. Porter and THOMAS MARSHALL. Proved in Cocke County, Tennessee Aug. Term 1804.

Same reference: Cocke County Tennessee, Feb. 5, 1799, John Nave, Sr. of Cocke County to John Nave Jr. of said County 100 lbs. of Virginia Money land on Pigeon River adjoining Henry Nave part of original grant of No. 1067 (Revolutionary War). This name was sometimes called "Neff."

Jefferson County May 14, 1796 John Nave of Jefferson County Tennessee to Jacob Nave of said County. Land on Pigeon River in Jefferson County adjoining Henry Nave's line.

Same reference: William Bell to John Nave. Jefferson County, Tennessee, Oct. 12, 1792, land in Jefferson County, Tennessee.

Joseph Mitchell, N. C. land warrant No. 197 private 274 acres March 7, 1786.

Vol. 7, page 10. . . . Warrant No. 4372 John Lovey, private in N. C. Line 640 A of land issued Dec. 20, 1796. Notation says, Hereby relinquish my whole title assignee to Bolony Laucius whom I purchased of Jesse Mitchell, D. Hall.

Hall also made notation Wake Co. Mar. 1, 1797 I do hereby relinquish my whole right and Boling Loveys of the within claim unto James Mitchell of Wake Co. N. C. June 3, 1797 to Ralph Williams in the presence of Jno. Terrell, Ralph Williams of Person Co. N. C. to Daniel Farmer June 20, 1797 in presence of Wm. Jeffreys, Farmer assigned it to Wm. Cocke as surety for payment for twenty one dollars in Person Co. N. C. Mar. 5, 1799.

James Mitchell, a lawyer of Blount County resembled Sam Houston, elected Congressman of that district, and later moved to Mississippi in 1834. Richard Mitchell Clerk about 1790 seems to have resided in Cocke County, served in Hawkins County.

Samuel Mitchell 1794 one of the corporators of Washington College. George Mitchell, Sheriff of Washington Co. 1784, State of Franklin,

Sarah Mitchell married about 1817 to John or Joshua Leming (Lemmons). But which of these men is what interests Sam K. Leming of Waldron, Ark. Any one with a record of this family should communicate with the Honorable Sam K. who has many interesting and valuable records in his possession. He has contributed more to this work than any other person save Edmund C. Burnett of Washington, D. C. and Mrs. Lucile Smith Walker of Chattanooga.

COUNTY COURT EXPENDITURES FOR THE YEAR OF 1950

J. P. Per Diem	$ 575.20
Officials' Bonds	1,362.86
County Physician	628.00
Telephone Bill for Court House	556.77
P. M. A. Rent	790.00
Drugs	425.58
Cocke Co. Poor Farm Com. Appropriation for Fertilizer	92.00
Tax Book—F. W. Parrott, Clerk	500.00
Appropriation for Cocke Co. Fair	500.00
Sessions Court Supplies	44.85
Inquest	85.95
Reg. Soldier Discharges and Official Bonds	54.00
County Attorney Fee	810.00
Judgements—Right of Way	1,084.57
Health Unit	4,326.54
Elections	5,564.90
Bridge Fund	4,591.83
Advertising Bonds	47.78
Comptroller-Treasury—Auditors	76.00
Juvenile Court Costs	69.20
West Tenn. T. B. Hospital	425.00
Postage for Court House	103.00
Dept. Conservation—Forest Fire Control	1,000.00
Clerk Overpaid to Trustee	6.30
Notary Seals	13.17
Special Bridge Fund	90,814.10
Jail and Turn Key	12,239.23
Court House Lights and Water	820.77
Jail and Court House Supplies	4,499.50
Insanity	379.15
Circuit Court Costs	7,747.94
Clerk Signing Bonds (Revenue Bonds)	100.00
Cocke County Library	500.00
Bank Charges—Trustee and County Court Clerk	46.07
Welfare—Rent and Lights	141.92
Eastern State Hospital	3,817.22
Chancery Court Costs	8.00

Salaries:

Viola Clark—Clerk & Master	1,337.10
Chairman's Salary	500.00
Janitor's Salary	1,562.50
County Agent	1,500.00
Asst. County Agent	1,200.00
Sessions Court Judge	2,664.65
Sessions Court Clerk	1,400.00
Tax Assessor	2,100.00
Vet. Assistant (Mary Willis)	300.00
Mrs. Art Fisher, Rent Welfare Bldg.	480.00
Ruth Tate, Home Demonstrator	700.00
Election Commission Salaries	350.00
Equalization Board	315.00

TOTAL EXPENDITURES	**$159,256.65**

County Court—Seated at desk, Chairman W. R. Nease; standing is Clerk J. Donald Cody; seated at table, Harmon Fancher; standing, BURNETT R. DAWSON, CLARENCE SCOTT, C. B. Proffitt, DEWEY STRANGE; next to wall, Benton Giles, E. T. Fowler, Jonah Buckner, Len Brown, Fuller Smith, Cecil Parrott, W. R. Miller, Thomas Phillips, T. S. Ellison, John Lewis More, Clayton Freeman, Burl McGaha and R. Walter Layman. Seated on first row are GUY E. FRESHOUR, CHARLES MANTOOTH, JAMES A. T. WOOD and ESTEL STOKELY. The woman in the picture is Mrs. Lagretta Cureton Parrott, Supt. of County Schools.

Index
Compiled by
Ella E. Lee Sheffield
and
Pauline Shields Walker